Commerce and Peace in the Enlightenment

For many Enlightenment thinkers, discerning the relationship between commerce and peace was the central issue of modern politics. The logic of commerce seemed to require European states and empires to learn how to behave in more peaceful, self-limiting ways. However, as the fate of nations came to depend on the flux of markets, it became difficult to see how their race for prosperity could ever be fully disentangled from their struggle for power. On the contrary, it became easy to see how this entanglement could produce catastrophic results. This volume showcases the variety and the depth of approaches to economic rivalry and the rise of public finance that characterized Enlightenment discussions of international politics. It presents a fundamental reassessment of these debates about "perpetual peace" and their legacy in the history of political thought.

BÉLA KAPOSSY is Professor of History at the University of Lausanne.

ISAAC NAKHIMOVSKY is Assistant Professor of History and the Humanities at Yale University.

RICHARD WHATMORE is Professor of Modern History at the University of St Andrews.

Commerce and Peace in the Enlightenment

Edited by

Béla Kapossy
University of Lausanne

Isaac Nakhimovsky
Yale University

Richard Whatmore
University of St Andrews

CAMBRIDGE
UNIVERSITY PRESS

CAMBRIDGE
UNIVERSITY PRESS

University Printing House, Cambridge CB2 8BS, United Kingdom

One Liberty Plaza, 20th Floor, New York, NY 10006, USA

477 Williamstown Road, Port Melbourne, VIC 3207, Australia

4843/24, 2nd Floor, Ansari Road, Daryaganj, Delhi - 110002, India

79 Anson Road, #06-04/06, Singapore 079906

Cambridge University Press is part of the University of Cambridge.

It furthers the University's mission by disseminating knowledge in the pursuit of education, learning and research at the highest international levels of excellence.

www.cambridge.org
Information on this title: www.cambridge.org/9781108416559
DOI: 10.1017/9781108241410

First published 2017

Printed in the United Kingdom by Clays, St Ives plc

A catalogue record for this publication is available from the British Library

ISBN 978-1-108-41655-9 Hardback

For István Hont (1947–2013)

Contents

Contributors

CHRISTOPHER BROOKE is University Lecturer in Political Theory in the Department of Politics and International Studies at the University of Cambridge, and a Fellow of Homerton College, where he is Director of Studies in Politics. He is the author of *Philosophic Pride: Stoicism and Political Thought from Lipsius to Rousseau* (Princeton, 2012), the co-editor (with Elizabeth Frazer) of *Ideas of Education: Philosophy and Politics from Plato to Dewey* (Routledge, 2013), and the editor of the new Penguin *Leviathan* (2017).

EDWARD CASTLETON is a researcher and lecturer at the University of Franche-Comté, Besançon. He has written numerous articles about Pierre-Joseph Proudhon and is editing the latter's manscripts for publication.

BÉLA KAPOSSY is Professor in Modern History at the University of Lausanne. He is the author of *Iselin contra Rousseau: Sociable Patriotism and the History of Mankind* (Schwabe Verlag, 2006) in addition to a number of works concerning political thought, political economy and moral philosophy in eighteenth-century and early nineteenth-century Europe.

DUNCAN KELLY is a Reader in Political Thought in the Department of Politics and International Studies at the University of Cambridge, and a Fellow of Jesus College, Cambridge. He is the author of *The State of the Political* (Oxford, 2003) and *The Propriety of Liberty* (Princeton, 2010), editor of *Lineages of Empire* (Oxford, 2009) and co-editor of the journals *Modern Intellectual History* and *Max Weber Studies*. He is currently writing an intellectual history of the First World War.

IAIN MCDANIEL is Lecturer in Intellectual History at the University of Sussex. He is the author of *Adam Ferguson in the Scottish Enlightenment: The Roman Past and Europe's Future* (2013).

ISAAC NAKHIMOVSKY is Assistant Professor of History and Humanities at Yale University. He is the author of *The Closed Commercial State: Perpetual Peace and Commercial Society from Rousseau to Fichte* (Princeton, 2011) and a new edition of Johann Gottlieb Fichte's *Addresses to the German Nation* (2013).

EVA PIIRIMÄE is Associate Professor of Political Theory at the Johan Skytte Institute of Political Studies, University of Tartu. Piirimäe specialises in eighteenth-century political thought, with a special focus on debates on patriotism, cosmopolitanism and philosophical histories of mankind. She is currently writing a book on Johann Gottfried Herder's political thought in the context of enlightenment Europe.

SOPHUS A. REINERT is Marvin Bower Associate Professor of Business Administration in the Business, Government and the International Economy Unit at Harvard Business School. He is the author of numerous works on the histories of capitalism and of political economy, including *Translating Empire: Emulation and the Origins of Political Economy* (Harvard, 2011).

MARK SOMOS is the Alexander von Humboldt Foundation Fellow at the Max Planck Institute for Comparative Public Law and International Law, Heidelberg, and Senior Visiting Research Fellow at Sussex Law School. He is the author of *Secularisation and the Leiden Circle* (Leiden: Brill, 2011). He is currently finishing two further monographs, *American States of Nature* and *The Republican Patronage of the World: Secularization, Commerce, and Provincial Authority in English Soft Imperialism*.

MICHAEL SONENSCHER is a fellow of King's College, Cambridge. His most recent books are *Before the Deluge: Public Debt, Inequality, and the Intellectual Origins of the French Revolution* (Princeton University Press, 2007) and *Sans-Culottes: An Eighteenth-Century Emblem in the French Revolution* (Princeton University Press, 2008).

KOEN STAPELBROEK is Associate Professor of the History of Political Theory at Erasmus University Rotterdam, Academy of Finland Research Fellow at the University of Helsinki and co-Director of the Helsinki Centre for Intellectual History. He is the author of *Love, Self-Deceit and Money: Commerce and Morality in the Early Neapolitan Enlightenment* (Toronto, 2008) and a range of articles and edited volumes on European eighteenth-century political thought. He is completing a monograph on European perceptions of the rise and fall of the Dutch trade republic.

RICHARD WHATMORE is Professor of Modern History at the
University of St Andrews and director of the St Andrews Institute of
Intellectual History. He is the author of *Republicanism and the French
Revolution* (Oxford, 2000), *Against War and Empire* (Yale, 2012) and
What is Intellectual History? (Polity, 2015).

Acknowledgements

The editors would like to thank Anna Hont and Michael Sonenscher for help with every aspect of this volume. The volume is one of two books dedicated to István Hont that engage with the work of the great intellectual historian – the second will appear with Harvard University Press in 2018. Additionally, thanks go to the organisers of the symposia that facilitated the development of the chapters, and especially two of the contributors, Alexander Schmidt and Doohwan Ahn, whose work has been published in other places. The book would not have been completed without the support of Mon Han Tsai, Masaya Kobayashi, Erik S. Reinert, The Other Canon Foundation, the Estonian Science Foundation (individual research grant No. 8887), the Center for Public Philosophy at Chiba University, the University of Lausanne, the Swiss National Science Foundation, the University of Tartu, King's College Cambridge, King's College Research Centre and the Cambridge History Faculty. Liz Friend-Smith has been the ideal editor at Cambridge University Press: we are extremely grateful for her labours and for the comments of independent referees.

One of István Hont's most remarkable gifts was to bring scholars from different places and backgrounds together, to direct their research and get them to work collaboratively. Although he would undoubtedly have been critical of the result, this book was developed in precisely such a Hontian fashion.

Introduction
Power, prosperity, and peace in enlightenment thought

Béla Kapossy, Isaac Nakhimovsky,
and Richard Whatmore

I

In the early 1780s, Benjamin Franklin was fascinated by the possibility of establishing a perpetual peace. In 1782, as an end to the War of American Independence began to appear on the horizon, he arranged for the translation and publication of a peace plan by a former galley slave, Pierre-André Gargaz.[1] Gargaz's plan for a union of European states, Franklin wrote, might "appear in some respects chimerical," but, he continued, "there is Merit in so good an Intention."[2] Towards the end of 1783 he was writing to the British MP David Hartley, a longstanding friend also involved in the Paris peace negotiations that ended the North American war, lamenting the stupidity of conflict. In the case of Britain and France there had been seven centuries of "mad wars" doing "one another mischief." Instead of wasting resources on war, Franklin asked, "how many excellent things might have been done to promote the internal welfare of each country? What Bridges roads, canals, and other useful public works, and institutions tending to the common felicity might have been made and established?" Franklin had a ready solution. He proposed to Hartley a collective treaty or "family compact" between Britain, France, and North America. North America, Franklin wrote, "would be as happy as the Sabine Girls, if she could be the means of uniting in perpetual peace her father and her husband."[3]

---

[1] [Pierre-André Garsaz], *Conciliateur de toutes les nations d'Europe, ou Projet de paix perpétuelle entre tous les souverains de l'Europe & leurs voisins* (n.p., 1782). See E. R. Cohn, "The Printer and the 'Peasant': Benjamin Franklin and Pierre-André Gargaz, Two Philosophers in Search of Peace," *Early American Studies: An Interdisciplinary Journal*, 8, no. 1 (2010): 146–72.
[2] Franklin to unnamed person, 22 May 1783, *Benjamin Franklin Papers*, Digital Edition, The Packard Humanities Institute.
[3] Franklin to David Hartley, 16 October 1783, *Benjamin Franklin Papers*.

Franklin's was an age obsessed with such transformative visions of perpetual peace. As this volume showcases, these discussions were closely connected to contemporary debates about political economy. They were centrally concerned with the rise of global commerce and its effects on both competition among European states and on Europe's relation to the rest of the world. It was evident to every eighteenth-century commentator that perpetual peace could never be established without dealing with the realities of economic competition among rival states and empires. In an undated fragment entitled "Plans for Perpetual Peace," part of a projected work on war and peace, Jeremy Bentham noted that "All plans of this sort written in the past were premature [because] they were put forth before the spirit of enlightenment had spread sufficiently to allow people to recognize the community of interests that exists among nations. This will not be accepted before the science of political economy is understood by the general public."[4]

Students of politics and of international relations have tended to ignore the variety and the depth of the approaches to the relationship between commerce and peace that characterized the Enlightenment. They have also tended to focus their attention on a small subset of the eighteenth-century literature on perpetual peace, which they have regarded primarily as a moral discourse, as a succession of attempts to provide a normative grounding for international relations. The best-known discussion of perpetual peace has long been the essay with that title published by Immanuel Kant in 1795.[5] However, the term "perpetual peace" had entered into wide circulation much earlier, thanks to the Abbé de Saint Pierre, whose continually revised and extended treatise on the subject first took shape during the diplomatic negotiations that resulted in the 1713 Treaty of Utrecht.[6] Among Saint-Pierre's most important readers in the eighteenth century was Jean-Jacques Rousseau, who spent an important period in the 1750s intensively studying Saint-Pierre's writings, producing among other things a widely read abstract

---

[4] Jeremy Bentham, undated fragment, Papers of Jeremy Bentham, The Bentham Project, Bentham MS Boxes 177 and 178, University College, London, 294–5.

[5] Immanuel Kant, *Zum ewigen Frieden: Ein philosophischer Entwurf* (Königsberg: Friedrich Nicolovius, 1795). On Kant's essay, see James Bohman and Matthias Lutz-Bachmann (eds.), *Perpetual Peace. Essays on Kant's Cosmopolitan Ideal* (Cambridge, MA: The MIT Press, 1997); Immanuel Kant. *Vers la paix perpétuelle*, ed. Max Marcuzzi (Paris: J. Vrin, 2007); for an anthology of German peace plans, see Anita and Walter Dietze (eds.), *Ewiger Friede? Dokumente einer deutschen Diskussion um 1800* (Leipzig and Weimar: Gustav Kiepenheuer, 1989); the continuing relevance of Kant's essay is discussed in, Reinhard Merkkel and Roland Wittmann (eds.), *"Zum ewigen Frieden." Grundlagen, Aktualität und Aussichten einer Idee von Immanuel Kant* (Frankfurt a.M.: Suhrkamp, 1996).

[6] Charles Irénée de Castel de Saint-Pierre, *Projet pour rendre la paix perpetuelle en Europe* (Utrecht: A. Schouten, 1713).

of his treatise on perpetual peace.[7] Saint-Pierre, Rousseau, and Kant represent a rather distinctive set of contributions to a much larger and more varied literature that extends back to the seventeenth century and proliferated after every major war in the eighteenth century, including the War of American Independence. By illuminating the contours of this wider literature about perpetual peace, and revealing the extent of its preoccupation with political economy, the chapters in this volume give us a better sense of these seminal Enlightenment debates and their historical legacies.[8]

The extent to which eighteenth-century writers were preoccupied with economic rivalry as a facet of intensifying political conflict is now well understood, thanks above all to the scholarship of Istvan Hont.[9] Hont himself found David Hume and Adam Smith to be particularly illuminating starting points for thinking about the relationship between commerce and peace because of their focus on, as he put it, "how the logic of commerce actually played itself out when superimposed upon the logic of war."[10] According to Hont, Smith's 'The' *Wealth of Nations* was not a treatise on "perpetual peace" in that it did not imagine a world without competition between states; on the contrary, Smith's work amounted to "a competitive economic strategy."[11] At the same time, however, Hont viewed Smith as developing a critical perspective on state behavior that was predicated on a cosmopolitan theory of globalization, or the spread of economic development around the world. The chapters in this volume take up and extend into new territory this important insight that "a cosmopolitan theory of commercial globalization" and a "competitive globalization strategy" were not necessarily mutually exclusive categories in eighteenth-century thought – though powerful tensions were generated by attempts to combine them. This volume is also indebted to Hont in an additional sense, since it represents an enduring collaboration that began in 2008 with a series of exploratory workshops he helped convene at King's College, Cambridge, on the theme of "Commerce and

[7] Rousseau's abstract of Saint-Pierre's treatise appeared in 1761 and became part of a particularly wide debate about perpetual peace in the context of the Seven Years War, but his accompanying judgment only became available posthumously, in 1782. The best modern edition is Jean-Jacques Rousseau, *Principes du droit de la guerre: écrits sur la paix perpétuelle*, ed. Blaise Bachofen and Céline Spector (Paris: J. Vrin, 2008).
[8] See further, Hans Blom, "The Republican Mirror. The Dutch Idea of Europe" and Biancamaria Fontana, "The Napoleonic Empire and the Europe of Nations," in Anthony Pagden (ed.), *The Idea of Europe. From Antiquity to the European Union* (Cambridge University Press, 2002), 91–115 and 116–28; Bo Stråth, *Europe's Utopias of Peace. 1815, 1919, 1951* (London: Bloomsbury, 2016).
[9] See above all Istvan Hont, *Jealousy of Trade: International Competition and the Nation-State in Historical Perspective* (Cambridge: Harvard University Press, 2005).
[10] Hont, *Jealousy of Trade*, 6.   [11] Hont, *Jealousy of Trade*, 8.

Perpetual Peace in the Eighteenth Century."[12] Although the title of this book is *Commerce and Peace in the Enlightenment*, it is not solely concerned with the eighteenth century, the argument being that we understand what happened after enlightenment, normally understood as ending with the French Revolution. *Commerce and Peace* underlines the extent to which enlightenment controversies continue to influence and illuminate politics and society today, the point being that we ought to seek to understand them and their various legacies.

The relationship between commerce and peace was a central concern for those involved in correspondence with Franklin – physiocratic and *philosophe* circles in Paris, dissenters and reformers across Britain, and members of the governing class in the new North American republic – all of whom perceived themselves to be living through a distinctive period in history, characterized by acute uncertainty about the future. From their perspective, the world had changed since commerce had become the central issue of national politics. The natural sociability of human beings was being thwarted, including in the relations between states. This was a shift that Hume had dated to the previous century. In the first edition of Hume's *Essays, Moral and Political* (1741), in the essay "Of Liberty and Despotism," a title that was changed to "Of Civil Liberty" in editions from 1758, Hume claimed that until the seventeenth century "trade was never esteemed an affair of state." Xenophon mentioned trade but doubted "if it be of advantage to a state." Plato "totally excludes it from his imaginary republic," and in more recent times "even the Italians [of the sixteenth century] have kept a profound silence with regard to it." More recently, by contrast, trade had become "the chief attention, as well of ministers of state, as of speculative reasoners." The cause of the new obsession with trade was evident to Hume: "the great opulence, grandeur, and military achievements of the two maritime powers [England and the Dutch Republic] seem first to have instructed mankind in the importance of an extensive commerce."[13]

Commerce brought uncertainty in the form of the flux of markets. This might lead to the decline of major and minor states, as shown by the cases of Spain in the seventeenth century and of the Dutch Republic in the eighteenth century. The former had neglected its domestic markets; the latter had seen the prices of its products undercut by the lower

[12] Follow-up workshops took place in Lausanne in 2013 and in Tartu in 2014.
[13] David Hume, *Essays Moral, Political, Literary*, Eugene F. Miller (Indianapolis: Liberty Fund 1987), 88–9.

wage costs of its competitors.[14] On top of this, states had begun to rely on national debts to fund the ballooning costs of warfare conducted by standing armies and large navies. The prevalent fear of unintended national bankruptcy, or monarch-inspired planned bankruptcy, was evoked most powerfully by Hume in his essay "Of Public Credit," which deployed the image of cudgel-playing in a china shop as a description of "princes and states fighting and quarrelling amidst their debts, funds and public mortgages."[15] Hume, like so many of his contemporaries, regarded the new system of war finance to be a dangerous innovation. Its tendency was to lock the power politics of internationally trading states into a mutually reinforcing degenerative spiral. As a cancerous growth it had to be excised altogether from modern economic life. Either the economy had to be made institutionally incapable of financing modern war, or war had to be stopped and global peace achieved.[16] The alternative was a world that was even worse than that of Thomas Hobbes's gladiator states jealously monitoring each other's preparedness for war. What Hume had called "jealousy of trade," in an essay of 1758, was identified as an intensification of earlier, purely political, antagonism – or jealousy – between states. Economic war was becoming a permanent condition.[17] In the view of Hume's close friend Adam Smith, such a development was a gross abuse of the old vice of "national animosity." Instead of "national friendship" between neighboring countries, "mercantile jealousy," Adam Smith wrote, "inflames, and is itself inflamed, by the violence of national animosity." It makes every nation "look with an invidious eye upon the prosperity of all the nations with which it trades, and to consider their gain as its own loss."[18]

---

[14] Istvan Hont, "The 'Rich Country – Poor Country' Debate in Scottish Political Economy," in *Jealousy of Trade*, 267–324; "The Rich Country – Poor Country Debate Revisited: The Irish Origins and French Reception of the Hume Paradox," in Margaret Schabas and Carl Wennerlind, eds., *Hume's Political Economy* (London: Routledge, 2007), 222–342.

[15] David Hume, *Essays Moral, Political, Literary*, 361–2.

[16] Istvan Hont, "The Rhapsody of Public Debt: David Hume and Voluntary State Bankruptcy," in *Jealousy of Trade*, 325–54; Michael Sonenscher, "The Nation's Debt and the Birth of the Modern Republic: The French Fiscal Deficit and the Politics of the Revolution of 1789," *History of Political Thought*, 18 (1997): 64–103, 267–325; Michael Sonenscher, *Before the Deluge. Public Debt, Inequality, and the Intellectual Origins of the French Revolution* (Princeton University Press, 2007).

[17] Istvan Hont, "The Political Economy of the 'Unnatural and Retrograde' Order: Adam Smith and Natural Liberty," in *Französische Revolution und Politische Ökonomie*, ed. Maxine Berg et al. (Trier, 1989), 122–49, and "Jealousy of Trade: an introduction," *Jealousy of Trade*, 1–156.

[18] Adam Smith, *An Inquiry Into the Nature and Causes of the Wealth of Nations* (London: A. Strahan and T. Cadell, 1776), 2 vols., II, Book IV, Chapter III, 82–3.

The response of numerous contemporaries was to condemn the new commercial world, or at least some of its most salient features. Victor Riqueti, marquis de Mirabeau, Jean-Jacques Rousseau, and Gabriel Bonnot de Mably all, in very different ways, advised the abandonment of industrial strategies seeking commercial dominion, on the grounds that they were ultimately self-defeating and would lead to the collapse of states. By contrast, Smith's 'The' *Wealth of Nations*, with its celebration of productivity, the division of labor, and machinery, was intended to destroy the idea that the wealth of modern nations could not last, but would decline like that of their ancient and early modern forerunners. National wealth could be preserved, Smith held, by implementing a national economic strategy of mass production, combined with mechanization, and constant technological innovation. Smith, like Jean-François Melon before him, suggested that it was technology and innovation, rather than wage rates, that would determine the outcome of competitive trade battles internationally. Smith's hope was that international relations could come to be characterized more by emulation, or economic competition conducted without envy and without involving all sorts of military and other power struggles over economic gains. Smith was convinced that there were kinds of economic competition that were instances of such noble rivalry. However, he was also far less sanguine than many of his contemporaries about the limits of the human capacity for judgment, and hence far more skeptical about the possibility of maintaining a stable distinction between emulation and envy, or engaging in economic competition while maintaining a cosmopolitan respect for the attainments of other nations.[19] It was difficult to see, in other words, how the race for prosperity could ever be fully disentangled from the struggle for power, and it was easy to see how the latter could pervert the former.

In the early 1780s, Franklin and his friends had become convinced that conditions had arrived in which the kind of emulation among nations described by Smith could be made a reality. With Britain exhausted by war and nearly bankrupt, and France in similar circumstances, the time was ripe for sociability and peace to be restored to Europe. Recent events had confirmed the irrationality and waste of war, and underscored the likelihood that corrupt commercial systems led to national defeat. The prominent Welsh dissenting minister Richard Price was convinced that "the empire of reason and virtue" was imminent, with nations abandoning the sword of conflict. The defeat of Britain in the American Wars proved that corrupt forms of commerce, exemplified by Britain's mercantile system, could not sustain states in the building of

---

[19] On Smith and emulation see Hont, *Jealousy of Trade*, 111–25.

commercial empires.[20] States able to recognize the benefits of commerce and the impossibility of establishing commerce without peace, were the future. Strategies to implement this cosmopolitan vision included the proclamation of free ports and leagues of armed neutrality against warmongers, commercial treaties between states, and agreement on an international code of law. In addition, the study of the classic texts concerned with perpetual peace was recommended, especially Saint Pierre's *Projet de paix perpetuelle*, usually "with Rousseau's remarks."[21] Franklin and his friends anticipated a world in which human beings collected in communities would become more sociable, rationally accepting the benefits of peace, or recognizing the need to live peacefully because the alternative of endless war and the collapse of civilization was too monstrous to accept.

The major problem, Franklin recognized, was that human sociability was insufficiently powerful to draw communities and states together into mutually beneficial peaceful relationships. However rational it might be to embrace peace, and to maintain it, the reality of individual and national behavior so often pulled in an opposite direction. States were always more than capable of pursuing a policy entirely at odds with their own interests and those of humanity. This was why, in 1784, Franklin was speculating about ways of forcing states to abandon military confrontation. One way to get to perpetual peace that aroused his interest for a time was the air balloon. Another of Franklin's friends, the Dutch natural philosopher Jan Ingenhousz, remarked in a letter of 2nd January 1784, that balloons were "one of the greatest discoveries of natural philosophy."[22] They had the capacity to force perpetual peace upon the world. Ingenhousz asked how an army could subsist if an enemy could "throw force and destruction upon their stores and magazines at any time?" Franklin replied on 16th January 1784, agreeing that balloons might very well "give a new turn to human affairs."[23] They would

---

[20] Richard Price, *Observations on the importance of the American Revolution, and the means of making it a benefit to the world* (London, 1784), 7.

[21] Saint-Pierre's *Projet* was republished several times in the final decades of the eighteenth century, and Rousseau's commentary many more times still. See, for example, "Projet de paix perpétuelle de M. l'abbé de Saint-Pierre" and "Analyse de J-J. Rousseau" in Jean-Antoine-Nicolas de Caritat Marquis de Condorcet, Charles de Peyssonnel, Isaac René Guy Le Chapelier, eds., *Bibliothèque de l'homme public; ou, Analyse Raisonnée des principaux ouvrages françois et étrangers, sur la politique en général, la législation, les finances, la police, l'agriculture et le commerce en particulier, et sur le Droit naturel et public*, Seconde année, Volume 5 (Paris: Buisson, 1791), 90–155.

[22] Jan Ingenhousz to Franklin, 2 January 1784, in Jan Ingenhousz, *The Ingenhousz-Jenner Correspondence*, (London: Janus, 1964), 541.

[23] Franklin to Ingenhousz, 16 January 1784, in Ingenhousz, *The Ingenhousz-Jenner Correspondence*, 545.

contribute to convincing sovereigns of "the folly of wars." Balloons were cheap; Franklin said that five thousand balloons carrying two men each would not cost more than five ships of the line. The technical problems associated with using balloons as a deterrent to war would be overcome, Franklin stated, once the English recognized their potential, because "they are such ingenious mechanicians." Franklin involved himself in the experiments to keep balloons steady in the air in the following months, forwarding his correspondence to the French *Académie des Sciences* in the hope that control over the movement of balloons might soon be perfected.[24]

Such inflated expectations of the 1780s were short-lived, as have been many subsequent hopes of engineering a technological means for ending war (including, for example, H.G. Wells's 1933 vision of a global peace ushered in by an Anglophone "Air Dictatorship").[25] The French Revolution seemed to many observers to have made a reality of Hume's vision of warlike states battling for imperial and economic ascendency. Though some retained Franklin's hopes of a federative future – notably Thomas Paine – for many the renewal of war between Britain and France, after barely a decade of peace, underlined the inevitability of war between leading commercial states. The problem was "the prevalence and extension of the war-system throughout Europe, supported as it has been by the universal adoption of the funding-system."[26] As George Chalmers put it, the renewal of "dreadful war" was accompanied by a train of evils, as "bankruptcy followed bankruptcy in rapid succession, our resources seemed to vanish, distrust and terror seized the mercantile world, and the Bank of England itself partook... of the general alarm." Against a background of Terror across France, the supporters of reform became mute: "the once sacred name of Liberty itself became offensive."[27] Chalmers believed that he could prove that despite war and bankruptcy, commerce thrived on peace, and that economic development would continue to occur in the face of the actions of states in making wars. Hume's argument that bankruptcy would destroy both politics and trade was

[24] Creuzé to Franklin, 24 December 1783, 4 January and 14 February 1784; Jean-Baptiste Le Roy to Franklin, 7 January and 18 February, 1784, *Benjamin Franklin Papers*.
[25] H.G. Wells, *The Shape of Things to Come* (London: Hutchinson & Co, 1933).
[26] Jasper Wilson [James Currie], *A Letter, Commercial and Political, Addressed to the Rt. Honble. William Pitt: in Which the Real Interests of Britain, in the Present Crisis, Are Considered, and Some Observations are Offered on the General State of Europe* (London: G. G. J. and J. Robinsons, 1793).
[27] Chalmers, *An Estimate of the Comparative Strength of Great-Britain. During the Present and Four Preceding Reigns, and of the Losses of Her Trade from Every War Since the Revolution* (London: John Stockdale, 1794), 14.

mistaken.[28] An alternative view was that war should be lauded as a means of revivifying the corruptions of national character that accompanied commerce. As John Brand wrote in 1797, drawing on Adam Ferguson's work, war would at least increase the "masculine energy which for more than half a century has been declining by a natural decay from the want of the necessity of exercising it, artificially accelerated by a mawkish and hypocritical system of petrifying [commercial] principles disseminated among us."[29]

For other observers of European politics, including Kant, modern history offered a different lesson on the subject of perpetual peace. On the one hand, Kant was an outspoken critic of the warlike behavior of contemporary commercial states. On the other hand, he insisted on defining rigorous ethical limits on the use of state power even for peacemaking purposes. In Kant's view, the only truly successful agent of peace making had been war itself. The march of reason or sociability could not be relied upon to put an end to war. Rather, perpetual peace had to be conceived in terms of the "unsocial sociability" (*ungesellige Geselligkeit*) that for Kant defined commercial society itself. According to Kant, the only stable peaceful equilibrium was one in which the destructive powers of states – particularly their fiscal capacities – were reined in by "republican" governments of consenting citizens who, exhausted by war, had come to dissent from violence. This equilibrium was defined in principle as the purely moral product of good will, as an (automatically peaceful) "ethical commonwealth" or Kingdom of Ends; but historically Kant claimed that it would be the product of unsociable, possibly near-fatal collisions among intelligent, self-loving selves, a process that would eventually foster an (perhaps reluctant, but peaceful) attachment to "culture" and to "right." One of the great tasks of philosophy, according to Kant, was to work out what a politics erected on this foundation would look like.

II

Eighteenth-century discussions of perpetual peace – especially Kant's – have continued to serve as a starting point for reflection about the normative structure of the international order. They have also been linked to contested claims about the ability of modern Western states to behave in a peaceful, self-limiting way, or to generate an international legal

---

[28] Chalmers, *An Estimate of the Comparative Strength of Great-Britain*, ix–x.

[29] Brand, *Considerations on the depression of the funds, and the present embarrassments of circulation: with propositions for some remedies to each* (London: Richard White and T. Longman, 1797), 64–9.

order and operate within its confines. Such claims are a key aspect of these states' identity, on a par with the claim that there is a particular affinity between their political institutions and a market-based economy (though one prominent explanation of this peaceful tendency is called the "democratic peace thesis," conspicuously referencing political institutions alone).[30] On the other hand, the development of an international legal order, like economic globalization, can be seen as the product of centuries of war-making by Western states and as the continuation of a long history of Western empire-building.[31] From this perspective, the flourishing of literature on the "democratic peace" since the 1980s looks like an echo of earlier imperial ideologies from the turn of the twentieth century, Anglophone ones in particular.[32] This is the same point of origin to which historians are increasingly inclined to trace the development of international organizations like the League of Nations and the United Nations.[33]

The chapters in this volume are contributions to a fundamental reassessment of Enlightenment debates about "perpetual peace" and their legacy in the history of political thought. They examine how eighteenth and nineteenth-century theorists of international order approached the conduct of the European states and empires of their time, particularly with regard to economic rivalry and the rise of public finance. The history of the idea of "perpetual peace" is most often told in terms of the classic juridical analogy that results from the idea of international relations as a state of nature, comparable to a state of nature among individual human beings.[34] In these terms, "perpetual peace" denotes a legal framework that puts an end to the anarchy of international relations. The result is an analytical typology that has often been

---

[30] On these aspects of the identity of the democratic state see particularly John Dunn's extensive investigations, most recently in *Breaking Democracy's Spell* (New Haven: Yale University Press, 2014). Also relevant is his "The Identity of the Bourgeois Liberal Republic," in *The Invention of the Modern Republic*, ed. Biancamaria Fontana (Cambridge University Press, 1994), 206–25. On "democratic peace" see, classically, Michael W. Doyle, "Kant, Liberal Legacies, and Foreign Affairs," *Philosophy and Public Affairs* 12, no. 3 (Summer 1983): 205–35; and Michael W. Doyle, "Kant, Liberal Legacies, and Foreign Affairs, Part 2," *Philosophy and Public Affairs* 12, no. 4 (Autumn 1983): 323–53.

[31] See e.g. Antony Anghie, *Imperialism, Sovereignty, and the Making of International Law* (Cambridge University Press, 2005); Costas Douzinas, *Human Rights and Empire: The Political Philosophy of Cosmopolitanism* (London: Routledge-Cavendish, 2007).

[32] Duncan Bell, "Before the Democratic Peace: Racial Utopianism, Empire and the Abolition of War," *European Journal of International Relations* 20, no. 3 (2014): 647–70.

[33] Mark Mazower, *No Enchanted Palace: The End of Empire and the Ideological Origins of the United Nations* (Princeton University Press, 2009).

[34] Cf. Theodore Christov, *Before Anarchy: Hobbes and his Critics in Modern International Thought* (Cambridge University Press, 2016).

projected into an opposition between "realist" theorists of international anarchy on the one hand, such as Machiavelli or Hobbes, and "liberal" theorists of perpetual peace like Kant on the other.[35] The persistence of such historical projections is perhaps a symptom of what David Armitage has referred to as the "fifty years rift" between the disciplines of history and international relations; only relatively recently have they been exposed to revision by historians of political thought.[36] A major impetus for such revision has come from the reinterpretation of Hobbes as a theorist of the international order – appropriately enough if he is in fact the ultimate ancestor of these typologies.[37] An approach to Enlightenment debates about perpetual peace that does not merely reproduce the twentieth-century reception of nineteenth-century sociology must set aside the projections generated by these later typologies and start instead with the eighteenth-century reception of Hobbes.

According to the view developed most powerfully by Richard Tuck, Hobbes's significance for eighteenth-century political theory was not just as the theorist of the absolutist state par excellence: he was also the animating force behind some of the most radical eighteenth-century critiques of the behavior of such regimes. Hobbes, on this view, was the purest practitioner of the new expression of natural jurisprudence that emerged in the seventeenth century and codified the principles of state behavior, or reason of state, in terms of a universal right to self-preservation.[38] Unlike many others, Hobbes did not leave room for appeals to a separate principle of sociability as a moral bulwark against the state's pursuit of its own preservation. Tuck has suggested, referring to Kant's famous criticism of international lawyers in his essay on perpetual peace, that such appeals to sociability always amount to "sorry comfort": such wishful thinking, in making the world seem more moral

[35] A variation on this approach tries to define a "third way" between these two positions. In this scheme, a "Kantian" notion of community or solidarity was not the only alternative to Hobbesian anarchy: there could also be a Grotian international society, a looser form of association among states. Hedley Bull, *The Anarchical Society: A Study of Order in World Politics* (New York: Columbia University Press, 1977).

[36] David Armitage, "The Fifty Years' Rift: Intellectual History and International Relations," *Modern Intellectual History* 1, no. 1 (2004): 97–109.

[37] Hont has suggested that such typologies are best understood as variations on a distinction between community and society that was elaborated in the nineteenth century by Ferdinand Tönnies, who as Hont stressed was not only a sociologist but a Hobbes scholar attuned to Hobbes's distinction between "union" and "concord." Istvan Hont, *Politics in Commercial Society*, ed. Béla Kapossy and Michael Sonenscher (Cambridge: Harvard University Press, 2015), 5–8.

[38] See Richard Tuck, "The 'Modern' Theory of Natural Law," in *The Languages of Political Theory in Early-Modern Europe*, ed. Anthony Pagden (Cambridge University Press, 1987), 99–119; and more generally *Philosophy and Government, 1572–1651* (Cambridge University Press, 1993).

than it really was, merely succeeded in furnishing legal justifications for aggressive behavior that Hobbes's more reductive approach had, in fact, succeeded in ruling out categorically.[39] For instance, Hobbes, unlike Locke, excluded justifications of imperialism in terms of a right to punish violators of natural law.

As a radical approach to perpetual peace, this Hobbesian minimalism took two forms in the eighteenth century. One possibility, taken up by the Abbé de Saint Pierre, was to complete the analogy suggested by Hobbes's account of the state of nature. Just as the state of war led individuals to create the state, so the state of war among nations would result in states submitting to a common judge with overwhelming power and authority (though Saint-Pierre envisioned this international Leviathan taking a federal form, as a "republic of sovereigns," as opposed to a single polity or "universal monarchy"). The other possibility was to fully break the Hobbesian analogy. If competitive trade was deemed inherently unsociable and warlike, then a peaceful world was one in which states withdrew from this activity. The most explicit and extreme articulation of this approach was Johann Gottlieb Fichte's theory of the "closed commercial state."[40] Fichte's *The Closed Commercial State* (1800) is often seen as the beginning of modern socialism and social democracy. In the first instance, however, it was an attempt to show that perpetual peace or the taming of state behavior involved reforming all the commercial relations of modernity. Kant, following the natural jurists, had described commerce as the only mechanism that could reunite humanity after its dispersion around the globe. Fichte denied that commerce could serve this unifying function because commercial interests were too heavily implicated in the unstable power dynamics of the European states system. He described market relations as a Hobbesian state of war and stipulated that states withdraw from competitive global commerce. Only a state with a balanced and mostly self-sufficient domestic economy could hope to re-establish commercial ties beyond its borders while remaining peaceful.

To many eighteenth and nineteenth-century writers, neither of these approaches constituted a genuine solution to the problem of international competition. A good guide to this sort of thinking is supplied by a review essay on theories of perpetual peace published in 1800 by the prominent diplomat Friedrich Gentz. In his view, neither Saint-Pierre's

---

[39] Kant's phrase served as the original title of Tuck's 1991 Carlyle Lectures at Oxford University, which became *The Rights of War and Peace: Political Thought and the International Order from Grotius to Kant* (Oxford University Press, 1999).

[40] Isaac Nakhimovsky, *The Closed Commercial State: Perpetual Peace and Commercial Society from Rousseau to Fichte* (Princeton University Press, 2011).

nor Fichte's approach to the state was compatible with the process of civilization that was driven by what Kant had called "unsocial sociability." Kant did not envision the elimination or suppression of the unsocial passions by the state, but rather gave these passions a constructive role in history. According to Gentz, it was war that was consolidating Europe's political landscape into the kinds of stable and powerful states that were capable of maintaining the rule of law. At the same time, the discovery of "true principles of political economy" in the eighteenth century ensured that wars among states would not prevent the global progress of civilization from continuing.[41] This process would create the conditions in which states could become capable of pursuing their interests peacefully, within legal limits. They could acquire the moral attributes of self-mastery or autonomy that he associated with the "true theory of the balance of power."[42] According to Gentz, Rousseau had been wrong to claim that if Saint Pierre's vision of an international federation could be created for a day, it would last forever.[43] What mattered, rather, were the conditions for its perpetuation. These conditions could not be supplied through a permanent legal apparatus such as Saint-Pierre had envisioned because there was no available source of agency for enforcing such legal judgments among states. It was only the historical process driven by cycles of war and the expansion of trade that could gradually bring about the moral transformation of state behavior. In other words, sociability among states was the outcome of this civilizing process, not its cause. The problem with the alternative kind of Hobbesianism promoted by Fichte, in Gentz's view, was that it cut off this possibility altogether.

Though Gentz's essay was shaped by its polemical purpose, it offers a particularly clear example of the kind of analytical framework that defined many eighteenth-century discussions of perpetual peace and continued to inform many nineteenth-century treatments of the subject.[44] The search for ways to harmonize the behavior of states with

---

[41] Friedrich von Gentz, "Über den ewigen Frieden," in *Zum ewigen Frieden: ein philosophischer Entwurf: Texte zur Rezeption, 1796–1800*, ed. Manfred Buhr and Steffen Dietzsch (Leipzig: Reclam, 1984), 287.

[42] Gentz, "Zum ewigen Frieden," 273.

[43] Jean-Jacques Rousseau, "Jugement sur la paix perpétuelle," in *Principes du droit de la guerre: écrits sur la paix perpétuelle*, 116.

[44] See e.g. Wilhelm Traugott Krug, "Ueber politisches Gleichgewicht und Uebergewicht, Universalmonarchien und Völkervereine, als Mittel, die Völker zum ewigen Frieden zu führen" [1818], *Krug's gesammelte Schriften* (Braunschweig: Friedrich Vieweg, 1834), 2:73–90; and Franz von Holzendorff, *Die Idee des ewigen Völkerfriedens* (Berlin: Carl Habel, 1882). For a recent collection of studies on the nineteenth century see Thomas Hippler and Milos Vec, *Paradoxes of Peace in Nineteenth Century Europe* (Oxford University Press, 2015).

the general interest of humanity (whether codified legally or not) is a unifying thread that runs through the essays in this volume. For all but the most radical writers, this alignment was not to be achieved in a purely reductive way, by reducing the state's interest to self-preservation. Rather, many sought to move away from the view that the role of the state was to suppress the political as well as economic impact of *amour propre*, or the desire for recognition, rather than finding a way for it to play a constructive role (or as Albert Hirschman famously put it, "harnessing" its power).[45] At the same time, by identifying the distinct courses of historical development that had given rise to different forms of human association, these writers sought to determine what kinds of political units were capable of participating in a harmonized international system, and what forms of military, diplomatic, legal, commercial, and financial relations among them might be regarded as instrumental to human fulfillment.

Viewed independently of Gentz's polemic, even the most Hobbesian eighteenth-century writers on perpetual peace were operating in these areas of theoretical activity at least to some extent. Saint-Pierre was, as recent literature has emphasized, a realist critic of the balance of power and a genuinely Hobbesian theorist of a supranational Leviathan.[46] At the same time, however, Saint-Pierre insisted that it was necessary to go beyond the reductive principle of negative justice proclaimed by the seventeenth-century natural law theorists (*"Abstine a malo"*).[47] Instead he sought to show how the right constitutional arrangements could transform the external behavior of the state, making it capable of exercising *"bienfaisance"* toward the rest of the world.[48] (Saint-Pierre's protégé, the Marquis d'Argenson, called this kind of regime "demo-cratic monarchy," and might therefore be considered a theorist of the

---

[45] Albert Hirschman, *The Passions and the Interests: Political Arguments for Capitalism Before its Triumph* (Princeton University Press, 1977).

[46] Olaf Asbach, *Staat und Politik zwischen Absolutismus und Aufklärung: Der Abbé de Saint-Pierre und die Herausbildung der französischen Aufklärung bis zur Mitte des 18. Jahrhunderts* (Hildesheim: G. Olms, 2005); Céline Spector, "L'Europe de l'abbé de Saint-Pierre," in *Les projets de l'abbé Castel de Saint-Pierre, 1658–1743: pour le plus grand bonheur du plus grand nombre*, ed. Carole Dornier and Claudine Poulouin (Caen: Maison de la recherche en sciences humaines, Université de Caen Basse-Normandie, 2011), 39–49; Bruno Bernardi, "L'idée d'équilibre européen dans le jus gentium des modernes: esquisse d'histoire conceptuelle," in *Penser l'Europe au XVIIIe siècle: commerce, civilisation, empire*, ed. Antoine Lilti and Céline Spector (Oxford: Voltaire Foundation, 2014), 19–46.

[47] Charles Irénée de Castel, Abbé de Saint-Pierre, *Ouvrajes de morale et de politique* (Rotterdam: Jean Daniel Beman, 1733–41), 6:129.

[48] Saint-Pierre, *Ouvrajes de morale et de politique*, 7:3.

"democratic monarchy peace thesis.")[49] Rousseau and Kant were condemned as all too Hobbesian by contemporary critics, but there was an important republican element to their respective theories of the state, though it was highly restricted or attenuated by comparison with those of their contemporaries. They too were engaged in efforts to find a substitute for seventeenth-century natural jurisprudence, and there was an important historicizing dimension to their thinking about the idea of perpetual peace, which they recast as the outcome of a historical process driven by unintentional consequences. Finally, while Fichte's Hobbesianism was perhaps the most extreme of all in its expression, his *Closed Commercial State* also drew on radical republican views of political economy to claim that the resources afforded by public credit might enable states to extricate themselves from international competition and engineer the moral transformation of modern economic relations.[50] At the same time, in contrast to Gentz, other contemporary readers also took Fichte's theory to represent a further specification of Rousseauian or Kantian philosophy of history, driven by a process of "unsocial sociability."[51]

The line traced by the chapters in this volume, then, does not set out from Hobbes's radically reductive approach to politics, and continue with its reception in the eighteenth and nineteenth centuries. Instead it begins with Hobbes's republican contemporary James Harrington, who imagined that the English commonwealth, its constitution reinvigorated by agrarian reform, could act as the benevolent liberator of Europe: by relying on an alliance with the Dutch banking republic, it could transform the corrupt and diseased regimes of seventeenth-century Europe into a new continental empire, thereby exercising "the patronage of the world."[52] Harrington's vision had an extensive reception in both Europe and North America – Harrington himself remarked that the first continental power (most likely France, in his estimation) to clear away the detritus of feudalism would rule the world.[53] For Voltaire and Frederick the Great, however, the very features of European monarchies that moralists condemned as corrupt and diseased – such as their

---

[49] René-Louis de Voyer marquis d'Argenson, *Considérations sur le gouvernement ancien et présent de la France* (Amsterdam, 1765). On d'Argenson see Nannerl O. Henry, *Democratic Monarchy: The Political Theory of the Marquis d'Argenson* (Ph.D., Yale University, 1968).

[50] Nakhimovsky, *The Closed Commercial State*, 103–29.

[51] Nakhimovsky, *The Closed Commercial State*, 164–5.

[52] See the contribution of Mark Somos.

[53] James Harrington, *The Commonwealth of Oceana* [1656], ed. J.G.A. Pocock (Cambridge University Press, 1992), 232–3.

consolidation of political authority and concentration of wealth – were instrumental in the emergence of a stabilized European balance of power that left room for the operation of commercial reciprocity. The moderated form that the Anglo-French rivalry had assumed after the War of the Spanish Succession supplied an alternative model of Europe's future to the Abbé de Saint-Pierre's vision of a European Union: a model that France could help project into Central Europe and beyond.[54] Voltaire's and Frederick's claims about the character of powerful eighteenth-century monarchies were extended by the Amsterdam financier Isaac de Pinto to apply even to their increasing reliance on public debt. Rather than fueling military rivalry and imperial expansion, modern finance could supply the means for achieving the Abbé de Saint-Pierre's vision of perpetual peace. Like Harrington, Pinto imagined a key role for the Dutch republic, whose influence on capital markets could help moderate competition among the great powers.[55]

For many eighteenth-century observers, the prospect that this competition was in fact spiraling out of control, and would prove lethal to the commercial bonds between states, evoked the historical case of ancient Carthage, which could be identified as a commercial republic overwhelmed by the military might of Rome.[56] The possibility that the modern European states system could produce a different outcome hinged on fundamental questions about human sociability: on the extent to which the "iron clamp of the state" (as Friedrich Nietzsche, referring back to Hobbes, later put it) was an indispensable condition for human flourishing, or on whether (or what types of) economic or cultural activity might be able to generate healthy and sustainable social relations independently of the state.[57] This is why, in eighteenth-century Italy, those who were confident that political economy could provide the answers for how to pacify the behavior of European states could be derided as "socialists," as the famous Milanese reformer Cesare Beccaria was in the 1760s.[58] One of the most important and far-reaching eighteenth-century discussions of sociability was undertaken by Johann Gottlieb Herder, who mounted a profound attack on the historical model underlying Voltaire's and Frederick the Great's model of Europe's future. Even Kant, in Herder's view, failed to provide a genuine alternative to that model because he retained the principle that the state was a fundamental condition for the

---

[54] See the contribution of Isaac Nakhimovsky.
[55] See the contribution of Koen Stapelbroek.
[56] See the contribution of Christopher Brooke.
[57] Friedrich Nietzsche, "The Greek State" [1871–72], in *On the Genealogy of Morality*, ed. Keith Ansell-Pearson (Cambridge University Press, 1994), 170.
[58] See the contribution of Sophus Reinert.

development of human sociability and economic progress. The possibility of an economically vibrant perpetual peace, Herder insisted, had to be detached from the relatively recent and contingent history of Europe's violent "state machines," and grounded instead in the historical development of its national cultures.[59] Kant's forceful rejoinder, however, was that any such attempt to get more morality into international relations would remain implicated in the power dynamics, imperialism, and warmaking from which it was supposed to provide an escape.

In his 1892 review essay, the German philosopher Moritz Brasch pointed out that the legacy of the eighteenth-century literature on perpetual peace for the development of international law in the nineteenth century was not limited to Saint-Pierre's scheme for the normative structure of international relations, which had been taken up by Kant and then by post-Kantian jurists; it also included insights into the principles of regularized, pacified state behavior that Brasch associated primarily with Bentham and his influential Genevan editor Étienne Dumont.[60] As we have seen, many other eighteenth-century writers on perpetual peace also shared this preoccupation, and the breadth and variety of perspectives on how to tame the behavior of the state extended into the nineteenth century. In the wake of Britain's defeat in the War of American Independence, for example, Scottish writers critical of British imperial power began reviving the "cosmopolitan republican" idea of a federation, which had been put forward at the beginning of the eighteenth century by Andrew Fletcher, a follower of Harrington who had been an outspoken critic of the Anglo-Scottish union of 1707.[61] To his late-eighteenth-century readers, Fletcher's political thought provided a touchstone for thinking about the possibility of a radical post-imperial reconfiguration of the United Kingdom itself; about the fate of the American and French republics in the 1790s; and even about the possibility that a benevolently imperial Anglo-American-Dutch alliance could impose a post-revolutionary peace on continental Europe and the Spanish empire (a type of arrangement that was attempted after the fall of Napoleon, though in the event this "holy alliance" was directed from Vienna and Saint Petersburg rather than London, New York, and Amsterdam).[62] To many other late-eighteenth-century observers, however, it seemed that the British state was successfully defying predictions that its rising labor

---

[59] See the contribution of Eva Piirimäe.

[60] Moritz Brasch, "Die Friedensidee und das Völkerrecht: Eine historische Skizze," *Die Waffen nieder!* 1, no. 4 (May 1892): 1–7; and *Die Waffen nieder!* 1, no. 5: 1–14.

[61] See the contribution of Iain McDaniel.

[62] Cf. Richard Whatmore, *Against War and Empire: Geneva, Britain, and France in the Eighteenth Century* (New Haven: Yale University Press, 2012), 260–75.

costs would price it out of export markets and that its ballooning national debt would undermine its political stability. Rather than succumbing to the fate of ancient Carthage, in this view, Britain was offering the only viable alternative to the instability and militarism being exported by revolutionary France. Genevan republicans in particular began to argue that Britain was not acting as a ruthless economic predator but rather as a benevolent cosmopolitan empire that would guarantee the liberty of small states because its own prosperity depended on securing them access to global markets.[63]

After the fall of Napoleon, a wide range of writers continued to investigate forms of association that had arisen independently of modern states – the various outcrops of what Georg Friedrich Wilhelm Hegel termed "civil society" – and that might therefore provide a solid foundation for liberty. Karl Ludwig von Haller is best known as a theorist of reactionary Prussian authoritarianism (though he was in fact a traditional Bernese republican), while Pierre-Joseph Proudhon is best known as a French anarchist. Both, however, regarded post-revolutionary liberal democracy as incompatible with liberty, and launched powerful attacks on Grotius, Hobbes, and Kant, and the international lawyers that had retained their idea of the state as the fundamental basis of social order. Calling for a "restoration" of pre-Hobbesian political science, Haller defended a Bernese model of political culture in which a patriarchal form of patriotism provided a source of sociability and served to rein in the centrifugal effects of *amour propre*.[64] Proudhon too rejected the legacy of Hobbes, Rousseau, and Kant, charging that their approach to the state had allowed war to be sublimated into a legal fiction by international lawyers. Instead, Proudhon outlined a historical trajectory of state development that ultimately opened up the possibility of perpetual peace, thanks to a radical rebalancing of the economy in conditions of scarcity that would eliminate the social and psychological pathologies caused by unbridled *amour propre*. Like Voltaire's in the previous century, Proudhon's hopes for Europe's future were premised on an Anglo-French model of the progressive pacification of the state – though what Proudhon envisioned was very different from the Cobden-Chevalier free trade agreement of 1860, which he criticized as combining the worst elements of English plutocracy with French militarism.[65]

As these nineteenth-century responses to the eighteenth-century literature on perpetual peace suggest, the joining of a Kantian approach to international law with a non-reductive theory of peaceful state behavior

---

[63] See the contribution of Richard Whatmore.
[64] See the contribution of Béla Kapossy.   [65] See the contribution of Edward Castleton.

under the banner of "liberalism" was not the only way to think about perpetual peace at the dawn of the twentieth century, or even the most obvious one. The joining of these two strands is illuminated by the case of Carl Friedrich, a German émigré who became an influential professor at Harvard. In the wake of the Second World War, Friedrich repositioned Kant, together with John Locke, as part of the intellectual genealogy of a peaceful postwar transatlantic democratic order. In fact, Friedrich's genealogy drew on early-twentieth-century discussions of how Germany might safely compete economically with its geopolitical rivals: discussions that had revolved around German reinterpretations of Locke not as a defender of the limitless prerogative of the executive power, but as a theorist of what Friedrich came to call "constitutional reason of state." For Locke and Kant to become liberal theorists of the normative foundations of international relations, in other words, they first had to be made into theorists of the self-limiting behavior of the state.[66] It is revealing, and perhaps appropriate, in this light, that more recent writers on the "democratic peace" have sometimes identified closer affinities to contemporaries of Kant whose political thought was in fact quite different from his, such as Thomas Paine.[67] One of the great puzzles in the history of political thought, as John Dunn has long emphasized, is how a regime that originally defined itself in opposition to "democracy" quite precipitously and irrevocably came to bear the name of its critics.[68] In the case of the democratic peace, too, it remains important not to confound Rousseau's and Kant's notably sceptical contributions to the eighteenth-century literature on perpetual peace with the real eighteenth-century ancestors of the "democratic peace" thesis.

[66] See the contribution of Duncan Kelly.
[67] See e.g. Thomas C. Walker, "The Forgotten Prophet: Thomas Paine's Cosmopolitanism and International Relations Theory," *International Studies Quarterly* 44, no. 1 (2000): 51–72; Daniel Deudney, "Publius Before Kant: Federal-Republican Security and Democratic Peace," *European Journal of International Relations* 10, no. 3 (2004): 315–56.
[68] John Dunn, *Setting the People Free: The Story of Democracy* (London: Atlantic, 2005).

1   Harrington's project
The balance of money, a republican constitution for Europe, and England's patronage of the world

*Mark Somos**

Our knowledge of Harrington's reception continues to grow apace. The extent and sense in which he was typical of seventeenth-century English republicanism is the subject of a long-running debate. Among the clear and explicit elements of Harrington's proposals are the distribution of land and the creation of citizen-soldiers in order to turn England into an expansionary, imperialist republic. Despite the lively interest and the undisputed core features of Harrington's thought, the question that has seldom been asked is: where did Harrington think England should expand? In light of the scale and importance of England's extra-European colonial and commercial expansion throughout the seventeenth century, the answer is surprising.

This chapter aims to show that Harrington had a rudimentary but coherent imperial project that began with the English conquest of Scotland and Ireland, continued with the conquest of France and the rest of Europe, and eschewed premature overseas expansion. The project involved the implementation of republican reforms under a doctrine Harrington called "the patronage of the world," a high degree of provincial autonomy, and eventual representation in Westminster. Another seldom discussed Harringtonian notion, the balance of money, and the logic of Harrington's imperialist republican scheme, suggest that he would have made an exception for Holland and perhaps Genoa from the agrarian laws to utilise their rare ability to remain stable on the balance of money and turn them into free ports for England's European empire. They would have circulated and harnessed the manufacturing and commercial energies of other European states, once those states were cured by England's benign intervention from the diseased mismatch between their non-monarchic balance of property and

* I am grateful to Hans Blom, Ioannis Evrigenis, Marketa Klicova, James Livesey, Gaby Mahlberg, Daniel Margócsy, Russell Muirhead, Andrew Sartori, and the editors for their comments. This chapter was researched and written thanks to a fellowship at the E.J. Safra Center for Ethics at Harvard University, and a Jack Miller Center fellowship at the Yale Center for the Study of Representative Institutions.

retrograde Gothic constitutions and became virtuous republics, immune to corrosive luxury and able to support further expansion.

I

To ask whether it bee lawfull for a commonwealth to aspire unto the Empire of the world, is to ask whether it be lawfull for her to do her duty; or to put the world into a better condition than it was before. (Harrington, Oceana)

James Harrington (1611–77) is best known today for *The Commonwealth of Oceana* (1656). References to his other works in the secondary literature are scarce by comparison. One of *Oceana*'s most astute critics was Matthew Wren (1629–72), a Hobbesian Anglican. Wren's objections in *Considerations on Mr. Harrington's Common-wealth of Oceana: restrained to the first part of the preliminaries* (1657), and the decline of Oliver Cromwell's health, explain several shifts of emphasis between Harrington's *Oceana* and *The Prerogative of Popular Government* (1657). One shift is the downplaying of *Oceana*'s benevolent Protector as the source of prudence, and Harrington's new emphasis on political scientists as experts with specialised knowledge unavailable to both people and princes.[1] Another shift of emphasis is from land, as the unit of analysing the balance of property, toward a mixed political economy that encompasses two types of states: those with their domestic stability and imperial ambition grounded in land, and states like Holland, the biblical Israel, Venice, and Genoa (although Harrington is inconsistent about these Italian cities) that illustrate the feasibility of substituting money for land in special circumstances.[2]

Three features distinguish states of the latter type.[3] They already have money at their founding moment; they are geographically small and prevented from territorial expansion; and their religion supports international trade and, due to its underlying secularising and republican morality, prevents both priestly encroachment on politics and

---

[1] Epistle to the Reader; Preface, 1–2. In the *Art of Law-Giving* (1659), Harrington gave up hopes of being employed, but reiterated the need for political scientists. Epistle to the Reader, and I.ii.20–1.

[2] While the famous "balance of property" in *Oceana* refers to land, there are already hints of this special case. E.g. *Oceana*, "Preliminaries," 5, the short heading "Ballance in money." Cromartie suggests another shift between *Oceana* and the *Prerogative*'s preoccupation with interest. Alan Cromartie, "Harringtonian Virtue: Harrington, Machiavelli, and the Method of the *Moment*," *The Historical Journal* 41:4 (1998), 987–1009, esp. 992–3.

[3] *Prerogative*, I.iii.13–15. The section begins with Harrington's explanation that he is enlarging the argument about the balance of money in response to Wren's point in *Considerations* that money is enough to build an empire.

the corruption of morals conventionally associated with trade and empire.[4] Such states based on the balance of money expand not via land, but banking and trade – yet they remain republican. In *The Prerogative* Harrington derives general rules from these exceptions, for instance that regulated lending and borrowing is good for large states,[5] or that banks create republics, and *vice versa*.[6] A sophisticated theory of necessary inequality also follows. States must have some, so that the rich can use economies of scale to innovate; but not so much as to provoke unrest.[7] One corollary is that levelling is not in the people's true interest. Harrington cautions against levelling not simply because of its short-term disruption of social order, but also because it would upset the balance of property that underpins not only the constitutional reform that is customarily associated with *Oceana*, namely a bicameral parliament with wide franchise and term limits, but also the aforementioned rules of political economy in Harrington's proposal.[8]

The project that unfolds when *Oceana* and *The Prerogative* are read together is best understood as a form of commercial republicanism. In my view, the commercialisation of Harrington's republicanism, dubbed "neo-Harringtonianism," begins with Harrington himself.[9] There is no "sudden and traumatic discovery of capital" between Harrington's and the eighteenth-century Court Whig positions.[10] We simply have

---

4   Harrington, *Prerogative*, I.xi.96–7. The Jews were fighters, but not merchants, until they first lost their land, then settled in too narrow a strip: Petrus Cunaeus, *The Hebrew Republic* ([1617] tr. P. Wyetzner, Shalem Press, 2007), I.4, 20–1. The smallness of republics prevents civil wars: Harrington, "Pour enclouer le Canon" (1659), 1.
5   *Prerogative*, I.iii.15. Borrowing must be more profitable than lending, therefore the rate should be capped, e.g. at 4%. This is good for large states, where land cannot be 'overballanced by money,' because it encourages industry, trade, and improvement.
6   *Prerogative*, I.iii.17. Steven Pincus, "Neither Machiavellian Moment nor Possessive Individualism: Commercial Society and the Defenders of the English Commonwealth," *American Historical Review* 103 (1998), 705–11, on banking schemes from the 1650s. On Toland's Harringtonian banking schemes, and praise of the Bank of England as Harringtonian, see Justin Champion, "'Mysterious Politicks': Land, Credit and Commonwealth Political Economy, 1656–1722," in ed. D. Carey, *Money and Political Economy in the Enlightenment* (Oxford, Voltaire Foundation, 2014), 117–62.
7   *Prerogative*, I.viii.45–6.   8   *Oceana*, 199–201, *Prerogative*, I.viii.44, etc.
9   J.G.A. Pocock, *The Ancient Constitution and the Feudal Law: A Study of English Historical Thought in the Seventeenth Century* (Cambridge University Press, 1957), 128–9. Pocock, "Machiavelli, Harrington and English Political Ideologies in the Eighteenth Century," orig. *William & Mary Quarterly* (1965), repr. in *Politics, Language and Time: Essays on Political Thought and History* (Chicago University Press, 1967), 104–47, 113, 115, 137, *passim*. Pocock, "Early Modern Capitalism: The Augustan Perception," in eds. Eugene Kamenka and R.S. Neale, *Feudalism, Capitalism and Beyond* (London, 1975), 62–83. Pocock, *The Machiavellian Moment: Florentine Political Thought and the Atlantic Republican Tradition* (1975, with new afterword, 2003, Princeton University Press), 406.
10 Pocock, *Virtue, Commerce, and History, Chiefly in the Eighteenth Century* (Cambridge University Press, 1985), 107–9. Also see *Machiavellian Moment*, chapter XIII. Pincus

not traced Harrington's reception well. There was no rediscovery, because he was not forgotten.[11] Harrington was read and cited by English colonisers and American colonists from the start.[12] Holland and

is right that there "was no consensus for or against capitalism." *1688: The First Modern Revolution* (Yale, 2009), 368. Other criticisms of the Harringtonian – neo-Harringtonian distinction include Paul Rahe, *Republics Ancient and Modern, Volume II: New Modes and Orders in Early Modern Political Thought* (North Carolina University Press, 1994); Gaby Mahlberg, "Henry Neville and English Republicanism in the Seventeenth Century" (Ph.D., University of East Anglia, 2006), chapter 9; Mahlberg, *Henry Neville and English Republican Culture in the Seventeenth Century* (Manchester University Press, 2009), 2, 155–6, 161–3. Pocock raises a problem his genealogy creates on *Virtue*, 259: "What remains not fully explained is how an ideology stressing Roman warrior – civic values and the independence that came best from real property possessed the appeal it visibly had for town dwellers..." The answer is that in one strand of republicanism, discussed below, agriculture was added to the warrior and civic values. The Renaissance and early modern reception of this strand brought colonialism into a unitary framework of political analysis; and with Harrington, via Cunaeus, it was transformed in special cases into commerce and banking. Highly relevant is the seamless transformation of the *laus urbis* genre to include commerce among the virtues of cities, including Antwerp, Amsterdam, and London. Somos, *Varieties of Secularisation in English and Dutch Public and International Law* (PhD, Leiden 2014), III.1.3. *Prerogative*, I.xi.96–9.

[11] Henry Neville, William Penn, John Toland, and Walter Moyle are well-studied conduits, but Anthony Ashley Cooper, first Earl of Shaftesbury, and William Petty require more work. For clues to Harrington's influence on Shaftesbury see Russell Smith, *Harrington*, 137–9, and Thomas Leng, "Shaftesbury's Aristocratic Empire," in ed. John Spurr, *Anthony Ashley Cooper, First Earl of Shaftesbury, 1621–1683* (Ashgate, 2011), 101–25. On Petty, see Smith, *Harrington*, 130–1. Another unrecognised Harringtonian political economist is Nehemiah Grew in the 1706–7 *The Meanes of a Most Ample Encrease of the Wealth & Strength of England in a Few Years* (Huntington mss., HM 1264; and ed. Julian Hoppit, Records of Social and Economic History, New Series 47, Oxford, 2012).

[12] Smith, *Harrington*, chapters VII and VIII. Charles Blitzer, *An Immortal Commonwealth: The Political Thought of James Harrington* (Yale University Press, 1960). Less frequently discussed texts fill in the gaps in the history of Harrington's uninterrupted reception. Jonathan Scott, *When the Waves Ruled Britannia: Geography and Political Identities* (Cambridge University Press, 2011), 120 cites Henry Sheres's 1691 Harringtonian analysis of England's relationship with Europe and Holland. Bernard Bailyn, *The Ideological Origins of the American Revolution* (enlarged ed., Belknap Press, 1992), 75n20 on Robert Hunter, Governor of New York and New Jersey, using Harringtonian arguments in 1711. James Abercromby's *An Examination of the Acts of Parliament Relative to the Trade and the Government of our American Colonies* (1752) and his 1774 *De Jure et Gubernatione Coloniarum, or An Inquiry into the Nature, and the Rights of Colonies, Ancient, and Modern* are both indebted to Harrington's system, ranging from extensive uses of Sigonius (already in the 1766 draft of *De Jure*, John Carter Brown Library, Codex-Eng.50) to details of Harrington's England's European empire. See e.g. *Magna Charta for America*, eds. J.P. Greene, C.F. Mullett, and E.C. Papenfuse, Jr. (Philadelphia, 1986), 45, 68–70, 175, 186, 198–202, 212–18, 245, 249–50, 257–60, 265, 282–3. Also see George Chalmers, *Letter to Lord Mansfield* (1780, John Carter Brown Library, Codex=Eng150), analyse in Harringtonian terms the operation and unique liberty of government in England's colonies, the industriousness of farmers, distant colonies' drive for independence, Britain's need to preserve the economic dependence of its colonies, and the effect of capturing the Dutch free port of New York on the governability of New England colonies. Like Abercromby and Chalmers, Thomas Bever also writes a Harringtonian history of empires in *The History of the Legal Polity of the Roman State* (1781), see e.g.

France produced several explicitly Harringtonian constitutional designs between the 1670s and the 1800s. In addition to the issues outlined above, I also suspect that the 1651 Navigation Act shaped Harrington's scheme, and Harrington's scheme in turn affected, even if indirectly, several Restoration laws, including the 1660 extension of the Navigation Act, paying off the New Model Army, and provisions for several proprietary and Crown colonies.[13] Thus, the project for a European empire that combined territorial with commercial considerations and claimed to spread liberty has been a valid alternative to extra-European expansion at least since Harrington, and is not an innovation of the "long eighteenth century." Harrington's invention of the balance of property, including the balance of money, is the key to unlocking this story.[14]

II

It is true that some formulations of virtue denounce all productive activities one had to pursue for a living (*negotium*); and some formulations opposed commerce, seaports, and the disassociation of money from tangible goods. Plato and Aristotle were among those who criticised the corrosive effect of working for hire, and of commerce, on civic virtue.[15]

---

xii, 21, 27, 46, 77–80, 109–115, 189–200. John H. Elliott, *Empires of the Atlantic World: Britain and Spain in America, 1492–1830* (Yale, 2006), 334–6. Yirush, *Settlers, Liberty, and Empire: The Roots of Early American Political Theory*, 1675–1775 (Cambridge 2011). 41–4 on relevant British-American legal continuities, including Chief Justices Matthew Hale and John Vaughan, and William Blackstone. Most of these discussions focus almost exclusively on *Oceana*.

[13] Smith, *Harrington*, 100–1, 103, and 122 on Harrington's lost scheme for Charles II.

[14] Harrington's claim that the balance of property is his invention, and the beginning of political science: *Prerogative*, I.iii.20.

[15] Plato, the Athenian Stranger's report on Crete in *The Laws*. IV.705a, XI.918d. Commerce and trades forbidden to citizens, confined to foreign residents: V.736e–741e, VIII.846d–847b, XI.918a–920c. As Nelson points out, Harrington explicitly invokes this part of *The Laws*. Eric Nelson, *The Greek Tradition in Republican Thought* (Cambridge, 2004), 115–17. Harrington also draws on Aristotle, e.g. *Politics*: craftsmen and laborers cannot be virtuous III.5.1278a20–1, cf. I.13.1260a38–b1. VII.9.1328b39–1329a2, cf. III.4.1277b3–7, VIII.2.1337b5–15. *Oceana*, 217, including: "Whereas I am of Aristotle's opinion, That a Common-wealth of Husband-men (and such is ours) must be the best of all others." Discussing Aristotle in response to Harrington, Peter Heylyn distinguishes between *populus*, the whole body of people who form the commonwealth, and *plebs*, "those of inferiour quality, as Laborers, Handicrafts, Artificers." Note that Heylyn does not include farmers among the plebs. *Certamen Epistolare* (1659), 235. Aristotle against money: *Politics*, I.9.1257b20–3. Against commerce: I.9.1257b23–8, I.10.1258b1–2. Against banking: I.10.1258b2–8. Good oligarchies exclude the *nouveau riche* engaged in trade: VI.7.1321a28–9, III.5.1278a25–6. Harrington also refers to Aristotle and others for this point: *Prerogative*, I.xi.85–6. See fn32 below for Harrington citing Aristotle's prefiguration of the key doctrine of the balance of property. On the corrupting influence of money as an abiding concern in English imperial projects

Cicero occasionally professed the same opinion.[16] Yet Machiavelli had a comprehensive and high-level theory of labour, which emphasised energy in the forms of agriculture, industry, or war, and identified idleness as the certain decay and death of any republic.[17] In Oceana, the agrarian multiplied industry and money, as well as fighting men;[18] and Harrington crafted commercial republicanism by linking banks to republics and by positing the balance of money in *The Prerogative*.[19] Harrington also favoured industry and commerce in England, since they were unlikely to outweigh the value produced by land, whether derived from agriculture or rent.[20] In sum, Machiavelli's and Harrington's misgivings about commerce, and their proposed solutions, are not in the same mould as most ancient contrasts between luxury and civic virtue.[21] Machiavelli and Harrington should be understood as reacting to and adapting a distinct strand of republicanism based on the ideal of *farmer*-soldier-citizens. This tradition goes back at least to Xenophon and Cicero and runs through Leon Battista Alberti, Lodovico Guicciardini, and Johannes Althusius to John Adams, Thomas Paine, St. John de Crèvecœur, and Thomas Jefferson. It was to this tradition that Carolus Sigonius (c. 1524–1584) added a provincial (Paduan, Bolognese) dimension, which, in contradistinction from Milanese and Florentine civic

---

and European rivalries: John Bargrave?, *A Treatise Shewing Howe to Erecte a Publique and Increasinge Treasurie for Virginia* (ca. 1633 mss, Huntington HM 962).

[16] Cicero, *De leg. agr.* in *Pro Quinctio. Pro Roscio Amerino. Pro Roscio Comoedo. The Three Speeches on the Agrarian Law Against Rullus* (tr. J.H. Freese, Loeb, 1930), 471: "It is not so much by blood and race that men's characters are implanted in them as by those things which are supplied to us by nature itself to form our habits of life, by which we are nourished and live. The Carthaginians were given to fraud and lying, not so much by race as by the nature of their position, because owing to their harbours, which brought them into communication with merchants and strangers speaking many different languages, they were inspired by the love of gain with the love of cheating." Harrington cites *De leg. agr.*, e.g. *Oceana*, 7, 57. See Christopher Brooke's chapter on Carthage.

[17] Somos, *Varieties*, chapter III. Harrington's adaptation: e.g. *Oceana*, 208, 217, *Prerogative*, I.viii. 44–5, *Art of Law-Giving*, I.i.6.

[18] *Oceana*, 106. Compare Harrington's account of England as a commerce-tolerant, but not commerce-driven, republic with Huet's view of Rome, as discussed in Christopher Brooke's paper.

[19] Even descriptions that predate Pocock and acknowledge that commerce had a role in Harrington's thought tend to neglect *The Prerogative*, and argue mainly from *Oceana*. H.F. Russell Smith, *Harrington and His Oceana: A Study of a 17th Century Utopia and its Influence in America* (Cambridge University Press, 1914), 35.

[20] *Prerogative*, I.iii.14–15: "in a Countrey where Merchandise is exercised, it is so far from being destructive, that it is necessary." Money must not be left to "rust unprofitably in private purses."

[21] See Champion, "Mysterious," esp. 150, 161. For the English appreciation of the *vita activa*, see Markku Peltonen, *Classical Humanism and Republicanism in English Political Thought, 1570–1640* (Cambridge University Press, 1995).

humanisms, emphasised agrarian laws, local government, and colonial projects as instruments for relatively small states to navigate the pernicious rivalries of large states. Sigonius also applied the ancient Athenian, Spartan, Roman, and feudal Italian categories of colonialism and local government, including division into tribes and a principle of subsidiarity to protect the jurisdiction of provincial courts against metropolitan encroachment that emerged from his systematic comparisons to the biblical Israel. This was the comparative framework that Petrus Cunaeus (1586–1638) extended by adapting Machiavelli's analysis of politics to the biblical Israel, which he presented as armed, agrarian, commercial, expansionary, and potentially immortal thanks to the political instrumentalisation of its religion by Moses, its Machiavellian prince.[22]

These were the components that Harrington, drawing on Sigonius and Cunaeus, combined in positing the balance of property (land) in *Oceana* as the foundation of all government, neutralised Israel as a model, and proposed a British and republican version of benign imperialism.[23] The idea behind the balance of property is not simply that money can take flight, and people without land have a partial or false interest in the common good.[24] The farming component of the *kalokagathia* of Xenophon's Ischomachus in *Oeconomicus*, popularised in works such as Leonardo Bruni's 1420 translation of the pseudo-Aristotelian *Oeconomicus*, Poggio Bracciolini's *De avaritia* (1428–29) and "De nobilitate," and Leon Battista Alberti's *I Libri della Famiglia*, matures by the time of Sigonius into a theory of educating ideal citizens who not only cherish individual economic independence and collective interdependence, but move readily between the sword and the plough whenever their republic embarks on a colonial adventure.[25] Further inspired by his Dutch experience and

---

[22] Somos, *Varieties*.
[23] On Cunaeus and Harrington: Nelson, *Greek Tradition*, 94n29. Lea Campos Boralevi, "James Harrington's 'Machiavellian' Anti-Machiavellism," in eds. Ioannis Evrigenis and Mark Somos, *Pact with the Devil: The Ethics, Politics and Economics of Anti-Machiavellian Machiavellism, Special Issue of the History of European Ideas* 37:2 (2011), 113–19. On Harrington's neutralisation of the biblical model: Somos, "Irenic Secularization and the Hebrew Republic in Harrington's *Oceana*," in eds. Mahlberg and Wiemann, *European Contexts for English Republicanism* (Ashgate, 2013), 81–103.
[24] *Prerogative*, I.iii.11; I.viii.37–40.
[25] For the relevant analysis of Sigonius' *Fragmenta Ciceronis* (1559), "Oratio de laudibus historiae" *in Orationes septum* (1560), *De antiquo iure civium Romanorum* (1560, 2nd ed. 1563), *De antiquo iure Italiae* (1560), *De lege curiata magistratuum et imperatorum* (1569), *De antiquo iure prouinciarum* (1567), and *De republica Hebraeorum* (1582) see Somos, *Varieties*, III.3. Harrington relies on Sigonius extensively. *Oceana*, Second Part of Preliminaries, 30f. on the Roman agrarian. *Oceana*, 57f., 265–6. *Prerogative*, I.xii.126, II.ii.12, 16, II.iii.33, *Art of Law-Giving*, III.iv. Also see Hont on Botero, *Jealousy of Trade: International Competition and the Nation-State in Historical Perspective* (Harvard University Press, 2010), 16–18.

readings,[26] and responding i.a. to Wren's challenge, this is the model that Harrington inherited and commercialised in *The Prerogative*.[27]

How does Harrington adopt this model to England, which differs from Venice in being (in Machiavelli's terms) a commonwealth for increase, as opposed to preservation – in other words, a state organised for expansion? And if England is a republic for increase, and that means territorial rather than commercial expansion,[28] then where would Harrington like to invade? *Oceana* begins with the assertion that the English are "the most martiall in the whole World."[29] Harrington cites Machiavelli and Francis Bacon that military success requires the right ratio of cavalry to infantry, in other words a proper balance between nobility and commoners, which in turn depends on instituting the correct balance of property.[30] In England's case this means that commoners must have enough land to be independent, but not enough to stop working the land themselves.[31] This is the best way to raise men fit for war, and in this England resembles the Roman Republic. Harrington here paraphrases Aristotle's *Politics*, VI.iv on farmers as the best citizens and leaders, in contrast with urban tribes in cities like Athens or Rome, which breed turbulence.[32] Given that England's balance of property already shifted from the nobility and clergy to the people, the corresponding shift in form of government is a Hobson's choice between collapse, or instituting a republic for increase.[33] Harrington's proposals for an English republic and empire are mutually reinforcing; neither is subordinate to the other. And just as every citizen will defend and expand England better when

---

[26] Pocock denies that Harrington's Dutch experiences and readings, and the politics of the United Provinces, had any formative influence on his writing. E.g. Pocock, "Introduction," in ed. Pocock, *The Political Works of James Harrington* (Cambridge University Press, 1977), 61. However, see i.a. *Oceana*, 39, 62, 94, 151, *Prerogative*, I.ix.64–6 and I.x.78.

[27] See e.g. *Oceana* 199–201. *Prerogative*, I.ii.11–17, I.viii.45, I.ix.63.

[28] *Prerogative* I.iii.18–19.   [29] Introduction, B.

[30] The rest of Bacon's "True Greatness" contradicts Harrington's line of reasoning. A similar citation of Bacon to the same effect is *Prerogative*, I.x.79–80. Lord Archon citing Bacon, Essay XIX, "Of Empire:" *Oceana*, 143.

[31] *Oceana*, Introduction. Note here that one cannot assume that "neo-Harringtonians" believe in the virtue of country gentlemen. Country virtue belongs to those who work the land. In exactly the same way, if the people are soldiers, they will rule. The nobility must become soldiers themselves, and not farm out this function, if they wish to retain some power. *Oceana*, 228–9.

[32] Harrington on Aristotle prefiguring the balance of property: *Oceana*, 7, 97. Echoes in *Prerogative*, I.xi.83, 85–6, 91.

[33] E.g. *Oceana*, 21, 177. The phrase, "Hobson's choice," after stable owner Thomas Hobson who offered customers the choice between the horse closest to the door or no horse at all, is used by Harrington in the 1659 *Valerius and Publicola* before Samuel Fisher's use in 1660, mistakenly given by the OED as the first occurrence.

he has a stake in it, England's empire must also be designed such that everyone feels its setbacks and triumphs equally.[34]

The Roman Republic had three sets of agrarian laws, Harrington explains: for land distribution at home, for new colonies' distribution of land seized from the enemy, and for distributing public money received for land. A recurring problem with the second category, designed particularly for empire-building, was the aristocracy's tendency to steal the land from veterans under some pretext or another. According to Harrington, it is only these cases that caused internal dispute and collapse. The on-going large-scale misappropriation of conquered land shifted the balance of property, and dismantled the Republic under Sulla.[35] It was replaced by feudalism or the "Gothic Balance," in which land granted in return for military service became hereditary. This brought down the Roman Empire. In England, as in most other European countries, the Gothic balance meant landownership for the nobility and the clergy.[36] In his battle with them, Panurgus (Henry VII) encouraged the people to obtain land. Coraunus (Henry VIII) shifted power from the church to the people, effectively completing another transition, this time to a republican balance of property. Since forms of government must follow the balance of property, the Civil War became inevitable.[37]

Although some of the secondary literature uses "gentry" for those who obtained land thanks to Henry VII and VIII,[38] in the *Prerogative* and the *Art of Law-Giving* Harrington prefers the term, "yeomanry" for this group. This instructively links him to earlier texts on English farmer-soldier-citizens, including the 1523 *Boke of Husbandire* by Anthony Fitzherbert (or his brother John, sometimes identified as the author). Fitzherbert explains that his book is vital because it helps the yeoman perform his duties, and it is yeomen who defend and maintain all other orders, and best represent their collective interest.[39] The *Boke*

---

[34] *Oceana*, 42, 46, 258, 267–8.

[35] *Oceana*, 30–3. *An Essay upon Two of Virgil's Eclogues* (1658), "A Note." Similar reports adapted from Livy: *Oceana*, 159–64.

[36] *Oceana*, 37–8. Harrington's source for British feudalism in *Oceana*, 34f. is John Selden's 1614 *Titles of Honour*.

[37] *Oceana*, 39–41. *Prerogative*, I.ix.54. This was a sudden shift in the balance of property, from monarchical to popular: *Art of Law-Giving*, III.i.26. Also see *Art of Law-Giving*, I.ii, where Harrington cites Bacon's analysis of the impact of Henry VII on land ownership structure. *Art of Law-Giving*, II.ii.40–1: good levelling is not done by the people but by some great man, as Moses, Joshua, Lycurgus; or as an unintended consequence, as in the case of Henry VII and Henry VIII.

[38] Hugh Trevor-Roper, "The Gentry, 1540–1640," *Economic History Review Supplement* 1 (1954). Pocock, *Ancient*, chapter 6.

[39] Compare Alexander Hamilton, *Federalist Papers* 35 (1788), on merchants as "the natural representatives" of all classes.

of Husbandire was reprinted often throughout the sixteenth century, and enjoyed a revival in the mid-seventeenth-century. It was almost always printed with Xenophon's *Oeconomicus*, showing the publisher's recognition of the connection between agriculture, household management, and participation in, and management of, the whole country's government and economy.

Another constitutional treatise that connects Harrington and the strand of ancient republicanism outlined above is *De Republica Anglorum* by Thomas Smith (1513–1577), first published in 1583. In Smith's view, a hallmark of a king, as opposed to a tyrant, is that the former "doth see the profit of the people as much as his owne."[40] In the service of Henry VIII, Smith made the Machiavellian point that papal influence on English law and character suppressed England's natural martial spirit,[41] and the kings of England owed no allegiance to the papacy.[42] Smith describes the household as resembling the government,[43] and colonisation as a natural extension of the family's growth.[44] Perhaps surprisingly, Smith considers rotation to be the natural political arrangement after the death of the first, founding *paterfamilias*. People, however, wish to become immortal through their posterity – hence the ambition for conquest. Both of these points are made in I.xiii on the rise of aristocracies, and echoed in Harrington's *Oceana*.[45]

Smith also praises yeomen, freeholders between gentlemen and labourers who "commonly live wealthily, keepe good houses, and doe their businesse and travell to acquire riches."[46] They farm gentlemen's lands, go to market, employ servants, shun idleness, and send their sons to university or raise them into gentlemen by other means. Then follow pages of praise for this new class, their ability to farm and to fight as archers and infantry and thereby save and expand England, unlike the equestrian French aristocracy, which continues to suffer defeats.

---

[40] *De Republica Anglorum*, I.vii.10. Note how this formulation of complementary interests differs from many others, from Plato to John of Salisbury or Aquinas, in which only the tyrant, not the king, has interests that are distinct from his people's interests.

[41] *De Republica Anglorum*, III.iii.212–13. Smith's account of mercenaries, the danger of wandering troops and *condottieri*, and the consequent rise in violent factionalism, is also Machiavellian. III.iv.216–17. Further insistence that England's spirit is strongly and primarily military: III.v.229, III.ix.246, *passim*. Smith discusses and offers conjectures about some constitutional continuities between the England of his time, and before conversion to Christianity, in III.xi.

[42] *De Republica Anglorum*, I.ix.18–19. All religious courts owed their authority to the king: III.xi.269.

[43] *De Republica Anglorum*, I.xi.25.   [44] *De Republica Anglorum*, I.xii.26–27.

[45] Arihiro Fukuda, *Sovereignty and the Sword: Harrington, Hobbes, and Mixed Government in the English Civil Wars* (Clarendon Press, 1997) describes other textual links between Smith and Harrington.

[46] *De Republica Anglorum*, I.xxiii.60.

When Smith explains that common law does not abide torture, but it allows the death penalty, he strongly hints that the free and tough yeomen best reflect, and perhaps determine, the ancient and new *mores* of England.[47] Finally, Smith speculates that the English "yeomen" comes from the Dutch "yonker."[48] Like Fitzherbert's, Smith's book underwent a remarkable revival and numerous editions in the middle of the seventeenth century.

Although he builds on an English version of the tradition of appreciating farmer-soldier-citizens as a uniquely powerful political and historical agent, vested in land yet able to both defend and expand the state, Harrington thought that the Civil War brought a rare opportunity. The Roman model, England's exceptional temporary advantage over other European countries under the Protectorate due to having adjusted its form of government to match its balance of property, and England's most martial character, combined to support the creation of a republican empire. "The Sea giveth law unto the growth of Venice, but the growth of Oceana giveth law unto the Sea."[49] The first question of the republican imperial agenda is how to settle England's conquering army. It is not possible to strengthen and control it by turning the newly conquered land into a monarchy, or by using military colonies the way the Roman emperors did. Turning the veterans' lands into hereditary holdings, whether with a popular or aristocratic dominion, creates a "Nationall interest" distinct from the motherland's. Trying to conserve the balance on the motherland's side by taxing the colonies is a non-starter. Taxes cannot raise enough money; they can only cause resentment.[50] The only option left is to conquer new lands, and settle the veterans with benefices. The next question is what current residents of the foreign lands in England's crosshairs will think of all this.

III

"If you have subdued a Nation that is capable of liberty, you shall make them a present of it." (Harrington, *Oceana*)

The republican empire, Harrington points out, begins at home. There is Scottish courage, but Scotland had too many noblemen, and fell to

---

[47] *De Republica Anglorum*, II.xvii.197.

[48] He makes a similar Dutch-English etymological connection between legal concepts in *De Republica Anglorum*, III.x.258–9.

[49] *Oceana*, Introduction. Compare the British maritime exceptionalism in Somos, "Selden's *Mare Clausum*: The Secularisation of International Law and the Rise of Soft Imperialism," *Journal of the History of International Law* 14:2 (2012), 287–330.

[50] *Oceana*, 44.

England.[51] Ireland is soft and cannot produce soldiers. The best thing would have been to repopulate it with Jews, who were excellent farmers in Canaan, and learned commerce in the diaspora.[52] They should have received freedom of religion, and been allowed to combine agriculture with trade, opening free ports in Ireland. England should have installed a provincial army for protection, and reaped the rewards from the customs that Ireland's Jewish agriculture and trade would have generated.[53] Since the opportunity to resettle Ireland with Jews has passed, Harrington offers a cautious scheme to encourage Ireland, the Anglo-Irish nobility, and new English settlers to approximate the Scottish state of development, in which a willingness to fight for England's empire will be rewarded with the kind of provincial autonomy that Sigonius found in ancient Rome. Once Scotland and Ireland are integrated, Harrington argues that England can field a huge army for foreign conquest, thanks to the agrarian, and to Scottish and Irish auxiliaries. Rome was right, and modern princes are wrong: wars should be fought with huge citizen armies, not mercenaries. Large citizen armies give the public a stake in the war and are likely to produce quick victories, thereby saving money.[54]

There are numerous passages in Harrington's works that deal with the history of imperialism, and describe his proposed international order for governing military, political, and commercial relations between the provinces, the mother country, and the metropolis.[55] The influence of Sigonius and the colonial strand of republican imperialism is ubiquitous.

---

[51] *Oceana*, Introduction. *Oceana*, 259–60: Scotland lost because it was successful at expansion, like England, and therefore had to be confronted.

[52] Harrington's reference to the missed opportunity of repopulating Ireland probably refers to the Rump Parliament's *Act for the Settling of Ireland* (August 1652), which proposed mass executions and sweeping land confiscation. Harrington on the Rump as a missed opportunity in general: Fukuda, *Sovereignty*, chapters 5, 6. Harrington notes that God instructed the Jews to expel all Canaanites before they settled down: *Art of Law-Giving*, II.ii.42; although they failed: II.iii.60–1. Given Locke's familiarity with Harrington, *Oceana*'s Introduction is a likely source for the comparison of the Roman and Jewish republican combination of agriculture with government in *Some Thoughts Concerning Education* (London, 1693), §205.

[53] *Oceana*, Introduction, B1–2. Compare the commonplace in eighteenth-century imperialist debates, used i.a. against George Grenville, that trade and demographic growth of the colonies provide a market and revenues from commerce that far outweigh the costs of military protection. Freedom of religion a key to Rome's imperial success: *Prerogative*, II.ii.19.

[54] *Oceana*, 233–4. For Cromwell's policy toward Scotland and Ireland in the context of republican imperialism see Jim Smyth, "Empire-Building: The English Republic, Scotland and Ireland," in eds. Ariel Hessayon and David Finnegan, *Varieties of Seventeenth- and Early Eighteenth-Century English Radicalism in Context* (Ashgate Publishing, 2011), 129–44.

[55] Including *Prerogative*, I.iv, and II.ii.20–22.

If a state or region meets two conditions, namely readiness to implement the appropriate agrarian and willingness to help England expand, it comes under England's protection, and eventually sets up its own parliament, and/or obtains representation in Westminster.[56] It is important to maintain a mismatch between the local government of an imperial province, and its balance of property. Otherwise it comes into its own as a state, and becomes independent. This is particularly probable when the province is far from the mother country: "for men like flowers or roots being transplanted take after the soyl wherein they grow."[57] Another precondition of stability is keeping the clergy without land. A clergy with property starts playing politics, and transforms religion into superstition to increase its own power. This corruption, in turn, causes wars of religion among states.[58] Among the benefits bestowed by Harrington's empire are protection and freedom of conscience (not merely freedom of religion), both of which are in turn essential for keeping the republican empire peaceful and perpetual. Harrington calls this package of secularising, soft imperialist policies "the patronage of the world."[59]

This system is introduced at the end of *Oceana* and developed in *The Prerogative*. Harrington explains that Rome's "Patronage, and in that the Empire of the World," came about through different methods during its imperial life cycle. It started with colonies, and moved to "unequal Leagues." It only created colonies in Italy, never too far from Rome. If a city rebelled, Rome conquered it, but preserved its liberties, and settled Roman citizens on some of the land taken. Thus Rome earned a reputation for spreading liberty, while it rewarded soldiers and gained new citizens. As Rome later moved to unequal leagues as an instrument of empire, a distinction was made between social and provincial unequal leagues. Social leagues were either by "Latinity" or "Italian Right." The

---

[56] *Oceana*, 268–70. In the *Art of Law-Giving*, III.iv.101–3, Harrington proposes a somewhat more stringent system of colonial councils, although with the right of "provincials" to appeal to Westminster against the colonial government.

[57] *Oceana*, 8. See *Oceana*, 38, on the Normans ceasing to be "forraigne Plants" some time after the Conquest, and embracing Anglo-Saxon rights and liberties as their own. The Harringtonian language on the unfairness of the artificial imbalance in favour of the mother country, maintained by measures like the Navigation Acts, coupled with the impossibility of perpetually imposing them on distant colonies, was readily transformed from guidelines for British imperialism into criticism in the American colonies.

[58] *Prerogative*, I.ix.56–7. In *Oceana*, Harrington insists that there were no wars of religion before Christianity.

[59] *Oceana*, 259, 271, *Prerogative*, II.ii.19, 21, etc. Somos, "Irenic," 96–7; "*Mare Clausum, Leviathan*, and *Oceana*: Bible Criticism, Secularisation and Imperialism in Seventeenth-Century English Political and Legal Thought," in eds. Carly Crouch and Jonathan Stökl, *In the Name of God: The Bible in the Colonial Discourse of Empire* (Brill, 2014), 85–132. For a relevant formulation of soft imperialism see Somos, "Selden's *Mare Clausum*."

former approximated the Romans' own rights, the latter was without suffrage. Both offered a considerable degree of self-government. Provincial leagues, by contrast, were governed by Roman administrators. This range of statuses formed a continuum. Ideally, a province would move gradually toward greater liberty and affinity with Rome. Rome led Macedon, for instance, benignly to a more republican condition by granting and implementing Italian rights.

This is the model that Harrington boldly recommends, even though the Macedonians rebelled, and their status was downgraded.[60] The first major task for England is to firmly occupy Scotland and Ireland, and impose the agrarian laws and other arrangements befitting republican provinces. The conquering troops can settle down, create their own laws and magistrates, and raise the revenue produced there so greatly that the occupied natives will hugely benefit. "I appeal unto any man, whether the Empire described, can be other than the Patronage of the world."[61] The benignity of this "patronage" brand of imperialism is its own justification.[62] Importantly, this empire is based on natural expansion, not debt.[63]

In my reading, Harrington's system in *The Prerogative* foreshadows projects and variables that we normally think of as long eighteenth-century innovations. One reason for our difficulty in recognising Harrington as the ancestor of these innovations may be that mid-seventeenth-century schemes are normally associated with

---

[60] *Oceana*, 265.   [61] *Oceana*, 271.

[62] *Oceana*, 261–6. Compare Defoe's argument that valiant Scotland can only escape poverty via union with England: *Caledonia* (1706), 27–31, cited in Laurence Dickey, "Power, Commerce and Natural Law in Daniel Defoe's Political Writings, 1608–1707," in ed. John Robertson, *A Union for Empire: Political Thought and the British union of 1707* (Cambridge, 1995), 63–96.

[63] *Oceana*, 269–72. Another scheme for Scotland and Ireland in the *Art of Law-Giving*, III.iv.99–101 is to set £2,000 per year revenue as the cap in Ireland, and £500 in Scotland. A £4,500 income from land in Ireland, Scotland, and England together "maketh a Provincial Citizen" (100). This can drain some greed from England to Ireland; stimulate martial valour in Scotland, making it a source of auxiliary troops; stop the concentration of wealth in the provinces from turning "provincials" into slaves; and when the empire expands, similar limits can be established and still make both conquerors and the conquered richer than even their own nobility was before the conquest. Scotland as an excellent source of auxiliary troops: *Art of Law-Giving*, III.iv.105–6. On provincial status and representation for Scotland and Ireland: *Aphorisms Political* (2nd enlarged ed., 1659), XLIX–LVI.

Not all imperial expansion is soft power and civilising mission. In *Art of Law-Giving*, III.iv.108–9, Harrington admits that it is impossible to remove all risk that the provinces will be tyrannised, as at the end of the day, provinces must be held by arms. As mentioned above, Harrington thought that failing to repopulate Ireland was a mistake. For the army and investors vying for land in Ireland see John Cunningham, "Divided Conquerors: The Rump Parliament, Cromwell's Army and Ireland," *English Historical Review* CXXIX:539 (2014), 830–61, esp. 847–8, 853–8.

extra-European commercial and colonial expansion. Virtually all major figures in early modern English economic thought write about the virtues, dangers, and means of occupying and holding more of the Indies, Jamaica, the Caribbean, America, and Africa. Harrington seldom does. Instead, he recommends that England puts its domestic arrangements in order by introducing tribes and divisions, voting arrangements,[64] minimum 5,000 lots,[65] a bicameral parliament, agrarian laws and rotation,[66] a freeholding citizen militia and a nobility that resumes its military function,[67] agrarian laws in Scotland and Ireland,[68] and so on. The reformed England will dominate Europe, and it will need Holland, as Machiavelli's Florence needed Venice, as an outlet to benefit from trade. This makes it possible for England to enjoy the benefits of republican expansion and virtue, and for the rest of Europe to contain the moral and social threat of luxury, thanks to England's benign patronage and Holland's unique ability to remain uncorrupted and stable despite commerce, given the balance of money as its foundation. Significantly, Harrington also warns that if England fails to follow this course, the country most likely to do so is France, which would make England a province in France's European empire. Once the aforementioned reforms are in place, Harrington therefore calls for the conquest of France.[69] He also considers the possibility that other European states correct their outdated Gothic balance first.[70]

Why would Harrington construct this basic, rudimentary European project? Allow me to suggest three possible, distinct but compatible reasons. First, Scotland and Ireland posed clear and constant military challenges to the Protectorate. If Harrington's scheme was to have any chance of being taken seriously, it had to address land ownership structure, the nobility, the revenues needed to send and maintain troops, and the question of a stable arrangement between England, Scotland, and Ireland.[71]

---

[64] *Oceana*, 60f.   [65] *Oceana*, 100.   [66] *Oceana*, 22–3.

[67] Praise of militia: *Prerogative*, I.ix.64–5. The nobility should fight: *Oceana*, 228–9.

[68] *Oceana*, 87, 111–12. Introducing the agrarian will be a shock to Scotland. It will create liberty, bestow land on the people, and make Scotland depend on England for protection. Englishmen looking for good land will settle and improve Ireland. England can gradually lead Scotland to become a republic by mini-elections: *Oceana*, 176–7. Similarly, the Roman Republic allowed popular assemblies in its conquered provinces. *Prerogative*, II.v.70, etc.

[69] *Oceana*, 272. *Prerogative*, I.ix.60. *Art of Law-Giving*, III.iii.93–4, III.iv.97. France unstable: Harrington, "The Stumbling-Block of Disobedience & Rebellion..." (1658), 3. England reformed will have the greatest army: *Art of Law-Giving*, III.iv.106.

[70] *Prerogative*, I.x.79.

[71] See Smyth, "Empire-Building," for how Algernon Sidney, Henry Vane, Henry Neville, Michael Hawke and others thought about Ireland in the 1650s.

Second, in Harrington's historical analysis of the modern prudence that followed the fall of Rome, the feudal and Gothic balance
that underpinned the Scottish and Irish problem in the first place
extended to the whole of Europe. To use Harrington's term, the
Gothic balance made all European states profoundly sick.[72] England,
with a government reformed by the Civil War to better align with
its balance of property, had three choices: catch the same disease
again from its neighbours; fall under the dominion of another state
that cures itself (most probably France); or expand its republican,
benign patronage to countries suffering because their governments –
mostly monarchies – were still based on a Gothic foundation that
no longer existed. This effectively meant Europe, with a few exceptions: Venice was viable as a republic for preservation, and Genoa and
the Dutch were stable on their balance of money. The Gothic balance
was not a plausible reason for extending the republican empire over
these countries; but co-operation seemed possible and desirable.[73]

Although Harrington does not suggest Holland as a model for England, he admires the young mercantile state because it threw off a king
before England did, it does not allow priests to meddle in politics, it
shook off mighty Spain, it is keen on universities but does not take
religion too seriously, it pays counsellors of state properly, and it has an
in-built agrarian, ancient liberties, excellent agricultural practices, and
neither high priests nor civil wars.[74] As long as foreign trade does not
come to outweigh the rest of the English economy, or the economy of the

---

[72] "If France, Italy and Spain, were not all sick, all corrupted together, there would bee
none of them so, for the sick would not bee able to withstand the sound, nor the sound
to preserve her health without curing the sick. The first of these Nations (which if
you stay her leasure, will in my minde bee France) that recovers the health of ancient
Prudence, shall assuredly govern the world." *Oceana*, 272.

[73] In response to Wren, Harrington locates Swiss and Dutch liberties in their Gothic past,
albeit without using the term. *Prerogative*, I.vii.32. He does the same with Genoese and
Dutch liberties: *Prerogative*, I.x.76.

[74] *Oceana*, 39: Holland overthrew a king before Oceana. One wonders whether Harrington's point that Holland borrowed a foreign prince (*Oceana*, 25) may have been of
interest during the Glorious Revolution. *Oceana*, Model: Holland shook off Spain, pays
counsellors of state well, and has the right policies toward universities and ministers
who try to meddle with affairs of state. Holland's (and Switzerland's) in-built agrarian: *Oceana*, 94, 148. *Prerogative*, I.ix.63–4: Holland fought Spain "with such Courage
and Disdain, as is Admirable unto the World." *Prerogative*, I.x.78: "The *Hollander*, who
under a potent Prince, was but a Fisherman, with the restitution of the popular government, is become the better Souldier; nor hath been matcht but by a rising Commonwealth." *Prerogative*, I.x: ancient liberties of Holland; and great Dutch agriculture. *Pian
Piano* (1656): no high priest in Holland. "Pour enclouer le Canon:" no civil war. The
Rump also noted God's blessings upon Venice, Switzerland, and Holland: Blair Worden, "Liberty for Export: 'Republicanism' in England, 1500–1800," in eds. Mahlberg
and Wiemann, *European Contexts*, 13–32, at 22.

English republican empire as it expands in pursuit of Harrington's vision, there is no reason not to cooperate with or even emulate the Dutch. Banks and republics go together well. Read this way, Harrington's balance of property is not a reactionary defence of landed aristocracy and the rural way of life, but a caution against financial speculation that can desert or turn against the national interest at the drop of a hat.[75] One might even conjecture that Harrington presented Holland as a republic stable on the balance of money in order to prevent competition with England, which he described as stable and expansionary on the balance of property. This allowed Harrington in the aftermath of the First Anglo-Dutch War to frame a scheme for collaboration between the two potentially complementary, non-competing states.[76] This interpretation would make sense of De la Court's 1671/2 letter to Harrington, written at Harrington's request and echoing Slingsby Bethel, which proposed a Dutch-English alliance *because* the two countries were different.[77] The unequal leagues of Rome that Harrington recommends as an instrument of English expansion could easily accommodate such an alliance.

The third reason why Harrington's writings contain the framework and many elements of a European project is that he saw overseas, extra-European empires as failing, and did not have a solution. Harrington considered it an axiom of political science that colonies should be close to the mother country, otherwise they develop their own national interest and seek independence.[78] Another such axiom was that the mother

---

[75] One could also consider some of the proposals for land banks, and other instruments for turning land into monetised credit, as intermediary steps between Harrington's scheme and schemes like Bethel's; especially if they played on the advantage of England over Holland in having monetisable landmass. E.g. Otis Little's 1748 "Proposals for a New Currency in America," John Carter Brown Library, mss Codex=Eng33.

[76] Joint Anglo-Dutch schemes were common in the 1650s, Milton's among them. *Defence of the People of England*, 1651. Less well known is the extraordinary royalist adaptation of Harrington's Anglo-Dutch model in ca. 1672 *Pax et obedientia* (Beinecke, Osborn fb234), esp. 154–66, 284–5, 291–4, 316–25. Jonathan Scott, *Commonwealth Principles: Republican Writing of the English Revolution* (Cambridge University Press, 2004). Freya Cox Jensen, *Reading the Roman Republic in Early Modern England* (Brill, 2012). For Dutch reactions see Helmer Helmers, *The Royalist Republic: Literature, Politics and Religion in the Anglo-Dutch Public Sphere, 1639–1660* (Cambridge University Press, 2015). In 1776 Isaac de Pinto argued that the Dutch and the English were natural allies, and had to stop American independence together by using Dutch commercial power and raising revenue from undervalued English land. *Letters on the American Troubles*, 48–52, 61–2. Also see Koen Stapelbroek's chapter.

[77] Weststeijn, "Why the Dutch," 117–18. For Harrington's influence on De la Court and Spinoza see Hans Blom, "Popularizing Government: Democratic Tendencies in Anglo-Dutch Republicanism," in Mahlberg and Wiemann, *European Contexts*, 121–35.

[78] *Oceana*, 8. Repeated in *Prerogative*, I.iv. Albeit in criticism of Harrington, Heylyn makes a similar point about distance from the mother country and the risk of developing a distinct identity and interest in *Certamen Epistolare* (1659), 237–8, citing the Anglo-Irish as an example.

country's task was to overbalance the colonies, but not through taxation. As a cautionary tale, Harrington repeatedly refers to Spain, drained due to misaligned political economies of the mother country and its empire in the Indies.[79]

Identifying Harrington as the precursor of the strategy for continental empire that emerged in the eighteenth century shows the limited utility of debating whether English republican imperialism was neo-Roman or neo-Greek,[80] and that the construction of the history of feudalism, as part of this republican imperialism, was not a justification for a clean break, but part of English self-understanding of the Civil War as a natural development, given the shift in the balance of property, and the drive inherent in the common law toward popular sovereignty.[81] Harrington used the tradition discussed here, accommodating agriculture, commerce, empire and the republican form, to develop a plan of transition for Britain. The transition was predicated on the assumptions that the balance of property in England had shifted since Henry VII, and Scotland and Ireland could enter a relatively stable alliance or state of dependence. This Harringtonian transitional blueprint involved neither a violent nor a clean break with England's feudal past.[82] Viewed

---

[79] *Oceana*, 9. Cannot do it through taxation: *Oceana*, 44. However, Oceana should retain a little revenue from the provinces to finance "publick work" and further expansion: *Oceana*, 269. This is in keeping with Harrington's commentary on the Agreement of the People (perhaps against John Wildman's 1659 *The Leveller*) in the *Art of Law-Giving*, III.iii.81–2: the citizen army should be unpaid in the home counties and paid in the provinces, including Scotland and Ireland. In his 1637 defence of John Hampden, Sir Oliver St. John interpreted English custom to favour the same arrangement. T.B. Howell, *A Complete Collection of State Trials* (London, 1816), III.887–9. Burgess contrasts the Levellers' impracticable insistence on consent with Harrington's reliance on constitutional design. Glenn Burgess, *British Political Thought, 1500–1660* (Palgrave, 2009), 347–9.

[80] I agree with Scott, *Commonwealth Principles*, that political thinkers were oblivious to neither Greek nor Roman sources, and their choice or mixture of sources does not in itself indicate ideological allegiance.

[81] To characterise Harrington's diagnosis of feudalism as an "inherently unstable" system is an oversimplification. Pocock, "Machiavelli," 120.

[82] E.g. *Oceana*, 203–4, on reasons to stop destroying country estates. Also see passages against levelling: *Oceana*, 199, *Prerogative*, I.viii.44–5, I.xi.84, *Art of Law-Giving*, III, Preface. Harrington had good reasons to dissociate himself from the Levellers, since his proposals seemed *prima facie* similar for instance to John Lilburne's agrarian in *Lilburne Revived* (1653), 6–23, or *The Upright Man's Vindication* (1653), 6–22; although see Rachel Hammersley, "Rethinking the Political Thought of James Harrington: Royalism, Republicanism and Democracy," *History of European Ideas* 39:3 (2013), 354–70, at 368. Henry Ferne referred to Harrington's agrarian as levelling: *Pian Piano*, 3–4. The break with feudalism is a healing process: *Oceana*, 272. It took a long time to shift the balance of property from aristocratic to popular: Harrington, *Pian Piano*, 52. The existence of a discourse on feudalism as a common denominator in the laws of England and Scotland, and thus a protection against violent breaks, is suggested by Alain Wijffels' description of Thomas Craig, "De unione regnorum Britanniae tractatus" (1605), "A British *Ius Commune*? A Debate on the Union of the Laws of Scotland and England during the

in terms of re-establishing the long-standing connection between land-holding and military service, Harrington was not so much scrapping feudalism as expanding it to a system of popular obligations and popular sovereignty.[83]

IV

European projects like Harrington's are familiar to us from England from the early eighteenth century, from France after the 1690s, and Germany from the mid-eighteenth century. A unified European empire is a dominant template for political discourse by the second half of the eighteenth century. How can France, how can Prussia, how can Britain become "the friend of man," the law-giver and arbiter of international relations, or occupy everything and create an enlightened absolutist super-state, federal only in name, but spreading virtue and light? These questions in these forms do not fit the current historiographical focus on the 1650s' preoccupation with extra-European imperialism and rivalry. A close and contextual re-reading of *The Prerogative* therefore has several benefits. The next question is whether there is an actual link between Harrington and the eighteenth-century schemes for reordering Europe, or if Harrington's is merely an unusual sort of imperialism for the mid-seventeenth-century.

I will not summarise the work on Harrington's reception. Smith, Robbins, Blitzer, Pocock, Hont, Worden, Mahlberg, Hammersley, and others have explored much of Harrington's influence, ranging from his contemporaries in England to France and the American colonies until the end of the eighteenth century.[84] Although not on European

First Years of James VI/I's English Reign," *Edinburgh Law Review* 6:3 (2002), 315–55, at 334–7.

83 The same train of thought appears in St John's (unsuccessful) defence of Hampden in 1637. Howell, *State Trials*, III.862–4.

84 For Harrington's influence on the 1780 Massachusetts constitution see Smith, *Harrington*. On Fletcher and Davenant: Hont, *Jealousy*, 65, 213, 262–3. On Smith and Hume: Hont, *Politics in Commercial Society: Jean-Jacques Rousseau and Adam Smith* (Harvard University Press, 2015), 80–1, 83. On a 1793 French constitutional draft: S.V. Liljegren (ed.), *A French Draft Constitution of 1792 Modelled on James Harringtons' Oceana* (Lund, 1932) and Rachel Hammersley, *The English Republican Tradition and Eighteenth-Century France: Between the Ancients and the Moderns* (Manchester University Press, 2010), 161–2. Also see Hammersley, 37 for a 1737 Huguenot review of Toland's edition, 74–8 on Montesquieu, 164f. on Harrington's influence on Sieyès, 189–94 on Rutledge, etc. See the studies in eds. Mahlberg and Wiemann, *European Contexts*. Pesante shows that John Adams borrowed Harringtonian points more straightforwardly than Pocock suggests. Maria Luisa Pesante, "Between Republicanism and the Enlightenment: Turgot and Adams," in eds. Manuela Albertone and Antonino De Francesco, *Rethinking the Atlantic World: Europe and America in the Age of Democratic Revolutions* (Palgrave, 2009), 61–79, at 73.

expansion, Harrington's proposals were seriously promoted by Henry Neville and Captain Baynes in Parliament in 1659.[85] His influence on Locke, Shaftesbury, Algernon Sidney, Walter Moyle, Trenchard and Gordon, Toland and Molesworth has also been discussed.[86] Adaptations by Andrew Fletcher, George Stuart, and Robert Watson of Harringtonian rationales for agrarian reform, civic militias, free ports, and reconstituting the relationship between England, Scotland and Ireland, and England and continental Europe, are best brought out by Iain McDaniel in this volume. Castleton's paper discusses the influence of Harrington's formulation of the balance of property on the thought of Proudhon, eighteenth-century views on Poland, and Molinari's book on Saint-Pierre. Here I would like to make a few complementary connections in order to broadly relate Harrington's project for the benign conquest of Europe by an England reformed as a commercial republic, to the history of political economy in the eighteenth century.

First of all, in addition to these readings and adaptations of Harrington's European scheme by Moyle, Molesworth, Fletcher, Stuart, and Watson, recovering the commercial and imperialist elements of Harrington's system allows us to reread texts like Neville's *Isle of Pines* (1668), Bethel's *A True and Impartial Narrative of the most Material Debates* (1659), revised as *Interest of the Princes and States of Europe* (1680), and even Defoe's "Standing Army" (1698), as adaptations of Harrington's analysis of the balance of property as a fundamental law that drives politics, commerce (as compatible with republican virtue, the balance of money as a special case of the balance of property), and pro-Dutch and anti-French English imperialism.[87] When the balance of money and the scheme for European empire are not neglected, Harrington's system emerges as closer to Bethel's and Defoe's, and the striking similarities noted in recent literature are no longer inexplicable.

In my interpretation, Harrington's Holland in *The Prerogative* also anticipates the model of a reformed state, Salentum, in François Fénelon's widely influential *Les aventures de Télémaque* (1694, 1699). To

---

[85] Thomas Burton, *Diary* (1656–9), ed. T.J. Rutt (London, 1828), III.133–4, 146–8. Harrington's circle submitted the Humble Petition of Divers Well-Affected Persons on 6 July 1659. Harrington prints his petition to Parliament, and the planned follow-up to the people, in *Valerius* (1659). Mahlberg's analyses of Neville's borrowings and transformations of Harringtonian arguments: *Neville*, 150–6, 159, *passim*. For Harrington's early influence also see Nelson, *Greek Tradition*, chapter 4.

[86] Pincus presents Molesworth's attempt, including the widely popular *Account of Denmark*, to reorientate England toward a European military and foreign policy "in defense of European liberty" in a way that looks quite Harringtonian. *1688*, 357–62.

[87] Scott, *England's Troubles*, 371. Mahlberg, *Neville*, 123–5 on *Isle of Pines*, and calling on England to follow the Dutch model. Defoe's link between liberty of conscience and commercial flourishing: Dickey, "Power," 93.

my knowledge, this continuity does not appear in the scholarly literature of the last few decades. Tracing this genealogy also explains why Fénelon rejected Claude Fleury's combination of the idealised republic of simple manners and no commerce with the biblical polity (*Mœurs des Israelites*, 1681) as a source of *Télémaque* in favour of a commercial republican model, patterned on Harrington (and perhaps on an intermediary like De la Court).[88] This model relies neither on the biblical template, which proved inherently divisive and irresolvably contentious and thus unable to frame constructive debate over reform, nor on the Roman republican one, which was almost equally contentious (and would have been certainly more dangerous to invoke in a morality tale for *le Petit Dauphin*). Instead, it invokes a fictional one, set in the Homeric world. *Oceana* links up with *Télémaque*. In choice of genre, fictional setting, and policy advice, Fénelon's choices become clearer in this light.[89]

Montesquieu's 1748 *Spirit of the Laws* may also owe more to Harrington than his oft-cited dismissive remark on Harrington's utopianism suggests.[90] For instance, the Republic of Marseilles under Rome, in Book XXI ch. 11, strongly recalls Holland in Harrington's European project. If one assumes that Montesquieu thought that commerce could not be suppressed, one also wonders whether Harrington's insistence on personal involvement in agriculture and fighting, and on the close connection between the smallness of the Genoese and Dutch republics and their ability to accommodate commerce without corruption, served as an inspiration for Montesquieu's point that republics had to remain small to survive. Furthermore, Montesquieu's account of the English system in Book XIX resembles Harrington's reform proposal for England, except the agrarian law takes the form of high taxes. According to Montesquieu, England is rich, industrial, and commercial, yet thanks to heavy taxes it has little room for idleness.[91] Montesquieu's view is that one cannot easily transplant this system, but one can globalise

---

[88] Blom, "Popularizing Government."

[89] Strategic irenicism is partly explained in Somos, "Irenic." For early eighteenth-century English appropriations of *Télémaque* to support Britain's "Right to set all Europe free," see Doohwan Ahn, "From Idomeneus to Protesilaus," in eds. C. Schmitt-Maass, S. Stockhorst, and D. Ahn, *Fénelon in the Enlightenment: Traditions, Adaptations, and Variations* (Rodopi, 2014), 99–128, at 104–6. For Fénelonian novels as political economy treatises see Somos, "The Lost Treasures of Sethos, Enlightened Prince of Egypt (1731)," in ed. Paschalis Kitromilides, *Athenian Legacies: European Debates on Citizenship* (Florence, 2014), 271–314.

[90] *The Spirit of the Laws* (eds. A.M. Cohler et al., Cambridge, 1989), Part II, 11.6, 166.

[91] Compare Adam Smith on the Dutch necessity of preferring business to idleness: *Wealth of Nations*, I.ix.108. Another possible inspiration may be Harrington's "Genius of the Nations," which he often invokes to explain different outcomes in otherwise identical circumstances. E.g. *Oceana*, 32.

the commercial spirit. Taxation, especially progressive or land tax, functions like Harrington's caps on land ownership. This link between Harrington and Montesquieu allows us to ask new questions, such as: how does public debt fit into the history of the agrarian? Is there an eighteenth-century discourse in favour of public debt not because of its industrial and military benefits but because it allows taxes to stay high, and thereby keep both luxury and idleness at bay?

While drawing out such implications is beyond this chapter's scope, it is useful to ask whether later readers understood that Harrington proposed a European imperialist project. A particularly strong test of this thesis is American colonial readings more than a century after *Oceana* and *The Prerogative* were first published. One would expect Harrington's relevance to consist mostly of American colonists and imperial administrators contesting specific criteria of English imperialism's benignity and the hallmarks of the colonies' maturity. Indeed, we find both numerous explicit invocations of Harrington and strongly Harringtonian language in texts concerning the representation of the colonies, counterproductive taxation, provincial strategies to escape entanglement in the pernicious rivalries of large states, the unfairness of the artificial imbalance in favour of the mother country, the natural tendency of distant colonies toward independence, and so on. Alongside the Harringtonian framework of these discussions, some direct textual references to Harrington in the American colonial literature are discussed in studies mentioned above, including Smith's and Blitzer's. Further evidence can be added, ranging from the dissemination of Harrington's works, through previously unrecognised Harringtonian references in Galloway, Dickinson, Paine, and others, to unusual forms of reception such as using Harrington as a pen name.[92] Crucially, some texts also show that the European focus of Harrington's imperialism was not yet forgotten.

Since Caroline Robbins' 1959 article, little attention has been paid to the thorough intellectual debt of Thomas Pownall, Governor of

---

[92] The 1737 version of Toland's edition of Harrington's *Works* appears in the 1741 catalogue of the Library Company of Philadelphia, the 1754 New York Society Library catalogue, and Thomas Hollis donated his annotated copy to Harvard in 1764 (Houghton Soc 730.1.2*). Representation and unfair trade: Joseph Galloway, "Candid Examination..." (1775), 35–9. John Dickinson and Charles Thomson, "To the Author of a Pamphlet, entitled 'A Candid Examination'..." (1775). Galloway, "Reply" (1775), 29–30. On the power of provincial governments: Galloway, "Candid Examination," 9, 20–1, 55. Union among unequals as a form of imperial government: Galloway, "Candid Examination," 58–9. A coherent use of Harrington to outline comprehensive British imperial reform is John Adams, Novanglus VII, 6 March 1775. As pen name, perhaps by Benjamin Rush: "Harrington, To the Freemen of the United States," *Pennsylvania Gazette*, 30 May 1787. *Oceana*, 80, 176, prefiguring Jefferson on periodic revolutions.

Massachusetts and later MP, to Harrington.[93] Pownall's *Principles of Polity* (1752), published the year before his first mission to America, is already full of enthusiastic endorsements of Harrington, whom Pownall finds more pragmatic and compelling than utopia-writers and other "Wild-shavers."[94] So are Pownall's later writings, including the *Administration of the Colonies* (1764), much discussed by Benjamin Franklin, John Adams, Thomas Paine, and others. James Otis, Jr.'s *The Rights of the British Colonies Asserted and Proved* (1764), among other things a direct response to Pownall's *Administration*, is an oft-cited source in histories of the American Revolution. Rights, property, and the state of nature are among its prominent themes.[95] Less famously, Otis praises "the great, the incomparable *Harrington*" and his demonstration in *Oceana* "and other divine writings, that Empire follows the balance of *property*," even though Otis disagrees with Harrington on this score and derives government from man's natural needs instead.[96] However, Otis agrees with Harrington that Rome fell due to its failure to balance the senate with the people, and its mismanagement of the provinces.[97] He also agrees that Britain is closest to perfection among European states, but vulnerable to challenges.

The *British* constitution in theory and in the present administration of it, in general comes nearest the idea of perfection, of any that has been reduced to practice; and if the principles of it are adhered to, it will, according to the infallible prediction of *Harrington*, always keep the *Britons* uppermost in *Europe*, 'till their only rival nation shall either embrace that perfect model of a commonwealth given us by that author, or come as near it as *Great-Britain* is. Then indeed, and not till then, will that rival and our nation either be eternal confederates, or contend in greater earnest than they have ever yet done, till one of them shall sink under the power of the other, and rise no more.[98]

Pownall and Otis understood that Europe was the primary context for Harrington's imperial calculations. The reception of Harrington's

---

[93] "An Active and Intelligent Antiquary, Governor Thomas Pownall," *Pennsylvania History* 26:1 (1959), 1–20.

[94] *Principles*, 29–30. Wholly Harringtonian arguments on 69–72, 139–41. Pownall donated a copy to Harvard, with a long note, in 1764 (Houghton *EC75.P8758.752p(A)).

[95] Somos, "From Rightless Savage to the Chosen Nation: The Founders' Response to European States of Nature," presented at *Reforming the European State in the Long Eighteenth Century*, Vadstena, Sweden, 12 September 2008.

[96] *Right*, 10. Otis also uses Harringtonian language about popular sovereignty and the "superstructures" of government (e.g. *Rights*, 17), and analogies between politics and cosmology (e.g. 20). Otis addressing Pownall's *Administration*: *Rights*, 61, 72, 74–5, 77, 79, 95–6, etc.

[97] *Right*, 78, has a strongly Harringtonian analysis of Roman emperors' colonial policies, and Gothic property relations.

[98] *Right*, 21. Also 61: "The cards are shuffling fast through all Europe. Who will win the prize is with God." The "next universal monarchy" should go to Britain.

scheme of republican patronage, with its provisions for advanced provinces' representation in Parliament, is one reason why Pownall, Otis and others were able to argue that the Grenville government violated the Colonies' right to representation, while they also disregarded facts, because the lack of parliamentary representation meant that details of colonial political economy could not be presented even when they affected the mother country or the whole empire.[99] Otis is of course most famous for rejecting the legitimacy of British taxation, both because it is illegitimate, and bad political economy.[100]

V

It may be time for a thoroughgoing reinterpretation of Harrington. Adding European imperialism and the balance of money to our reading brings new questions into focus. Harrington's commercial republicanism now emerges as an influential precursor to the eighteenth-century idea of benign, land-based republican empire. Harrington's project lives on, for example, in the language and reasoning of American colonial objections to taxation without representation, as well as in projects to turn the mixed political economy of European alliances against France.[101] His scheme also provoked specific counter-schemes, such as endorsements of public debt as a means for war finance, or the development of complex financial services disconnected from land. Finally, Harrington's mixed political economy of the English balance of property and the Dutch balance of money was transformed into early-eighteenth-century debates over the balance of trade and currency. What changed was not the discovery of capital, but the conflation of the two sides of Harrington's imperial vision.

[99] *Right*, 53–4; and 65–6 for another Harringtonian train of thought: unlike the Colonies, Ireland is a conquered country. Even then, they can earn the right to freedom. Pownall wrote to Thomas Hutchinson from London on 9 September 1767 that the colonists will fail to gain exemption from taxation, but should and ought to strive for and win representation at Westminster. *Collections of the Massachusetts Historical Society* vol. 1, series 3 (Boston, 1825), 148–9.

[100] *Rights*, 81–3, 103–5. On Otis and John Adams praising and following Harrington see Smith, *Harrington*, chapter VIII. Another important means of transmission between Harrington and the Founders is *Cato's Letters* (1720–23) by John Trenchard and Thomas Gordon. See e.g. Letter 35, "Of publick spirit," 1721, in *Cato's Letters*, ed. Ronald Hamowy (Liberty, 1995), I.253 on the agrarian, Letter 106 (1722), II.748–9 on the Harringtonian system of colonies to settle veterans or to advance trade, and 750 on soft imperialism.

[101] See Isaac Nakhimovsky's chapter in this volume.

2 The enlightened prince and the future of Europe

Voltaire and Frederick the Great's Anti-Machiavel of 1740

Isaac Nakhimovsky

Frederick of Prussia's joint venture with Voltaire, the *Anti-Machiavel* of 1740, has often been taken to be a disingenuous, or at best misleading declaration of the primacy of virtue and justice in politics.[1] By the end of 1740, its newly crowned but still anonymous author had already invaded Silesia, engulfing Europe in war. At the turn of the twentieth century, the *Anti-Machiavel* was influentially cast by the historian Friedrich Meinecke as emblematic of a broader eighteenth-century failure to overcome the tension between its enlightened values and its genuinely Machiavellian power politics: the *Anti-Machiavel*, in this view, proclaimed the former while affirming the necessity of the latter.[2] Meinecke's interpretative framework leaves unexplained what it was that the *Anti-Machiavel* was designed to do, and more recent attempts to connect the political theory articulated in the *Anti-Machiavel* to Frederick's subsequent manner of exercising power have not supplied a convincing answer to that question.[3]

In fact, this chapter will show, the *Anti-Machiavel* sought to explain how to participate in a new kind of international order: a new kind of balance of power that, as Voltaire put it, had turned Europe into "a great

---

[1] Or, in Thomas Babington Macaulay's words, as "an edifying homily against rapacity, perfidy, arbitrary government, unjust war, in short, against almost every thing for which its author is now remembered among men." "Frederic the Great," in *Critical and Historical Essays, Contributed to The Edinburgh Review*, vol. 2 (London: Longmans, Green and Co., 1866), 2:250.

[2] Friedrich Meinecke, *Machiavellism: The Doctrine of Raison D'état and Its Place in Modern History*, trans. Douglas Scott (New Haven: Yale University Press, 1957), 272–342.

[3] See Theodor Schieder's 1983 biography, *Frederick the Great*, trans. Sabina Berkeley and H.M. Scott (Harlow: Longman, 2000), 75–89; Massimo Mori, "Federico II e Machiavelli: Una reinterpretazione," *Etica & Politica* 17, no. 3 (2015): 9–31.

republic divided into many states."[4] This vision of a "great republic" did not amount to a vision of "perpetual peace" as articulated by the Abbé de Saint-Pierre, in which an institutionalized legal order above states allowed the reciprocity of *doux commerce* to definitively supersede military competition.[5] Nor, however, did the *Anti-Machiavel* regard commerce solely as an arena for power politics, as it had been by writers like the Bristol merchant John Cary, who saw an empire to monopolize trade as a means for overcoming a rival power: a "neo-Machiavellian" perspective that David Hume labeled "jealousy of trade."[6] Rather, the *Anti-Machiavel* joined Hume in claiming that commerce could exert a moderating influence on competition among European states. It would not serve as a substitute for a balance of power, but as a means of stabilizing its operation. Such attempts to define a stable middle ground between perpetual peace and power politics cannot match the analytical clarity of either Cary's or Saint-Pierre's understanding of the balance of power. As the most interesting recent literature has emphasized, it is in fact the latter's cosmopolitan critique of the idea of a balance of power that offers the most clear-sighted treatment of that concept.[7] The aim of this chapter is to locate the *Anti-Machiavel*'s vision of Europe's future in this context, and to identify its significance for modern international political thought.

As this chapter will also show, this vision of Europe shaped the *Anti-Machiavel*'s engagement with Machiavelli's *The Prince*. The *Anti-Machiavel* was a chapter-by-chapter commentary on Machiavelli's text

---

[4] Voltaire, *Le siècle de Louis XIV*, in *Oeuvres historiques*, ed. René Pomeau (Paris: Gallimard, 1968), 620.

[5] On "doux commerce" see Albert Hirschman, *The Passions and the Interests: Political Arguments for Capitalism Before Its Triumph* (Princeton University Press, 1977).

[6] David Hume, "Of the Jealousy of Trade," in *Essays: Moral, Political, and Literary*, ed. Eugene Miller, Rev. ed (Indianapolis: Liberty Classics, 1987), 327–31. On "jealousy of trade" in Enlightenment thought and on "neo-Machiavellian political economy" see Istvan Hont, *Jealousy of Trade: International Competition and the Nation-State in Historical Perspective* (Cambridge: Harvard University Press, 2005). On John Cary in this context see Sophus A. Reinert, *Translating Empire: Emulation and the Origins of Political Economy* (Cambridge: Harvard University Press, 2011).

[7] See especially Bruno Bernardi, "L'idée d'équilibre européen dans le jus gentium des modernes: esquisse d'histoire conceptuelle," in *Penser l'Europe au XVIIIe siècle: commerce, civilisation, empire*, ed. Antoine Lilti and Céline Spector (Oxford: Voltaire Foundation, 2014), 19–46. On Saint-Pierre's "réalisme" see also Olaf Asbach, *Staat und Politik zwischen Absolutismus und Aufklärung: Der Abbé de Saint-Pierre und die Herausbildung der französischen Aufklärung bis zur Mitte des 18. Jahrhunderts* (Hildesheim: G. Olms, 2005); Céline Spector, "L'Europe de l'abbé de Saint-Pierre," in *Les projets de l'abbé Castel de Saint-Pierre, 1658–1743: pour le plus grand bonheur du plus grand nombre*, ed. Carole Dornier and Claudine Poulouin (Caen: Maison de la recherche en sciences humaines, Université de Caen Basse-Normandie, 2011), 39–49.

that Frederick undertook in 1739 with Voltaire's encouragement and guidance.[8] Contrary to Meinecke's view, the *Anti-Machiavel*'s moral condemnations of Machiavelli, and its claim to have superseded the politics of *The Prince*, did not amount to the claim that moral virtue, as opposed to self-interest, ought to guide the conduct of the prince. In fact, as its title ultimately indicated, the *Anti-Machiavel* constituted a revision rather than a rejection of the idea of reason of state – an idea closely associated in the eighteenth century with Machiavelli. In Voltaire's editorial hands, the title of Frederick's original manuscript, the *Réfutation du Prince de Machiavel*, became the *Anti-Machiavel, ou essai de critique sur le Prince de Machiavel, publié par M. de Voltaire*.[9] At the same time, however, the *Anti-Machiavel* was also a critical intervention in a literature that sought to articulate a moral alternative to reason of state: a literature that includes, most importantly for Frederick and Voltaire, the Archbishop Fénelon's celebrated epic *The Adventures of Telemachus, son of Ulysees*.[10]

The first part of this chapter shows how Frederick and Voltaire positioned the *Anti-Machiavel* in relation to Machiavelli's politics – especially as interpreted by the late-seventeenth-century critic Amelot de la Houssaye – as well as Fénelon's. As we shall see, the *Anti-Machiavel*'s attempt to define an enlightened form of reason of state was not grounded solely in moral claims about the nature of kingship. Rather, it also drew on Voltaire's contributions to a much broader set of early-eighteenth-century discussions concerning political economy and the nature of a

---

[8] Frederick announced his intention to undertake such a project in March 1739, having previously objected to Voltaire's inclusion of Machiavelli in a list of great figures of his age in a draft of what became the *Age of Louis XIV*. Frederick of Prussia to Voltaire, 31 March 1738, in François Marie Arouet de Voltaire, *Correspondence and Related Documents*, ed. Theodor Bestermann, Oeuvres Complètes de Voltaire (Geneva: Institut et musée Voltaire, 1969-), vol. 89, D1476; and 22 March 1739, in *Correspondence*, Oeuvres Complètes 90, D1950. On the correspondence between Voltaire and Frederick and the many twists and turns in their relationship see Christiane Mervaud, *Voltaire et Frédéric II: une dramaturgie des lumières, 1736–1778*, Studies on Voltaire and the eighteenth century 234 (Oxford: The Voltaire Foundation at the Taylor Institution, 1985).

[9] Werner Bahner and Helga Bergmann, "Introduction," in *Anti-Machiavel*, by François Marie Arouet de Voltaire, Oeuvres Complètes 19 (Oxford: Voltaire Foundation, 1996), 94–5.

[10] On Fénelon and reason of state theory see Albert Chérel, "L'Anti-Machiavélisme de Fénelon et la 'Conversion' du Roi," in *Mélanges Albert Dufourcq* (Paris, 1932), 181–93; Lucien Jaume, "Fénelon critique de la déraison d'Etat," in *Raison et déraison d'Etat*, ed. Yves Charles Zarka (Paris: Presses Universitaires de France, 1994), 395–422. On Fénelon as educator see Jacques Le Brun, "Du privé au public: l'éducation du prince selon Fénelon," in *Le savoir du prince: du Moyen Age aux Lumières*, ed. Ran Halévi (Paris: Fayard, 2002), 235–60. On Fénelon's importance for eighteenth-century thought see Albert Chérel, *Fénelon au XVIIIe siècle en France (1715–1820) Son prestige – Son influence* (Fribourg: Imp. Fragnière frères, 1917); Christoph Schmitt-Maaß, Stefanie Stockhorst, and Doohwan Ahn, *Fénelon in the Enlightenment: Traditions, Adaptations, and Variations: With a Preface by Jacques Le Brun* (Rodopi, 2014).

distinctively modern form of monarchical government.[11] The remainder of the chapter then shows how these discussions in turn formed the basis for a vision of Europe's future that amounted to a controversial substitute for the Abbé de Saint-Pierre's perpetual peace project. The resulting debate, including the subsequent responses to the *Anti-Machiavel* by Saint-Pierre and his admirers and defenders (the most interesting and formidable of whom was Jean-Jacques Rousseau), reveals a recurring pattern in modern international political thought.

"Anti-Machiavellianism" is a notoriously diffuse category. For Voltaire, as for Pierre Bayle and others, it referred to critical commentaries on Machiavelli's *The Prince*, beginning with Innocent Gentillet's *Anti-Machiavel* of 1576.[12] However, many of these commentaries can just as plausibly be described as "Machiavellian": though they might purport to restore moral content to the concept of self-interest, or in classical terms to reassert the compatibility of the *utile* with the *honestum* (the advantageous with the honorable), in fact many served to legitimate as "true" reasons of state the tactics that Machiavelli had advocated.[13] Voltaire was breezily dismissive of this earlier literature, advising Frederick not to bother with it.[14] Instead, Voltaire used his editorial preface to launch a sharp attack on Amelot de la Houssaye, the ex-diplomat turned historian

---

[11] On the scope of these discussions see above all Michael Sonenscher, *Before the Deluge: Public Debt, Inequality, and the Intellectual Origins of the French Revolution* (Princeton University Press, 2007), chap. 2. On the failure of many discussions of Frederick's "enlightened absolutism" to distinguish sufficiently between a form of government and a style of rule see Simone Zurbuchen, "Theorizing Enlightened Absolutism: The Swiss Republican Origins of Prussian Monarchism," in *Monarchisms in the Age of Enlightenment: Liberty, Patriotism, and the Common Good*, ed. John Christian Laursen, Luisa Simonutti, and H.W. Blom (University of Toronto Press, 2007), 240–66.

[12] François Marie Arouet de Voltaire to Frederick of Prussia, 1 June 1740, in Voltaire, *Correspondence*, Oeuvres Complètes 91, D2214; Pierre Bayle, "Machiavel," in *The Dictionary Historical and Critical of Mr. Peter Bayle*, vol. 4 (London, 1737), 10–17. On this tradition see José A. Fernández-Santamaria, "Reason of State and Statecraft in Spain (1595–1640)," *Journal of the History of Ideas* 41, no. 3 (September 1980): 355–79; Robert Bireley, *The Counter-Reformation Prince: Anti-Machiavellianism or Catholic Statecraft in Early Modern Europe* (Chapel Hill: University of North Carolina Press, 1990); Alain Dierkens, ed., *L'antimachiavelisme de la renaissance aux lumières*, Editions de l'Université de Bruxelles 8, 1997; H. Höpfl, "Orthodoxy and Reason of State," *History of Political Thought* 23, no. 2 (2002): 211–37.

[13] On this pattern see "Pact with the Devil: the Ethics, Politics and Economics of Anti-Machiavellian Machiavellism," a collection of essays edited by Ioannis D. Evrigenis and Mark Somos, and their introduction, "Wrestling with Machiavelli," *History of European Ideas* 37, no. 2 (2011): 85–93. On "true" reasons of state see Richard Tuck, *Philosophy and Government, 1572–1651* (Cambridge University Press, 1993).

[14] Voltaire to Frederick of Prussia, 1 June 1740, in Voltaire, *Correspondence*, Oeuvres Complètes 91, D2214.

who, Jacob Soll has claimed, was "the only Frenchman openly defending Machiavelli in late seventeenth-century Paris."[15]

The *Anti-Machiavel's* engagement with Amelot was not straightforward. In 1739 Frederick reported to Voltaire that Amelot had come to his attention because someone to whom he had disclosed his plan to refute Machiavelli had told him that this would be a wasted effort, since Amelot had already produced a "complete refutation" of the *Prince* in his commentary on Tacitus's history. Upon investigation, Frederick told Voltaire, he did not find that Amelot had refuted "the work as a whole" (*l'ouvrage en corps*) but only "some maxims of that dangerous and detestable politics."[16] Though Frederick himself originally used a different edition of *The Prince* – a French translation by Henri Desbordes published in 1696 – Voltaire went to considerable lengths, at Frederick's instigation, to ensure that Frederick's commentary was bound together with Amelot's 1683 translation of *The Prince* into French, complete with the preface and notes in which Amelot had elaborated his interpretation of Machiavelli.[17] Arranging the two texts side by side, Voltaire explained in his preface, was supposed to bring together the poison with the antidote.[18] However, as Soll has pointed out, in making the *Anti-Machiavel* into a multilayered commentary on a commentary, this strategy preserved an important formal link to the humanist reason of state literature that Amelot himself was instrumental in reviving in the final decades of the seventeenth century.[19] In taking this form, the *Anti-Machiavel* differentiated itself in a significant way from the most formidable contemporary statement of a moral alternative to reason of state, namely Fénelon's *Télémachus*, which first appeared in 1699 and was published in full in 1715. The *Anti-Machiavel's* relationship to Fénelon's famous work is spelled out in an anonymous review of the *Anti-Machiavel* – a review that Voltaire wrote himself in 1740:

The author [Jean Terrasson] of a novel, entitled *Séthos*, said that if the well-being of the world could arise from a book, it would arise from *Télémachus*. May it be permitted for us to say that in this regard the *Anti-Machiavel* surpasses even the *Télémachus*. The one is principally made for young people, the other for men.

---

[15] Jacob Soll, *Publishing the Prince: History, Reading, & the Birth of Political Criticism* (Ann Arbor: University of Michigan Press, 2005), 96.

[16] Frederick of Prussia to Voltaire, 6 November 1739, in Voltaire, *Correspondence*, Oeuvres Complètes 91, D2214.

[17] For a full discussion see Charles Paul Fleischauer, "Voltaire and the Anti-Machiavel of Frederick the Great" (Ph.D., Harvard University, 1952), 15.

[18] François Marie Arouet de Voltaire, *Anti-Machiavel, ou essai de critique sur le prince de Machiavel, publié par M. de Voltaire*, Oeuvres Complètes 19 (Oxford: Voltaire Foundation, 1996), 106.

[19] Soll, *Publishing the Prince*, 116.

The pleasant and moral novel *Télémachus* is a tissue of incredible adventures, and the *Anti-Machiavel* is full of real examples, taken from history. The novel inspires an almost ideal virtue, and principles of government made for a fantastical age, which one might call heroic. It wants, for example, to divide citizens into seven classes: it gives each class distinctive clothing, it entirely bans luxury, which is perhaps the soul of a great state, and the principle of commerce. The *Anti-Machiavel* inspires a practical virtue, and its principles are applicable to all the governments of Europe.[20]

This review, which was printed together with several subsequent editions of the *Anti-Machiavel*, shows that the aim of the project was to supersede Fénelon's politics as well as Amelot's. It sought to translate the moral message of the former into the historical idiom promoted by the latter. The *Anti-Machiavel* emerges from Voltaire's review as a synthesis of Fénelon's moral tale with the Tacitist reason of state literature represented by Amelot: it sought to transfer Fénelon's ideals from the realm of classical fantasy to the real historical circumstances of modern European monarchies, just as, by taking the form of a commentary on Machiavelli, it translated them into the conventions of Tacitist reason of state literature.[21]

At the most basic level, the *Anti-Machiavel* aspired to replace Machiavelli's advice book with a very different account of the interests that ought to govern a prince. Its chief target in this enterprise was not so much Machiavelli's *The Prince* itself, however, as the conception of reason of state that Amelot had articulated in his commentary on that text. "He speaks much of reason of state in his dedicatory epistle," Voltaire wrote of Amelot, "but a man, who, having been secretary of an embassy, did not have the secret to rescue himself from poverty, poorly understands reason of state, in my opinion."[22] Voltaire and Frederick's distaste

---

[20] Voltaire, *Anti-Machiavel*, 497–8. This review was published by Pierre Paupie, the house that published the authorized version of the *Anti-Machiavel* in 1740, and subsequently appeared in other editions as well. For evidence of Voltaire's authorship see Bahner and Bergmann, "Introduction," 55–6. On Jean Terrasson and his novel *Sethos* see Mark Somos, "The lost treasures of Sethos, Enlightened Prince of Egypt (1731)," in *Athenian Legacies: European Debates on Citizenship*, ed. Paschalis Kitromilides (Florence: Leo S. Olschki, 2014), 271–314.

[21] The same form was adopted by some critics of the *Anti-Machiavel*, including Saint-Pierre; the result was a commentary on a commentary on a commentary. See Charles Irénée Castel de Saint-Pierre, *Réflexions sur l'Antimachiavel de 1740* (Beman, 1741); Ludwig Hess, *Historische und politische Anmerkungen über den Antimachiavel* (J.A. Berger, 1751).

[22] Voltaire, *Anti-Machiavel*, 108–9. The same criticism appears in Voltaire's "Catalogue de la plupart des écrivains français" in his *Le siècle de Louis XIV*: Voltaire, *Oeuvres historiques*, 1133. Voltaire's remark reflects an old trope about the mysteries of state. In fact, Amelot too had observed in the dedicatory letter to his edition of *The Prince* that "there are so few who know what reason of state is"; he attributed criticism of Machiavelli

for Amelot's politics was widely shared by contemporaries such as the Scottish commonwealthsman Thomas Gordon and the Huguenot printer Prosper Marchand.[23] The common denominator was a rejection of the severe Augustinianism that characterized much late-seventeenth-century moral theory.[24] Amelot had defended Machiavelli by presenting him as a faithful disciple of Tacitus who had correctly perceived the need for a distinct political morality and identified "certain maxims of state whose practice has become almost absolutely necessary because of the evil and perfidy of men."[25] According to Amelot, The Prince was a good guide for princes that showed them how to conduct themselves in a corrupt world where genuine virtue remained beyond the capacity of self-interested, fallen humanity. Machiavelli's The Prince had suggested that it was sufficient for princes to give the appearance of virtue.[26] Amelot, who defined political science as the science of reconciling reason of state with religion, interpreted this claim in a markedly Augustinian spirit.[27] In a world thoroughly corrupted by self-love, it would be prudent for

to this ignorance, and concluded that "one must be a prince, or at least a minister, in order to know, I do not say the usefulness, but the absolute necessity of these maxims." Abraham-Nicolas Amelot de La Houssaye, "Epitre," in Le prince de Nicolas Machiavel, ed. Abraham-Nicolas Amelot de La Houssaye (Amsterdam: Henry Wetstein, 1684). Cf. Machiavelli's own preface to The Prince, where he says that commoners have a better view of mysteries of state than those who practice them. By contrast, in encouraging Frederick, Voltaire emphasised the prince's unique authority to write about the mysteries of statecraft: "it is for a prince like you to instruct princes." Voltaire to Frederick of Prussia, 15 April 1739, Correspondence and Related Documents, Oeuvres Complètes 90, D1978.

23 Thomas Gordon, "Discourses upon Tacitus," in The Works of Tacitus, vol. 1 (London, 1737), 54. Voltaire recommended Gordon's discourses to Frederick: Voltaire to Frederick of Prussia, c. 25 July 1739, in Voltaire, Correspondence, Oeuvres Complètes 90, D2051. Though he was likewise no supporter of Amelot, the Huguenot printer Prosper Marchand found Voltaire's attack in the preface to the Anti-Machiavel distasteful and even wondered if someone else had written it: "It is a very amusing, not to say very ridiculous thing, that such a reproach appears at the head of an Anti-Machiavel. If it is true, as it is pronounced, that Mr de Voltaire must be the minister of the king of Prussia here, it is enough to imply that he will use reason of state more skilfully than the simple imbecile Amelot de la Houssaye; and that he will know at least as well to refute the wise lessons of his master in fact, as he knew to praise them by writing." Prosper Marchand, "Anti-Machiavel," in Dictionaire historique ou mémoires critiques et littéraires concernant la vie et les ouvrages de divers personnages distingués, particulièrement dans la république des lettres, vol. 1 (La Haye: Pierre de Hondt, 1758), 44.

24 On Amelot's Augustinianism see Luc Foisneau, "Le machiavélisme acceptable d'Amelot de la Houssaye ou la vertu politique au siècle de Louis XIV," Corpus, revue de philosophie 31 (1997): 189–206. On late-seventeenth-century moral theory more generally see Nannerl O. Keohane, Philosophy and the State in France: The Renaissance to the Enlightenment (Princeton University Press, 1980).

25 Amelot, "Preface," in Le prince de Nicolas Machiavel.

26 Niccolò Machiavelli, The Prince, ed. Quentin Skinner and Russell Price (Cambridge University Press, 1988), 55.

27 Amelot, "Epitre," in Le prince de Nicolas Machiavel.

princes who lacked genuine virtue at least to simulate it, rather than incite resistance by displaying their faults openly.[28]

Amelot's approach to Machiavelli produced a form of political criticism that many eighteenth-century critics found excessively opaque and irredeemably compromised.[29] Amelot's theory was designed to exclude attempts to give a moral content to self-interest, while showing that even rulers who were incapable of genuine virtue (like Louis XIV) could still approximate its effects by following their personal self-interest. The famously outspoken challenge to Louis XIV's reign posed by Fénelon was fundamentally different in nature.[30] Fénelon had served as the tutor of the Duc de Bourgogne, Louis XIV's grandson and the successor to French throne, and he had composed *Telemachus* in the hope that his pupil's reign would be nothing like his grandfather's. In *Telemachus* as well as his other writings, Fénelon held out an alternative ideal of kingship that reversed Machiavelli's view of the people as easily deceived and too self-interested to be bound to the prince by love instead of fear.[31] This moral message was articulated as an explicit attack on Machiavelli's *The Prince* by Fénelon's close collaborator and fellow tutor Claude Fleury.[32] In his *Reflections on the works of Machiavel*, Fleury observed that the principles of politics elaborated in *The Prince* "complemented the corruption of the human heart."[33] Though most people might live badly and in error, Fleury insisted that Machiavelli was wrong to deny the existence of a moral standard or of truth, and to advocate self-interest and dissimulation in their place. Fleury claimed that the pursuit of self-interest was self-defeating, for its discipline could only guide a prince to tyranny and hence provoke resistance, while the practice of dissimulation would necessarily generate distrust. The "goal of true politics," Fleury insisted, was the good of the people, and pursuing this goal demanded spiritual renewal from the prince.[34]

---

[28] Foisneau, "Le machiavélisme acceptable," 200–1.

[29] Its opacity remains sufficient for Amelot to have been identified as a panegyrist of Louis XIV by Luc Foisneau and as a crypto-republican by Jacob Soll.

[30] Lionel Rothkrug, *Opposition to Louis XIV: The Political and Social Origins of the French Enlightenment* (Princeton University Press, 1965).

[31] Machiavelli, *The Prince*, 59, 62.

[32] On Fleury and Fénelon see Chérel, "L'anti-machiavélisme de Fénelon et la 'conversion' du Roi"; A.T. Gable, "The Prince and the mirror: Louis XIV, Fénelon, royal narcissism, and the legacy of Machiavelli," *Seventeenth-Century French Studies* 15, no. 1 (1993): 243–68.

[33] Claude Fleury, "Réflexions sur les oeuvres de Machiavel," in *Oeuvres de l'abbé Fleury*, ed. Louis Aimé-Martin (Paris: Auguste Desrez, 1839), 564. Fleury thought better of the *Discourses on Livy*: "Voilà des belles maximes."

[34] Fleury, "Réflexions sur les oeuvres de Machiavel," 565.

In line with Fleury's attack on Machiavelli, Fénelon's *Telemachus* redefined the interest of the prince by showing that princes could attain
true glory only by serving their subjects. Fénelon attributed Louis XIV's
quest for glory and imperial conquest to selfish pride, rather than a
principle of legitimate government. By contrast, he promised, a prince
who subordinated his own interests to the "true needs of the state" and
ensured the people's security and prosperity would earn their love as
well as true glory.[35] So long as a ruler sought to earn the love of his
people rather than dissimulating his personal ambition, Fénelon's tale
promised, he would enjoy much greater power than Louis XIV: "He can
do anything to the people; but the laws can do anything to him. He
has an absolute power in doing good, but his hands are tied from doing
wrong."[36] Fénelon was not the only admirer of Fleury to employ this
evocative formula to describe virtuous kingship: it also appears in John
Locke's *Second Treatise on Government*. In his depiction of the dynamics
of royal prerogative, Locke described an unlimited "power to do good"
whose scope would keep expanding insofar as it was manifestly exercised
in service of the people's welfare by a good king, but find itself hemmed
in by constitutional restrictions if trust should evaporate.[37] The same
formula would reappear in a number of early-eighteenth-century texts
connected to Voltaire, including the *Anti-Machiavel*.

Fénelon's claims about the power and security of a virtuous king were
grounded in economic and military analysis as well as in moral claims
about the nature of glory and love. A virtuous king was more powerful and secure not only because of the immense authority he would be
granted by his grateful subjects, but because the policies that would earn

---

[35] Fénelon preferred the language of "true needs" to that of interest: Jaume, "Fénelon
critique de la déraison d'Etat," 403. See, e.g., Fénelon's contrast between the "true
needs of the state" and the prince's own "pretentions" in his "Examen du conscience
sur les devoirs de la royauté," in *Oeuvres complètes de Fénelon*, vol. 22 (Paris: Gauthier
frères, 1830), 237.

[36] François de Salignac de La Mothe Fénelon, *Telemachus, Son of Ulysses*, ed. Patrick Riley
(Cambridge University Press, 1994), 61.

[37] "For as a good Prince, who is mindful of the trust put into his hands, and careful of
the good of his People, cannot have too much *Prerogative*, that is, Power to do good: So
a weak and ill Prince, who would claim that Power, which his predecessors exercised
without the direction of the Law, as a Prerogative belonging to him by Right of his
Office, which he may exercise at his pleasure, to make or promote an Interest distinct
from that of the publick, gives the People an occasion to claim their Right, and limit that
Power, which, whilst it was exercised for their good, they were content should be tacitly
allowed." John Locke, *Two Treatises of Government*, ed. Peter Laslett (Cambridge University Press, 1988), 377 (sect. 165). See also sect. 42: "that Prince who shall be so wise
and godlike as by established laws of liberty to secure protection and incouragement to
the honest industry of Mankind against the oppression of power and narrownesse of
Party will quickly be too hard for his neighbours."

him this love would significantly enhance the state's economic and military capacity. The primary target of this argument was Jean-Baptiste Colbert, the finance minister who had sought to pay for Louis XIV's wars by accelerating the development of French trade in competition with the Dutch and English. In Fénelon's estimation Colbert's policy had only succeeded in impoverishing the state, damaging the moral character of its people, and funding wars of conquest that served only Louis XIV's appetite for personal glory. In fact, heavy taxation and the growth of the luxury trade had undermined the true foundations of the state's power by distorting its economy, depopulating the countryside and crippling agricultural productivity. Accordingly, Fénelon's alternative ideal of kingship was closely linked to a sweeping program of political and economic reform.

The most important element of Fénelon's reform proposal was to thoroughly purge France of "luxury" by imposing an elaborate regime of sumptuary laws and reorienting the economy toward agricultural production (though it would retain a commercial port, isolated from the rest of the economy and modeled on Holland, whose revenue would fund an armaments industry).[38] As Fénelon had argued in his letters to Louis XIV as well as in *Télémaque*, the elimination of luxury and the revitalization of agriculture would actually increase "real wealth" by eliminating "false needs."[39] The result would be a powerful monarchy that was able to take advantage of the military as well as economic benefits of agricultural self-sufficiency and population growth. As Fénelon explained to the Duc de Bourgogne, his reform program supplied an alternative path to restoring French power without reigniting the disastrous wars of Louis XIV: an alternative that Jean-François Melon would later capture in his distinction between the "spirit of commerce" and the "spirit of conquest."[40] The pursuit of territorial expansion was self-defeating because it imposed the necessity of resistance on others, and resulted in wars that inflicted tremendous damage on the constitution and economy of even a victorious state. Instead, Fénelon concluded, the best policy was to seek to maintain a stable balance of power militarily and territorially, while pursuing aggrandizement only through internal economic development. In this vision, the revitalization of France would go hand

[38] On luxury and Fénelon's reform proposal see above all Istvan Hont, "The luxury debate in the Early Enlightenment," in *The Cambridge History of Eighteenth-Century Political Thought*, ed. M. Goldie and R. Wokler (Cambridge University Press, 2006), 379–418.
[39] Fénelon, *Telemachus*, 59–60.
[40] Jean-François Melon, *A Political Essay upon Commerce* (Dublin: Philip Crampton, 1738), 136.

in hand with the emergence of a more stable and peaceful European order.

The *Anti-Machiavel* was the product of a re-examination of Fénelon's anti-Machiavellism as much as it was a response to Amelot's Machiavellism. Frederick had been enthralled by Fénelon's *Telemachus* since the age of nine, but he had been deeply affected by Voltaire's ideas as well. The crown prince of Prussia was particularly influenced by Voltaire's *The Henriade*, the epic poem that had made Voltaire a celebrity at age twenty-five, and after he drew Voltaire into correspondence in 1736 he received many other writings including *Le Mondain* and an early draft of what became *The Age of Louis XIV*.[41] Amidst the flowery flattery that filled their early correspondence, Frederick's declaration in his first letter that Voltaire's poetry had been "a course in morals" that had taught him "the idea of true glory" seems relatively sincere.[42] Three years later, while composing what would become the *Anti-Machiavel*, he wrote that "What I am planning against Machiavellism, is properly a continuation of *The Henriade*. It is upon the grand sentiments of Henry the Fourth that I am forging the lightening bolt that will crush Cesar Borgia."[43]

Fénelon's vision of an anti-Louis XIV and his model of an anti-Machiavellian monarchy had inspired several decades of debate over how much of Fénelon's model should be retained in the aftermath of the Sun King's reign. Voltaire was an important figure in this debate.[44] The *Anti-Machiavel* was in fact one of several texts connected to Voltaire that emerged in the late 1730s, and were concerned to reassess Fénelon's critique of Louis XIV's reign and the French monarchy. One of these was a manuscript treatise on monarchy, by René Louis de Voyer de Paulmy, Marquis d'Argenson. Voltaire praised d'Argenson's treatise in 1739 as a real-life, new and improved version of Fénelon's *Telemachus* – the same terms he later used in his review of the *Anti-Machiavel*.[45]

---

[41] Bahner and Bergmann, "Introduction," 4.

[42] Frederick of Prussia to Voltaire, 8 August 1736, in Voltaire, *Correspondence*, Oeuvres Complètes 88, D1126.

[43] Frederick of Prussia to Voltaire, 26 June 1739, in Voltaire, *Correspondence*, Oeuvres Complètes 90, D2036.

[44] See Patrick Neiertz, *Voltaire et l'économie politique* (Oxford: Voltaire Foundation, 2012), chap. 4; Sonenscher, *Before the Deluge*, chap. 2; Hont, "The luxury debate in the Early Enlightenment," 412–418; Florian Schui, *Early Debates about Industry: Voltaire and His Contemporaries* (Basingstoke: Palgrave Macmillan, 2005). These discussions have superseded an older literature that was more concerned with Voltaire's skepticism and deism: e.g. Peter Gay, *Voltaire's Politics: The Poet as Realist* (New Haven: Yale University Press, 1988).

[45] Voltaire wrote that "I find all my ideas in your work" and claimed that "it can be said more justly of this work than of *Télémaque*, that if a book can give birth to the well-being

Voltaire even asked d'Argenson if he could share the closely guarded manuscript with Frederick, then still crown prince of Prussia, but his request was denied.[46] Another close parallel is Viscount Bolingbroke's *The Idea of a Patriot King* (1738), which, like Fénelon's *Télémaque*, was originally intended to instruct an heir to the throne (in this case, Frederick the Prince of Wales) on how to recover from the policies of the current regime (Walpole's ministry). Though Bolingbroke's text is usually discussed in the context of English party politics, its discussion of an enlightened form of reason of state, and its views on the political and economic character of a modern monarchy, were also closely related to Voltaire's re-evaluation and development of Fénelon's anti-Machiavellian ideas.[47]

Like Saint Pierre, d'Argenson, Bolingbroke, and others, Voltaire challenged the strict dichotomy between a genuinely selfless virtue and an inherently corrupt self-love that had been asserted by Jansenist and Calvinist theologians.[48] Instead Voltaire joined those such as the Huguenot pastor Jacques Abbadie who sought to identify a more flexible and complementary relationship between self-love and morality, and to establish the possibility of a more accessible and worldly type of virtue.[49] Voltaire's anonymous review of the *Anti-Machiavel* referred to

of humankind, it would be this book [. . .] This is not any longer the colony of Salentum where Mr de Fénelon wants there to be no pastry-chefs, and seven modes of dress. Here is something very real, which experience proves in a most striking manner." Voltaire to René Louis de Voyer de Paulmy, Marquis d'Argenson, 8 May 1739, in Voltaire, *Correspondence*, Oeuvres Complètes 90, D2008. Though Voltaire encouraged d'Argenson to publish the manuscript treatise, it was only published, partially, in 1764.

[46] Voltaire to d'Argenson, 21 June 1739, and d'Argenson to Voltaire, 7 July 1739, in Voltaire, *Correspondence*, Oeuvres Complètes 90, D2035 and D2041. See Nannerl O. Henry, "Democratic monarchy: the political theory of the Marquis d'Argenson" (Ph.D., Yale University, 1968), 75.

[47] Bolingbroke's relationship with Voltaire was complex: Voltaire once referred to him as "one of the most brilliant geniuses and the most eloquent man of his age," but their relations subsequently cooled. François Marie Arouet de Voltaire, *Histoire de Charles XII*, in *Oeuvres historiques*, 241. For the English context see Christine Gerrard, *The Patriot Opposition to Walpole: Politics, Poetry, and National Myth, 1725–1742* (Oxford: Clarendon Press, 1994). On Bolingbroke's involvement in French intellectual circles during his period of exile there see D.J. Fletcher, "The fortunes of Bolingbroke in France in the eighteenth century," *Studies on Voltaire and the Eighteenth Century* 47 (1966): 207–32; and Nick Childs, *A Political Academy in Paris, 1724–1731: The Entresol and Its Members* (Oxford: Voltaire Foundation, 2000).

[48] See Keohane, *Philosophy and the State in France*; Dale Van Kley, "Pierre Nicole, Jansenism, and the morality of enlightened self-interest," in *Anticipations of the Enlightenment in England, France, and Germany*, ed. Alan Charles Kors and Paul J. Korshin (Philadelphia: University of Pennsylvania Press, 1987), 69–85; Patrick Riley, *The General Will before Rousseau: The Transformation of the Divine into the Civic* (Princeton University Press, 1986); R.R. Palmer, *Catholics and Unbelievers in Eighteenth Century France* (Princeton University Press, 1939).

[49] See Isaac Nakhimovsky, "The enlightened epicureanism of Jacques Abbadie: *L'art de se connoître soi-même* and the morality of self-interest," *History of European Ideas* 29 (2003):

this conception of virtue as "practical virtue," and the text presented it as a middle ground between Fénelon and Machiavelli. "Compare Fénelon's prince with Machiavelli's," Frederick wrote. "If in reading M. de Fénelon's *Telemachus* it seems as if our nature approaches that of the angels, it appears to approach the demons of hell when one reads the *Prince*."[50] In his *Traité de metaphysique* (1736), Voltaire had held that virtue might be associated with a healthy kind of love of esteem that was grounded in but transcended the self.[51] As Bolingbroke later put it in *The Idea of a Patriot King*, the attention to "decorum" or "civility" that characterized such action was not a deceptive veneer that concealed a true nature lacking in virtue; rather it was the quality that made virtue inherently pleasurable and admirable to behold, and distinguished it from purely self-seeking dissimulation, or a mask of deceit that no prince could keep in place forever.[52] Accordingly the *Anti-Machiavel* did not condemn the self-interest of the prince but sought to moderate it.[53] A prince whose love of esteem led him to serve the best interests of the people would be rewarded with the object of his desire. Voltaire condensed Frederick's characteristically scattered pronouncements on this theme in his original *Réfutation* into one concise argument: "one wants princes to have enough self-love in order to love glory, to do great acts, and that at the same time to be indifferent enough to renounce their tastes for the sake of their work; the same principle ought to push them to deserve praise, and to reject it."[54]

The *Anti-Machiavel* also reflects the challenge that Voltaire leveled against Fénelon's reform program. Voltaire accepted Fénelon's basic argument that a prince would gain real power and true glory by encouraging internal growth and development rather than pursuing conquest. However, he challenged the claim that this development required the exclusion of luxury from a monarchy and the imposition of an austere asceticism on its prince and subjects. Instead Voltaire worked to

1–14. For another helpful discussion of such arguments see Thomas Ahnert, *Religion and the Origins of the German Enlightenment: Faith and the Reform of Learning in the Thought of Christian Thomasius* (Rochester: University of Rochester Press, 2006).

50 Voltaire, *Anti-Machiavel*, 147.

51 François Marie Arouet de Voltaire, *Traité de metaphysique*, ed. W.H. Barber, Oeuvres Complètes 14 (Oxford: Voltaire Foundation, 1989), 468–81.

52 Henry St. John Viscount Bolingbroke, "The idea of a patriot king," in *Political Writings*, ed. David Armitage (Cambridge University Press, 1997), 280–1. On the importance of Ciceronian *decorum* in eighteenth-century moral thought see James Moore, "Utility and humanity: the quest for the honestum in Cicero, Hutcheson, and Hume," *Utilitas* 14, no. 3 (2002): 365–86; Michael Sonenscher, *Sans-Culottes: An Eighteenth-Century Emblem in the French Revolution* (Princeton University Press, 2008), chap. 1.

53 " . . . no man is without passions. When they are moderated, they are the soul of society; but when they are unleashed, they are the cause of its destruction." Voltaire, *Anti-Machiavel*, 139.

54 Voltaire, *Anti-Machiavel*, 235.

rehabilitate the legacy of Colbert: in *The Henriade*, Henry IV – the image of the virtuous king and the antithesis of Louis XIV – was granted a vision of France's future, only to discover (in a line Voltaire added to the 1737 edition) that his posterity was ensured by none other than Fénelon's bête-noir: "Colbert, it is on your heels that happy abundance, / the daughter of hard work, comes to enrich France."[55] Voltaire elaborated this defense of luxury in *Le Mondain* (1736), which viciously satirized Fénelon's view of luxury as inherently antithetical to virtue, and mocked the austere reforms he had proposed in order to insulate the domestic economy of a monarchy from luxury and foreign trade.[56] Voltaire's poem infamously stressed that the simple life of Adam and Eve was not particularly virtuous, it was just bestial and poor. The message was that the pursuit and enjoyment of luxury was not necessarily equivalent to corruption and vice, and that trade could promote rather than hinder agricultural improvement. In fact, Voltaire held, the spiritual dimensions of life could not be accessed without the cultivation of the arts. Only the arts made it possible to develop a taste for virtue, just as one could never develop a taste for living well if every day of one's life was a struggle for bare survival. Without the veneer created by the luxury and arts of a developed society, human nature would hardly be characterized by moral purity and the selfless love of one another.[57] The expression of natural morality was the result of substantial social development, which was itself contingent upon a certain condition of material abundance. In short, as Voltaire put it in *The Age of Louis XIV*, the problem with more severe moralists was that they failed to appreciate how it was only the development of the arts that distinguished the "age of Louis XIV" from the "age of Attila"; to reverse this development in the name of "austerity" would not yield a golden age of virtuous simplicity.[58] Such moralists "who cry out against what is called luxury," Voltaire wrote in

---

[55] François Marie Arouet de Voltaire, *La Henriade*, ed. O.R. Taylor, Oeuvres Complètes 2 (Geneva: Institut et Musée Voltaire, 1970), 528. On the image of Henry IV and its emergence as a rival to that of Louis XIV see Neal Johnson, *Louis XIV and the Age of the Enlightenment: The Myth of the Sun King from 1715 to 1789*, Studies on Voltaire and the Eighteenth Century 172 (Oxford: Voltaire Foundation, 1978). In the preface he later wrote for *La Henriade*, Frederick claimed that Voltaire was better than Homer because Henri IV's dream was more realistic: *La Henriade*, 347–8.

[56] François Marie Arouet de Voltaire, "Le Mondain," in *Writings of 1736*, ed. H.T. Mason, Oeuvres Complètes 16 (Oxford: Voltaire Foundation, 2003), 295–303.

[57] As Voltaire later elaborated in his article on "love" in his *Philosophical Dictionary* (1764), it was the arts, and the wealth they produced, that gradually allowed sexual desire to develop into a desire to love and be loved. François Marie Arouet de Voltaire, "Amour," in *Dictionnaire philosophique*, ed. Christiane Mervaud, vol. 1, Oeuvres Complètes 35 (Oxford: Voltaire Foundation, 1994), 323–7.

[58] Voltaire, *Oeuvres historiques*, 893.

a letter to Frederick, were "nothing but wretches with a poor sense of humor."[59]

These claims about morality and the arts stood behind the *Anti-Machiavel*'s aspiration to identify a middle ground between Fénelon and Machiavelli. The *Anti-Machiavel*'s account of monarchy was based on a contrast between the way of commerce and the way of conquest that recalls Fénelon's. As Frederick put it, "There are two manners by which a prince can aggrandize himself: one is that of conquest, when a warrior prince extends the limits of his dominion by the force of his arms; the other is that of good government, when a hard-working prince makes all the arts and sciences flourish in his states, rendering them more powerful and civilized." This point, he noted, was entirely lost on Machiavelli, whose book "is full of reasoning on only the first manner of self-aggrandizement" rather than "the second, which is more innocent, more just, and just as useful as the first."[60] However, the *Anti-Machiavel* rejected Fénelon's further claim that the alternative to conquest entailed the elimination of luxury. It was true that "luxury would cause the death of a small state," Frederick argued, but the opposite was true of a large monarchy: "The luxury which comes from abundance, and which makes riches circulate through all the veins of a state, makes a great kingdom flourish. It is what maintains industry, and what multiplies the needs of the rich, in order to bind them by these needs to the poor. If it occurred to some incompetent politician to banish luxury from a great empire, that empire would begin to languish." It was thus "an indispensable rule for all politicians never to confound small states with great ones, and it is in this that Machiavelli grievously sins in this chapter."[61]

In addition to their ability to produce vast amounts of wealth, the political stability of eighteenth-century monarchies set them apart from small states. "In the time of Machiavelli," Frederick wrote, "the great and the nobles were still seen in France as little sovereigns who shared the power of the prince in some manner; this gave rise to divisions, fortified factions, and fermented frequent revolts."[62] The long process of political centralization had eliminated this instability by elevating royal authority. The *Anti-Machiavel* aligned itself with the royalist historiography of the French monarchy promulgated by the Abbé Dubos as well as Saint-Pierre, Voltaire, and d'Argenson. In France, in Frederick's admiring view, Cardinals Richelieu and Mazarin had consolidated authority so successfully that the crown had become the sole representative power

---

[59] Voltaire to Frederick of Prussia, 10 January 1737, in Voltaire, *Correspondence*, Oeuvres Complètes 88, D1251.
[60] Voltaire, *Anti-Machiavel*, 225–6.   [61] Voltaire, *Anti-Machiavel*, 192–3.
[62] Voltaire, *Anti-Machiavel*, 131.

and no longer faced any meaningful opposition from the *parlements*.[63] Machiavelli's analysis of the threat to the prince posed by the nobility therefore no longer applied because their wealth and status had come to depend so thoroughly on the sovereign.[64] Frederick shared d'Argenson and Voltaire's skepticism about the merits of a system of ranks: since it was in a prince's interest to avoid creating divisions among his population, Frederick observed, "a prince must treat all the orders he commands in his state equally well, without making distinctions that would cause jealousies disastrous for his interests."[65] To a considerable extent, in fact, the *Anti-Machiavel* envisioned that the subjects of a monarchy could come to resemble the citizens of a republic. Like Saint-Pierre, d'Argenson (who labeled this ideal "democratic monarchy"), and Bolingbroke, Frederick presented the commercial prowess and republican spirit of the Dutch as a model for large monarchies.[66] Though Frederick deemed republics ungovernable, he was full of praise for that republican "spirit of independence and pride which has produced so many great men in the world."[67] In one of its most radical moments, the *Anti-Machiavel* declined to assign the nobility any distinctive political or military function: in effect, the only role that remained for them was to consume the luxury that drove economic development. Though he stopped well short of explicitly advocating a limited monarchy for himself, Frederick did repeat Fénelon's description of the king as the first servant of the people (Voltaire upgraded the title from *domestique* to *magistrat*); and he followed Voltaire as far as praising England as an ideal constitution that embodied Fénelon's ideal of virtuous government: "It seems to me that if there is a government which in our days could be proposed as a model of wisdom, it is that of England. There the parliament is arbiter between the people and the king, and the king has all the power to do good; but he has none to do evil."[68]

Voltaire had previously echoed Locke and Fénelon's anti-Machiavellian formula for virtuous kingship in his *Letters Concerning the English Nation* (1733), where he praised England for having "at last

---

[63] "Today," Fredrick wrote, "this body is no more than a phantom, which still occasionally imagines that it might well be a body, but which is ordinarily made to repent of this error." Voltaire, *Anti-Machiavel*, 133.
[64] Voltaire, *Anti-Machiavel*, 121.   [65] Voltaire, *Anti-Machiavel*, 214.
[66] On "democratic monarchy" see Henry, "Democratic monarchy: the political theory of the Marquis d'Argenson."
[67] Voltaire, *Anti-Machiavel*, 158. In another passage toned down by Voltaire, Frederick's *Réfutation* matched Bolingbroke's sentiment that "The height of glory would be to restore liberty to a people having rescued it." Frederick of Prussia, "Réfutation du Prince de Machiavel," in *Anti-Machiavel*, by François Marie Arouet de Voltaire, Oeuvres Complètes 19 (Oxford: Voltaire Foundation, 1996), 293.
[68] Voltaire, *Anti-Machiavel*, 119, 211.

establish'd that wise Government, where the Prince is all-powerful to do good, and, at the same time, is restrain'd from committing evil."[69] The same formula also appears in Bolingbroke's *The Idea of a Patriot King*.[70] From this perspective, the *Anti-Machiavel* can be seen as an attempt to join this ideal of virtuous kingship to a new understanding of monarchy as a form of government, with a new political economy based in "luxury" and a new historiography that celebrated the consolidation of royal authority. What this synthesis implied was that the interests of an eighteenth-century monarchy could hardly be compared to the concerns of a small Renaissance principality constantly struggling just to survive. Because state power had become so dependent on the development of trade, Frederick argued, it was no longer sufficient for a prince to focus exclusively on military matters, as Machiavelli had advised.[71] Modern princes would have to expand their portfolios to include the promotion of trade and economic development. "The surest mark that a country is under a wise and felicitous government," Frederick observed, echoing Voltaire, "is when the fine arts are born under its care; these are flowers which grow in rich soil and under a clear sky; but which die in a drought or under the heavy breathing of noses. Nothing makes a reign more illustrious than the arts that flourish under its wing."[72]

The *Anti-Machiavel* deemed Machiavelli's *The Prince* to be outdated in its analysis of military and diplomatic matters as well. Departing from Fénelon, Frederick claimed that the transformation of warfare by modern military tactics, resources, and technologies had actually enhanced rather than diminished the security of contemporary states, to a level that could scarcely have been imagined in the principalities of Renaissance Italy. "Since the time that Machiavelli wrote his *Prince*," Frederick asserted, "the world has changed so much, that it is almost no longer recognizable. If some skillful captain of Louis XII reappeared in our days,

---

[69] François Marie Arouet de Voltaire, *Letters Concerning the English Nation*, ed. Nicholas Cronk (Oxford University Press, 1999), 34. Voltaire also wrote to d'Argenson that England was "existing evidence of the wisdom of your ideas": Voltaire to d'Argenson, 8 May 1739, in Voltaire, *Correspondence*, Oeuvres Complètes 90, D2008.

[70] "The limitations necessary to preserve liberty under monarchy will restrain effectually a bad prince, without being ever felt as shackles by a good one. Our constitution is brought, or almost brought, to such a point, a point of perfection I think it, that no king, who is not, in the true meaning of the word, a patriot, can govern Britain with ease, security, honour, dignity, or indeed with sufficient power and strength. But yet a king, who is a patriot may govern with all the former; and, besides them, with power as extended as the most absolute monarch can boast, and a power, too, far more agreeable in the enjoyment as well as more effectual in the operation." Bolingbroke, "The Idea of a Patriot King," 233–4.

[71] Machiavelli, *The Prince*, 51–2.   [72] Voltaire, *Anti-Machiavel*, 228.

he would be entirely disoriented."[73] Above all, Frederick claimed, the large standing armies maintained by modern princes increased the security of their states by restraining the ambition of others: they were "naked swords, which keep those of others in the scabbard."[74] The dependence of modern monarchies on commerce meant that the standing armies, which formed the basis of their security, could not be composed of patriotic citizen soldiers, as Machiavelli (and Fénelon) had advised. However, Frederick argued, the risks Machiavelli had attributed to a reliance on mercenaries and foreign auxiliaries could be greatly mitigated so long as they were properly assimilated into the national army and brought to a high level of discipline using barracks and other innovations unknown in Machiavelli's time.[75] Although Machiavelli was undoubtedly correct that "the best troops of a state are the national ones," Frederick allowed, no major European state enjoyed this military advantage.[76] The military self-sufficiency that Machiavelli had advocated was also no longer feasible: if even Louis XIV had not been able to sustain himself without allies during the War of the Spanish Succession, then no lesser prince could possibly aspire to survive without alliances, let alone aspire to "universal monarchy" or the recreation of Roman hegemony.[77] However, the *Anti-Machiavel* claimed, the development of the treaty system and the creation of diplomatic channels between the courts of Europe had made it possible to maintain the balance of power more effectively.

The central claim of the *Anti-Machiavel*, as Voltaire's anonymous review indicated, was that the possibility of realizing the "practical virtue" of the prince was linked to some of the same historical developments that Fénelon had condemned as the essence of Louis XIV's Machiavellism. On the contrary, Voltaire and Frederick argued, it was these very developments that now made it possible for the prince of a "great state" to avoid making recourse to Machiavelli's ruthless tactics. Reversing these developments as Fénelon had proposed meant not escaping from a Machiavellian world but destroying what had made an escape possible. Frederick memorably concluded that Machiavelli had

---

[73] Voltaire, *Anti-Machiavel*, 161.
[74] Voltaire, *Anti-Machiavel*, 121.   [75] Voltaire, *Anti-Machiavel*, 129.
[76] The only exception was Sweden: "It is only the Swedish troops, who are burghers, peasants, and soldiers at the same time; but when they go to war, almost nobody remains in the interior of the country in order to work the land: thus, they cannot do anything for long, without ruining themselves more than their enemies." Voltaire, *Anti-Machiavel*, 174–5. On eighteenth-century concerns about the implications of a revival of ancient military virtue in modern Europe see Iain McDaniel, *Adam Ferguson in the Scottish Enlightenment* (Cambridge, Mass.: Harvard University Press, 2013).
[77] Voltaire, *Anti-Machiavel*, 163, 257–8.

become obsolete: "The princes of whom Machiavel speaks," Frederick wrote, "are properly no more than hermaphrodites of sovereigns and [private] individuals; they play the role of sovereign only in a very small theater."[78] On the other hand, Frederick wrote,

what would Machiavelli himself say if he could see the new form of the European body politic [*corps politique de l'Europe*], so many great princes who now figure in the world but amounted to nothing then, the power of kings solidly established, the manner in which sovereigns negotiate, and that balance which establishes in Europe the alliance of some important princes in order to oppose the ambitious, with no other goal than the tranquility of the world?[79]

The "new form of the European body politic" had drastically reduced the need for and applicability of the ruthless politics that Machiavelli had deemed a matter of constant necessity: "All these things have produced a change so general and universal that they render most of Machiavelli's maxims inapplicable to our modern politics."[80] The *Anti-Machiavel*, then, represents a revision, not refutation of reason of state theory. The true interests of modern states demanded that sovereigns abandon their pursuit of false glory through conquest and devote themselves to promoting the industry and prosperity of their subjects. At the same time, the enhanced resources of modern states and the established authority of their sovereigns made them far more secure. In this way, the harsh imperatives of reason of state were diluted by a kind of politics based primarily on practical virtue rather than necessity. Where Machiavelli's prince was tasked with resisting the effects of chance or *fortuna*, the *Anti-Machiavel* asserted both that the modern prince faced a changed set of historical circumstances and that these were, to a significant degree, intelligible; those who grasped the nature of these changes best would distance themselves the most from the world of Machiavelli's *The Prince*.[81] Machiavellian tactics could not be ruled out when the necessity of survival did impose itself on sovereigns, but eighteenth-century Europe was increasingly no longer a world in which dire necessity had to be the solitary interest governing the prince, leaving room for the practice of virtue and the operation of commerce. For the most part – a significant caveat, as we shall see – princes of large commercial monarchies could be virtuous and follow the greater, more enlightened interests of their subjects. They could make their people prosperous and happy by pursuing the

---

[78] Voltaire, *Anti-Machiavel*, 164.
[79] Voltaire, *Anti-Machiavel*, 162.   [80] Voltaire, *Anti-Machiavel*, 162.
[81] Voltaire, *Anti-Machiavel*, 394. Cf. Reinhart Koselleck, "Chance as a motivational trace in historical writing," in *Futures Past: On the Semantics of Historical Time*, trans. Keith Tribe (Cambridge, Mass.: MIT Press, 1985), 117–19.

interests of their peoples within a more stable and peaceful international system.

These claims about the radically enhanced capabilities of modern monarchies are perhaps more familiar as Hume's concept of the "civilized European monarchy," which he introduced in his famous essay "On civil liberty," first published in 1741 (one year after the *Anti-Machiavel*).[82] Hume pursued a comparable line of argument: he claimed that a large monarchy like France was nearly as capable as small republics of fostering the kinds of behavior that had hitherto been possible only in the latter. The arts and sciences flourished, property was secure, and above all commerce thrived in such a monarchy. Hume concluded that these transformations had profoundly altered the political constraints faced by these states: "Machiavel was certainly a great genius; but having confined his study to the furious and tyrannical governments of ancient times, or to the little disorderly principalities of Italy, his reasonings especially upon monarchical government, have been found extremely defective; and there scarcely is any maxim in his *prince*, which subsequent experience has not entirely refuted."[83] The *Anti-Machiavel*, like Hume's account of "civilized European monarchy," had no time for the contractual underpinnings of Locke's theory, but it retained the view that the trust earned through utility and encoded in public opinion served as the measure of the prince's prudence. Like Hume, too, the *Anti-Machiavel* detached the Lockean ideal of "constitutional reason of state" from an exclusively national context.[84] Whereas Locke's account of royal prerogative operated within the parameters of English constitutional history, the *Anti-Machiavel* substituted a general

---

[82] The original title was "Of liberty and despotism"; it was changed beginning with the edition of 1758.

[83] David Hume, "Of civil liberty," in *Essays: Moral, Political, and Literary*, ed. Eugene Miller, Rev. ed (Indianapolis: Liberty Classics, 1987), 88, 92–4. On Hume's complex engagement with Machiavelli see Frederick G. Whelan, *Hume and Machiavelli: Political Realism and Liberal Thought* (Lexington Books, 2004). Hume's attempt to distinguish Machiavelli from Machiavellism, and his defense of the former as a precursor of a modern science of politics, are also discussed in "Hume's knaves and the shadow of Machiavellianism," Istvan Hont's unpublished contribution to a conference on "Anti-Machiavellian Machiavellism" convened by Ioannis Evrigenis and Mark Somos at the University of Sussex in 2010.

[84] Cf. Duncan Forbes, "The European, or cosmopolitan, dimension in Hume's science of politics," *British Journal for Eighteenth-Century Studies* 1 (1978): 57–60; John Robertson, "Universal monarchy and the liberties of Europe: David Hume's critique of an English Whig doctrine," in *The Languages of Political Theory in Early-Modern Europe*, ed. Anthony Pagden (Cambridge University Press, 1987), 349–73. On "constitutional reason of state" see, in conjunction with Duncan Kelly's contribution to this volume, Carl J. Friedrich, *Constitutional Reason of State: The Survival of the Constitutional Order* (Providence: Brown University Press, 1957).

European history with the French monarchy as its archetype: a historiography that it exported as a model for Prussia.[85]

In his anonymous review of the *Anti-Machiavel*, Voltaire claimed that its vision of politics was "applicable to all the governments of Europe." In Prussia the *Anti-Machiavel* did in fact become a touchstone for debates about the nature of monarchical government and political economy, and it remained one into the nineteenth century. For Jacob Friedrich Bielfeld and Thomas Abbt in the 1750s and 1760s, for example, The *Anti-Machiavel* continued to represent an attractive alternative to the theory of monarchy put forward in Montesquieu's *The Spirit of the Laws* (1748): though Montesquieu also famously proclaimed the eclipse of Machiavellism, and described a fundamental affinity between monarchy and a political economy based on luxury, he also insisted that monarchies required a system of ranks and seemed to deny that the patriotism of a republican citizen could be matched by the subject of a monarchy. Though Frederick himself had abandoned his bid to sideline the nobility, Bielfeld and Abbt appealed to the *Anti-Machiavel* in order to defend a vision of what d'Argenson had called "democratic monarchy."[86]

What made the *Anti-Machiavel* particularly controversial, however, was the vision of Europe and of the European balance of power that it articulated. As J.G.A. Pocock has shown, Voltaire's image of "a great republic divided into many states" was embedded in an "Enlightened narrative" whose premise was that Europe was no longer haunted by the specter of "universal monarchy" and that international politics since the Treaty of Utrecht in 1713 had transcended the confrontation between

---

[85] "He that will look into the history of England . . . " Locke, *Two Treatises of Government*, 377 (sect. 165). One figure who may have had a part in this historiographical shift was the Abbé Jean-Baptiste Dubos, a personal friend of Locke's (and a correspondent of Fénelon's) whose history of the French monarchy was much admired by Voltaire. On Dubos see Thomas Kaiser, "The Abbé Dubos and the historical defense of the French monarchy in early eighteenth-century France," *Studies in Voltaire and the Eighteenth Century* 267 (1989): 77–102; Sonenscher, *Before the Deluge*, chap. 2; Dan Edelstein, *The Enlightenment: A Genealogy* (University of Chicago Press, 2010).

[86] On these debates see Eva Piirimäe, "Thomas Abbt's Vom Tode für das Vaterland (1761) and the French debates on monarchical patriotism," *TRAMES: A Journal of the Humanities & Social Sciences* 9, no. 4 (December 2005): 326–47; Eva Piirimäe, "Dying for the Fatherland: Thomas Abbt's theory of aesthetic patriotism," *History of European Ideas* 35, no. 2 (June 2009): 194–208; Zurbuchen, "Theorizing enlightened absolutism: The Swiss republican origins of Prussian monarchism." A classic work remains Horst Dreitzel, *Monarchiebegriffe in der Fürstengesellschaft: Semantik und Theorie der Einherrschaft in Deutschland von der Reformation bis zum Vormärz* (Köln: Böhlau, 1991). On Frederick's own readings and annotations of Montesquieu see B. Hemmerdinger, "Montesquieu et Frédéric le Grand," *Studi Francesi* 36 (1992): 505–12.

Louis XIV and the Anglo-Dutch led alliance.[87] Europe was no longer
divided by a quest for continental hegemony on one side and a quest
for a maritime trading empire and control of the seas on the other.[88] On
the contrary, Britain and France had locked themselves into a stable system of treaties and commercial relations that did not exclude wars but
precluded a repetition of the historical trajectory of classical antiquity:
the consolidation of a "universal monarchy" followed by its decline and
fall. However, Pocock further observed, this post-Utrecht vision of a stabilized balance of power operating according to the logic of commerce
lasted only as long as the Anglo-French compromise over the Spanish
succession. By the Seven Years' War, it had become entangled in and
overtaken by intensified imperial rivalries far beyond the Anglo-French
core, in North America and South Asia as well as in Central Europe.[89]

The *Anti-Machiavel* embraced this post-Utrecht historiography of
the balance of power and backed it up with its Fénelonian description
of internal development as a peaceful mechanism for maintaining the
balance of power. What the *Anti-Machiavel* added to this Fénelonian
vision, besides linking it to a radically different political economy
that prioritized industrial rather than agricultural development, was a
proposal to extend its scope through the territorial reorganization of
Central Europe. Far from reflecting the narrow geographical limits of
Voltaire's "Enlightened narrative," then, the *Anti-Machiavel* represents
an effort to extend it into the space that later, tendentiously, came to
be called *Mitteleuropa*.[90] To observers like d'Argenson, the key problem
with the balance of power in continental Europe was that it still revolved
to a great extent around the dynastic rivalry between the houses of

---

[87] J.G.A. Pocock, *Barbarism and Religion, Vol. 1: The Enlightenments of Edward Gibbon,
1737–1764* (Cambridge University Press, 1999), 109–23; J.G.A. Pocock, *Barbarism and
Religion, Vol. 2: Narratives of Civil Government* (Cambridge University Press, 1999). On
"enlightened narrative" see also Karen O'Brien, *Narratives of Enlightenment: Cosmopolitan History from Voltaire to Gibbon* (Cambridge University Press, 1997); and, more generally, Edelstein, *The Enlightenment: A Genealogy*.

[88] On the historiography of land and sea empires see also David Armitage, *Foundations of
Modern International Thought* (Cambridge University Press, 2012), chap. 3.

[89] Pocock, *Enlightenments of Edward Gibbon*, 130.

[90] The *Anti-Machiavel* therefore qualifies Pocock's claim that "As the Enlightened Europe
of Utrecht was a construct of France and the Maritime Powers, so its scheme of history
was both Latin and Atlantic, with little room for German history." Pocock, *Enlightenments of Edward Gibbon*, 111–12. For a projection of this claim into the nineteenth
century see J.G.A. Pocock, "Enlightenment and counter-enlightenment, revolution and
counter-revolution: a Eurosceptical enquiry," *History of Political Thought* 20(1999):
126–39. Contrast the engagement with the maritime world described in Alison Frank,
"Continental and maritime empires in an age of global commerce," *East European Politics & Societies* 25, no. 4 (2011): 779–84. For the tendentious view of a *Mitteleuropa*
set apart from the economic world of the maritime powers see Friedrich Naumann,
Mitteleuropa (Berlin: G. Reimer, 1916).

Bourbon and Habsburg – an arrangement that seemed too outdated to serve as the framework for an enlightened politics of reason of state. The relative backwardness of the Empire and the Habsburg dominions ensured that so long as the balance remained in its current form, it could not be governed by peaceful aggrandizement through commercial development alone. Nor was the Empire equipped with the resources needed to prevent it from falling under the sway of the German clients of a foreign power (in particular, d'Argenson and others were saying in the 1730s, of Britain). In short, the political circumstances and interests of the Habsburgs, Emperors over the monstrously decentralized and fragmented Holy Roman Empire, were unlike those of the kind of prince described by Frederick and Voltaire. An increasingly powerful faction at the French court, centered around figures like the Duc de Richelieu and the Comte de Belle-Isle, argued that a war directed by France was the only way to stabilize the political landscape of Germany.[91] To them, the long-anticipated death of Emperor Charles VI in 1740, and the contested succession of his daughter Maria Theresa, presented the opportunity to transform Germany and bring the European balance of power up to date with eighteenth-century realities. According to d'Argenson, who rehearsed this scenario several times, the goal of such a war was not to aggrandize France itself, but to end the obstructive influence of the Habsburgs and restructure the territory of the Empire: "To chase the new House of Austria out of Europe and send it back to Hungary, to make us the distributors of its hereditary states for a new division that equalized the possessions of the third part of Europe, and to take nothing for us."[92] Following this plan "involves no less than executing the famous plan of Henry IV which is discussed in the *Mémoires de Sully*" – the legendary peace plan described by the Duc de Sully which Saint Pierre had claimed as the inspiration of his own writings on "perpetual peace." In this manner, d'Argenson claimed, France would be able to bring about the pacification of Europe, achieving the aims of Saint-Pierre's system of international arbitration singlehandedly.[93]

---

[91] See François Labbé, "La rêve irénique du marquis de la Tierce: Franc-Maçonnerie, lumières, et projets de paix perpétuelle dans le cadre du Saint-Empire sous le règne de Charles VII (1741–45)," *Francia* 18, no. 2 (1991): 47–69; Peter Robert Campbell, *Power and Politics in Old Regime France, 1720–1745* (London: Routledge, 1996), 156–76.

[92] René-Louis de Voyer de Paulmy d'Argenson, *Journal et mémoires du marquis d'Argenson*, ed. E.J.B. Rathery, vol. 4 (Paris: Mme V. Jules Renouard, 1862), 223. Cited in Labbé, "La rêve irénique," 53. The passage cited appears to vary in different published editions of d'Argenson's journal: in some versions, for example, Austria is to be chased out of Germany, not Europe.

[93] René-Louis de Voyer de Paulmy d'Argenson, *Journal et mémoires du marquis d'Argenson*, ed. E.J.B. Rathery, vol. 1 (Paris: Mme V. Jules Renouard, 1859), 371. See also Édouard

The unnecessary wars of succession caused by the present dynastic confusion of Germany would be eliminated, and the "tyrannical commerce" of the English could be confronted by the rest of Europe.[94] The result would be the transformation of Central Europe into economically viable, politically centralized, modern states capable of participating in a more stable and peaceful form of a balance of power, one that was disentangled from the complicated problems of dynastic politics.

This political context suggests a reading of Frederick's *Anti-Machiavel* as an overture to pro-war factions at the French court, and perhaps as an offer to serve as a client whose enlarged and consolidated kingdom of Prussia would help France liberate Germany from Habsburg domination, preserve it from British influence, and extend the post-Utrecht order eastwards into central Europe.[95] From this perspective, Frederick's insinuations that the petty princes of Germany – modern examples of the "hermaphrodite" sovereigns of Machiavelli's day – had no place in modern politics take on added meaning: in his *Réfutation* he explicitly counseled them to abandon their miniature armies and pretensions to power and opt instead "to figure in the world only as well-to-do private individuals."[96] Frederick's commentary on Machiavelli's principles of conquest is also instructive in light of the French aspirations to reorganize Germany by military means: he claimed that a ruler did not need to reside in the states he had conquered, as Machiavelli had advised, and that it was not necessary to kill vanquished former princes. In a similar vein, colonies were not necessary to preserve conquests; the best strategy was to garrison troops in the new cities and to ensure that they were well-disciplined enough not to impose on the local population.[97]

The *Anti-Machiavel* expanded Voltaire's revision of the Fénelonian ideal of monarchy into a vision of a stabilized European order, and projected that vision into central Europe. The tensions in this enterprise,

Goumy, *Étude sur la vie et les écrits de l'abbé de Saint-Pierre* (Paris: P.A. Bourdier, 1859), 60–2.

[94] René-Louis de Voyer marquis d'Argenson, *Considérations sur le gouvernement ancien et présent de la France* (Amsterdam, 1765), 323–5.

[95] Frederick had already made such an overture to the French: in 1734, when his father fell gravely ill during the Polish succession crisis, Frederick secretly offered his services as a "Gustavus Adolphus or Charles XII." See Ernest Lavisse, *Le Grand Frédéric avant l'avènement* (Paris: Hachette, 1893), 327–8. On the recurrence of this idea during the Napoleonic Wars see Isaac Nakhimovsky, *The Closed Commercial State: Perpetual Peace and Commercial Society from Rousseau to Fichte* (Princeton University Press, 2011), chap. 2.

[96] Frederick of Prussia, "Réfutation du Prince de Machiavel," 313. I have borrowed the translation of this remark from *The Refutation of Machiavelli's Prince: Or, Anti-Machiavel*, ed. Paul Sonnino (Athens: Ohio University Press, 1981), 77.

[97] Frederick of Prussia, "Réfutation du Prince de Machiavel," 277–80.

of conquering in the "spirit commerce," are reflected in the negotiations between author and editor about publishing the *Anti-Machiavel*. Whatever his other ambitions at the time (they were many, and seem to have included the prospect of heading Frederick's new academy of sciences), Voltaire does seem to have entertained the hope that the publication of Frederick's avowal of an anti-Machiavellian politics would act as a constraint both on Frederick and on other sovereigns – particularly once Frederick had acknowledged his authorship. Voltaire expressed this hope in a verse he planned to add to the edition of *The Henriade* that Frederick had intended to publish (it never appeared, though Frederick's preface later did, and Voltaire withdrew the verse):

> And you, young hero, always guided by [Truth]
> Disciple of Trajan, rival to Marcus Aurelius
> Citizen on the throne, and model of the North
> Be my dearest aid, be my greatest support
> Let the other kings, those false terrestrial gods
> Bring deception or war everywhere:
> They ravage the world, and you must enlighten it."[98]

For his part, Frederick did not commit himself to Voltaire's publication plan for the *Anti-Machiavel*, even after he had sent Voltaire the manuscript, and pursued other options in England; he only left Voltaire in charge of the project when his succession to the throne made it impossible for him to remain involved any longer.[99]

The tensions inherent in the French project to reorganize Germany by force are also reflected in Voltaire's editorial efforts to temper Frederick's more expansive remarks about just war. Frederick's manuscript dismissed wars of personal ambition and wars of religion as unnecessary and therefore unjust. However, while the circumstances of modern monarchies had reduced the incidence of truly unavoidable necessity, Frederick stressed that they did not entirely eliminate it:

The world would be happy if there were no other means than that of negotiation for maintaining justice and for re-establishing peace and good harmony among nations. Arguments would be employed instead of arms, and people would only debate each other, instead of slaughtering each other; an unfortunate necessity obliges princes to have recourse to a much more cruel means. There are occasions when it is necessary to defend by arms the liberty of a people whose oppression is unjustly sought, when it is necessary to obtain by violence that which iniquity refuses to mildness, when sovereigns must commit the cause of

---

[98] Voltaire, *La Henriade*, 366.
[99] For a guide to the resulting proliferation of authorized and unauthorized editions, see Bahner and Bergmann, "Introduction," 10–13.

their nation to the fate of battles. It is in such cases that the paradox becomes true, that a good war yields and affirms a good peace.[100]

Frederick's typology of just wars extended well beyond defensive wars. It also included "preventive wars" to maintain the balance of power, wars undertaken to meet treaty obligations, and more generally, wars to "repulse usurpers, maintain legitimate rights, guarantee the liberty of the world, and avoid the oppression and violence of the ambitious."[101] Voltaire significantly downplayed Frederick's discussion of such wars, which he labeled *guerres d'intérêt*: he omitted Frederick's assertion that "Since there is no tribunal superior to kings and no magistrate in the world to judge their disputes, combat decides their rights and judges the validity of their reasons," and that such wars were a "sacred and indispensible" means of securing justice.[102] Finally, Voltaire also omitted Frederick's argument that there was a place for conquest in anti-Machiavellian politics so long as it was justly undertaken and in the interests of the people rather than the product of ambition.[103]

These discrepancies suggest more than an impending rift between a secretly bellicose young prince and a well-meaning philosopher. Frederick's broader endorsement of wars in the public interest, and Voltaire's efforts to tone it down, also reflect the fault lines between two closely related but competing visions of the future of Europe after the Treaty of Utrecht. These fault lines were exposed in the controversy generated by two pamphlets responding to the *Anti-Machiavel*, authored in 1741 by the 82-year-old Abbé de Saint-Pierre. In his commentary Saint-Pierre fulsomely endorsed the moral discourse of the *Anti-Machiavel* and echoed its distinctions between true and false glory, between the spirit of conquest and the spirit of commerce.[104] Saint-Pierre's own views on monarchical government and political economy were also quite close to Voltaire's and Frederick's.[105] However, Saint-Pierre rejected the notion that realigning Germany territorially and modernizing it politically would reduce instability sufficiently to ensure that the balance of power could operate primarily through trade rather than military action. Saint-Pierre had always maintained that the Utrecht settlement would

---

[100] Voltaire, *Anti-Machiavel*, 256.

[101] Frederick of Prussia, "Réfutation du Prince de Machiavel," 402–3.

[102] Compare Voltaire, *Anti-Machiavel*, 256; Frederick of Prussia, "Réfutation du Prince de Machiavel," 402.

[103] Frederick of Prussia, "Réfutation du Prince de Machiavel," 277.

[104] Charles Irénée de Castel de Saint-Pierre, *Reflexions sur l'antimachiavel de 1740* (Rotterdam: J. D. Beman, 1741), 22–4, 47–8.

[105] See for example his favorable response to Voltaire's *Histoire de Charles XII*: Charles Irénée Castel de Saint-Pierre to Voltaire, 2 October 1739, in Voltaire, *Correspondence and Related Documents*, *Oeuvres Complètes* 91, D2085.

remain unfinished without the creation of a permanent and comprehensive federation of states, formed to deter aggression and ensure access to international markets. In Saint-Pierre's view, in other words, the image of Europe as a "great republic of states" had to become less like a metaphor and much more like an actual republic with a federal government. Only the irresistible military force controlled by this federal republic of sovereigns could ensure that territorial expansion was no longer an option for particular princes; as a result they would have no choice but to pursue "the other kinds of aggrandizement, which may result from good policy, the perfection of laws, useful establishments, the progress of arts and sciences, the augmentation of commerce."[106] Though he had, and has long retained, a reputation for utopianism and irrepressible optimism, at the end of his life it was Saint-Pierre who accused Voltaire and Frederick of entertaining an unrealistic view of the balance of power. "The way of wars is the great obstacle to the progress of universal reason," he wrote. "It is clear that as long as the infancy of the world endures, that is to say, as long as war or the superiority of force, skill, and treachery, remain the means for deciding the differences between sovereigns, there is hardly any point in hoping for improvement through political proofs in order to augment human happiness."[107] The only way Frederick could redeem the *Anti-Machiavel* and prove he was not another conqueror in pursuit of false glory like Charles XII of Sweden, Saint-Pierre lectured, was to admit that his invasion had been a youthful mistake.[108]

Though he shared a great deal with Voltaire intellectually, the publication of the *Anti-Machiavel* found Saint-Pierre in rather different company politically. A tireless promoter of his peace plan, Saint-Pierre had seized an opportunity in January 1740 to urge it once again upon the aging Cardinal Fleury, whose control over French policy was fading together with his hopes of keeping France out of the escalating Anglo-Spanish colonial war.[109] Saint-Pierre then travelled to Berlin following Frederick's coronation in May, with an introduction from the Saxon minister Count Brühl to Count Manteuffel, the Saxon ambassador in

---

[106] Charles Irénée de Castel de Saint-Pierre, *Projet pour rendre la paix perpétuelle en Europe*, ed. Simone Goyard-Fabre (Paris: Fayard, 1986), 32–3.

[107] Saint-Pierre, *Reflexions sur l'antimachiavel*, 62.

[108] Saint-Pierre, *Reflexions sur l'antimachiavel*, 28.

[109] On Saint-Pierre's exchange with Fleury see Goumy, *Étude sur la vie et les écrits de l'abbé de Saint-Pierre*, 67–9. Saint-Pierre also contributed a proposal for Franco-Dutch mediation in the Anglo-Spanish conflict, as a vehicle for introducing his scheme of permanent arbitration. His "Idées pacifiques sur les demelez entre l'Espagne et l'Angleterre" was published by Antoine-Augustin Bruzen de la Martinière in *État politique de l'Europe*, vol. 3 (La Haye: Adrien Moetjens, 1740).

Berlin.[110] Manteuffel had been a fixture of Berlin's literary establishment in the 1730s and helped engineer Frederick's reinstatement of the exiled philosopher Christian Wolff. Manteuffel represented a network of Wolffians competing for influence over Frederick against Voltaire and his compatriots: their efforts even produced a Wolffian counterpart to the *Anti-Machiavel*, a French popularization of Wolff's discussion of virtuous kingship, dedicated to Frederick and published immediately following his coronation.[111] The lines between these philosophical camps were not as rigidly drawn as Voltaire's famously outspoken skepticism about metaphysics would suggest: the edition of Wolff's lecture took its epigraph from Voltaire's *The Henriade*, and Frederick tried unsuccessfully to recruit both Voltaire and Wolff for his new Academy of Sciences.[112] In the end, though, the rivalry between Voltaire and Manteuffel merged with diplomatic intrigue between France and Saxony, and collided with Frederick's invasion plans. Manteuffel was summarily expelled from Berlin in November 1740, and Saint-Pierre was not treated more delicately. In April 1741, as the Comte de Belle-Isle made his way across Germany to negotiate an offensive alliance with Frederick, Saint-Pierre amplified his criticism in a second pamphlet, which deemed the *Anti-Machiavel* the work of a "political enigma": it openly accused Frederick of hypocrisy, claiming that his conquest of Silesia represented the very kind of Machiavellan politics he had written against. The only way for Frederick to vindicate the claims of his treatise, Saint-Pierre insisted, was to submit his claim to Silesia to international arbitration. A year later, as the war dragged on in Moravia and pressure on Frederick to submit to British diplomatic mediation increased, Frederick noted to Voltaire that Saint-Pierre "honors me with his correspondence" and had sent him a "bel ouvrage" – presumably *l'Enigme politique*. Frederick immediately commissioned a response from Jean Henri Samuel Formey, the Prussian-born Huguenot who later became the perpetual secretary of the new Berlin Academy. Formey's pamphlet, *L'Anti St. Pierre, ou refutation de l'enigme politique de l'Abbé de St. Pierre,*

---

[110] Johann Gustav Droysen, "Über die Schrift Anti-St. Pierre und deren Verfasser," in *Monatsberichte der königlich preussischen Akademie der Wissenschaften zu Berlin: Aus dem Jahre 1878* (Berlin, 1879), 713.

[111] Christian Wolff, *Le philosophe-roi et le roi-philosophe: La théorie des affaires publiques, pièces tirées des oeuvres de Monsieur Chr. Wolff* (Berlin, 1740). On Manteuffel and his role see Johannes Bronisch, *Der Mäzen der Aufklärung: Ernst Christoph von Manteuffel und das Netzwerk des Wolffianismus* (Walter de Gruyter, 2010).

[112] Adolf von Harnack, *Geschichte der Königlich Preussischen Akademie der Wissenschaften zu Berlin* (Berlin: Reichsdruckerei, 1900), 1:249–54. See also James E. McClellan, *Science Reorganized: Scientific Societies in the Eighteenth Century* (New York: Columbia University Press, 1985), 73.

appeared in June 1742 and ridiculed its elderly target, notably employing allusions to Fénelon's *Telemachus* to cast Saint-Pierre as an impractical dreamer.[113] Saint-Pierre's many volumes were good only for battles of books or lecterns, Formey charged, whereas the *Anti-Machiavel* was destined for immortality.[114]

Voltaire's response to Saint-Pierre's challenge was less clear cut. His taste for jokes at the good Abbé's expense is well known.[115] However, his correspondence with Frederick after the publication of the *Anti-Machiavel* expresses French dissatisfaction with the course of the war and reflects the tensions that Saint-Pierre had identified. In March 1742, weeks before Frederick reported that Saint-Pierre had sent him his *Enigme politique*, Voltaire wrote to Frederick mocking him as "the image of the divinity; and a very thinking and very active image" – so active that Voltaire professed not to know which battlefield to address the letter. In an echo of the withdrawn additional verse to *The Henriade* that had praised Frederick, he went on to question whether the war could in fact yield peace and stability: "Will you ever cease, you and your fellow kings, to ravage this earth, which, you say, you desire so much to render happy?" Voltaire asked. "Instead of this horrible war / Whose blows are felt by everybody, / Why do you not address yourselves / to the good Abbé de Saint-Pierre?" Paris was full of rumours about Belle-Isle and Frederick, Voltaire noted, yet Saint-Pierre "would grant you everything as easily as Lycurgus divided the lands of Sparta, and as easily as equal portions would be given to monks. He would establish the fifteen dominions of Henry IV."[116] Perhaps fearing he had gone too far, in subsequent letters Voltaire took pains to clarify that he held no illusions about the practicality of Saint-Pierre's ideas or the arbitration arrangement he was advocating, and assured Frederick that "the philosopher king knows perfectly well that which the philosopher who is not king tries in vain to guess."[117] Shortly after Prussia's important victory over

[113] Saint-Pierre was likened to "Mentor" and "le Nestor Politique": Jean Henri Samuel Formey, "Anti St. Pierre, ou refutation de l'enigme politique de l'Abbé de St. Pierre," in *Monatsberichte der königlich preussischen Akademie der Wissenschaften zu Berlin: Aus dem Jahre 1878* (Berlin, 1879), 738, 740.

[114] Formey, "Anti St. Pierre," 745.

[115] See Merle Perkins, "Voltaire and the Abbé de Saint-Pierre on World Peace," *Studies in Voltaire and the Eighteenth Century* 18 (1961): 9–34; Patrick Riley, "The Abbé de St. Pierre and Voltaire on Perpetual Peace in Europe," *World Affairs* 137, no. 3 (1974): 186–94.

[116] Voltaire to Frederick of Prussia, c. 15 March 1742, in Voltaire, *Correspondence*, Oeuvres Complètes 92, D2596.

[117] Voltaire to Frederick of Prussia, 15 May 1742 in Voltaire, *Correspondence*, Oeuvres Complètes 92, D2605.

the Austrians at Chotusitz on 17 May 1742, Voltaire told Frederick he would be as celebrated as Louis XIV:

I think of humanity, sire, before thinking of you yourself; but after having become an Abbé de Saint-Pierre and crying over humankind whose terror you have become, I abandon myself to all the joy which your glory gives me. This glory will be complete if your majesty forces the queen of Hungary to accept peace, and the Germans to be happy. Now you are the hero of Germany, and the arbiter of Europe. You will be its pacifier, and the prologues of our operas will only be for you.[118]

Though he thereby reaffirmed his support for the war (over which the French had rapidly lost control), Voltaire's remarks about Saint-Pierre are telling. The balance of power continued to operate according to the principles of necessity and war, rather than being stabilized according to the principles of peaceful commerce, as the *Anti-Machiavel* had envisaged.

The *Anti-Machiavel*'s vision of this new kind of balance of power in Central Europe remained beyond the reach of Frederick's Prussia. Frederick's attempt to begin participating in global commerce by creating a Prussian East Asia company in 1750 was immediately suppressed by the British and Dutch.[119] Frederick's secret *Political Testament* of 1752 notoriously conceded that "Machiavelli is right": a state surrounded by ambitious powers would perish unless it continued to expand.[120] Significantly, however, the only means of growth that Frederick went on to discuss were conquest and succession: the Fénelonian ideal of internal economic growth had disappeared from the picture.[121] In practice, over the course of Frederick's reign, the aspirations articulated by the *Anti-Machiavel* were largely sacrificed to the imperative of maximizing revenues to support the army.[122] Nonetheless, the *Anti-Machiavel*'s claims about the stabilization of the continental balance of power did have an enduring legacy. They were revived and reworked by others, including by the Prussian subject turned Saxon diplomat Emer de Vattel in his

---

[118] Voltaire to Frederick of Prussia, 26 May 1742, in Voltaire, *Correspondence*, Oeuvres Complètes 92, D2611.

[119] Florian Schui, "Prussia's trans-oceanic moment: the creation of the Prussian Asiatic Trading Company in 1750," *The Historical Journal* 49, no. 1 (2006): 143–60.

[120] Frederick of Prussia, *Die politische Testamenten Friedrich's des Grossen*, ed. Gustav Berthold Volz (Berlin: Reimar Hobbing, 1920), 59.

[121] Frederick of Prussia, *Die politische Testamenten Friedrich's des Grossen*, 59.

[122] T.C.W. Blanning, "Frederick the Great and Enlightened Absolutism," in *Enlightened Absolutism: Reform and Reformers in Later Eighteenth-Century Europe*, ed. H.M. Scott, Problems in Focus Series (Basingstoke, Hampshire: Macmillan, 1990), 265–88. For a famous indictment leveled at the conclusion of Frederick's reign see Honoré-Gabriel de Riqueti de Mirabeau, *Lettre remise à Frédéric-Guillaume II, Roi Regnant de Prusse, Le jour de son Avénement au Trône* (Berlin, 1787).

famous treatise *The Law of Nations* (1758).[123] At the same time, however, Saint-Pierre's challenge to that vision of Europe's future continued to carry a great deal of force.

The force of Saint-Pierre's challenge reverberates in the reading of the *Anti-Machiavel* conducted by the "Société du Comte de la Lippe," a reading group convened in Lausanne in the 1740s to help educate the teenage heir of the German principality of Lippe, which recorded a remarkable transcript of its discussions.[124] In one sense the *Société* used the *Anti-Machiavel* as it was designed, as an advice book for enlightened princes that superseded Machiavelli's *The Prince*. The spirit of the discussion is captured by one participant who concluded: "The *Anti-Machiavel* successfully refuted the author [i.e., Machiavelli] in saying that a prince must be sensitive to praise; because the desire to win the esteem of men and to acquire reputation is a powerful motive for princes to fulfill their duties."[125] However, in limiting their interest in the book to its statement of moral values, these readers were silently rejecting its politics. The *Anti-Machiavel*'s vision of replacing the "hermaphrodite" sovereigns who populated the landscape of Germany with modern monarchies on the French model left no political future for a prince like Lippe. Tellingly, when the *Société* did turn to questions of just war and the balance of power, they were much more interested in the writings of the Abbé de Saint-Pierre, which they discussed in detail over the course of several sessions. Far from regarding Germany's fragmented political landscape as incompatible with modern commerce and in need of radical restructuring, Saint-Pierre regarded the Holy Roman Empire as a prototype for a future European Union and one of its historical antecedents; his peace plan was premised on freezing the territorial status quo.

The most explicit and forceful restatement of Saint-Pierre's challenge to the *Anti-Machiavel*, however, was Jean-Jacques Rousseau's. Rousseau had met Saint-Pierre at the end of the latter's life, in 1742 or 1743; in 1756 he began an arduous and frustrating effort to edit Saint-Pierre's

---

[123] See Isaac Nakhimovsky, "Vattel's theory of the international order: commerce and the balance of power in the law of nations," *History of European Ideas* 33 (2007): 157–73. On Voltaire's sceptical response to Vattel's treatise see Dan Edelstein, "Enlightenment rights talk," *The Journal of Modern History* 86, no. 3 (2014): 533–8.

[124] Société du comte de la Lippe, "Extrait des conférences de la société de M. le Comte de la Lippe" (Lausanne, 1742–45), *Bibliothèque cantonale et universitaire Lausanne*, Ms. BCUL 2S 1386/1–2, now transcribed and published online at http://lumieres.unil.ch/projets/5/.

[125] Société du comte de la Lippe, "Assemblée XIX. Lecture du chapitre XXIII de l'Anti-Machiavel 'Comment il faut fuir les Flatteurs,'" in "Extrait des conférences de la société de M. le Comte de la Lippe," 30 March 1743, 1:215, transcribed at http://lumieres.unil.ch/fiches/trans/534/. The remark is attributed to Lieutenant Ballival De Bochat.

prodigious writings.[126] Saint-Pierre had doubted whether European states could be reformed and their leaders animated by the "spirit of commerce" absent the establishment of a European Union or system of permanent arbitration; Rousseau greatly amplified this scepticism while also denying the availability of Saint-Pierre's solution.[127] From this perspective, the vision of Europe articulated by the *Anti-Machiavel* was an absolute travesty. Rousseau, who later defended Machiavelli's *The Prince* as "the book of republicans" and its author as "an honest man and a good citizen,"[128] identified Frederick as the real Machiavellian in a 1758 letter:

> I can neither esteem nor love a man without principles, who tramples every law of nations, who does not believe in virtue, but regards it as a decoy for toying with idiots and who began his Machiavellism by refuting Machiavelli. I confess that I would always like to keep the diameter of the earth between me and that man, I think I could sleep more comfortably there.[129]

Rousseau later made this condemnation public, and cast the *Anti-Machiavel* as the antithesis of Fénelon's ideals, in his best-selling novel *Emile, or On Education* (1762). At the very end of the novel, it is finally time for Emile to exit his pedagogical cocoon and learn about the real world. Following Rousseau's exposition of his political philosophy, "the true principles of political right" of the *Social Contract*, Emile's tutor takes him on a tour of Europe, with Fénelon's book as his guide:

> Then I make him read *Telemachus* while proceeding on his journey. We seek the happy Salente and the good Idomeneus, made wise by dint of misfortunes. On our way we find many Protesilauses, and no Philocles. Adrastus, king of the Dorians, is also not impossible to find. But let us leave the readers to imagine our travels – or to make them in our stead with *Telemachus* in hand; and let us

---

126 On Rousseau's engagement with Saint-Pierre see Olaf Asbach, *Die Zähmung der Leviathane: die Idee einer Rechtsordnung zwischen Staaten bei Abbe de Saint-Pierre und Jean-Jacques Rousseau* (Berlin: Akademie Verlag, 2002); and Jean-Jacques Rousseau, *Principes du droit de la guerre: écrits sur la paix perpétuelle*, ed. Blaise Bachofen and Céline Spector (Paris: J. Vrin, 2008).

127 Rousseau's scepticism in this regard is explored in Richard Tuck, *The Rights of War and Peace: Political Thought and the International Order from Grotius to Kant* (Oxford University Press, 1999), chap. 7; Béla Kapossy, *Iselin Contra Rousseau: Sociable Patriotism and the History of Mankind* (Basel: Schwabe, 2006); Sonenscher, *Before the Deluge*, chap. 3; Richard Whatmore, *Against War and Empire: Geneva, Britain, and France in the Eighteenth Century* (New Haven: Yale University Press, 2012), chap. 3.

128 Jean-Jacques Rousseau, *The Social Contract and Other Later Political Writings*, ed. Victor Gourevitch (Cambridge University Press, 1997), 95.

129 Jean-Jacques Rousseau to Toussaint-Pierre Lenieps, 4 December 1758, in Jean-Jacques Rousseau, *Correspondance complète de Jean Jacques Rousseau*, ed. R.A. Leigh, vol. 5 (Geneva: Institut et musée Voltaire, 1967), no. 748.

not suggest to them invidious comparisons that the author himself dismisses or makes in spite of himself.[130]

As contemporaries well understood, and as Rousseau later spelled out in his *Confessions*, "invidious comparisons" were precisely the point here: the remark about Adrastus was a reference to Frederick.[131] In Fénelon's thinly-veiled allegory, Idomeneus's Salente stood for a reformed France. Idomeneus, unlike Louis XIV, was persuaded to abandon his misguided quest for false glory through conquest; he then joined the alliance that had formed to resist his unjust ambitions (an alliance that promised to become the permanent foundation of international peace) in order to combat the real menace to all, namely Adrastus, King of the Dorians, "who despised the gods, and sought only to deceive mankind."[132] In *Emile*, Rousseau rounded off his attack on the *Anti-Machiavel* and its author by implicating its editor as well. "Besides," concluded Rousseau, echoing Voltaire's review of the *Anti-Machiavel* while accusing him of hubris, "since Emile is not a king and I am not a god, we do not fret about not being able to imitate Telemachus and Mentor in the good that they did for men."[133]

The *Anti-Machiavel* no longer figures in discussions of Europe's destiny or in debates about the nature of a stabilized international order, though Frederick makes a brief appearance in John Rawls's *Law of Peoples* (1999), where he serves as an archetype for Machiavellism.[134] In the nineteenth-century, however, Frederick could still represent the possibility of superseding Machiavelli's politics. For the prominent Swiss international lawyer Johann Caspar Bluntschli, for example, it was important to establish that the emergence of modern political life was not to be traced back to 1789 or 1688, nor to the Renaissance or the Reformation, but rather to 1740, because Frederick's reign represented the taming of powerful post-Renaissance monarchies like Louis XIV's and their transition into constitutional regimes that could coexist in a stable international order.[135] Of course, not all nineteenth-century writers on international law were so sanguine about Frederick's legacy. But even Henry Wheaton, the American diplomat who served as Ambassador to

---

[130] Jean-Jacques Rousseau, *Emile, or On Education*, trans. Alan Bloom (Basic Books, 1979), 467; Jean-Jacques Rousseau, *Oeuvres complètes*, ed. Bernard Gagnebin and Marcel Raymond (Paris: Gallimard, 1964), 4:849.
[131] Rousseau, *Oeuvres complètes*, 1:593.   [132] Fénelon, *Télemachus*, 214.
[133] Rousseau, *Emile*, 467; Rousseau, *Oeuvres complètes*, 4:849.
[134] John Rawls, *The Law of Peoples* (Cambridge: Harvard University Press, 1999), 26.
[135] Johann Caspar Bluntschli, *The Theory of the State*, trans. P.E. Matheson, R. Lodge, and D.G. Ritchie (Oxford: Clarendon Press, 1885), 55.

Berlin in the 1830s and 1840s, retained a fine sense of the nature of the ambition that animated the *Anti-Machiavel*, even as he named Frederick a warmonger. Voltaire and Rousseau alike would have recognized the work that he glossed in his celebrated *History of the Law of Nations in Europe and America* (1845):

These sentiments, worthy of a Fenelon in the benevolent spirit they breathe, and at the same time not too refined to be capable of practical application by the ruler of a state, did not prevent Frederick from reviving an antiquated claim of the house of Brandenburg to several duchies in Silesia [...] His real motives are avowed in his private correspondence, which discloses the love of glory, ambition, the desire of employing the army and treasure his father had bequeathed to him, in the aggrandizement of Prussia, as the secret springs by which he was moved.[136]

The *Anti-Machiavel* was animated by the prospect of stabilizing the balance of power, by a vision of independent states capable of substituting commerce for war without relying on the degree of consensus required to establish an institutional order above themselves. Whenever the latter has appeared beyond reach, visions of this sort have tended to return to the fore, however incisively the tensions they harbor have been exposed by the likes of Saint-Pierre or Rousseau. It is overly hasty, therefore, to claim that "it was Adam Smith [...] and not Frederick II, who with *The Wealth of Nations* wrote the true *Anti-Machiavel* of the Age of Enlightenment."[137] In fact, as Istvan Hont recognized, the *Anti-Machiavel* and *The Wealth of Nations* shared a good deal in common in their respective efforts to rework the idea of reason of state for an age of commerce that was something less than an age of perpetual peace: not to resolve the fundamental tension between the way of commerce and the way of war, but to determine how, and how far, the politics of necessity could be curbed by commerce.[138]

[136] Henry Wheaton, *History of the Law of Nations in Europe and America: From the Earliest Times to the Treaty of Washington, 1842* (Gould, Bank & Company, 1845), 170.
[137] Michel Senellart, "La Raison d'Etat Antimachiavelienne," in *La Raison d'Etat: Politique et Rationalité*, ed. Christian Lazzeri and Dominique Reynié (Paris: Presses universitaires de France, 1992), 32.
[138] Istvan Hont, "Introduction," in *Jealousy of Trade: International Competition and the Nation-State in Historical Perspective* (Cambridge: Harvard University Press, 2005), 8, 22–30, 78–81.

3   From jealousy of trade to the neutrality
     of finance
     Isaac de Pinto's "system" of luxury and
     perpetual peace

     Koen Stapelbroek

     I

"A spectre was haunting the modern world, wrote the Neapolitan
Ferdinando Galiani in 1751, the spectre of 'luxury'".[1] When Istvan
Hont reminded his readership of Galiani's phrase from *Della moneta*,
which would echo in the opening lines of a much more famous text, the
Communist manifesto, he immediately stressed the existence of two different eighteenth-century luxury debates: one between "ancients" and
"moderns" – on whether inequality was an unequivocal political problem and the idea of luxury represented moral vice – and the other among
"moderns" – where the issue was how to channel human nature as
it was onto a course of morally and politically sustainable economic
growth. It was the latter debate among moderns that Hont argued
ran from Fénelon and Mandeville to Adam Smith to which virtually all eighteenth-century political writers in some way contributed.
This debate connected the somewhat differently oriented natural law,
property and sociability debates of the seventeenth century to the discourses of classical political economy, the "social question" and economic nationalism of the nineteenth century. In between, as Hont's
entire oeuvre suggests, the eighteenth century formed a historical hinging point that saw the escalation of "Jealousy of trade," the first global
trade wars and major financial crises, but that was also the period in
which what are still the most advanced reflections on the options for
stabilising modern politics were developed. The theme of luxury, within
the architecture of these reflections, connected any particular writer's
positions on self-interest, commerce, finance, foreign trade, population

[1] Istvan Hont, "The Early Enlightenment Debate on Commerce and Luxury," in: *The
Cambridge History of Eighteenth-Century Political Thought*, eds. Mark Goldie and Robert
Wokler (Cambridge University Press, 2006), 379–418: 379; Ferdinando Galiani, *Della
moneta e scritti inediti*, eds. A. Caracciolo and A. Merola (Milan: Feltrinelli, 1963), 241,
also 282. Marx was an avid reader of Galiani's works, particularly *Della moneta*.

growth, international law and the history of trade and political institutions and as such provided an index of the range of positions on all eighteenth-century debates on peace and trade. This was the shared eighteenth-century template typical for the political thought of Rousseau, Smith and many others.[2]

The argument of this chapter shows how this template functioned in the case of the Amsterdam financier and political writer Isaac de Pinto, who, like Galiani, operated in the same domain as the writers who have been discussed more extensively by Hont in his published works. What is special about Pinto's political thought is that through his specific theories of luxury, the development of global trade "circulation" and his inclusion of modern financial institutions into the "constitutional" workings of the modern state, he engaged both with Harringtonian distinctions about the reform of modern government and with the legacy of the Peace of Utrecht. What has hitherto not been recognised is that a lot of what Pinto argued in the eighteenth century, and what was then highly controversial, became included into the constitutional politics that were fundamental to the Vienna order as was established in the early nineteenth century.

Pinto is mostly known now as an opponent of David Hume's thoughts on public credit or as a defender of the British government in the outbreak of the War of the American Independence.[3] Starting from his ideas on luxury, quickly compared with Galiani's, and mapping these onto the wider dimensions of eighteenth-century political thought that are covered by his writings a more comprehensive view emerges. One of the best connected figures in the worlds of trade, finance and actual politics in eighteenth-century Europe, a reconstruction of what Pinto called "my system" ultimately provides opportunities for better understanding the political dangers of the time and how they might be neutralised.

II

What was remarkable about Galiani's "Digression on luxury" in *Della moneta* was his critique of Jean-François Melon on the subject of luxury.

[2] On Rousseau and Smith, Istvan Hont, *Politics in Commercial Society: Jean-Jacques Rousseau and Adam Smith* (Cambridge, MA: Harvard University Press, 2015). The general template, Istvan Hont, *Jealousy of Trade. International Competition and the Nation-State in Historical Perspective* (Cambridge, MA: Harvard University Press, 2005), esp. 1–156.

[3] On Pinto the intellectual biography by I.J.A. Nijenhuis, *Een Joodse Philosophe, Isaac de Pinto (1717–1787)* (Amsterdam: NEHA, 1992) is the best introduction. See also J.L. Cardoso and A. de Vasconcelos Nogueira, "Isaac de Pinto (1717–1787). An Enlightened Economist and Financier," *History of Political Economy* 37 (2005), 264–92. On Hume on finance, Hont, *Jealousy of Trade*, pp. 325–53. Pinto and Hume are compared in my forthcoming "Trade, Treaties and Political Virtue: The Machiavellian Legacy at the End of the Republic."

Most arguments advanced in *Della moneta* were in agreement with and followed Melon's *Essai politique*, whose influence on Neapolitan political economy (notably on Galiani's teachers Celestino Galiani and Bartolomeo Intieri) right after gaining sovereign independence in 1734 is well known.[4] Underneath the rhetorical presentation of the *Dialogues on the grain trade*, published in 1770, directed against physiocracy still lay everything that Melon had argued about grain policy in the *Essai politique*. In his earlier work Galiani agreed with Melon's measured defence of the use of monetary devaluations. Bearing in mind the detrimental effects on credit if devaluations were used too often, under circumstances in which a devaluation was necessary for the public good everyone would accept it as "justice," Galiani claimed.[5]

Galiani's Italian contemporaries were astounded to find that in *Della moneta* he restated some of Melon's highly contentious favourable positions on the *alzamento* and that in some parts of his discussion of public debts and paper money he stayed quite close to John Law. Had they looked in closer detail at Galiani's position on luxury they might have been even more puzzled. There Galiani was not the radical "modern" they believed him to be, but instead showed himself very wary of luxury and saw it as a restriction to economic growth.

The most important difference between Melon and Galiani was their basic attitude to the politics of luxury. Melon defined it as the "business of the State to make an Advantage of" luxury.[6] Luxury was the key to economic growth and should be cultivated, explored and exploited in Melon's version of neo-Colbertism.[7] It destroyed sloth and idleness and was "an additional incitement" for people to "enjoy an easy, voluptuous life." It was present in every "well-governed society."[8] Galiani, by contrast, held that luxury might be regulated and "converted into a state

---

[4] See Vincenzo Ferrone, *Scienza, natura, religione: mondo newtoniano e cultura italiana nel primo Settecento* (Naples: Jovene, 1982), John Robertson, *The Case for the Enlightenment: Scotland and Naples 1680–1760* (Cambridge University Press, 2005), Koen Stapelbroek, *Love, Self-Deceit and Money: Commerce and Morality in the Early Neapolitan Enlightenment* (University of Toronto Press, 2008).

[5] Galiani, *Della moneta*, 201.

[6] Jean-François Melon, *A political essay upon commerce* (Dublin, 1738), 194, 174.

[7] Melon's ideas on luxury are often placed in the same bracket as Mandeville's, but this is crucially wrong. While the essence of Mandeville's self-liking is the impossibility of distinguishing between needs and luxuries, Melon, perfectly following Colbert, sharply differentiated these kinds of goods, not so much as reflecting personal desires, but in the realm of foreign trade management. Trade in subsistence goods could relatively easily be established even between Britain and France. Once manufactured goods were involved it became more complicated. Still, this was no reason for *not* making manufactured goods an object of politics through the conclusion of an Anglo-French commercial treaty, Melon felt.

[8] Melon, *Political essay*, 177.

in which it is not harmful."[9] Yet, by its very nature it was a danger to society and a sign of imminent decline.

The core of the disagreement between Melon and Galiani on luxury lay in the moral philosophies from which the two positions were developed and in how these influenced their general politics. Melon's theory of political economy was rooted in a neo-Augustinian notion of sinful man.[10] Luxury was an engine of growth, not a complex parameter in the social fabric of economic productivity and political stability. The young Galiani instead, had found himself engaging with Paolo Mattia Doria's concept of *amor proprio*, which Galiani redeveloped into a principle of "self-deceit," a socialising force generating new forms of self-love and ultimately the possibility of a socially shared value system from which the institution of money could emerge.[11] Being able to explain the emergence of money functioned as a litmus test to all rival theories of commercial sociability and Galiani himself, balancing on the shoulders of a previous generation of Neapolitan thinkers, was the only one who passed it. From this decidedly non-contractual basis Galiani fiercely criticised Locke, Montesquieu and all others whose ideas about the nature of money, financial and economic policy were based on an imperfect theory of sociability. Ultimately, this could only have disastrous political consequences.

Galiani's explanation of how politics required a theory of human "self-deceit" shadowed Giambattista Vico's handling of fear, self-interest and idolatry in his *Scienza nuova*.[12] In their historical dimension both their theories of human development rejected the conjectural schemes put forward by natural law thinkers and reconstructed primitive law and property along the lines of Roman civil law.[13] What Vico did in his *Scienza nuova* the young Galiani had planned to do in his "Arte del governo": provide an institutional overview of the history of humankind. The "Digression on luxury" in *Della moneta* was directly taken from this combined historical and moral philosophical manuscript. It explained by

[9] Galiani, *Della moneta*, 242.
[10] For Melon's moral philosophy, cf. Antonella Alimento, "Entre range et mérite: la réflexion économique de l'abbé Duguet," *Il pensiero gerarchico in Europa (XVIII–XIX secolo)*, eds. Antonella Alimento and Cristina Cassina (Florence: Olschki, 2002), 11–30.
[11] Doria (with his concept of *amor proprio* and his tripartite division of principles of government, first developed in his *La vita civile* of 1709) was to the young Galiani what Rousseau and Montesquieu were to a later generation of European writers. See Stapelbroek, *Love, Self-Deceit and Money*, 90–106.
[12] See Stapelbroek, *Love, Self-Deceit and Money*, 106–26.
[13] In his autobiography Vico ecstatically cited lengthily from LeClerc's review of his early work where LeClerc recognised the novelty of Vico's inversion of the structure of natural law theory. Cf. Hont, *Politics in Commercial Society*, pp. 69–73 on Smith's take on Roman law and natural liberty as the root difference between Smith and Rousseau.

which mechanisms medieval luxury destroyed the overconsuming aristocracy and fueled the creation of a bourgeois class. In the same way *Della moneta* described how in Genova the *Casa di San Giorgio* had corrupted the trade republic and how in Rome and to a degree in modern Britain class politics sabotaged the public good: "in this way, in our day the poor have become the usurees of the rich, and the rich the administrators of the rents of the poor."[14]

The "Arte del governo," however, was no argument against inequality but an inquiry into how modern politics might contain its risks and preserve commercial liberty. The analysis of how a theory of sociable "self-deceit" fit with the development of early "commercial society" at the time of the Trojan war and how the discovery of America had created new wealth and population growth were fundamental steps towards demarcating the scope of "good government" from "tyranny."[15]

Galiani's bigger picture of the history of trade, human nature, law and politics, in which luxury was an analytical variable broke off into a distinction with a Harringtonian ring to it: "good government" and "justice" were those political actions that confirmed the providential regularity in the history of commerce. The backbone of this theory of politics was the concept "utility," a measure of the intrinsic capacity of a society to satisfy the natural and accrued moral desires of its members. "Tyranny," sometimes dictated by private interest, was the state in which political decision-making tended to a collapse of society into "despotism" and "military government." It was the latter prospect that Galiani in his *Dialogues on the grain trade* held in front of his French audience when he called France a "nation des joueurs." Treating the politics of grain as an issue directly related to the constitution[16] Galiani represented the grain debate as the challenge of going from a situation in which war was "the luxury of the monarchy" to France becoming a commercial monarchy capable of peaceful competition with Britain.[17]

Whatever Galiani's exact positions were on how to stabilise modern politics, domestically and at the interstate level, is not at stake here, but their character was recognised by contemporary critics – and rightly so – as similar to the positions adopted by Isaac de Pinto who published his main work in 1771. Triggered by Pinto's praise for Galiani's *Dialogues*

[14] Galiani, *Della moneta*, 241–4, 326, 109, 236.
[15] Galiani, *Della moneta*, 351–79, 390–2.
[16] Galiani stated this in correspondence with J.B. Suard. Ferdinando Galiani, *Correspondance avec Mme d'Epinay, Mme Necker, Mme Geoffrin, &c. Diderot, Grimm, d'Alembert, De Sartine, d'Holbach, &c* (II Vols. eds. Lucien Perey & Gaston Maugras, Paris: Lévy, 1881), I: 193.
[17] Inverting Fénelon's logic the phrase "war is the luxury of the monarchy" was the only one to feature both in *Della moneta* and the later *Dialogues*. Stapelbroek, *Love, Self-Deceit and Money*, 43.

on the grain trade, the physiocrat Baudeau lumped together Pinto and Galiani as representatives of the same system of "false politics." Tapping the same reservoir of false principles ostensibly geared towards "peace" and "universal prosperity," Baudeau ranted, Pinto and Galiani also held similar views of luxury.[18]

III

With what exact purposes Pinto intervened in the luxury debate when he published his *Essai sur le luxe* in 1762 is unclear.[19] At the outset of his *Essai* he stated that it was the most important theme in modern politics and that a "person of consideration" had inquired about "the causes of commercial decline of a certain state" (probably the Dutch Republic), which Pinto had suggested lay in luxury. This while "some first order minds" had judged luxury "as necessary and even useful in a large Kingdom."[20] Rather than a delayed critique of these appraisals by Melon, Voltaire and Montesquieu, the authorship of the *Encyclopédie* entry *Luxe* and the political debates of the Seven Years' War provide the contexts for Pinto's argument.

In the wake of a bankruptcy during the Seven Years' War, Pinto left Amsterdam for Paris where he quickly built up a political and intellectual network – including Voltaire, Diderot, Hume, Mirabeau and possibly Galiani who was a Neapolitan diplomat in Paris in these years – and was involved in the Peace negotiations at Fontainebleau.[21] These years also saw the publication of a few small works by Pinto, including the text on luxury.[22] Significantly, as he wrote in the introduction to the later *Traité*: "The first part of this Essay was written in France in the year 1761. I

---

[18] *Éphemerides du Citoyen* vol. 10 (1771), 67, 98.

[19] See Richard H. Popkin, "Isaac de Pinto's criticism of Mandeville and Hume on luxury," *SVEC* 154 (1976), 1705–14. Nijenhuis, *Een Joodse Philosophe*, 104–12. Hont, *Jealousy of Trade*, judged Pinto a "protagonist of [. . .] luxury" but his international reputation, in the words of Accarias de Serionne, was that he was an "enemy of luxury *tout court*" (Nijenhuis, 107). The title of the Dutch translation in the *Vaderlandsche Letter-Oefeningen* of 1763 emphasised its "harmful effects on the public good" ["nadeelige uitwerkselen voor het gemeen"].

[20] Isaac de Pinto, *Essai sur le luxe* (Amsterdam, 1762), 3.

[21] Richard H. Popkin, "Hume and Isaac de Pinto," *Texas Studies in Literature and Language. A Journal of the Humanities* 12 (1970), 417–30; Richard H. Popkin, "Hume and Isaac de Pinto, II. Five new letters," *Hume and the Enlightenment. Essays Presented to Ernest Campbell Mossner*, William B. Todd ed. (Edinburgh University Press, 1974), 99–127. In 1777 Pinto became the object of a slander campaign waged by the *Gazette des Deux-Ponts*, which branded him a traitor of the Dutch (francophile) interest. Pinto's own dossier of the affair is in Ets Haim – Livraria Montezinos Amsterdam, BEH 48A19 (nrs. 5, 6, 8).

[22] Notably, Isaac de Pinto, *Apologie pour la nation juive: Réflexions critiques sur le premier chapitre du VIIe tome des oeuvres de M. Voltaire* (Amsterdam, 1762) signalled his entrance into *philosophe* circles.

thought it necessary therefore to enter into a detail of various particulars respecting the English funds, with which the French were unacquainted. Several persons took copies of it at Paris. Some English noblemen, whom I saw there after the peace, did me the same honor."[23] Pinto had long believed that public finance systems were decisive in modern politics and the possibility of creating a lasting peace. When credit and the strength of the British public funds became a topic in French pamphleteering, Pinto intervened by writing a first version of what later became his main work and spread it among the Anglo-French elites gathered in Paris.

Likewise, his argument on luxury responded to dangerous political misconceptions of the time. To see how contemporaries understood Pinto's luxury argument – he became known as "the author of the *Essai sur le luxe*" – it is useful to compare it to the *Encyclopédie* entry on *Luxe* edited by Saint-Lambert. Certainly, in these years more short writings on luxury appeared that in style and content are comparable to the *Encyclopédie* entry and it is known that the article had a complex authorial history.[24] The text that was edited by Saint-Lambert bore some significant resemblances to Pinto's and may have been inspired by it to some degree. It even appeared in English translation in 1766 with "Mr. Pinto" as the author mentioned on the title page. Yet, the differences are more instructive.

The starting point of both texts was that the word luxury was indeed something of a spectre. It had always been criticised in history as a moral danger to the state and was recently excessively praised for its capacities to enhance economic productivity, stimulate population growth, increase circulation of goods and level material inequalities. The standard-bearers of the latter argument were Melon, Voltaire, and Hume. The problem in Pinto's words was that it was impossible to "accept this system without large restrictions" and that luxury still needed to be "methodically analysed" to understand its political effects.[25]

Saint-Lambert's longer text included numerous examples that differentiated between various states in history and how their characteristics

---

[23] Isaac de Pinto, *Traité De La Circulation Et Du Crédit: [...] & Suivi D'une Lettre Sur La Jalousie Du Commerce, Où L'on Prouve Que L'interêt Des Puissances Commerçantes Ne Se Croise Point* (Amsterdam, 1771). References are to the English translation Isaac de Pinto, *An essay on circulation and credit: in four parts; and a letter on the jealousy of commerce* (London, 1774), xv.

[24] For context on comparable texts by Auffray, Forbonnais, Sain-Lambert and others see François Moureau, "Le manuscrit de l'article Luxe ou l'atelier de Saint-Lambert," *Recherches sur Diderot et sur l'Encyclopédie* 1 (1986), 71–84. [Saint-Lambert], *Essay on Luxury written originally in French by Mr. Pinto* (London, 1764).

[25] Pinto, *Essai sur le luxe*, 3.

responded to degrees of material inequality. While "the desire of enriching one self is, and ought to be considered as one amongst the many springs of every government, that is not founded on the equality and community of goods" it depended on "the principal objects of government, considered in general" whether luxury "should ever ruin a state."[26] The problem was not so much those "passions which introduce luxury" but their coupling with "private interest" that could turn into a political problem.[27] Saint-Lambert analysed the nature of "despotism" as the epitome of corrupt government and concluded that "the arbitrary power of a single man over a great number, by the help of a small number" relied on the corruption of the few whose luxury was often, though not necessarily the vehicle by which private interest "occasioned such changes to be made in the constitution of a state."[28] To prevent luxury from becoming the vehicle of corrupt private interest sometimes oldfashioned sumptuary laws could be very adequate, while sometimes luxury was innocent and in balance with another register of passions of patriotic "public spirit" that together determined whether "good order is maintained."[29]

Pinto did not hold this same moral philosophy of balancing centrifugal and centripetal passions that Saint-Lambert copied from Shaftesbury and was also shared by Galiani's Neapolitan contemporary Genovesi.[30] Instead, Pinto saw an evolving interplay in human nature between the realms of the physical and the moral.[31] Like for Galiani, the key concept was error. Humans, Pinto explained in a manuscript from the early 1740s, were capable of productive moral self-deceit in the field of commerce when they attributed between each other new imagined values to previously less useful things and nourished desires to own these things. Luxury, *amour propre* and vanity, thus understood, were neither virtues nor "necessary vices" (here Pinto engaged with Mandeville), but signs of a developing social system of opinion and exchange that required new forms of accommodation in order not to collapse.[32] To understand

---

[26] [Saint-Lambert], *Essay on Luxury*, 30.   [27] [Saint-Lambert], *Essay on Luxury*, 15–16.
[28] [Saint-Lambert], *Essay on Luxury*, 15–18: cit. 16–17.
[29] [Saint-Lambert], *Essay on Luxury*, 32.
[30] For Shaftesbury, Hont, "Commerce and Luxury." For Genovesi, Koen Stapelbroek, "Preserving the Neapolitan state: Antonio Genovesi and Ferdinando Galiani on commercial society and planning economic growth," *History of European Ideas 32* (2006), 406–29.
[31] As he argued in the later chapters of Isaac de Pinto, *Précis des Arguments Contre les Matérialistes* (The Hague, 1774) in which he discussed natural philosophy, religion and free will.
[32] BEH 48A19 (nr. 11) entitled "Paradoxe soutenu de plusieurs Exemples Pour prouver Que la Vérité nous conduit souvant à l'erreur et l'Erreur à la Vérité." See also nr. 10 an early version of his critique of philosophical materialism.

amour propre in commercial society as a centrifugal individual passion that required new integrative codes of virtue was fundamentally misconceived. Shared error itself essentially increased social integration, but needed to be sustainable, at which level the moral quality of motives (the ideas of which were itself socially conditioned) and social effects of spending tended to correlate. Here, against the moral relativism that Voltaire's luxury argument tended to, Pinto reconciled his view of morality as grounded in error with the idea that people's intuitions about good and bad usually were correct.[33]

Commercial morality offered new possibilities. As he argued in his *Letter to Diderot on card-playing*, "both in the natural and moral state of man" – the latter was built upon the former – "there results a new system of manners, temper, and constitution."[34] Card-playing had civilised human manners and the comprehensive way in which it spoke to the human passions was representative of the progress as well as the dangers to commercial society. It made no sense to try to separate the virtues and vices of commercial society. What mattered in comparing previous compounds of human emotions to the present was that "humankind has gained more than it has lost" and that while states no longer could rely on patriotism, the self-deceptive conditioning of the passions made man fit for commercial society, which needed an altogether different style of politics. In "my system," Pinto reasoned, "the infatuation of a frivolous amusement, which deceives and eludes the effect of the passions [. . .] means the virtues are often lopped of their growth; but then the vices [. . .] are still more".[35] This was the essence of commercial liberty that still had to be thought through properly to "operate on the government, and on manners."[36] While the modern history of mankind had seen three crucial revolutions, the demise of feudalism, the discovery of America and the invention of printing and progress of arts and sciences, which together conspired to the rise of civil liberty, population growth and "a greater equality among man," the fourth was still incomplete. Even if "spiritual Machiavelism" had lost its supporters, there remained many "errors political and moral" that still had to be "exhausted" before human civilisation would be securely lifted to a higher level.[37]

---

[33] The same theory, developed by his uncle Celestino, was held by Ferdinando Galiani, Stapelbroek, *Love, Self-Deceit and Money*, 56–87.

[34] Isaac de Pinto, *On Card-Playing. in a Letter from Monsieur de Pinto, to Monsieur Diderot. with a Translation from the Original, and Observations by the Translator* (London, 1768), 20.

[35] Pinto, *On Card-Playing*, 22.

[36] Pinto, *On Card-Playing*, 24.   [37] Pinto, *On Card-Playing*, 25–8.

At this stage in the argument Pinto and the *Encyclopédie* seemingly converged again. Saint-Lambert noted that "almost all over Europe, the emulative passion for appearing rich, and a respect for riches" had arisen "independently of [..] natural causes." While previously under the "feodal law" there was "no opulence but in landed property" the "progress of commerce" had created "a new kind of property." Pinto and Saint-Lambert agreed that these new kinds of property needed to be carefully incorporated into the political order of modern states. Like Galiani they both used the terms "tyranny" and "despotism" to denote a lapse into the causes that had brought down Rome and many other states in history.[38] "Luxury" in this discourse was an analytical variable that beyond the notion of unproductive consumption hollowed out the state. Yet the ways in which Saint-Lambert and Pinto argued this point differed slightly.

Despite arguing that luxury and corruption were not a direct function of each other and their relation was mediated by the specific constitution of the state (itself a response to the natural development process of states from simplicity to refinement), Saint-Lambert still defined luxury as a moral constant.[39] Saint-Lambert copied from Forbonnais, the intended author of the luxury entry, and indeed indirectly from Melon, that "luxury is the use which we make of riches and of industry, in order to procure an agreeable existence."[40] From this perspective of luxury as a useful vice, it was important to avoid "attacking luxury" fiscally or by other redistributive means and risk a relapse into simplicity, but also to reform it, as disorderly luxury dried up its own channels. The task of politics, Saint-Lambert offered his solution, was to contain the socially divisive aspects of commercial society through an "implicit reform" of new moral codes that would promote the re-circulation of capital and enhance productivity.[41] In this way the incorporation of new kinds of property, like national debts – which Saint-Lambert valued very negatively[42] – into dangerously urbanised modern states might hopefully be kept from overwhelming their constitution.

IV

For Pinto, luxury was an altogether different phenomenon. Human nature was not greedy, anti-social and requiring correction, but fundamentally error prone and increasingly hyper-social as the edifice of

[38] [Saint-Lambert], *Essay on Luxury, passim.*
[39] [Saint-Lambert], *Essay on Luxury*, 13–16.   [40] [Saint-Lambert], *Essay on Luxury*, 1.
[41] [Saint-Lambert], *Essay on Luxury*, 58; 44, 80–6: 81.
[42] [Saint-Lambert], *Essay on Luxury*, 52.

shared artificial values and desires in modern societies rose. The political challenge of luxury, from this perspective, lay not in balancing the passions, but in managing the moral structures of exchange, value and esteem. The precarious character of commercial society itself was what made luxury a danger. Pinto did not call for a return to simplicity and frugality, even though he emphasised that excessive luxury was the prime cause of the decadence of states.[43] He accepted the political economic argument that more labourers might be fed through the luxury consumption and circulation of capital owned by a small share of society. But in order to capitalise on this prospect, which carried huge risks, it was essential that the fabric of desires and capital investment remained linked to agricultural productivity and population growth.[44] If this took place luxury indeed could stimulate economic productivity in real terms and produce the benign effects that Hume, Melon, and Voltaire envisaged while underestimating the risks involved.

Luxury however was much more likely to announce an irreversible loss of wealth if not a lapse into military government and simplicity. Commercial society was a structure that produced new forms of artificial wealth based on artificial ideas. These could and should feed into the creation of true wealth, at which point luxury could serve as a "thermometer" of wealth and truly be "the symptom of power, riches, industry and opulence of a state." It was therefore a major mistake to see luxury as the *cause* of wealth, as human nature was always inclined to err and which Hume, Voltaire and Melon had mistakenly turned into a political principle. Luxury and artificial desires fuelled vanity and self-love and "prompt[ed] many to run into expenses, beyond what their circumstances will admit, by the respect attached to it." Likewise, on a political level taking luxury for the cause of wealth and power was "to sap a commodious edifice in order to build a larger, which we can never erect." Following a sensation of "violent fevers [...] which seem to increase the natural strength" soon "the state loses the house and does not gain the palace."[45] Pinto invoked the metaphor used by Montesquieu of the natives of Louisiana who harvested fruit by axing the tree and likewise compared a state that engaged in mistaken trade policies to "a body that devours its own limbs."[46]

The standard trajectory Pinto identified for a commercial state to set up its own decline ran via the development of an unbalanced economy. Here Pinto criticised the supporters of democratic luxury, like

---

[43] Pinto, *Essai sur le luxe*, 24.   [44] Pinto, *Essai sur le luxe*, 11, 23.

[45] Pinto, *Essai sur le luxe*, 11–12; Galiani, *Della moneta, passim* deployed the same metaphors.

[46] Pinto, *Essai sur le luxe*, 13,15, 19, 22.

Forbonnais, and specifically echoed both Galiani's concept of "utility" in *Della moneta* and the historical and moral developmental sketches in Rousseau's *Discourse on inequality*[47]:

It is the quantity of consumers, who regularly make an honest, well-supported and permanent expense, which augments industry, circulation, commerce, manufactures, and all the useful arts. But when excessive luxury causes, that the arts are lucrative in the inverse ratio of their utility, the most necessary become the most neglected.[48]

Should the profitability of labour employed within different sections of the economy become overly skewed, all the accrued notions of value attached to immaterial objects in a commercial society would collapse. Not only would the commodities owned by the nation fall into the hands of others, but a much larger and irreversible destruction of social capital would follow:

it is the number of individuals-in easy circumstances, which create its wealth [of the nation]. But it is absolutely false, that those possessions are found in the mass of the public; if the possession of each individual consisted in silver, this might be so; but property for the most part is fictitious or artificial: industry, credit, opinion, form a great part of the riches of each individual, which vanish, and are annihilated with the ruin of his former possessions, and are forever lost with respect to the state.[49]

Pinto was aware that this was not to begin with a political and economic problem, but a moral one. Human nature was the "martyr of opinion." The esteem of others was the "spectre that surrounded it, at the risk of becoming its victim."[50] The fate of those tempted by luxury and outward appearance bore a "resemblance to those unfortunate victims of love."[51] How then to approach this issue through politics?

The answer lay in policies that were fine-tuned to impinge upon exactly what luxury was. If the "political vice" that Pinto saw lay in that unattended "luxury destroys the means that render it salutary," the right policies were geared towards the promotion of sustainable capital reinvestment. Pinto explained what he meant through the example of public debts. In contrast with Saint-Lambert's negative connotations with state

[47] Rousseau as interpreted by Hont, *Politics in Commercial Society*.
[48] Pinto, *Essai sur le luxe*, 15; cf. Pinto, *Essay on Circulation and Credit*, 106: "They, who have undertaken to apologise for luxury, have run into another extreme. Their view of that multiplied circulation, which encourages industry and commerce, has not been complete. They did not consider, that circulation is maintained by a daily expence, permanent, solid, and constantly kept up."
[49] Pinto, *Essai sur le luxe*, 14.   [50] Pinto, *Essai sur le luxe*, 29.
[51] Pinto, *Essai sur le luxe*, 18. Cf. Galiani on "Platonic love," Stapelbroek, *Love, Self-Deceit and Money*, 143–52.

debts and modern finance, Pinto argued that "the Creation of public funds, when made opportunely and as long as they do not exceed the sphere of their power is a realised Alchemy, of which even those who operate it often do not know the mystery." Pinto believed that the mechanisms of credit and the monetisation of state debts were a potential solvent, channelling the reinvestment of unequal property and profits into new terrains from where the connection with the basic production factors of land and labour and the social bases of economic development remained intact.

There were others ways too in which cleverly designed policies managed modern wealth and inequality. Differently from Saint-Lambert, Pinto's definition of luxury as a "political vice" and its impact on "the corruption of manners" regarded not primarily the mixing of corrupt human nature with private interest.[52] That was only a secondary manifestation of the real problem. The root causes of corruption lay in the realm of social imagination and the institutional accommodation of investment opportunities for unequal wealth. The direct way to take the sting out of luxury would be to implement new social codes that made wealth accumulation and reinvestment, not spending the object of admiration. But such projects carried the inherent risk of tending to "tyranny." A more promising approach that was "easier in practise than one imagined and prodigiously useful" lay in the legal creation of personal spending regimes to be managed by banks issuing loans to the profligate victims of luxury in order to save their honour and credit and prevent social capital leakages. Next to this idea of financial re-education, Pinto in the late 1740s had proposed numerous projects, such as a national lottery, to Stadholder William IV and his advisors that all had the aim to use broad social-financial schemes to "turn vice into virtue."[53]

Politics for Pinto was the management of the human imagination, not the exploitation or patriotic balancing of human weakness. The problem of luxury accordingly went beyond the unproductivity of capital, but regarded the collapse of commercial society. The political challenge of modern politics was to make opinion work *for* the state rather than against it. Intriguingly, modern finance came into this perspective as

---

[52] Pinto, *Essai sur le luxe*, 10, 18.

[53] BEH 48A19 (nrs. 7, 9), Isaac de Pinto, "Tribut patriotique présenté avec le plus profond respect à Son Altesse Sérénissime Monseigneur le Prince d'Orange et de Nassau," particularly the "Essai sur le credit" and the "Essai sur les finances en general," Nationaal Archief Den Haag, 2.21.005.39 (Gogel collection), inv. 165; see also "Reflexions politiques, Au sujet d'une Augmentation de Taxe qu'on propose de mettre sur chaque Action de la Compagnie des indes Orientales sous le Titre d'Amptgeld," NADH, 1.10.29 (Fagel collection), inv. 2204.

a positive agency rather than a threat to society and the state. More fundamentally, in coming to these insights Pinto developed his political thought from very different building blocks from the principles held by Locke, Mandeville, Melon, Voltaire, and Hume.

V

Pinto's ideas on luxury ran parallel to his outlook on the history of the modern state. In an unpublished manuscript he declared that his later main work that was published in 1771 and that circulated in an early version in the early 1760s in France and Britain in fact grew out of earlier writings from the late 1740s.[54] Exactly at the time of the restoration of the Stadholder in 1748, Pinto reflected on the fate of the United Provinces and the scope and requirements for its successful economic regeneration and put forward a series of reform proposals. The nature of the underlying reflections is worth looking into.

In his manuscripts from the late 1740s Pinto sketched how the development of the American and Asian trade by European states and their East India Companies had given rise to a peculiar global system of economic development.[55] The Dutch in particular, Pinto explained, by way of their East India Company were the first to almost accidentally tap into a major resource for changing the face of the earth through trade. It was by means of this company that one had found the "secret" of how a sterile country could survive and flourish, after which geographical situation became a key factor in international politics. Many people still failed to understand the sheer impact of this discovery, Pinto asserted. Numerous philosophers and politicians ventured to argue with dry eyes that the mines of Peru and Mexico had not enriched Europe, but that the abundance of gold and silver only made subsistence goods and manual labour more expensive. Although in a simple sense they were right, the consequences of their views were absolutely false. After the discovery of America and the development of intercontinental currents of capital and goods streams, Europe had become infinitely richer and become universally opulent. While these particular riches were like other forms of commerce in that they both created immense fortunes and a lot of misery, Pinto admitted, it was still the case that without the abundance of gold and silver Amsterdam could only have 20,000 inhabitants rather than 220,000.

---

[54] BEH 48A19 (nr. 7), "Transactions auxquelles M. Is. de Pinto a eu part, pendant le dernier Stadhoudérat de Guilllaume IV," c. 20.
[55] Isaac de Pinto, *Tribut patriotique*.

Within the natural system of its economy, commerce for the Dutch Republic was "comme un fruit natural du pays." Whereas elsewhere trade was a secondary economic activity, it was a sort of "denrée chez nous." Following through this argument Pinto argued that the Dutch by means of trade, rather than through political alliances, were tied to the territory of other states whose reliance on the Dutch for their trade gave the Dutch state a special function and viability in interstate politics.[56] This conclusion was very similar in tone to the one of the text of the famous 1751 *Proposal* (drawn up by contacts of Pinto) for turning the entire Republic into a limited freeport, which confidently stated with regard to the attitude of other states towards a fiscal reform strengthening the Dutch capacity to attract trade, that "neighbouring Nations will be more or less concerned, in the Conservation of our Trade, as their commerce chiefly consists in the Vending of their own Products; and will therefore rather protect than obstruct ours, which has such a Connection with their own, that it may not improperly be called a Part."[57]

But Pinto was highly critical of this position if it was not included in a wider perspective on trade competition and public finance. Trade was only the beginning, not the end, of the development of the modern state and here Dutch policies had neglected to further cultivate their original advantage. Particularly following the "facheux" Peace of Utrecht Dutch politicians had failed to adapt the fiscal, financial and commercial structures of the state to the evolving requirements of the interstate commercial system.[58]

There was something normative about Pinto's argument. The discovery of America led to a primitive international trade society, but one that was dominated by fierce rivalries and injustices. Still, it was to be seen as a historical turning point that had to be seized to perfect the system of international trade. Here, Pinto echoed and contributed to a tradition of thought as well as diplomatic practice that around the War of the Spanish Succession engaged with the challenge of institutionally restructuring global trade (notably the Spanish South-America trade) to create a durable European system of commerce and "Perpetual Peace."[59] Just

---

[56] Pinto, *Tribut patriotique*.
[57] *Proposals made up by His late Highness the Prince of Orange [. . .] for redressing and amending the Trade of the Republick* (London, 1751), 59.
[58] Pinto, *Tribut patriotique*.
[59] This tradition of analysing Dutch trade as an embryonic case for the regulation of international commerce, inequality and finance is the object of my forthcoming study "Carthage must be preserved: the neutrality of trade and the end of the Dutch Republic." For now see Koen Stapelbroek, "'The long peace': commercial treaties and the principles of global trade at the Peace of Utrecht," *The 1713 Peace of Utrecht and its enduring effects* (ed. A.H.A. Soons, Leiden: Brill, 2017) and Koen Stapelbroek,

like luxury created "new kinds of property" that needed to be incorporated into the structure of society so global trade and circulation of goods
created "nouvelles valeurs" that had to be made sustainable.

Pinto's writings from the 1760s and 1770s shifted the perspective from
that of the Dutch Republic to that of the modern commercial state in
general and the dynamics of international competition. Intercontinental
flows of goods and capital through trade were a basis for the further
developmental stages of a functioning global trade system.[60] The starting
point, thus, was the same as in the 1740s (with the Spanish monarchy in
the role of the Dutch East India Company):

The world seemed to enlarge under the power of the Spanish monarchy, and
in many respects altered its form. A general opulence introduced by the gold
and silver of the new world, the multitude of hands employed to supply the new
wants and luxury of America, have created new means of subsistence. When the
political machines, like the elements of commerce, grew more extensive, vast
and complicated, they required springs stronger and more numerous. It became
necessary to multiply the circulation of paper, by which the numerary wealth was
increased. This was done as it were by instinct, but with fear and trembling. We
scarce knew what we were doing, or for what reason. Gold and silver having lost
three fourths of their value, a great quantity was required to represent so many
things, and to keep the same machines going which money had set in motion.
Means of all sorts were to be trebled. Without an augmentation of the signs of
value, which form an artificial wealth, neither commerce nor luxury could have
subsisted. It is the discovery of America, which, by an extraordinary increase
in the mass of gold and silver, has extended commerce, luxury, navigation, and
manufactures. There required a greater rapidity of circulation; and by a singular
paradox, as money multiplied and grew common, it required so many more signs
to represent it. Public funds, paper and stocks, became necessary, sometimes to
absorb an excess of specie, and sometimes, like a spunge, to be pressed and
give it back again. They fix, increase, and collect the numerary in one quarter,
while the specie itself circulates in another. The nation is really richer, because
it appears so, and furnishes government with greater supplies upon critical and
decisive occasions; without precluding, however, the use of proper expedients to
relieve the distress that must result from too great a swell of the national debt.[61]

The outcome of Pinto's "stages" theory of the commercial state – from
trade, to public debts, to credit – was the realisation of a fully-fledged
beneficial luxury regime, pretty much as Voltaire and others had naively
sketched from what Pinto believed were mistaken principles. Just like the
discovery of trade had been accidental to start with, but by nature was

"Between Utrecht and the War of the Austrian Succession: The Dutch Translation
of the British Merchant of 1728," *History of European Ideas* 40 (2014), 1026–43.
[60] Isaac de Pinto, *Letters on the American Troubles Translated from the French* (London,
1776), 44, 63–4, 73, 80–9.
[61] Pinto, *Essay on Circulation and Credit*, 29–30.

inevitable in the build-up of commercial states, so the same logic covered the accidental discovery of credit and state debts, which in reality were inevitably part of a fully developed commercial state. It was true that the financial contraction of the state led to an unequal distribution of "the taxes, drawn from the public to pay the interest" back to the public. Yet, commercial justice was not about levelling:

> This inequality is still corrected by the money which the proprietors of the funds spend themselves, and enable others to spend. A great part of their revenue is employed in favor of industry. Thus every account is balanced, the numerary phantom of artificial riches continues to subsist, produces its effect, supports the proprietors, and is beneficial to others. The mass of representative signs supplies the place of a real, solid property.[62]

In this way, clever politics and a fortuitous course of history led to the potential taming by humankind of the spectre of the human imagination. Overseas commerce had triggered within Europe the invention of new production methods and had allowed for the major increase of manufacturing improvement, parallel to which the "intrinsic power" of states had become linked with the management of public credit.[63] The connections that had thus arisen between "circulation" and "credit" acted as checks to the development of complementary exchange relationships between states, each drawing upon its own characteristics and relative competitive strengths in international trade.

It was telling in this regard to eighteenth-century observers of the luxury debate that Pinto's analysis of the development of commercial society was remarked by its translator to "have inverted the natural order of" production factors. "The first state of improvement depends on population and agriculture. The progress of commerce forms the second. The augmentation of specie, or balance of trade, is the last object of the three," so the Translator corrected Pinto's listing.[64] Yet, this was a deliberate inversion. Just like the Dutch Republic as a trade-based entity accidentally discovered the key to modern wealth, so Pinto presented credit as a solvent of primitive forms of inequality. In his main work Pinto repeated his dictum from the luxury essay that "the public funds

---

[62] Pinto, *Essay on Circulation and Credit*, 31. Cf. 175–6 on commercial justice in contrast with the politics of inequality in antiquity (and a blast against Voltaire's understanding of usury in ancient Israel).

[63] Pinto, *Essay on Circulation and Credit*, 26–30, 44–7. Pinto, *Letters on the American Troubles*, 44, 63–4, 73, 80–9. Compare Hont, *Jealousy of Trade*, 36–7, 52.

[64] Cf. Smith's "unnatural and retrograde order" in Hont, *Jealousy of Trade*, 354–88 and Smith's inversion of natural law theory adhered to by Locke and Rousseau in Hont, *Politics in Commercial Society*, 69–73.

are a realised alchemy."[65] It was this "alchemy" that enabled Pinto ultimately to agree with Montesquieu (as did Galiani) that wealth was not always what it seemed:

"Among commercial nations," says Montesquieu, "that, which possesses the most money, is not the richest and the strongest; but that which has the most money circulating in property and real commodities, by means of representative signs.

VI

In the same period in which Pinto's manuscript of the later *Traité* circulated and he produced his *Essai sur le luxe* another influential work was attributed to him.[66] Published by the same printer who published the text of the *Encyclopédie* and gave Pinto as its declared author in 1764, in 1765 a curious pamphlet entitled *An Essay on the Constitution of England* saw the light.[67]

A review of the pamphlet, in a journal edited by the *philosophe* Jean-Baptiste Suard, commented on the profile of the anonymous author, who "has taken from Harrington and from Hume's history" and seemed to have "observed more than read and thought more than observed." There was something idiosyncratic about what was really a revisionist neo-Harringtonian reading of English history and commercial liberty.[68] The method of the piece, the "supplemental Preface" to the second edition stated, was:

To trace the actual progress of English liberty, from its lowest ebb to that glorious height to which it has arrived; to shew that this encrease was constant and gradual, not arising from any providential laws or contrivances of men; but from a certain tide of things which flowed, not only against the means that were contrived to prevent it, but sometimes flowed the faster by those very means.[69]

This history of the English constitution was an abstract way of revealing the unintended consequences in the creation of laws that led to modern liberty.[70] Its simple aim was to "remedy [..] the imbecility" of seeing

---

[65] Pinto, *Essay on Circulation and Credit*, p. 44.

[66] It was generally attributed to Allan Ramsay. Cf. Michael Sonenscher, *Sans-culottes: an eighteenth-century emblem in the French Revolution* (Princeton University Press, 2008), 41–3, 308–12.

[67] [Allan Ramsay], *An Essay on the Constitution of England* (London, 1766). Printed by T. Becket and P.A. De Hondt, quotations below are from the second edition of 1766.

[68] *Gazette littéraire de l'Europe* 5 (March–May 1765), 242–53, 285–95. I owe this reference to Michael Sonenscher.

[69] *Essay on the Constitution of England*, v–vi.

[70] E.g. *Essay on the Constitution of England*, 19, also v–vi, xiii.

Magna Charta as the cause of British liberty.[71] "What is now called the *natural liberty of mankind*" then was "only meant to ascertain the privileges of a small part of the nation."[72] Laws themselves in fact were not what they were thought to be. They were always a reflection of the power and property distribution of the period:

The laws being not the makers, but the creatures of the constitution and of the constituents of government, who either make or abolish, alter or explain, as best pleases them.[73]

It was this relation between the "constituents" and the "constituted" that determined what government cared about, which was the key to proper political analysis.[74] As such the essay served:

..to put us in mind that *liberty* is only another word for *power*; that the extention of *political liberty* can signify nothing else but the extention of the circle of government and of its constituents; and that every extension of this circle must be deemed a change in the constitution, either for the better or the worse.[75]

Looked at in this way the classical divisions between forms of government were naïve and superficial political theory. Despotism, much as the *Encyclopédie* article also argued, was not the government by a single *"Autocrator"* but a dual relation of power and property by which "a power [was] delegated during pleasure, by the *major vis* of the community to one man." While this form of government, in contrast with the classical *Autocrator* idea *was* a historical reality, moreover, "it will be perhaps found to be the nature of all governments under the sun."[76]

The idea that original forms of government were all inherently despotic and always retained some of this character was the starting point of the analysis of the "extention of *political liberty*." The liberty that now seemed "natural" did not come from an intentionally conceived ancient constitution. Instead, from an intended and stipulated "aristocratical privilege" ultimately "the benefits of this clause [..] extended to all Englishmen" against "the contemplation of those who penned Magna Charta [..] but from causes deeply rooted in the nature of things, and of which Magna Charta itself was only a symptom.'[77]

---

[71] *Essay on the Constitution of England*, v.
[72] *Essay on the Constitution of England*, 11.   [73] *Essay on the Constitution of England*, 7.
[74] On the role of this conceptual vocabulary in Italian small states in the late eighteenth century Koen Stapelbroek and Antonio Trampus, "Vattel's Droit des gens und der Europäischen Handelsrepubliken im achtzehnten Jahrhundert," *Der moderne Staat und "le doux commerce" – Staat, Ökonomie und internationales System im politischen Denken der Aufklärung* (ed. Olaf Asbach, Baden-Baden: Nomos Verlagsgesellschaft, 2014), 181–204.
[75] *Essay on the Constitution of England*, vi.
[76] *Essay on the Constitution of England*, 3.   [77] *Essay on the Constitution of England*, xiii.

The essay accordingly was a combined political-economic descriptive account of the processes by which a primitive "government of men" transformed slowly into a "government of laws." As the *Gazette's* reviewer noted, Harrington's dictum that the balance of power follows the balance of property here had been thoroughly redeveloped into a constitutional principle and analytical tool for explaining political-economic change. The turning point in the descriptive account of the essay, and the main reason why the piece would have been attributed to Pinto, was the nature of the identification of William III as the constitutional saviour of British liberty. At a time when Britain threatened to lapse into military government and was dominated by fiscal crises and faction politics, William III, whose hands were tied, introduced a new form of voluntary contributions to the state. Through the use he made of the loans he transformed Britain into a new Rome. Without realising what they were doing, the essay argued, the government of William III had engineered the inclusion of a new set of "constituents" through the creation of a new kind of property and thereby changed the constitution. The fictional wealth that was involved depended entirely upon opinion, but was solid. The policies and institutions involved set the new norm for aspiring commercial states.[78] While, the *Gazette* noted, all English political writers declaimed against the national debt, the opinion of the writer of the essay to identify public credit as the principle of power and opulence was truly different.[79]

These same ideas making Britain the norm for modern politics were deployed by Pinto from the 1740s onwards in a Dutch context. Pinto's proposals of the late 1740s, in a series of writings addressed and dedicated to stadtholder William IV and high officials, that the United Provinces should reform its company trade institutions, its public finance and fiscal system can be seen as an attempt to refuel the power of the "constituent" class of merchants and financiers in Dutch politics.[80] Pinto also went to great lengths in the 1760s when he defended the strength of British public finance and explained the nature of credit in relation to the commercial state in the circulating early version of his later *Traité*. Most directly, Pinto countered the rise of Dutch patriotism and anti-British sentiment in a series of pamphlets written during the War of the American Independence by arguing that the British constitution, citing

---

[78] *Essay on the Constitution of England*, 77–81; *Gazette littéraire*, 245–6.
[79] *Gazette littéraire*, 293. There remained a sense of ambiguity at the end of the Seven Years' War in the essay's concern about whether a nation that was geared towards being the new Rome might use the credit revolution to routinely convert warfare into commerce, *An Essay on the Constitution of England*, 81–3; cf. *Gazette littéraire*, 292–3.
[80] BEH 48A19 (nr. 7), "Transactions" provides a good overview of Pinto's projects.

Delolme and Montesquieu, had an in-built parliamentary ability to filter partial self-interested political opinions and accommodate the nation's interest. In this same context Pinto defended the British regulation of neutral shipping in wartime introduced during the Seven Years' War, which was developed from principles going back to Bynkershoek and further again to Harrington.[81]

In these pamphlets, accompanied by the *Letter on the Jealousy of Commerce* (to be discussed below) Pinto further developed his "system" of how European trade and power relations might be balanced once put on the foundation of the modern commercial state. Here the idea of the "constituens" gave rise to new concepts such as the "intrinsic power" of the state and the "right to trade."[82]

VII

When Pinto first circulated his ideas on credit and modern finance in the Seven Years' War he intervened in the polarised debate about the solidity of the British funds, particularly the publication of the *Bilan de l'Angleterre*, a piece of anti-British propaganda.[83] In the introduction of his main work Pinto also referred to the *Essay on the Constitution of England* identifying it as a major adaptation of his "own principles".[84] From the point at which "some well-informed Englishmen told me at Paris, that my system, so far as it concerns the national debt, was entirely new," Pinto's realised that "my ideas began to be received in England; and, considering the number of manuscript copies that have been taken within these three years, I am not surprised at it." While the *Essay on the Constitution of England* could be read as proof of the present greatness of Britain as a commercial society, Pinto commented that its author had "not proved his system by the same kind of arguments."[85] Instead, Pinto

[81] Koen Stapelbroek, "The Dutch debate on commercial neutrality 1713–1830," *Trade and War: The Neutrality of Commerce in the Inter-State System*, ed. Koen Stapelbroek, special issue of *COLLeGIUM: Studies Across Disciplines in the Humanities and Social Sciences published by the Helsinki Collegium for Advanced studies* (Helsinki Collegium for Advanced Studies, 2011), 114–42.

[82] On these terms Koen Stapelbroek, "Dutch Decline as a European Phenomenon," *History of European Ideas*, 36 [2] (2010), 139–52 and Stapelbroek, "Dutch debate on commercial neutrality."

[83] Vivant de Mezagues, *Bilan général et raisonné de l'Angleterre, depuis 1600 jusqu'à la fin de 1761* (Paris, 1762). The *Journal de Commerce* (February 1761), 19–20, likewise countered a circulating manuscript (possibly, William Wallace's *Characteristics of the Present Political State of Great Britain*, 1758) that explained British wealth through William III's financial revolution by arguing British artificial wealth was disconnected from nature and would inevitably collapse.

[84] Pinto, *Essay on Circulation and Credit*, xiii–xiv.

[85] Pinto, *Essay on Circulation and Credit*, xiv.

argued, his own perspective was geared towards finance as an instrument of peace. Britain and France:

are formed to esteem each other, and to live in peace; yet, unfortunately, they quarrel about supposed interests, which at the bottom perhaps are misunderstood. Jealousy of commerce, and competition for power, create enmity between nations as well as between individuals. [..] If princes could be persuaded, that the real interests of commercial powers do not clash (as I shall endeavour to show hereafter) peace and the happiness of mankind might possibly be established on a durable foundation.[86]

Later editions and translations of the *Traité de la Circulation et du Crédit* contained in appendix the *Lettre sur la Jalousie du Commerce*, in which Pinto put the eighteenth-century political idea of a project for perpetual peace in relation to the realm of trade politics and finance. It is crucial to recognise that the *Traité* too, even though Pinto had already gained a reputation as an apologist of state debts, was written to confront this same topic. This is what Pinto's remarks about Hume in the intro were really concerned with. Pinto emphasised that between Hume and himself there were "friendship and affection" as they met at Paris and in their political writings "both aim at the same object." As it happened, Pinto was concerned that his 1761 manuscript "seemed exactly a refutation of" Hume's "*Essay on Public Credit*, which I had not seen when I drew up the first part of my *Essay on Circulation*."[87] Hume read Pinto's manuscript on public credit:

some time after at Paris, together with the Letter in which I have endeavoured to prove that the jealousy of commerce is ill understood, and that the true interests of princes are not at variance; and he was pleased to express his approbation of the two essays in terms which I cannot venture to repeat. That sublime genius had also touched the subject of the jealousy of commerce.[88]

Pinto judged that "if he had unfolded the principles of his system more at large, I should have suppressed my letter." But clearly Hume had not. Likewise, Hume might "be right in a certain sense, when he foretells, that either the nation must destroy public credit, or public credit will destroy the nation." But Hume was crucially and fundamentally mistaken, Pinto suggested, when he considered the consequences of a voluntary bankruptcy in Britain being the commercial society it was. The "natural death" of public credit was not a matter of sacrificing the interests of "thousands [..] to the safety of millions." The damage done

---

[86] Pinto, *Essay on Circulation and Credit*, xv.
[87] Pinto, *Essay on Circulation and Credit*, xix, 103.
[88] Pinto, *Essay on Circulation and Credit*, 103–4.

to the nation through the general recession that would thus be caused would be much greater than Hume envisaged and, in the words of Istvan Hont, amount to his own "worst case scenario (the loss of independence through conquest by foreign powers)."[89]

However, this was not where the argument stopped. "Pinto's famous criticism of Hume's voluntary bankruptcy plan," as Hont pointedly defined it, was not what it seemed. It was not just a disagreement on the politics of public finance, but a comprehensive criticism of Hume's understanding of commercial society. Much like Galiani criticised all rival political writers for misunderstanding money and being incapable of explaining it from a valid logic of commercial sociability, so Pinto effectively put Hume in the category of the "Machiavellians," political writers whose logic of commercial society was inconsistent and who conflated ancient and modern techniques of government[90]:

> Mr. Hume observed, that multiplying the representative signs lowered the value of specie. But he did not consider the necessity of having such signs to represent the multitude of things, which the abundance of gold and silver has in some measure rendered necessary. Let us new model our manners; let us go twenty centuries back; let us reduce human nature to its primitive condition; let us banish those factitious wants which we have changed into necessities; let us be philosophers, and with Diogenes reject the earthen vessel, and drink out of the hollow of the hand; let us be poor and virtuous, and Mr. Hume's principles may then be applied. But since there is no likelihood of such an alteration for some centuries, we may as well pursue our course, and endeavour to correct abuses. [...] We must not attempt to govern a corrupted people by the same laws which suit a virtuous people.[91]

Pinto inverted Hume's opinions about luxury, wage levels and public credit from his combined perspective on the development of the commercial state and his moral philosophy. On the one hand, as we saw, he was very critical of Hume's negligent take on luxury: if the relative profitability of the arts and the production of subsistence goods in relation to their relative utility was not political accommodated luxury could transform into the greatest threat to society. On the other hand, Hume the excessive defender of luxury, as Pinto had exposed him in his *Essai sur luxe* was an "ancient" in disguise despite himself. Hume was inconsistent in his thinking about the integration of new artificial desires and new

---

[89] Pinto, *Essay on Circulation and Credit*, 104–6. See also Hont, *Jealousy of Trade*, 339.

[90] Cf. above note 37. Pinto used "Machiavellism" as an organising category in his political thought, see below (and Stapelbroek, "Trade, Treaties and Political Virtue"). See also Pinto, *Letters on the American Troubles*, 10.

[91] Pinto, *Essay on Circulation and Credit*, 104. Cf. Galiani *Della moneta*, 45 for the same argument citing Diogenes.

modes of property and their concomitant wage level effects. You could not have Hume's luxury, high wages (which Hume himself struggled with) and *not* have modern finance. Pinto stressed that public credit was not a problem of commercial society, but a core manifestation of its full development. For this reason Pinto called it a "necessity." It was badly understood, badly managed and therefore a potential inlet for abuse. Yet, to suggest that state debts might be gotten rid of was bad political reasoning that presaged a lapse into antiquity.

Engaging with Hume in this way opened up onto the problems of international trade and commercial rivalry. Pinto's positions on luxury and trade were the perfect opposite of a Fénelonian downscaling of inequality and artificial desires through a moral and institutional reform of society. The aim of Pinto's "system," like Fénelon's, was to follow through these positions so that they matched with a working system of complementary international exchange relations. This was exactly why he chose Hume as a friendly opponent: they shared the same final aim, but Pinto believed Hume's principles of the commercial state were faulty.

In contrast to Fénelon's and Hume's "systems," Pinto thought it not illogical to contemplate a structure by which a domestically oriented national economy operated within a system of very limited foreign exchange as an "insulated state."[92] Yet, as he wrote, "such a state, though not repugnant to nature, from which we have too far departed, is incompatible with our manners."[93] The global economy had given rise to so many different products and artificial desires that this option was immediately irrelevant. This left the development of complementary exchange relationships as the only remaining route to peace.

The way Hume approached "Jealousy of Trade" in his essay of that title was highly similar to the message of Pinto's *Letter on the Jealousy of Commerce*. Hume famously criticised "our narrow and malignant politics" designed to "reduce all our neighbouring nations to [. . .] sloth and ignorance" and instead preferred to "pray [..] as a BRITISH subject [. . .] for the flourishing commerce of GERMANY, SPAIN, ITALY, and even FRANCE itself." In other essays he criticised British national rivalry and depicted France as a civilised monarchy.[94] Pinto shared the

---

[92] Pinto, *Essay on Circulation and Credit*, 193, cf. Isaac Nakhimovsky, *The Closed Commercial State: Perpetual Peace and Commercial Society from Rousseau to Fichte* (Princeton University Press, 2011).

[93] Pinto, *Essay on Circulation and Credit*, 193.

[94] For context, Hont, *Jealousy of Trade*, 75–6. Likewise Smith (*Wealth of nations*, book IV chapter 7, par. 13) deemed the colonies of Spain and Portugal useful for all European states. Cf. Hume's phrasing with Pinto, *Jealousy of Commerce*, 191 ("Our neighbours, reduced to misery [..] Such a devouring commerce would destroy itself").

same views. Following the Peace of Utrecht there was simply no valid reason left for "Jealousy of Trade" to exist[95]:

If the harmony of the political picture of commercial Europe be attended to, it will be found, that it is no way incompatible with the common interest of all parties, that the mines of Peru should belong to Spain, those of Brazil to Portugal, the spice trade and herring fishery to Holland; the sugars, indigo, and other produce of St. Domingo, Martinique, and Guadeloupe, as well as a share in the great fisheries, to France; and that England, at the same time, may and ought to preserve a universal command over all the commence of which North America, Jamaica, and the Great Indies (except the Moluccas and Ceylon) are the basis.[96]

The principle that "a particular commercial advantage, almost useless to one nation, is necessary and essential to the preservation of another" created a "connection of interests inseparable in a commercial system." Within that system even the greatest rivals were mutually dependent: "the more France shall flourish, and the more plentiful her harvests are, at so much the cheaper rate will she be able to afford her commodities; and the happiness of France will revert upon England."[97] In Pinto's opinion, the division of territories and advantages at Utrecht was optimal by approximation and any jealous war to alter it always cost more than it could ever win. Here Pinto cited the manifestos of modern politics Voltaire's *Siècle de Louis XIV* and Rousseau's *Jugement du Projet de paix perpétuelle* in support of his position.[98] One had better leave intact the current "balance of Europe, purchased with the blood of our ancestors [that] is now so well established." Any attempt to conquer "commerce [,] the apple of discord" would involve the "destruction of trade" itself.[99] This did not mean Pinto adhered to the principle of balance of power:

Every age has its system of politics, as well as philosophy. The new discoveries in Asia and America succeeded to the crusades; then came the wars of religion; and afterwards the pretended system of equilibrium, or balance of power.[100]

The weight-bearing element in modern politics was commercial reciprocity. Engaging in global trade was not even a prerequisite for profiting from it, Pinto held. France did not need a great navy for its preservation, nor for its economic development. It could easily develop its wealth without too many overseas possessions and a merchant fleet, as long as it could exchange its domestically produced goods in peace with other

---

[95] Pinto, *Jealousy of Commerce*, 221–2; also 191–2.   [96] Pinto, *Jealousy of Commerce*, 221.
[97] Pinto, *Jealousy of Commerce*, 192, 196.   [98] Pinto, *Jealousy of Commerce*, 223.
[99] Pinto, *Jealousy of Commerce*, 228.   [100] Pinto, *Jealousy of Commerce*, 235.

states: "France, within her own bosom, has a lucrative and superior commerce [. . .]. The vineyards are a real Peru to that country."[101] Once this attitude took hold it should reinforce itself:

When the present picture of Europe shall be well understood, every power may find its preservation and prosperity therein, provided they do not thwart each other for imaginary interests. Every commercial power has employment for at least twenty years, to re-establish and improve its internal administration, and that commerce which lies, within the sphere of its strength. Until all these objects are accomplished, and every possible advantage made of them, distant objects, which by their extent go beyond the sphere of strength, are foreign and hurtful to commerce, and to the real interest of nations; this is a truth demonstrated by the event of almost all our wars.[102]

To counteract those remaining passions, prejudices and interests that persisted Pinto contemplated an alternative scheme that prominently involved the Dutch Republic. "Europe being a family," Pinto argued, "it is impossible to destroy one of them without damage to the rest; and Holland is the power, to which this principle most manifestly applies."[103] It was important to fix the Dutch privileges of the herring fishery, the spice trade and the carrying trade.[104] Protecting the Dutch state had a reason. Should the present system of global exchange of precious metals and spices reach its expiry date, the Dutch capital market played a key role in the new situation that set much tighter limits to European economies to prevent collapse.[105] These agreements were part of the establishment of a political confederacy:

There is a system, or rather a plan of geometrical politicks, which would make the happiness of Europe, if the powers the most interested in it would adopt it. This plan appears to me founded on incontestable principles. This is its outlines. 1st. Amongst all the nations of Europe Spain, England, Portugal, of France, and Holland have the largest possessions, and the most considerable and valuable establishments in America, Asia, and Africa. 2d. I think I have demonstrated elsewhere that these powers reciprocally participate more or less in the advantages of the possessions of their neighbours; that the jealousies and rivalry betwixt them are detrimental, because ill understood; and that their real interests do not clash so much as it is imagined. 3d. I believe, likewise, that means might be found to settle things on all sides, in such a manner as to render the truth of these principles palpable; they might still be rendered more solid and more manifest by small exchanges and certain conventions betwixt these powers, for their reciprocal interests. 4th. If then these five powers were to form a confederacy, mutually

101 Pinto, *Jealousy of Commerce*, 228–36; 235.   102 Pinto, *Jealousy of Commerce*, 237.
103 Pinto, *Jealousy of Commerce*, 192   104 Pinto, *Jealousy of Commerce*, 220–1.
105 Pinto, *Letters on the American Troubles*, 41–5; Pinto, *Jealousy of Commerce*, 197–214; 220–1.

to protect their possessions, they would be rendered solid, durable, and permanent, as long as least as the human eye can penetrate into the gloom of futurity – this security would be reciprocal – all Europe would feel the good effects of it.[106]

Yet, this confederacy would be hard to establish, Pinto admitted, "I very much fear that this will never happen. [...] At present there are too many prejudices to overcome, and too many passions the fermentation of which must be evaporated by time and experience."[107] The next best alternative thus was to fix the commercial system that existed and let the forces of peace do their work over time.

An intimate alliance with the commercial powers, a solemn and mutual guarantee of colonies, possessions, and commercial privileges, founded upon common interest and the general good, might establish confidence, and erect a new system, which would be the happiness of mankind, and the glory of the age. These powers acting always in concert, and with good faith to each other, might contribute to appease, or prevent a rupture among the rest. Twenty years peace would be sufficient to make every nation happy.[108]

If Pinto thought that "Jealousy of Trade" was groundless and public finance a solvent of inequality and integral part to the commercial state, why did he need a confederacy or alternatively call for political restraint and agreements?

VIII

In the aftermath of the Peace of Utrecht the abbé de Saint-Pierre had already come to a similar conclusion as Pinto when he declared that European states lived in a state of a "terrible dependence" upon one another.[109] Although "Arts & Commerce" had brought European societies "all the certainty, security, conveniences and enjoyments of life," still "their happiness would increase at the same rate within twenty years, as would the happiness of a family of savages in the same space of time were they transported from the soil of a Canadian forest and put in some rich and well administered European city."[110] The centrality of the

---

106 Pinto, *Letters on the American Troubles*, 52–3.
107 Pinto, *Letters on the American Troubles*, 53.
108 Pinto, *Jealousy of Commerce*, 237. Compare the paraphrase of this passage by Johann Gottfried von Herder, "Letters for the Advancement of Humanity. Tenth Collection," *Political Writings*, ed. Michael N. Forster (Cambridge University Press, 2002), 407. On Herder see the chapter in this volume by Eva Piirimäe.
109 Charles-Irénée Castel de Saint-Pierre, *Projet pour render la paix perpetuelle en Europe* (Utrecht, 1713–17, 3 vols.), II:362 (part of the *Récapitulation*).
110 Saint-Pierre, *Projet pour render la paix perpetuelle en Europe* II:361–2: cf. Voltaire, *Histoire De La Guerre De mil sept cent quarante & un* (Amsterdam, 1755), I:28: "Chaque peuple répara ses pertes pendant les vingt années qui suivirent la paix d'Utrecht."

Utrecht settlement for Pinto's understanding of European politics was further underscored by his idea that Europe seemed to be caught up in a "paradox" of modern politics. The paradox was that even while the division of comparative advantages made at Utrecht had created a situation in which "each European power enjoys more or less the possessions of its neighbours" – effectively there *was* a joint European trading system that extended to the entire world, still it was the case that "chimerical commercial jealousies," as Pinto called them, prevailed and caused repeated warfare.[111] Based on Pinto's own idea that the Utrecht settlement should be a sufficient condition for dissolving jealousy of trade, and did not need a European confederacy, already in 1713 it should have become "possible to reconcile the separate interests of every nation with the common and reciprocal advantage of them all. From that moment the system of the Abbé de St. Pierre would cease to be considered as the dream of an honest man."[112] The "paradox" was that this had not happened.

Like Saint-Pierre, Pinto believed that the Peace of Utrecht was incomplete and a missed opportunity.[113] The motivation for his *Traité*, later published in conjunction with the *Letter on the Jealousy of Commerce*, was to present British financial institutions and fiscal arrangements as a model for France and their adoption by France a requirement for European peace. In general, all of Pinto's writings engaged with the remaining obstacles to peace that kept the just mentioned "paradox" intact. The concrete occasion for writing the *Letter on the Jealousy of Commerce* had been the French reduction of Dutch trade privileges following the Seven Years' War, which confirmed trade as a function of war.[114] Sovereign states had the right to design their own commercial policies and both the British Navigation Acts and the Methuen Treaty were as perfectly rightful as they had been successful.[115] Yet, tinkering with tariffs and market access was precisely the kind of "mercantile" jealous politics that did not

---

[111] Pinto, *Letters on the American Troubles*, 40–1.   [112] Pinto, *Jealousy of Commerce*, 189.

[113] Stapelbroek, "The long peace" reconstructs this 'incompleteness' as a missed opportunity, recognised by a range of figures from Saint-Pierre to the diplomat Mesnager, to reorganise global trade (notably Spanish the South-America trade, but also the East Indies). Pinto in diplomatic practice too played with ideas of partially merging chartered companies, primarily the Dutch and English – a plan developed with Thomas Hope – and supported Anglo-French integration before and territorial "conciliation" at Fontainebleau, with a view to a more secure durable peace. See also BEH 48A19 (nr. 6), cc. 13–18 and John Shovlin, "Turning from Empire: Treaty Negotiations between the French and English East India Companies, 1753–1755," *Balance of Power, Balance of Trade: The Politics of Commercial Treaties in the Eighteenth Century*, Antonella Alimento and Koen Stapelbroek eds. (Basingstoke: Palgrave, 2017).

[114] Pinto, *Letters on the American Troubles*, 49.

[115] *Essay on Circulation and Credit*, 222. Pinto's discussion of the Navigation Acts was included in a piece that was eliminated from the English translation, see Pinto, *Traité De La Circulation Et Du Crédit*, 7.

just fuel war but interrupted patterns of global circulation of capital and goods. These policies profoundly affected the very essence of commercial societies as entities within which sustainable luxury, high wages and credit had developed out of more primitive forms of trade.

The root of the problem of "mercantile" jealousy was, however, not politics itself, Pinto suggested at the beginning of his *Letter on the Jealousy of Commerce* and at the end of the *Essai sur le luxe*: "Private interest usually assumes the masque of public good [and] the essential interests of commercial powers [..] would not clash [..] if private interests did not frequently intervene."[116] The protectionist elements of commercial treaties, such as those concluded at Utrecht, tended to preserve pockets of privilege and personal profit that held political sway and that frustrated the integration of national economies. The challenge was to find structures, such as Pinto's light confederacy, that facilitated the breaking down of established monopolies and "despotic" private interests that affected the common interest of Europe.[117] Once the existing system of commercial privileges that had survived Utrecht was bracketed, the "reciprocal reverberation of mutual interest" as Pinto called it would drive out "misguided covetousness [that] defeats its own purpose."[118]

If getting rid of "Jealousy of Trade" by perfecting the Utrecht settlement was Pinto's solution for dealing with the remnants of the "despotic" politics of the past, by the late 1770s Pinto was concerned with a new threat to the international system of fully developed commercial societies. Within Pinto's system a distinctive set of rules existed for modern finance to function as an attendant monitor to peaceful economic development of an integrated trade system. The problem at the time of the Seven Years' War had been that politicians did not yet know these rules, grasp their inevitability and had not learned how to manage them properly. By the 1770s the political understanding of public credit similar to luxury and wage levels as part of the challenge of upholding the moral edifice of the commercial state was still fragile. Pinto, notwithstanding his interest in John Law's scheme and citing of Berkeley disapproved of financial schemes as political reform projects. The irony of Pinto's unfortunate expression that "the Creation of public funds" represented a "realised Alchemy" was that he meant that these new institutions had semi-unintentionally arisen through the murky practices of naïve political will as a new stage in the development of the commercial state. Their

---

[116] Pinto, *Jealousy of Commerce*, 189; cf. *Essay on Circulation and Credit*, 107: there was a causal link through which "excessive luxury, by disordering the various springs" disbalanced "the fortunes of individuals" and inspired policies that both held back economic development and spurred unrestrained war-finance.

[117] Pinto, *Jealousy of Commerce*, 189.   [118] Pinto, *Jealousy of Commerce*, 196.

discovery should not invite grand projects. Britain following the Glorious Revolution and John Law had tapped into a new reservoir of political development. Now the challenge was to demystify and transform financial politics, parallel to luxury, into a regular set of rules and principles and remove it from oscillating between the poles of Voltaire's delirium of unchecked luxury and Fénelonian post-property levelling schemes.[119]

Seeing financial politics as a moral choice between ancients and moderns and thereby lapsing into "Machiavellism" was exactly what Pinto witnessed during the War of the American Independence. Partly swayed by French pamphleteering campaigns, John Adam's diplomacy and Franco-British debates about the rights of neutral trade in wartime and strength of respective state debts, the Dutch state was brought into a crisis involving a capital strike on the British public debt. Back in his role from the Seven Years' War of policing these debates and make people see the bigger picture of global trade and the commercial state, Pinto ridiculed the idea that the British government might be capable of controlling public credit, cited Delolme and Bynkershoek and agitated against the appropriation of levelling revolutionary discourses in British party politics and by Dutch *Patriotten*.[120] For Pinto it was merely logical that tampering with the neutrality of finance ate away at the foundations of the commercial state more profoundly than privately interested jealousy of trade ever could. This was exactly what happened when John Adams almost sealed a five per cent interest loan where France paid seven per cent. It was absurd, Pinto fulminated, as he added "I will ask Mr Necker... if these colonies already believe they deserve more credit than these Powers [i.e. France]."[121]

While Pinto's name remained attached until the Napoleonic era to polarised usages of state debts,[122] Friedrich von Gentz and Dugald

---

[119] For Voltaire on Law, Michael Sonenscher, *Before the Deluge: Public Debt, Inequality, and the Intellectual Origins of the French Revolution* (Princeton, 2007), 116–18. John Law in his "demystified" form was also the only author referenced in the 1751 *Proposals for redressing the Trade of the Republick*, 60–1.

[120] Pinto, *Letters on the American Troubles*, "Second Letter," *passim* and 57. See also the unpublished manuscript, dated 1779, Archivio di Stato di Torino, inv. 100, 2a addizione, OLANDA, mazzo 4 addizione, fascicolo 2 and a different version entitled "Examen impartial des intérêts actuels de la République par rapport à une alliance" held by the Dutch Royal Library, van Goens Collection (130 D3/J, dated 1783).

[121] Isaac de Pinto, *Discours d'un bon Hollandois a ses compatriotes, sur différents objets intéressants* (s.l., 1778), 41. Ironically, Pinto proudly coined J.F. van Hogendorp's suggestion that in 1748 when the Republic was threatened by a French proxy-invasion and Pinto helped raise a cheap public loan, he had "saved the state," BEH 48A19 (nr. 7), "Transactions," c. 19v.

[122] A 1778 review of Karl August von Struensee's German adaptation mentioned that "jeder Politiker [..] lobt, tadelt, widerlegt, vertheidigt und oft nicht versteht" Pinto's

Stewart in different contexts included him in their syntheses of classical political economy. Alongside the canonisation of Adam Smith's system of natural liberty, Pinto was rehabilitated by Gentz and Stewart as the person in the eighteenth century who had best understood the nature of public finance – and his monetary policy used to correct Smith and Hume.[123] Pinto's contribution to the history of political thought was his integration of credit into his "system", a general plan for trade and perpetual peace. The point here is not the originality or truth-value of Pinto's ideas, but the suggestion that at the beginning of the nineteenth century when a new classical orthodoxy in political concepts crystalised that may be recognised in the Vienna settlement, Pinto's "system" was implicated in the design.

IX

Pinto's and Galiani's critiques of modern politics built-up from their moral philosophies and histories of humankind, with luxury as a crucial node, ran perfectly parallel to Smith's critique of the mercantile system in book IV of the *Wealth of Nations*. Fundamentally, there was not that much in Smith that was not in Galiani and Pinto, despite their divergence on state debts and chartered companies. As far as political and economic reform was concerned they all agreed that the way forward was not the way out. However corrupted the "mercantile system" might be, it needed not to be attacked but perfected, respecting the causes that led to its emergence along with modern wealth and inequality. Hont's reminder that Smith (and the same goes for Pinto and Galiani) was deeply sceptical about proto-social and political science and theory-based human intervention was not merely based on Smith critique of physiocracy and its attempt to "heal" the political body.[124] The most

---

Traité. Nijenhuis, *Een Joodse Philosophe,* 48–50, 126–32, *cit.* 49. On Struensee also Nakhimovsky, *Closed Commercial State,* 121–2.

[123] Dugald Stewart, *Lectures on Political Economy* (Edinburgh, 1856), ii:218–20: called Pinto "the most ingenious and best informed writer who has hitherto appeared as an advocate for the policy of our national debt" and contrasted Smith's remarks "particularly directed against the theory of Pinto" with Ivernois' judgement of Pinto's *Traité* as "the first work in which the true theory of National Debts was unfolded." Stewart believed Pinto might have convinced Hume of his errors and thought Pinto's remarks on population remarkably prescient, quoting them and his thoughts on circulation and taxation at length (i:203–4; 375, 378–9; 429–31, 438–40; ii:237). Likewise, Friedrich von Gentz, *Essai sur l'état actuel de l'administration des finances et de la richesse nationale de la Grande Bretagne* (London, 1800), 118 cited Pinto once, but side-stepping his usual track of following Adam Smith, largely adopted Pinto's theory of state debts along with a conjectural history of the commercial state triggered by the discovery of America.

[124] Hont, *Politics in Commercial Society.*

refined eighteenth-century thinkers adopted principles like self-deceit, error and unintended consequences to account for how primitive forms of society, morality, law and exchange historically emerged and developed. They did so not because of intellectual fashion but out of a profound sense of urgency that this was what it took to avoid the poles of ancients and moderns and prevent the collapse of modern Europe into military government, a fate whose misery lay far beyond that of mere economic or moral decline.

From this perspective it becomes possible to look in a new way at the main political and economic projects and institutional arrangements of the 1760s, 1770s, and 1780s: such as the Bourbon Family Pact, the first League of Armed Neutrality and the Eden-Rayneval Treaty of 1786. What needs to be done is connect a genealogy of thinking about commercial liberty, from the level of moral philosophy to the politics and practices of trade regulation, to the actual plans that were discussed in these decades. Galiani actively promoted Neapolitan accession to the League of Armed Neutrality and wrote an intriguing treatise on the topic. Pinto and Smith also, directly and indirectly, in writing and through personal relations, were involved in these schemes.[125] Understanding how the most refined political writers of the later eighteenth century analysed these projects is an indispensable basis for grasping how their ideas could be canonised and implicated in a new geopolitical design in the early nineteenth century.

The period of the eighteenth and early nineteenth century, the scepticism of its political economic thought and the specific characteristics of its institutional designs, still merits to be further unlocked. Doing so would be one way to develop Hont's legacy, rather than consume his intellectual inheritance, and resist the persistent risk of defaulting into a polarised and dysfunctional opposition between ancients and moderns while facing the political challenges of our time.

---

[125] Pinto, *Letters on the American Troubles*, 89 in 1776 perhaps hinted that Smith adopted his ideas. Declaring the aim of all his writings, notably the *Letter on the Jealousy of Commerce*, had been to cure national hatred Pinto had seen "some celebrated authors adopt and improve upon the principles there established."

4   Eighteenth-century Carthage

Christopher Brooke

In the years following the Glorious Revolution, Charles Davenant – in J. G. A. Pocock's words, "the most ambitious neo-Machiavellian thinker of the early Augustan period"[1] – was one of those who was beginning to apply the perspective of *raison d'état* to the politics of international commerce. Trade was now a "matter of state," not just a "conveniency, or accidental ornament," and the old logic that "riches always follow power, and that iron brings to it the gold and silver of other places" was being inverted.[2] Machiavelli may have been right once upon a time to argue that money was not the sinew of war, but this was no longer the case, given just how extraordinarily expensive warfare had become.[3] As Steven Pincus has argued, furthermore, "Party political dispute in the late 17th and early 18th centuries was as much about political economy as it was about religion and the constitution."[4] A part of Davenant's contribution was towards the fashioning of what Pincus has called "the tory theory of empire."[5] England – later Britain – had on this view to buy cheap and sell dear, importing commodities from the East and West Indies, where they had been produced with either low-waged or slave labour, and selling them at profit in European markets. Overseas possessions were to be regulated from the imperial centre, which would aim to secure an adequate supply of slave labour to the tobacco and sugar colonies, and these would remain "dependent upon their Mother country," which would not permit "those laws upon any account, to be loosened, whereby they are

---

[1] J. G. A. Pocock, *The Machiavellian Moment: Florentine Political Thought and the Atlantic Republican Tradition* (Princeton University Press, 1975), p. 437.

[2] István Hont, *Jealousy of Trade: International Competition and the Nation-State in Historical Perspective* (Cambridge, MA: The Belknap Press of Harvard University Press, 2005), pp. 212, 213, quoting Charles Davenant, *The Political and Commercial Works* (London: R. Horsefield *et al.*, 1771), vol. 1, pp. 89, 349.

[3] Niccolò Machiavelli, *Discourses on Livy*, Harvey C. Mansfield, Jr. and Nathan Tarcov, trans. (University of Chicago Press, 1996), II.10, pp. 147–50.

[4] Steven Pincus, "Addison's Empire: Whig Conceptions of Empire in the Early 18th Century," *Parliamentary History*, vol. 31, no. 1 (2012), p. 101.

[5] Ibid., p. 102.

tied to it."[6] The whigs, by contrast on Pincus's account, "advocated an integrated commercial empire in which the key to prosperity and power was human labour," one that focused on manufacturing rather than on the long-distance carrying trade, and envisioned a much less hierarchical relationship between England and her various overseas territories.[7]

As the late István Hont demonstrated across the course of his career, this application of *raison d'état* to the sphere of international trade transformed European political thought. It also changed the ways in which European theorists of politics and economics thought about the dynamics of the classical world, and the aim of this chapter is to reconstruct in light of the new political theories of commerce, colonies and war the eighteenth-century conversation concerning the ancient rivalry between Carthage and Rome, which were widely held to be the greatest commercial and the greatest military imperial powers from antiquity respectively, from Pierre-Daniel Huet's work on ancient commerce in 1716 down to the publication of Adam Smith's *Wealth of Nations* in 1776.

As just indicated, the most common contrast in the political thought of what we might call the very long eighteenth century – starting, say, with the publication of Hobbes's *Leviathan* in 1651 – involved the juxtaposition of Roman martial virtue with the commercial instincts of the Carthaginians. So, James Harrington in *Oceana* (1656) observed that

if Carthage or Venice acquired any fame in their arms, it is known to have happened through the mere virtue of their captains, and not of their orders; wherefore Israel, Lacedemon and Rome entailed their arms upon the prime of their citizens, divided (at least in Lacedemon and Rome) into youth and elders, the youth for the field and the elders for defence of the territory.[8]

For Nicholas Barbon in his *Discourse on Trade* (1690),

And therefore the ROMANS who made War (the only Way to Raise & Enlarge their Dominion) did in the almost Infancy of their State, Conquer that Rich and TRADING City of CARTHAGE, though Defended by HANIBAL their General, one of the greatest Captains in the World: so that, since TRADE was not in those days useful to provide Magazines for Wars, an Account of it is not to be expected from those Writers.[9]

For Jean-Jacques Rousseau, in *The Social Contract* (1762),

In a word, besides the principles that apply to every nation, there is in each people some cause why they should be applied in a particular manner, making its

---

[6] Davenant, *Works*, vol. 2, p. 24, in Pincus, "Addison's Empire," p. 103.
[7] Ibid., p. 105.
[8] James Harrington, *The Commonwealth of Oceana, in The Commonwealth of Oceana and A System of Politics*, J. G. A. Pocock, ed. (Cambridge University Press, 1992), p. 76.
[9] Nicholas Barbon, *A Discourse of Trade* (London: Thomas Milbourn, 1690), Preface, p. 6.

legislation suitable for it alone. Thus the Hebrews in ancient times, and the Arabs recently, have made religion their primary concern; the Athenians, culture; Carthage and Tyre, trade; Rhodes, its navy; Sparta, war; and Rome virtue. The author of *The Spirit of Laws* has given a multitude of examples showing the skill with which a legislator directs a system of law towards each of these aims.[10]

And for Adam Ferguson, in his *Essay on the History of Civil Society* (1767),

The Roman people, destined to acquire wealth by conquest, and by the spoil of provinces; the Carthaginians, intent on the returns of merchandise, and the produce of commercial settlements, must have filled the streets of their several capitals with men of a different disposition and aspect. The Roman laid hold of his sword when he wished to be great, and the state found her armies prepared in the dwellings of her people. The Carthaginian retired to his counter on a similar project; and, when the state was alarmed, or had resolved on a war, lent of his profits to purchase an army abroad.[11]

The first significant attempt to disrupt this binary identification of Carthage with wealth and of Rome with virtue came from Pierre-Daniel Huet, who had studied once upon a time with Samuel Bochart,[12] in the history of ancient commerce that he published in 1716. The book had in fact been written long before then – indeed, it had originally been written at the request of the French finance minister Jean-Baptiste Colbert, who had himself died in 1683. Paul Cheney has suggested that one of Huet's remarks about the Phoenicians could be read as a "swipe against Louis XIV and his repeated failures to subdue the Dutch," and that this may explain why the book was not published until after the king's death in 1715.[13] Although it was basically right, according to Huet, that the "Romans had little regard to Commerce in the Wars they undertook," whereas "Traffick was the chief Aim of the Carthaginians," he argued against the prevailing view that denied the Romans any real knowledge of commercial life. A "People of their Wisdom," he insisted, "could not be ignorant how much Riches were necessary to bring about their Designs; and that Commerce was the surest means whereby they might acquire Wealth."[14] Contact with their neighbours in Italy, such as the cities of

[10] Jean-Jacques Rousseau, *The Social Contract*, Christopher Betts, trans. (Oxford University Press, 1993), II.11, p. 88.
[11] Adam Ferguson, *An Essay on the History of Civil Society*, 5th ed. (London: T. Cadell, 1782), IV.3, pp. 318–19.
[12] See April G. Shelford, *Transforming the Republic of Letters: Pierre-Daniel Huet and European Intellectual Life, 1650–1720* (University of Rochester Press, 2007), pp. 27–29, 35–6.
[13] Paul Cheney, *Revolutionary Commerce: Globalization and the French Monarchy* (Cambridge, MA: Harvard University Press, 2010), p. 29.
[14] Pierre-Daniel Huet, *The History of the Commerce and Navigation of the Ancients* (London, B. Lintot, 1717), ch. 21, p. 73.

Magna Graecia, would have given the Romans "many Proofs of the great Advantages arising by Commerce"; and

even their Necessities constrain'd them to it, for the Country they liv'd in was not fertile enough to furnish them with Provisions. And although they profess'd an extraordinary Frugality, and seem'd to despise Riches, yet were they obliged by all the Rules of Prudence and Policy, to provide against Poverty and Want.[15]

The main battle was fought, however, on the terrain of Polybius studies. On the one hand, Huet noted, Polybius "tells us positively, that before the first Punick War, the Romans had not thought of the Sea," and that they were only able to construct a fleet after capturing "a cover'd Galley from the Carthaginians" which "they made of... as a model."[16] But on the other hand, Huet was able to dig evidence out of Polybius, which pointed towards a different trajectory. In 509 BCE, 250 years before the first Punic war, the Romans had signed a treaty with Carthage, in which they undertook not to "navigate beyond the Cape of Carthage on the North side, which was called the Fair Promontory, unless Necessity urg'd them to it."

The Voyages which were undertaken by them on account of Trade, as well to Africa and Sardinia, as that part of Sicily which was possess'd by the Carthaginians, are expressly regulated and distinguish'd by particular Clauses in this Treaty.[17]

Huet considered subsequent treaties, from 348 and 279, using the evidence provided by both Polybius and Livy, whose terms again made little sense without the assumption that Rome and her allies were regularly trading across the Mediterranean; and he also noted the occasion in 338, still long before the outbreak of the first Punic war, when the Romans seized the twenty-two galleys that made up the fleet of the Antiates, burnt the six that were "armed with Beaks," and brought the rest back to Rome.[18] According to Huet, then, the Romans "apply'd themselves to Navigation from the Time of their Kings, first with regard to Trade, and afterward much more on account of War"; but the many years of warfare in Italy kept them busy and "constrain'd them to neglect the Sea, 'till the Time of the first Punick War," whereupon they

had such extraordinary Success in their Navigations, that all they had done before might pass for nothing in comparison of what they now understood and practiced: And it is in this Sense we must understand and explain Polybius.[19]

---

[15] Ibid., p. 74.   [16] Ibid.   [17] Ibid., p. 75.   [18] Ibid., p. 76.   [19] Ibid., p. 78.

If the Romans had successfully managed to combine commercial wealth and military virtue, perhaps they could continue to serve as a practical model for France to emulate?

Those who were critical of French policy, and hostile to the ambition for universal monarchy, continued to prefer the older approach that emphasised the contrast between Carthage and Rome. One of these was Jean-François Melon, who explained the opposition between "the spirit of conquest" and "the spirit of commerce" in his 1734 *Political Essay upon Commerce*. These "mutually exclude each other, in a Nation," and Melon indicated his preference for the spirit of commerce. As soon as a conquering nation stopped conquering, he argued, "it is soon subdued," whereas "the Spirit of Commerce, is always accompanied by the Wisdom necessary for Preservation."[20] The outcome of the Punic wars therefore posed an obvious problem for his analysis – since Carthage was not so much preserved but destroyed – and so Melon sought to explain it away. Insofar as the Carthaginians had earlier "obtained . . . the greatest Advantages over the Romans," it was through their employment of mercenaries; similarly, insofar as the Romans eventually prevailed, it was "by Means of particular Circumstances," rather than owing to anything to do with "the different Forms of their Government."[21] As if to acknowledge that this on its own was not really a detailed enough argument to persuade a sceptic, Melon added that in those days, "the Spirit of Commerce and Preservation, were, as it may be said, in their Infancy, and had not time to grow perfect."[22] If the Carthaginians had fortified their frontiers, for example, "the Romans would have been no more to them, in the first Punick War, than a Gang of Banditti."[23] This reflection on Carthage was followed immediately by a more general analysis of Rome. Prior to the Principate, the city was "more a Camp, than a Town," and no kind of "Civil Society"; the Emperors subsequently "owed their Elevation to the Soldiers," and "were Generals, always perplexed in restraining the Insolence of those Soldiers, upon whom they were dependent," who "neither thought, of securing their Frontiers, nor, of introducing Civil Polity into their State, where People attained to Honours and Riches, by War alone."[24] The inevitable result was that,

When Time, and want of Discipline, had softened the Spirit of Conquest, they were easily subdued by the Northern Nations, who were of the same fierce

[20] Jean-François Melon: *A Political Essay upon Commerce*, David Bindon, trans. (Dublin: Philip Crampton, 1738), ch. 7, p. 136. See also Sophus Reinert, *Translating Empire: Emulation and the Origins of Political Economy* (Cambridge, MA: Harvard University Press, 2011), p. 20.

[21] Melon, *Political Essay*, p. 136.   [22] Ibid., pp. 136–7.
[23] Ibid., p. 137.   [24] Ibid., p. 137.

Nature, with the first Romans; and these new Conquerors, became, in some Time, the Conquest of others, who, were like themselves.[25]

Montesquieu was another writer who disagreed sharply with Huet.[26] "A central objective of M's modern 'science of politics,'" Iain McDaniel has written, "was to undermine the relevance of ancient Rome as a model for modern European states."[27] Rome's wealth did not derive from commerce, Montesquieu argued, but rather from conquest and pillage, and in a modern world in which it was no longer plausible to envisage one state prevailing by war over all the others, the Roman original could no longer be copied.[28] But if that were the case, then what about Carthage? One contemporary admirer was Daniel Defoe, who celebrated the Carthaginian contribution to exploration, colonisation and commerce in his 1725–6 *General history of discoveries and improvements, in useful arts, particularly in the great branches of commerce, navigation, and plantation, in all parts of the known world.* "And here two things are very remarkable, with relation to Trade," he wrote there:

I. That, had the Carthaginian Government remain'd we have Reason to believe that we had found many noble Settlements and populous Cities, and perhaps Nations, upon all the Western Coasts of Africa, from Cape Spartel, quite away to the Cape of Good Hope; and which had still been more considerable, we had found a civiliz'd, industrious, trading People, every where planted; prepare'd for Commerce, and furnish'd with a Product fit for making their Returns for all the Manufactures, and Merchandizes of Europe, when we had come to trade with them.

II. As this did not happen, but that the Carthaginian State was overthrown and destroy'd all these Settlements died in their infancy for want of those supplies; and when we, in so many Ages of Time, came to discover those Coasts, we found them either Desolate and Barren, and almost without Inhabitants; or those Inhabitants untaught, wild, and naked Savages, the remembrance of former People being quite

---

[25] Ibid., p. 138.

[26] Duncan Kelly, *The Propriety of Liberty: Persons, Passions, and Judgement in Modern Political Thought* (Princeton University Press, 2010), p. 74.

[27] Iain McDaniel, *Adam Ferguson in the Scottish Enlightenment: The Roman Past and Europe's Future* (Cambridge, MA: Harvard University Press, 2013), p. 15.

[28] For a summary of Montesquieu's argument, see István Hont, "The early Enlightenment debate on commerce and luxury," in Mark Goldie and Robert Wokler, eds. (Cambridge University Press, 2006), pp. 407–9. See also Kostas Vlassopoulos, "Imperial encounters: discourses on empire and the uses of ancient history in the eighteenth century" in Mark Bradley, ed., *Classics and Imperialism in the British Empire* (Oxford University Press, 2010), pp. 34–5.

lost and sunk out of their Minds, nor so much as any civilized remains
left among them.[29]
A specific connection was forged when he described Hanno as 'the
Carthaginian Sir Walter Raleigh, as afterwards Sir Walter Raleigh
was call'd the English Hanno'.[30] And whereas the Romans sent out
colonies 'for Conquest', 'we' – i.e., the English, but reminiscent of the
Carthaginians – 'planted for Commerce; they planted to extend their
Dominion, we to extend our Trade; and as the last is the best Foundation, so it is the surest Possession...'.[31] Broadly similar discussions
were presented in two works published in 1728, his *Plan of the English
Commerce*,[32] and the *Atlas Maritimus & Commercialis*, in which Defoe
remarked that 'it had been much happier for Mankind in general, but
especially for the Trading Part of the World, if Carthage had stood, and
the Roman Empire had been destroyed'.[33]

Like Defoe, and like Melon, Montesquieu was a strong critic of Rome.
Also like Defoe, there is reason to think that Montesquieu was thinking about Britain when he was writing about Carthage, indeed, thinking
about Britain as being a sort of non-dysfunctional modern version of
Carthage.[34] But Montesquieu never became any kind of simple apologist for the Carthaginian cause. In his *Considerations on the Causes of the
Greatness of the Romans and of their Decline*, published in 1734, the same
year as Melon's *Political Essay*, Montesquieu suggested some of the reasons why the Romans had prevailed. 'As the Carthaginians grew wealthy
sooner than the Romans, so they were sooner corrupted'.[35] Whereas

[29] Daniel Defoe, *A general history of discoveries and improvements, in useful arts, particularly
in the great branches of commerce, navigation, and plantation, in all parts of the known world*
(London: J. Roberts, 1725–6), pp. 104–5.

[30] Defoe, *General history*, pp. 105–6; also quoted in Jonathan Scott, *When the Waves Ruled
Britannia: Geography and Political Identities, 1500–1800* (Cambridge University Press,
2011), p. 131.

[31] Defoe, *General history*, p. 169, quoted in Howard D. Weinbrot, *Britannia's Issue: The Rise
of British Literature from Dryden to Ossian* (Cambridge University Press, 1993), p. 257.

[32] Defoe, *A Plan of the English Commerce, Being a Compleat Prospect of the Trade of This
Nation, As Well the Home Trade As the Foreign* (London, Charles Rivington, 1728),
pp. 312–17.

[33] John Harris, John Senex, and Henry Wilson, *Atlas Maritimus & Commercialis, or, A
general view of the world, so far as relates to trade and navigation* (London: James & John
Knapton *et al.*, 1728), p. 265, quoted in Weinbrot, *Britannia's Issue*, p. 256.

[34] Paul A. Rahe, 'The book that never was: Montesquieu's *Considerations on the Romans*
in historical context', *History of Political Thought*, vol. 26, no. 1 (Spring 2005), esp.
p. 82. Also, at greater length, Rahe, *Montesquieu and the Logic of Liberty: War, Religion,
Commerce, Climate, Terrain, Technology, Uneasiness of Mind, the Spirit of Political Vigilance,
and the Foundations of the Modern Republic* (New Haven, CT: Yale University Press,
2009), ch. 2.

[35] Montesquieu, *Grandeur and Declension of the Roman Empire*, in *Complete Works* (London:
T. Evans and W. Davis, 1777), vol. 3, p. 19.

'in Rome, war immediately united the several interests', in Carthage it pulled them apart. The 'two prevailing factions in Carthage were so divided, that the one was always for peace, and the other always for war; by which means it was impossible for that city, either to enjoy the one, or engage in the other to advantage'.[36] In law-governed Rome, 'the people entrusted the senate with the management of affairs'; whereas in Carthage, 'which was governed by fraud and dissoluteness, the people would themselves transact all things'.[37] Carthage faced the further difficulty that although the Carthaginian currency of 'gold and silver may be exhausted', the 'virtue, perseverance, strength, and poverty' of their Roman adversaries were 'inexhaustible'.[38] The Carthaginian rule in Spain, furthermore, was 'vastly oppressive'.

They had trampled so much upon the Spaniards, that, when the Romans arrived among them, they were considered as their deliverers; and if we reflect upon the immense sums it cost the Carthaginians to maintain, in that country, a war which proved fatal to them, it will appear that injustice is very improvident, and is not mistress of all she promises.[39]

Although Hannibal carried the war to Italy, he 'did not receive any succours from Carthage, either by the jealousy of one party, or the too great confidence of the other'.

So long as he kept his whole army together, he always defeated the Romans; but when he was obliged to put garrisons into cities, to defend his allies, to besiege strong holds, or prevent their being besieged, he then found himself too weak, and lost a great part of his army by piecemeal. Conquests are easily made, because we achieve them with our whole force; they are retained with difficulty, because we defend them with only a part of our forces.[40]

In the later *Spirit of the Laws*, published in 1748, Montesquieu extended his analysis. In his treatment of colonies, he observed that in Europe, 'it remains a fundamental law that any commerce with a foreign colony is regarded as a pure monopoly enforceable by the laws of the country' – the kind of approach to empire as hierarchical dependence that Davenant had advocated for Britain – before noting, first, that the ancients treated their colonies differently on this score, but, second, in a footnote, that the exception to this rule was 'the Carthaginians, as seen in the treaty ending the First Punic War'.[41] His subsequent

---

[36] Ibid., p. 20.   [37] Ibid., p. 21.   [38] Ibid.

[39] Ibid., p. 23. The problems generated by empire are emphasised by McDaniel, *Adam Ferguson in the Scottish Enlightenment*, pp. 18–19.

[40] Montesquieu, *Grandeur and Declension*, pp. 28–9.

[41] Montesquieu, *The Spirit of the Laws*, Anne M. Cohler, Basia Carolyn Miller, and Harold Samuel Stone, trans. (Cambridge University Press, 1989), 21.21, p. 391 fn. 144. Note

discussion made the analogy between ancient and modern colonisation explicit:

The Carthaginians, in order to make the Sardinians and the Corsicans more dependent, prohibited them from planting, sowing, or doing anything of the like on penalty of death; they sent them their food from Africa. We have come to the same point without making such harsh laws. Our colonies in the Antilles are admirable; they have objects of commerce that we do not and cannot have; they lack that which is the object of our commerce.[42]

When it came to the Punic wars, his basic framework for understanding the conflict was the same as it had been in the earlier book. 'The Romans were never notable for jealousy over commerce', he observed, and 'it was as a rival nation and not as a commercial nation that they attacked Carthage'. 'Moreover, their genius, their glory, their military education, and the form of their government', he asserted, 'drew them away from commerce'.[43] This time around, however, Montesquieu explicitly considered counterfactuals. Had the Carthaginians explored just a bit further down the African coast, he observed, they would have reached the Gold Coast.

They would have engaged in a commerce there of an importance quite different from that of the present, when America seems to have depreciated the wealth of all the other countries; they would have found treasures that could not have been taken away by the Romans.[44]

And in a chapter significantly entitled 'on a republic that conquers' Montesquieu noted that had the Carthaginians won the war, their victory would have led to the destruction of the republic. A 'democracy' which 'conquers a people in order to govern it as a subject... will expose its own liberty, because it will entrust too much power to the magistrates whom it sends out to the conquered state'.

What danger would not the republic of Carthage have run if Hannibal had taken Rome? Having caused so many revolutions in his own town after his defeat, what might he not have done there after that victory?[45]

As has now been extensively discussed in the literature, the period of the Seven Years' War was a significant one for the use of these ancient

that the particular treaty Montesquieu mentions in that note, which is the one pre-sented at Polybius 3.27, says nothing about commerce. He is probably thinking of the earlier treaty between Carthage and Rome described at Polybius 3.24. (There is similar confusion at 21.11, p. 378.)

[42] Ibid., p. 392.   [43] Ibid., 21.14, p. 381.
[44] Ibid., 21.11, p. 376.   [45] Ibid.,10.6, p. 143.

analogies and identifications.[46] Although in the seventeenth century it had been common to identify the Dutch as the modern Carthaginians, the decline of the United Provinces and the rise of Great Britain increasingly led French commentators to analogise the English with the Carthaginians, being both perfidious (*Punica fides*), maritime, and commercial. The identifications, unsurprisingly, were more popular in France, since they implied that the story would end with the total destruction of Carthaginian power. But they were not absent from England, most strikingly in Edward Wortley Montagu's 1759 *Reflections on the Rise and Fall of the Ancient Republicks Adapted to the Present State of Great Britain*. Wortley there disagreed with 'the sententious Montesquieu' about Carthage: its problem, as it happened, was the same that he diagnosed in modern Britain, which was the absence of a national milita – for just as the Carthaginians had been terrified by Agathocles, so too London had been thrown into panic in 1745 'at the approach of a poor handful of Highlanders, as much inferior even to the small army of Agathocles in number, as they were in arms and discipline'.[47]

Two other republican references to Carthage from the 1760s are worthy of note – especially in light of the modern republics that would soon appear on either side of the Atlantic. John Dickinson ended the second of his *Letters from a Farmer in Pennsylvania to the Inhabitants of the British Colonies* in 1767 with a reflection on the Carthaginians' control over Sardinia, in order to elucidate 'the nature of the necessities of dependent states, caused by the policy of a governing one, for her own benefit'.

[T]hey made a decree, that the Sardinians should not raise corn, nor get it any other way than from the Carthaginians. Then, by imposing any duties they would upon it, they drained from the miserable Sardinians any sums they pleased; and whenever that oppressed people made the least movement to assert their liberty, their tyrants starved them to death or submission. This may be called the most perfect kind of political necessity.

From what has been said, I think this uncontrovertible conclusion may be deduced, that when a ruling state obliges a dependent state to take certain commodities from her alone, it is implied in the nature of that obligation; is essentially requisite to give it the least degree of justice; and is inseparably

---

[46] Edmond Dziembowski, *Un nouveau patriotisme français, 1750–1770: la France face à la puissance anglaise à l'époque de la guerre de Sept Ans* (Oxford: Voltaire Foundation, 1998), e.g. pp. 83–6, 238–40, 244–6. Rahe, *Montesquieu and the Logic of Liberty*, p. 58. Edward Arnold, *Imperial Republics: Revolution, War, and Territorial Expansion from the English Civil War to the French Revolution* (University of Toronto Press, 2011), p. 50.

[47] Edward Wortley Montagu, *Reflections on the Rise and Fall of the Ancient Republicks Adapted to the Present State of Great Britain* (London, A. Millar, 1759), p. 194. Arnold, *Imperial Republics*, p. 64.

united with it, in order to preserve any share of freedom to the dependent state; that those commodities should never be loaded with duties, FOR THE SOLE PURPOSE OF LEVYING MONEY ON THE DEPENDENT STATE.[48]

Gabriel Bonnot de Mably's *Phocion's Conversations*, from 1763, had its fourth-century BCE protagonist prophesy the fall of Carthage, 'for there will be on earth some people eager to make war on opulent nations, and riches, as corrupting the manners, have in all ages, down to our days, fallen into the hands of courage and discipline'.[49] A footnote, reminiscent of Harrington's forecast of consequences of the recovery of 'ancient prudence',[50] extended the argument to modern times, calling Phocion's prophecy 'the horoscope of trading states'.

All the powers of Europe are now becoming commercial; and this defect in their politics being general, none of them feel the inconveniences of it, with regard to their enemies: they fight on equal terms; but should a republic be formed, on the Roman system, what would become of such commercial states?[51]

Mably was still working with the old contrast between commercial Carthage and virtuous Rome. Voltaire, by contrast, sought to break with it. In his 1764 *Philosophical Dictionary*, in the entry on the spirit of the laws, and with precise reference to Montesquieu's comment about how Rome 'attacked Carthage as a rival, not as a commercial nation', he remarked that it 'was both as a warlike and as a commercial nation, as the learned Huet proves in his "Commerce of the Ancients", when he shows that the Romans were addicted to commerce a long time before the first punic war'.[52] And it is when we turn to Adam Smith's analysis of the Punic wars, that we find the most developed argument about Rome and Carthage, which presented them as qualitatively similar regimes. Three of Smith's discussions of Carthage have come down to us: first, in the notes of the lectures on jurisprudence from Glasgow in early 1763, the discussion of 28 February continuing on to 1 March. Second, in some further remarks that survive in the record of the 1766 version of the same lecture course. Third, in Book V of

---

[48] John Dickinson 'Letters from a Farmer in Pennsylvania to the Inhabitants of the British Colonies', #2, in *The Writings of John Dickinson*, Paul Leicester Ford, ed. (Philadelphia, PA: The Historical Society of Pennsylvania, 1895), vol. 1, p. 321.

[49] Gabriel Bonnot de Mably, *Phocion's Conversations, or, the Relation between Morality and Politics*, William MacBean, ed. (London: Dodsley, 1769), pp. 161–2.

[50] Harrington, in *Oceana*, Pocock, ed., p. 232.

[51] Mably, *Phocion's Conversations*, p. 287. See also McDaniel, *Adam Ferguson in the Scottish Enlightenment*, p. 106.

[52] Voltaire, 'Laws (spirit of)', in *A Philosophical Dictionary* (London: John and Henry L. Hunt, 1824), vol. 4, p. 334.

The Wealth of Nations, from 1776. I shall take each of these discussions in turn.

Where earlier analyses presented Carthage and Rome as quite distinct types – the republic of wealth, and the republic of virtue – Smith in 1763 argued that they were the same. The republics of the ancient world fell into two varieties, he maintained, the 'defensive republick', of which the several states of Greece will serve for examples', and the 'conquering republick' – the same category that we had earlier found in Montesquieu – 'of which Rome will serve us for an example, and Carthage also', for, as he went on to note, 'as I shall shew by and by Carthage would have shared the same fate as Rome had it not been overrun by the latter'.[53]

The point on which Smith focused his attention when he turned to the fate of the conquering republick was the social composition of the army. Peace and tranquility at home 'gives great room for the cultivation of the arts, and opulence which follows on it', and 'Commerce too will naturally introduce itself, tho' not, as now, particularly studied and a theory laid down'.[54] With the development of 'arts and luxury', 'the rich and the better sort of people will no longer ingage in [military] service'. This was the case in Rome after Marius, and it was the case at Carthage, too. Such an army of 'freed men, or liberti, of run–a–way slaves, deserters, or the lowest of the mob' would after several campaigning seasons become dependent for 'all that they were worth in the world' on its commander, who, if he were 'affronted at home, or any way discontented', would be able to challenge the government of the state. Smith's Roman examples were the usual suspects: Sulla and Marius, Pompey and Caesar, Antony – 'and at last Augustus alone, on the throne'. 'And the same will be the case in all conquering republicks where ever a mercenary army at the disposall of the generall is in use'.[55] Cromwell was cited as a modern example of the same phenomenon. 'But the same thing was feared and must have happened at Carthage', Smith continued, 'had the project of Hanniball succeeded, and he made himself master of Italy'. Together with his brother's army in Spain, 'these two armies would probably have enslaved their country' – and the 'scanty allowances he had plainly show how jealous' the rest of the Carthaginian aristocracy was of him, 'nor does it appear that they ever intended his project should succeed'. Indeed, 'perhaps they would choose rather to be conquered by a foreign enemy than by one of their

[53] Adam Smith, *Lectures on Jurisprudence*, Ronald L. Meek, Ronald, D. D. Raphael, and Peter Stein, eds. (Oxford: Clarendon Press, 1978), 28 February 1763.
[54] Ibid., 1 March 1763.   [55] Ibid., 28 February 1763.

own body', for 'they would be grieved to see their equal raised above them'.[56]

In the report of the 1766 series of lectures, Smith covered broadly similar ground, and, as Montagu had done before him, juxtaposed the Jacobite rebellion with the history of Carthage. A few thousand 'naked unarmed Highlanders took possession of the improved parts of this country without any opposition from the unwarlike inhabitants', Smith noted, and 'had they not been opposed by a standing army they would have seized the throne with little difficulty'. 'Our ancestors', he explained, 'were brave and warlike, their minds were not enervated by cultivating arts and commerce, and they were already with spirit and vigor to resist the most formidable foe'. The general point he was seeking to establish was that

A commercial country may be formidable abroad, and may defend itself by fleets and standing armies, but when they are overcome and the enemy penetrates into the country, the conquest is easy.

The Punic wars offered an example of the same phenomenon: 'The Carthaginians were often victorious abroad, but when the war was carried into their own country they had no share with the Romans'. 'These', Smith remarked, 'are the disadvantages of a commercial spirit', and 'To remedy these defects would be an object worthy of serious attention'.[57]

Finally, in *The Wealth of Nations*, Smith offered his overall explanation of Carthaginian defeat in the second Punic war. After many campaigning seasons, 'the army which Annibal led from Spain into Italy must necessarily, in those different wars, have been gradually formed to the exact discipline of a standing army'. The Roman armies Hannibal encountered had not 'been engaged in any war of very great consequence; and their military discipline, it is generally said, was a good deal relaxed'. Thus, what was effectively a Carthaginian standing army thumped the Roman militia at Trebia, Thrasymenus, and Cannæ.[58] But thereupon the tables were turned. Hannibal in Italy 'was ill supplied from home', and the 'Roman militia, being continually in the field, became in the progress of the war a well disciplined and well exercised standing army'. Hasdrubal led his standing army into Italy, and was beaten by an equivalent military force, which enjoyed the benefits of home advantage.

---

[56] Ibid., 1 March 1763.   [57] Ibid., Report of 1766, 'Of Police'.
[58] Adam Smith, *An Inquiry into the Nature and Causes of the Wealth of Nations*, R. H. Campbell and A. S. Skinner, eds. (Oxford: Clarendon Press, 1979), V.i.a, vol. 2, p. 702.

What Hasdrubal left behind in Spain was merely a militia, which Scipio overcame – and 'in the course of the war, his own militia necessarily became a well-disciplined and well-exercised standing army', which in turn invaded Africa, 'where it found nothing but a militia to oppose it'. Hannibal's army was recalled to Africa, where it was destroyed at Zama. 'The event of that day determined the fate of the two rival republicks'.[59]

Although there were certainly similarities between Smith and Montesquieu's respective analyses of the contest between Rome and Carthage – in particular, both thought that the Carthaginian republic could not have survived Hannibal's counterfactual victory in the second Punic war, but would have become a personal dictatorship – it is the differences that stand out. By insisting that Rome and Carthage were instances of the same broader type, the commercial, conquering republick, Smith was able to do two things. First, he had an argument for what the eventual fate future of Carthaginian power would have had to be, had the Punic wars gone the other way. Carthage, like Rome, was a conquering republick, and Carthage, like Rome, would have fallen victim to barbarian invasions (or 'shepherds', to use the categories of the four-stages theory) for the same reasons that ultimately did for the Roman emperors. The ancient republics – of both varieties, for the Greek defensive republicks were also overwhelmed by their shepherd neighbours – could not, according to Smith, have sustained themselves indefinitely into the future.

A second implication of Smith's account was that Montesquieu's argument about the fall of Rome that he offered in his *Considerations* could not be correct. According to Montesquieu, in the absence of commerce, Rome could only become wealthy through conquest and pillage; the expansion of the republic through such conquest and pillage led to inequality; but she never developed either the commercial habits that could bring an end to the need for further conquests, in order to satiate an impossible demand for luxury goods at home, nor the kind of political institutions of modern monarchy that could stabilise a radically unequal society. When the army itself developed a taste for luxury, cheaper foreign soldiers were substituted for more expensive Roman citizens, the long run of military success finally came to an end, and Roman power was ultimately doomed. For Smith, however, the Romans had long been actively engaged in commerce – if for not quite as long as she had been on Huet's account – and the problem such a society faced was that it was

[59] Ibid., p. 703.

insufficiently warlike – hence the need, in the end, to outsource military protection to the shepherds. Commerce and the luxury to which it gave rise made Carthaginian territory easy to invade. And in the end, it did the same for Rome.[60]

[60] For further discussion of Smith's analysis of the fate of ancient republicanism, see István Hont, *Politics in Commercial Society: Jean-Jacques Rousseau and Adam Smith*, Michael Sonenscher and Béla Kapossy, eds. (Cambridge, MA: Harvard University Press, 2015), Lecture 4: 'Histories of Government: Republics, Inequality and Revolution'.

5   Enlightenment socialism
Cesare Beccaria and his critics

Sophus A. Reinert

Of the ceaseless debates animating the long eighteenth century in Europe, and the period colloquially referred to as 'The Enlightenment', few were more vocal – and more consequential – than that which raged over the vexing question of human sociability.[1] The anxieties and assumptions motivating this debate often crystallized in a famous Manichean opposition, one popularized centuries earlier by the Renaissance humanist Erasmus of Rotterdam, between the Roman playwright Titus Maccius Plautus' trenchant observation that *'lupus est homo homini* [man is a wolf to man]' and the Stoic philosopher Seneca's more hopeful *'homo, sacra res homini* [man is something sacred to man]'.[2] Were men wolves to one another, or were they sacred? Was peaceful sociability a fragile, hard-fought victory to be vigilantly defended against man's predatory passions, or was it the blessedly spontaneous and orderly result of instinctive camaraderie or countervailing self-interests? By the mid seventeenth century, the English political philosopher Thomas Hobbes

---

[1] On this debate see, among many, many others, Istvan Hont, *Jealousy of Trade: International Competition and the Nation-State in Historical Perspective*, Cambridge, MA: Harvard University Press, 2005, pp. 37–51, 159–84 and John Robertson, 'Sacred History and Political Thought: Neapolitan Responses to the Problem of Sociability after Hobbes', *The Historical Journal*, vol. 56, no. 1, 2013, pp. 1–29. What precisely the 'Enlightenment' was remains an issue of great contention. For introductions see among others John Robertson, *The Case for the Enlightenment: Scotland and Naples, 1680–1760*, Cambridge University Press, 2005 and Anthony Pagden, *The Enlightenment: And Why It Still Matters*, New York: Random House, 2013. On the question see also Sophus A. Reinert, 'In margine a un bilancio sui lumi europei', *Rivista storica italiana*, vol. 118, no. 3, 2006, pp. 975–86.

[2] Plautus, *Asinaria*, 495; Lucius Annaeus Seneca, *Epistulae morales ad Lucilium*, XCV, 33. In his *Adagia*, I.1.69 and I.1.70. Erasmus of Rotterdam reformulated these classical phrases and gave them the form by which they would become best known in early modern Europe: 'homo homini deus [man is a god to man]' and 'homo homini lupus [man is a wolf to man]'. See William Barker (ed.), *The Adages of Erasmus*, University of Toronto Press, pp. 37–41. This was further popularized by Thomas Hobbes, *On the Citizen* [*De Cive*], eds. Richard Tuck and Michael Silverthorne, Cambridge University Press, 1998, p. 3. On this see also François Tricaud, '"Homo homini Deus," "Homo homini lupus": Recherche des deux formules de Hobbes', in Reinhart Koselleck and Roman Schnur (eds.), *Hobbes-Forschungen*, Berlin: Duncker und Humblot, 1969, pp. 61–70.

could argue in *De Cive*, or *On the Citizen*, that the emergence of states had made 'citizens' sacred to each other, while the relationship between 'commonwealths' remained lupine. Leviathans had arisen from the depths of time in the form of modern states, but they could be terrible to behold; time had socialized *people*, but not yet *peoples*.[3]

Was Hobbes right? If so, why, how had it happened, how durable might the success of establishing a political community be, and what, if anything, could one do to expand the thresholds of sociability further? To what extent could the competing and often warring states of the world be brought together in a process of peaceful, worldly melioration – not unlike what Immanuel Kant soon would call the project for 'perpetual peace' – and how should one proceed in one's quest for it?[4] These questions, seemingly perennial in nature, had long been the domain of theology and political philosophy. In the early modern period economic affairs undeniably rose to a position of prominence in international relations, and they increasingly claimed the attention of sovereigns, laymen, and the political and economic reformers populating and so profoundly characterizing the European Enlightenment.[5] The substantial incongruity between states and markets, and the ways in which economic and political concerns mutually affected one another, offered both concrete challenges and fertile grounds for intellectual debate.[6] Not fortuitously it was at the intersection of these worlds, the divine and the secular, the ideal and the practical, that the neologism 'socialism' made its first appearance in debates around the nature and future of human sociability.

The term 'socialism' – quite distinct from the countless proto-socialist writings and regimes populating the historical record, dating back at least to the teachings of the Zoroastrian prophet Mazdak[7] – did not originate, as is often argued, in British and French Utopian Socialism of the 1820s, among the Owenites, the Fourierists, and the Saint-Simonian prophets

---

[3] Hobbes, *On the Citizen*, pp. 3–4. On the process of state-formation see still Charles Tilly, "Reflections on the History of European State-Making," in id. (ed.), *The Formation of National States in Western Europe*, Princeton: Princeton University Press, 1975, pp. 3–83. On *people* and *peoples* see John Rawls, The Law of Peoples Cambridge, MA: Harvard University Press, 1999, p. 23.

[4] Immanuel Kant, 'Perpetual Peace: A Philosophical Sketch', in id., *Political Writings*, ed. Hans Reiss, 2nd ed., Cambridge University Press, 1991, pp. 93–130.

[5] On the rise to prominence of economic concerns see Sophus A. Reinert, 'Rivalry: Greatness in Early Modern Political Economy', in Philip J. Stern and Carl Wennerlind (eds.), *Mercantilism Reimagined: Political Economy in Early Modern Britain and its Empire*, Oxford University Press, 2013, pp. 348–70.

[6] Hont, *Jealousy of Trade*, p. 155.

[7] Mansour Shaki, 'The Social Doctrine of Mazdak in Light of Middle Persian Evidence', *Archiv Orientální*, vol. 46, no. 4, 1978, pp. 289–306.

of industrial civilization.[8] Rather, it emerged more than half a century earlier in the tumultuous smaller states of Germany and, particularly, the Italian peninsula.[9] This is not to say that these socialisms are entirely unrelated, only that the term, when first conjured, was protean enough to justify, in Reinhart Koselleck's elegant phrase, multiple 'futures past'.[10] And there are good reasons why this earliest socialist moment has largely been overlooked. 'Socialism' was a rare and derogatory term, and just as no eighteenth-century 'socialist' proclaimed himself to be one (at the time they were, alas, as far as we know, all men), none even acknowledged having been called one.

Notably, the term was used to criticize the Milanese coterie of mostly noble writers and reformers known as the *Accademia dei pugni*, The *Academy of Fisticuffs*, the most important members of which were the brothers Pietro and Alessandro Verri and the young Cesare Beccaria.[11] And it was Beccaria's 1764 publication of *Dei delitti e delle pene*, or *On Crimes and Punishments*, that first merited the moniker 'socialist' in vernacular print.[12] The short pamphlet remains one of the most famous

8 On these movements, see among others Emile Durkheim, *Socialism and Saint-Simon*, ed. Alvin W. Gouldner, London: Routledge, 2009; Gregory Claeyes, *Machinery, Money and the Millennium: From Moral Economy to Socialism, 1815–1860*, Princeton University Press, 1987; Jonathan Beecher, *Charles Fourier: The Visionary and His World*, Berkeley: University of California Press, 1990; Robert Wokler, 'Ideology and the Origins of Social Science', in Mark Goldie and Robert Wokler (eds.), *The Cambridge History of Eighteenth-Century Political Thought*, Cambridge University Press, 2006, pp. 688–710.

9 Given the German and Italian context of this specific debate over 'socialism', it fell outside of the boundaries of André Lichtenberger's *Le socialisme au XVIIIᵉ siècle: Etude sur les idées socialistes dans les écrivains français du XVIIIᵉ siècle avant la Révolution*, Paris: Félix Alcan, 1895. The classic treatments of the origins of 'socialism' in Enlightenment Italy remain Franco Venturi, 'Contributi ad un dizionario storico: "Socialista" e "socialismo" nell'Italia del Settecento', *Rivista storica italiana*, 75, 1963, pp. 129–40, truncated in id., *Italy and the Enlightenment: Studies in a Cosmopolitan Century*, ed. Stuart Wolf, trans. Susan Corsi, London: Longman, 1972, pp. 52–62, and Giorgio Spini, *Le origini del socialismo: Da utopia alla bandiera rossa*, Turin: Einaudi, 1992, pp. 347–349, developed in id., 'Sulle origini dei termini "socialista" e "socialismo"', *Rivista storica italiana*, 105 (1993), 679–97, republished in id. *Dalla preistoria del socialismo alla lotta per la libertá*, Milan: FrancoAngeli, 2002, pp. 31–49.

10 Reinhart Koselleck, *Futures Past: On the Semantics of Historical Time*, translated by Keith Tribe, New York: Columbia University Press, 2004.

11 On the group, see Sophus A. Reinert, 'Patriotism, Cosmopolitanism, and Political Economy in the *Accademia dei pugni* in Austrian Lombardy, 1760–1780', in Koen Stapelbroek and Jani Marjanen (eds.), *The Rise of Economic Societies in the Eighteenth Century: Patriotic Reform in Europe and North America*, Basingstoke: Palgrave Macmillan, 2012, pp. 130–56.

12 For ease of reference I quote from Cesare Beccaria, *On Crimes and Punishments and Other Writings*, ed. Aaron Thomas, trans. Aaron Thomas and Jeremy Parzen, University of Toronto Press, 2008. For the critical edition see Luigi Firpo and Gianni Francioni (eds.), *Edizione Nazionale delle Opere di Cesare Beccaria*, 16 vols., Milan: Mediobanca, 1984–2015 [henceforth *ENOCB*], vol. I: *Dei delitti e delle pene*, ed. Gianni Francioni, pp. 215–368.

and influential publications of the eighteenth century, and certainly the most lionized work to emerge from the Italian Enlightenment. Beautifully written, it engaged with a wide array of sources and intellectual traditions to present an impassioned plea for penal reform, most famously against torture and capital punishment. Through this lens, Beccaria touched upon most aspects of human life, suggesting a new interpretation of the social contract, in which individuals were never forced to give up their right to life, from which most of his penological suggestions derived, as well as a guiding definition of justice as sociability that underscored the practical limits of material inequality viable in a polity and even trumped considerations of private property.[13] But if one accepts the vague if commonplace equation of the eighteenth-century idiom 'commercial society' with the modern concept of 'capitalism', an assumption on which much scholarship on the phenomena rightly or wrongly rests, then an inescapable proposition emerges: the first 'socialists' were at the time Europe's greatest proponents of 'capitalism'.[14] 'Socialists' were, in the final instance, those bold enough to believe that political economy trumped theology as a matrix for social organization.[15]

What follows will shed new light on the etymological origins of socialism, the role it played in contemporary economic debates, and its relevance as a prism for understanding Beccaria's never fully formulated project for pacifying peoples as well as people through trade in his lectures, administrative work, and the fragments constituting his unpublished *Ripulimento delle nazioni,* or *Refinement of Nations,* which was ostensibly meant to redraw the history and, perhaps, future of civilization through the lens of political economy.[16] Even though commerce

---

[13] Beccaria, *On Crimes and Punishments,* pp. 10–12. See also Madeleine van Bellen, 'Die Begriffe *giustizia* bei Cesare Beccaria und den Brüdern Pietro und Alessandro Verri', in Helmut C. Jacobs and Gisela Schlüter (eds.), *Beiträge zur Begriffsgeschichte der italienischen Aufklärung im europäischen Kontext,* Frankfurt am Main: Peter Lang, 2000, 151–64, particularly p. 153. The ur-source for Beccaria's argument might well be Samuel von Pufendorf, *On the Duty of Man and Citizen According to Natural Law,* ed. James Tully, translated by Michael Silverthorne, Cambridge University Press, 1991, pp. 35–36: 'all that necessarily and normally make for sociality is understood to be prescribed by natural law. All that disturbs or violates sociality is understood as forbidden'.
[14] E.g. Gregory Blue and Timothy Brook, 'Introduction', in id., (eds.), *China and Historical Capitalism: Genealogies of Sinological Knowledge,* Cambridge University Press, 1999, 1–9, p. 4.
[15] A sentiment expressed clearly in Ferdinando Facchinei, 'Brevi note da porsi in pie' di pagina al libro dei Delitti e delle pene 1764', Archivio di Stato di Venezia, Venice, Italy, *Miscellanea di atti diversi manoscritti, no. 71,* ff. 15v and 16v.
[16] On these fragments see Gianni Francioni, 'Il fantasma del "Ripulimento delle nazioni": Congetture su un'opera mancata di Cesare Beccaria', *Studi Settecenteschi,* vol. 5, 1984, pp. 131–73, which appropriately reads them through the contemporary lens of stadial theories of history, for which see still Ronald L. Meek, *Social Science and the Ignoble Savage,* Cambridge University Press, 1976. What follows will offer complimentary

was one of the centrifugal civilizing forces affecting mankind in Beccaria's scheme, there was no necessary corellation between trade and peace in his political economy; for him, unless relationships between states and markets were carefully calibrated, world trade could just as easily reproduce centripetal patterns of war and dependence.[17]

Societies had of course long contained markets, but the brave new world of early modern Europe increasingly saw the emergence of market societies per se, in which, in the words of Italy's first professor of political economy Antonio Genovesi, people approached the world 'with the eyes of a merchant'.[18] Yet the nexus among the social, the economic, the political, and the spiritual out of which 'socialism' emerged remained deeply contentious. Derivatives of the Latin 'socius' – 'ally' or 'partner' – such as 'social' abounded in Europe at the time. The 1741 edition of the great *Vocabolario* of the *Accademia della Crusca*, or *Academy of the Bran*, a Florentine academy established in 1583 to defend the Italian language as derived from the Tuscan dialect, defined the varieties of sociability thus:

SOCIABLE. *Adj. Social, Companionable.* Lat. *sociabilis.*Gr. κοινωνικός.

Varch. Ercol. 31. Man is the most sociable, or companionable animal of all. *And below:* Many other animals which, if not civil etc. are at least sociable. *Gell. Let. 2 'lez. 9.191.* Man, being a sociable animal that loves living with those of its own species, rejoices in the happiness of others.

SOCIAL. *Adj. Who loves company.* Lat. *sociabilis, socialis.* Gr. κοινωνικός

Mor. S. Greg. Obviously he who loathes patience soon abandons social life from impatience. *Buon. Fier. intr.* I. That I am a far more social person.[19]

rather than contradictory readings of Beccaria's unfinished project. The phrase 'ripulimento delle nazioni' first appeared in Pietro Verri, 'Elementi del commercio', in *Il Caffè, 1764–1766*, eds. Gianni Francioni and Sergio A. Romagnoli, Turin: Bollati Boringhieri, 1993, 30–38, p. 37, when Verri discusses 'that luxury, which is never divorced from the universal culture and refinement [*ripulimento*] of nations'. On this piece, see Reinert, 'Patriotism, Cosmopolitanism, and Political Economy'.

[17] On the trope of peace through trade, and its massive historiography, see Reinert, *Translating Empire: Emulation and the Origins of Political Economy*, Cambridge, MA: Harvard University Press, 2011, p. 17 and passim.

[18] Antonio Genovesi, *Storia del commercio della Gran Brettagna*, 3 vols., Naples: Benedetto Gessari, 1757–8, vol. I, p.11n. On Genovesi's political economy see Reinert, *Translating Empire*, pp. 186–232. On this transition see still Karl Polanyi, *The Great Transformation: The Political and Economic Origins of Our Time*, ed. Fred Block with an introduction by Joseph E. Stiglitz, Boston: Beacon Press, 2001.

[19] *Vocabolario degli Accademici della Crusca*, 5 vols., Venice: Francesco Pitteri, 1741, vol. IV, pp. 371–72. This was a private reprint of the 4th Florentine edition. On this remarkable collaborative enterprise, see among others Edgar Zilsel, *The Social Origins of Modern Science*, Dordrecht: Kluwer, 2003, p. 163. Though I have used more recent editions, the references are, in order of appearance, to Benedetto Varchi, 'L'Ercolano, ovvero Agli alberi, dialogo', in id., *Opere di Benedetto Varchi*, 2 vols., Trieste: Lloyd Austriaca, 1858–1859, vol. II, 7–183, p. 25; Giovanni Battista Gelli, 'Lettura seconda *Letture edite*

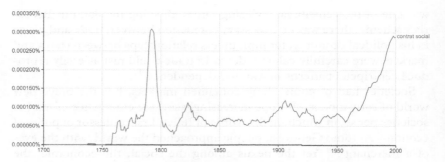

Figure 5.1 Google Ngram of the Phrase 'Contrat Social' in French
Publications, 1700–2000

That the Crusca drew on the examples of the sixth-century Pope Gregory the Great, the humanist Giovanni Battista Gelli, and the artistic
polymath Michelangelo Buonarroti is telling with regards to the relative
antiquity of the term and the sort of literature favored by the Academy.
And Benedetto Varchi's *L'Hercolano*, one of the late Renaissance's premier dialogues on the Tuscan dialect written by a troubled historian of
the Medici Grand Duchy, clearly established that sociability was a step
on the ladder towards civility.[20]

This relationship between the social and the civil was also a leitmotif
in the immense historiography on the so-called *'guerra sociale italica'*, or
the Roman Social War or Allied War of 88–91 BCE, the great civil war
through which, in the Roman historian Appian of Alexandria's phrase,
'all the Italians became part of the Roman state'.[21] Appian's equation
of social and civil wars – society and the polity – would reverberate
through the ages and throughout Europe in related terms like 'social
love', 'social chain', 'social laws', and finally 'social contract', particularly
following the publication of Jean-Jacques Rousseau's eponymous work.
[Figure 5.1]. This contractarian current also emphasized the interrelationship between the social and the civil to the point of conceptual confusion, for example when Rousseau echoed Cicero in speaking of 'the

e inedite di Giovan Battista Gelli sopra la commedia di Dante, ed. Carlo Negroni, 2 vols.,
Florence: Fratelli Bocca, 1887, vol. I, p. 285; St. Gregory the Great, *Morals on the
Book of Job*, 3 vols., Oxford: John Henry Parker, 1845, vol. II, Book XXI, comment
on Job 31:22, p. 542; Michelangelo Buonarrotti, *La fiera: commedia*, ed. Pietro Fanfani,
Florence: Le Monnier, 1860, p. 13. I have corrected the translations where appropriate.
20 Varchi, 'L'Ercolano', p. 25.
21 Eg. Giovanni Botero, *Della ragion di stato*, Ferrara: Baldini, 1589, p. 255 all the way to
Nicola Fortunato, *Discoverta dell'antico regno di Napoli col suo presente stato a pro della
sovranita e de' suoi popoli*, Naples: Giuseppe Raimondi, [1766], p. 56fA and beyond;
Appian, *The Civil Wars*, translated by John Carter, London: Penguin, 1996, I.53, p. 29.

social state, where everything is under the authority of the laws', and other times suggested one led to the other.[22] But large parts of the early modern debate over sociability revolved around attempts by Protestant theorists of natural law, and particularly by Samuel von Pufendorf, to restrict natural law to the technologies of '*socialitas*' necessary to pacify human relations, encourage ever denser civil states, and 'teach one how to conduct oneself to become a useful member of human society' without reference to a hypothetical afterlife.[23]

Looking back at earlier centuries, this was precisely the sort of relationship identified by the Paduan Franciscan lawyer and political economist Giacomo Giuliani, whose 1803 *Antisocialismo confutato*, or *Antisocialism Confuted*, marks one end-point of this particular tradition of 'socialism' animating eighteenth-century debates of sociability. At his 1808 inaugural lecture on criminal law, he lamented the survival of gristly forms of torture even in an age of 'culture and societal civilizing'.[24] Civilization depended on socialization, polity on humanity, every step of the way from individuals, to people, and finally to peoples. As he later would put it, 'the civilizing process is the effect of social perfectibility', and political economy was the key to its realization.[25] Ultimately, these debates all revolved around attempts to delineate, improve, and expand a sphere of human activity ever more distant from the state of nature, cemented by various interpretations and depictions of sociability independent of nature or theology.

From its Latin roots, terminological variations on sociability had spread across the European vernaculars. The semantic drift from the venerable 'social' to the neologistic 'socialist' was in this context rather short, and for example occurred, seemingly independently and without

---

[22] Jean-Jacques Rousseau, 'Of the Social Contract', in id., *The Social Contract and Other Later Political Writings*, ed. Victor Gourevitch, Cambridge University Press, 39–152, p. 46.

[23] Pufendorf, *On the Duty of Man*, p. 35, as well as 36–37, 117. See also Ian Hunter, *Rival Enlightenments: Civil and Metaphysical Philosophy in Early Modern Germany*, Cambridge University Press, 2001, pp. 157–58 and, generally, on Pufendorf's 'programme for detranscendentalising moral philosophy', pp. 176–77. See for variations also id., *The Secularization of the Confessional State: The Political Thought of Christian Thomasius*, Cambridge University Press, 2007, pp. 89–99 and *passim*.

[24] Giacomo Giuliani, *Orazione inaugurale*, Padova: Penada, 1808, p. 33; Giacomo Giuliani, *L'antisocialismo confutato; opera filosofica di Giacomo Giuliani conventuale vicentino*, Vicenza: Bartolommeo Paroni, 1803. On Giuliani, see Nazzarena Zanini, 'Note bibliografiche sul giurista dell'Universita di Padova Giacomo Giuliani (1772–1840) gia minore conventuale', *Il Santo*, vol. 33, no. 1–2, 1993, pp. 151–68.

[25] Giacomo Giuliani, '*Scienze politiche*', no date early 1830s, Biblioteca Antoniana, Padua [henceforth BA], scafale 23, MS 772, vol. II, 20r; id., '[*Lezioni*] *Della economia politica*, 1828–1829', BA, scafale 23, MS 774, 2v.

much consequence, when an anonymous London pamphleteer of the early 1790s employed the word 'socialist' as the antonym of a 'savage':

> But these, we are told, are more enlightened days. Man, alas! in savage or in social life, is still the same selfish, restless, sanguinary being; in savage life, his wants are fewer, and his power of doing mischief more contracted; in social life his wants are insatiable, and his means of devastation boundless. A very slender vocabulary enables the savage to transact the business of life. Voluminous dictionaries enable the socialist to misinterpret the transactions of his neighbour.[26]

The pamphleteer's point was to ridicule those who bewailed the horrors of the French Revolution by underscoring 'the depravity of human nature' everywhere. The word 'socialist' was, as such, ironically invented to undermine itself. But these were rather loose semantic spasms around the core problem of sociability, and what is striking about the earlier Germano-Italian tradition is that it seems to have gelled, for a period of several decades, into a coherent theoretical critique of 'socialism', understood to mean something quite specific and, seemingly, dangerous to the status quo of early modern Europe.

In light even of new technologies that have come to radically facilitate lexicographical archaeology in recent years, it seems likely that the first version of the term 'socialist' to ever appear in print did so in the form '*socialistae*' in Anselm Desing's 1753 *Juris naturae larva detracta...*, or *Natural Law Unmasked*.[27] A stout Catholic of the Bavarian Benedictine Congregation, Desing railed against the impious writings of Protestant theorists of natural law in the tradition of Grotius and Pufendorf.[28] Though Desing did not bother stopping to explain his neologisms, which probably already existed in the oral, and perhaps manuscript culture of the Benedictine international, '*Socialistae*' and '*naturales socialistae*' were pejorative terms for those who believed social life on this earth was the ultimate end of politics and that something like civic interests might prevail over spiritual considerations and the supremacy of revelation.[29]

---

[26] Anonymous, *Fact without Fallacy; or, constitutional principles contrasted with the ruinous effects of unconstitutional practices*, London: J.S. Jordan, [1793], p. 41.

[27] Anselm Desing, *Juris Naturae larva detracta compluribus libris sub titulo Juris Naturae prodeuntibus ut Puffendorffianis, Heineccianis, Wolffianis etc....*, Munich: Gastl, 1753.

[28] Leticia Cabrera, 'Anselmo Desing o la rehabilitacion de la ciencia juridical en la ilustracion alemana', *Revista de Estudios Historico-Juridicos*, XIX (1997), 169–86, p. 172. On Desing and his life see Ildefons Stegmann, *Anselm Desing, abt von Ensdorf, 1699–1772: Ein Beitrag zur Geschichte der Aufklärung in Bayern*, Munich: Kommissions-Verlag R. Oldenbourg, 1929; Hans Müller, *Ursprung und Geschichte des Wortes Sozialismus und seiner Verwandten*, Hannover: Verlag J.H.W. Dietz Nachf. GmbH, 1967, pp. 30–35; Michael Printy, *Enlightenment and the Creation of German Catholicism*, Cambridge University Press, 2009, pp. 117–18; Ulrich L. Lehner, *Enlightened Monks: The German Benedictines, 1740–1803*, Oxford University Press, 2011, pp. 171–74.

[29] Spini, *Dalla preistoria del socialismo*, p. 34.

While both Pufendorf and Christian Wolff had argued religion to be a society within the state, Desing countered that it rather was the other way around, with 'state and society' being 'states *within* the religious state'. Worldly laws and politics remained inescapably subject to the higher laws of religion.[30] Desing even included the term '*Socialistae*' in his work's analytical index, with the subfields 'they exclude the Gospel from natural law against their interest [*contra suum interesse excludunt a jure naturae evangelium*]' and, strikingly, 'they differ little from Hobbesians [*ab Hobbianis parum different*]'. Socialists were, in the widest sense, irreligious secularists for Desing and the tradition he represented, and their governing preoccupation with the preservation and expansion of society spoke to the very core of contemporary political philosophy.[31]

Desing's dense work met with notable success, and, though seemingly unnoticed until now, the terms '*socialistae*' and even '*socialistarum*', or 'of socialists', reappeared frequently in the work of the German Benedictine and Salzburg Professor of Philosophy Ulrich Huhndorff.[32] Desing was further praised, among others, by his friend the Benedictine Cardinal Angelo Maria Querini, former head librarian of the Vatican, and his concerns were mirrored by likeminded Catholics across Italy.[33] Though

---

[30] Desing, *Juris Naturae larva detracta*, pp. 4–5.

[31] Desing, *Juris Naturae larva detracta*, p. 236. See, for the Protestant equation of Pufendorf with Hobbes on ironically similar grounds at the time, Richard Tuck, 'The "Modern" Theory of Natural Law', in Anthony Pagden (ed.), *The Languages of Political Theory in Early-Modern Europe*, Cambridge University Press, 1987, 99–119, pp. 102–03. Though he never spelled this out, Istvan Hont wrote of how Pufendorf's 'followers were described as the school of "socialists" (or society-ists)', see his *Jealousy of Trade*, p. 45.

[32] Ulrich Huhndorff *et al.*, *Ius naturae in suo principio cognoscendi expensum...*, Augsburg: Pingizer, 1755, pp. 96, 107, 112, 121, 124. Very little is known of Huhndorff, but see Johan Friedrich von Schulte, *Die Geschichte der Quellen und Literatur des Canonischen Rechts von der Mitte des 16. Jahrhunderts bis zur Gegenwart*, Stuttgart: Enke, 1880, entry 139, pp. 192–93. See also Richard Bruch, *Ethik und Naturrecht im deutschen Katholizismus des 18. Jahrhunderts: Von der Tugendethik zur Pflichtethik*, Tübingen: A. Francke Verlag, 1997, p. 94 and, for Huhndorff as part of a larger reaction against Pufendorfian theories of sociability, p. 256.

[33] Lehner, *Enlightened Monks*, p. 174; Johann Baptist Schneyer, *Die Rechtsphilosophie Anselm Desings O.S.B. (1699–1772)*, Kallmünz: Lassleben, 1932, pp. 42–47; Herbert Schambeck, "Anselm Desings Kritik an der Vernunftsrechtslehre", in René Marcic et al. (eds.), *Internationale Festschrift für Alfred Verdross: Zum 80. Geburtstag*, München: Wilhelm Fink Verlag, 1971, 449–78, pp. 458–59. On Desing's travels to Italy, including a visit to Querini in Brescia, see Klaus Kempf, 'La visita del benedettino Anselm Desing alla biblioteca queriniana (12 agosto 1750)', in Ennio Ferraglio and Daniele Montanari (eds.), *Dalla libreria del vescovo alla biblioteca della città: 250 anni di tradizione della cultura a Brescia*, Brescia: Grafo, 2001, pp. 201–11. On Querini's German connections and visits to Benedictine monasteries, see also Mario Bendiscioli, 'La Germania protestante tra ortodossia, pietismo, Aufklärung, nell'età e nella corrispondenza del cardinale Angelo Maria Querini', in Gino Benzoni and Maurizio Pegrari (eds.), *Cultura religione e politica nell'età di Angelo Maria Querini*, Brescia: Morcelliana, 1982, 23–31, p. 31.

Natural Law Unmasked remained untranslated, Desing's fame was great enough to warrant a 1769 Ferrarese edition, in Italian, of his *Opuscoli*, or *Pamphlets*. The term 'socialists' did not make an appearance in these Italian writings, but they eloquently summarized his fundamental attack on modern natural law for having sought the 'foundations of human society' in 'vile, carnal' causes rather than by 'raising' man's 'gaze' towards the heavens. It seemed strange to Desing that everyone spoke of 'the spirit of the laws' in wake of Montesquieu's *magnum opus*, yet conveniently forgot the semantic origins of the phrase: 'If I am not mistaken, the spirit of the laws is something spiritual; divine is the Sovereign reason of that Supreme Being who arranges and regulates everything'. There was a very real danger, Desing thought that 'reformers' would think '*reason alone*' could suffice as a tool for achieving worldly melioration.[34]

The fraught relationship between society and religion, state and church, was one of the most political expressions of this debate, and Italian translators also published Desing's *Le ricchezze del clero utili, e necessarie alla repubblica*, or *The Wealth of the Clergy Useful and Necessary to the Republic* in 1768, in which he quoted his *Natural Law Unmasked* explicitly to again champion the supremacy of religion in the world against those who argued that the Church was 'a state within the state': 'I have confuted this monstrous division by Pufendorf in a book entitled *Larva detracta*, in which, I think, it has been demonstrated that . . . the Church is not *a state within Realms*, but that these are *states within the Church*'.[35] Where the German historical school economist Gustav von Schmoller would later identify early modern 'natural law' as an intellectual movement to return some sense of community to mankind after the fall of Rome and the fragmentation of organized religion, Desing's argument against the 'socialists' rested on a resolute rebuttal of its very premises.[36] There was no need for a new source of cohesion for Desing, for that source had to remain the Catholic Church, within whose sprawling halls human history unfolded.

---

[34] Anselm Desing, *Opuscoli*, Ferrara: Giuseppe Rinaldi, 1769, pp. 90, 201, 259 and *passim*, criticizing the reception of Charles Louis de Secondat, Baron de la Brède et Montesquieu, *The Spirit of the Laws*, eds. Anne M. Cohler, Basia C. Miller and Harold S. Stone, Cambridge University Press, 1989. On the Italian translations of Desing's work see Franco Venturi, *Settecento riformatore*, 5 vols. in 7, Turin: Einaudi, 1969–1990, vol. II, pp. 199–202.

[35] Anselm Desing, *Le ricchezze del clero utili, e necessarie alla repubblica*, Ferrara: Gianantonio Coatti, 1768, p. 8. On the variations of this volume and their original context, see Printy, *Enlightenment and the Creation of German Catholicism*, pp. 76–81.

[36] Gustav von Schmoller, *The Mercantile System and its Historical Significance*, New York: The Macmillan Company, 1897, pp. 70–71.

In fact, the same year that Beccaria clandestinely sent his *On Crimes and Punishment* to press in Livorno, the Dominican friar Bonifacio Finetti published *De principiis juris naturae et gentium adversus Hobbesium, Pufendorfium, Thomasium, Wolfium, et alios*, or *The Principles of the Law of Nature and of Nations against Hobbes, Pufendorf, Thomasius, Wolff, and Others* in Venice. Known even in England as 'the most astonishing linguist . . . that ever existed', Finetti was an academically inclined monk who 'scarcely ever stirred from his cell', in which he received 'all sorts of books and manuscripts' from 'all the corners of the world'. Yet he was, nonetheless, a man of his times, the vast library he collected including not only grammars, dictionaries, and bibles for his research on the historical linguistics of Hebrew and other languages, but also numerous '*treaties of peace and commerce*'.[37] Finetti is today best remembered for his vitriolic critiques of the Neapolitan historian and philosopher Giambattista Vico, whose conception of 'Providence' he felt could have belonged to 'a mere naturalist or fatalist'. And, though a Dominican, Finetti was also an important agent for the dissemination of German Benedictine scholarship in Italy. He both quoted Desing positively and railed against the '*socialistae*' who, like Hobbes and Spinoza, had fallen 'into the principle of utility' alone, which he wholeheartedly 'condemned'.[38] Finetti's passionate defense of Catholic dogma against the dangers of a secularized sociability and the imperatives of worldly 'utility' was reprinted in 1777 and 1781, in Venice and Naples, and doubtlessly helped paint the backdrop against which Beccaria revolted and against which *On Crimes and Punishments* was received.

---

[37] Giuseppe Marco Antonio Baretti, *An Account of the Manners and Customs of Italy; with Observations on the Mistakes of some Travellers, with Regard to that Country*, 2 vols., London: T. Davies, 1768, vol. I, pp. 206–08, emphasis added, republished also in Anonymous, 'Some Account of Father Finetti, a Dominican Friar', in section 'characters' of *The Annual Register, or a View of the History, Politics, and Literature, for the Year 1768*, 6th edition, London: Woodfall, 1800, pp. 37–40.

[38] Bonifacio [Germano Federico] Finetti, *De principiis juris naturae et gentium adversum Hobbesium, Pufendorfium, Thomasium, Wolfium, et alios*, 2 vols., Venice: Tommaso Bettinelli, 1764, vol. I, p. XVnA and vol. II, p. 26. On Finetti see the supplementary materials to his *Difesa dell'autorità della sacra scrittura contro G.B. Vico*, ed. Benedetto Croce, Bari: Laterza, 1936, particularly pp. 89–91 and Venturi, *Settecento riformatore*, vol. II, pp. 251–52. On his polemic with Vico see also Giuseppe Mazzotta, *The New Map of the World: The Poetic Philosophy of Giambattista Vico*, Princeton University Press, 1999, p. 236 and Jonathan Israel, *Enlightenment Contested: Philosophy, Modernity, and the Emancipation of Man 1670–1752*, Oxford University Press, 2006, p. 532. On the connection between *honestum* and *utile* in Pufendorf and Grotius, see among others Tuck, 'The "Modern" Theory of Natural Law', p. 105. Strikingly, though in the context of Enlightenment socialism, Desing, Huhndorff, and Finetti were discussed together for similar reasons in Bruch, *Ethik und Naturrecht*, p. 258.

A mere year after Beccaria published his book, Ferdinando Facchinei, a Benedictine operating in Venice and attuned to the vagaries of German scholarship, harnessed Desing's and Finetti's vocabulary in the now infamous *Note ed osservazioni sul libro intitolato "Dei delitti e delle pene"*, or *Notes and Observations on the Book Entitled "On Crimes and Punishments"*.[39] The Tuscan jurist and philosopher Cosimo Amidei wrote to Beccaria that Facchinei 'deserves to be punished with infamy, as he already has been punished in the tribunal of reason', a statement which turned out to be remarkably prophetic.[40] History has not been kind to Facchinei, who complained late in life of having been 'hated and defamed', not to mention forced into 'silence, slandered and oppressed' for his *Notes and Observations*.[41] One of his more inventive critics even described him as having 'a truly amphibious and hermaphroditic head', and it has been argued that Facchinei became 'almost proverbial as a symbol of obtuse fanaticism'.[42]

Yet Facchinei was hardly a throwback to some hypothetical Dark Ages. He struggled against contemporary canons of censorship like many of his ostensibly more forward-looking contemporaries, claiming he 'studied secretly' in the monastery to avoid being 'stoned'. Probably a 'heretic and deist' in his youth, he was eventually jailed and perhaps tortured for his radical interests in the 'never sufficiently praised Mr. Newton'.[43]

---

[39] Ferdinando Facchinei, *Note ed osservazioni sul libro intitolato "Dei delitti e delle pene"*, N.P. [Venice]: n.p., 1765. Facchinei was very much attuned to developments in German scholarship, see for example, Ferdinando Facchinei, *Lettera intorno alla cagione fisica de' sogni*, Turin: Nella stamperia Mairesse, 1762. His engagement with Christian Wolff, in particular, was also noted by his contemporaries, see Giuseppe Baretti, *La frusta letteraria*, Milan: Società tipografica de' classici italiani, 1838, pp. 246–53. On Facchinei see Antonio Mambelli, 'Il padre Ferdinando Facchinei: poligrafo e polemista del Settecento', *Deputazione di storia patria per le province di Romagna*, 1961, pp. 221–46. On Facchinei's connection to the German publishing world, see furthermore Venturi, *Settecento riformatore*, vol. II, p. 252. On the origins of the Vallembrosan Order, see Francesco Salvestrini, *Disciplina caritatis: Il monachesimo vallombrosano tra medioevo e prima età moderna*, Rome: Viella, 2008.

[40] Cosimo Amidei to Beccaria, 21 April 1766, in *ENOCB*, vol. IV: *Carteggio (parte I: 1758–1768)*, 290–93, p. 292.

[41] Ferdinando Facchinei, *Miscellanea che può servir anche di aggiunta al Saggio di un nuovo metodo per insegnar gli elementi delle scienze a' fanciulli*, Bergamo: Dal cittadino Antoine, 1797, p. xiii.

[42] [Gian Vincenzo Bolgeni], *L'accusatore convinto reo delle colpe falsamente apostate all'innocente*, Milan: Galeazzi, 1768, p. 37; Carlo Scognamiglio Pasini, *L'arte della ricchezza: Cesare Beccaria economista*, Milan: Mondadori, 2014, p. 100.

[43] Ferdinando Facchinei to Giovanni Lami, 10 January 1750/51 and 14 November 1762, Biblioteca Riccardiana, Florence, Italy [henceforth BR], *Mss. Lami*, n. 3724, 2r–3v and 117v; Ferdinando Facchinei to Francesco Antonio Zaccaria, 11 April 1763, Archivo Histórico de la Casa de Loyola, Sanctuary of Loyola, Azpeitia, Spain [henceforth AHCL], *Fondo Zaccaria*, b. 19, 1r. For the unpublished manuscript see Ferdinando Facchinei, *Vita di Newton*, Biblioteca Nazionale Centrale di Firenze, I, I, 98 (D113),

And he was no model Benedictine, at least considering his private correspondence: 'a pox on whoever invented [religious] brothers! . . . if only I could speak!' he complained in the early 1750s.[44] A decade later, he still lamented the years spent 'discussing wine, rice, and illnesses'.[45] Foulmouthed and with a peculiar sense of humor, he considered himself 'made to be, or live like, a Jesuit', one of the 'Christian Philosophers', and the length to which he 'joked' about being upset by his rebuttal suggests he might have been upset after all.[46] Franco Venturi argued that Facchinei's youthful rebellion eventually turned into conservative cynicism, but he continued to engage with rather mainstream 'Enlightenment' topics in the 1760s, among other things teaching 'experimental physics' and engaging with the perennial questions of public happiness and agricultural reform, praising not only Montesquieu and Jean le Rond d'Alembert, co-editor of the *Encyclopédie*, but also the Tuscan polymath Bartolomeo Intieri and his protégé Antonio Genovesi.[47]

There is indeed something tragic about Facchinei, and the way in which he so eagerly wished to partake in the eighteenth-century movements for reform. As he wrote in private correspondence the year before Beccaria published *On Crimes and Punishments*, 'I am only 36 years old; I am very healthy; I am filled with the desire to study, and to do good; and I could, and I will, write something useful to the public'.[48] This was not far off from the sentiment of Beccaria's mentor Pietro Verri: 'would that I could say something useful! Would that I could *do* something!'[49] What exactly the two imagined something *useful* to be, however, lay at the core of the tragedy soon to unfold, for Facchinei was adamant that the *Fisticuffs* had mistakenly put their faith in the '*bouleversant* liberty' of

---

ff. 255–314. On this manuscript see Richard Davies, 'Newtoncini tra lumi e tenebre: Beccaria e Facchinei', in Richard Davies and Persio Tincani (eds.), *Un fortunato libriccino: L'attualità di Cesare Beccaria*, Milan: Edizioni l'ornitoronco, 2014, 79–127, p. 111 and *passim*.

44 Ferdinando Facchinei to Giovanni Lami, 20 September 1751 and 24 September 1751, BR, *Mss. Lami*, n. 3724, 94v–r and 98v.

45 Ferdinando Facchinei to Francesco Antonio Zaccaria, 17 January 1763, AHCL, *Fondo Zaccaria*, b. 19, 1v. Underlining in original.

46 Ferdinando Facchinei to Francesco Antonio Zaccaria, 11 April 1763, AHCL, *Fondo Zaccaria*, b. 19, 2r. See also Facchinei to Zaccaria, 17 April 1763, AHCL, *Fondo Zaccaria*, b. 19, 1r–1v.

47 See for example the list of his manuscripts in Mambelli, 'Il padre Ferdinando Facchinei', pp. 234–42; Venturi, 'Contributi ad un dizionario storico', pp. 130–31; for his teaching of 'experimental physics' see also Facchinei to Zaccaria, 25 August 1763, AHCL, *Fondo Zaccaria*, b. 19, 1r.

48 Facchinei to Zaccaria, 24 November 1763, AHCL, *Fondo Zaccaria*, b. 19, 2r.

49 Pietro Verri, *Meditazioni sulla economia politica*, Livorno: Stamperia della Enciclopedia, 1771, p. 4.

the 'ultramontanes'.[50] For all his commitment to, and interest in, the learning of his time, he could not let go of a higher mooring. 'Is it perhaps a sin to desire this Paradise here on earth? I remit, and adore Providence'.[51] And he seemed equally torn about the role of monasteries, wishing to prove that 'religious communities' were 'not only useful to the Catholic Religion spiritually, as one already argues against all the desperate fanatics, but also very useful temporally, against the author of the book = Affairs of France Poorly Understood', probably a reference to an anonymous, deeply anti-monastic work by the French spy and adventurer Ange Goudar.[52] Facchinei's faith in Providence was unshakable:

[T]he religious economy is assisted by the economic hand of God [*mano economica di Dio*], which has taught the way to build many houses and religious hospitals to the benefit and ornament of the public.[53]

Perhaps by 'religious economy' Facchinei meant the domestic management of monastic life, perhaps he meant something grander with regards to the larger household management of the Catholic Church, though there is no doubt that 'economia' by this time also had come to signify something very close to our modern conception of 'the economy'.[54] In any case, his defense of Catholic economic administration was based on its ostensible success, explained by divine intervention through 'the economic hand of God', that is the creator's continuing and beneficial interference in economic administration. There is even a hint of imperialism in his incensed letter, suggesting, however opaquely, that the Church best manages the household not only of monastic life but also of creation itself, and therefore should be entrusted with the world's reins.

---

[50] Facchinei to Zaccaria, addendum to letter of 17 April 1763, AHCL, *Fondo Zaccaria*, b. 19, 2v.

[51] 26 April 1762, 1v.

[52] Facchinei to Zaccaria, addendum to letter of 17 April 1763, AHCL, *Fondo Zaccaria*, b. 19, 1v, plausibly reacting to Ange Goudar, *Les Intérêts de la France mal entendus, dans les branches de l'agriculture, de la population, des finances, du commerce, de la marine, & de l'industrie. Par un citoyen*, 3 vols., Amsterdam [but Avignon]: Jacques Coeur, 1756, vol. II, pp. 189–209, echoed in Facchinei, *Note ed osservazioni*, pp. 79–85. On Goudar see Jean-Claude Hauc, *Ange Goudar: Un aventurier des Lumières*, Paris: Honoré Champion, 2004. For similar debates over the role of Church wealth in society in German lands, including Desing, see Printy, *Enlightenment and the Creation of German Catholicism*, pp. 72–81.

[53] Facchinei to Zaccaria, addendum to letter of 17 April 1763, AHCL, *Fondo Zaccaria*, b. 19, 1v.

[54] See, for example, how it was used in the Habsburg administration of Milan in Gian Rinaldo Carli to Wenzel Anton von Kaunitz, 18 July 1766, in Umberto Marcelli (ed.), 'Il carteggio Carli-Kaunitz', *Archivio storico italiano*, vol. CXIII, 1955, 388–407, 552–81, vol. XCIV, 1956, 118–35, 771–88, vol. CXIII, pp. 406–07.

Though historiography seems to have overlooked this fact, Facchinei had confided already in January of 1763 that he was about to complete a 'letter regarding the sum of pleasures and pains', in which he hoped to show that 'it is only schmucks [*minchioni*] who don't find more pleasures than pains in this world as well [as in the next world]'. The sudden appearance first of Verri's anonymous *Meditations on Happiness*, followed closely by Beccaria's also anonymous *On Crimes and Punishments*, therefore upset him deeply, perhaps also for careerist reasons.[55] These works, seemingly written by the same author, hiding behind a screen of anonymity, went not only against his understanding of religion, but against his perception of authorship as well – it was sedition of the most cowardly sort. 'I want to be a writer', Facchinei had written shortly before embarking on his critiques, 'not masked, nor transformed, but as a gentleman'.[56] Yet, in spite of all his righteous erudition, there was something crude about Facchinei's literary manners, and something so violent about his critiques, that broke with the silent code of conduct in the eighteenth-century republic of letters, even with regards to inherently touchy subjects such as that of human sociability. And one of the first reactions to his writing would, painfully, proclaim them 'unworthy of a gentleman'.[57]

Bottom line, Facchinei's problem with the *Fisticuffs* was their failure to appreciate the 'practical consequences of their actions', which by virtue of their naïve sedition would lead to 'certain ruin'. Facchinei's *Notes and Observations*, Venturi concluded, were 'a desperate and extreme defense of the traditional world'.[58] Yet it was not that Facchinei disagreed with everything Beccaria had argued. He approved, for example, of the sentiment that luxury was a relative term and that the timely pursuit of it contributed to the welfare of a society, not to mention that 'power' ultimately derived from 'wealth'.[59] The essential problem was that Beccaria, though his authorship remained unknown to Facchinei, 'transcended, and was contrary to, Religion, and good sense', being a 'false Christian' and 'true Epicurean'. *On Crimes and Punishments* was, as such, the 'true daughter of *Rousseau's Social Contract*'.[60]

Following Rousseau, Facchinei suggested, Beccaria had argued that 'civil societies' had been 'formed by the consensus of free and isolated men, united together to secure their own lives, and that for that purpose

---

[55] Ferdinando Facchinei to Francesco Antonio Zaccaria, 17 January 1763, AHCL, *Fondo Zaccaria*, b. 19, 1v.

[56] 3 November 1764, 2r. Facchinei, *Note ed osservazioni*, p. 188.

[57] [Bolgeni], *L'accusatore convinto reo*, quoted and embellished upon quite colorfully in Ciro Caversazzi, 'Una lettera di Luigi Piccioni in difesa di un frate antibarettiano', *Bergomum*, vol. XIV, no. 1, 1940, 23–26, p. 26.

[58] Venturi, 'Contributi ad un diszionario storico', p. 132.

[59] Facchinei, *Note ed osservazioni*, 74.   [60] Facchinei, *Note ed osservazioni*, pp. 4, 37, 41.

also had formed some Laws, and elected various persons (doubtlessly from their own ranks) to be depositaries, and executors of said Laws', a theory that was 'contrary to religion, contrary to the Right of Sovereignty of all the states of our World, and contrary to true religion'. This, in short, was what the *'socialists'* argued, seemingly calling for worldwide revolution, but such imaginary societies had 'never existed'.[61] Studying the history of the

origins of Republics, and of Empires, and regarding their enlargement, as well as their revolutions, and their decline, the Law of the strongest has always prevailed, but because of such circumstances, and such combinations, that one sees (judging correctly) the work, and the contribution of an invisible hand, yes, but a very powerful one.[62]

The Thrasymachian definition of justice as 'what is good for the stronger' here received divine approbation, suggesting Facchinei's reaction to the *Fisticuffs* was fuelled by something far more specific than mere conservatism.[63] Faith in the providential order of the universe raged underneath the surface of his arguments like a subterranean current, only occasionally breaking the surface in an explicit reference to 'the economic hand of God' or a 'very powerful' if 'invisible hand' guiding human affairs.[64] Encouraging agricultural productivity was one thing; challenging the very structures of worldly authority was something entirely different.

Though scholars have recently downplayed the historical relevance of Adam Smith's metaphor of the 'invisible hand', Facchinei's use of the idiom was closer to the mythical one of economics and serves to remind us that what is at stake in current debates over spontaneous order also loomed large in the eighteenth century.[65] God's hand – sometimes invisible, sometimes not – was literally involved in the management of the household of creation, and challenging the Providential order – challenging, in short, the social and institutional *status quo* – was tantamount to sacrilege. Existing systems of sovereignty ultimately derived from 'the

---

[61] Facchinei, *Note ed osservazioni*, pp. 7–9.   [62] Facchinei, *Note ed osservazioni*, p. 9.
[63] Plato, *The Republic*, 338c, ed. G.R.F. Ferrari, translated by Tom Griffith, Cambridge University Press, 2000, p. 15.
[64] Facchinei to Zaccaria, addendum to letter of 17 April 1763, AHCL, *Fondo Zaccaria*, b. 19, 1v; Facchinei, *Note ed osservazioni*, p. 9.
[65] See, emphasizing the metaphor's joking, sarcastic, or even wrongheaded nature, among others Hont, *Jealousy of Trade*, pp. 39, 91, 113; Emma Rothschild, *Adam Smith, Condorcet, and the Enlightenment*, Cambridge, MA: Harvard University Press, 2001, pp. 116–56; Alessandro Roncaglia, *Il mito della mano invisibile*, Bari-Rome: Laterza, 2005, p. 19; Warren Samuels with Marianne F. Johnson and William H. Perry, *Erasing the Invisible Hand: Essays on an Elusive and Misused Concept in Economics*, Cambridge University Press, 2011, pp. 290–91.

true system of the creation of man'.[66] And God had not intended power to be equally distributed; nobles, clergy, kings and parents ruled for a reason, and the less people knew of the basis of law and order the better. An enlightenment program of public education regarding the laws, like that argued for by Beccaria, would ultimately 'multiply crimes'.[67] Similar attempts at equalizing fortunes had historically failed, at times with unintended negative consequences. For had not 'slaves' been treated far better than ostensibly free 'domestic servants'?[68] There was simply no doubt in Facchinei's mind that 'society has the right to free itself of a villain in any way it deems most expedient'.[69] He disagreed with practically all of Beccaria's assumptions regarding capital punishment, for killing was so evidently part of God's plan.[70]

I ask the most prejudiced Socialists: if a man, finding himself in his primitive natural state of liberty before having entered any Society, I ask does a free man have the right to kill another man who wishes in any way to take his life? I am certain that all Socialists this time will respond yes.[71]

If people had a right to kill, which Facchinei argued even a 'socialist' would agree they had under certain conditions, obviously capital punishment was based on, and justified by, natural law, not to mention divine will. The charge was, however, curious, in that it extended well beyond the critique of a 'socialist' as being an adherent of the theory of social contracts. Indeed, Facchinei employed the term to shed light on Beccaria's conjectural history of the state of nature, seemingly by default outside of the purview of eighteenth-century socialism. And it suggests that a 'socialist' for Facchinei also was someone who cared, however vaguely, about social relations in general, and about what sorts of natural laws bound men even before the advent of the social contract and society as such.

Curiously, a 'socialist' for Facchinei was not someone who believed in the inherent, innate sociability of man but the very opposite. A socialist was someone who believed in secular socialization through a social contract and subsequent legal reforms, which itself was an impossibility to him; 'because man is a social animal ... naturally so proud and so driven to liberty and independence, it is inconceivable that he would spontaneously subject himself and obey other men'.[72] Facchinei was misreading Beccaria, who repeatedly emphasized the hard-fought and far from

---

66 Facchinei, *Note ed osservazioni*, p. 14.
67 Facchinei, *Note ed osservazioni*, pp. 14, 19, 26.
68 Facchinei, *Note ed osservazioni*, p. 29.
69 Facchinei, *Note ed osservazioni*, p. 61. 70 Facchinei, *Note ed osservazioni*, pp. 87, 99.
71 Facchinei, *Note ed osservazioni*, p. 100. 72 Facchinei, *Note ed osservazioni*, p. 101.

spontaneous origins of society and man's harrowing 'original sociability', but the intellectual baggage he brought to the discussion and the lenses through which he contemplated the larger debate go a long way towards explaining it. As Facchinei recently had put it in private correspondence:

... I will certainly not hang around consulting Puffendorf [sic]; because I have never let my conscience depend on lawyers, nor casuists, but only on the Gospel, interpreted my way, which is that of the Pope, which to me is the most perfect plan, and system of Natural Laws.[73]

Facchinei felt socialists were so misguided because they had read the wrong books and drawn the wrong lessons from history. There was something inherently civilizing about 'the Wolf's bite', he thought, and without such harshness and cruelty men would still have 'lived in the forests, and the deserts, the way Bears and Lions live'.[74] Far from Beccaria's gradual view of how civilization and sensibilities developed, Facchinei underscored that 'fear conserves realms'.[75] Spectacles of torture and public execution were necessary to maintain a state of fear in society, but the ultimate social glue – the real issue at stake in the term socialism – was the role played by religion. Cloying jeremiads like Beccaria's didn't convince him at all, yet not for socialist reasons in the modern sense.[76] 'The Social Contract is an impossible Chimera', Facchinei declared, but this did not mean he was opposed to natural law, far from it. *His* natural law, however, which he believed to be far better equipped to defend key Old Regime institutions such as private property ('a natural right . . . to some extent as necessary as life') and the 'holy Tribunal of the Inquisition'.[77] Neither he, nor the 'socialists', then, believed in man's natural sociability, what differed was their external mechanism for socialization: providence or the gradually expanding sphere of secular law.

In the end, Facchinei argued, *On Crimes and Punishments* based itself on the fatal assumption that human society could be experienced, understood, and reformed on its own terms. 'If our Politics is not a visible part of the true Religion', he thundered, 'it will never be a good Politics, but a vague, broken Philosophy'. One could simply not consider this world in isolation from the next, a mere 'part' compared to the 'whole' of 'eternity'.[78] As such, Beccaria's pamphlet was nothing less than 'the greatest and most blasphemous sedition ever encountered against the

[73] Facchinei to Zaccaria, 25 August 1763, AHCL, *Fondo Zaccaria*, b. 19, 1r.
[74] Facchinei, *Note ed osservazioni*, p. 106.   [75] Facchinei, *Note ed osservazioni*, p. 164.
[76] Facchinei, *Note ed osservazioni*, pp. 111–12.
[77] Facchinei, *Note ed osservazioni*, pp. 122–23, 148.
[78] Facchinei, *Note ed osservazioni*, pp. 159–63.

sovereign rulers and against the Christian religion from the most impious heretics and from all the irreligious, ancient and modern alike'.[79] It amounted to the vain ramblings of someone who deeply wished to be 'thought the *Rousseau* of the Italians'.[80]

However ludicrous later historians have found Facchinei's arguments, Verri and Beccaria took them most seriously. Indeed, his attacks seemed all the more worrisome because of their place of publication, the most Serene Republic of Venice. Suspecting the anonymous author of *On Crimes and Punishments* to be Venetian, local authorities there had banned the book on the grounds that Beccaria had offered a veiled critique of one of the republic's most iconic institutions, the use of 'secret accusations'.[81] Initially belligerent, co-authoring an anonymous *Reply* to Facchinei with his brother Alessandro in a mere week, Pietro Verri soon wrote cautious letters to his then friend Gianrinaldo Carli, noting that 'the law of St. Mark must be respected everywhere you can find arsenic or an assassin'. And he had good reason to fear the wrath of Venice; at the time, *La Serenissima* frequently deployed extra-territorial assassins to dispatch its real and imagined enemies in the early modern equivalent of drone attacks.[82]

Facchinei was relentless, however, and soon published a critique also of Pietro Verri's anonymous *Meditazioni sulla felicita*, or *Meditations on Happiness*, believing the book to be by the same pen, two 'monstrous twins' by an author he now considered 'truly the Rousseau of Italy'.[83]

---

[79] Facchinei, *Note ed osservazioni*, p. 187.   [80] Facchinei, *Note ed osservazioni*, p. 188.

[81] Facchinei in effect reacted at length to Beccaria's writings regarding secret accusations, and about Venice, see his *Note ed osservazioni*, pp. 51–58, 188. See on this affair Gianfranco Torcellan, 'Cesare Beccaria a Venezia', *Rivista storica italiana*, vol. 76, no. 3–4, 1964, pp. 720–48.

[82] [Pietro and Alessandro Verri], *Risposta ad uno scritto che s'intitola Note ed osservazioni sul libro Dei delitti e delle pene*, Lugano: Agnelli, 1785, on which see Gian Paolo Massetto, 'Pietro e Alessandro Verri in aiuto di Cesare Beccaria', in Carlo Capra (ed.), *Pietro Verri e il suo tempo*, Bologna: Cisalpino, 1999, pp. 289–351; Pietro Verri to Gian Rinaldo Carli, 8 February 1765, in Francesco De Stefano, 'Cinque anni di sodalizio tra Pietro Verri e Gian Rinaldo Carli (1760–1765) con XXIV lettere inedite di Pietro Verri', *Atti e memorie della Società istriana di archeologia e storia patria*, vol. 45, 1933, 43–103, p. 78. On Venice's bloodcurling secret services, see Gaetano Cozzi, 'Authority and the Law in Renaissance Venice', in John Rigby Hale, *Renaissance Venice*, London: Rowman & Littlefield, 1973, pp. 293–334 and generally Paolo Preto, *I servizi segreti di Venezia: Spionaggio e controspionaggio ai tempi della Serenissima*, Milan: Il Saggiatore, 1994.

[83] Ferdinando Facchinei in Pietro Verri, *Meditazioni sulla felicità con note critiche [Ferdinando Facchinei] e risposta alle medesime d'un amico piemontese [Francesco Dalmazzo Vasco]*, Milan: Galeazzi, 1766, pp. 2–4. That said, even the Livornese publisher marketed the two volumes as having been written by the same anonymous author, see Cesare Beccaria to Giuseppe Aubert, 8–9 December 1764, in *ENOCB, vol. IV: Carteggio (parte I: 1758–1768)*, eds. Carlo Capra, Renato Pasta, and Francesca Pino Pongolini, Milan: Mediobanca, 1994, pp. 83–86, see particularly p. 84n2 for a discussion of the misunderstanding.

This sparring between Facchinei and his anonymous, hydra-like opponent produced less analysis than it did bile, on both sides of the equation, and the word 'socialism' did not appear again in their exchanges. Yet the term – and what it had begun to signify to contemporaries – lay at the very core of their polemic. Pietro Verri had arrived even at straightforwardly conflating 'virtue' with 'utility', stating that the 'end of the social contract is the welfare of every individual who concurs to form society, which resolves in public happiness, that is the greatest happiness possible shared with the greatest equality possible'.[84] To Facchinei's sensibilities, there was something unnervingly boundless about the *Fisticuffs'* vision for reform and the possibilities of worldly melioration. Verri had written of how technological progress made contemporaries 'more Enlightened' than their forerunners. 'It seems', Facchinei ridiculed his opponent, that 'he wished to write, that perhaps someday man will even arrive at flying', to which the *Fisticuffs's* Piedmontese ally Dalmazzo Francesco Vasco replied that, well, yes, why not?[85]

Having been picked up on by neither Beccaria nor the Verri brothers in their direct reply to Facchinei, however, the term 'socialism' would not play a major part in the vast literature to emerge out of *On Crimes and Punishments* until the nineteenth century, by which time the word had acquired its modern meaning and inspired reactions to different (yet related) aspects of the text. Particularly, 'socialist' readings would highlight passages questioning the extent to which economic disparities could be tolerated given the fundamental equation of justice and sociability, in other words the degree of inequality societies actually could absorb. Before then, however, the Desingian signification of 'socialistae' galvanized by Beccaria would, continue to make sporadic appearances in eighteenth-century Italy, and again in ways that can shed light on the crucial contemporary debate over human sociability, peace, and the necessity – and possibility – of regulation in worldly affairs.[86]

Beccaria never responded to the criticisms directly, but, even in the absence of assassins, Facchinei nonetheless did his damage. Pietro Verri had hoped Beccaria could launch the Milanese Enlightenment – and

---

[84] Verri, *Meditazioni*, pp. 79, 83–84.

[85] Verri, *Meditazioni*, pp. 54, 105, and Facchinei's note 17. For the reply see Dalmazzo Francesco Vasco, 'Meditazioni sulla felicità di Pietro Verri con note critiche di Ferdinando Facchinei e risposta alle medesime d'un amico piemontese (Dalmazzo Francesco Vasco) (1766)', in id., *Opere*, ed. Silvia Rota Ghibaudi, Turin: Fondazione Luigi Einaudi, 1966, 51–105, pp. 77–78n17.

[86] See for example Appiano Buonafede, *Della restaurazione di ogni filosofia ne' secoli XVI, XVII, e XVIII*, 3 vols., Venice: Graziosi, 1785–1789, vol. III, pp. 52–57. For his praise of Desing see pp. 150–51, 242.

himself – to international fame, and when that project failed to materialize he actively began undermining his former protégée. The thick web of rumours surrounding these events is hard to penetrate, but many factors contributed to making what Alessandro Verri could soon call '*il tristissimo affare Beccaria*'.[87] Rumour began spreading that Beccaria might have taken credit for the Verri brothers' *Reply* to Facchinei while on a visit to Paris, and soon Alessandro Verri sought to convince the *philosophes* in Paris that Beccaria had merely supplied 'the style and organization' to their own 'material' in his *On Crimes and Punishments*.[88]

Though the Verri brothers avoided making their polemic too public, mostly because they were too worried of making 'another scene, like that between Hume and Rousseau', a reference to the perhaps strangest and certainly most famous public quarrel between intellectuals in eighteenth-century Europe, they did what they could to harm Beccaria's standing in the Italian republic of letters.[89] Principally, this involved undermining Beccaria's authorship of *On Crimes and Punishments*, summarized in the caustic statement by the jurist and political economist Giovan Battista Freganeschi that 'what is good in it is not his' and 'what is his is not good'.[90] Extraordinarily, however, the Verri brothers themselves went to some length looking for the textual sources of *On Crimes and Punishments*, in everything from Seneca to Pufendorf and Rousseau, suggesting they privately knew that though they might have provided an impetus, Beccaria himself had done more research than they might have liked

---

[87] Alessandro Verri to Pietro Verri, 13 March 1767, in *CV*, vol. I.1, 297–307, p. 299; Alessandro Verri to Pietro Verri, 29 December 1766, quoted and discussed in Vianello, *La giovinezza*, p. 182. See also Gianni Francioni, 'A Parigi! A Parigi! Gli illuministi milanesi e la Francia', in Maria Bettetini and Stefano Poggi (eds.), *I viaggi dei filosofi*, Milan: Raffaello Cortina, 2010, pp. 113–33.

[88] Pietro Verri to Paolo Frisi, 21 January 1767, in *Viaggio a Parigi e Londra*, pp. 467–69; Pietro Verri to Alessandro Verri, 30 March 1767, in *CV*, vol. I.1, 313–17, p. 314; Pietro Verri, 'Memorie sincere', p. 147. On this see also Vianello, *La giovinezza*, p. 182.

[89] For an obvious example of Pietro Verri undermining Beccaria's authority, see his letter to Paolo Frisi, 21 January 1767, in *Viaggio a Parigi e Londra*, pp. 467–69. On Rousseau and Hume see Alessandro Verri to Pietro Verri, 4 March 1767, in *CV*, vol. I.1, 290–93, p. 291. This is merely one of several letters regarding the affair in their correspondence. Interestingly, they tended to think the criticism of Rousseau exaggerated, see for example Alessandro Verri to Pietro Verri, 19 October 1766, in *CV*, vol. I.1, 19–27, p. 26 and Pietro Verri to Alessandro Verri, 24 January 1767, in *CV*, vol. I.1, 171–74, pp. 172–73. The infamous quarrel between Hume and Rousseau has recently seen a resurgence of interest, see among others Robert Zaretsky and John T. Scott, *The Philosophers' Quarrel: Rousseau, Hume, and the Limits of Human Understanding*, New Haven: Yale University Press, 2010. For an insightful contemporary take on the problem, see Adam Smith to David Hume, 6 July 1766, in Ernest Campbell Mossner and Ian Simpson Ross (eds.), *The Correspondence of Adam Smith*, Indianapolis: Liberty Fund, 1987, pp. 112–14.

[90] This was how the myth was channeled by Verri's close friend Giovan Battista Freganeschi's letter to Isidoro Bianchi, 18 January 1783, quoted and discussed in Vianello, *La giovinezza*, p. 181.

to admit.[91] As the Verri brothers put it, Beccaria would have to write a 'second, equal book' to truly prove his merit.[92] Beccaria knew this well, and indeed planned, between 1764 and 1770, a major work tentatively entitled the *Refinement of Nations*, a sustained study of the history of human progress that he eventually abandoned – leaving only sundry manuscripts – in favor of his university lectures on political economy and policy work.[93] Between Beccaria's lectures and his fragmentary writings, however, one can adumbrate his unfulfilled vision of the history of human sociability and the means – however hard fought – of expanding it ever further, of socializing not merely the relations between people but between *peoples*; the way, that is, of making international trade a peaceful force in the world.

In one of the few surviving fragments of the *Refinement of Nations*, entitled *Thoughts on the Barbarism and Culture of Nations and the Savage State of Man*, Beccaria had suggested a conceptual matrix for analyzing nations at all stages of their historical development. On one axis he proposed a spectrum stretching from barbarism to culture, a measure of a nation's 'ignorance of things that are useful to it' and the best 'means' of achieving 'individual happiness'. The other axis stretched from savagery to sociability, gauging the degree of a nation's distance 'from the greatest union that can exist between men, and from the greatest absolute happiness possible divided among the greatest possible number'. A nation, Beccaria concluded, 'can be savage and barbarian, it can be savage and non-barbarian, it can be very barbarian and very sociable at the same time'.[94] Like Rousseau, he identified the engine of social development in individual needs, but he rejected the notion that social developments could be somehow 'unnatural', not to mention that they were by necessity infelicitous.[95] 'All man's sentiments, in any state he finds himself, are always natural', Beccaria underscored, doubtlessly drawing on the mechanistic physiology and moral philosophy of the *Fisticuffs* and, as needs and sociability developed hand in hand, man's wants increased alongside

---

[91] Pietro Verri to Alessandro Verri, 20 September 1780, in *CV*, vol. X, pp. 147–54.

[92] Alessandro Verri to Pietro Verri, 21 January 1769, in *Carteggio di Pietro e Alessandro Verri*, eds. Greppi et al., 12 vols., Milan: L. F. Cogliati; Milesi & figli; Giuffrè, 1910–1942, vol. II, p. 135.

[93] Francioni, 'Il fantasma del "Ripulimento delle nazioni."'

[94] Cesare Beccaria, 'Pensieri sopra la barbarie e coltura delle nazioni e su lo stato selvaggio dell'uomo', in *ENOCB, vol. II: Scritti filosofici e letterari*, eds. Luigi Firpo, Gianni Francioni, and Giammarco Gaspari, Milan: Mediobanca, 1984, 284–92, p. 284.

[95] The locus classicus in Beccaria's oeuvre on the historical role of needs is in his 'Inaugural Lecture' in political economy, p. 133, but see also id., *Elementi di economia pubblica*, first published in 1804 as vols. XI and XII in *Scrittori classici italiani di economia politica*, ed. Pietro Custodi, 50 vols., Milan: Destefanis, 1803–1816, vol. XI, p. 26, with rather Malthusian musings around, p. 60.

his capacity to satisfy them. Socialized men changed over time, leading in turn to a 'change' in the 'nature of sociability itself' and its causes as societies had expanded from the earliest villages to the states-system of early modern Europe. An important corollary of this dynamism affected the character of legislation and political economy alike, which, far from being written in stone (literally, for some), had to be endlessly dynamic and adaptive to changing circumstances.[96]

The moral philosopher sees the present advantages, the progress of the science of living happily, and finds them [to be the] effects of ancient disorders, and dares to predict that today's evils are necessary movements and agitations, after which the peoples [of the world] will move back to a final, very remote state of equality and happiness.[97]

Again, juxtaposition with Rousseau can shed light on Beccaria's larger project. Rousseau had argued in *The Social Contract* that a hypothetical coastal country of 'nothing but nearly inaccessible rocks' should 'remain barbarous and fisheaters', and that by so doing its people would 'live the more tranquil for it, perhaps the better, and certainly the happier'.[98] And even if one accepted the theorem that man was 'naturally wicked', which, for the record, he did not, the polemical Genevan admitted that 'some good might happen to come of the sciences at their hands; but it is perfectly certain that they will lead to far more harm: Madmen should not be given weapons'.[99] Beccaria thought the greatest happiness was yet to come, and that it was only through the arming of humanity – however madcap – with the arts and sciences that it could be achieved. Where Rousseau's political project came to revolve around damage-control in wake of civilization and the end of the halcyon state of nature, Beccaria's unwritten *Refinement of Nations* would have carried a very different practical payload; it would have suggested political economy, and what his critics called 'socialism', as a means of explaining and continuing the history of man's socialization, from people to peoples, to reclaim lasting 'equality and happiness' in a civilized, technological world.

---

[96] Beccaria, 'Pensieri sopra la barbarie', pp. 286–87. He was, needless to say, here merely formalizing a very widely held belief in early modern political economy, expounded even in 'Observations by Jean-Jacques Rousseau of Geneva on an Answer made to his Discourse', in id., *The Discourses and Other Early Political Writings*, 32–51, p. 51. See on this tradition more widely, Reinert, 'Rivalry', pp. 357–58.

[97] Beccaria, 'Pensieri sopra la barbarie', pp. 286–87.

[98] Rousseau, 'The Social Contract', p. 79.

[99] Rousseau, 'Last Reply', in id., *The Discourses and Other Early Political Writings*, 63–85, p. 69.

Many of the preoccupations that had animated Beccaria's earliest writings would continue to inspire his more mature work, including the dangers of economic inequality in a polity, but he would never spell out the full spectrum of his ideas, nor the complex role he saw for private property in the history of human progress. But as fate would have it, and much to the satisfaction of the Verri brothers, Beccaria's project for the *Refinement of Nations* never materialized. Overcome by practical duties, plausibly also a convenient excuse, Beccaria would instead channel his reformist impulse into his university lectures and practical work for the Habsburg administration. As Joseph A. Schumpeter would put it, 'Beccaria, almost certainly more richly endowed by nature, gave to the public service of the Milanese "state" what A[dam] Smith reserved for mankind'.[100]

Early on in his lectures on *Public Economy*, delivered for the first time in 1769, Beccaria recast his earlier praise of legislators in the more general guise of 'supreme directors', who with 'arms and laws steer the internal operations of society, defend it against external assaults, and excite movement and activity in the quotidian indolence of men'. The 'multitude' therefore had to 'furnish' these 'directors' with the 'means' of so doing in the form of '*tributes*'. Much as men in the state of nature gave up a part of their liberty to empower sovereignty with the capacity to safeguard them, in other words, so they gave up a part of their material resources to similarly empower 'directors' to structure, defend, and invigorate commercial societies. Human welfare in its entirety depended on successful 'policing', a noble endeavor ever at odds with 'the limits of human capacity and the inexorable law of pain'.[101]

Yet their role was simply to direct and channel the work of the polity's citizens, for 'the wealth of nations doesn't really emerge from anything but by the labor of individuals'.[102] Not all labor was the same, however, in that some activities were more conducive to economic development than others, and the role of 'directors' was therefore cardinal in perfecting development.[103] In an ideal world, Beccaria was clear, 'absolute liberty' should be the aim of political economy, or rather what he referred to as the 'non system' peddled by many economic theorists, but in real life

---

[100] Joseph A. Schumpeter, *History of Economic Analysis*, Oxford: Oxford University Press, 1954, p. 180. On Smith and Beccaria see furthermore Peter Groenewegen, 'Turgot, Beccaria and Smith', in id., *Eighteenth-Century Economics: Turgot, Beccaria and Smith and their Contemporaries*, London: Routledge, 2002, pp. 3–47.

[101] Beccaria, *Elementi di economia pubblica*, vol. XI, pp. 21–23, 31–32, 36; Beccaria, *On Crimes and Punishments*, p. 10.

[102] Beccaria, *Elementi di economia pubblica*, vol. XII, p. 114.

[103] Beccaria here drew on a venerable Italian economic historiography dating back to the Middle Ages, on which see Reinert, 'Greatness'.

there were endless complications geographical, political, and economic to consider, not to mention human nature itself. 'Partisans of liberty' challenged the 'difficulty of fixing limits of annual consumption', preferring dogmatic absolutes to the dangers of purposeful action in the economy, but Beccaria embraced the challenge of vigilantly and relentlessly tailoring economic policies to endlessly changing conditions.[104] Legislators *could* style the economic architectures of their polities, and some industries – particularly high-value-added manufactures – deserved the 'attention of political economists', who ideally should 'encourage' certain trades on the one hand and 'slow down ruinous commerce' on the other.[105] The real difficulty lay not in successfully pursuing economic policies, but rather in aligning domestic economic needs with the ideals of international sociability, the final part of the 'socialist' project attacked by his critics.

The language Beccaria adopted to describe the anarchic world of international trade was far from peaceful. A wide variety of economic activities, he argued, were a useful defense against the 'reciprocal obstacles that nations impose on each other in the always spirited war of industry and of profit'.[106] Legislation was clearly about encouraging what he called 'the entire chain of affairs and of economic actions of the state'.[107] But these great chains of national affairs and activities were in turn intertwined through the inexorable incongruence between states and markets characterizing the early modern world. '*The political boundaries of a state are almost never the same as its economic boundaries*', Beccaria observed, and countries, '*however divided by sovereignty and reciprocally independent with respect to their political laws*' were thus '*really a single nation tightly united by physical laws and dependent one on the other through their economic relations*'.[108] As such, 'the division of nations' was 'a matter of fact, not something established by the nature of things'.[109] There was nothing permanent or Providential about the commercial competition of the Westphalian states-system, and much of Beccaria's work indeed aimed at its gradual overcoming, at the slow socialization of the international sphere through purposeful political economy.

But the chains of interconnectivity could all too easily become shackles of dependence for Beccaria, and a cardinal task of legislation lay in

---

[104] Beccaria, *Elementi di economia pubblica*, vol. XI, pp. 161, 173, 184, 196–97, 256, 289, 307; vol. XII, p. 90.
[105] Beccaria, *Elementi di economia pubblica*, vol. XI,
[106] Beccaria, *Elementi di economia pubblica*, vol. XI, p. 277; vol. XII, p. 96.
[107] Beccaria, *Elementi di economia pubblica*, vol. XI, p. 323.
[108] Among other places Beccaria, *Elementi di economia pubblica*, vol. XI, pp. 34–35.
[109] Beccaria, *Elementi di economia pubblica*, vol. XI, p. 44.

negotiating that 'spirited war of industry and profit' to avoid becoming
'dependent' on other nations.[110] Trade was war by other means, and
though he in no way envisioned international trade as necessarily peaceable or even mutually beneficial, he saw it as uniquely offering a means
of neutering the most violent forms of competition. Commerce was not
a failsafe means of achieving peace, but it *could* be conducive to it. And,
in line with his historicist approach to political economy, the past – and
particularly the tempestuous one of the Italian city-states – served as
Beccaria's roadmap in realizing this ideal. After abandoning conquest
with the ruins of Rome, for example, they had 'turned its disquiet activity towards the peaceful but no less domineering [*signoreggianti*] arts,
and if not with such quick success and with such despotic influence, at
least with greater and more placid and less dangerous security'.[111] Trade
risked, for Beccaria and for many of his contemporaries, being an alternative form of imperialism. He was namely quite adamant that *someone*
always gained in any exchange. In domestic trade, this meant the balance of gains and losses remained in equilibrium, but once one considered international interactions, differential gains could quickly achieve
systemic importance. The 'profits of external commerce' could be 'to
the advantage of the citizenry at the expense of the non-citizenry, so that
the sum of value increases for the members of the state, without the loss
of any members of said state'.[112] So how could trade contribute to peace
and the expansion of human sociability?

Though it was evident that 'up to a certain point a nation can prosper at the expense of another', Beccaria suggested that 'beyond a certain
point our true prosperity produces the prosperity of others, given man
was not given an exclusive happiness or misery'. This was 'a clear indication', he thought, that there existed 'a secret communion of things' and
that 'nature wished' for a 'brotherhood of the human species'.[113] This
was as close as he got to Facchinei's 'economic hand of God', to the
idea, in short, that the process of sociability was driven by some expansive telos. Yet, given his failure to produce a more coherent account of
this momentum in the *Refinement of Nations*, it remained an elusive ideal

---

[110] Beccaria, *Elementi di economia pubblica*, vol. XI, p. 229. Yet Beccaria never flirted with radical alternatives to a social order based, on some level, on an interdependent division of labor the way Rousseau did on multiple occasions, among others in his 'Preface to *Narcissus*' and 'Second Discourse', in id., *The Discourses and Other Early Political Writings*, 92–106, pp. 100 and 111–222, p. 159, respectively.
[111] Beccaria, *Elementi di economia pubblica*, vol. XI, p. 236.
[112] Beccaria, *Elementi di economia pubblica*, vol. XII, pp. 83–84.
[113] Beccaria, *Elementi di economia pubblica*, vol. XI, p. 172. This might well be a veiled reference to David Hume's essay 'Of the Jealousy of Trade', in id. *Political Essays*, ed. Knud Haakonssen, Cambridge University Press, 1994, pp. 150–53.

in his lectures. Adopting the venerable vocabulary of active and passive commerce, and of the balance of trade, Beccaria embraced the possibility that a fair international exchange of manufactures might pave the way to a pacification of the world system.[114] Not all countries could harbor all manufactures, and the 'introduction' of certain goods could be 'opportune to open an exit for our things, and a communication with other nations', thus gradually, incrementally, socializing relations.[115] He adumbrated, in short, the possibility of a world order based on commercial rather than military competition, but one that ironically required the constant commitment of legislators to furthering their own nation's causes in international trade.

The crux of his retort to the 'non-system' of invisible hands lay in man's capacity to legislate his own and others' actions. To achieve, in short, intended consequences. This was greatly facilitated by his understanding of human beings in rigorously materialist terms of biological machines involved in a perennial calculus of pleasures and pains, thus making them to a certain extent programmable actors in an environment woven into existence by laws.[116] Regulation, as such, was not merely economic but existential in nature. But it depended, entirely, on the knowledge and expertise of legislators and legislatees alike. Beccaria's call for popular enlightenment in 'this century of light and research' was grounded in very specific assumptions about human nature and the mechanisms of socialization.[117] Enlightenment, as such, was Beccaria's reply to the doctrine of the invisible hand; it epitomized his faith in humanity and its capacity to improve itself in *this world*; it was a resolutely man-made project of international economic socialization dependent on political economy rather than theology or, even, military might, remaining determinedly 'socialist' in the word's original signification.

It is curious that Beccaria's project so often has been derided with the moniker 'utopian'. The venerable ideals of 'the good life' as related to 'the common good', of individual flourishing in a quintessentially social world, found one of their most eloquent mouthpieces in his writings and lectures, but he had little patience for utopias. His very choice of epitaph for *On Crimes and Punishments* speaks for itself:

In all negociations of difficulty, a man may not look to sow and reap at once, but must prepare business, and so ripen it by degrees. (Francis Bacon, *Essays*, 47)[118]

[114] Beccaria, *Elementi di economia pubblica*, vol. XI, p. 340, vol. XII, pp. 88–89.
[115] Beccaria, *Elementi di economia pubblica*, vol. XI, pp. 264–65.
[116] Beccaria, 'Sulla materia', *ENOCB*, vol. II, pp. 308–09.
[117] Beccaria, *Elementi di economia pubblica*, vol. XI, pp. 108, 152.
[118] Beccaria, *On Crimes and Punishments*, p. 4, quoting Francis Bacon, 'Of Negotiating', in id., *The Essays*, ed. John Pitcher, London: Penguin, 1986, 103–04, p. 104.

However revolutionary Beccaria's ideals might have been, he was ever the Fabian, whether in his work on the Council of Commerce in Austrian Lombardy or in his anonymous calls for action.[119] Voltaire got him right: 'we are seeking to perfect everything in this century; so let us seek to perfect the laws on which our lives and fortunes depend'.[120] But perfection took time, and Beccaria's calls for 'Enlightenment' and gradual economic integration were as far from the trauma of revolution as could be imagined in eighteenth-century Europe.[121] It is perhaps fitting that 'socialism', invented to critique gradual secular reformism, with time would come to signify revolutionary change; while 'social science', originally a transcendental discipline of worldly regeneration, became an intellectual armory of the status quo.[122] History may be a 'tool of skeptics', as Istvan Hont once wrote, but it is also a school of irony.[123]

Beccaria's temperament was not one at ease with shock therapies, and utopia for him was less a plan to be realized than a light to lead the way. As such his project to promote human sociability and economic development fit John Rawl's definition, in his Harvard lectures, of 'political philosophy' as 'realistically utopian', as a means of '*probing the limits of practicable political possibility*'.[124] Earthly perfection might remain beyond man's grasp, but this did not exclude small steps towards it, what Immanuel Kant described as the 'infinite process of gradual

---

[119] Though at times critical of private property, Beccaria was no 'communist', if one accepts its equation with 'a desire to dig up the foundations of society and rebuild', see Robert Service, *Comrades: A History of World Communism*, Cambridge, MA: Harvard University Press, 2007, p. 13.

[120] Voltaire, 'Commentary on the Book On Crimes and Punishments', in id., *Political Writings*, ed. David Williams, 1994, 244–79, p. 279.

[121] On contemporary apprehensions regarding revolution, see among others Reinert, *Translating Empire*, p. 132 and *passim*; id., 'Lessons on the Rise and Fall of Great Nations'; Sonenscher, *Before the Deluge*. For other examples from Beccaria's circle, see Gianrinaldo Carli to Giuseppe Gravisi, 15 August 1765, in *Trecentosessantasei lettere*, pp. 123–24 and Giovan Stefano Conti to Ruđer Josip Bošković, 13 September 1769, in *Giovan Stefano Conti: Lettere a Ruggiero Giuseppe Boscovich*, ed. Edoardo Proverbio, 2 vols., Rome: Accademia nazionale delle scienze, 1996–1998, vol. I, 231–33, p. 232. On Conti see Tommaso Trenta, 'Origini, Progressi, e vicende dell'Accademia degli Oscuri', Biblioteca Governativa di Lucca, Lucca, Italy, *MS 557*, 381–405.

[122] On the case of social science, see Wokler, 'Ideology and the Origins of Social Science', pp. 707–09. For earlier statements of unease with this transition of social science, see Giuseppe Romanazzi, *Note e considerazioni sull'affrancazione de' canoni e sul libero coltivamento del tavoliere di Puglia*, Naples: Tramater, 1834, p. 104; John Hobson, quoted and discussed in Gregory Claeys, *Imperial Sceptics: British Critics of Empire, 1850–1920*, Cambridge University Press, 2010, p. 272; Mark Mazower, *Governing the World: The History of an Idea*, London: Penguin, 2012, pp. 95–100, 292.

[123] Hont, *Jealousy of Trade*, p. 156.

[124] John Rawls, *Lectures on the History of Political Philosophy*, ed. Samuel Freeman, Cambridge, MA: Harvard University Press, 2007, pp 10–11. Emphasis in the original.

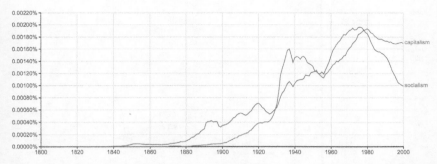

Figure 5.2 Google Ngram of the words 'Capitalism' and 'Socialism' in English Publications, 1800–2000

approximation' in his *Perpetual Peace*.[125] As it were, Beccaria never proposed a plan for 'perpetual peace' as such, though his lectures, publications, and manuscript fragments point the way to an ideal of ever-expanding human sociability based on carefully calibrated laws and economic policies aimed at neutralizing man's urge to dominate others, within polities and between them, by conquest as well as by commerce.[126] Between people the pivot was penal reform; between peoples it was regulating international trade. From this perspective, *On Crimes and Punishments* and his abandoned *Refinement of Nations* engaged with different aspects of the same basic problem of human sociability in the world, something hinted at by the great Risorgimento-era historian Cesare Cantù when, in his magisterial study of Beccaria, he bewailed those 'austere spirits' who 'smile as mirthlessly at the abolition of the death penalty as they do at projects for perpetual peace'.[127] It was a remarkably astute observation; one that cut to the very core of Beccaria's project and the nature of Enlightenment 'socialism' alike.

Though 'socialism' eventually gained a new meaning in the early nineteenth century, doubling down on certain aspects of its original signification, the word remained deeply indebted to eighteenth-century concerns with the role of international political economy, with inequality, with private property, and with man's ability to purposefully improve life in this

---

[125] Kant, 'Perpetual Peace', p. 130.
[126] For a similar later project, see Thomas Hopkins, 'The Limits of "Cosmopolitical Economy": Smith, List, and the Paradox of Peace through Trade', in Thomas Hippler and Miloš Vec (eds.), *Paradoxes of Peace in Nineteenth Century Europe*, Oxford University Press, 2015, 77–91, p. 91.
[127] Cesare Cantù, *Beccaria e il diritto penale*, Florence: Barbèra, 1862, p. 311. On this work, see among others Cesare Mozzarelli, 'Riforme istituzionali e mutamenti sociali nella Lombardia dell'ultimo Settecento', in Romagnoli and Pisapia (eds.), *Cesare Beccaria tra Milano e l'Europa*, 479–94, pp. 481–82.

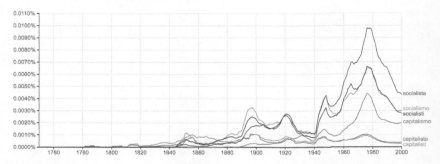

Figure 5.3 Google Ngram of Variations of 'Capitalism' and 'Socialism' in Italian Publications, 1750–2000

world. The story of how 'socialism' as the science of 'commercial society' became something close to its own antonym as the bogeyman of 'capitalism' remains to be told. Judging from the changing fortunes of both 'socialism' and 'capitalism' in recent decades [Figures 5.2 and 5.3], the time may now be right to do so. Perhaps Minerva's owl has already taken flight.

6 State-machines, commerce and the progress of *Humanität* in Europe

Herder's response to Kant in *Ideas for the Philosophy of History of Mankind*

Eva Piirimäe[1]

In the second half of the 1780s, Johann Gottfried Herder became involved in a protracted philosophical controversy with Immanuel Kant concerning universal history. Herder's *Ideas for the Philosophy of History of Mankind* were published in four instalments (1784, 1785, 1787, 1791). Kant's *Idea for a Universal History with a Cosmopolitan Purpose* appeared in November 1784, and his reviews of the first and second instalment of Herder's *Ideas* were published in January and November 1785 respectively.[2] From the second instalment, Herder answered Kant's challenges, mostly implicitly, while Kant continued to respond to Herder in a series of writings.[3] Although there were a number of common elements in their philosophies, the former academic teacher and his student vehemently disagreed about the methodology of philosophy of history, and held contrasting views about the relationship between

[1] The research for this chapter has been funded by the Estonian Science Foundation Grant No. 8887 and institutional research funding IUT20–39 of the Estonian Ministry of Education and Research. I am grateful to Wolfgang Proß for his very helpful comments on an earlier version of this chapter.

[2] Immanuel Kant, 'Reviews of Herder's *Ideas on the Philosophy of Mankind*', in idem, *Political Writings*, edited by Hans S. Reiss and trans. by H.B. Nisbet, 2nd, enlarged edition (Cambridge, 2000), 201–220. On these reviews, see Rudolf Haym, *Herder nach seinem Leben und seinen Werken* (Berlin, 1958 (reprint of 1885)), 275, 279; Hans S. Reiss, 'Introduction to Reviews of Herder's *Ideas on the philosophy of mankind* and *Conjectures on the beginning of human history*', in Kant, *Political Writings*, 250–272 (195).

[3] See Immanuel Kant, 'Conjectures on the Beginning of Human History', in idem, *Political Writings*, 221–234 and idem, *Critique of Judgement*, trans. James Creed Meredith (Oxford, 1992), 92–100. On the importance of Herder's work for Kant's concerns with history, see John H. Zammito, *The Genesis of Kant's Critique of Judgement* (Chicago, 1992) and Karl Ameriks, 'The Purposive Development of Human Capacities', in *Kant's Idea of a Universal History with a Cosmopolitan Aim. A Critical Guide*, edited by Amélie Oksenberg Rorty and James Schmidt (Cambridge, 2009), 46–67.

nature and culture, about the course and possible goal of human history, and about the role of the modern state.[4]

This chapter revisits the Kant-Herder debate by focusing on Herder's response to one of the central themes of Kant's *Idea*, the philosophical history of human culture and political government and his corresponding assessment of the prospects for achieving international peace. I argue that Herder not only rejected Kant's ideas about sociability, morality and the modern state, but offered a penetrating critique of Kant's proposed solution to the problem of war in universal history, a strong federation of states with coercive powers. This critique – including Herder's famous remark on the 'most natural state' being 'One nation' [Ein [sic!] Volk] – in turn must be understood against the background of his alternative vision of universal and European history. Herder passionately disagreed with Kant's view of modern territorial states as the best environment for achieving freedom, morality and happiness; Herder contrasted modern states with ancient polities in which political government rested on, and supported, the morals [*Sitten*] and national character of the people. Nevertheless, Herder, too, detected processes in European history that pointed to some positive prospects for greater peace in Europe and in the world. Although he rejected Kant's argument that the realisation of international peace was necessary for the development of human freedom, morality and the highest kind of happiness, he regarded peace as an inherently valuable ideal. He also sought to offer his own account of the possible trajectory of Europe's pacification and explored the ways in which the philosophy of history could contribute towards this goal.

While earlier studies have focused on Kant's critique of Herder's method and dissected their diverging understandings of humanity, human nature, cultural agency, morality, happiness and historical progress,[5] no previous interpretation has reconstructed Herder's

---

[4] The classic study of the controversy is Hans Dietrich Irmscher, 'Die geschichts-philosophische Kontroverse zwischen Kant und Herder,' in *Hamann, Kant, Herder. Acta des vierten Internationalen Hamann-Kolloquiums im Herder-Institut zu Marburg 1985*, edited by Bernhard Gajek (Frankfurt/Main, 1987), 111–192 (reprinted as 'Die Kontroverse zwischen Kant und Herder über die Methode der Geschichtsphilosophie', in: Hans Dietrich Irmscher, *Weitstrahlsinniges Denken: Studien zu Johann Gottfried Herder*, edited by Marion Heinz and Violetta Stolz (Würzburg, 2009), 295–334); see also Sharon Anderson-Gold, 'Kant and Herder', in *A Companion to the Philosophy of History and Historiography*, edited by Aviezer Tucker (Oxford, 2008), 457–467.

[5] See Marion Heinz, 'Kulturtheorien der Aufklärung: Herder und Kant', in *Nationen und Kulturen. Zum 250. Geburtstag Johann Gottfried Herders*, edited by Regine Otto (Würzburg, 1996), 139–152; Sonia Sikka, *Herder on Humanity and Cultural Difference: Enlightened Relativism* (Cambridge, 2012), 44–84; Allen Wood, *Kant's Ethical Thought* (Cambridge, 1999), 229–249; Sankar Muthu, *Enlightenment against Empire* (Princeton, 2003), 210–258; Michael L. Frazer, *The Enlightenment of Sympathy. Justice and the Moral Sentiments in the Eighteenth Century and Today* (Oxford, 2010).

critique of Kant's hypothetical account of the trajectory of universal history in sufficient detail, or laid out Herder's own 'history of mankind' as a conscious alternative to Kant's.[6] There is an age-old debate about Herder's putative nationalism and his views on the relationship between the state and the nation,[7] but in this debate, too, little attention has been given to Herder's engagement with this question in the framework of his controversy with Kant, or indeed against the background of his philosophical history of civil society and political government.[8] One reason for this relative neglect of Herder's ideas on the history of civil society is probably Herder's own sustained emphasis on the lesser importance of political government as a factor in history, and his critical remarks on the four stages theory of civilisation embraced by various Scottish historians of civil society. Indeed, one of Herder's self-proclaimed goals was to understand and appreciate the individuality of the societies and cultures of historical peoples.[9] Yet, as recent scholarship has emphasised, this goal by no means committed him to a single methodology of 'empathetic understanding' [einfühlendes Verstehen] in all his works.[10] Particularly in the *Ideas*, Herder sought to offer genetic as well as causal explanations for the rise and history of different kinds of historical societies and

---

[6] In analysing Herder's theory as an alternative to Kant's, I do not wish to claim that Kant's was the only theory of history that Herder opposed and sought to answer in *Ideas*. For a broader typology of eighteenth-century philosophies of history including Herder's, see Wolfgang Proß, *Geschichte als Provokation zu Geschichtsphilosophie: Iselin und Herder, in Isaak Iselin und die Geschichtsphilosophie der europäischen Aufklärung* (Basel, 2011), 201–265.

[7] See e.g. Frederick M. Barnard, 'Introduction', in *J. G. Herder on Social and Political Culture*, translated, edited and introduced by F. M. Barnard (Cambridge, 1969), 7–9; 57–60; idem, *Herder on Nationality, Humanity, and History* (Montreal and Kingston, 2003), 48–49 and passim; Horst Dreitzel, 'Herders politische Konzepte', in *Johann Gottfried Herder, 1744–1803*, edited by Gerhard Sauder (Hamburg, 1987), 266–298 (295–296); Frederick C. Beiser, *Enlightenment, Revolution and Romanticism: Genesis of Modern German Political Thought* (Cambridge, MA, 1992), 211–213; Wulf Koepke, 'Der Staat – die störende und unvermeidliche Maschine', in *Nationen und kulturelle Vielfalt in Herders Geschichtsphilosophie*, edited by Regine Otto (Würzburg, 1996), 227–238; Dominic Eggel, Andre Liebich and Deborah Mancini-Griffoli, 'Was Herder a Nationalist?', *The Review of Politics*, 69 (2007), 48–78; Alan Patten, 'The Most Natural State: Herder and Nationalism', in *History of Political Thought*, XXXI (2010), 658–689.

[8] Compare, however, Istvan Hont's highly suggestive remarks on Herder in 'The Permanent Crisis of a Divided Mankind: "Nation-State" and "Nationalism" in Historical Perspective', in: idem, *Jealousy of Trade: International Competition and the Nation-State in Historical Perspective* (Cambridge, MA, 2005), 447–528 (505–507).

[9] Johann Gottfried von Herder, 'This Too a Philosophy for the Formation of Humanity: A Contribution to Many Contributions of the Century', in *Johann Gottfried von Herder: Philosophical Writings*, edited and trans. by Michael N. Forster (Cambridge, 2002), 272–358 (291–293; cf. 299).

[10] On Herder's notion of *Einfühlung*, see Hans Adler, *Die Prägnanz des Dunklen: Gnoseologie, Ästhetik, Geschichtsphilosophie bei J. G. Herder* (Hamburg, 1990), 166–172.

cultures.[11] In so doing, he drew on various Enlightenment approaches to history. As Wolfgang Proß has pointed out, Herder's philosophy of history can be seen as a 'combined elaboration [. . .] of the "three histories" of Enlightenment, that is, of natural history, the history of the human mind, and the history of society'.[12] To this list, perhaps also 'sacred history' could be added, insofar as Herder in Book Ten attempted to incorporate a distinctive philosophical interpretation of the Biblical account of Genesis into his history of mankind.[13] The main focus of this chapter is Herder's philosophical history of human culture and civil society in the *Ideas* in particular; I also briefly touch upon his interpretation of Genesis in explaining the origins of human antagonism and wars.

By exploring Herder's answer to Kant and his alternative version of the history of civil society, my intention is to dispel some of the ambiguities still surrounding his political thought. In particular, I suggest that it is crucial to appreciate the differences between Herder's views on commerce, morality and politics in his early and mature philosophy of history. Herder's distinctive history of political government and international relations in the *Ideas* was based on a considerable qualification of his own earlier critique of the 'enlightened narratives', tracing the rise of modern large commercial monarchies as preconditions for the future progress of political liberty, prosperity, morality and peace in *This Too a Philosophy of History for the Formation of Humanity* (1774). Not that Herder in the *Ideas* fully embraced a version of such a narrative; he continued criticising modern 'state-machines'. What changed, I will argue, was his view of their origins, as he now located these in the

[11] Frederick C. Beiser, *The German Historicist Tradition* (Oxford, 2011), 98–167 (135–136). On Herder's genetic method, see Hans Dietrich Irmscher, 'Aspekte der Geschichtsphilosophie Johann Gottfried Herders', in *Herder und die Philosophie des deutschen Idealismus*, edited by Marion Heinz (Amsterdam, 1997), pp. 5–47 (36–39); for the central role of naturalist anthropology and his aim to explain historical phenomena, see Wolfgang Proß, 'Die Ordnung der Zeiten und Räume. Herder zwischen Aufklärung und Historismus', in *Vernunft – Freiheit – Humanität. Über Johann Gottfried Herder und einige seiner Zeitgenossen. Festgabe für Günter Arnold zum 65. Geburtstag*, edited by Claudia Taszus (Eutin, 2008), pp. 9–73 (48–53); see also John Zammito, 'Herder and Historical Metanarrative: What's Philosophical about History?', in *A Companion to the Works of Johann Gottfried Herder*, edited by Hans Adler and Wulf Koepke (Rochester, NY, 2009), 65–91 (70–80).
[12] Wolfgang Proß, 'Naturalism, Anthropology, Culture', *The Cambridge History of Eighteenth-Century Political Thought*, edited by Mark Goldie and Robert Wokler (Cambridge, 2006), 218–247, 235.
[13] It was in answer to this book specifically that Kant wrote his *Conjectures on the Beginning of Human History* (1786), hence offering his own playful version of a sacred history, one he characterised as a 'pleasure trip' guided by reason. For the term and genre of 'sacred history', as connected to debates on sociability and history of civil society, see John Robertson, 'Sacred History and Political Thought: Neapolitan Responses to the Problem of Sociability after Hobbes', *The Historical Journal* 56:1 (2013), 1–29.

Carolingian period, as well as his understanding of the nature and utility of commerce, and its relationship to the modern state. Aware of the various abuses of modern commerce, Herder founded his hopes upon the emancipatory potential of commerce and upon the human ability to learn from past mistakes.

The chapter consists of two sections. In the first, I will contrast Herder's and Kant's philosophical histories of culture, morality and political government. I begin by laying out the basic features of Herder's naturalism and his account of the natural foundations of morality and *Humanität* in the first instalment of the *Ideas*, proceeding then to discuss Herder's critical response to Kant's 'a priori rule' of universal history as proposed in the latter's *Idea*. I will attempt to link this response to Herder's overall understanding of the development of political government and 'state-machines' in human history, as developed in the third and fourth instalment of the *Ideas*. In the second section, I turn to Herder's alternative vision of the development of culture and *Humanität* in Europe, discussing his theory of the role of commerce in European history and his vision of the possible pacification of Europe in the future. Since my main goal will be to elucidate Herder's position, I will not be defending Kant against Herder's reading of his ideas, nor will I be able to discuss Kant's responses to Herder in any detail.

I

In contrast to *This Too a Philosophy*, which emphasised the limits of the human ability to understand the aims and course of Providence in history, Herder's *Ideas* were a systematic theodicy, departing from the suppositions that 'God is in all his works', and that a proper study of the perceptible phenomena created by divine forces [Kräfte] could reveal God's plan for the world.[14] For Herder, however, this physico-theological starting point was compatible with, and served to legitimate, what Wolfgang Proß has characterised as Herder's novel and 'radically naturalist' interpretation of human culture and history: for Herder, the latter were

---

[14] Johann Gottfried Herder, *Outlines of a Philosophy of History of Man*, trans. by T. Churchill (London, 1800), ix (henceforth abbr. as *Outlines*); Johann Gottfried Herder, *Ideen zur Philosophie der Geschichte der Menschheit* [1784–1791], in: *Werke*, vol. III/1, edited by Wolfgang Proß (Munich, Vienna: Carl Hanser Verlag, 1989) (henceforth abbr. as *Ideen*), 15. Since *Outlines* is the only complete English translation, I am standardly referring to this edition. However, I have had to modify the translation on several occasions and where possible, I am also using F. M. Barnard's translation in Johann Gottfried von Herder, 'Ideas for a Philosophy of History [1784–1791]', in *J. G. Herder on Social and Political Culture* (henceforth abbr. as *Ideas*), which contains excerpts from books 3–9.

an integral part of one single process of nature in which the basic living force was diversifying itself so as to reach a state of stability in organised forms of various degrees of complexity.[15] Drawing on the most recent approaches in natural science, Herder posited the laws of attraction and repulsion as the fundamental principles of the activity of this force, viewing each organic whole as consisting a specific kind of organised hierarchy and balance between its internal forces.[16] The inner organisation of an organism, and its position in the hierarchy of organisms, for Herder was revealed through its material shape.[17] This entailed the deployment of an empiricist methodology when studying organisms. Relying on comparative anatomy and physiology, Herder also arrived at a specification of humanity's place in the cosmos, and more narrowly in the animal world, from which he further derived humans' specific capacities and forces.[18]

Crucially, Herder in the *Ideas* categorised the human being as a 'middle creature among the animals of the earth', emphasising the specific organisation of the human skull and the upright position of the human body as making possible his 'finer senses' as well as also constituting the basis for the human ability for art. The latter, in turn, was activated by 'the divine gift of speech', that is, the human capacity for language and symbolic cognition (religion).[19] Reason, Herder argued, was to be 'learned' and 'acquired', being essentially a product of humans' propensity to compare the impressions and ideas of their finer senses 'according to the[ir] delicacy, accuracy and frequency', so as to best serve their self-preservation, on the one hand, and to contribute to their

---

[15] Wolfgang Proß, 'Nachwort', in *Herder: Werke*, vol. 3/1: *Ideen zur Philosophie der Geschichte der Menschheit* (1987), ed. Proß, pp. 839–1040 (984–1006). See also Wolfgang Proß, 'Herder-Handbuch: Ideen zur Philosophie der Geschichte der Menschheit', *Herder-Handbuch*, edited by Heinrich Clairmont, Stefan Greif and Marion Heinz (Paderborn, 2015) (I am most grateful to Professor Proß for allowing me to read this piece in manuscript first); John H. Zammito, Karl Menges, Ernest A. Menze, 'Johann Gottfried Herder Revisited: The Revolution of Scholarship in the Last Quarter Century', *Journal of the History of Ideas*, 71: 4 (2010), 661–684, 664; Beiser, *The German Historicist Tradition*, 149–154.

[16] For a discussion, see Beiser, *The German Historicist Tradition*, 151–152.

[17] Herder, *Ideas*, 260–261; 265; Outlines, 84–85; 92; *Ideen*, 124–126; 132.

[18] See Proß, 'Nachwort', 998–999; cf. Proß, 'Herder-Handbuch'. A still useful discussion of Herder's comparative anatomy and physiology and Kant's unsympathetic reading of and response to it can be found in Irmscher, 'Die Geschichtsphilosophische Kontroverse', 128–133.

[19] Herder, *Ideas*, 263; Outlines, 87; *Ideen*, 128. The continuity between Herder's early naturalist theory of the origins of language in his *Treatise on the Origins of Language* with his later account emphasising the ultimately divine origins of language has been demonstrated by Wolfgang Proß in 'Das "göttliche Geschenk der Rede" – Hat Herder die Sprachursprungstheorie der *Abhandlung* in den *Ideen* revoziert?', in *Sprachsplitter und Sprachspiele*, edited by Jürg Niederhauser and Stanislaw Szlęk (Bern, 2000), 223–233.

self-constitution as 'sons of Gods', on the other.[20] Thus locating even
reason within nature, Herder at the same time proceeded to link it to
freedom, characterising humans as the only beings who can learn from
experience so as to make judgements about true and false, good and evil,
and hence consciously choose between the latter.[21] Thanks to this distinctive capacity, humans were also able to pursue the realisation of pure
immortal humanity, the goal never to be achieved fully in this life.[22] This
destiny Herder famously captured with the term *Humanität*:

I wish I could include in this word *Humanität* everything that I have said so
far about the noble formation [Bildung] of man for reason and freedom, finer
senses and impulses, the most delicate and most robust health, the realization of
the purpose of the world and the control over it. For man has no nobler word for
his destiny than that which expresses the essence of himself as a human being,
and which thus reflects the image of the Creator of our earth. We need only
sketch his structure and constitution [Gestalt], to trace his noblest duties.[23]

Moral duties, hence, were also ultimately derived from the
human constitution and original capacities. For Herder, human self-
determination built on, reinforced and corrected humans' natural sociability. In a stoic vein, Herder maintained that natural human drives could
be reduced to two fundamental principles: the one of self-preservation,
on the one hand, and sympathy and communication with other sentient
beings, and particularly with other human beings, on the other.[24] Thanks
to these principles, humans' natural disposition was towards peace, voluntary mutual commitment between two people of the opposite sex,
parental love and a general sympathy through 'voice and language' in
particular.[25] Humans' necessarily partial and biased natural sociability, further, could and also had to be corrected by the 'rule of justice
and truth', which originated in human reason itself, since human reason
necessarily searched for truth and beauty in imitating God's reason. As
such it was also able to perceive unity and symmetry, which in practical

---

[20] Herder, *Ideas*, 264–265; *Outlines*, 91–92; *Ideen*, 134–135.
[21] Herder, *Ideas*, 264–265, 91–92; *Outlines*, 91–92; *Ideen*, 134–135.
[22] Herder, *Ideas*, 280–281; *Outlines*, 127–131; *Ideen*, 179–184.
[23] Herder, *Ideas*, 267–268; *Outlines*, 98; *Ideen*, 142–143. For discussion of Herder's concept of *Humanität*, see Hans Adler, 'Herder's Concept of Humanity', in *A Companion
to the Works of Johann Gottfried Herder*, edited by Adler and Koepke, 93–116.
[24] Herder, *Ideas*, 268–269 (I have slightly modified the translation.); *Outlines*, 98–99;
Ideen, 143. Later he comes to support the idea that all human drives derive from the
single self-feeling or self-love (one including also the feeling (and loving) of others),
see Johann Gottfried Herder, *Sämmtliche Werke* (henceforth abbr. as SW), edited by
Bernhard Suphan (33 vols, 1877–1913), vol. 18, 344.
[25] Herder, *Ideas*, 268–269; *Outlines*, 99–101; *Ideen*, 143–145.

contexts led it to recognise and to pursue the 'great law of equity [Billigkeit] and reciprocity [Gleichgewicht].[26] Essentially, this rule taught human beings to '*not [do] unto others what you would not wish them to do unto you*; but *what you expect others to do unto you, do unto them too*'.[27] However, although this rule was inherent in reason, or, as Herder also argued, even in 'the breast of a human monster', humans had to learn to apply it through accumulated experience, based on trial and error in specific natural and cultural contexts; this was the specific moral aspect and calling of *Humanität*.[28] Furthermore, as Herder sought to show in the second part of the book, the entirety of human history was a learning process, while it was the noble task of the philosophy of history to assist humans in achieving knowledge of the laws of the cultural and historical world.

Kant's *Idea* was published shortly before his first, devastating review of the first instalment of Herder's *Ideas*.[29] But Kant was already aware of Herder's work and sought to provide an alternative to it.[30] As opposed to Herder, Kant posited a strict dualism between the phenomenal realm of natural causality and the noumenal one of the freedom of the will and morality. Although Kant, too, discussed the purposive order of nature and proposed nature's (possible) plan for mankind, he qualified it as an 'idea ... which to some extent follows an *a priori* rule'.[31] For Kant, this *a priori* idea consisted in the historical development of the human species towards a condition of the greatest possible civil freedom under external laws, the full realisation of which ultimately depended on the establishment of an international federation of states with coercive powers. Civil liberty and international peace, he argued, were both necessary conditions for enabling humans to fully develop their reason and attain moral freedom, as a result of which they would also achieve happiness 'as far as is possible on earth'.[32]

[26] Herder, *Ideas*, 270; *Outlines*, 101–102; *Ideen*, 147. I have modified the translation here, so as to bring out the juridical origins of this term, cf. Proß, *Anmerkungen*, 301–304.
[27] Herder, *Ideas*, 270; *Outlines*, 102; *Ideen*, 147.
[28] Adler, 'Herder's Concept of Humanity', 101.
[29] Immanuel Kant, 'Reviews of Herder's Ideas on the Philosophy of the History of Mankind', *Political Writings*, edited by H.S. Reiss and trans. H.B. Nisbet, 2nd, enlarged edition (Cambridge, 2000), 201–220 (210).
[30] Kant heard about Herder's *Ideas* from Johann Georg Hamann in August 1784. Kant's *Idea* was published in November 1784, and his review of the first instalment of Herder's *Ideas* in January 1785, Rudolf Haym, *Herder nach seinem Leben und seinen Werken* (Berlin, 1958 (reprint of 1885)), 275, 279; Reiss, 'Introduction to Reviews', 195.
[31] Immanuel Kant, 'Idea for a Universal History with a Cosmopolitan Purpose', in idem, *Political Writings*, 41–53 (53).
[32] Kant, 'Idea', 43. On the importance of Herder's work for the evolution of Kant's views on history, see Zammito, *The Genesis* and Karl Ameriks, 'The Purposive Development of Human Capacities', in *Kant's Idea of a Universal History*, 46–67.

Herder learned about Kant's essay and review of the first instalment of his *Ideas* simultaneously in early 1785. In letters to his friends Johann Georg Hamann and Friedrich Heinrich Jacobi, Herder maintained sarcastically that Kant's argument in his essay was essentially that 'man was made for the species and the most perfect state-machine at the end of all times'.[33] This idea was not just ridiculous but also detestable. Explaining the development of human forces [*Kräfte*] through 'political antagonism and the most perfect monarchy, indeed, the co-existence of many most perfect monarchies that are ruled by pure reason *in corpore*', Kant's essay breathed 'wretched ice-cold, slavish enthusiasm [hundelende Eiskalte, Knechtsschwärmerey]'.[34]

Although Herder's bitter reaction to Kant was influenced by his disappointment about Kant's critical review of his own work, he rightly detected that Kant's hypothesis of a 'natural mechanism' for achieving peace and morality rested on a sceptical theory of human unsocial sociability,[35] and affirmed a fundamentally Hobbesian account of sovereignty.[36] While human cultural agency[37] was triggered by need as well as mutual competition and antagonism, the best conditions for it were created in states coming closest to realising the external freedom of all. Yet this condition of freedom was to be guaranteed by a strong sovereign authority. 'Living among others of his species', Kant argued, 'man [was] an *animal who needs a master*', that is, a powerful agent who would force him to obey 'a universally valid will under which everyone can be free'.[38] Kant, just like Hobbes, could not imagine any constitutional limits to sovereign power. Yet he voiced the need for restraining the sovereigns at the international level. The states, he famously argued, remained in a state of nature among themselves, and wars and preparation for war constantly interrupted and interfered with the development of culture, and the process of *enlightenment*, which was necessary for moral education and for achieving a fully free civil constitution. In order not to 'abandon all practical principles', it thus was necessary for

---

33 Herder to Hamann 14 February 1785 in Johann Gottfried Herder, *Briefe. Gesamtausgabe*, edited by Wilhelm Dobbek and Günter Arnold, 14 vols. (Weimar, 1977–2009), vol. 5 (September 1783–1788)(1979), 106. All translations are mine unless otherwise stated.

34 Herder to Jacobi, 25 February 1785, in Herder, *Briefe. Gesamtausgabe*, 109. I am grateful to Wolfgang Proß for suggesting this translation to me.

35 On this account and its relationship to moral autonomy, see J.B. Schneewind, 'Good Out of Evil: Kant and the Idea of Unsocial Sociability', in *Kant's Idea of a Universal History*, 94–112; cf. Allen Wood, 'Kant's Fourth Proposition: the Unsociable Sociability of Human Nature', in *Kant's Idea of a Universal History*, 112–128.

36 Kant, 'Idea', 44–45.

37 I am borrowing Muthu's apt term here, see Muthu, *Enlightenment against Empire*, 7.

38 Kant, 'Idea', 45.

humans to maintain hope, and hence Kant suggested further ways in which things might improve. Modern commerce, Kant argued, was creating new conditions in international politics, forcing rulers to refrain from interfering with the civil liberty of their subjects. The mounting public debt, further, would make rulers regard wars as ever more dubious enterprises.[39] The increasing interrelatedness of modern states would thereby ultimately lead to the establishment of informal mediating institutions between states, and finally, to that of a 'great federation' (*Foedus Amphictyonum*) in which 'each state, even the smallest, could expect to derive its security and rights not from it own power or its own legal judgement . . . but from a united power and law-governed decisions of a united will'.[40] Hence Kant essentially recommended that empirical historians would trace the ruptured, yet in broad outline 'regular process of improvement in the political constitutions of our continent'. It would be worthwhile, he argued, to further determine how this factor, and the laws and the mutual relations among states 'by virtue of the good they contained' have 'served to elevate and glorify nations'.[41] In developing this argument Kant notably did not express any criticism of European colonialism, suggesting instead that 'our continent will probably legislate eventually for all other continents'.[42]

Herder seized the opportunity to answer Kant's vision of the possible political and moral progress in history in the second instalment of his *Ideas*. The overall topic of this part of his work was the physical and cultural diversification of the human species into different nations under varying external conditions (climate, geographical habitat, mode of life [Lebensart]) and through 'traditions of education'. Books Eight, Nine and Ten in particular dealt with themes highly relevant for making the case against Kant's idea for a universal history. In Book Eight, Herder offered a detailed account of the epistemological and moral-psychological foundations of human sociability and cultural agency (human sensuality [Sinnlichkeit], imagination, practical reason, sentiments and drives), while also explaining the diversity of national characters and conceptions of happiness by tracing the creative unfolding of the human forces [Kräfte] in different external conditions. In Book Nine, provoked by Kant's third proposition according to which man 'should produce everything out of himself',[43] Herder proceeded to discuss the role of various kinds of tradition (language, political government, arts and sciences and religion) in the education of humanity

---

[39] Kant, 'Idea', 49.   [40] Kant, 'Idea', 47.
[41] Kant, 'Idea', 52.   [42] Kant, 'Idea', 52.
[43] Cf. Beiser, *The German Historicist Tradition*, 157; see also Proß, 'Anmerkungen', 491–493.

(understood as the sum of the generations of human beings, organised into families and nations).[44]

Although Herder in Book Nine was primarily interested in the positive contribution of different traditions to educating humanity and the relationship of these traditions to each other, he also tried to account for the possible aberrations from the human striving for *Humanität* in certain forms of tradition. Political government for him represented a distinctive and highly mutable form of tradition. It is here, too, that Herder's most direct answer to Kant's political ideas can be found, being mostly developed in his notorious Chapter Four on governments. Herder himself regarded this chapter as a *caput mortuum*.[45] As he complained to Hamann, he had revised and shortened it a number of times in order to properly answer 'Mr Immanuel [Kant] and the public of universal history for whom everything in miserable history [leidige Geschichte] is hinging on it [government]'.[46] The final published version turned out in some ways to be even more opaque than the earlier ones, and much of Herder's critique of Kant's political cosmopolitanism, including an entire section on the 'imperfection of all ways of the human formation [Bildung] on earth', was omitted from the published version.[47] The philosophical history of political government that Herder presented there was highly fragmentary and can only be understood in combination with his philosophical elaboration of sacred history in Book Ten as well as in his empirical history of the political government of different nations, that he developed in the last two instalments of the *Ideas*. In what follows I will reassemble this critique by focusing on the themes of Book Eight and Nine successively.

In Book Eight, Herder targeted the premises of Kant's legitimation of the modern state: his theory of unsocial sociability, cultural agency and civilisation. A major theme in this book was Herder's defence of natural sociability. More clearly than in his earlier account of natural sociability in his *Treatise on the Origin of Language* (1770/1772), which was primarily directed against Rousseau,[48] Herder here emphasised the pacific nature of humanity. Although humans did seek self-preservation and happiness, he argued, this was in itself no source of antagonism between them either

---

[44] Herder, *Outlines*, 251–256; *Ideen*, 340–347.
[45] *Caput mortuum* (dead head) was the term alchemists used for referring to the worthless residue of a chemical process.
[46] Herder to Hamann, 23. April 1785, *Briefe. Gesamtausgabe*, 121.
[47] Herder, SW 13, 464–470; reprinted also in Herder, *Ideen*, 1135–1139.
[48] On this account, see Eva Piirimäe, 'Sociability, Nationalism and Cosmopolitanism in Herder's Early Philosophy of History', *History of Political Thought* Vol. XXXVI:3 (2015), 521–559.

individually or even in groups: since nature had secured widely diverse kinds of enjoyments for the 'diverging species' of humanity, the chances that the self-preservation and pursuit of happiness of different human groups would collide with each other were minimal.[49] In terms of their physical and physiological make-up, mental capacities and the circumstances of birth and infancy, humans were a sociable species designed to live in peace with each other.[50] The feelings of love of a mother and father for the children, and the necessarily weaker love of the latter for their parents, constituted the very basis of human sociability, while the broader groups of tribes, and finally nations, originated in the education fathers sought to give their sons.[51] Even the fierce tribal wars which had often been regarded as the disgrace of humanity in fact originated in one of the noblest forms of human feeling, that of companionship and friendship among those participating in common perils and endeavours, from which the feeling of wounded tribal honour or hurt tribal friendship was derived.[52] Pervasive antagonism between individual human beings emerged only at a higher stage of civilisation [*Cultur*], that is, with nations that had invented agriculture and thereby thoroughly transformed their natural environment and their entire mode of life.[53]

Fortunately, there was no predetermined progression towards this condition in human history. Herder cautioned against simplistic applications of the standard division of nations into hunters, fishers, pastoralists and agriculturalists for determining the rank of a people in a single hierarchy of civilisation [Cultur] or when it was assumed that one or other way of living would automatically bring about a higher level of civilisation.[54] There was a significant diversity in the morals, customs and arts of different peoples falling into the same category in this scheme, one resulting primarily from their varying living conditions (climate and geography). In many cases, there simply existed no impetus for progress to a further level of civilisation. Clearly, a human being living on an isolated island with a mild climate and 'feeding on roots, herbs, and fruits' would remain 'contented under his necessities' once natural indolence and this contentment had 'begotten the child called convenience'.[55] Instead, different external causes had to combine in order to propel the

---

[49] Herder, *Ideas*, 305; *Outlines*, 209–211; *Ideen*, 286–287.
[50] Herder, *Ideas*, 304; *Outlines*, 209; *Ideen*, 284–285.
[51] Herder, *Ideas*, 305–306; *Outlines*, 211–218; *Ideen*, 288–296.
[52] Herder, *Ideas*, 306; *Outlines*, 217; *Ideen*, 296. Herder here reiterated the argument which he had made, relying on Ferguson's ideas, in *Of the Origin of Language* and *This Too a Philosophy*, see my 'Sociability, Nationalism and Cosmopolitanism', 543–544.
[53] Herder, *Ideas*, 304; *Outlines*, 210; *Ideen*, 286.
[54] Herder, *Ideas*, 302; *Outlines*, 202; *Ideen*, 276–277.
[55] Herder, *Ideas*, 302; *Outlines*, 202; *Ideen*, 277.

development of civilisation, among which Herder particularly emphasised the proximity of men and animals on 'our large continents', and
the resulting practices of hunting and the domestication of animals.[56]

Herder's final and most important point in Book Eight, was that man's
happiness was in no way enhanced by the development of civilisation.
Kant agreed, of course, that there was no linear growth of morality
and happiness in universal human history. Rather, Kant had hinted that
unsocial sociability under the conditions of stable political government
would foster the development of moral freedom by activating our 'crude
disposition' for moral discrimination – one consisting in humans' ability
to restrain themselves, although not for moral purposes as yet. So far in
human history, however, the outcome had been ever more 'mere' civilisation. Kant's hope was that this might change, once stable civil freedom
was achieved and humans would properly have a chance to enlighten
themselves, thereby moving closer to a situation in which they could also
become aware of moral freedom and the ideal of moral happiness resulting from everyone's acting on the basis of the moral law.

Herder passionately rejected this understanding of moral happiness.
Emphasising humans' active forces of the mind as the source of their
cultural agency, Herder associated happiness with the natural exercise
of these very forces and a simple sensation of existence accompanying
it in all natural and cultural conditions.[57] Thus, he argued, 'large,
complex state-machines' were by no means the necessary preconditions
for achieving virtue or happiness. On the contrary, they instead created substantial obstacles to realising these goals. Here Herder again
reiterated his earlier argument, developed first in his *Treatise on the
Origin of Language*, that thanks to the ever greater division of labour in
human societies, the forces of the soul were not used in total any more,

[56] Herder, *Ideas*, 302–304; *Outlines*, 202–208; *Ideen*, 276–284. For a discussion of Herder's
comparison between Eurasia and the Americas in terms of the number of animals available for domestication and the resulting differences between the development of civilisation (and ultimately the ability of self-defence) in these two parts of the world, see
Muthu, *Enlightenment against Empire*, 240–241. However, as will become evident below,
I do not agree with Muthu's claim that for Herder, agriculture as such rendered nations
bellicose, see ibid., 242.

[57] Herder, *Ideas*, 307–311; *Outlines*, 218–224; *Ideen*, 298–305. For discussion, see
Wolfgang Proß, '"Natur" und "Geschichte" in Herders "Ideen zur Philosophie der
Geschichte der Menschheit" (Nachwort)', in *J. G. Herder: Werke*, edited by Proß,
III/1: *Ideen zur Philosophie der Geschichte der Menschheit* (1987), 839–1040 (912–925)
and Sikka, *Herder on Humanity*, 53–58; cf. Allen Wood, *Kant's Ethical Thought*, 226–
233. For Herder's very similar ideas on this subject already in the 1760s, see Marion
Heinz, 'Die Bestimmung des Menschen: Herder contra Mendelssohn', in *Philosophie
der Endlichkeit: Festschrift für Erich Christian Schröder zum 65. Geburtstag*, edited by Beate
Niemeyer and Dirk Schütze (Würzburg, 1991), 263–285.

which led to a significant decrease of the original intensity of sensation, and finally to servility and inertness, which in turn paved the way for despotism and empty moral cosmopolitanism.[58] Drawing on this theory, in *This Too a Philosophy* Herder had further launched a devastating attack on the notion of modern sovereignty, associating its rise with the progress of technology and luxury which had made certain key human virtues redundant and facilitated the transformation of the entire society into a 'machine' led by one individual.[59] In the *Ideas* Herder, too, ironically associated this political ideal with the increased happiness of being able to 'serve in this machine as an unthinking component'; Herder memorably contrasted the happiness of the intellectually over-refined 'citizen of the world', who was in love with the 'name' of mankind, with that of a savage who actively exercised his powers in loving his wife, children and in being active for his tribe and who as such was willing to 'receive a stranger in his poor hut as his brother, and with a calm benevolence'.[60]

In Book Nine, Herder famously mounted a direct attack on what he took to be Kant's morally repulsive Hobbesianism:

The maxim that 'man is an animal who needs a master when he lives with others of his species, so that he may attain happiness and fulfil his destiny on earth', is both facile and noxious as a fundamental principle of a philosophy of history. The proposition, I feel, ought to be reversed. Man is an animal as long as he needs a master to lord over him; as soon as he attains the status of a human being he no longer needs a master in any real sense. Nature has designated no master for the human species, brutal vices and passions render one necessary. [–] A father who brings up his children in a manner which keeps them under age for the rest of their lives and hence in need of a tutor and guardian, is rightly considered a bad father. [–] Let us apply this line of reasoning to the educators of mankind, to fathers of fatherlands and their pupils. Either the latter are incapable of improvement or it must have become perceptible during the thousands of years that they have been governed as to what has become of them, and to what purposes they have been trained by their teachers.[61]

Previous scholarship has mainly focused on the first half of this quotation, discussing the question as to whether Herder was rejecting all

---

[58] Herder, *Ideas*, 309–311; *Outlines*, 207–209; 220–221; *Ideen*, 283–284; 300.
[59] Herder, *This Too a Philosophy*, 319; for discussion, see my 'Sociability, Nationalism and Cosmopolitanism', 536.
[60] Herder, *Ideas*, 310; *Outlines*, 222–223; Ideen, 304. (The translation of the phrases is mine.)
[61] Herder, *Ideas*, 323 (I have extensively modified the translation.); *Outlines*, 249; *Ideen*, 336–337.

political government, or perhaps only modern absolute monarchies.[62] The ambiguity of Herder's meaning is further exacerbated by Herder's following remarks: 'Nature educates families, the most natural state [der natürlichste Staat], therefore, is also *One nation* [Ein [sic!] Volk], with One national character [mit Einem [sic!] Nationalcharakter]. This it retains for thousands of years and can be developed most naturally, if the princes belonging to the same nation only wish so.'[63] But as a careful reading of Herder's argument in the previous quoted section suggests, Herder did not regard it as possible to answer the question about political obligation and the aims of political government in the abstract only: he instead made a call for the study of the empirical history of political government. Therefore, before we can determine what Herder may have had in view in criticising Kant, it is important to try to understand in what way Herder explained the origins of different kinds of political government in human history, and how he construed the history of European states in particular.

Altogether, Herder in Book Nine distinguished three 'degrees of government'.[64] The first two were 'natural', while the third was invented. The first consisted simply in the 'ties of the law of nature' as constituted through human natural sociability and as expressed in family relations.[65] The second was also natural and characteristic of hunters, fishers and shepherding nations, who because of their mode of life did not need much of each other's assistance for most of the time, yet had to elect leaders for their common undertakings. Even 'the elected judges of a community', Herder argued, emerged at this stage of government.[66] This form of authority was originally temporary and lasted only as long as was necessary for carrying out the specific joint venture.[67] At the end of this stage of development, however, humans reached a crucial crossroad at

---

[62] See e.g. Beiser, *Enlightenment, Revolution and Romanticism*, 211–213; Eggel et al., 'Was Herder a Nationalist?'.

[63] Herder, *Ideas*, 324; *Outlines*, 249; *Ideen*, 337. The translation is entirely my own here.

[64] It has gone unnoticed so far that Herder's account of the rise of political government had significant parallels with that of Hume in his *Treatise of Human Nature*. For Hume, too, political government was an artifice upon which men had come under specific conditions only. It originated in rivalry between societies, which in turn was spawned by their geographical proximity and inequality of resources, David Hume, *The Clarendon Edition of the Works of David Hume: A Treatise of Human Nature*, edited by D.F. Norton and M.J. Norton (Oxford, 2007), T.3.2.8.2; 540–541. For an intriguing recent reconstruction of Hume's views on political obligation, see Paul Sagar, 'The State without Sovereignty: Authority and Obligation in Hume's Political Philosophy', *History of Political Thought* XXXVII: 2 (2016), 271–305.

[65] Herder, *Ideas*, 317–319; *Outlines*, 244–245; *Ideen*, 330–331. (The translation of the term 'Grad der Regierung' is from *Outlines*.)

[66] Herder, *Ideas*, 318; *Outlines*, 244; *Ideen*, 331.

[67] Herder, *Ideas*, 318; *Outlines*, 244–245; *Ideen*, 330–331.

which they were forced to invent political institutions. 'Nature extended the bonds of society only to families', Herder wrote, while 'beyond that, she left mankind at liberty to knit them, and to frame their most delicate work of art, the state, as they thought proper. If they framed it well, happiness was their reward; if they chose, or endured tyranny and bad forms of government, they had to bear their burden'.[68] Human nature certainly did not necessitate political government, let alone a monarchical or despotic form of government. No nation knowingly gave away its freedom. Sometimes it occurred through loss of vigilance or even laziness, while in most cases despotism originated in conquests.[69] Hereditary government [Erbregierung] or the right to dominate [herrschen] was based not on natural right, but on 'forcible conquests' and tradition.[70]

What was the cause of wars for Herder? To this question a symbolic answer can be found in Book Ten, in which Herder attempted to shore up his thesis of natural sociability by offering a philosophical interpretation of the Biblical story of the Fall. Rejecting accounts of any kind of 'state of nature' by reference to humanity as a creative species, which always already had some degree of culture, Herder suggested turning to different older 'traditions' describing the origins of mankind. Among them, he argued, only the Mosaic one proved to be truly original, that is, 'philosophical, symbolic and profound', while others reflected particular features of national imagination and heritage. The Mosaic tradition showed that God had endowed humanity with distinctive capacities (language and governing reason), which, however, were to be developed in interaction with the external conditions and through education and tradition.[71] The original condition in which God placed man was a garden, since in a garden humans could follow their original 'mild' way of life as opposed a 'wild' one; yet when humans left this 'garden' – which Herder located in a valley in Cashmere – they also developed different passions, and 'impelled by necessity, climate, and the habitual sway of some passion', began to imitate the beasts in their 'knowledge of evil': it was the 'blood of animals', Herder argued, which gave humans their bellicose disposition,[72] to which, at a later stage, also the 'mischiefs of civil society' were added.[73]

---

[68] Herder, *Ideas*, 322; *Outlines*, 248; *Ideen*, 335. The translation is mine, combining phrases from *Ideas* and *Outlines*.
[69] Herder, *Ideas*, 320–321; *Outlines*, 246; *Ideen*, 334. I am using the translation of *Outlines* here.
[70] Herder, *Ideas*, 319–320; *Outlines*, 245–246; *Ideen*, 332.
[71] Herder, *Outlines*, 285; *Ideen*, 384.
[72] Herder, *Outlines*, 282–284; *Ideen*, 380–382.
[73] Herder, *Outlines*, 282 (I have modified the translation); *Ideen*, 380.

Herder's ideas on the underlying logic of the empirical history of political government can be reassembled from his discussion of different nations and their cultures in the third and fourth instalments of the *Ideas*; in the rest of this section, I will attempt to bring out some of the most relevant ideas in this vastly complex discussion. Right at the beginning of Part Three, Herder made clear that it was the 'half-savage hunters and nomads' in the harsh climate and 'cold, steep, broken land' of Northern Asia that first developed bellicose dispositions.[74] It was also in this context that ideas of leadership and submission soon degenerated into crude hereditary-based nomadic despotism, the paradigmatic example of which was the Tartarian war-lordship. In the South, by contrast, the story unfolded very differently: here 'migrating colonies, led chiefly by the rivers, gradually drew towards the sea, and assembled in towns and countries [Länder], while a milder climate awakened in them more refined ideas'.[75] In the South where there was more leisure, men's drives were also more stimulated, awakening the passions (and one might add, inventiveness leading to new modes of life such as agriculture), which however led to individual conflicts and necessitated the establishments of laws and various kinds of institutions, political and religious.[76] Yet since many of these countries soon degenerated through luxury and despotism, they were an easy prey for Northern nomads.

At the same time, Herder posited a stark contrast between South and East Asia, on the one hand, and the Near East (West Asia and Egypt), on the other. In South and East Asia, geography supported the formation of stable national borders, and hence 'national characters' – morals, customs, distinctive ways of thinking of the population – were fixed and fortified at an early stage. National characters were here supported and cultivated by political leaders, yet these states were also bound to be stuck at a certain stage of civilisation. The greatest kingdom of East Asia – China – developed from a semi-Tatar despotism into a rigid 'state-machine' built on a strict kind of subordination and 'childish obedience' reinforced by moral maxims.[77] Yet being contained in natural geographic borders, it did not pursue aggressive expansion. Only one single people, the Mongols, were a threat to China, and even if they conquered the

---

[74] 'Necessity and the circumstances of the country rendered men barbarous: a thoughtless way of life, once become habitual, confirmed itself in the wandering tribes, or those that separated from them; and fashioned amid rude manners that almost eternal national character, which so completely discriminates all the Northern asian tribes from the nations of the South.' Herder, *Outlines*, 289 (I have modified the translation); *Ideen*, 392.

[75] Herder, *Outlines*, 289; *Ideen*, 392.   [76] Herder, *Outlines*, 289; *Ideen*, 392.

[77] Herder, *Outlines*, 290–292; *Ideen*, 392–396.

172   *Eva Piirimäe*

Chinese state for a period, they did not alter the Chinese constitution or national character.[78]

In the Near East, by contrast, various empires arose in the proximity of mountains from which numerous primitive nomadic nations continuously descended to attack and overrun these empires, to found new ones themselves. In the Near East, hence, most nations developed a particularly bellicose mind-set, combining an originally nomadic form of government and wandering disposition with flourishing arts and trade; as a result there was constant shifting of borders, one empire being replaced by another.[79] There were also 'states springing up of one root' in the Near East. These were states that 'rested on themselves and were able to maintain themselves for ages': such states, Herder argued, could be subdued, 'but the nation preserves itself', remaining true to the old morals of their fathers – such were the Hebrews and the Egyptians.[80] Like China, the ancient kingdoms of these nations had originally ascribed great importance to the formation of morals [Sitten] through education, understanding that this was 'the spring of their internal strength'. This was in stark contrast to modern European states which were based only on money or mechanical political arts, while the early kingdoms drew on religion as a particularly suited 'drive' at this level of civilisation.[81] Yet since it was typical of all human inventions, whether political and religious, that they necessarily stagnated and degenerated after a few generations, these state religions, too, were turned into vehicles of oppression and ignorance in due time,[82] rendering these states prey to aggressive empires in their neighbourhood.

In discussing ancient republicanism, Herder posited a strong contrast between Greek and Roman republicanism. The Greeks, who as a nation were formed in a specific coastal and insular geographic environment, represented the first example of an open culture in which, thanks to the impact of multiple cultural sources, a unique national character was formed. Although Herder was no uncritical admirer of Greek republicanism, he celebrated its fundamental tendency: 'the period of Greek republics', he argued, was the first step towards the maturity of the human spirit [Mündigkeit des menschlichen Geistes] in the important matter of how humans should govern humans.'[83] Using this unmistakably Kantian terminology against Kant himself, Herder corrected Kant's emphasis on modern monarchies as the most suitable environment for

[78] Herder, *Outlines*, 296; *Ideen*, 400.
[79] Herder, *Outlines*, 316–317; 323; *Ideen*, 425–427, 434.
[80] Herder, *Outlines*, 350 (I have modified the translation.); cf. 325; *Ideen*, 468; cf. 436.
[81] Herder, *Outlines*, 350; *Ideen*, 468.   [82] Herder, *Outlines*, 351–352; *Ideen*, 469–470.
[83] Herder, *Outlines*, 373 (I have modified the translation); *Ideen*, 497.

political debate: the origins of critical philosophical reflection about politics, clearly, lay in Greek republics. Furthermore, the Greeks had invented and tested, although not fully achieved, two key principles of political obligation: first, that of patriotism as the voluntary submission to the laws as cherished in Sparta, and second, that of the *enlightenment* about civic matters as pursued by the Athenians.[84]

Crediting the Greeks with the first invention of the ideal of the 'government of humans by humans', Herder drew a sharp distinction between Greek and Roman republicanism. Rome was a military state through and through, fundamentally a 'rudely composed living machine... within the walls of one city',[85] which through its artificial division in different classes, and an ever increasing number of various superior offices and honours was geared towards external military conquests and empire, and which finally collapsed under its own weight.[86] Furthermore, the celebrated Roman law was suitable for governing the city of Rome only; as soon as it was applied in a wider area, it corrupted the original character of the conquered nations and became an instrument of oppression.[87]

For Herder, a similar process had also taken place when the Germanic peoples had established new states on the conquered territories of the Romans. The Germanic peoples that conquered the Roman territories were fundamentally European 'Tartars', barbarous and bellicose peoples who had devised a distinctive ideal of government known as 'Germanic peoples' government' [*Deutsche Völkerverfassung, Gemeinverfassung*] for governing themselves; furthermore, those Germanic peoples which had already served in the Roman army added a Roman type of militarism to their original national character. Basically, Herder argued, European states originated in the unhappy modifications of the original Germanic type of government.[88] Originally, the Germanic tribes were 'free nations', choosing leaders for the accomplishment of specific tasks only. Also the territories conquered remained in the common possession of the nation as a whole. Yet, when conquering and settling down in the vast territories of the Roman Empire, most people became 'landholders [*Landeigentümer*] on their newly acquired possessions', while continuing

---

[84] Herder, *Outlines*, 375; *Ideen*, 499–500.   [85] Herder, *Outlines*, 404; *Ideen*, 538.
[86] Herder, *Outlines*, 404–405; *Ideen*, 538.   [87] Herder, *Outlines*, 433; *Ideen*, 574.
[88] This constituted a major revision compared to Herder's earlier views. In his early philosophy of history, he had contrasted large modern monarchies with the widely despised 'small islands' and 'subdivisions' of the earlier, Gothic period, attempting to highlight the positive virtues such as manliness and reliance on oneself as being nourished and cultivated by this system of government, Herder, *This Too a Philosophy*, 308. In the *Ideas* Herder located the origins of modern European state-machines in the period of Carolingians.

to owe specific duties, particularly military service and council, to the state. They soon lost their common spirit, no longer participated in the assemblies of the nation, and began to hire 'knights' to serve in the military instead of them, which gradually led to the freemen's loss of rights and possessions. Since knights were rewarded by the kings with land, their power gradually increased both relative to the kings, who were soon impoverished, as well as to the common people, so that finally there were only 'noblemen' and their 'servants' [*Knechte*].[89]

Herder made it clear that the Germanic peoples originally had no concept of the territorial state, conceiving of the relationship of the king and his people as a personal one. While Charlemagne continued to rely on these 'Germanic' elements of personal loyalty in his administration, he also strengthened royal and imperial authority, building a central power structure like that of Rome. For governing vast territories, 'viceroys, dukes, and counts' were needed. A state-machine was thereby emerging, while the king was seen as an 'abstract token' exemplifying the idea of the 'artificial machine' [*Kunstmaschine*] of the state. As an extraordinary figure, Charlemagne was for a moment capable of really breathing life into the imperial structure thus created and had made use of this structure in keeping away external danger. After his death, however, the latter soon fragmented into feuding islands of 'satrapism'.[90]

Simultaneously, a 'singular metamorphosis' also happened, essentially consisting in a 'monstrous' combination of Tartarian and Roman elements of political government. In a Tartarian form of government, the king's dignity was also transferred to the members of his household – his satellites, domestics and servants. This was also the case with the Germans. Yet in the post-Carolingian states, the idea of the king's dignity was turned into a 'naked reality'; 'the household of the regent was made the sum and substance of the kingdom'.[91] The various kinds of personal service to king were turned into hereditary dignities and offices, and celebrated as those to the state, while the household members[*Knechts*] themselves began to claim to represent the body of the nation. A singular kind of 'barbarous pomp', further, came to surround them all. These claims, Herder stipulated, were totally absurd, since 'no free member of [this body] had been [the king's] servant, but only a comrade and co-fighter, and could not allow himself to be represented by any of the king's domestics'. It was also a form of government of which 'neither

---

[89] Herder, *Outlines*, 558–559; *Ideen*, 737–738.
[90] Herder, *Outlines*, 542–545; 558–559; *Ideen*, 717–721; 738–739.
[91] Herder, *Outlines*, 560; *Ideen*, 740.

Greeks nor Romans, neither Alexander nor Augustus', had known anything of.[92]

Returning now to Herder's critique of Kant, it is evident that his famous remark about the 'most natural state' being 'one people [*Volk*], with one national character'[93] aimed to contrast the modern European externally-oriented, expansive and aggressive monarchies with internally-oriented and self-contained ancient kingdoms in which 'compatriot [*mitgeborene*] prince[s]' cultivated the 'national character' of the people.[94] Although he certainly preferred the latter to modern states in this respect, Herder was not setting up any of these ancient kingdoms specifically as models for modern political communities, finding much to criticise in them, too. Contrary to a widespread reading of this passage, thus, he was not suggesting a 'new' ideal of a 'nation-state' in this context either. His main goal in making this remark was to buttress the idea that modern state-machines grounded in, and geared towards, foreign conquest were fundamentally unstable in themselves:

Nothing therefore appears so directly opposite to the end of government as the unnatural enlargement of states, the wild mixing of various human races [Menschen-Gattungen] and nations [Nationen] under one sceptre. The human sceptre is far too weak and slender for such incongruous parts to be engrafted upon it: glued together indeed it may be into a fragile machine, called state-machine [*Staatsmaschine*], but destitute of internal life and sympathy between parts. [–] Like Trojan horses these machines get close to each other, mutually promising eternity, yet without national character [*National-Charakter*], there is no life in them and for those thus forced together it is only the whim of fate that dooms them to immortality: since precisely the art of politics [*Staatskunst*] that brought them about, is also the one that plays with peoples and humans as with lifeless bodies.[95]

One of Herder's main points against Kant, hence, concerned the stability of the modern state, and by implication, the possibility of heightened cultural agency in it. While Kant, too, had criticised modern monarchies for their bellicosity, he nevertheless seemed to think that internally they offered the best chance for the development of culture. Herder disagreed, making clear that European monarchies were still continuing the tradition of barbarous government. They hampered the cultural energies

---

[92] Herder, *Outlines*, 538–545; *Ideen*, 717–721.
[93] Herder, *Ideas*, 324; *Ideen*, 337; *Outlines*, 249 (I have modified the translation).
[94] Herder, *Ideas*, 324; *Ideen*, 338; *Outlines*, 249. Proß suggests that the term 'national' refers to 'Gemeingeist' (public spirit) here, Proß, 'Herder-Handbuch', 40.
[95] Herder, *Ideas*, 324 (I have extensively modified the translation); *Outlines*, 250; *Ideen*, 338.

of their populations, while also denying them any proper representation, let alone political participation.

Herder also clearly distanced himself from the ideal of enlightened paternalist monarchism. It is impossible to tell whether he also, and mistakenly, read Kant as supporting this idea.[96] In any case, in voicing this critique Herder revealed his own republican and constitutionalist sympathies. He passionately emphasised that the people itself had to be active in seeking enlightenment and happiness, and not only by engaging in public debate but by taking active responsibility for their situation.[97] He cautioned against evaluating constitutions on the basis of the rulers' capacity to contribute to public enlightenment and happiness, regarding this as an 'arbitrary' aspect of their rule.[98] The only essential point of view from which all citizens should and would view forms of government instead, Herder argued in a draft version, was to what extent the constitution enabled limiting the possible 'damage to the machine' that a bad ruler might do.[99] At the same time, Herder left it open as to what these limitations exactly could consist of.

In criticising the idea that modern monarchs would come to appreciate their true self-interest in international affairs and join into a strong international federation, however, Herder was again clearly targeting Kant's theory. Considering Kant's emphasis on enlightenment and maturity, Herder was astonished that he envisioned the emergence of an international federation as a likely or indeed, desirable, prospect in this situation. In a section he ultimately omitted from publication, he directly invoked the abbé de Saint-Pierre as his ally against Kant:

The abbé de Saint-Pierre, one of the most philanthropic dreamers who has ever written with truly-good purposes, and whom new and worse [authors] have repeatedly copied, wanted to get rid of war in Europe and tirelessly continued making proposals for a European Diet; yet he was not enough of a dreamer

---

[96] While Kant indeed did not see the possibility of establishing constitutional limits to the power of monarchs, he did not demand that monarchs would directly promote their subjects' moral virtue and happiness. Also, Kant acknowledged that a 'perfect solution' to the master's possible abuse of power did not exist, see Kant, *Idea*, 46–47, see also Kant's defence of his own views in his 'Review of Johann Gottfried Herder, *Ideas for a Universal History of Mankind* (Part Two) (Riga and Leipzig, 1785)', idem, *Political Writings*, 219.

[97] Herder, SW, 453–454, 456; reprinted in Proß, *Anmerkungen*, 509–510.

[98] Herder, SW 13, 453. While this was not a Kantian idea, Gottlieb Hufeland, a young professor at the University of Jena had sought to show that on Kantian premises it was the duty of rulers to promote their subjects' moral virtue and enlightenment, see Reidar Maliks, *Kant's Politics in Context* (Oxford, 2014), 32–35. It is possible that Herder was here trying to answer Hufeland's ideas in particular.

[99] Herder, SW 13, 453.

to hope his perpetual peace to be achieved by the political state-machines simply, but made hundreds of other suggestions in all his writings to show how
the evil passions of the high and low-positioned people might be extinguished,
active education improved and general reason made truly effective; had this happened, perpetual peace would have been achieved even without a European
Diet.[100]

As Herder's resentment in his private letters reveals, what most disturbed him about Kant's account was precisely his self-avowedly
'*chiliastic*' expectation that 'the purpose of nature is at least fairly well
safe-guarded (if not actually furthered) even by the ambitious schemes of
various states' and by European colonialism.[101] Herder did not dispute
Kant's view of the increasing interdependence of European monarchies.
He too acknowledged that a standard version of despotism as 'unbound
license' [*ungebundene Willkühr*] had become impossible in European
states that found themselves in 'a most artificial condition in respect to
each other'.[102] As Herder's draft versions reveal, however, he rejected the
union of state-machines as a solution to the Kantian problem (without
directly mentioning Kant), labelling it ironically as 'Achaean league[s]
of the rulers of the world'.[103] For Herder, the danger of the abuse of
power by the strong central authority of such a league was evident,
while it was not clear how a less strong union could be kept together.
Either there was one 'ruler of the world' or this league was bound to
collapse through internal disagreements. While modern monarchies
were 'rubbing against each other' like huge machines or lifeless Trojan
horses within Europe,[104] they gave full vent to their aggressive disposition in colonial politics.[105] Fortunately, however, the formation of such
a 'league' seemed to be an impossible goal thanks to Nature's wonderful
arrangement in which nations were separated from each other:

... not only by woods and mountains, seas and deserts, rivers and climates, but
also more particularly by languages, inclinations and characters ... No Nimrod
has yet been able to drive all the inhabitants of the World into one Park for
himself and his successors; and though it has been for centuries the object of
united Europe to erect itself into a despot, compelling all the nations of the Earth
to be happy in her way, this happiness-dispelling deity is yet far from having
obtained her end.[106]

Nonetheless, as we have seen, Herder's discussion of the history of
political government was not altogether negative. Ancient kingdoms had

---

[100] Herder, SW 13, 468; Proß, 'Dokumentarischer Anhang', 1138.
[101] Kant, *Idea*, 50.   [102] Herder, SW 13, 455.   [103] Herder, SW 13, 455.
[104] Herder, SW 13, 456.   [105] Herder, SW 451, 455.
[106] Herder, *Outlines*, 224; *Ideen*, 305.

achieved stability, although at the cost of internal dynamism. The Greeks had discovered the principles of patriotism and civic enlightenment, giving an important example of a 'government of humans by humans'. Also with a view to contemporary challenges, Herder claimed that it was to a certain extent possible for the subjects of modern monarchies to 'undo the damage' resulting from the barbaric 'art of politics' using the positive means [*Hülfsmittel*] that human culture provided.[107] But in the present situation, Europeans were to adopt the maxim of serving the state only if it was strictly necessary, while using every opportunity for directly 'serving the freedom, enlightenment and happiness of man'.[108] 'We are certainly tied to a chain of tradition binding so many centuries [...]', Herder boldly and at this point cryptically insisted in a draft version, 'yet humankind [*Menschheit*] with all its rights and duties remains eternally young [...], shakes off the old prejudices and learns, even if against its will, reason and truth'.[109] Therefore, it was highly unlikely that modern European state-machines would be able to preserve themselves for long any more. A look at the history of human societies demonstrated that such 'instruments of human pride were made of clay' and were hence bound to collapse sooner or later.[110] This, however, did not mean that humans were to passively complain, let alone envision abstract utopian fantasies; what truly helped humanity was true (civic) enlightenment and 'active human help' in concrete situations.[111]

II

In his classic intellectual biography, Rudolf Haym presented Herder as having changed his mind about modernity and historical progress in the last two volumes of the *Ideas* in response to the critique of his ideas by Kant, and largely in agreement with Kant's alternative vision in *Idea* and *Conjectures*.[112] Although recent scholarship has not endorsed this view,[113] it has remained somewhat elusive as to whether and how the relative optimism about modern developments as expressed in the last book of Herder's third instalment (Book Fifteen) can be reconciled with the vehement critique of modern state-machines (and Kant) that Herder developed in the second one. My goal in the remainder of this chapter is to clarify some of this ambiguity by reconstructing Herder's

---

[107] Herder, SW 13, 456.   [108] Herder, SW 13, 456.   [109] Herder, SW 13, 457.
[110] Herder, *Ideas*, 324; *Outlines*, 250; *Ideen*, 337–338.
[111] Herder, SW 13, 469; reprinted in Proß, 'Dokumentarischer Anhang', 1138.
[112] Haym, *Herder*, vol. 2, 289–291.
[113] See, most importantly, the very different and highly instructive interpretation by Proß, 'Anmerkungen', 722–746.

argument about modern commerce and politics in Book Fifteen and Herder's vision of European history in the fourth instalment. I will argue that despite his critique of Kant's vision of universal history, Herder, too, believed in the possibility of achieving a more pacific European order, while his understanding of the distinctive features of this order and of the processes leading towards it was different. First, he continued to reject Kant's view of the core of historical progress as consisting in an asymptotic approximation to the period of 'moralisation' (as opposed to mere 'civilisation') thanks to the development and implementation of ever more enlightened ideals of political government in human history. Yet he by no means wished to deny the numerous relative achievements of modern Europe in comparison to ancient societies, including even Greek ones, invoking a certain notion of enlightenment himself.

In this respect, Herder considerably qualified his earlier views in *This Too a Philosophy*. Second, while remaining highly critical of modern European state-machines, Herder in the fourth instalment of the *Ideas* set out to explore the foundations of European culture and Europe's 'higher rank among other parts of the world' in non-political factors.[114] Europe, for Herder, was both a geographical and cultural concept, while he also invoked the widespread eighteenth-century notion of the 'European republic'.[115] Yet in contrast to the standard use of this term, Herder did not mean Europe's distinctive states system, but rather a 'union of nations' [*Nationen-Verein*] grounded in a certain 'general spirit' [*Allgemeingeist*].[116] A key question for him was whether this spirit could again be strengthened in modern Europe, so as to replace the military spirit of the existing state-machines.

In his review of the second instalment of Herder's *Ideas* and in direct response to Herder's critique of his own *Idea*, Kant reiterated his earlier view that the only morally encouraging way of making sense of human history was to posit, and empirically illustrate, humanity's ability to work its way towards a new political condition in which the development of moral freedom in each individual human being would become possible:

But what if the true end of Providence were [. . .] the ever continuing and growing activity and culture which are thereby set in motion, and whose highest possible expression can only be the product of a political constitution based on concepts of human right, and consequently an achievement of the humans

---

[114] Herder, *Outlines*, 631 (I have modified the translation); *Ideen*, 829.
[115] Herder, *Outlines* (I have modified the translation), 468; *Ideen*, 624.
[116] Herder, *Outlines*, 488; *Ideen*, 649; cf. Herder, *Outlines*, 628; *Ideen*, 825.

themselves? [–] Does the author really mean that, if the happy inhabitants of Tahiti, never visited by more civilised nations, were destined to live in their peaceful indolence for thousands of centuries, it would be possible to give a satisfactory answer to the question of why they should exist at all, and of whether it would not have been just as good if this island had been occupied by happy sheep and cattle as by happy human beings who merely enjoy themselves?[117]

We saw in the previous section that Herder vehemently rejected the idea that a refinement of the art of political government as such could contribute towards heightened cultural activity, and thereby, ultimately, moral perfection and happiness. In Book Fifteen, Herder again reiterated these views in response to Kant's continuing disagreement with him, emphasising that each people pursued *Humanität* in its distinctive way, and that there was no increase of cultural agency, let alone approximation of morality or universal happiness in history, human nature itself ever remaining the same mixture of good and bad.[118] In this concluding book of the part dealing with ancient history, Herder now turned his attention to the meaning and logic of the overall historical process. Given that the rise and fall of the different ancient peoples amply testified to the transient and evanescent quality of all political *and* cultural formations in human history, was it possible to talk about the moral education of humanity at all?[119] In order to answer this question, Herder elaborated his theory of the 'natural laws' of history.

It is possible to sketch the gist of this theory only in brief; nor will I be able to offer any substantial insight into the difficult question of how and whether, Herder solved the question of the relationship of the necessity of natural laws and human freedom and responsibility in history.[120] For our purposes, it suffices to show that Herder's key move here was to maintain that in history, just like in nature in general, order arises out of chaos, while humans, as opposed to the rest of the creation, are able to learn about the laws of this process and hence to knowingly contribute to order.

Assuming again the strongly moralising tone characteristic of the chapter on government in Book Nine, Herder now set out to evaluate morally the historical developments that he so far had mainly sought to explain, attributing to nations the responsibility for their achievements and errors, while still maintaining the idea that *Humanität* was

---

[117] Kant, 'Review of Johann Gottfried Herder', 219–220.
[118] Herder, *Outlines*, 437; *Ideen*, 578.
[119] Herder, *Outlines*, 436–438; *Ideen*, 577–579. Cf. Proß, 'Anmerkungen', 733.
[120] On this issue and the inspiration of Kant's early natural philosophy and Spinoza's (and Lessing's) philosophical theology for Herder's argument, see the discussion of Proß, 'Anmerkungen', 723–746; cf. Beiser, *The German Historicist Tradition*, 163–165.

sought and achieved everywhere. As cultural and moral beings, Herder argued, humans were everywhere pursuing both self-preservation and self-constitution, in accordance with what was possible for them in their 'time and place'.[121] Yet they were not fully tied to any of the traditions they created. Particularly the Greeks and Romans were shining examples that it was possible to 'shake off the yoke of ancient forms of government and traditions' in pursuing the best form of *Humanität* possible.[122] In this respect they provided inspiration for modern times, encouraging moderns to pursue ever 'purer and nobler' forms of *Humanität*.[123] Times had moved on, creating much more favourable conditions for such a pursuit. Just like the laws of attraction and repulsion that produced order out of chaos in nature, Herder argued, so were human societies moving towards a greater degree of order both within *and* between themselves. Even if humans' destructive powers would never entirely disappear, they 'must not only yield in the course of times to preserving powers, but must ultimately serve the formation [*Ausbildung*] of the whole'.[124] The number of destructive demons in history was decreasing, both at the individual and state level, which made it possible collectively to defeat them. Likewise, the perfection of the arts and sciences (inventions) enabled humans increasingly to master unruly natural elements like fire and oceans, while even the wildest human activities like war had been transformed into ordered and systematic practices.[125]

Herder also attempted to justify this vision by describing it in terms of a mathematical theory of nature according to which a certain maximum or minimum of some characteristic was necessary for all natural objects to achieve a harmony or equilibrium of their internal powers in order to sustain themselves. Human societies, too, were striving for the highest possible harmony of various kinds of 'cooperative powers', anchored in a certain maximum that best sustains this society (e.g. the political morality of the Chinese or the 'maximum of sensual beauty both in arts and manners, in science and in political institutions in Greece').[126] Next to these maxima, however, there could be significant shortcomings in other respects, e.g. in the form of government of a society. The happiness of society, Herder argued, depended only on the 'most perfect bond of union' of forces achieved in it.[127] As soon as societies internally went out of balance, mainly due to the passions of powerful individuals, they were bound to oscillate from one extreme to the other, which destroyed

---

[121] Herder, *Outlines*, 438–442; *Ideen*, 580–585.   [122] Herder, *Outlines*, 441; *Ideen*, 583.
[123] Herder, *Outlines*, 441; *Ideen*, 583.   [124] Herder, *Outlines*, 443; *Ideen*, 585.
[125] Herder, *Outlines*, 447–450; *Ideen*, 591–595.
[126] Herder, *Outlines*, 451–452; *Ideen*, 597.
[127] Herder, *Outlines*, 453; *Ideen*, 599; cf. idem, *Outlines*, 451; *Ideen*, 597.

the overall balance between them, too: 'Thus Rome had disturbed the peace of the Globe for more than a thousand years; and half a World of savage nations was requisite for a slow restoration of its quiet'.[128] The historical process, Herder emphasised, could by no means be expected to resemble the 'peaceable progress of an asymptote', but rather the course of a pendulum striking from one extreme to another, finally achieving a state of balance.[129]

Making this argument, Herder qualified his earlier scathing critique of enlightened narratives celebrating the refinement and mildness of modern manners and the growth of knowledge in the modern period,[130] now praising 'the growth of reason' in human history, as assisted by humans' aesthetic, compassionate as well as 'calculating' judgement of history:

The more reason increases among men, the more will one learn from early youth to understand that... it is more laudable... to form, than to ravage a nation, to establish, rather than destroy cities. Industrious Egyptians, ingenuous Greeks and commercial Phoenicians not only come across as more beautiful, but they also enjoyed a much more pleasant and useful life than the destructive Persians, conquering Romans and stingy [*geizige*] Carthagineans.[131]

At the present level of culture, Herder argued, it was possible to see that nations had achieved longevity and brilliance in human history by pursuing pacific industry and internal harmony, while dire consequences necessarily followed from the destruction of balance and order within or between societies.[132] It was in this context, too, that Herder discussed commerce. European commerce was in every respect incomparably larger than that of earlier nations,[133] and although still widely believed to be 'the greatest self-interest [grösseste Eigennutz]', it was in reality a major vehicle of communication, exchange and interaction between nations.[134] Here Herder was probably drawing on the abbé de Raynal's highly critical, but not entirely pessimistic analysis

---

128 Herder, *Outlines*, 456; *Ideen*, 603.
129 Herder, *Outlines*, 456; *Ideen*, 603; cf. *Outlines*, 451; *Ideen*, 596.
130 In *This Too a Philosophy*, Herder had rejected the idea that modern civilisation and enlightenment constituted true moral progress, underlining the fundamentally unsociable foundations of various forms of civil behaviour and hence the ambivalent impact of increasingly abstract human thinking on moral sentiments. Developing some of Adam Ferguson's insights, Herder had highlighted the connections between increasing pacification of humanity, on the one hand, and modern despotism and imperialism, on the other, see my 'Sociability, Nationalism and Cosmopolitanism'.
131 Herder, *Outlines*, 445; *Ideen*, 589; cf. *Outlines*, 454; *Ideen*, 601.
132 Herder, *Outlines*, 445–446; *Ideen*, 589; cf., *Outlines*, 441–442, 462–467; *Ideen*, 584–585, 612–619.
133 Herder, *Outlines*, 459; *Ideen*, 607.
134 Herder, *Outlines*, 446; *Ideen*, 590. The translation of the phrase is mine here.

of modern commercial politics: in his *History of the Two Indies*, Raynal had laid bare the causes of the decline of various formerly successful modern commercial polities, while continuing to emphasise the beneficial nature of commerce rightly pursued.[135] 'Every commercial nation [handelnde Nation] in Europe', Herder argued in the same vein, 'is now bitterly lamenting, and will do so even more in the future, what they formerly destroyed out of superstition or jealousy'. Subscribing to the widespread contemporary critique of overseas' trading companies and maritime commercial powers, Herder voiced a more positive hope that these policies would soon to be abandoned because of their ultimately self-defeating consequences, thus 'conquering seafaring' giving way to 'commercial' one, one 'based on reciprocal justice [*Gerechtigkeit*] and leniency [*Schonung*], on a progressive emulation to excel in arts and industry, in short, on humanity and its eternal laws'.[136]

Even in terms of the principles of war and politics in modern times, Herder believed it possible to determine that a certain new 'level of culture' had been reached in Europe over time. Nations had been brought closer to each other, even if through the destructive power of war at first. Since Romans, Herder argued, no civilised [*cultivierte*] European nation had built its entire organisation [*Einrichtung*] on wars and conquests, and the rude German settlers also gradually learnt to value 'arts-based industry [*Kunstfleiss*], farming [*Landbau*], commerce and sciences'.[137] Now echoing ideas developed in David Hume's, William Robertson's and Isaak Iselin's enlightened narratives, Herder argued that the 'growing true enlightenment' [*wachsende wahre Aufklärung*] was even reflected in the increasing 'reasonableness' [*Vernunft*] and 'mildening' [*Milderung*] of the art of war and politics.[138]

---

[135] On Raynal's analysis of modern commercial politics, see Iain McDaniel, 'Enlightened History and the Decline of Nations: Ferguson, Raynal, and the Contested Legacies of the Dutch Republic', *History of European Ideas* 36:2, 203–216 (211–215). Herder's early engagement with Raynal is pointed out by Wolfgang Proß, 'Anmerkungen [Auch eine Philosophie der Geschichte]', in *Herder: Werke, vol. 1: Herder und der Sturm und Drang 1764–1774*, ed. Proß (Munich, Vienna, 1984), 850 and 862–863; cf. Dreitzel, 'Herders politische Konzepte', 276–277.

[136] Herder, *Outlines*, 446; *Ideen*, 590. I have modified the translation. I am grateful to Wolfgang Proß for suggesting this translation to me.

[137] Herder, *Outlines*, 446; *Ideen*, 590.

[138] Herder, *Outlines*, 448–450; *Ideen*, 592–595. Herder's debts to Hume in his 1775, 1778 and 1780 contributions to essay contests is emphasised by Alexander Schmidt, 'Scholarship, Morals and Government: Jean-Henri-Samuel Formey's and Johann Gottfried Herder's Responses to Rousseau's *First Discourse*', *Modern Intellectual History* 9 (2012), pp. 249–274 (265–268); for the importance of Hume's *Essays* for early Herder, see my 'Philosophy, Sociability and Modern Patriotism: Young Herder between Rousseau and Abbt', *History of European Ideas* 41:5, 640–661.

Herder thereby aligned himself with the theories he had earlier criticised and mocked in *This Too a Philosophy*, while continuing to argue
that a greater degree of reasonableness and order in society did not mean
greater happiness or virtue for individuals. His main theoretical target
of criticism in the *Ideas*, however, continued to be Kant's distinctive
version of Europe's history. Not the gradual improvement of political
constitutions and the growing chances for men to enlighten themselves,
but the 'natural laws of history' fostered hopes for a more harmonious
international order. While for Kant human 'natural instincts' had
so far continued to rebel against the demands of morality, and only
a 'crude disposition to morality' was activated through civilisation,
Herder sketched an optimistic vision of a broader learning process
well under way in European history. This learning process in his view
made it possible to hope for a 'natural' non-political solution to the
problem of war. As we shall see in the next subsection, however, Herder
at the same time continued to insist that this solution involved the
transformation or indeed, dismantling of modern state-machines from
within.

Although the fourth instalment of Herder's *Ideas* was published in 1791,
its manuscript was finished already by 1788 and hence preceded the
French Revolution.[139] Also, since it concluded with the period of the
Reformation and Renaissance, it did not directly address contemporary
politics; in consequence, Herder's original views on modern developments can only be distilled from his sketch of the overall plan of the
work.[140] Nevertheless, since in Herder's analysis the period of *Völker-
wanderungen* and the era of Germanic conquest had laid the foundations
for subsequent developments, it provided important information about
Herder's views on the trajectory of Europe's history and its future
prospects.[141] Here, Herder was particularly interested in the contingent
intersections between various chains of events and tendencies. Quite
expectedly, political developments played a rather ambivalent, and certainly not a central role, in his narrative of the formation of the European
common spirit, while he singled out Europe's distinctive geography and
climate, the impact of the common religion of Christianity, the cultivation of the arts and sciences, and above all, freedom and commerce
in cities as the key factors in this process. In what follows I will briefly

---

[139] Proß, 'Nachwort', 1012.
[140] Proß, 'Anhang zum *Nachwort*', 1157f. On this plan, see below.
[141] For Herder, in Europe now constituted a new centre of humanity's development, taking over from the ancient states, which ended in a *stasis* (China) or downfall (Egypt,
Rome, etc.), Proß, 'Nachwort', 1013.

highlight his view of the contribution of commerce to Europe's common spirit in particular.

For Herder, the foundations for the emergence of the distinctive culture and spirit of the 'European republic' were laid by the fusion of the 'ancient' Mediterranean civilisation and the northern 'barbarian' cultures, which in turn had been made possible by Europe's distinctive geography.[142] In Herder's vision there was a continuous 'descending plane' from the 'vast, elevated region, Asiatic Tartary' westwards towards the sea, which explained Europe being exposed to the 'pressure' and influx of various kinds of northern-eastern peoples.[143] Internally, however, Europe possessed a particularly rugged terrain and intersected geographical space, with various rivers, lakes, seas, coastlands, which contributed simultaneously to national diversity, on the one hand, and communication and commerce between various regions and peoples within Europe, on the other, while also connecting Europe to the world. All of this, Herder argued, led to highly distinctive processes of ethnogenesis in Europe, so that instead of 'strong national characters' characteristic of ancient nations, the emerging European nations developed 'milder' forms of national identities, which enabled the rise of a 'European common spirit'.[144] Through appropriation of the remnants of the Mediterranean ancient civilisation, and the new universalistic religion of Christianity, Europe hence had unique chances for developing a new kind of international ethic.

The realisation of this potential, however, was hampered by two distinct types of developments: first, the continuing relevance of the Roman imperial structures and law for the development of the ecclesiastical hierarchy, and second, the transformation of the original Germanic system of government based on common property and freedom into a 'Tartarian imperial constitution' in the large post-Roman 'cultivated' or 'miscultivated' space.[145] These developments brought along what Herder called the 'phantom monarchies' of the spiritual

---

[142] Europe's geographical space and climate, Herder argued, were determined by a 'huge mound of rocks, known by the names of Mustag, Altai, Kitzigtag, Ural, Caucasus, Taurus, Haemus, and farther on by the Carpathian mountains, the gigantic Alps and the Pyrenees'. The climate in Europe was milder than at the other side of Ural and Altai, yet nevertheless there was a distinctive continuity between Northern Europe and 'Tartary', explaining the Germanic nations' and 'Tartarians' rather similar 'vandal-gothic-scythian-tartarian way of life' in the early period (one distinct from other, less adventurous nations such as Slavs or Fennic peoples which hence also easily fell prey to the former). Herder, *Outlines*, 468; 479–480; 481–484; 487 (I have modified the translation); *Ideen*, 623; 637–638; 640–643; 647–648.

[143] Herder, *Outlines*, 479–480; *Ideen*, 637–638.

[144] Herder, *Outlines*, 488 (I have modified the translation); *Ideen*, 649.

[145] See the previous section of this chapter.

and lay kind, or as he also put it, a 'double barbarism' of the Germanic kings and knights, on the one hand, and of Roman popes and priests, on the other.[146] Modern monarchies, as we saw in the previous section, originated in this system of government and had preserved its core element: the 'artificial' and 'outward-projected' (i.e. aggressive) structure which was not in any way suited for energising the common people. Likewise, the popish government in no way managed to fulfil the universalistic and impartial role it should have assumed as a spiritual authority.

We saw above that Herder had deemed the transferral of the original Germanic constitution to the vast conquered territories in southern Europe to have been a disaster.[147] Nevertheless, he maintained that thanks to the specific balance of power that had emerged between the lay and spiritual phantom-monarchies, Europe could avoid the two extremes of rude despotism and an ecclesiastical state.[148] Furthermore, in the long run, this fortunate balance of powers enabled the rise of cities as havens of industry and commerce, bringing along 'a third estate' [*den dritten Stand*], the one of 'science, of useful activity, of emulative industry in the arts', which alone could be the 'life-blood of this great active body' of Europe.[149] Herder believed that cities constituted the specific context in which the principles of Germanic constitution had been applied and developed with success.[150] European cities, he argued, were essentially 'aristocratic-democratic bodies, the members of which watched over each other, were often mutual enemies and opponents, and on this very account unavoidably promoted common security, emulative industry and common exertion'.[151] It was in cities that the nobles as well as commoners enjoyed the first title of common liberty, citizenship [*Bürgerrechts*].[152] Furthermore, emerging luxury awakened industry, and encouraged not only trade and the establishment of manufactures, but also agriculture in the surrounding countryside.[153]

Like William Robertson and Adam Smith, Herder emphasised the pivotal role of the southern European towns in preserving and developing the Roman arts and trade following the German conquest, and undermining the power of the nobility through emerging luxury, yet ultimately also degenerating into tyranny or falling prey to conquest because of

---

[146] Herder, *Outlines*, 560; *Ideen*, 740.   [147] Herder, *Outlines*, 561; *Ideen*, 742.
[148] Herder, *Outlines*, 631–632; *Ideen*, 830.   [149] Herder, *Outlines*, 632; *Ideen*, 830.
[150] Herder, *Outlines*, 561; *Ideen*, 742.
[151] Herder, *Outlines*, 627–628; *Ideen*, 824–825.
[152] Herder, *Outlines*, 627; *Ideen*, 824–825.   [153] Herder, *Outlines*, 604; *Ideen*, 795.

it.[154] In this context, Herder saw the development of the chivalric spirit in European monarchies as a welcome countervailing development,[155] while squarely rejecting William Robertson's view that crusades had unintentionally contributed to freedom in cities and to the liberation of serfs in the countryside.[156] Herder did not deny that crusades had led to the widening of horizons and cultural contacts, but deemed their over-all impact to have been highly negative. It was crusades in particular that had contributed to increased rivalry among European princes, had nour-ished the taste for luxuries both among rulers and their subjects and had even led to a reckless aggressive competition for any kinds of resources at the global level.[157]

A different process unfolded, however, in Northern Europe. Although there, too, crusades played an important role in leading to the German conquest and colonisation of the North-Eastern regions, there had also emerged a distinctive commercial culture in the cities of this region. Like their southern counterparts, Northern cities contributed to the rise of industry, the rule of law and security of property. By uniting in the Hanseatic League they had furthermore established a 'true com-mercial state based on genuine principles of mutual aid and security', which as such served as a 'model of the future situation for all trading European peoples [*Völker*]', exemplifying the principles that Europe as a common system [*Gemeinwesen*] was truly based on.[158] Going beyond all national and religious differences, the Hanseatic cities had 'grounded a union of states in mutual utility, emulating industry, honesty, and order'.[159]

---

[154] Herder, *Outlines*, 604–605; *Ideen*, 795–796; cf. Istvan Hont's brilliant reconstruction of Smith's ideas (which, as Hont suggests, were in turn were borrowed and popu-larised by Robertson), 'Adam Smith and the Political Economy of the "Unnatural and Retrograde" Order', in idem, *Jealousy of Trade*, 354–388.

[155] Herder, *Outlines*, 605; *Ideen*, 796.

[156] On the central importance of this idea in Robertson's narrative, see J. G. A. Pocock, *Barbarism and Religion, vol 2: Narratives of Civil Government* (Cambridge, 1999), 281.

[157] '... on this holy theatre Europeans got better acquainted with each other, though not in a manner much to be praised. With this more intimate acquaintance kings and princes for the most part brought home an implacable enmity: in particular the wars between France and England derived from it fresh fuel. The unfortunate experiment that a Christian republic could and might contend in unison against infidels, formed a precedent for similar wars in Europe, which have since extended to other parts of the globe. [—] Everyone was desirous of wealth, trade, conveniences, and luxuries; as an uncultivated mind is prone, to admire these in strangers, and envy them in the hands of another', Herder, *Outlines*, 619; *Ideen*, 814.

[158] Herder, *Outlines*, 600; *Ideen*, 790.

[159] Herder, *Outlines*, 623 (I have modified the translation); *Ideen*, 825.

The development of modern European trade and the concomitant rise of the European 'third estate' were to serve as the central themes of the final, fifth instalment of the *Ideas*. Herder intended an entire book in this volume to focus on the relationship of the arts, letters and sciences to the idea of the balance of power and law of nations, while the following book was to discuss the relationship of the general spirit of industry and trade to money, luxury and taxes concomitant with it. As a sequel to this, a book focusing on Europe's different 'others' was planned, starting with Russia, and finishing with a general European 'colonial system'.[160] The concluding book, finally, was supposed to show the growth of *Humanität* 'at the individual level, in respect of religion', as well as in respect of 'state constitutions, trade, arts, sciences'.[161]

Since this final volume never materialised, we cannot lay out in any detail what Herder's view of the development of European politics might have been. There are, however, a few hints concerning his likely thoughts. Despite his growing optimism about the progress of *Humanität* in Europe, it was clear that Herder did not think that European monarchies would be able to sustain themselves for long. Furthermore, it was precisely commerce that he saw as undermining the existing 'state-machines', despite the arts of war and government becoming more 'mild'. Curiously, it has not been noticed that in predicting the 'awakening' of the Slavic nations and the eventual collapse of Europe's empires, Herder emphasised the emancipatory potential of trade and international commerce more broadly:

The wheel of changing time would continue to revolve, and as these nations inhabit for the most part the finest region of Europe, if it were completely cultivated and its trade opened; while it cannot be supposed, but that legislation and politics in Europe, instead of a military spirit, must and will more and more promote quiet industry, and peaceful commerce [ruhige Verkehr] between different peoples [Völker], these now deeply sunk, but once industrious and happy people, will awake from their deep and long slumber, will be freed from their chains of slavery and will use their beautiful areas from Adriatic sea to Carpathian mountains, from Don to Muldaw as their property and can celebrate on them their old festivals of peaceful industry and trade.[162]

Any more specific guidance as to how this might happen, whether it would involve violence, maybe even wars, and what kind of future form of government these peoples should establish on their newly-liberated historical territories, Herder did not give in the *Ideas*; just as he did not

[160] Herder, *Ideen*, 1157.   [161] Herder, *Ideen*, 1158.
[162] Herder, *Outlines*, 483–484 (I have slightly modified the translation); *Ideen*, 643.

specify what their relationship to the descendants of their former conquerors was to look like. It remained a suggestive hint only.[163] Instead of moving on to discussing modern politics in the final volume of the *Ideas*, Herder began to work on a different kind of project in the new political situation created by the French Revolution – the final title of this project came to be *Letters for the Advancement of Humanity* (1793–1797).

This chapter has reconstructed Herder's response and alternative to Kant's philosophical history of human culture and political government, as developed in the latter's *Idea* and reviews of Herder's first two instalments of the *Ideas*. Herder passionately disagreed with Kant about modern territorial states as the hitherto most favourable environment for the development of human culture, and by implication, morality and rejected Kant's proposed solution to the problem of war in international relations (a strong federation of states with coercive powers). Instead, Herder offered alternative naturalistic explanations for the development of culture and morality, on the one hand, and for the rise of individual, social and international antagonism, on the other. Herder also accordingly rejected Kant's central focus on the history of political government in discussing the prospects for peace in Europe. He emphasised the uniqueness of each distinct national culture, exploring the interplay of different genetic and environmental factors in the formation of these cultures and the corresponding divergent ways of realising the universal ideal of *Humanität*. Nevertheless, he did embrace a highly sympathetic view of the Athenian civic enlightenment, focusing on how *humans could govern humans*, and shared Kant's commitment to international peace, voicing hopes that Europeans would soon attempt to reform their traditions of political government.

In contrast to Kant, Herder did not identify the origins of the flourishing of European commerce in early modern monarchs' economic policies, but in Europe's distinctive political and geographic situation. Herder's key argument about European history in the *Ideas* was twofold: first, he located the origins and foundations of modern European 'state-machines' in a distinctive type of political government developing after the Germanic conquest of Roman territories and in the Carolingian period specifically; second, he emphasised the much more long-term

[163] It was of course widely picked up by Herder's nineteenth-century Slavic readers in Habsburg empire, on this reception, see Peter Drews, *Herder und die Slaven: Materialien zur Wirkungsgeschichte bis zur Mitte des 19. Jahrhunderts* (Munich, Sagner, 1990) and Holm Sundhaussen, *Der Einfluß der Herderschen Ideen auf die Nationsbildung bei den Völkern der Habsburger Monarchie* (Munich: Oldenburg, 1973).

development of commerce in Europe in pre-Germanic times already. Combining various themes from Hume's comparisons of ancient and modern politics in his *Essays*, and Hume's, Robertson's and Smith's 'enlightened narratives' of Europe's history, Herder claimed that the interplay between civil and clerical authorities in the post-Carolingian period enabled the relatively autonomous growth of cities, which in turn had established the rule of law and security of property in their territories, hence becoming havens of industry, commerce and even mutual aid and security. Particularly the Hanseatic League, developing in Northern Europe, served as a great example for Herder in the latter respect, and in his view could and ought to be emulated by all modern trading nations in Europe.

Both these sets of arguments constituted a significant revision of Herder's position in *This Too a Philosophy* published in 1774. In the latter, Herder's main emphasis was the development of the human mind and division of labour in society, while modern commerce for him was primarily a sign and vehicle of the rising social fragmentation and egoism in European states, which in turn supported a specific kind of despotic government and imperialism. In the *Ideas*, he remained critical of the morals of modern large societies, yet was now highly sympathetic towards various trading nations in human history, emphasising the role of commerce in supporting invention, industriousness and international communication. In Europe, too, commerce had substantially contributed to the rise of a certain 'general spirit of Europe'. Although Herder continued to be highly critical of modern 'state-machines' and the new type of competitive and monopolistic trade that had emerged in the post-Renaissance period, he now put forward a theory of the natural laws of history that enabled him to express confidence in humanity's providentially guaranteed ability to restore the natural tendency of commerce to promote harmony among nations in the long run.

Herder also made an original point in arguing that an increasing understanding of the true 'art of government' and growing international trade would gradually empower the colonised and subdued peoples in Europe. This, he proposed, would ultimately undermine and dismantle the existing multinational state-machines, possibly leading to a far-going restructuring of the whole political landscape in Europe. This was Herder's cursory, yet highly suggestive hint in the *Ideas*. In an early draft of what became *Letters for the Advancement of Humanity*, written in a very different context, Herder further broadened his theory of Europe's positive future prospects by voicing hopes about the possible overcoming of the barbarian foundations of European politics both in Europe's internal as well as external relations.[164] These were cautious hopes, and Herder continued denying the possibility of finding a final solution to the problem of war. As opposed to the *Ideas*, however, his main concern in the (post-)French revolutionary period was not 'wretched ice-cold, slavish enthusiasm', but a warmer kind of 'dazzling phantom... [which] blinds with the names of "freedom", "enlightenment", "highest happiness of peoples"'.[165] Once again, however, one of his main theoretical adversaries turned out to be his former academic mentor – Immanuel Kant. This is a theme for another chapter.

---

[164] Herder, 'Letters concerning the Progress of Humanity (1792) [excerpts on European politics]', in *J. G. von Herder: Philosophical Writings*, 361–369 (361–365).

[165] Herder, 'Letters for the Advancement of Humanity (1793–1797) – Tenth Collection', in *J. G. von Herder: Philosophical Writings*, 380–424 (413).

7   Peace, commerce and cosmopolitan
      republicanism
      The legacy of Andrew Fletcher in
      late-eighteenth-century Scotland

      Iain McDaniel

                          I

In his wide-ranging introduction to *Jealousy of Trade* (2005), Istvan Hont
described the political thought of Andrew Fletcher of Saltoun (1655–
1716) as an example of what he termed "cosmopolitan republicanism."
In Hont's reconstruction, Fletcher's republicanism was distinguished
by a concern for maintaining peace in Europe by creating republics of
small extent, linked in an intricate system of federal unions modelled on
the ancient Achaean League. As Hont summarised Fletcher's position:
"Only popular governments, that is, republics, could be peaceful, thanks
to their unique ability to reconcile their national interest with the interest
of mankind."[1] Fletcher's advocacy of a federal union and a civic militia
was, from this perspective, not purely a product of his patriotic opposition to English reason of state and the damage to Scotland's flourishing
that an incorporating union with England – as occurred in 1707 – would
entail.[2] More generally, it was an aspect of a more far-reaching cosmopolitan perspective on international relations that viewed the establishment of republican constitutions across Europe as a mechanism for
neutralising jealousy of trade, mitigating "universal wars," and bringing

---

[1] Istvan Hont, *Jealousy of Trade: International Competition and the Nation-State in Historical
Perspective* (Cambridge, MA, 2005), 64–66. Fletcher apparently followed Harrington's
Oceana, with its suggestion that "the interest of popular government, comes, the nearest
unto the interest of mankind"; see James Harrington, *The Commonwealth of Oceana and
A System of Politics*, ed. and trans. J. G. A. Pocock (Cambridge, 1992), 22. Fletcher also
featured extensively in Hont's 1990 essay on Neo-Machiavellian political economy; see
Hont, "Free Trade and the Economic Limits to National Politics: Neo-Machiavellian
Political Economy Reconsidered," in Hont, *Jealousy of Trade*, 258–66.
[2] On Fletcher's contribution to the debates surrounding the Union, see especially John
Robertson, "An elusive sovereignty. The course of the Union debate in Scotland 1698–
1707," in Robertson, ed., *A Union for Empire: political thought and the British Union of
1707* (Cambridge, 1995), 198–227.

the interest of distinct communities back into alignment with the interest of mankind.[3] It was also a way of thinking about the properties of
republics that distinguished Fletcher's thought from that of Machiavelli,
who had firmly linked the *grandezza* of republics to their capacity for
expansion.

Although Fletcher's own political thought has been the subject of some
incisive scholarship, the reception of his ideas among subsequent generations of Scots has been studied less fully. This omission is partly
explained by the widespread assumption that Fletcher's unusual blend
of patriotic, civic republican and cosmopolitan commitments had little impact on the subsequent Scottish Enlightenment, whose major
representatives adopted a thoroughly "Anglo-British" perspective on
the Union and offered a more confident assessment of the stability of
Europe's civilized monarchies.[4] Yet there was a significant revival of
what might be termed the Fletcherian perspective upon peace, empire,
Britain and Europe among a younger generation of eighteenth-century
Scots. After Britain's defeat in the War of American Independence,
several Scottish thinkers devoted sustained attention to reconceptual-
ising Britain's future as a post-imperial power which, properly reformed,
would contribute towards the creation of a more stable and more pacific
international order. Convinced that Britain's pursuit of commercial
hegemony since 1688 had been a principal obstacle to international
peace, these writers argued that Britain now needed to abandon its
"jealousy of trade," renounce the pursuit of empire and instead achieve
a more balanced economy, a more stable political system and a more
pacific foreign policy.[5] It was in this context that a number of Scottish Whigs and radicals sought to revive the cosmopolitan perspective
on republican government and international relations that had characterised Fletcher's *Account of a Conversation of the Right Regulation of Governments for the Common Good of Mankind* (1704) and some of his other
writings, an effort most visible in the various biographies and editions of

---

[3] For these passages, see Andrew Fletcher, "An Account of a Conversation Concerning a Right Regulation of Governments for the common Good of Mankind" [1704],
in Fletcher, *Political Works*, ed. John Robertson (Cambridge, 1997), 193, 201–2, 206.

[4] See especially Colin Kidd, *Subverting Scotland's Past: Scottish Whig Historians and the
Creation of an Anglo-British Identity 1689–1830* (Cambridge, 1994); J. G. A. Pocock,
Barbarism and Religion: Volume II. Narratives of Civil Government (Cambridge, 2002).

[5] In identifying Britain as the principal obstacle to international stability, these Scottish
writers echoed French and other continental European critics of the destructive effects
of Britain's eighteenth-century pursuit of commercial empire. For a French perspective,
see Richard Whatmore, "War, trade, and empire: the dilemmas of French liberal political
economy, 1780–1816" in Helena Rosenblatt and Raf Geenens, eds. *French Liberalism
from Montesquieu to the present day* (Cambridge, 2012), 169–91.

Fletcher's writings that appeared in the 1790s.[6] More generally, several thinkers adopted Fletcherian ideas about republican institutions, federal unions and peaceful commerce as resources for mapping out an alternative, morally-grounded trajectory for Britain after almost a century of debt-fuelled wars for commerce and empire.[7]

The wider purpose of this chapter is to reconstruct several Scottish perspectives upon the larger eighteenth-century debate about republican government and international peace, a topic most often associated with Immanuel Kant's famous 1795 sketch on "Perpetual Peace."[8] Most of the writers examined here shared a number of key presuppositions about the connection between republican constitutions and the establishment of a more peaceful international order. Some of these, such as a commitment to civic militias as vehicles of international peace, or to the establishment of a more equal system of property and representation, looked back to the central ideas of the British commonwealthman tradition. These writers also shared a critical perspective on the history of Great Britain since the Glorious Revolution, which they, in contrast with Enlightenment historians like William Robertson, saw as an incomplete settlement, which had forged a dangerously unstable and expansionist polity. Some shared Fletcher's interest in utilising federal institutions as a means of neutralising military expansion, while others set out a conjectural vision of Europe's future as a pacific republic of small states engaged in the peaceful exchange of economic surpluses. This cosmopolitan perspective upon republican institutions and commerce stands in sharp contrast with a better-known preoccupation among eighteenth-century Britons with reconciling liberty with empire.[9]

---

[6] These include David Stewart Erskine, Earl of Buchan, *Essays on the Lives and Writings of Fletcher of Saltoun and the Poet Thomson* (London, 1792), and Andrew Fletcher, *The Political Works of Fletcher of Salton; with notes &c. to which is prefixed a sketch of his life, with observations, moral, philosophical and political,* ed. R. Watson (1798).

[7] Fletcher's republican ideas were sometimes utilised by those in the Scottish parliamentary reform movement of the early 1790s; see e.g. *An Illustration of the Principles of the Bill, Proposed to be Submitted to the Consideration of Parliament* (Edinburgh, 1787); *The Address of the British Convention, Assembled at Edinburgh, November 19, 1793, to the People of Great Britain* (Sheffield, 1794), 14, which cited the "neo-Roman" suggestion that "Not only is that Government tyrannical which is tyrannically exercised, but all Governments are tyrannical which have not, in their Constitution, a sufficient security against the arbitrary power of the Prince."

[8] For useful assessments of Kant's understanding of republicanism and peace, see Pauline Kleingeld, *Kant and Cosmopolitanism: The Philosophical Ideal of World Citizenship* (Cambridge, 2013), Ottfried Höffe, *Kant's Cosmopolitan Theory of Law and Peace,* trans. Alexandra Newton (Cambridge, 2006), 177–88.

[9] On this, see especially David Armitage, "Empire and Liberty: A Republican Dilemma," in Quentin Skinner and Martin van Gelderen, eds., *Republicanism: A Shared European Heritage* (Cambridge, 2002), 2:29–46.

But it should also be noted that the participants in this Scottish debate drew upon a range of intellectual resources from beyond the British commonwealthman tradition. Some echoed an alternative tradition of monarchical pacifism that had roots in Archbishop Fénelon's *Telemachus* (1699) and was revived periodically by Tory and Jacobite writers in eighteenth-century Britain.[10] Another, more recent, reference point was the discussion of war, empire and mercantile jealousy set out in Smith's *Wealth of Nations* (1776). Smith's book was deemed particularly relevant to discussions of international peace after 1776 because of its emphasis on eradicating mercantile jealousy ("the most fertile source of discord and animosity") through the implementation of free trade among European states.[11] One of the themes in what follows is the effort to construct a more cosmopolitan, morally-guided political economy in which Smith's ideas about fostering peace through the promotion of domestic prosperity and free trade were combined with republican ideals about constitutional reform and the rebalancing of civil-military relations.

II

Although reflection upon the dangers posed by Britain to international stability by no means began in the 1780s, the period following the American War of Independence witnessed renewed speculation about the possibility of correcting Britain's tendency towards war, debt and empire. Some of these concerns can already be detected in Smith's comments during the war about the dangers of a British victory and his emphasis on the "real futility of distant dominions."[12] Major British thinkers writing after the war, ranging from Richard Price to Josiah Tucker, followed Smith's lead in advocating the construction of a more balanced and less bellicose polity. This intersected with the continuing debate about Britain's relationship with Ireland and the consequences of legislative independence in 1782, a debate which drew on Smith's ideas about legislative union and free trade, but which also raised the legacy

---

[10] On Fénelon's legacy in eighteenth-century Britain and Europe, see Christoph Schmitt-Maaß, Stephanie Stockhurst and Doohwan Ahn, *Fénelon in the Enlightenment: Traditions, Adaptations, and Variations* (Amsterdam, 2014).

[11] Adam Smith, *An Inquiry into the Nature and Causes of the Wealth of Nations*, ed. R. H. Campbell and A. S. Skinner, 2 vols. (Oxford, 1976), IV.iii.c.9. For the way in which Smith's ideas were developed by the Shelburne circle in this period, see Richard Whatmore, *Against War and Empire: Geneva, Britain and France in the Eighteenth Century* (New Haven, CT. 2012), 177–205.

[12] See Smith's "Thoughts on the State of the Contest with America" (February 1778), and Adam Smith to Sir John Sinclair, 14 Oct 1782, both in Adam Smith, *The Correspondence of Adam Smith*, ed. Ernest Campbell Mossner (Oxford, 1987), 380–85; 262.

of the Anglo-Scottish union and its consequences.[13] The idea of neutralising commercial animosity between Britain and Ireland was related to wider projects for the establishment of international peace in the first half of the 1780s, most visibly in Lord Shelburne's promotion of pacific free trade between Britain and France.[14] The middle years of the 1780s seemed, in short, an auspicious moment for the construction of a more modern, pacific polity in Britain.

An interesting Scottish contribution to these discussions was John Knox's *A View of the British Empire*, a work first published in 1784. Although Knox is best remembered today as a Highland improver, he actually advocated a more comprehensive overhaul of Britain's political and military institutions as a way of correcting jealousy of trade and expansion, and hence serving the cause of international peace. As he noted, the most urgent task facing British statesmen in 1783 was to "allay the jealousies, dissipate the resentments, and secure the friendship of an offended world."[15] He claimed that Britain's true interests had been "sacrificed to expensive schemes of conquest and empire," and praised both William Eden and Josiah Tucker for recognising the damage done by territorial annexations.[16] The purpose of the book was thus to propose an alternative to the "old delusive system of politics" that had characterised Britain's eighteenth-century history. Knox made two main suggestions as to how this could be achieved. The first was the eradication of public credit, which he described as the most effectual invention "for the destruction of the human species."[17] The second was the expansion of internal trade between England and Scotland, coupled with policies designed to revive Scottish agriculture, fishing and industry. The purpose of promoting internal trade was not simply to foster

---

[13] The best guide to the debates about British-Irish relations in the period is James Kelly, *Prelude to Union: Anglo-Irish Politics in the 1780s* (Cork, 1992); on Smith's and Tucker's influence on Pitt's 1785 Commercial Propositions see also Bernard Semmel, *The Rise of Free Trade Imperialism: Classical Political Economy, the Empire of Free Trade and Imperialism 1750–1850* (Cambridge, 1970), 30–38. For the "vaguely felt sympathy" among reformist Scots for Irish legislative independence, see Nicholas Phillipson, "Scottish Public Opinion and the Union in the Age of the Association," in N. T. Phillipson and Rosalind Mitchison, eds., *Scotland in the Age of Improvement: Essays in Scottish History in the Eighteenth Century*, 2nd ed. (Edinburgh, 1996), 125–47.

[14] Whatmore, *Against War and Empire*, 177–205.

[15] John Knox, *A View of the British Empire, more especially Scotland; with some Proposals for the Improvement of that Country, the extension of its fisheries, and the relief of its people* (London, 1784), xxxviii.

[16] Knox, *View of the British Empire*, xxx–xxxi. Knox later (p. lxvii) quoted Tucker's criticisms of war, colonies and conquests more fully; the reference is to Josiah Tucker, *The Case of Going to War, for the sake of procuring, enlarging, or securing of trade* (London, 1763), 31.

[17] Knox, A *View of the British Empire*, iv–vii.

Scotland's economic prosperity, but also to counterbalance the British state's tendency to launch wars for commercial advantage. One of the subtexts here – made explicit in the "Preliminary Discourse" to the third (1785) edition of the work – was Knox's scepticism towards the alleged economic benefits accruing to Scotland from the Union of 1707. Although Knox praised the Union's political effects – it "secured the constitution, religion, and laws on the most permanent foundation" – he rejected the widespread assumption that Union had worked in Scotland's economic favour.[18] Echoing Fletcher's prediction that incorporating union would subordinate Scotland's economy to the interests of the metropole, Knox devoted much of his "Preliminary Discourse" to explaining how Scotland's eighteenth-century economy had suffered as a consequence of its entanglement with English state interest.[19] His cosmopolitan politics thus centred on the problem of eradicating England's traditional "phrensy of conquest," and focusing instead on the maintenance of peace, the fostering of domestic trade and the establishment of non-competitive commerce with neighbouring states.

A more extensive, but surprisingly rarely studied, Scottish analysis of the connections between constitutional reform and international peace appeared in George Stuart's *Reflections, Moral and Political*, a two-volume work published anonymously in 1787. Stuart, who was Professor of Humanity at Edinburgh University between 1741 and 1775, and the father of the better-known historian Gilbert Stuart, proposed a comprehensive reconfiguration of Britain's domestic and foreign politics. The context was Britain's inevitable decline as an empire in the aftermath of American independence, political instability after the Dutch Patriot revolution of 1787 and the developing financial crisis in France, which Stuart observed keenly. According to him, England's pursuit of grandeur on an unprecedented scale had led to the creation of a disastrously overgrown territorial empire as well as to the distortion of relations between the component nations of the British composite monarchy. He drew upon Montesquieu, and probably Hume, to demonstrate that the preservation of a free state was incompatible with the attainment of empire.[20]

All the three countries [i.e. England, Scotland and Ireland] have been too deeply sacrificed to wild schemes of ambition, the fleeting pageantry of triumphs in the eastern and western hemispheres. If our unparalleled constitution so happily escaped the contagion of the riches of South America, in the rejection by Henry VII of the proffered services of Christopher Columbus; the constitutional liberty

---

[18] John Knox, *A View of the British Empire, more especially Scotland; with some proposals for the improvement of that country*, 3rd ed. (London, 1785), xxvi.
[19] Knox, *A View of the British Empire*, 3rd ed., vii–xl.
[20] [George Stuart], *Reflections, Moral and Political*, 2 vols. (London, 1787), 1:57, 124–25.

there escaped only, while the eve of national bankruptcy was reserved for us in North America.[21]

Stuart's work is interesting in drawing eclectically upon several different strands in the eighteenth-century discourse on peace. Some of his arguments borrowed from Bolingbroke's *Idea of a Patriot King* (1738), which Stuart praised as a model of popular – even democratic – but virtuous and philosophical kingship, and for its recommendation that Britain avoid expensive continental commitments (a traditional theme in Tory criticisms of Whig foreign policy).[22] Other passages echoed the cosmopolitan language of Fénelon's *Telemachus*, with its emphasis on the amity and concord of mankind. A further intellectual underpinning of Stuart's reform programme was a revised conception of "political œconomy" as a kind of moral science that provided standards of rectitude for states and kingdoms:

Political œconomy, when considered in the enlarged and completely ennobled view of things, may be ranked among the sciences. It is in respect of states, what morality is in relation to individuals, and both are intimately connected. The standard of politics, as of the fine arts, should be nature; all should be a faithful imitation of her. The same moral rectitude that ought to regulate the actions of men, should, all things equal, influence the conduct of kingdoms towards each other.[23]

The key institution necessary for bringing about this morally-guided foreign policy was to be a virtuous monarch on the model of Bolingbroke's "patriot king." In the "Moral Essay" that Stuart annexed to his first volume, he suggested that monarchs should be "fathers of their people, and crowned citizens, their authority adding to the common good."[24] There was a hint of Plato's *Republic* behind his call for a reunification of "virtue and the diadem." He later added that the king of Britain ought to emulate the virtues of a Trajan or a Vespasian.[25] Stuart believed that this sort of patriotic prince would be the key to establishing a union of morals and politics and, by extension, the pacification of the international order. Describing the international realm as a kind of potential republican federation, he argued that a virtuous prince would also lead to the replacement of jealousy of trade by peaceful commercial emulation:

---

[21] Stuart, *Reflections*, I.263.
[22] Stuart, *Reflections*, I.173, 148–49. For further emphasis on the democratic foundation of the constitution, and his Bolingbrokean distrust of "faction," see Stuart, *Reflections*, I.139, 185–86.
[23] Stuart, *Reflections*, I.1.
[24] Stuart, "Moral Essay," in *Reflections*, I.49–50 [separate pagination].
[25] Stuart, *Reflections*, I.139.

It is for want of philanthropic princes and statesmen, that political science aspires not to those sublime speculations, that might consider the world as one great republic, composed of several subdivisions, all linked together in one common federal bond of union, adopting their several salutary laws and institutions, supplying each others' wants with their respective superfluities, rivals only in industry, and the arts of peace, supplanting all distrusts and jealousies and commerce with an honest and laudable emulation, in conformity to the maxims of sound policy, the dictates of natural liberty; swords beat into plough-shares and spears into pruning-hooks. It is in the degeneracy of politics that nations adopt that selfish system, which teaches, that each can only effect its own good, in proportion to the injuries it occasions to its neighbours.[26]

The other significant aspect of Stuart's programme was the need to reconfigure the union between England, Scotland and Ireland. He saw a window of opportunity in contemporary debates about Anglo-Irish commercial and political union to argue for a revision of Scotland's position within the union. Stuart was opposing contemporary critics of federal union such as Jean-Louis Delolme, whose *British Empire in Europe* (1787) advocated ever-closer legislative union between Britain and Ireland, based on the perceived success of the Anglo-Scottish Union.[27] Stuart recognised the need for British union for resisting French aggression in Europe. But, like Fletcher, he severely criticised the incorporating union that had taken place between England and Scotland in 1707. He claimed that union had distorted Scotland's natural "œconomy," pushing it on the path to commerce and luxury before it had established natural agricultural foundations. He went on to reject a full incorporating union as the model for Anglo-Irish union after 1787. Indeed, the real basis for a revival of Britain's strength had to be a reconfigured federal union, the re-establishment of the Scottish parliament and the retention of a separate legislature in Ireland. Here Stuart joined a tiny group of Scottish authors who were interested in models of federal union as a solution to Anglo-Irish relations in the 1780s.[28] Stuart argued that the restoration of a Scottish parliament would have positive effects in neutralising London, the engine of English imperialism, while simultaneously helping to maintain a more equal distribution of wealth and industry over the entire country.

---

[26] Stuart, *Reflections*, I.6–17.

[27] Jean-Louis Delolme, *The British empire in Europe: part the first, containing an account of the connection between the kingdoms of England and Ireland, previous to the year 1780. To which is prefixed, an historical sketch of the state of rivalry between the kingdoms of England and Scotland, in former times* (Dublin, 1787).

[28] The Aberdeen-based William Ogilvie also advocated federal union in 1782; see the discussion in Kelly, *Prelude to Union*, 47–49.

By such a federal union, all the three contracting parties have every thing to gain, and nothing to lose; they become a firm, compact solid body, their motto *Tria juncta in uno*. A free state of too great extent, can neither guard against hostile attacks from without, nor frustrate despotic attacks from within, any way so well as by subdividing itself into several federal states under one head. There is an urgent necessity for such a triple union, to oppose the triple league that is formed on the continent against the objects of it, by that power that ever has been ready to foment divisions in the Island of Great Britain, and take advantage of them when fomented; and that ever will be ready to encourage the same divisions between the two Islands themselves, and adopt the maxim, *divide et impera*, with which the world was conquered.[29]

Two further components of Stuart's programme were aimed specifically at Scotland. The first was the rejuvenation of Scotland's fisheries, which he saw as a counterweight to England's economic domination of Scotland and as a way of encouraging maritime habits and the navy.[30] The second was the "extension of a militia to the northern part of the united kingdom."[31] This combination of arguments about federation, Scottish economic prosperity, and the moral regulation of foreign policy make it legitimate to see Stuart as adapting aspects of Fletcher's legacy to Britain's situation at the end of the 1780s.

III

While Stuart's thinking about replacing the politics of war and empire with a morally-guided, cosmopolitan foreign policy echoed Fénelon and Bolingbroke as well as Fletcher, a more firmly Fletcherian vision was articulated by David Steuart Erskine, the 11th Earl of Buchan. Buchan, who was a supporter of Charles James Fox and adhered to many aspects of Fox's programme (including his support for the American and French revolutions), was active in the revival of a distinctively Scottish "country Whiggism" between the 1770s and 1790s.[32] He is a central figure in the story about Fletcher's reception in late-eighteenth-century Scotland for two reasons. First, Buchan was at the heart of a loose group of thinkers (often with family connections) who were consistently critical of English reason of state politics. Buchan was the nephew of Sir

---

[29] Stuart, *Reflections*, I.198–99.
[30] Stuart, *Reflections*, I.276.   [31] Stuart, *Reflections*, I.279–80.
[32] Buchan has been little studied by modern scholars, but he is briefly discussed in Colin Kidd, *Subverting Scotland's Past: Scottish whig historians and the creation of an Anglo-British identity, 1689-c. 1830* (Cambridge 1993), 214, 239, 245; Bruce Lenman, "Aristocratic 'country' whiggery in Scotland and the American Revolution," in Richard B. Sher and Jeffrey R. Smitten, eds., *Scotland and America in the Age of the Enlightenment* (Princeton, NJ, 1990), 180–92.

James Steuart, author of the 1767 *Principles of Political Oeconomy*, and, more importantly, was a friend of Aberdeen-based philosopher William Ogilvie, author of the significant *Essay on the Right of Property in Land* (1781).[33] Buchan also discussed the topics of peace and international relations in correspondence with George Washington. Peace, federation and international stability were, then, key topics in Buchan's intellectual circle. Second, Buchan was instrumental in recovering Fletcher's republicanism as a guideline for the reform of the British state in the early 1790s. The most important evidence for this interest in Fletcher was Buchan's *Essays on the Lives and Writings of Fletcher of Saltoun and the Poet Thomson* (1792), a work which contained a "Historical Sketch of Liberty in Scotland," a biography of Fletcher, and a collection of Fletcher's speeches during the parliamentary debates of 1703. Describing Fletcher as a civic thinker inspired by the patriots of ancient Greece, Buchan drew on Fletcher (as well as George Buchanan) as intellectual resources in his programme for the reform of the British state.

Buchan's starting point, like Stuart's, was a picture of a dangerously extended empire that was teetering on the brink. Buchan referred to Montesquieu's famous "prophecy" about the termination of the British constitution. Although there was a slight ambiguity in Buchan's attitude to empire – he occasionally voiced nostalgia for Britain's "wide-extended dominion" under George II – he was emphatic that by 1792 Britain had become a militarily and financially precarious imperial state, characterised by a "system of corruption," that would certainly collapse under pressure of yet another war:

Let us consider what hold we have *now* of the two Indies, of Canada, and our other lucrative dependencies. A blow may be struck, a blow will be struck, that shall reach the vitals of public credit, and it is an event which nothing but political insanity can induce public ministers not to provide against. But no provision can be made against this event, except that which has been pointed out by the finger of the genius of Britain's welfare.[34]

One other significant feature of Buchan's text was the language of ancient constitutionalism, which served to orient his demands for reform. A serious interest in Scotland's "ancient constitution" had, in fact, been one of the motivations behind his setting up of the Society of Antiquaries of

---

[33] For Buchan's referring to Ogilvie as his friend, see Earl of Buchan to George Washington, 28 June 1791, in Mark A. Mastromarino, ed., *The Papers of George Washington: Presidential Series*, 16 vols. (Charlottesville: University Press of Virginia, 1999), VIII, 305–08. On Ogilvie, see Michael Sonenscher, "Property, community, citizenship," in Mark Goldie and Robert Wokler (eds.), *The Cambridge History of Eighteenth-Century Political Thought* (Cambridge, 2006), 465–96.

[34] Buchan, *Essays*, xxxviii–xxxix. The "genius of Britain's welfare" was Adam Smith.

Scotland in 1778, which was partly designed as an intellectual counter-weight to the royalist historiography of William Robertson.[35] Buchan had sought to enlist the historian, Gilbert Stuart, as an ally in this endeavour, suggesting that Stuart had the credentials for reconstruct-ing the "constitution of the antient assemblies or parliaments of Scot-land," and hence inspiring "us with sentiments more congenial to the free and noble nature of the people with whom we are now united."[36] This theme reappeared in Buchan's texts on Fletcher. Following one of Fletcher's own parliamentary speeches, but also drawing from the political ideas contained in George Buchanan's famous *De Iure Regni apud Scotos* (1579), Buchan described Scotland prior to the regal union of 1603 as a limited monarchy, whose history was marked by regular, legitimate expressions of resistance to arbitrary kingship.[37] Buchan used Buchanan's account of Scottish popular sovereignty – the primacy of the *populus* – as the basis for the reform of the modern system of parliamen-tary representation:

But the Scots had no notion of such a monstrous organ of power for their king, as a separate house for his servants and chaplains, to stop the progress of laws in favour of the rights of the people, before they should come to receive the royal assent. As to the idea of a perfect constitution being to consist of three parts, this was a trinity in which the Scots did not believe; and they satisfied themselves with holding the doctrine of the unity, the majesty, and uncontroulable power of the legislative authority.[38]

Buchan also joined the contemporary Scottish debate about the nature of the Scottish peerage, a debate that included Gilbert Stuart and Alan Maconochie (author of a 1788 "Essay on the Origin and Structure of the European Legislatures").[39] As part of his project for reform of the elec-tion of Scottish peers, he insisted that the Scottish legislature had been based on property, rather than birth. Finally, Buchan lamented that the Glorious Revolution had not effected a more fundamental transforma-tion of the British state. The two main planks of his reform programme were the equalisation of the franchise and the abolition of primogeniture

---

[35] On the critique of Robertson, see Kidd, 214, 245. For details, see William Smellie, "An Historical Account of the Society of the Antiquaries of Scotland," in *Transactions of the Society of the Antiquaries of Scotland* (Edinburgh, 1792), vol. 1, p. v.

[36] [D. S. Earl of Buchan], *Discourse, delivered by the Right Honourable the Earl of Buchan, at a meeting for the purpose of promoting the institution of a society for the investigation of the history of Scotland, and its antiquities, November 14, 1778* (London, 1778), 13–14.

[37] Buchan, *Essays*, 82.   [38] Buchan, *Essays*, 58, n.

[39] Buchan, *Essays*, 57, n. Allan Maconochie, "Essay on the Origin and Structure of the European Legislatures," in *Transactions of the Royal Society of Edinburgh*, 1 (Edinburgh, 1788), 3–42, 133–80.

in private succession.[40] Yet he acknowledged that it would only be in the long run that the principles of Buchanan and Fletcher could be realised as foundations for a reformed system of government.

Although these intricate considerations about the history of the Scottish and British constitutions may appear to have little relevance to questions about international peace, it is important to see how the issue of constitutional reform was connected to Buchan's parallel programmes for the reform of the military and his hopes for a more stable international order. The link between the two was Buchan's idea of a free state or commonwealth. In the year following the publication of the *Essays on Fletcher and Thomson*, Buchan published his *Letters on the Impolicy of a Standing Army, in Time of Peace* (1793). The central theme of the *Letters* was the incompatibility of professional armies with the maintenance of what Buchan called a "free state." Echoing Harrington, he noted that "the sword and sovereignty always march hand in hand," and referred to a long tradition of free states or commonwealths (ancient Israel, Athens, Thebes, Rome, etc.) that had established regulations against the reliance on standing armies.[41] Buchan drew partially upon the "admirable Fletcher" in making these arguments, citing (for instance) Fletcher's claim that the "possession of arms is the distinction between a Freeman and a Slave."[42] But Buchan also made the significant point that standing armies were a kind of stimulus to warfare: "a large Standing Army, has ever proved in all countries, a strong stimulus and incentive to the Ruling Powers of the State possessing it, to go to War, that inhuman, bloody and destructive vortex, whose devouring and insatiable maw, never knows when to be glutted with the lives and treasure of the unfortunate and unhappy people, who are drawn or forced into it."[43] Republican militias were in this sense vehicles of international peace.

Perhaps the most intriguing evidence of Buchan's interest in establishing a more peaceful international order emerges from his correspondence with George Washington in the early 1790s. This exchange took place in the early years of Washington's presidency (1789–97), and sheds considerable light on Buchan's understanding of the United States as a novel type of peaceful republic. Buchan had been a firm supporter of the Americans' struggle for independence since the 1770s, and

---

[40] Buchan, *Essays*, 41.
[41] Buchan, *Letters on the Impolicy of a Standing Army, in Time of Peace. And, on the unconstitutional and illegal measures of barracks; with a postscript, illustrative of the real constitutional mode of defence for this island* (London, 1793), 18.
[42] Buchan, *Impolicy of a Standing Army*, 76.
[43] Buchan, *Impolicy of a Standing Army*, 54.

wrote, under his pseudonym Albanicus, a brief assessment of America's future prospects as a modern, morally-grounded republic in 1791.[44] The emphasis in that piece fell on the need to establish a comprehensive system of national education as a means of safeguarding America's moral future and remedying the loss of virtue already apparent in the early 1790s.[45] In his correspondence with Washington, Buchan outlined more fully his vision of America's future as a pacific republic that would continue to stand apart from the wars and rivalries of Europe:

I wish your America to be like a thriving happy Young family and to be little heard of in the great world of Politics and nothing seems so likely to produce this prosperity & happiness as agricultural & mechanical improvements accompanied by moderate desires and virtuous affectations enlightened and cherished by the dissemination of Science and literature in the mass of the people.[46]

Washington responded to this in the spring of 1793 by confirming the sincere wish of the Americans "to have nothing to do with the Political intrigues, or the squabbles of European nations; but on the contrary, to exchange Commodities & live in peace & amity with all the inhabitants of the earth . . . ".[47] On receipt of this letter, Buchan wrote on the reverse:

On the 18th of June 1793 I wrote to Mr Washington on the happy prospects America might entertain if by any means it could abstain from mingling in European Politics. I laid before him the Vanity & folly of preferring the indulgence of National Pride, Vanity & Resentment to the slow but certain benefits to be permanently obtained by Peace & internal prosperity & I flattered him the view of the Bankruptcy & misery of the old warlike System of Nations leading to a better order of Political policy. I ventured also to recommend two great objects to the Executive of America Peace & Union with the Red Natives & attention to National Education.[48]

Buchan answered Washington again in June 1793, when he emphasised the importance of agriculture and the avoidance of luxury for maintaining the stability of America. Recognising the difficulties that would inevitably face "a new State raised up after great fermentations," Buchan suggested that nothing was "more likely to produce this desirable tranquility & concert than Agricultural establishments and improvements

---

[44] Albanicus, "On America," in *The Bee, or Literary Weekly Intelligencer*, no. 21 (4 May 1791), (Edinburgh, 1791), vol. 3, pp. 96–102.

[45] Albanicus, "On America," 98–100.

[46] Buchan to George Washington, 22 October 1792, in *The Papers of George Washington*.

[47] George Washington to the Earl of Buchan, 22 April 1793, in The Papers of George Washington, Presidential Series vol. 12, ed. Christine Sternberg Patrick and John C. Pinheiro.

[48] George Washington to the Earl of Buchan, 22 April 1793, 471.

with manufactures of real use an *a Commerce of Œconomy* not leading to internal Luxuries that may have ill Physical effects on the health of the People and ill moral ones upon their national character."[49] Buchan thus placed his hopes for America in the avoidance of luxury, the stimulation of agricultural and mechanical improvements, a carefully-constructed system of national education, and the avoidance of European military entanglements. But he may also have thought that European nations had something to learn from the infant republic in reconstructing their own domestic economies, political systems and military establishments.

IV

A further example of the cosmopolitan reading of Fletcher appeared in an edition of his writings published in 1798. The editor of this volume appears to have been Robert Watson (1746?–1838), a shadowy but strangely intriguing figure who moved in late-eighteenth-century republican circles, in Britain and subsequently in continental Europe.[50] Born in Elgin, Scotland, in the late 1740s, Watson had moved to London by 1780, where he involved himself in radical politics, actively campaigning against the Militia Act and marking himself out as a committed defender of the French Revolution. After a period in prison in the mid-1790s (apparently after inciting a riot), Watson fled in 1798 to continental Europe and played a variety of roles in revolutionary France and Napoleonic Europe.[51] Despite his colourful life, Watson's edition of

---

[49] Buchan to Washington, 30 June 1793, vol. 13, ed. Christine Sternberg Patrick (Charlottesville, 2007). 162–64. The distinction between commerce of "economy" and "luxury" can be found in Montesquieu's *Spirit of the Laws*.

[50] The article on Robert Watson in the Oxford Dictionary of National Biography, written by Professor Malcolm Chase, makes no reference to the Fletcher volume. However, there is fairly good circumstantial evidence for the attribution. Both the Fletcher volume and Robert Watson's *Life of Lord George Gordon* (London, 1795), were published by the same London publisher, H. D. Symonds of Paternoster Row, who published other radical literature (for example, by Thomas Paine). Furthermore, there is a significant overlap in the content of the Fletcher volume and Robert Watson's *Life of Lord George Gordon*: both manifest a visceral hostility to primogeniture, both advocate militias, and both call for the establishment of a more popular form of republican government. Both Watsons also appear on the title pages of these works as "M. D." – either an assumed or authentic medical qualification. I'm grateful to Malcolm Chase for correspondence on this issue.

[51] Some of the more colourful stories about his life are that he served as Napoleon Bonaparte's English tutor, and stole an archive of materials on Jacobite rebellions from the Vatican in the early nineteenth century, which he then sold to Castlereagh. On these details, see Malcolm Chase, "Watson, Robert (1746?–1838)," *Oxford Dictionary of National Biography* (Oxford, 2004); online edn, Jan 2008 [http://www.oxforddnb.com/view/article/28862, accessed 16 Dec 2014]. On Watson's "romantic life and miserable death," see Alex Forbes, "Some Account of Robert Watson," *Proceedings of the Society of Antiquaries of Scotland*, 7 (1866–68), 324–34.

Fletcher – replete with a biography of Fletcher and detailed commentary on many of Fletcher's major pieces – offered a coherent reworking of the themes of equal citizenship, property, military organisation and cosmopolitan international relations. In this sense, Watson's edition provides us with a glimpse of how Fletcher's ideas were received within radical circles at the end of the 1790s. Signalling his intentions in the "Dedication," Watson suggested that the publication of Fletcher's works might contribute "to the emancipation of our enslaved country" and to the replacement of the "hereditary" by the "representative" system.[52] He highlighted the urgent need to replace the corrupt aristocratic system of war and empire that had characterised British politics for more than a century with a more benign system of government that would be compatible with international peace and fraternity. Watson looked forward to a time "when man shall every where meet a brother."[53]

The most important feature of Watson's argument was the connection he drew between domestic social and political arrangements, on the one hand, and the system of war and conquest, on the other. War, he stressed, was not an inevitable product of human nature, but rather an artificial consequence of "partial laws."[54] The key drivers of war and expansion were unequal property relationships and, in particular, a social system based upon primogeniture. Watson had already made this connection in his earlier *Life of Lord George Gordon* (1795): "To keep up a tyrannical government, whose principle had been conquest, which had spread calamity and destruction over the European world, amongst an innumerable variety of unjust laws, fatal to the interests of us all, it was found necessary to cherish the infernal, unnatural principle of primogeniture [. . .]."[55] He continued to attack "the cruel and unnatural law of primogeniture" in his "Life of Fletcher."[56] He also claimed that the establishment of militias would foster a more truly cosmopolitan system of international relations: "if [Britons] wish to live in fraternity at home, and in peace and friendship with the neighbouring nations, it is absolutely necessary that the whole body of the people be armed, and resume their original importance in the scale of existence."[57] In connecting equal property and martial virtue with the pacification of the international realm, Watson was echoing themes in earlier Scottish texts like

[52] Watson, "Dedication to William Boswell of Yorkshire," in Andrew Fletcher, *The political works of Fletcher of Saltoun; with notes, &c. To which is prefaced a sketch of his life, with observations, moral, philosophical and political*, ed. R. Watson (London, 1798), iii, v.
[53] Fletcher, *The political works*, viii.   [54] Fletcher, *The political works*, 247–48.
[55] Robert Watson, *The Life of Lord George Gordon: with a philosophical review of his political conduct* (London, 1795), 3.
[56] Fletcher, *The political works*, 20.   [57] Fletcher, *The political works*, vii.

William Ogilvie's *Essay on the Right of Property in Land* (1781), although he also looked back to George Buchanan (the author to whom "Europe is indebted for the little liberty she enjoys").[58] The upshot of Watson's analysis was that the establishment of free commonwealths, grounded on militias, an equal division of the soil and an equal representation, would serve to realise the fraternity of nations as well as political liberty at home.[59]

The most egregious example of the connection between faulty political arrangements and the addiction to war and conquest was, unsurprisingly, Great Britain. Britain's passion for conquest "may be traced to the materials of which our government is composed."[60] Like the other writers I have been considering, Watson was highly critical of the Glorious Revolution, which left political power in the hands of a corrupt aristocratic monarchy. Citing some of the leading eighteenth-century authorities on English policy in the East Indies (including Alexander Dow, author of the famous *History of Hindustan*), Watson argued that Britain's conquests were leading to its own political slavery:

Little did the inhabitants of Great Britain think they were preparing fetters for themselves, when rejoicing at the victories obtained in the east and west Indies. They did not attend to this sublime truth, that the great body of the people are never enriched by conquests, and that no nation ever enslaved its neighbours, and preserved its own liberty at the same time. Had the government employed the men and money, in improving the country, which have been consumed in cruel wars, Britain would have contained twice the number of her present inhabitants, and ten times her present wealth.[61]

Watson reserved some of his fiercest criticism for the 1707 Act of Union, which he described as a "shameful transaction" that had sealed Scotland's "political death."[62] Like Buchan, he believed that Scotland had enjoyed a "very considerable share of political liberty" prior to 1603.[63] The Union of 1707, an unprecedented act of betrayal on the part of Scottish elites, simply sealed Scotland's post-1603 status as an unfree, dependent province:

[58] For the reference to Buchanan, see Fletcher, *The political works*, 85.

[59] Watson also made some interesting remarks about the legitimacy of military intervention, claiming that intervention was justified if undertaken to free a people from despotism, but that no state had the right to impose any form of government on an independent nation. Fletcher, *The political works*, 234–35.

[60] Fletcher, *The political works*, 234.

[61] Fletcher, *The political works*, 235. Watson cited Alexander Dow, *The History of Hindostan, from the death of Akbar, to the complete settlement of the empire under Aurungzebe* (London, 1772).

[62] Fletcher, *The political works*, 89.   [63] Fletcher, *The political works*, 83–84.

By this shameful transaction, which is equally disgraceful to both nations, the whole power of Scotland was thrown into the hands of an aristocratic faction, dependent on the English ministers. The parliament of Scotland had assembled to transact the common business of the nation, and they betrayed their trust, for personal considerations, while the English court bought the sovereignty of a country from those who had no right to dispose of it. The one acted as brokers in stolen goods, the others as receivers. It was the ruin of Scotland, which may be considered in the light of a province, and England was not benefited by it; for although it gave the cabinet a great preponderance in the political scale, yet owing to a variety of causes, the advantages resulting from it, instead of being extended to the whole body of the people, have been confined to a few. That Scots interest, which sold their own country, has proved the willing instruments of every minister, and is equally injurious to the liberty of both nations. The modern representation of Scotland is a mere mockery; and nine-tenths of the people hardly know when the nomination for members of parliament takes place.[64]

As an alternative to this combustible mixture of unequal property arrangements and imperial monarchy, Watson presented a vision of the future as characterised by pacific commerce between small-scale republican societies. Significantly, he conceived of commerce as a force for the dissolution of national enmities and for uniting mankind. This was to redescribe one aspect of Fletcher's legacy as a theory of true commercial exchange, separated from the ruinous monopolies and jealousies that currently characterised economic relations between states. On Watson's account, ideas of "natural enemies" were disappearing with the progress of reason, "and the period is not very distant when the whole family of man will exchange the superfluities of their industry with one another, upon terms of mutual advantage without the dread of pirates, or prohibitory laws."

Without commerce our apples would degenerate into crabs and our wheat into rye. Our knowledge would be local – our ideas narrow and confined. And yet commerce, the source of so much enjoyment, like many other blessings, has frequently been turned to the injury of society: by being placed, in the hands of a few privileged companies, it has furnished them with weapons for oppressing their fellow citizens. This has induced many superficial observers to exclaim against commerce in general, without perceiving, that, it is only monopoly which is dangerous to liberty. They might, with the same plausibility, condemn agriculture, or any useful manufacture. Fletcher reasoned more accurately. He saw, that communication of thought was conducive to public and private happiness; and that without commerce, there could never be an extensive circulation of opinion.[65]

---

[64] Fletcher, *The political works*, 90–91.   [65] Fletcher, *The political works*, 66–67.

This distinction between free and monopolistic commerce was mirrored in the distinction Watson drew between two "species of colonization," one harmful and one beneficial. Conquest was a "direct robbery," subordinating justice to brute force, yet to "cultivate the earth, and multiply human beings, is to serve the end of our creation."[66] This meant, Watson argued, that Fletcher had been right to propose the creation of a free port in Darien, "thus connecting the east and west Indies, and benefiting the world at large."[67] Darien's failure was a direct consequence of English jealousy of trade. Following Smith, Watson advocated the complete liberalisation of trade, a measure that he saw as having the potential to alleviate the famines and poverty caused by commercial regulations.[68]

Towards the conclusion of his commentary, Watson offered the optimistic prediction that the large states of the world would gradually be replaced by smaller entities engaged in the peaceful, non-competitive exchange of surpluses:

In the present state of things, it would have been extremely improper in the Americans and French to have divided their country into small states; for the confederacy might have been broken, and the whole destroyed, whilst each was employed in its domestic concerns. Yet in the progress of civilization, when a few individuals will neither have the ambition nor the power, to disturb the repose of mankind, it is highly probable, the world will be divided into a great number of independent states, exchanging the superfluities of their respective industry, and living on terms of fraternity with one another.[69]

As this suggests, Watson's critique of contemporary political realities was balanced by a more optimistic vision of the future in which small republics would replace competitive imperial monarchies. Explicitly citing Fletcher's suggestion that it was possible to construct governments that would neutralise the dynamics of expansion and aggrandisement, he added that once "men become more enlightened they will discover that their interest consists in cultivating the arts of peace; and a dispute between nations will be as easily settled, as a dispute between individuals."[70] In this way Watson presented Fletcher's ideas as crucial resources for the achievement of perpetual peace in the 1790s.

[66] Fletcher, *The political works*, 68–69.
[67] Fletcher, *The political works*, 68–69.   [68] Fletcher, *The political works*, 72.
[69] At this point, Watson was engaging in the long-running debate about whether republican government could be reconciled with an extensive territory; he implied (siding with Harrington against Montesquieu) that territorial extent was *not* the main cause of the decline of Greece and Rome, but rather the neglect of the "political balance." Fletcher, *The political works*, 246–47.
[70] Fletcher, *The political works*, 248.

V

One of the texts upon which the Earl of Buchan had relied in reconstructing Fletcher's activities during the 1680s and 1690s was Sir John Dalrymple's *Memoirs of Great Britain and Ireland* (1771; new material incorporated 1788). Yet although Buchan spoke highly of Dalrymple – referring to him as a "kinsman" – the two authors were poles apart politically.[71] Dalrymple emphatically rejected the idea that a revived federal union could provide a viable structure for Anglo-Scottish (and Irish) relations in the late eighteenth century. He also took a much firmer line on the question of American independence, and his ingrained suspicion of France meant that he had little sympathy for the cosmopolitan perspectives of Stuart, Buchan or Watson.[72] Nevertheless, Dalrymple's text is an important part of the story of Fletcher's reception in this period. The first volumes, published in 1771, contained a wealth of historical material relating to the Glorious Revolution and the Darien venture; these were sources for Buchan's account of Fletcher's involvement in the Monmouth Rebellion of 1685.[73] But it was in a later, separate volume, published in 1788, that Dalrymple included the text of Fletcher's *State of the Controversy betwixt United and Separate Parliaments* (1703), as well as a paper of his own recommending a strict incorporating union between England and Ireland.[74] The immediate context of Dalrymple's 1788 volume was the international crisis generated by the 1787 Dutch Revolt, which he feared might provoke Britain into yet another continental war.[75] The text provides us with a radically different perspective on Fletcher's intellectual legacy, on the advantages and disadvantages of federal unions, and on the foundations of international political stability in the late 1780s.

In the body of his text Dalrymple wrote quite positively about Fletcher, describing him as an intelligent Scottish patriot and characterising his *Discourse of Government in Relation to Militias* as "one of

---

[71] Buchan, "Life of Fletcher," 46.

[72] See his anonymously published *Address of the People of Great-Britain to the Inhabitants of America* (London, 1775).

[73] John Dalrymple, *Memoirs of Great Britain and Ireland, from the Dissolution of the last Parliament of Charles II until the Sea-battle off La Hogue*, 2nd edition (London, 1773), vol. 2, 136 (Appendix 1, separate pagination).

[74] Historians disagree on whether this really was the work of Fletcher; see John Robertson, "The Union Debate in Scotland, 1698–1707," in Robertson, ed. *A Union for Empire: Political Thought and the Union of 1707* (Cambridge, 1995), 217, n. However, the work is attributed to Fletcher in Allan I. Macinnes, *Union and Empire: The Making of the United Kingdom in 1707* (Cambridge, 2007).

[75] John Dalrymple, *Memoirs of Great Britain and Ireland, from the Battle off La Hogue till the Capture of the French and Spanish Fleets at Vigo* (Edinburgh, 1788), vi.

the finest compositions in the English language."[76] Yet in Dalrymple's own paper on federal and incorporating unions he rejected the ideas set out in the *State of the Controversy betwixt United and Separate Parliaments*, which called for a federal union under a single monarch, coupled with strict limitations on the Crown (the reduction of the Crown's powers of veto and the civil list), annual parliaments, and the establishment of a militia.[77] Dalrymple briskly dismissed the viability of a federal union between England and Scotland, claiming that it must inevitably have resulted in war between the two nations.[78] This underlined the urgency of establishing an incorporating union between Ireland and Britain, whose relationship was now analogous to that between England and Scotland before 1707. Like many other participants in the argument about Irish union after 1780, Dalrymple believed that economic competition between neighbouring nations, producing roughly similar commodities and manufactures, had the capacity to generate intense jealousy of trade.[79] The only "engine" capable of breaking such jealousy was "an incorporated union; by which, I repeat, I mean an union of Parliaments, trade and taxes."[80] Incorporating union was thus seen partly in terms of establishing peace (at least within the boundaries of the British Isles) because of its capacity to neutralise the economic enmities between states. This pacific intent is exemplified in the following passage:

And the distinction between Irishmen and Englishmen being lost in the high character of citizens of the British Islands, it would signify little, except to a few individuals, from what part of those Islands the persons came, who were entrusted with power, civil and military; because those persons would have all the inducements of common service and common interest, to make them use with discretion the powers committed to their charge, and none to abuse them. – But above all, the suspicions and animosities, which continually prevail in separate assemblies of separate nations, would cease in the united assembly of one nation, even when the bitter truth was alternately explained, that partial evil is sometimes general good.[81]

The second part of Dalrymple's paper set out a proposal for the creation of a federal union between Britain and America. There is of course something rather ludicrous about this proposal – published five years after the Peace of Paris in 1783 – but it should also be remembered that Dalrymple's arguments reflected conventional eighteenth-century assessments about the prospects for stability in extensive republics. Repeating arguments made since the mid-1770s by Scottish critics of the American

[76] Dalrymple, *Memoirs* (1788), 126.   [77] Dalrymple, *Memoirs* (1788), 38.
[78] Dalrymple, *Memoirs* (1788), 39.   [79] Dalrymple, *Memoirs* (1788), 40–41.
[80] Dalrymple, *Memoirs* (1788), 41–42.   [81] Dalrymple, *Memoirs* (1788), 42.

struggle for independence like Kames, Alexander Carlyle, and Adam Ferguson, Dalrymple asserted that union with a "friendly protecting great state" (i.e. Britain) would be necessary if the Americans were to avoid the scenes of the Peloponnesian war being repeated "on the plains of America."[82] This was standard stuff among the Scottish critics of American independence: large republics were always vulnerable to civil war and disintegration. At the same time, a federal union would serve Britain's interests in holding onto her Caribbean possessions, which – Dalrymple conjectured – would otherwise fall victim to an expanding US empire.[83] Even more oddly, Dalrymple proposed that the executive officer of the newly constructed federation should be nominated by Britain. This idea was designed to furnish the supreme executive power in America with the power and authority that Dalrymple felt it lacked:

It is no secret to mankind, that the lightness of the American states in the scale of nations, at a time when they should have felt their weight the most, in the hour immediately after victory and glory, arises from their supreme power, being possessed neither of authority nor of force. They present a new spectacle in history; a great empire, possessed by a great people, who acknowledge no government, and obey no law. The consequence of which is, that all modern nations stand aloof from them, as the ancient nations did from the rocks of Scylla and Charybdis. But their supreme power would, by a federal union with Britain, be strengthened in the imaginations of their subjects; and being entitled, by the terms of it, to ask assistance equally against enemies and rebels, they could command that reality of power to protect their constitution, and enforce its regulations, without which no government, at least no great government, ever did, or ever can stand.[84]

These arguments were tied to a larger vision of the appropriate mechanisms for establishing international peace and stability in the post-war world. Writing in the aftermath of the Dutch revolt of 1787, Dalrymple believed that the time was ripe for an alliance between Britain and Holland, which would build upon his proposed unions with Ireland and the United States. His key idea was for a kind of grand alliance that would give Britain (with Ireland), the United States, and the Dutch a kind of joint hegemony over the international order. This would guarantee the perpetual subordination of the French and Spanish monarchies, the "disturbers of mankind":

If an incorporated union of Britain with Ireland, a federal union with America, and a league offensive and defensive of all the three with Holland, were to be

---

[82] Dalrymple, *Memoirs* (1788), 45.
[83] Dalrymple, *Memoirs* (1788), 47.   [84] Dalrymple, *Memoirs* (1788), 43.

accomplished, then the modern would return to the condition of the ancient world, in which the nations that were free, commanded the fate of those who were not free.[85]

Dalrymple's paper thus culminated in the expression of a striking alternative to the Fletcher-inspired programme for reigning in Britain's imperial proclivities as set out by Buchan, George Stuart, or Robert Watson. In place of their more genuinely cosmopolitan visions of a world made up of small-scale, equal, and peacefully-trading republics, Dalrymple was promoting a paternalist picture of Anglo-Dutch-American hegemony as a kind of permanent alliance of global empires. This vision fitted closely with some of Dalrymple's other texts, which had proposed the demolition of Spain's empire in South America, and argued for making Egypt and the Suez Canal the centrepiece of a revived British global commercial empire.[86] These ideas, Dalrymple concluded, could "force those two nations [France and Spain] to submit for ever, or at least as long as those unions, and that league lasted, to the peace of human kind, and to their own happiness."[87] But the idea of achieving peace through an alliance of great empires was not what Fletcher's Scottish disciples had in mind when they wrote about perpetual peace.

VI

This Scottish debate about Fletcher's legacy in the 1780s and 1790s provides an intriguing perspective upon a much broader debate about

---

[85] In broad outline, this was not entirely dissimilar from the Triple Alliance of Britain, Prussia and the United Provinces set up in the summer of 1788; see H. M. Scott, *The Birth of a Great Power System* (Longman), 242–43. Dalrymple, II, 52.

[86] Dalrymple called for a British onslaught on Spanish possessions in Mexico and Honduras in the first appendix to the 1788 volume, a project that "would shake the whole Spanish monarchy in those parts of the world, at a less expence to the public, than is required to maintain a war for only one month in Germany or Flanders"; Dalrymple, *Memoirs* (1788), 36. In his near-contemporary *Queries Concerning the Conduct which England should follow in foreign politics in the present state of Europe*, written in October 1788, Dalrymple advocated a British-Russian alliance (chiefly with the aim of containing a resurgent France) and the reconstruction of the Suez Canal as a means of connecting Britain's European and Indian dominions. Dalrymple's idea, in the tradition of Charles Davenant, was to use India as the centre for a revived empire of free trade, by which Britain "could throw open the possessions of England in India to all nations, and encourage all merchants to trade with them, and in them; because, from the industry and wealth which that trade would create in her dominions, she might draw great taxes, and yet retain her own superiority in trade . . . ". See John Dalrymple, *Queries Concerning the Conduct which England should follow in foreign politics in the present state of Europe* (London, 1789), 75–84.

[87] Dalrymple, *Memoirs* (1788), 52.

the possibility of pacifying Europe through the construction of republican constitutions. These Scottish thinkers were preoccupied by the questions of Britain's future as a post-imperial state after 1782–83, its domestic constitutional arrangements, and its relationships with Ireland, the United States, and Europe. In this context, Fletcher's ideas proved to be significant resources in the construction of a coherent cosmopolitan-republican perspective on international relations that emphasised the pacific qualities of civic militias, the dangers of public debts and standing armies, and the possibility that a more balanced distribution of property – through the abolition of primogeniture – might contribute to the construction of a more stable state with a more pacific, morally-guided foreign policy. Fletcher's ideas were also implicated in debates about British-Irish union, and this was also true for some Irish thinkers.[88] The larger implication is the existence of a distinctively cosmopolitan strand within the late-eighteenth-century rehabilitation of the British commonwealthman tradition. In contrast with those who assumed that republican ideas provided resources for projects of war and expansion – a view most crisply expressed by Edmund Burke when he wrote that the French revolutionaries "had continually in their hands the observations of *Machiavel on Livy*" – the texts discussed here reveal an alternative perspective that centred on the compatibility between the republican idea of a "free state" and a more peaceful international order. The Earl of Buchan's correspondence with Washington and Jefferson on precisely these issues is a tantalizing indication of one of the broader legacies of Fletcher's cosmopolitan republicanism.

One final Scottish indication of the fate of this cosmopolitan perspective on republican "free states" can be found in James Mackintosh's *Vindiciae Gallicae* of 1791. Mackintosh referred positively to Fletcher in the *Vindiciae*, describing him as an author who "maintained the cause of his deserted country with the force of ancient eloquence, and the dignity of ancient virtue."[89] He placed Fletcher in a wider Anglo-Scottish pantheon of civic theorists, including George Buchanan, John Milton, James Harrington, Algernon Sidney, John Locke and William Molyneux. Implicitly, Mackintosh was also situating his own arguments against Burke, and in defence of the French Revolution, in this tradition. Moreover, his endorsement of French political developments between 1789 and 1791 rested partly on the claim that the establishment of a modern

---

[88] For positive reference to Fletcher's legacy from an Irish critic of incorporating union, see e.g. Robert Orr, *An Address to the People of Ireland, against a Union* (Dublin, 1799), 30–31, 46.

[89] James Mackintosh, *Vindiciae Gallicae and other writings on the French Revolution*, ed. Donald Winch (Indianaopolis, 2006), 135–36.

constitution opened up a viable path towards the pacification of Europe. Since the "European Commonwealth" was characterised by a remarkable unity of manners among its distinct populations, the French Revolution would spark peace through a kind of sympathetic "propagation of sentiment."[90] Republican politics was connected to the renunciation of conquest, the repudiation of the languages of necessity and reason of state, and the abandonment of France's "cumbrous and destructive" colonies.[91]

Yet Mackintosh's stance towards the idea of the pacific republic became much more ambiguous from as early as 1792, when he began to doubt the compatibility of French revolutionary republicanism with the establishment of international peace. By the time he penned his famous retrospect on the entire revolutionary period, in his 'On the State of France in 1815,' he had abandoned his early faith in the pacific properties of republics and instead moved closer to Burke's perception that republican revolutions were more likely to incite popular passions for war and conquest.[92] Mackintosh's continued wrestling with this question was a significant Scottish example of the much broader European debate about the peacefulness of republics that intensified in the wake of the French Revolution. But his abandonment of his earlier faith in the pacific properties of democratic republics, and his turn to the languages of natural rights and the "Law of Nature and Nations," may be indicative of some of the difficulties Scottish thinkers faced in maintaining a commitment to a cosmopolitan understanding of republicanism during the period of the French Revolution.

[90] Mackintosh, *Vindiciae*, 158–59.   [91] Mackintosh, *Vindiciae*, 122.
[92] Mackintosh, 'On the State of France in 1815', in Mackintosh, Vindiciae Gallicae, 259–73. For detailed discussion, see Anna Plassart, The Scottish Enlightenment and the French Revolution (Cambridge, 2015), 94–98.

8   Liberty, war and empire
Overcoming the rich state-poor state problem, 1789–1815

Richard Whatmore

I

History plays tricks on the dead. An author's thoughts are always manipulated by subsequent generations and often twisted to address issues a world away from an original subject. More rarely the terms of an argument change radically, following contemporary events, in ways that would have been inconceivable to those living even a year before. History played an especially malevolent trick upon some of those who were coming to the end of their lives in the 1790s. This process can be illustrated by considering the final years of two giants of eighteenth-century thought, Edward Gibbon and Edmund Burke. Both men died convinced that the world they inhabited had all but been destroyed. The social and political orders they supported were breaking down across Europe. Each expressed palpably the view that the world they had lived in was being lost. They blamed the French Revolution. The Revolution, they were convinced, had initiated a war against society as presently constituted and against human history itself. Yet the revolutionaries saw themselves as being capable of restoring the entire world to peace in perpetuity and were fighting in the name of peace. As Burke put it, the revolutionaries 'pretend that the destruction of Kings, Nobles and the Aristocracy of Burghers and Rich Men is the only means of establishing an universal and perpetual peace'.[1] The result was a world newly addicted to war. History, for Gibbon, taught that perpetual peace could only be established by 'the wand of a legislator and a sage', the pursuit of 'the innocent and placid labours of agriculture', or religious inspiration; that the latter brought peace was always 'the illusion, perhaps the artifice, of the moment'. War tended to return because the 'sense of interest' was always so strong that states might be tempted to take advantage of a weaker power; equally, 'the

---

[1] Edmund Burke, *A letter from the Right Hon. Edmund Burke to His Grace the Duke of Portland, on the conduct of the minority in Parliament* (London: J. Owen, 1797), 53.

love of arms and rapine' was commonplace.[2] Projectors who promised peace were rarely if ever to be trusted. Burke called the revolutionaries 'the projectors of deception'.[3] They had come to dominate politics and neither man could see an easy way of challenging their dominion.

Soon after the deaths of Gibbon and of Burke, however, traditional understandings of war, revolution and politics were suddenly revived. The inauguration of Bonaparte's consulate enabled commentators to argue, often with an evident sigh of relief, that the French Revolution was an event explicable and not at all novel, having been through stages of popular rebellion, demagogic leadership and civil and international war before succumbing to a Caesar figure, as had so many revolutions before it.[4] The association of liberty and discord was explicable to contemporaries. The Revolution could be likened to a brain fever, moving through increasingly aggressive stages to 'the reign of Anarchy', when 'the frantic wretch' attacked everyone and everything. Such a fever demanded the medicine of 'armed despotism', when the patient was prevented from doing further harm through the extinction of liberty. This explained the transition after the Directory from 'a proud Triumvirate to a perpetual Dictatorship, and from that to a sudden introduction of an Imperial Crown, and Sceptre of Iron.'[5] Bonaparte could be presented as a French tyrant of the traditional kind, seeking 'an unlimited empire on the wrecks of civilized society' and dedicated to the destruction of Britain.[6]

The most surprising fact about the era of the revolutionary and Napoleonic wars ceased to be derived from events in France. Rather, for those interested in what might be on the horizon, the shocking phenomenon was the stability of the British state. Britain had ended the 1780s in turmoil, having lost the North American colonies and suffered defeat in war, having experienced the crisis of the Regency after George III was pronounced mad and facing an ever-increasing national debt. Into the 1790s the established jeremiad literature continued to

---

[2] Edward Gibbon, *The History of the Decline and Fall of the Roman Empire* (London: A. Strahan and T. Cadell, 1788), 2nd edn., six vols., V, Ch. Xliv, 113–114.

[3] Burke, *A third letter to a Member of the present Parliament: on the proposals for peace with the regicide directory of France* (London: F. and C. Rivington, 1797), 100.

[4] Gustav von Schlablendorf, *Bonaparte and the French People under his Consulate*, translated from the German (Tipper and Richards: London, 1804), preface.

[5] Felix Freeman [Anon.], *A View of the Present State of France; With a Retrospect of the Past; Wherein the True Interests of the Continental Powers, and the Blessings of our Constitution, are clearly demonstrated* (Edinburgh: Oliver and Co., 1807), 4–9.

[6] William Cobbett, *A collection of facts and observations: relative to the peace with Bonaparte, chiefly extracted from the Porcupine, and including Mr. Cobbett's letters to Lord Hawkesbury* (London: Cobbett and Morgan, 1801), 11. Cobbett went on to say that if peace was established 'Vattel would be superseded by Cocker; and the law of nations would shrink before the table of interest' (17).

predict that the British Carthage was about to succumb to the French Rome.[7] After the French Republic declared war at the end of February 1793, Britain fought wars constantly across the globe until 1814, with the brief respite of the Peace of Amiens between March 1802 and May 1803. Economic circumstances became so constrained in an era where fear of invasion was constant that in February 1797 the Bank of England suspended specie payments. By 1815 the debt level was at 200% of GDP, the highest figure in British history. Yet ministers in London survived the creation of a domestic revolutionary movement inspired by France. An aborted revolution in Ireland occurred in 1798, leading to the Acts of Union of 1800 that brought together the Kingdom of Great Britain and the Kingdom of Ireland. Seven successive coalitions against France between 1793 and 1815 were sustained by British funds. Republican and then imperial France was defeated, leaving Britain the dominant global economic power.

None of the luminaries of the enlightenment era had foreseen that Britain would be able to weather such political and economic storms. From Fénelon to Rousseau to Kant and to Fichte, numerous observers had anticipated political revolutions because of commerce and public credit.[8] Britain was seen across Europe as an aggressive, predatory, commercial and imperial state. Even those who admired Britain, and stated that the British enjoyed more liberty than any other people in history, were pessimistic about Britain's prospects. Montesquieu continues to be seen today as an author whose *De l'esprit des lois* (1748) inspired Anglophilia into the nineteenth century. Contemporaries were aware, however, of Montesquieu's prophecy: a state that began the century as 'a republic hiding under the form of a monarchy' would end it as 'a popular state or else a despotic state'.[9] No author writing before the French Revolution anticipated the success of Britain's constitutionalism and commercial society. Acknowledgement of Britain's success had

---

[7] David Hartley, *Arguments on the French Revolution and the Means of Peace* (Bath, 1794), 5, 80–82; Anon., *A Query whether certain political conjectures and reflections of Dr Davenant... be or be not applicable to the present crisis* (London, 1795), 89–90; William Morgan, *Facts addressed to the serious attention of the people of Great Britain respecting the Experience of the war and the state of the National Debt* (London, 1796); John Bowlder, *Reform or Ruin: Take your choice* (London, 1798) and *Sound an Alarm to all the inhabitants of Great Britain, from the least to the greatest* (London, 1798).

[8] Michael Sonenscher, *Before the Deluge: Public Debt, Inequality, and the Intellectual Origins of the French Revolution*; Isaac Nakhimovsky, *The Closed Commercial State: Perpetual Peace and Commercial Society from Rousseau to Fichte*.

[9] Montesquieu, *De l'esprit des lois*, Book XX, Chapter 7; XI, 6; II, 4; XX, 21–2; 'Notes sur l'Angleterre', *Œuvres complètes* (Paris, 1951), p. 334. See further Paul Rahe, *Montesquieu and the Logic of Liberty* (Newhaven, Conn.: Yale University Press, 2009).

significant consequences for perspectives on the relationship between commerce and peace.

The failure of the French Revolution to create a republic in a large state, and the ultimate success with which Britain fought Napoleon, changed the terms of political argument. Parties on either side of the British-French divide claimed that they were establishing empires for wealth and liberty, which were special because they overcame the traditional antagonism between rich and poor states. Perspectives upon Britain changed comprehensively during the period of the revolutionary and Napoleonic wars. Political argument had to begin from different premises to those of the enlightenment era. The aim of this chapter is to outline some of these new premises and the nature of the controversies they generated. The first argument of this chapter is to underline how surprising the stable character of British politics was after the American War and into the nineteenth century. The second is to explain how difficult it was for the reform-minded in Britain, the friends of liberty and of the French Revolution in its early years, to accept Britain's success. The third is to reveal a new argument in politics at the end of the century: that Britain was the first state in history to have resolved the rich country-poor country problem. This gave rise, fourthly, to a new image of nineteenth-century Britain as an empire for trade and for peace, which was a cosmopolitan empire that could be trusted to foster and to protect the interests of the smaller and weaker states it engaged with. Proof that Britain was a new kind of empire derived from relations between the constituent elements of the United Kingdom, where the poorer and weaker parts, and Scotland more especially, was thriving despite the wealth and power of England. The chapter reveals that the Napoleonic Wars saw the end of established hopes for a world purged of war through commerce working as a means to international friendship or as a solvent to empires. In its place, the idea of a cosmopolitan empire arose, that was predisposed towards peace, but that might have to go to war to prevent restrictions upon trade or wars for trade undertaken by other states.

II

Burke's *Reflections on the Revolution in France*, first published in November 1790, was ultimately an optimistic book. Events in France might be dreadful. The forms of barbarism on display at Paris were likened to the excesses of former ages of rudeness and savagery; but Burke foresaw an end point. A Pandora's Box of malignant ideas had been opened. One of the aims of Burke's book was to help to close it, to underscore what was healthy about European society and what France needed to do to reconstitute itself.[10] In other words, Burke was convinced that the Revolution would be over before too long. The bloodshed that had attended the transformation of politics and the collapse of the social and religious orders of society had weakened France; the institutions of government and the public culture that had hitherto maintained the state were now gone. But the domestic violence, ceaseless political intrigues and upheavals and the more general instability that accompanied them, could not be sustained. In subverting the acknowledged principles of politics and property the revolutionaries would see 'the ruin of their country'; their legacy would be 'a melancholy and lasting monument of the effect of preposterous politics, and presumptuous, short-sighted, narrow-minded wisdom'.[11] Gibbon agreed with Burke's analysis: 'the last revolution of Paris appears to have convinced almost every body of the fatal consequences of Democratical principles, which lead by a path of flowers into the Abyss of Hell'.[12] The Revolution would end, it was anticipated, through foreign troops, whose arms the disorganized French would never be able to withstand. When the Duke of Brunswick, commanding the united forces of Austria and of Prussia, invaded France at the end of July 1792, he quickly captured Longwy and Verdun before heading west towards Paris. Gibbon summarised the view of many in writing that 'On every rational principle of calculation he must succeed'.[13] For Burke, it was 'the most important crisis that ever existed in the world'.[14]

Yet Brunswick was heavily defeated at the Battle of Valmy on 20 September. Kellerman, in command of the French forces, reported after the battle that 'the best disciplined soldiers cannot excel [sic] those who have devoted themselves to the defence of liberty'.[15] Burke was horrified, declaring that professional troops had been vanquished by 'a troop of strolling players with a buffoon [Charles-François du Périer Dumouriez] at their head'. Unexpectedly, 'vigour and decision, though joined with crime, folly and madness, have triumphed.' French forces

---

[10] Edmund Burke, *Reflections on the Revolution in France, and on the proceedings in certain societies in London, relative to that event* (London: J. Dodsley, 1790), 7th edn., 362.

[11] *Edmund Burke, Reflections on the Revolution in France*, 360.

[12] Gibbon to John Holroyd, August 23 1792, J. E. Norton, ed. *The Letters of Edward Gibbon* (London: Cassell, 1956), 3 vols., III, 268.

[13] Gibbon to John Holroyd, 12 September 1792, *The Letters of Edward Gibbon*, III, 267–270.

[14] Burke to William Wyndam Grenville, 1st Baron Grenville, 19 September 1792, *The Correspondence of Edmund Burke. Volume VII. January 1792–August 1794*, ed. P. J. Marshall and John A. Woods (Cambridge University Press, 1968), 217.

[15] François Christophe de Kellermann to the Minister of War, 21 September 1792, *The Political State of Europe for the Year M. DCC. XCII* (London: J. S. Jordan, 1792), 2 vols., II, 523.

in the south then quickly took Nice and Savoy. Dumouriez proceeded to invade the Austrian Netherlands, over-running the territory within a month after the battle of Jemappes on 6 November. For Burke, all of Europe was threatened. Nothing was likely to stop the revolutionary armies; it was even the case that 'their mountains will not protect the Swiss'.[16]

One fervent supporter of France noted that nationalities were being broken down across Europe with the spread of liberty. The invasion of the realms of Joseph II, for example, was justified because his subjects might have been Austrians under the rule of kings, but 'they are French under the empire of liberty'.[17] In the journal *La Feuille Villageoise*, summaries were supplied of speeches in the National Convention declaring that revolutionary France would never be defeated, and indeed could easily put an end to British power, because of the overwhelming desire of the citizens, all of whom were necessarily soldiers, to sacrifice themselves for the greater good of the state. A new kind of armed citizen had been created because 'republican equality exists in the military camps just as it does in the cities'.[18] This republican soldier would establish 'the empire of liberty', no matter how many tyrants might 'vomit up new battalions' to fight against France.[19] French patriots were waging a new kind of warfare. Their numbers were vast, supplemented by citizens from every country they liberated. Welcomed by the oppressed, the poor and lovers of liberty, no military power on mainland Europe could stand against the revolutionary soldiers, once their cosmopolitan nature and revolutionary mission had been revealed. Burke and Gibbon were convinced that the power balance between Europe's states had been drastically altered as a result. Perpetual peace, which the revolutionaries vaunted, translated into reality into the most oppressive kind of empire, that of French democrats and republicans.

Gibbon, living at Lausanne since 1783, wrote to his friend John Baker Holroyd, 1st Baron Sheffield, that French troops were moving towards Geneva. He watched them arrive at the gates of the city in October 1792, certain that the tiny republic could put up little resistance.[20] Expecting to be 'eaten by cannibals' in 'hurricane latitudes', Gibbon became

---

[16] Burke to Richard Burke, 17 October, 1792, *The Correspondance of Edmund Burke. Volume VII. January 1792-August 1794*, 271–272.

[17] Joseph Lavallée, *Voyage dans les départemens de la France* (Paris: Brion et al., 1792), 5.

[18] Anon., 'La convention nationale aux Peuples Français', *No. 22 et vingt-deuxième semaine de la troisième année de la Feuille Villageoise, jeudi 28 Février 1793* (Paris: Cercle Social, 1793), 520–526.

[19] Anon., 'Chanson Patriotique', *Récréations décadaires, ou hommages à la raison* (Paris: Franklin, s. d.), 46.

[20] Gibbon to John Holroyd, 5 October 1792, *The Letters of Edward Gibbon*, III, 276–277.

depressed about the future. He anticipated 'a Democratical revolution' accompanied by Terror.[21] Within three months of Gibbon's letter the French had conquered Savoy, invaded the Italian states and the Austrian Netherlands, taken Mainz and pushed up the Rhine towards Frankfurt. Gibbon thought that Britain, 'the last refuge of liberty and law', too might fall before 'the Gallic dogs' because 'the whole horizon is so black'. The British people, seeing the 'most insolent prosperity' of the French, might 'eat the Apple of false freedom'.[22] Alternatively, if war broke out, Gibbon could not see how the British would be able to defy French arms for long. He called France the 'new Sparta'. Any fight would entail the death of either state. Gibbon likened the likely experience to 'plunging headlong into an abyss, whose bottom no man can discover'.[23]

Burke was equally of the opinion that France and the Revolution changed when the First French Republic was declared in September 1792. Like Gibbon, Burke then became suddenly fearful about the future. The certainties of the *Reflections on the Revolution in France* were gone. Burke, the least circumspect of authors, felt a grave doubt and apprehensiveness, perhaps for the only time in his public career. As he wrote to his friend the Member of Parliament French Laurence, 'the times are so deplorable, that I do not know how to write about them'.[24] The reason for Burke's worry was that he did not understand why the Revolution was not only surviving but thriving and spreading. A new force had been created in politics and the acknowledged rules of political life were being torn up. The invasion of the states of Europe by French soldiers should have been embattled, rather than being welcomed by the newly subject peoples. A bankrupt state whose economy was in tatters should not have been able to wage war, let alone mount new campaigns in numerous theatres. The monarchs, noble ranks and clerical orders of the continent should have been able to combat the revolutionaries, rather than crumbling, seemingly accepting that they were outdated and illegitimate. For the first time in the history of Europe an imperial power bent on dominion was being called liberator and friend to mankind. In a magnificent summary passage Burke identified the change in the world and his incomprehension, followed by a reiteration of his fear that Britain would embrace the gorgon by making peace with the French Republic:

[21] Gibbon to John Holroyd, 13 October 1792, *The Private Letters of Edward Gibbon*, II, 317–318.
[22] Gibbon to John Holroyd, 27 October and 10 November 1792, *The Letters of Edward Gibbon*, III, 282–286, 290–292.
[23] Gibbon to John Holroyd, 25 November 1792, *The Letters of Edward Gibbon*, III, 303.
[24] Edmund Burke to French Laurence, 12 May 1797, *Letters of Edmund Burke: a selection*, ed. Harold J. Laski (Oxford University Press, 1922), 414–415.

The Republic of Regicide with an annihilated revenue, with defaced manufactures, with a ruined commerce, with an uncultivated and half depopulated country, with a discontented, distressed, enslaved, and famished people, passing with a rapid, eccentric, incalculable course, from the wildest anarchy to the sternest despotism, has actually conquered the finest parts of Europe, has distressed, disunited, deranged, and broke to pieces all the rest; and so subdued the minds of the rulers in every nation, that hardly any resource presents itself to them, except that of entitling themselves to a contemptuous mercy by a display of their imbecility and meanness.[25]

Burke was not just worried that British ministers exhausted by war and concerned about bankruptcy would give up. He believed that powerful politicians, including Charles James Fox and William Petty, had already been seduced. The British people were more than likely to follow suit. Burke was not surprised in April 1797 at news of the Spithead mutiny, when the sailors of the Royal Navy created a miniature republic on the Solent off Portsmouth Harbour. He called it 'the first nidus and hot-bed of their [French] infection'. It might well be a prelude to a French invading force 'convoyed by a British Navy to an attack upon this kingdom'.[26]

Gibbon was as concerned with the small states of Europe as he was with Britain. He spent sixteen years in Switzerland during his life, at certain moments considered himself to be Swiss or French rather than English, and owed his engagement with Swiss, Dutch, French, and Italian discussions of classical literature, erudition, antiquarianism, Protestant apologetic, history, and philosophy to his life at Lausanne, the most important town of the Pays du Vaud, then occupied by the republic of Bern.[27] In his *Memoirs* he made the point that 'such as I am in Genius or learning or in manners, I owe my creation to Lausanne; it was in that school, that the statue was discovered in the block of marble.'[28] On 9 May 1793, his 57th birthday, he left Lausanne, avoided the armies in the path of northern travellers, and arrived in London via Brussels and Ostend. He continued to lament the tenor of the times and especially the fate of the Swiss. By the time of his death, in January 1794, revolutionary philosophy had taken hold at Geneva and massacres were taking place.

---

[25] Edmund Burke, *Two Letters Addressed to a Member of the Present Parliament on the Proposals for Peace with the Regicide Directory of France* (London: F. & C. Rivington, 1796), 7.

[26] Edmund Burke to French Laurence, 12 May 1797, *Letters of Edmund Burke: a selection*, 414–415.

[27] J. G. A. Pocock, *Barbarism and Religion. Volume 1. The Enlightenments of Edward Gibbon, 1737–1764* (Cambridge: Cambridge University Press, 2001), 50–71, 167–274; Henri Vuilleumier, *Histoire de l'Eglise réformée du Pays de Vaud sous le régime bernois* (Lausanne: La Concorde, 1927–1933), vol. IV.

[28] Gibbon, *Memoirs of My Life. Edited from the Manuscripts by Georges A. Bonnard* (London: Thomas Nelson, 1969), 86.

It was only in 1798 that Gibbon's concerns about the military decline of the Swiss were confirmed, when French forces overran the cantons in a matter of days.

For Burke there was a chink of light. If British patriotism, commercial power and military strength could be fully mobilized, then the French might yet be defeated. This was the message of Burke's *Letters on a Regicide Peace* (1796). Burke employed the example of John Brown's *Estimate of Manners*. This book was received as a work of Pythagorean certainty in 1758 and 1758 yet had wrongly predicted defeat in war against France because of the growth of a frivolous effeminacy in Britain. Equally, Burke held that the jeremiad voices of the 1790s might be proved false because 'the heart of the citizen', being 'a perennial spring of energy to the state', could bring the British to victory. Convincing the British people of what was at stake, of the importance of making every possible sacrifice to defeat France, and that death in the cause of ruining the French Revolution was the ultimate moral act, were the goals of Burke's final publications and private letters. War was vital to kill the French infection. Burke was under no illusion about the power of France and the temptation that revolutionary doctrines presented to those who desired to restore the world to a state of perfect justice. Ireland was a particular weak point for Britain, because it was in Ireland that the British could straightforwardly be presented as tyrannical brutes and the French philosophy a means to a better life in terms of liberty and wealth. Burke called Ireland 'a melancholy infirmary'.[29] Like Gibbon, Burke died depressed, expecting the French Revolution to make further gains and perhaps to destroy Britain itself.

III

Within eight years of Gibbon's death and within six years of Burke's, everything had changed. Britain was isolated in the late 1790s. The Dutch Republic had become the Batavian Republic in January 1795. Prussia had left the war in April 1795 and Spain followed in July. The final collapse of the First Coalition was the Treaty of Campo Formio in October 1797, which confirmed the defeat of the Holy Roman Empire in Italy and the Rhineland and put an end to Venetian independence. An attempted invasion of Britain had taken place in February 1797 at Fishguard in Wales, and a greater assault was expected at any time. Britain, however, survived every crisis. There were victories against

[29] Edmund Burke to Thomas Keogh, 17 November 1796, *Letters of Edmund Burke: a selection*, 391–395.

French, Spanish, and Danish fleets, and Bonaparte's manoeuvres in Egypt were thwarted. The continued instability of the French Republic was a fundamental problem that politicians at Paris were forced continuously to address. The most renowned constitutional architects, such as Emmanuel Sieyes, and every ambitious young author, such as Benjamin Constant and Jean-Charles-Léonarde Simonde de Sismondi, strove to resolve the most pressing intellectual problem of the day, how to create a republic in a large state. This led to the establishment of the Consulate, which it was hoped would reconcile revolutionary republicanism and public order. The consular constitution was initially welcomed as the most remarkable political experiment in modern history, bringing praise from advocates and critics of republicanism. Rather than being the epitome of republican doctrine in modern times, however, the Consulate ultimately sounded the death-knell of European republicanism because Bonaparte, as First Consul, turned the republic into a monarchy, proclaiming the First French Empire and crowning himself on 2 December 1804; Bonaparte made monarchs of his relations in Holland, Tuscany, Westphalia, Naples and Spain. Although Bonaparte was always respectful of the term 'republic', and portrayed himself as the inheritor rather than the enemy of the French Revolution, it was evident that in his eyes the republican experiments of the 1790s had failed to bring sufficient peace, prosperity, order or glory.

The effects of the rise of Bonaparte to supreme power were profound for republicans and for revolutionaries. Bonaparte had for many years been a hero to republicans.[30] Thomas Paine, who had been due to accompany Bonaparte in invading Britain, praised him as the ultimate republican general, someone who would avoid rapine and allow any liberated people to determine the form of their government. Writing in 1804 from America, Paine condemned William Pitt for violating the Peace of Amiens and for causing all of the instabilities of the French Revolution. Still anticipating a popular uprising, he advised Britons to

---

[30] Anon., *Épître à Napoléon Bonaparte, premier Consul; par un Soldat de l'Armée d'Italie* (Paris: Renard, An X [January 1802]); Charles-Yves Cousin d'Avallon, *Bonapartiana ou recueil des réponses ingénieuses ou sublimes, actions héroiques et faits mémorables de Bonaparte* (Paris: Pillot, 1801); L.-A. Legendre, *Ode au général Bonaparte, premier consul* de la *République* française, *sur le prochain retour de la paix* (Baudelot & Ebenhart: Paris, 1801); Philip Dwyer, 'Napoleon Bonaparte as Hero and Saviour: Image, Rhetoric and Behaviour in the Construction of a Legend', *French History*, 18/4 (2004), 379–403; Cyril Triolaire, 'Fêtes officielles et culte du héros Bonaparte en province entre Directoire et Consulat', in Serge Bianchi, ed., *Héros et héroïnes de la Révolution française* (Paris: CTHS, 2012), 159–176; Pierre Serna, *La république des girouettes, 1789–1815 et au-delà: une anomalie politique: la France de l'extrême centre* (Paris: Champ Vallon, 2005), 449–453.

look to America, because 'the new world is now the preceptor of the old'.[31] Richard Carlile expressed his disappointment that 'Bonaparte fell from the great height of a successful republican general, that had crushed or might have crushed the whole of the monarchy of Europe'.[32] When Bonaparte turned out to be the solvent to republican aspiration, silence was often the response. The surest case of this was Sieyes himself; the great advocate of the equality of productive ranks in society was made a count of the empire by Bonaparte and given extensive lands at Crosne in northern Paris. Having seen all of his constitutional experiments fail, Sieyes ceased to write about politics although he lived until 1836.[33] That the most influential theorist of republican constitutionalism of the French Revolution took such steps speaks volumes. Thomas Paine stated in 1802 that of the six persons involved in creating a republican constitution in 1793 only three were alive, himself, Bertrand Barrère and Sieyes. With characteristic self-regard, Paine noted that 'Sieyes and myself have survived – he by bending with the times, and I by not bending'.[34] Yet Paine too ultimately gave up on French republicanism. He wrote to Jefferson at the end of 1802, advocating the purchase of Louisiana, that the 'French Treasury is not only empty, but the Government has consumed by anticipation a great part of the next year's revenue'.[35] He was no more optimistic about North America, despite his advice to Paineite Britons, and identified a reign of Terror in both countries that had tarnished modern republicanism. In North America, the terrorists or would-be tyrants were George Washington and John Adams. Constant and Sismondi left their work on large republics in manuscript. Neither was published until the late twentieth century.[36]

Historians have made significant strides in recent times in describing the 'lost generation' of radicals in Britain, who were subject to the

---

[31] Thomas Paine, *A Letter to the English People, on the invasion of England* (W. T. Sherwin: London, 1817), 7–10.

[32] Richard Carlile, *The Republican*, No. 6, Vol. 11, February 11, 1825 (R. Carlile: London, 1825), Vol. 11, 166.

[33] Paul Bastid, *Sieyès et sa pensée* (Paris: Hachette, 1939); Michael Sonenscher, *Sans-Culottes: An Eighteenth-Century Emblem in the French Revolution* (Princeton University Press, 2008).

[34] Paine, 'Thomas Paine to the Citizens of the United States', *The National Intelligencer*, in Moncure Daniel Conway, *The Life of Thomas Paine: With a History of His Literary, Political, and Religious Career in America, France, and England* (New York and London: G. P. Putnam's Sons, 1893), 2 vols., II, 131.

[35] Paine to Thomas Jefferson, 25 December 1802 in Moncure Daniel Conway, *The Life of Thomas Paine*, II, 313.

[36] Benjamin Constant, *Fragments d'un ouvrage abandonné sur la possibilité d'une constitution républicaine dans un grand pays*, ed. Henri Grange (Paris: Aubier, 1991); Simonde de Sismondi, *Recherches sur les constitutions des peuples libres: texte inédit*, ed. Marco Minerbi (Genève: Librairie Droz, 1965).

Treasonable Practices Act and the Seditious Meetings Act of 1795, who were spied upon and suffered endless restrictions upon their liberties, who had looked to France for succour and wondered where to turn next, and who suddenly found that even private conversations might result in public prosecution, being branded republicans, atheists, cosmopolitans, Francophile traitors and revolutionaries.[37] Those who were not attracted by the proliferating Association for the Preservation of Liberty and Property against Republicans and Levellers also had to address a gargantuan intellectual problem. How could republican reform or revolution take place without an accompanying terror, that would avoid the rise of a republican general and that would not result in the reintroduction of aristocracy and monarchy after a prolonged period of domestic disorder? The turn to Toryism was an explicable path, and one taken by sometime radicals including the poets Robert Southey, William Wordsworth and Samuel Taylor Coleridge. The question in turn for those who 'wooed liberty as a youthful lover', as Hazlitt put it about Southey, but became patriotic opponents of radicalism and republicanism, was how to justify post-revolutionary Britain?[38] If the French Revolution had created a 'spirit of despotism' in Britain, as Vicesimus Knox, the headmaster of Tonnbridge School, wrote in 1795, in what ways could Britain be said to be superior to revolutionary or imperial France?[39] If liberty had been destroyed in states that embraced or that abhorred the French Revolution, were there any grounds for optimism about future politics and social life? Furthermore, were there any prospects for a sustainable peace?

IV

One perspective that became prominent in public argument across Europe was that Britain was remarkable because it had solved the problem of the relationship between rich states and poor states. Britain

---

[37] Greg Claeys, 'The Origins of the Rights of Labour: Republicanism, Commerce, and the Construction of Modern Social Theory in Britain, 1796–1805', *The Journal of Modern History*, 66 (1994), 249–290; John Mee, 'Anxieties of Enthusiasm: Coleridge, Prophecy, and Popular Politics in the 1790s', *The Huntington Library Quarterly*, 60 (1997), 179–203; John Barrell, *Imagining the King's Death: Figurative Treason, Fantasies of Regicide, 1793–1796* (Oxford University Press, 2000) and *The Spirit of Despotism: Invasions of Privacy in the 1790s* (Oxford University Press, 2006); Michael T. David and Paul A. Pickering, eds., *Unrespectable Radicals? Popular Politics in the Age of Reform* (Farnham: Ashgate, 2007); Kenneth R. Johnston, *Unusual Suspects: Pitt's Reign of Alarm and the Lost Generation of the 1790s* (Oxford University Press, 2013).

[38] William Hazlitt, 'Mr Southey' in *The Spirit of the Age: Or Contemporary Portraits* (London: Henry Colburn, 1825), 369.

[39] Vicesimus Knox, *The Spirit of Despotism* (London: W. Hone), 1795.

had become a true empire for liberty in the sense that it protected states inferior in size and strength, and had worked out how to maintain their cultural autonomy, secure their religious identity, and foster their economic development, while avoiding tyrannical rule from the London metropolis or ministerial dominion over their trade. Somehow the odd composite monarchy established after the Union of 1707 had managed to combat the flux, inconstancy and upheaval traditionally associated with commitment to trade. Trade within an empire also entailed peace, and the most vocal supporters of Britain argued that perpetual peace once more became a possibility in politics by following the British example. Every one of these claims was contested. The old argument that in Britain 'where all is self . . . the mind is contracted and debased, and the nation declining from that cause' was echoed by Thomas Paine's *Decline and Fall of the English System of Finance* (1796).[40] Those who remained friends to France reminded readers of the conquest of an England in decline by the Normans, the decrepit nature of contemporary Britain, and of the imminence of the defeat of Britain by France.[41] The view that Britain was addicted to war and about to collapse, having a 'miserable prospect before its eyes', was as prominent as ever in national argument.[42] Others embraced Bonaparte as a new Charlemagne who was recreating a Catholic empire a millennium on.[43] Bonaparte's

---

[40] Batista Angeloni [John Shebbeare], *Select letters on the English nation by Batista Angeloni, a Jesuit, who resided many years in London. Translated from the original Italian* (Dublin: Williamson, 1763), 58; Thomas Paine, *Décadence et chute du système des Finances de l'Anglererre* (Paris: Cercle Social, 1796).

[41] Anon, *Souvenirs du roi d'Angleterre pendant sa maladie, traduits sur la XIIIe. Edition de l'ouvrage dans lequel sont traces les principaux evenemens de son règne . . . et l'influence de M. Pitt sur les affaires de l'Europe* (Paris: Fuchs et al., An IX); Anon, *Plan d'une descente décisive en Angleterre, par un ami de sa patrie* (Paris: Rousseau, 1804); Claude-Auguste Dorion, *Bataille d'Hastings, ou l'Angleterre conquise: poème en dix chants* (Paris: Le Normant, 1806).

[42] Thomas Paine, *The Decline and Fall of the English System of Finance* [1796], *The Writings of Thomas Paine* (London, 1899), 3 vols., III, 311; Daniel Malthus to Thomas Robert Malthus, 14 April 1796 in *The Crisis: a View of the Present Interesting State of Great Britain, by a Friend of the Constitution*, T. R. Malthus, *The Unpublished Papers* (Cambridge University Press, 1997), 62; William Godwin, *The Enquirer* (London, 1797), ix, 291; Joseph Priestley to George Thatcher, 10 March 1798, 'Letters of Joseph Priestley', *Massachusetts Historical Society Proceedings*, ser. 2,3 (1886–7), 18–19 and *The Theological and Miscellaneous Writings of Joseph Priestley* (London, 1817–31), i, 398; Thomas Spence, 'A letter from Ralph Hodge, to his cousin John Bull' [1795], *The Political Works of Thomas Spence* (Newcastle-upon-Tyne, 1982), 22.

[43] On Bonaparte as Charlemagne see François Xavier Pagès, *Histoire du Consulat de Bonaparte: contenant tous les évènemens politiques et militaires.* (Paris: Testu, 1803), 2 vols., II, 512; Charles Théveneau de Morande, *Plan du poëme de Charlemagne* (Paris: Courcier, 1804), 325; 'Melancthon' [Thomas Lewis O'Beirne], *A Letter to Dr. Troy, Titular Archbishop of Dublin, on the Coronation of Bonarparte, by Pope Pius the Seventh* (London: Hatchard, 1805), 35–36; William Burdon, *The life and character of Bonaparte: From his*

coronation was modelled on that of Charlemagne, with a parade of virgins and imperial regalia, including the adoption of Charlemagne's symbol of the bee. Within the *respublica Christiana*, communities were to be protected by an emperor devoted to religious and political diversity and toleration.[44] Lucien Bonaparte tellingly composed the epic poem 'Charlemagne', dedicated to Pope Pius VII, once he had become estranged from his brother Napoleon; there could be no greater insult than to underline the differences between the emperors medieval and modern.[45]

The view of Britain as a new kind of state, and one that ought to be a model polity, was asserted especially among those who perceived France in the 1790s to have been continuing its ancient imperial adventures on mainland Europe under the veil of an aspiration to republican liberty. In great detail such observers as Jacques Mallet du Pan, François d'Ivernois, Thomas Brooke Clarke and Friedrich Gentz described the dismemberment of Europe's old republics, and charted the effects of the loss of sovereignty and the loss of civil liberty that accompanied French rule. D'Ivernois' work is illustrative in seeking to combat the creation of two Europes, the Christian continent of independent states characterised by morality, liberty and property, and the revolutionary empire of barbarism, irreligion and massacre. Even a culture as entrenched as Calvinism at Geneva had disintegrated in the face of revolutionary doctrine:

... the moral character of the most virtuous nation [Geneva], affords no security whatever, that revolutionary doctrines, if suffered to be propagated in it, will have a less pernicious influence upon its manners, than upon those of any other nation. It is impossible that those doctrines can take root in any such nation, without producing a complete, and radical change in its character. It is barely two months since the Genevese deservedly possessed the reputation of a brave and humane people. One single night of revolution [19 July 1794], by putting the arms which had been wrested from the people of property, into the hands of those who possessed nothing, instantly changed the former into dastardly cowards, and the latter into ferocious beasts of prey.[46]

---

birth to the 15th of August, 1804 (Newcastle-upon-Tyne: K. Anderson, 1805), 2nd edn., 214–217.

[44] Bancamaria Fontana, 'The Napoleonic Empire and the Europe of Nations', in Anthony Pagden ed., *The Idea of Europe from Antiquity to the European Union* (Cambridge University Press, 2002), 116–228.

[45] Lucien Bonaparte, *Charlemagne; ou l'église délivrée* (London: Longman et al., 1814).

[46] D'Ivernois, *La Révolution française à Genève: tableau historique et politique de la France envers les Genevois, depuis le mois d'Octobre 1792 au mois de Juillet 1795* (London: Vernor and Hood et al., 1795), 95–96. The translation is from *An account of the late revolution in Geneva; and of the conduct of France towards that republic, from October, 1792, to October, 1794; in a series of letters, to a citizen of Philadelphia* (Philadelphia: Francis C. King, 1798), 66.

D'Ivernois concluded that old Geneva was gone. There was no foresee-able way back. The city 'that was once so distinguished among the cities of the earth . . . the seat of religion, of morality, of art and of commerce, but above all, of sacred liberty . . . is irrecoverably lost: peace, security, and happiness, have for ever abandoned her'. An exodus for North America had commenced because Europe was on the brink of a new dark age.[47] After the creation of the Cisalpine Republic in northern Italy in 1797, and after Switzerland was transformed into the Helvetic Republic and Geneva annexed to France in 1798, d'Ivernois' compatriot Jacques Mallet Du Pan's *Essai historique sur la destruction de la Ligue & de la liberté helvétiques* (1798) came to the conclusion that the French were destroying Europe, stating that the French destruction of Switzerland had left 'only rocks, ruins, and demagogues'. A frontispiece from the *Emblemata politica* of 1618 accompanied the English translation of 1799. It showed a republican leopard astride the carcass of a magnificent stag, entitled 'havoc and spoil and ruin are my gain'. The hope for old Europe was altogether Britain. Britain was described as the state that was alone capable of defeating imperial France and of restoring peace to the globe. Its economy and financial power was stronger than ever.[48] It was also something new in the world in terms of the nature of its empire. It was an empire for liberty because it perceived its own interests to be identical to the interests of the weak and small states of Europe, which had been dismembered by revolutionary France. The creation of this empire for liberty was more significant than the French Revolution. It would prove to be longer lasting, and more determinant of the future of Europe.

V

The work of Istvan Hont is seminal here in charting what he termed the 'rich country-poor country' debate.[49] In fact, as Hont explained in his second major article on the subject, the controversy was bet-ter described as facilitating comparative analysis of the economic well-being of states and of evaluating their likely destinies as commercial

---

[47] D'Ivernois, *La Révolution française à Genève*, 165; *An Account of the late revolution*, 41, 53, 61–67.

[48] Frederic Gentz, *Essai sur l'état actuel de l'administration des finances et de la richesse nationale de la Grande Bretagne* (London: J. Debrett, 1800), dedication to Sir Francis d'Ivernois, 3.

[49] Istvan Hont, 'The "Rich Country-Poor Country" Debate in the Scottish Enlighten-ment', in *Jealousy of Trade: International Competition and the Nation State in Historical Perspective*, 267–322.

societies.[50] The commonplace view throughout the eighteenth century
was that rich commercial societies would sooner or later face upheaval
and decline because their trade would be undermined by competitors in
poorer states, which could easily undercut the wage costs faced by industries in rich states. This meant that commercial societies could never
expect to be stable states in terms of their wealth or their politics. Hont
showed that the origin of this argument could be traced to English fears
about the trade of Ireland, where the price of labour was much lower.
For John Locke it was obvious that Irish woollen manufactures had to be
'restrained and penalized'. In the view of Charles Davenant Ireland had
to be denied 'a capacity to ruin England'. For Richard Cantillon, 'States
who rise by trade do not fail to sink afterwards'.[51] Hont showed that such
views echoed through the eighteenth century, with David Hume's essay
'Of Money' being seen as the classic statement of the rich country-poor
country argument. The contention that the trade of rich states would
be undermined by the cheapness of labour in poor states led large numbers of French works, including Victor-Riqueti de Mirabeau's *L'Ami des
homes* (1756), Claude-Adrien Helvétius' *De l'Esprit* (1758) and Etienne
Bonnot, abbé de Condillac's *Le Commerce et le Gouvernement, Consid-
érés Rélativement l'un à l'Autre* (1776) to anticipate the decline of Britain.
More particularly, the nature of the English empire had to be tyrannical,
because otherwise the cheaper labour of the Welsh, the Scots and the
Irish would undermine English merchants and thereby English power.
High wage costs also opened the door to luxury, generating a spirit of
effeminacy which authors from John Brown's *Estimate of Manners* (1757)
to Vicesimus Knox's *Spirit of Despotism* (1795) was held to be the reason
for Britain's military decline relative to France.

Hont noticed that the consequence of many readings of Hume's 'Of
Money' was to portray him as an enemy of the union between England and Scotland in 1707. Scotland, being a poor country, would
undermine English trade; this would never have been acceptable to
the English, would have created conflict between the countries and

---

[50] Istvan Hont, 'The "Rich Country-Poor Country" Debate Revisited: The Irish Origins
and French Reception of the Hume Paradox', in Margaret Schabas and Carl Wennerlind eds., *David Hume's Political Economy* (London: Routledge, 2008), 243–323.

[51] Istvan Hont 'The "Rich Country-Poor Country" Debate Revisited', citing Locke 'Irish
Trade Proposal for the Board of Trade', Accepted August 24, 1697, in Henry Richard
Fox Bourne, *The Life of John Locke* (London: King, 1876), 2 vols., II, 263–272, Charles
D'Avenant, 'An Essay upon the Probable Methods of Making a people Gainers in the
Ballance of Trade', in *The Political and Commercial works of that Celebrated Writer Charles
D'Avenant, LL.D.*, ed. Sir Charles Whitworth (London: R. Horsfield, 1771), 5 vols., II,
252–254, Richard Cantillon, *Essai sur la nature du commerce en general* (London: Fletcher
Gyles, 1755), 235.

undermine any union. As his friends well knew, Hume was an arch-advocate of union, and his correspondence revealed a different view of the relationship between England and Scotland to the one implied by some of the passages in 'Of Money'. Hont revealed that William Petty, 2nd Earl Shelburne, gave permission to Thomas Brooke Clarke in 1800 to publish in his *A Survey of the Strength and Opulence of Great Britain* (1801) one of Hume's private letters to the political economist Henry Home, Lord Kames and a response from Josiah Tucker.[52] The letter to Kames showed that far from worrying that Scottish poverty would undermine English riches, Hume believed that 'we in Scotland also possess some advantages, which may enable us to share with them [the English] in wealth and industry.' Hume went on to say that he was going to publish a new essay refuting the jealousy of trade between states, which destroyed so much commerce and led to war and corruption:

My principle is levelled against the narrow malignity and envy of nations, which can never bear to see their neighbours thriving, but continually repine at any new efforts towards industry made by any other nation. We desire, and seem by our absurd politics to endeavour to repress trade in all our neighbours, and would be glad that all Europe were reduced to the same state of desolation as Turkey: the consequence of which must be, that we would have little more than domestic trade, and would have nobody either to sell or buy from us.[53]

Hume was increasingly pessimistic about Britain's future prospects, despite his belief that the Anglo-Scottish union had been a success. He was especially concerned that unnecessary wars were being fought, that foolish antagonisms between states were leading to war, and that the British nation was addicted to debt levels that would ultimately cause a bankruptcy, however prosperous the British state appeared to be. When Hume's friend the publisher William Strahan expressed a note of optimism Hume crushed him, reiterating his belief that a road to ruin was being followed:

I wish I could have the same Idea with you of the Prosperity of our public Affairs. But when I reflect, that, from 1740 to 1761, during the Course of no more than 21 Years, while a most pacific Monarch sat on the Throne of France, the Nation ran in Debt about a hundred Millions; that the wise and virtuous Minister, Pitt, could contract more Incumbrances, in six months of an unnecessary War, than we have been able to discharge during eight Years of Peace; and that we persevere in the same frantic Maxims; I can forsee nothing but certain and speedy Ruin either to the Nation or to the public Creditors. The last, tho' a great Calamity,

---

[52] Thomas Brooke Clarke, *Survey of the strength and opulence of Great Britain* (London: T. Cadell & W. Davies, 1801), 22–27.
[53] David Hume to Henry Home, Lord Kames, 4 March, 1758, *The Letters of David Hume*, ed. J. Y. T. Greig (Oxford University Press, 1932), 2 vols., I, 270–272 (Letter 144).

would be a small one in comparison; but I cannot see how it can be brought about, while these Creditors fill all the chief Offices and are the Men of greatest Authority in the Nation. In other Respects the Kingdom may be thriving: The Improvement of our Agriculture is a good Circumstance; tho' I believe our Manufactures do not advance; and all depends on our Union with America, which, in the Nature of things, cannot long subsist. But all this is nothing in comparison of the continual Encrease of our Debts, in every idle War, into which, it seems, the Mob of London are to rush every Minister. But these are all other Peoples' Concerns; and I know not why I should trouble my head about them.[54]

Such attitudes contributed to the sense of crisis that prevailed at the outbreak of the French Revolution across Britain. One clear lesson was to follow the French in their reforms; another was that the corrupt state of Britain could never defeat French arms. In other words, Hume's view led to the perspective of Gibbon and Burke, that Britain was facing dangers greater than it had ever faced before and that Europe was being transformed. Hont recognized the difficulty of arguing between 1793 and 1812 that Britain could maintain itself militarily and economically. Such claims flew in the face of the remarkable tenacity of the French in maintaining their European conquests, from the Revolution to the Empire. Hont also acknowledged the ambition of the Anglophiles in stating that Britain was an empire for liberty, having resolved the rich country-poor country problem and abandoned the jealousy of trade. In so doing, they were going against Hume himself, Adam Smith's scepticism about the possibility of establishing a non-mercantile empire and all of the political economists, from Locke to Condillac, for whom trade was a form of war in the contemporary world and for whom Britain was the most mercantile of modern states, with policies characterised by the jealousy of trade. In short, the Anglophiles' ambition and political imagination was singular in circumstances of crisis and uncertainty about the future of Europe, in part because they believed the example of Britain's composite monarchy led to peace, while revolutionary republicanism or Bonaparte's imperialism led to perpetual war.

VI

The starting point of the argument that Britain ought to be a model for Europe was not the eleventh book of Montesquieu's *L'Esprit des lois*. Rather, it was Burke's *Reflections*. Burke was the most historically-minded of authors because he recognised the specific and uniquely fortunate circumstances that had established what he revered as, 'the

[54] David Hume to William Strahan, 11 March 1771, *The Letters of David Hume*, II, 235–238 (Letter 454).

constitution of this kingdom and the principles of the glorious Revolution of 1688'. At the same time he felt that lessons could be gleaned for other nations from British experience, partly positive and partly negative. The positive lesson was the need to adhere to the 'firm but cautious and deliberate spirit which produced the [Revolution] and which presides in the [Constitution]'. The negative message was the need to avoid enthusiasm, the passionate 'wandering from true principles' and the abandonment of moderation in favour of 'metaphysic propositions which infer universal consequences'.[55] Burke was afraid of the Constitutional Societies and Revolution Societies that had sprung up across Britain because he considered them to be directed by fools like Richard Price, the dissenting minister and radical Whig, whose sermon at the Old Jewry on 4 November 1789, entitled 'A Discourse on the Love of Our Country', drew parallels between contemporary events in France, events in North America after 1776, and the revolution in England a hundred years before. For Price, such revolutions, all unfinished, were necessary to the generation of universal benevolence on earth, the end-point of true religion and reformation that he saw as a 'blaze that lays despotism in ashes, and warms and illuminates Europe.'[56] For Burke, it was already clear from French events that to anticipate prophetically the perfection of mankind, and the establishment of universal rights, was to open the door to 'dashing Machiavellian politicians' and to fanatics, among whom 'Catiline would be thought scrupulous and [Publius Cornelius] Cethegus a man of sobriety and moderation'.[57] The result for France was 'universal anarchy, joined to national bankruptcy', the destruction of a nation through 'servitude, anarchy, bankruptcy and beggary'.[58]

In sincerely wishing that his countrymen would 'recommend to our neighbours the example of the British constitution, than to take models from them for the improvement of our own', Burke was identifying what he termed 'an invaluable treasure', a free country where politics might not be perfect, but where wisdom, virtue and moderation could be found in abundance, a solvent to 'epidemical fanaticism'.[59] Burke's stance was adopted by many of those who fell out of favour during the early course of the Revolution. Jean-Joseph Mounier, the prominent member of the National Assembly, and Jacques Necker, Louis XVI's finance minister, adopted the view that the volatility of the Revolution

---

[55] Burke, *Reflections on the Revolution in France*, 2–3, 326–327.
[56] Richard Price, *A Discourse on the Love of Our Country* (London: T. Cadell, 1789), 2nd edn., 7–9, 50–51.
[57] Burke, *Reflections on the Revolution in France*, 12, 101.
[58] Burke, *Reflections on the Revolution in France*, 80, 275.
[59] Burke, *Reflections on the Revolution in France*, 79, 140, 226, 326.

would have been avoided if British political life had been imitated at Paris.[60] A much stronger argument had to be made, however, to convince Europeans to have faith in Britain as a model, because of the commonplace accusation that Britain, however liberal its politics appeared to be, was a corrupt mercantile system and rotten to the core. As the years of war with revolutionary France passed, this viewpoint was asserted ever more vociferously by Britain's enemies. A high point came with the publication in October 1800 of Alexandre Maurice Blanc de Lanautte, comte d'Hauterive's *De l'état de la France, à la fin de l'an VIII*. This work emphasised the control exercised by mercantile interests over British politics.[61] Any link between the British constitution, the public good and liberty was entirely spurious. Politics existed to serve the small group of merchants and bankers who dominated Britain. Britain was a kleptocracy where a tiny minority lived in grotesque luxury and the many were treated like and lived like brutes. Rich tyrants dominated everyone else. Britain was among the most corrupt states in history and pitiful in consequence. The sole object of British foreign policy was to extend this dominion abroad. Britain had caused most of the wars of the century in consequence.[62] The supporters of France portrayed themselves as advocates of a free Europe characterised by civil and political liberties never imagined by previous generations. France alone could prevent the rapacious British commercial empire from dominating the economy of Europe, and in consequence the politics of every European state. The 'universal empire of maritime commerce' was not compatible with the self-government of fellow trading nations; nor was it compatible with maintaining peace.[63] Britain was a nation whose populace was motivated by pride and an aristocratic lust for power. The result was

[60] Jean-Joseph Mounier, *Considérations sur les gouvernements, et principalement sur celui qui convient à la France* (Paris: Badouin, 1789), 36–41; Jacques Necker, *Du pouvoir exécutif dans les grands états* (n.p. [Paris], 1792) 2 vols., I, 399–404; *De la Révolution française* (Paris: n.p., 1796), 4 vols., IV, 44–95.
[61] Otto Karmin, *Sir Francis D'Ivernois, sa vie, son œuvre et son temps* (Geneva: Bader and Mongenet, 1920), 322–396; Murray Forsyth, 'The old European States-system: Gentz versus Hauterive', *The Historical Journal*, 23 (1980), 521–538; Günther Kronenbitter, *Wort und Macht: Friedrich Gentz als politischer Schriftsteller* (Berlin: Duncker and Humblot, 1994); Emma Rothschild, 'Language and Empire, c. 1800', *Historical Research*, 78 (2005), 208–229; Marc Belissa, *Repenser l'ordre européen (1795–1802): De la société des rois aux droits des nations* (Paris, 2006); Isaac Nakhimovsky, 'The 'Ignominious Fall of the European Commonwealth': Gentz, Hauterive, and the Armed Neutrality of 1800', in Koen Stapelbroek, ed., *Trade and War: The Neutrality of Commerce in the Interstate System* (Helsinki: Collegium: Studies Across Disciplines in the Humanities and Social Sciences, Volume 10, 2011).
[62] Alexandre Maurice Blanc de Lanautte, comte d'Hauterive, *L'Etat de la France à la fin de l'an VIII* (Paris: Henrics, 1800), 27, 58–66, 183, 215.
[63] Hauterive, *L'Etat de la France à la fin de l'an VIII*, 149–152, 274.

Machiavellianism in international politics and the seeking of monopoly in trade.[64]

One of the reasons why Friederich Gentz's work proved so popular at the turn of the century was because he grasped the weight and power of Hauterive's assault, taking seriously the claim that 'the commercial sovereignty of the English is made the foundation of their political despotism, and England becomes more and more the lawgiver and tyrant of Europe'.[65] Britain was either a monster state and responsible for the evil and war in the world or there were other causes at work. Gentz ridiculed Hauterive by showing that there was nothing peculiar about the rise of Britain as a commercial society, that British trade had grown through the use of machinery and new inventions, and that the French alternative, a Europe of federal relationships, would result in the loss of liberty and a general reduction in wealth.[66] France rather than Britain was truly a mercantile system. Proof lay in the 'deplorable misery' that prevailed among the people and the depreciation of a currency that few trusted because they recognised the extent of commercial corruption.[67]

VII

Asserting that Britain was not a mercantile system but rather an empire altogether supportive of smaller and weaker states required evidence. This tended to come from the history of Scotland. European perceptions of Scottish authors were not limited to Smith's critique of the British economy, however vocal that register was proving to be in France.[68] Rather, Scotland was associated with a vibrant intellectual life and the creation of a philosophical school that was so great as to rival ancient authority. Negativity about the future was not the lesson to be derived from Scotland. It was a success story of commercial progress and the resolution of ancient conflicts, whether between Highlanders and Lowlanders, Jacobites and Hanoverians or Presbyterians and Episcopalians.

---

[64] Jean L. Ferri de Constant, *Londres et les Anglais* (Paris: Fain Jeune, 1804), 179, 288–290, 339–340.

[65] Friedrich von Gentz, *On the State of Europe Before and After the French Revolution*, trans. John Charles Herries (London: J. Hatchard, 1802), 337.

[66] Friedrich von Gentz, *On the State of Europe Before and After the French Revolution*, 322–353.

[67] Anon, Review of Pierre-Samuel Dupont de Nemours, *Sur la banque de France, 1806, The Anti-Jacobin Review and Magazine; Or, Monthly Political and Literary Censor: From September to January (Inclusive) 1807* (London: B. McMillan, 1807), Vol. XXV, 464.

[68] Richard Whatmore, 'Adam Smith's contribution to the French Revolution', *Past and Present*, 175 (2002), 65–89.

Thomas Brooke Clarke conveyed this view in numerous publications at the turn of the century. Brook Clarke was an indefatigable supporter of a union between Britain and Ireland. He employed the history of eighteenth-century Scotland to support an argument that Britain had resolved the rich country-poor country problem. Scotland, desperately impoverished and suffering economic decline, had thrived since 1707. Brooke Clarke quoted Henry Dundas, 1st Viscount Melville, the War Secretary, that the union had not only established liberty for Scotland but had 'broken asunder the bands of feudal vassalage'.

In Ireland as in Scotland union would 'give power to rights, wealth to poverty, extent to liberty, and happiness to all'. Britain was a unique state because poor nations that were united with it experienced economic growth far greater than that of England.[69] The kinds of faction that were characteristic of poor states, which Brooke Clarke called Scotland's 'distractions, divisions and clanship', ceased with the union and 'the industry of the inhabitants was awakened'. The result was an explosion of the population, the formation of great cities and the growth of the kinds of politeness and civility that characterised cosmopolitan commercial societies.[70]

Such a view of Scotland was particularly marked among the smaller states of Europe that had lost their independence during the French Revolution. The case of Geneva is illustrative. Connections between Britain and Geneva were increasing despite the years of war. Although he had espoused a different opinion only two years earlier, Sismondi noted in 1814 that the people of Geneva spoke and wrote in French but 'think in English'.[71] Increasing numbers of Genevans were completing their education at the University of Edinburgh.[72] The *Bibliothèque Britannique* was established as a monthly journal in 1796 by Marc-Auguste Pictet, his brother Charles Pictet de Rochemont and their friend Frédéric-Guillaume Maurice. It epitomised Anglo-Genevan connections by translating and publishing extracts from British periodicals,

---

[69] Thomas Brooke Clarke, *Misconceptions of Facts, and Misstatements of the Public Accounts, by the Right Hon. John Foster, Speaker of the Irish Parliament* (Dublin: J. Milliken, 1800), 41–45, 60.

[70] Thomas Brooke Clarke, *The Political, Commercial, and Civil, State of Ireland* (Dublin: J. Milliken, 1799), 48–59.

[71] Sismondi, *Considérations sur Genève, dans ses rapports avec Angleterre et les États protestantes* (London, 1814), 7. On Sismondi's Anglophilia see Norman King, 'Sismondi et les libéraux anglais', *Atti del Colloquio internazionale sul Sismondi. Pescia, 8–10 settembre* (Rome, 1970), 103–126; *Genève, Lieu d'Angleterre, 1725–1814*, ed. Valérie Cossy, Béla Kapossy and Richard Whatmore (Geneva: Slatkine, 2009).

[72] Olivier Perroux, *Tradition, vocation et progrès: Les élites bourgeoises de Genève, 1814–1914* (Geneva: Slatkine, 2006).

memoirs, transactions of learned societies and the work of prominent authors.[73] Through the pages of the *Bibliothèque Britannique* the writings of a number of English, Irish and Scottish authors, including Jeremy Bentham, Maria Edgeworth and Dugald Stewart, were communicated across Europe.[74] Contributions to the *Bibliothèque Britannique* underlined the health of public culture in Britain and reinforced an impression of moderation, order, a respect for law and evidence of toleration and the love of liberty. As Charles Pictet noted in his study of North America, it was because the American Revolution had been founded upon British political mores that the republican constitution was respectful of liberty and property.[75] Scotland was not perfect. The *Bibliothèque Britannique* reported Thomas Douglas, the Earl of Selkirk's decision to transport 800 highlanders to Prince Edward Island in 1803.[76] The point was, however, that without violence and rapine problems of penury and backwardness were acknowledged and addressed. The benefits of a long-standing peace were being enjoyed. This was the message of Marc-Auguste Pictet's visit to Scotland in 1801, where he was astonished at the philosophical life, commercial progress, use of machinery and establishment of canals.[77]

The most significant purveyor of the view that Europe ought to learn from Scotland was Pierre Prévost, professor of theoretical philosophy at the Genevan Academy from 1793. Prévost considered Scottish intellectual life to be so important that he translated a large number of works by Scottish authors, and composed prefaces that underscored the vibrancy

[73] David M. Bickerton, *Marc-Auguste and Charles Pictet, the 'Bibliothèque Britannique' (1796–1815) and the Dissemination of British Literature and Science on the Continent* (Geneva: Slatkine, 1986); Jean Cassaigneau and Jean Rilliet, *Marc-Auguste Pictet ou le rendez-vous de l'Europe universelle, 1752–1825* (Geneva: Slatkine, 1995).

[74] Dugald Stewart to Alexandre-Louis Prévost, 30 March 1808 in Claire Etchegaray, Knud Haakonssen, Daniel Schulthess, David Stauffer and Paul Wood, 'The Correspondence of Dugald Stewart, Pierre Prevost and their Circle, 1794–1829', *History of European Ideas*, 38/1 (2012), 19–73. See further Daniel Schulthess, 'L'école écossaise et la philosophie d'expression française: le rôle de Pierre Prevost (Genève, 1751–1839)', in *Annales Benjamin Constant*, 18–19 (1996), 97–105; Michel Malherbe, 'The Impact on Europe', in *The Cambridge Companion to the Scottish Enlightenment*, ed. Alexander Broadie (Cambridge University Press, 2003), 298–315; László Kontler, *Translations, Histories, Enlightenments. William Robertson in Germany, 1760–1795* (London: Palgrave Macmillan, 2014).

[75] Charles Pictet, *Tableau de la situation actuelle des États-Unis d'Amérique* (Paris: Du Pont, 1795), 2 vols., I, 23–36.

[76] Anon., 'Economie Politique. Observations on the Present State of the Highlands of Scotland', *Bibliothèque Britannique... Tome Trente Cinquième. Douxième Année. Littérature* (Geneva: Bibliothèque Britannique, 1807), 273–275.

[77] Marc-Auguste Pictet, *Voyage de trois mois, en Angleterre, en Écosse, et en Irlande pendant l'été de l'an IX* (Geneva: Bibliothèque Britannique, 1802), 53–88.

of Scottish culture. He maintained an extensive correspondence, especially with Dugald Stewart, and was elected fellow of the Royal Society at Edinburgh on 27 June 1796. In Prévost's view it could not be denied that there was a Scottish school of authors 'so ingenious and so profound' that their writings were being venerated 'across all of Europe'.[78] The school derived from Francis Hutcheson, the 'master and predecessor of Smith', whose goal had been to moralise the world and to promote virtue. Following Hutcheson was Hume, 'less well known on the continent as a subtle metaphysician than as the immortal historian', Adam Ferguson 'the Stoic', Hugh Blair, Dugald Stewart and Thomas Reid. The latter were so brilliant as to be 'apostles of the public good'.[79] For Prévost there was no basis to the accusation that Britain was a mercantile system destructive of liberty, culture and wealth. Since the union Scotland, a puny, unknown and backward country, had become the epicentre of the philosophical study of society.

In his translation of Benjamin Bell's *Essays on agriculture with a plan for the speedy and general improvement of land in Great Britain* (1802), Prévost's preface underlined his disagreement with Bell's claim that Britain was addicted to a manufacturing system that fostered excessive commerce, urbanisation and the love of luxury. Fortunately, principles that were 'wise and liberal' had become 'the accepted maxims of administration and politics' because of the influence of Smith's *Wealth of nations*. The mercantile system had thereby been combatted and its ill effects modified. In his introduction Prévost supplied a list of the positive lessons of Smith's doctrines for modern states and welcomed Bell's particular prescriptions for the improvement of agricultural production. At the same time he warned his readers that Bell's description of food shortages in Scotland should not be taken for the current reality. The fact was that Britain was leading the way in production and political economy, and ought to be followed by other nations.[80]

Jacques Mallet du Pan was also of the opinion that the Scottish example should be imitated by small states. Mallet du Pan did more than any other author to track the effects of the French Revolution upon Europe's independent republics. Following Virgil, he called the French Republic a 'monster frightful, formless, immense, with sight removed [Monstrum

---

[78] Pierre Prévost, *Cours de rhétorique et de belles-lettres, par Hugues Blair, . . . traduit de l'anglais par M. Pierre Prévost* (Manget and Cherbuliez: Geneva, 1808), 4 vols., I, xvi.

[79] Pierre Prévost, 'Réflexions sur les Œuvres Posthumes d'Adam Smith', in *Essais philosophiques; par Adam Smith . . . précédé d'un précis de sa vie et de ses écrits par Dugald Stewart* (Paris: Agasse, 1797), 2 vols., II, 232–242.

[80] Pierre Prévost, 'Préface', *De la Disette, par Benjamin Bell . . . Traduit par P. Prevost* (Geneva: J.-J. Paschoud, 1804), v–xv, xxv–xl.

horrendum, informe, ingens, cui lumen ademptum]'. A democracy of vampires had been created, addicted to pillage and assassination.[81] Events in France had not been seen before in history because 'no organised confederacy was ever organised against a government or against the essential order of society to such an extent, so systematically, and with such means of execution as those of Jacobins. There were no such beings as Jacobins previous to the Revolution'. The natural consequence of Jacobinism was empire, in the sense of the initiation of rebellion in every state, with the goal of the creation of 'republican despotism'. Of French activity in Venice, Mallet du Pan wrote, 'in no country have those ravagers been more pitiless, more greedy of plunder, or more abhorred'.[82] At the end of the century Mallet du Pan was concerned that Jacobinism was spreading across Ireland through the medium of the United Irishmen. It was clear to him that the solution to the problem of Ireland had to be union with Britain, because the example of Scotland proved that Britain had overcome the rich country-poor country and large state-small state problem. Since the Union of 1707, religion, liberty and property had been secured in Scotland at the same time as the animosities that had riven the nation had diminished. The benefits for small states were clear; an increase in wealth and the reduction of the kinds of factionalism and turmoil that bedevilled democracies and popular states:

If experience and facts were enough to convince men, to silence the passions, and to direct the determinations of statesmen, the view of the effects, which have resulted from the Union of Scotland with England, would be a sufficient guide on the present [Irish] question. Nothing is more striking than the situation of Scotland before the Union, compared with its present prosperity.[83]

François d'Ivernois agreed that the key to the future of Geneva was to learn from the Scottish case. For d'Ivernois, Scotland had been transformed economically since the Union of 1707. Those who argued that Scotland had been incorporated into an English empire ignored the fact that the Scottish economy had grown at a far faster rate than England itself. Further proof came from Ireland during the short time it had been incorporated into the United Kingdom in 1801. Again, economic growth had been remarkable:

81 Mallet du Pan, *Correspondance politique, pour servir à l'histoire du républicanisme français* (Hamburg: P. F. Fauche, 1796), epigraph from *The Aeneid* (III, 658), 30–35; see further Mallet du Pan's *Essai historique sur la destruction de la ligue et de la liberté helvétiques [sic]*. *Extrait du Mercure britannique* ([London]: n.p., 1798).
82 Mallet du Pan, *The British Mercury; or, Historical and critical views of the events of the present times. Volume 2. Number IX* (London: T. Cadell et al., 1798), 482–483, 289.
83 Mallet du Pan, *The British Mercury; or, Historical and critical views of the events of the present times. Volume 2. Number IX* (London: T. Cadell et al., 1798),

Since the Union, the extension of the trade of Ireland has been so rapid, and has so far outstripped that of England and Scotland that if, in the former period, one hundred was an adequate number of representatives, she is now entitled to one hundred and thirty three.[84]

The broad point that d'Ivernois was seeking to make was that if Bonaparte sought to prevent trade with Britain, through the Continental System established by the decrees of Berlin and Milan in 1806 and 1807, the result would be the impoverishment of smaller nations across Europe. The lesson was that small states were a lot better off if they were united with benevolent and cosmopolitan empires like Britain, rather than being the pawns of tyrannies like the First French Empire. France's bleeding of Geneva since the annexation of 1798 demonstrated this.[85] Scottish history since the Union and the contemporary evidence of the vibrancy of Scottish culture and intellectual life proved that the mercantile system did not impoverish poor states. As such, Scotland offered an alternative future for many of the states of Europe. Those involved in the *Bibliothèque Britannique* continued their analysis of the British model of commercial society up to the point at which Geneva became a canton, and therefore part of Switzerland, in 1815; precisely the process of union that Scotland had experienced in 1707. In 1815 a special issue of the *Bibliothèque Britannique* was published devoted to British agriculture, including Sir John Sinclair's *An Account of the Systems of Husbandry Adopted in the More Improved Districts of Scotland* (1813).[86]

When the French soldiers left Geneva in 1814, d'Ivernois and Charles Pictet were the leading negotiators at the Congress of Vienna responsible for determining the future of the formerly independent republic. After his travels in Scotland and Ireland Charles Pictet continued to extol the virtues of Scotland and the remarkable transformation of the country in his massive *Cours d'Agriculture Anglaise* of 1810.[87] He undoubtedly had Scotland in mind when he worked for a union between Geneva and Switzerland in 1815, and indeed for the creation of a constitution at Geneva that would entrench forms of political moderation that had

---

[84] François d'Ivernois, *Effects of the continental blockade upon the commerce, finances, credit and prosperity of the British Islands* (London: J. Hatchard et al., 1810), 3rd edn., xxi, 121–137.

[85] François d'Ivernois, *Exposé de l'exposé de la situation de l'Empire français et des comptes de finances: publiés à Paris en février et en mars 1813* (Paris and Geneva: J.-J. Pascoud, 1813), 153–154.

[86] *Bibliothèque Britannique. Agriculture Anglaise. Tome Vingtième* (Geneva: Bibliothèque Britannique, 1815).

[87] Charles Pictet, *Cours d'Agriculture Anglaise, avec les développement utiles aux agriculteurs du Continent* (Geneva: J.-J. Pascoud, 1808–1810), 10 vols., IV, 163–210.

been altogether lacking during the previous century, and more especially during the previous quarter of a century. Pictet was upset that the
British diplomats, Robert Stewart, Viscount Castlereagh and the Duke
of Wellington, were so narrow-minded, being unwilling to stand up for
the smaller powers against the great. Castlereagh in particular he found
exasperating because of his indifference to the Genevan cause. Despite
the fact that its ministers' politics were 'too narrow', Pictet reaffirmed his
longstanding devotion to the British cause against 'the tyrant of the continent', confessing to 'a particular predilection' for 'this beautiful political machine'.[88]

Pictet's great hope was that the Swiss would play the role that the
English evidently had towards the Scots, supporting a Genevan renaissance of culture and intellect through the nineteenth century. He confided to his daughter a profound concern, however. While the British had
resolved the problem of small and large states domestically, through the
policy of union, they had yet to apply their principles to the international
arena. Their recent policies had been brutal, towards the North Americans during the recent war, and more generally in failing to support the
weak against the strong at Vienna. In making this point he likened the
British to the Greeks, once renowned for their civilisation and philosophy, but now more likely to employ religion to facilitate robbery. In so
doing, Pictet employed exactly the Anglophobic rhetoric of the mercantile system that had pervaded the years of war:

Britain appears to be charged by Providence to maintain the public law of the
civilized world; yet its admirals announce to the Americans that they will burn its
ports and ravage its coasts! Is this the same nation that has so recently abolished
the slave trade? The British are like the modern Greeks who make the sign of the
cross with one hand and steal with the other. Poor humanity![89]

Such rhetoric continued to be marked across the continent. Just as a
feeling of a return to normal politics had been felt when the French Revolution failed, so many observers anticipated the collapse of Britain in
accordance with the predictions of the political economists of the eighteenth century. Many followers of Adam Smith, including Jean-Baptiste
Say, expressed this view on the grounds that Britain remained a mercantile system whose politicians were stooges of commercial interests;

[88] Pictet to Albert Turrettini, 30 October, 1815, *Genève et Les Traités De 1815: Correspondance Diplomatique De Pictet De Rochemont Et De François D'Ivernois* (Geneva: Libr.
Kündig, 1914), ed. Lucien Cramer, 2 vols., II, 185–186.

[89] Charles Pictet to Amélie Pictet de Lancy, 10 October, 1814, *Charles Pictet de Rochemont
(1755–1824), Lettres écrites à sa famille pendant ses missions diplomatiques à Bâle, Paris,
Vienne, Paris et Turin (1814–1816)* (Geneva: Fondation des archives de la famille Pictet,
2010), 52.

as such it remained a likely source of war across Europe.[90] Say in the 1810s was close to Jeremy Bentham, newly converted to republicanism and democracy, and cited Bentham in the third edition of his *Traité d'économie politique* (1817) in describing the parlous state of Britain. Bentham's perspective on the likely future of Britain and Europe was very different to that expressed by Etienne Dumont in his editions of Bentham's manuscripts that appeared in the *Bibliothèque Britannique* and in 1802 as *Traité de legislation pénale*.[91] In other words, the battle for Europe that resulted in the defeat of France did not result in the acceptance of Britain as an empire for liberty and peace. Rather, the extent to which Britain was a novel state, had overcome the rich country-poor country problem, and ought in consequence to take a stand internationally in support of the weaker powers of Europe, continued to be asserted, especially by Scots and Romantics, but also continued to be questioned.[92]

[90] Jean-Baptiste Say, *De l'Angleterre et des Anglais* (Paris, 1815).

[91] Etienne Dumont, 'Lettre aux Rédacteurs de la Bibliothèque Britannique sur les ouvrages de Bentham', v (1797), 155–164. On Bentham and Say see Richard Whatmore, *Republicanism and the French Revolution. An Intellectual History of Jean-Baptiste Say's Political Economy* (Oxford University Press, 2000) and Emmanuelle de Champs, *Enlightenment and Utility. Bentham in French. Bentham and France* (Cambridge University Press, 2015).

[92] Anna Plassart, *The Scottish Enlightenment and the French Revolution* (Cambridge University Press, 2015), 187–224; Paul Stock, *The Shelley-Byron Circle and the Idea of Europe* (London: Palgrave Macmillan, 2010).

9   Karl Ludwig von Haller's critique of liberal peace

Béla Kapossy[1]

I

Rousseau's name was from the outset associated with the exploits and failures of the French Revolution. By 1790 his bust, together with a copy of his *Social Contract*, adorned the General Assembly. In 1794, while the Terror was raging in Paris, his body was ceremoniously brought from Ermenonville to the Panthenon and laid to rest amongst the Greats of France. For many Jacobins, Rousseau was undisputedly a saintly figure who singlehandedly provided the blueprint for a society in which any potential threat to the citizens' liberty would be eliminated indefinitely.[2] In light of the intensity with which his political ideas were discussed in the assemblies and committees, and the religious veneration that was bestowed upon him by those in charge of organising some of the bloodiest episodes of the revolutionary civil war, it seemed inevitable that Rousseau should bear the brunt of the anti-revolutionary backlash in the late eighteenth and early nineteenth century. When visiting Ermenonville in 1800 Napoleon Bonaparte is said to have remarked: "He was a mad man, your Rousseau; it is he who brought us to where he are now".[3] The counter-revolutionary writer Louis-Gabriel-Ambroise de Bonald accused Rousseau of having committed the "great political error" of

---

[1] For their valuable comments and editorial assistance, I would like to thank Edward Castleton, Isaac Nakhimovsky, Michael Sonenscher, and Richard Whatmore. Earlier versions of this chapter were presented in Besançon, Cambridge, Jena, Lausanne, and Tartu. I am grateful to those present for convincing me of the importance of Haller for understanding the variety of modern political thought.

[2] Bernard Manin, « Rousseau », in François Furet and Mona Ozouf (eds.), *Dictionnaire critique de la révolution française* (Paris 1988), 872–885. For recent surveys of the nineteenth-century French reception of Rousseau, see Raymond Trousson, *Rousseau. Mémoire de la critique 1800–1912* (Presses de l'université Paris-Sorbonne, 2012); Avi Lifshitz, ed., *Engaging with Rousseau. Reaction and Interpretation from the Eighteenth Century to the Present* (Cambridge University Press, 2016).

[3] Pierre-Louis Roederer, *Œuvres du comte P.L. Roederer*, ed. A. M. Roederer, 8 vols., Paris: Firmin Didot Frères, 1853–1859, Vol. 3, p. 336.

confusing the *volonté générale* with the *volonté collective*,[4] while the Abbé Barruel, in his history of the intellectual origins of Jacobinism, dedicated an entire chapter to "The System of Jean-Jacques Rousseau", claiming that by advocating the principles of small republics like Geneva for large nations, he had effectively set the road for the collective tyranny of the Parisian revolutionary masses.[5] Benjamin Constant, too, described the *Social Contract* in his novel *Adolphe* as the gateway to all forms of tyranny, "to that of a single person, to that of a few, to that of all, to legally constituted oppression, or to that exercised by popular fury".[6] Taken in by Rousseau's admiration for ancient Rome, "our reformers", Constant wrote, had wished to exercise public authority in the same way as it was done in the free states of Greece and in Rome. They believed "that everything had to give way to a collective authority and that any restrictions to individual freedom would be resolved through taking part in popular sovereignty".[7]

Critical engagement with Rousseau and his legacy was a common fixture in late and post revolutionary political thought, not only in France, but also and especially in Germany and Switzerland. In France, Rousseau was often held responsible for the confusion that marked the constitutional debates during the revolution, notably over how the constituting powers, the legislature and the government ought to be seen to be related to one another. The German as well as the Swiss debates on Rousseau were similar to those in France, although no one in Switzerland mistook Rousseau for a *philosophe* or advocate of materialism. Moreover, the Swiss experience of the revolution was different and this also affected responses to Rousseau. The territory of the Swiss Confederation was invaded in 1798 by French revolutionary troops on the grounds that the exploitative and oligarchic regimes of the Swiss city-states presented a systematic violation of the principle of human rights. The loosely aligned federation of late-medieval communes, principalities, and cities was transformed into a single and unified Helvetic Republic following the French model.[8] Swiss commentators were in no doubt as to who

---

[4] Louis-Gabriel-Ambroise de Bonald, *Essai analytique sur les lois naturelles de l'ordre social*, Paris: [s.n.], 1800, p. 139.

[5] Augustin de Barruel, *Mémoires pour servir à l'histoire du Jacobinisme*, 5 vols., Hamburg: P. Fauche, 1798–1799, Vol. 2, pp. 100–123.

[6] Benjamin Constant, *Adolphe. Anecdote trouvée dans les papiers d'un inconnu*, Paris: Charpentier, 1842, p. 295.

[7] Ibid., p. 300.

[8] See Alain Jacques Crouz-Tornare, ed., *Quand Napoléon Bonaparte recréa la Suisse: la genèse et la mise en œuvre de l'Acte de médiation*, Paris: Société des études robespierristes, 2005; Mario Turchetti, ed., *La Suisse de la Médiation dans l'Europe napoléonienne (1803–1814): actes du Colloque de Fribourg (2003)*, Academic Press Fribourg, 2005.

was to blame for setting in motion the dynamic that lead to the fall of the old Confederation. Recalling a conversation he had with Napoleon in 1797, the Bernese political theorist and writer Karl Viktor von Bonstetten stated that Bonaparte had "praised the advantages of revolutions entirely in the tone of the *Contrat social*".[9]

The German states fared no better than the Swiss. After the radical rearrangements of the southern German states into the Confederation of the Rhine in 1806, the Prussian army was defeated at Jena and Auerstätt in October 1806, leaving Napoleon free to enter Berlin at the end of November. From a German or Swiss perspective, accordingly, the French Revolution was marked not only by its notorious instability and by what it did to its own people, but also by its propensity to export revolution beyond its borders by military means.[10] It followed that Rousseau's legacy was bound up with the problem of republican war as much as with the problem of social unrest and constitutional crisis.

The first two decades of the nineteenth century saw an explosion of German and Swiss political writing in which those advocating constitutional reforms and unification faced the task of trying to disentangle what they saw as Rousseau's more cryptic or impracticable ideas of the *volonté générale* and to provide his theory of the state with a coherent and workable theory of representation. They likewise felt compelled to address Rousseau's dire predication that the lawlessness of inter-state relations might make it impossible to maintain the rule of law within states. German thinkers recognised Kant's indebtedness to Rousseau.[11] Both Kant and Rousseau, in turn, were seen to have been responding directly to Hobbes. As a result, German discussions of Rousseau were often woven into debates about Kant's perpetual peace and Hobbes' association of the realm of international relations with the state of nature; Fichte's *Closed commercial state* was probably the most famous of the many attempts to grapple with the Hobbesian and Rousseauean legacy for theories of perpetual peace.[12]

In what follows I want to elaborate on the German-speaking reception of Rousseau within the context of debates on perpetual peace by

---

[9] See Bonsettiana. Briefkorrespondenzen Karl Viktor von Bonstettens und seines Kreises, (eds.) Doris and Peter Walser-Wilhemn, Vol. 7, Bern: Peter Lang, 1997, p. 1119.

[10] Jacques Godechot, *La grande nation: l'expansion révolutionnaire de la France de 1789 à 1799*, Paris: Aubier Montaigne, 1983.

[11] See Richard Tuck, 'How Rousseau was read in the eighteenth and nineteenth centuries' in Béla Kapossy, Isaac Nakhimovsky, Sophus Reinert, and Richard Whatmore (eds.), *Morals, Markets and Politics*, Harvard University Press, forthcoming.

[12] Isaac Nakhimovsky, *The Closed Commercial State: Perpetual Peace and Commercial Society from Rousseau to Fichte*, Princeton University Press, 2011.

focusing on one of the most influential texts of the German Restauration[13] period, one that not only gave the period its name, but that also earned its author, the self-taught jurist Karl Ludwig von Haller, the title of "Rousseau of the Restauration" and "Anti-Rousseau" at the same time.[14] The nineteenth-century political economist Wilhelm Roscher claimed that Haller was "without doubt the most honest, the most consistent and [intellectually] ruthless" of all German reactionaries.[15] No one else provided such a "grandiose, consistent and systematic reaction".[16] The legal scholar Johann Caspar Bluntschli came to a similar conclusion, arguing that "in the same way as Rousseau became the prophet and instigator of revolution, Haller became the teacher and champion of the Restauration".[17]

Haller's main work, *Restauration of Political Science, or Theory of the natural state of sociability opposed to the chimerical and artificial state of civil society*, was first published in German in six volumes between 1816 and 1834.[18] Together with his essays on the Spanish Cortes, his letter to his family explaining his conversion to Catholicism, and his studies of the language of Liberalism, it evoked extensive polemical responses and made him a hated figure within European liberal circles.[19] At the

[13] See 'Reaktion, Restauration' in Otto Brunner et al. (eds.), *Geschichtliche Grundbegriffe. Historisches Lexikon zur politisch-sozialen Sprache in Deutschland*, Stuttgart: Klett-Cotta, 1972–1997, vol. 5, pp. 179–230.

[14] See especially Karl Riedel, *Karl Ludwig von Haller's staatsrechtliche Grundsätze. Nach dessen Restauration der Staatswissenschaft bearbeitet und beleuchtet*, Darmstadt: C.W. Leske, 1842, xiv–xv.

[15] Wilhelm Roscher, *Geschichte der National-Oekonomik in Deutschland*, München: Oldenbourg, 1874, p. 779

[16] Roscher, Ibid., p. 1025.

[17] J.C. Bluntschli and K. Brater, *Deutsches Staats-Wörterbuch*, vol. 4, Stuttgart und Leipzig: Expedition des Staats-Wörterbuchs, 1859, p. 622.

[18] Karl Ludwig von Haller, *Restauration der Staatswissenschaft, oder Theorie des natürlich-geselligen Zustands, der Chimäre des künstlich-bürgerlichen entgegengesetzt, von Carl Ludwig von Haller, des souverainen wie auch des geheimen Raths der Republik Bern, der Königl. Gesellschaft der Wissenschaften zu Göttingen correspondirendem Mitglied etc.*, 6 vols., Winterthur: Steinersche Buchhandlung, 1816–1834. All references are to the second edition 6 vols., Winterthur: Steinersche Buchhandlung, 1820–1834, reprinted 6 vols., Aalen: Scientia, 1964. On Haller, see Ronald Roggen, '*Restauration*' – *Kampfruf und Schimpfwort*, Freiburg i.Ü.: Universitätsverlag Freiburg, 1999; Kurt Guggisberg, *Carl Ludwig von Haller*, Frauenfeld/Leipzig: Huber & Co., 1938; Wilhelm Hans v. Sonntag, *Die Staatsauffassung Carl Ludwig v. Hallers, ihre metaphysische Grundlegung und ihre politische Formung*, Jena: Gustav Fischer, 1929; Ewald Reinhard, *Karl Ludwig von Haller, der Restaurator der Staatswissenschaft*, Münster: Wirtschafts- und Sozialwissenschaftlicher Verlag, 1933. For a full bibliography, see Albert Portmann-Tinguely, 'Haller, Karl Ludwig von', in *Biographisch-Bibliographisches Kirchenlexikon*, vol. 17, Herzberg: Bautz, 2000, pp. 587–614.

[19] Karl Ludwig von Haller, Über die Constitution der Spanischen Cortes, [Winterthur]: s.n. 1820.

Wartburgfest in 1817, a gathering of liberal students rallying for German unification, the first book of Haller's *Restauration* was burned as a symbol of the reactionary politics of the German courts. While some dismissed Haller as a sleeper who had just awoken from medieval slumber,[20] others took him far more seriously. Adam Müller demanded that every German university should have a chair dedicated to the development and dissemination of Haller's ideas. Had it not been for his conversion to Catholicism in 1820 Haller would probably have been offered a professorship in political science in Berlin and in all likelihood would have ended up as a colleague of Hegel.[21] Despite his failure to get an academic appointment at a German university, Haller's *Restauration* had a lasting impact. It remained crucial to the development of German constitutional and medieval political history, informing discussions of the history of the origins of the German state, especially the distinction between private and public law, and the political status of medieval corporations from Romeo Maurenbrecher, Johann Caspar Bluntschli, Robert von Mohl, right up to Otto von Gierke, Hugo Preuss, Georg von Below, Max Weber, and Otto Brunner.[22]

Most studies of Haller's theory of the patrimonial state have focused on his involvement in Prussian anti-constitutionalist circles and the French ultra-Catholic monarchist movement.[23] Given Haller's considerable influence at the court of Frederic William IV in Berlin and the backing he received from the Prussian landed nobility defending the institution of manorialism, the Prussian context, as Friedrich Meineke

[20] Wilhelm Roscher, *Geschichte der National-Oekonomik in Deutschland*, p. 779.

[21] On Hegel's critique of Haller, see Walter Kämpfer, 'Die Kritik Hegels an der Staatsaufassung Karl Ludwig von Hallers', in *Festgabe Max Obrecht, herausgegeben vom solothurnischen Juristenverein*, Solothurn: Union Druck, 1961, pp. 3–20; Lionel Ponton, « L'opposition de Hegel au conservatisme de Charles-Louis de Haller », *Laval théologique et philosophique*, 51 (1995) 323–334.

[22] Romeo Maurenbrecher, *Die deutschen regierenden Fürsten und die* Souverainität, Frankfurt a.M.: Franz Varrentrapp, 1839; Robert von Mohl, 'Karl Ludwig von Haller', in *Die Geschichte und Literatur der Staatswissenschaften*, vol. 2, Erlangen: Verlag Ferdiand Enke, 1856, pp. 529–560; Ibid., *Encyklopädie der Staatswissenschaften*, Tübingen: H. Laupp, 1859, p. 298ff., where he distinguishes 'Patriarchal State', 'Patrimonial Rule', 'Theocracy', 'Classic State', and 'Legal State'; Johann Caspar Bluntschli, *Geschichte des allgemeinen Staatsrechts und der Politik, seit dem sechzehnten Jahrhundert bis zur* Gegenwart, Münschen: Literarisch-artistische Anstalt, 1864, pp. 494–502; Hugo Preuss, *Gemeinde, Staat, Reich als Gebietskörperschaften: Versuch einer deutschen Staatskonstruktion auf Grundlage der Genossenschaftstheorie*, Berlin: J. Springer, 1889; Georg von Below, *Der deutsche Staat des Mittelalters*, Leipzig: Quelle und Meyer, 1914; Max Weber, *Wirtschaft und Gesellschaft, Max Weber-Gesamtausgabe*, vol. 1/23, Tübingen: Mohr Siebeck, 2013, Chapter 3: 'Typen der Herrschaft', pp. 449–591; Otto Brunner, *Land and Lordship* (1939), Philadelphia: University of Pennsylvania Press, 1992, pp. 124–127.

[23] See, J.J. Oechslin, *Le mouvement ultra-royaliste sous la Restauration. Son idéologie et son action politique*, Paris: R. Pichon, 1960.

revealed, is indeed very illuminating.[24] The Prussian context is all the more revealing as some of the most substantive criticisms of Haller's thought were formulated by Prussian liberal academics; a leading example is the work of Kant's successor at Königsberg, Wilhelm Traugott Krug, several of whose writings, including *The Science of Politics in the process of Restauration* of 1817 and the *History of Liberalism* of 1823 took direct aim at Haller.[25] This emphasis on the Prussian context is not, however, unproblematic. For one, Haller was not Prussian, nor can he be seen to be part of the Romantic Movement, as has often been claimed.[26] The same applies to Haller's association with the likes of Bonald or de Maistre.[27] While Haller later did stylise himself as a spokesman of the Catholic anti-liberal international, defending the Catholic Church as the only institution capable of providing the European state system with a universal moral grounding, there is little in his works to suggest that he shared the position of German Idealism that men had a calling to aspire to a higher level of personal freedom, and that religion constituted a necessary part within that process.[28] There was no fundamental distinction between what he called divine order and natural order, a point that was duly noted by Haller's many Protestant critics who question his true motives for converting to Catholicism. The return to the Catholic faith was a logical step of his political conversion to Patrimonialism.[29]

[24] Friedrich Meineke, *Cosmopolitanism and the Nation State* (1908), Princeton University Press, 1970, esp. Chapter 10; Robert M. Berdahl, *The Politics of the Prussian Nobility: The Development of a Conservative Ideology, 1770–1848*, Princeton University Press, 1988.

[25] Wilhelm Traugott Krug, *Die Staatswissenschaft im Restaurazionsprozesse der Herren von Haller, Adam Müller und Konsorten* (Leipzig: Fleischer, 1817); *Geschichtliche Darstellung des Liberalismus alter und neuer Zeit* (Leipzig: Brockhaus, 1823); *Dikäopolitik oder neue Restaurazion der Staatswissenschaft mittels des Rechtsgesetzes* (Leipzig: Hartmann, 1824).

[26] See Jakob Baxa, *Einführung in die romantische Staatswissenschaft*, Jena: Gustav Fischer, 1931, p. 235; O. Friedländer, *C.L. von Haller und die Gesellschaftslehre der Romantik*, Diss. Freiburg i.B., 1922; and especially Herbert R. Liedke, « The German Romanticists and Karl Ludwig von Haller's Doctrines of European Restauration », *The Journal of English and Germanic Philology*, Vol. 57, No. 3 (Kuly 1958), pp. 371–393.

[27] David, Klinck, *The French conterrevolutionary theorist Louis de Bonald (1754–1840)*, New York: Peter Lang, 1996.

[28] See K.G. König, 'Karl Ludwig von Haller, zubenannt 'der Restaurator'', in J. C. Bluntschli, *Kritische Überschau der deutschen Gesetzgebung und Rechtswissenschaft*, vol. 3, München: Literarisch-artistische Anstalt, 1856, pp. 89–104. Haller's earlier attempt to derive political theory from scripture was largely ignored by contemporaries and lacked the philosophical ambition of the *Restauration*; see, Haller, *Politische Religion oder biblische Lehre über die Staaten*, Winterthur: Steiner, 1811.

[29] See, for example, Jean Louis Henri Manuel, *Observations adressées à M. Ch. L. de Haller, sur la lettre par laquelle il annonce à sa famille son retour à l'église de Rome*, Lausanne: Henri Fischer, 1821; Wilhelm Traugott Krug, *Apologie der protestantischen Kirche gegen die Verunglimpflichungen des Herrn von Haller in dessen Sendschreiben an seine Familie*, Leipzig: Rein'sche Buchhandlung, 1821; Heinrich Gottlieb Tzschirner, *Der Uebertritt*

Haller was first and foremost a Swiss, and more precisely, a Bernese political thinker who, as he himself repeatedly pointed out, drew his insights into the fundamental weaknesses of Liberalism from his experience working at the state chancellery and through the debates surrounding the fall and subsequent occupation of the old Bern by the troops of revolutionary France.[30]

Seeing Haller as a Swiss, rather than a German or French reactionary thinker has direct implications for understanding his critique not only of Liberalism but also and especially of Rousseau. Most importantly, it suggests that Haller's opposition to Rousseau has less to do with monarchism versus republicanism, or Catholicism versus atheism, as Barruel argued in his *Mémoires pour servir à l'histoire du jacobinisme*. Instead, it is primarily a conflict between two contrasting visions of republican politics, in this case Rousseau's neo-roman political theory versus the republicanism of the old and pre-modern Swiss city-states that had been swept away in 1798.

Born in 1768, Haller was only one year younger than the famous liberal theorist Benjamin Constant. Although they both came from similarly privileged backgrounds and were both through their families early on exposed to debates on the modernisation of the Swiss republics, they eventually came to occupy opposite poles of the political spectrum.[31] The fact that Constant grew up in Lausanne and was therefore formally a subject of the sovereign city of Bern, while Haller was a member of one of Bern's leading families, would undoubtedly have played a considerable role in shaping their respective intellectual trajectories.

Haller, like Constant, was initially drawn to the French revolutionary cause; he professed a deep admiration for Sieyès, even in his *Restauration*, and when visiting Paris in 1790 he expressed sympathies for the Girondin position.[32] In the years prior to the French invasion, he thus

---

des Herrn von Haller zur katholischen Kirche, Leipzig: F.C.W. Vogel, 1821; Johann Gottlieb Rätze, *Die Constitutionsscheu des Herrn von Haller oder dessen inspirirte Ansichten vom Staate und von der Kirche*, Leipzig: Hartmann, 1821.

[30] In the *Restauration*, Haller explicitly and repeatedly referred to the significance of his Bernese background for the development of his theory of the patrimonial state. See e.g. *Restauration*, Vol. 1. x–xi, xxxii–xxxiii. The Bernese dimension of Haller's theory is central to Guggisberg, *Carl Ludwig von Haller*, passim.

[31] See Gustave Rudler, *La jeunesse de Benjamin Constant, 1767–1794. Le disciple du XVIIIᵉ siècle. Utilitarisme et pessimisme. Mᵐᵉ de Charrière*, Paris: A. Colin, 1909; Kurt Kloocke, *Benjamin Constant: une biographie intellectuelle*, Genève: Droz, 1984; and Biancamaria Fontana, *Benjamin Constant and the Post-Revolutionary Mind*, New Haven and London: Yale University Press, 1991.

[32] Ewald Reinhard and Adolphine Haasbauer, eds. 'Aufzeichnungen Karl Ludwig von Hallers über seine Jugendjahre 1768–1792', *Berner Zeitschrift für Geschichte und Heimatkunde*, 23 (1961) 27–67. For a survey of his early writings, see Christoph Pfister,

would probably have been rather sympathetic to the young Hegel, whose first publication was a German translation of an anti-Bernese tract and who later, in § 258 of his *Philosophy of Right*, launched a personal attack against Haller and his notion of a Patrimonial state, which he criticised for lacking any transcendent idea of the state.[33] By 1798 Haller seems to have given up any hope that political Liberalism could provide a sufficient answer to Rousseau, even though his last-ditch attempt to appease the invading French army by penning a liberal republican constitution for Bern in March 1798 shows he was fully in command of the juridical and political debates of the Directoire.[34] The fall of the old republic and the establishment of a unitary Helvetic Republic under French control forced Haller into exile, first to Southern Germany, then in 1801 to Vienna. After the act of Mediation, which spelled the end of the Helvetic Republic, Haller returned to Bern where he was elected professor in public law at the local academy. In a series of articles written from exile, in his inaugural lecture, *On the necessity of establishing a different general foundation of public law* of 1806, and finally in his *Handbook on general politics* of 1808, Haller sketched out the arguments that later formed the backbone of his *Restauration of Political Science*.[35] Many of the arguments Haller later presented against Rousseau were therefore first developed in the years after his return to Bern, where he lobbied against the new liberal movements in the city's former subject territories and called for a full return to the status quo before the revolution.[36] After his conversion to Catholicism in 1820, the Bernese government stripped him of his seat in the council and barred him from holding office for the rest of his life. Shortly after, Haller moved to France where he was welcomed by the ultra-royalist set. Having briefly served in the ministry of foreign affairs under Poligniac, in 1830 Haller had to move once more. He finally settled in the small Swiss catholic town of Solothurn from where he disputed the ideas of Liberalism and political Protestantism up to his death in 1854.

Die Publizistik Karl Ludwig von Hallers in der Frühzeit 1791–1815, Bern: Herbert Lang, 1975. On Sieyès, see Emmanuel Joseph Sieyès, *Political Writings*, Michael Sonenscher (ed.), Indianapolis and Cambridge: Hackett, 2003, 'Introduction'.

[33] G.W.F. Hegel, *Elements of the Philosophy of Right* (1821) ed. by Allen W. Bloom, Cambridge University Press, 1991, § 258, pp. 275–281.

[34] Karl Ludwig von Haller, *Project einer Constitution für die Schweizerische Republik Bern. Angefasst im Merz 1798, auf die Voraussetzung, dass solche einstweilen Platz haben könne*, Bern Typographische Buchhandlung, 1798.

[35] Karl Ludwig von Haller, *Ueber die Nothwendigkeit einer andern obersten Begründung des allgemeinen Staats-Rechts. Eine Inaugurations-Rede bey Antretung des Prorektorats an der Akademie zu Bern, gehalten am 2. November 1806 von Carl Ludwig von Haller, Professor der Staatskunde und Geschichte*, Bern Typographische Gesellschaft, 1807.

[36] Haller, *Restauration*, Vol. 1, xxiv.

In his *Handbook*, and later in the *Restauration*, Haller framed his critique of Liberalism and of liberal visions of peace as a dispute over the correct reading of Rousseau.[37] Although he acknowledged the Liberals' critical stance towards Rousseau, Haller claimed that they laboured under the mistaken belief that the basic tenets of Rousseau's political theory could be salvaged and adapted to the requirements of the societies of post-revolutionary Europe by emphasising the compatibility of the *Contrat Social* with the idea of political representation. While Rousseau's love of paradoxes left parts of his work open to interpretation, Haller maintained that Rousseau had been perfectly clear on the fundamental issues. One was that all law emanated from a social contract that established civil society. Another was that sovereignty and government were two fundamentally distinct institutions in politics. Sovereignty remained at all times with the people and could not be represented. The so called Representative System that promised to put an end to the instrumentalisation of Rousseau's idea of the *volonté générale* presented a step in the wrong direction in that it underplayed, or wilfully ignored, the radically democratic nature of Rousseau's political theory.[38]

According to Haller, Liberals were self-delusional at best when professing their belief that a modern representative republic would prove sufficiently stable to banish the spectre of reoccurring terror and civil war. Haller aimed the same charge against the various projects of perpetual peace. The "curious proposal endlessly put forward by so many philosophers of a universal republic, a state of all states or of all world citizens, a ribbon uniting all of mankind that would bring about perpetual peace" was obviously a "beautiful idea". Yet, Haller argued, none of its proponents were able to make a convincing case for how peace could be achieved otherwise than at the price of the "utter destruction of liberty and complete servitude of all".[39]

Nowhere, Haller claimed, was this more obvious than in Kant's peace plan, which he likened to the "peace of the grave". Although Kant, whom Haller saw as a staunch follower of Rousseau, had avoided the mistake of associating the state of nature with a state of unsociability, accepting instead the possibility of natural societies based solely on natural and private laws. Yet, by simultaneously declaring the natural social state to be "law-less, *justitia vacuus*, a state of injustice" from which even

---

[37] See also, Ch. Ph. Graf Dijon de Montenon, *Die 'Entzauberung' des Gesellschaftsvertrags. Ein Vergleich der Anti-Sozial-Kontrakts-Theorien von Carl Ludwig von Haller und Joseph Graf de Maistre im Kontext der politischen Ideengeschichte*, Frankfurt: Peter Lang, 2007.

[38] For a more detailed account, see Richard Tuck, *The Sleeping Sovereign. The Invention of Modern Democracy*, Cambridge University Press, 2016.

[39] *Restauration*, vol. 5, pp. 369–370.

current societies had to escape in order to transform conditional private laws into full civil laws, Kant held up Rousseau's idea of a civil state as an ideal that humans were obliged to strive for.[40] Kant's claim that societies should "leave their current state reveals the most sublime, deceitful and most dangerous kind of Jacobin poison, for it obviously aims at the destruction of all existing states, to kill them with *aqua tofana*, in order to introduce a so-called *civil* [rechtliche], that is, revolutionary constitution".[41] This left little ground for feeling hopeful about any prospect of perpetual peace. For if the conditional status of private law in natural societies could be overcome only through the establishment of civil society, it was difficult to see how a just and rightful international regime could exist outside the setting of a single universal state, despite Kant's advocacy of a federal model.

Other authors were no more convincing in their defence of a Rousseauean ideal of civil society, whether such a defence was based on man's anthropological disposition, making the establishment of civil society, as Friedrich Buchholz suggested, the necessary outcome of a general social law, or whether, as in the case of Haller's critic Krug, it took the form of a History of Mankind, presenting a modern liberal state as the moral culmination of a cultural development that could be traced back to Antiquity.[42] Nor did Haller think much of the latter's attempt to separate what he called 'true Liberalism' from both 'anti-Liberalism' and militant 'ultra-Liberalism'. Even though Liberals displayed considerable ingenuity when it came to forging a new political vocabulary, they remained fundamentally wedded to the conceptual framework of the *Contrat social*.[43] This alone suggested that Liberalism, instead of bringing to a close the repeated cycle of civil war and violence, simply perpetuated revolution, either unintentionally, or openly, as in the case of the Spanish Cortes.[44] Rather than calling them liberals, Haller concluded in his *De quelques denominations de partis* of 1822, they should be named for what their actions really amounted to: 'revolutionaries' and 'jacobins'.[45]

---

[40] *Restauration*, vol. 1, pp. 73–75, also xxviii.   [41] Ibid, p. 75.

[42] See especially Friedrich Buchholz, *Darstellung eines neuen Gravitationsgesetzes für die moralische Welt* (Berlin: J.F. Unger, 1802), and *Der neue Leviathan* (Tübingen 1805); Wilhelm Traugott Krug, *Geschichtliche Darstellung des Liberalismus alter und neuer Zeit. Ein historischer Versuch* (Leipzig: Brockhaus 1823). For a systematic overview of the semantics of early nineteenth-century European Liberalism, see Jörn Leonhard, *Liberalismus. Zur historischen Semantik eines europäischen Deutungsmusters* (München: Oldenbourg, 2001).

[43] See esp. Chapters 4 and 5 of Vol. 1 of the *Restauration*.

[44] Karl Ludwig von Haller, Über die Constitution der Spanischen Cortes, [Winterthur]: s.n. 1820.

[45] Karl Ludwig von Haller, *Quelques dénominations de partis, pour servir à l'intelligence des journaux et de plusieurs autres écrits modernes* (Genève: Guers, 1822).

II

For Haller this was more than simple name-calling. Rather, it pointed to what he perceived to be a common trait of much of European political thought since the middle of the seventeenth century. Moreover, it helped to better capture the underlying ideological causes that had placed modern Europe onto a trajectory of continuous revolution. From this perspective, he argued, even Rousseau appeared as a mere contributor to the malaise rather than being the actual instigator of a wider and more deep-seated contemporary pathology. In his *Restauration*, Haller acknowledged the role that the system of European debt finance played in destabilising the pre-revolutionary monarchies, just as he readily joined the choir of Catholic anti-revolutionaries like Barruel, Bonald, and de Maistre who denounced the Enlightenment attack on religion as a contributing factor to bringing about the events of 1789.[46] Neither of these phenomena, however, was sufficient in itself in order to explain the fall of the old regime. Both on the institutional and on the economic level, European nations had been in no more of a crisis in the 1780s than they had been in the past. Far more important, Haller argued, were the dynamics that had been set off by the radical change in political terminology due to the widespread reception of Roman law and its ready adaptation into modern Natural Law.[47]

When the first volume of Haller's *Restauration* was published, the German critique of Roman law was of course nothing new. It was already contained in eighteenth-century German patriotic literature, such as in the writings of Justus Möser, as well as in academic legal treatises, like in the *Specimen iuris publici gentium medii aevi: De instauratione imperii romani sub Carolo M. et Ottone M. facta eiusque effectibus* of 1784, where the Göttingen law professor Johann Stephan Pütter had studied how the reception of Roman law under Charles the Great had helped to revive the office of Emperor.[48] More generally, during the eighteenth century,

[46] Haller dealt with the issue of public debt at some length in Volume 3 of the *Restauration*, p. 21ff. Haller summarised his view on the connection between the attack on religion and revolution in *Satan und die Revolution. Ein gegenstück zu den Paroles d'un croyant*, Luzern: Gebrüder Räber, 1834. He subsequently extended his critique to include the Protestant Reformation; see *Histoire de la révolution religieuse, ou de la réforme protestante dans la Suisse occidentale*, Paris: Auguste Vaton, 1837.

[47] For a recent discussion of the reception of Roman Law in modern Natural Law, see Benjamin Straumann, *Roman Law in the State of Nature. The Classical Foundations of Hugo Grotius' Natural Law*, Cambridge University Press, 2015. Also, Richard Tuck, *Philosophy and Government, 1572–1651*, Cambridge University Press, 1993; Timothy Hochstrasser, *Natural law theories in the early Enlightenent*, Cambridge University Press, 2000.

[48] On J. Möser, see *Jonathan B. Knudsen*, Justus Möser and the German Enlightenment, Cambridge University Press, 1986; Fredrick C. Beiser, *The German Historicist Tradition*, Oxford University Press, 2011, pp. 63–97.

German jurists drew on the idea of a patrimonial state in order to establish juridical foundations for territorial particularism that could not be explained with reference to the Roman legal notion of *Imperium*.[49] Closer to home, and perhaps more importantly to Haller, in 1765 the Bernese law professor Gottlieb Walther argued in his study on the history of Bernese law that the city had maintained its distinctive character due to its refusal to adopt Roman law: "We can be assured that the true origins of our local laws are entirely German. Bern never accepted Roman law; never did foreign customs change or replace our local customs". Bern's opposition to Roman law, Walther claimed, was illustrated by the fact that members of the legal profession commonly traded the names of the fourteenth-century Italian jurists Bartolus and Baldus as insults.[50] Haller could not have agreed more. Nowhere, he claimed, had the true, non-roman, theory of state law been better preserved than in the old Swiss Confederation.[51]

During the first half of the nineteenth century the critical discussion of the dissemination of Roman law became a central issue in the writings of the Germanist branch of the German Historical School centred around Karl Friedrich Eichhorn, Jacob Grimm, and Georg Beseler.[52] Haller explicitly referred to the works of Pütter, Möser, Eichhorn and others, yet he was probably the first political theorist who made the reception of Roman law and its contribution to the idea of a social contract the focal point of his critique of Enlightenment political thought.[53]

As Haller reminded his readers, first in his *Handbook* of 1808 and then in more detail in Volume One of the *Restauration*, it was only due to the spread of Roman Law that scholars began rejecting the idea of divine right and replacing it with the equally-erroneous idea of an original contract as the source of legitimate political authority. The first inconvenience of Roman law, Haller argued, was that it contained "almost

[49] See Otto Brunner, *Land and Lordship*, p. 125. For traces of patrimonial thinking in German legal thought, see Fritz Hartung, *Deutsche Verfassungsgeschichte. Vom 15. Jahrhundert bis zur Gegenwart*, Stuttgart: K.F. Koehler Verlag, 1954, passim; and more generally, Konrad Beyeler, 'Patrimonalstaat', in *Staatslexikon der Görres-Gesellschaft*, 5. Ed., Freiburg: Herder, 1931, p. 75ff.

[50] Gottlieb Walther, *Versuch zu Erläuterung der Geschichten des Vatterländischen Rechts*, Bern [s.n.] 1765, pp. 39–40.

[51] Haller, *Restauration*, Vol. 1, p. xxxiii.

[52] See for example Eichhorn's contributions to the first volume of the newly founded *Zeitschrift für geschichtliche Rechtswissenschaft* Berlin 1815), where he insisted on the Germanic origins of the constitutions of German towns, « Ueber das geschichtliche Studium des Deutschen Rechts » (124–146), and « Ueber den Ursprung der städtischen Verfassung in Deutschland » (147–247). For a study of the wider context of his Medievalism, see Mack Walker, *German Home Towns. Community, State, and General Estate, 1648–1817*, Ithaca, New York: Cornell University Press, 1971.

[53] See for example Haller comment on Eichhorn, *Restauration*, Vol. 1, p. 96, note 22.

exclusively a republican terminology", which was then applied indiscriminately to any form of political society, irrespective of whether these states were principalities or republics. In a telling passage Haller described the ensuing confusion in the following manner:

Just as the citizens of Rome constituted a community [Gemeinde], a citizenry, a genuine *societas civilis*: all other forms of human association and relations, too, had to be called *societas civilis* or civil societies. Soon all forms of states, even principalities had to be called *civitates* or *respublicas* (republics, commonwealths), the aggregate of serviceable people was called *populum liberum* (a free people), individual subjects who amongst themselves did not form any corporation and who were not in any particular way legally bound to one another were now called *cives* (citizens), the estates, servicemen who were called into council, and vassals were called *comitia* (popular assemblies) where the majority should carry the vote; princely domains were called *patrimonium populi* (public or state domains), the treasure of an individual lord became an *aerarium publicum*, private services owed to powerful and mighty lords were called *munera publica* (public offices) etc.[54]

This, he claimed, was how scholars gradually became accustomed to using an inappropriate language and to describing existing social and legal relations in terms that historically referred to very different circumstances. "The erroneous use of language", Haller claimed, "the imperfection of signs was and remains even today a source of endless errors. The meaning of falsely applied words was forced onto things, whereas the terms ought to have been adapted to fit new circumstances".[55]

A further problem that ensued with the reception of Roman law was that when scholars and political advisers turned to ancient history in search of political models for Europe's early modern monarchies, they did not study the early Roman republic, or the ancient kingdoms. Instead, they focused exclusively on the Roman Empire without giving sufficient thought to the fact that the Empire at the time when the legal codes were established found itself, in a shocking condition; as Haller put it the Roman Empire was, "in this unnatural, monstrous phase of incomplete usurpation. Neither monarchy, not republic, it contained parts of each, but was no longer couched on any solid foundation. The institutions and the vocabulary of the old republic (eadem magistratuum vocabula) were still in place, yet it was founded on nothing but limitless and arbitrary military power".[56] Unlike in the case of the old Roman kings, who merely ruled over their own domain, the emperors

---

[54] Ibid., pp. 89–91.   [55] Ibid., p. 91.
[56] Ibid., p. 93. On the reception of classical notions of monarchy in early-modern Europe, see Peter Stacey, *Roman Monarchy and the Renaissance Prince*, Cambridge University Press, 2007.

laid claim to what formerly had belonged to the republic, and the people of Rome thereby acquired unprecedented power and wealth. Due to this admiration for the Roman Empire and the legal code it had produced, early modern scholars also forgot about the fundamental distinction ancient writers had drawn between republics and monarchies, thereby importing *nolens volens* into their own institutions the confusion that had marred imperial rule.[57] Classical authors, Haller insisted, would have been abhorred seeing their own terminology applied to states of the early modern period. The original Roman republic had been an independent, exclusive community of legally equal citizens who jointly ruled over their commonly held property and the people they had subjected. The very institution of monarchy ruled out the existence of any community of equals, in the same way as it ignored the possibility of a king claiming a right to dispose of what was not strictly his. Despite these differences, ancient republics and monarchies were compatible to the extent that both institutions, Haller claimed, required an appropriate economic base in the form of territory.[58] Early modern legal and political scholars and those who followed them seemed to have forgotten this basic historical fact.

If the use of Roman law was initially restricted to the community of legal scholars, according to Haller, its terminology soon found its way into the chancelleries, princely councils and ministerial offices and eventually ended up becoming the dominant political language that even sovereigns themselves relied on for defining their relationship, both to other members of their own society, as well as to other sovereigns.[59] According to Haller, the simultaneous reception of Roman law and the widespread admiration of the politics and institutions of the Roman Empire proved simply too strong for alternative, historically more accurate, political theories to be heard: "It was in vain that several clear eyed legal scholars tried to rally against this fundamental error; they were powerless in the face of this common idolatry of Roman Law".[60]

There were obvious reasons, Haller explained, why early-modern monarchs would want to declare themselves head of a *respublica*:

By calling themselves the highest officers of the people, their wars became legally speaking national wars [Volks-Kriege], their debts became national debts, their

---

[57] Haller, *Restauration*, Vol. 1, p. 94.
[58] Haller, *Restauration*, Vol. 5, p. 5: « [republics, properly understood] are nothing else but free commonwealths, independent communities or corporations, and to the extent that their independence, like that of an individual lord, is maintained through landed property and sufficient power, one can call them rich and powerful communities subject to no-one. »
[59] Haller, *Restauration*, Vol. 1, p. 93.   [60] Haller, Restauration, Vol. 1, p. 92.

own needs became those of the nation; conscriptions, arbitrary taxes, mandatory services of all sorts could easily be put forward and justified through the idea of a commonwealth and an imagined popular sovereignty. Private laws and private contracts with individuals and corporations were no longer valid, once the so-called national goals or the interest of the majority or the presumed popular will was declared the origin of all law.[61]

No longer finding their political actions limited by the confinements of their *patrimonium*, early-modern sovereigns, now turned quasi-emperors, could conceive of financial instruments that were linked to a projected public wealth, rather than the monarch's domain, and hence initiate military adventures on a scale previously deemed unimaginable.[62]

The downside of projecting a Roman imperial model onto the social and institutional realities of the European monarchies was that, while it granted sovereigns the prerogatives of a republican Emperor, it also led to what Haller called the "steady erosion of their power".[63] Here, too, the spread of the republican vocabulary of Roman law played a decisive role. For one, the monarch's own originally private domains could now be described as '*bona publica*, property belonging to the state or the nation'. Moreover, it meant that that the new Roman-style monarchs, at least in principle, no longer ruled over subjects but over *cives*, citizens. Given the rate of illiteracy amongst the common people, Haller conceded that this subtlety was probably lost on most inhabitants of rural Europe. Likewise, it was of little consequence that the absolutist king of Prussia, Frederick II, decided foolishly to declare himself, "the first servant and magistrate of the state", thereby potentially opening up a discussion over the origins of monarchical authority.[64] In other situations, however, especially where the sovereign's position was not as undisputed as in Prussia, the dissemination of a Roman republican language had a noticeably destabilising effect. One such case, as Haller recalled in an essay from 1799, was his own hometown of Bern.[65] Republics tended to have greater difficulties maintaining power over their subjects and for these reasons were particularly sensitive to the language used in their official documents, especially their correspondence with lawyers and notaries from their subject territories. It was for these reasons that the Swiss republics for a long time refused to use the term *respublica* in their official seals, preferring instead that of 'free city' or 'free city community'.[66] It was only at the end of

---

[61] Haller, *Restauration*, Vol. 1, p. 178.
[62] Haller, *Restauration*, Vol. 1, p. 178, Vol. 3, p. 31f.
[63] Restauration Vol. 1, p. 179.   [64] Haller, *Restauration*, Vol. 1, p. 190.
[65] Karl Ludwig von Haller, 'Karakteristik der Verfassung der Schweiz vor der durch das französische Direktorium bewirkten Revolution', *Deutsches Magazin*, August 1799, pp. 97–131.
[66] Haller, *Restauration*, Vol. 6, p. 4, note 5.

the seventeenth century, when *respublica* had become a standard term describing the independence of a state, that cities like Bern and Zurich began calling themselves 'city and republic' [Stadt und Republik].[67] Following Haller's account, this moment of vanity was to cost them dearly, for over the course of the following century the term *respublica*, which the Bernese had intended as a mere adjective asserting the city's independence from the Holy Roman Empire, was interpreted as applying to the Canton as a whole, thus effectively relegating the sovereign city of Bern to the rank of a mere administrative and political capital. The dispute over the right meaning of republic and consequently over the meaning of "citizen" did indeed constitute a central topic in the anti-Bernese tracts written by Vaudois lawyers during the 1790s.[68] But for Haller the tragedy went deeper, for well before 1789 members of the government of Bern had become confused over their own position: during council meetings "the small and great council of Bern was labelled the national government, or at least was thought of in this way".[69]

The explosive nature of this highly normative political language, that bore no relation to the social realities of seventeenth- and eighteenth-century Europe, was finally revealed during the French Revolution. Having been relabelled citizens, it seemed inevitable, Haller claimed, that the people finally demanded the rights and privileges they had come to associate with this new status. What followed was the bloody spectacle of the neo-Roman republic in action. Without any common property to bind them together into a real citizenry, they were incapable of forming the reasoned and moderate civic culture that came with the responsible guardianship of an entail or *fideicommiss*. Instead, they were left with little but the fictitious right to consider themselves part of a collective sovereign incapable of expressing itself. The successive revolutionary governments in turn fully confirmed the volatile nature of the neo-Roman state. While their role as mouthpiece and executor of the general will gave them authority over the wealth and collective force of the new *civitas*, they lacked their own resources to enforce their policies except by means of brute force, terror and by generating a particularly vicious form of patriotism directed against both internal and external enemies.

---

[67] This reading is largely confirmed by Thomas Maissen, *Die Geburt der Republic. Staatsverständnis und Repräsentation in der frühneuzeitlichen Eidgenossenschaft*, Göttingen: Vandenhoeck & Ruprecht, 2006.

[68] Many of these claims were summarised in Jean-Jacques Cart's, *Lettres de Jean-Jacques Cart à Bernard de Muralt, trésorier du Pays de Vaud, sur le droit publique et les événements actuels* Paris: Imprimerie du Cercle Social 1793. Hegel subsequently published an annotated translation under the title *Vertrauliche Briefe über das vormalige staatsrechtliche Verhältniss des Waadtlandes (Pays de Vaud) zur Stadt Bern* Frankfurt am Main: Jagersche Buchhandlung, 1798.

[69] Haller, 'Karakteristik', p. 110.

However much Rousseau might have contributed to bringing about this sequence of events, Haller argued that the real initiator was in fact Hobbes, whom he labelled "the true forefather of all Jacobins, of all revolutionary errors, even though this was clearly not what he intended".[70] As Haller put it, in a genuinely "republican fashion, like Rousseau later on, [Hobbes] had not recognised any contract between the prince and the subjects, but only one true *contrat social* between the individuals themselves (pactum sociale inter singulos)".[71] By arguing that the existence of society depended upon the prior establishing of a state, Hobbes, Haller argued, had also rejected the independence of private law in the state of nature. The only real difference between Hobbes and Rousseau was that:

... while [Hobbes] after the act of a *contrat social* wants to delegate the original popular sovereignty to a prince or a senate, [Rousseau] wishes to keep it with the entire popular assembly. According to the former, the will of the prince is the general will, whereas the latter believes that the people expresses [the general will] directly. In both cases, however, the general will commands everything and is infallible. In both systems all private will, all privately held right, all private judgement had to be ceded, here to one or to several, there to the collective or to an arbitrary majority.[72]

III

Haller seemed convinced that his own work, the *Restauration of political science* provided a radical and conclusive answer to both Rousseau and Hobbes. The reason he believed why he had succeeded, where all others had failed, was that he dismissed the entire conceptual framework their respective political theories were built upon, by avoiding the republican language of Roman Law altogether. Here, Haller claimed, lay the difference between his own way of dealing with Rousseau's legacy and that of the Liberals. The solution was not to provide Rousseau's theory of the state with a theory of representation, but to show instead how sovereignty, which Rousseau had rightly insisted could not be represented, might be explained without having to fall back onto the idea of a social contract or a neo-Roman *societas civilis*. Restoring political science meant just that, showing how states could legitimately be formed from the top down, rather than from the bottom up.[73]

---

[70] Haller, *Restauration*, Vol. 1, p. 43. On Hobbes, see ibid., pp. 40–43, 76–77. On Rousseau as a follower of Hobbes, see Richard Tuck, *Rights of War and Peace. Political Thought and the International Order from Grotius to Kant*, Oxford University Press, 1999, ch. 7.
[71] Haller, *Restauration* Vol. 1, p. 41.
[72] Haller, *Restauration* Vol. 1, p. 121.   [73] Haller, *Restauration*, Vol. 1, p. x.

For Haller, sovereignty was fundamentally an attribute of real personal independence, not only materially, in the sense of the control one might have over the management of physical needs, but also spiritually: "the so called sovereignty or highest power consists in nothing else but the personal independence of the prince".[74] There was therefore no real difference between how a sovereign ruled his estate and the people who depended upon him, and the way in which any other lord governed his land and his people. The same applied also to republics and other communes. What set sovereign princes and republics apart from the myriad of similar social formations that could be encountered throughout European history was simply the absence of any further superior. Ultimately, for Haller, the rise of certain communes to the status of republics and of lords and chieftains to that of sovereign princes could only be explained historically, representing the "greatest possible gift of fortune". Whatever its origin, sovereign power was perfectly legitimate and could be explained through the natural law of first occupation and the agreements that were formed between private individuals. Haller's *Patrimonial State*, understood as the outgrowth of earlier forms of the household, could thereby be described entirely in terms of private law. What modern theorists called public law were in truth private service agreements between the powerful and those unable to satisfy their individual needs for security, food, shelter and so forth. Haller's move was made clear in the subtitle of the *Restauration*: «theory of the state of natural sociability opposed to the chimera of an artificial civil state». Its ambition, as he put it, was to provide a political theory *sine societas civilis*: "this work can be called a general theory of all sociable relations, but one that places special emphasis on the powerful and the free, whom I call states, and where all other social relations are only mentioned in passing and for the sake of illustration and confirmation".[75]

Accordingly, most of Hobbes' errors, and in a different way also those of Rousseau, stemmed from their defence of civil society as the only solution to the precariousness of life in the state of nature. The first error here was to assume that the state of nature was an unsociable state and that society consequently could flourish only after the establishment of civil society. As Haller pointed out, the Hobbesian claim about the natural unsociability of man had been dismissed by virtually all subsequent

---

[74] Ibid, p. x. See also, *Handbuch* p. 41: « The state is not an association of legal insurance [Rechtsversicherungs-Anstalt], or a society of free men for securing strict justice, as most political thinkers seem to believe. Instead, it is nothing else but a natural, sociable relationship between the free and the servants, which distinguishes itself from other similar societies through the fact that its head is independent. »

[75] Haller, *Restauration*, Vol. 1, xlvi.

natural law thinkers. Rather than following Hobbes, they instead sub-scribed to Pufendorf's notion of *socialitas* derived from the idea of men's general neediness and inability to survive without the support from others. By placing greater emphasis upon a utility-driven human *socialitas*, Pufendorf had been able to insert a new conceptual space between the Hobbesian state of nature and civil society. Humans could be seen to barter, set up families, extend households and even create institutions of lordship and servitude without, as Haller put, there ever arising the need for any voluntary association or Hobbesian union.[76]

Most thinkers, Haller claimed, in fact recognised the existence of natural societies, some of them like Locke, Boehmer and Pufendorf even "seemed to prefer them to artificial or so called civil societies".[77] Grotius spoke of "patrimonial states, of natural lordships that maintain themselves by their own power".[78] Hobbes, too, Haller argued, "speaks at one moment of a *civitas naturalis*."[79] Pufendorf, Haller claimed, "traces the natural origins of monarchies", and even "lists the innumerable difficulties of a voluntary association and the setting up of a civil society, he even traces the natural and rightful origin of a monarchy through individual private contracts".[80] Pufendorf was thus perfectly right to conclude "that the sociable state came first and that the non-social state emerged only afterwards through the breaking up of the family unit".[81] Given this general consensus regarding man's sociable nature and his ability to form social institutions solely on the basis of private law, Haller seemed at a loss when having to explain why none of the eighteenth-century thinkers "grabbed the pearl, no one tried to hold on and develop the truth that was right in front of them".[82] Several of them, notably Kant and Sieyès, seemed to have come close, but they too in the end reverted back to defending the need for civil society. The only way to explain this abandonment of the study of the natural state in favour of the study of "Roman style citizenry" was that eighteenth-century authors had lacked the courage to dismiss the neo-Roman arguments entirely: "they didn't open their eyes to see that even today there exist no other form of

---

[76] On Pufendorf's notion of socialitas in relation to Hobbes, see Istvan Hont, "The Language of Sociability and Commerce: Samuel Pufendorf and the Theoretical Foundations of the 'Four-Stages' theory", in *Jealousy of Trade. International competition and the Nation-State in historical perspective*, Cambridge MA: The Belknap Press of Harvard University Press, 2005, pp. 159–184.

[77] Haller, *Restauration*, Vol. 1, p. 349.

[78] Haller, *Restauration*, Vol. 1, xxix, p. 39.   [79] Haller, *Restauration*, Vol. 1, xxix, p. 43.

[80] Haller, *Restauration*, Vol. 1, p. 50. On Locke, see p. 46, Böhmer, p. 52.

[81] Haller, *Restauration*, Vol. 1, p. 342.

[82] See, Stefan Breuer, *Sozialgeschichte des Naturrechts*, Wiesbaden: Springer, 1983; especially Chapter 3 'Naturrecht und Patrimonialstaat', pp. 124–215.

society and that [a general theory of social relations] was entirely sufficient in order explain the nature of states". Even the law of nations, which underpinned Kant's peace plan, could be defined in terms of private law:

Had Kant separated private law into two categories, non-social and social, the latter then into service relations and communal relations; and if he had then recognised the law of nations (the law between states) as a modified version of non-social private law and state law (the law of princes and republics) as a modification of the latter, that is to say as an application of sociable private law to independent persons and closed social arrangements: he would have been the true reformer of natural law.[83]

As it stood, Kant was to be credited only with having imported the socially explosive features and terminological confusions of Romanist Natural Law into the Law of Nations, thus setting the stage for continuing international civil war. In so doing, Kant seemed to surpass even his teacher Hobbes, for while the latter "still occasionally recognises divine laws, Kant in [the *Groundwork of the Metaphysics of Morals*] does not; Hobbes considers a former imagined state as the state of perpetual war, while Kant sees the current state as the state of war; Hobbes thinks that this state has already been left behind, Kant holds that it still needs to be overcome."[84]

It was only by overcoming these confusions that the possibility of lasting international and domestic peace could arise.[85] A more dedicated study of natural society, Haller claimed, would have revealed a few general principles of this general science of social relations.[86] One such principle was that individuals who distinguished themselves through intellectual, spiritual or physical superiority naturally attracted those in need of protection, moral guidance or education. From this, one could deduce as a first general principle that the stronger or in any way superior should rule over the weak.[87] At one level, this principle simply reflected the varying degree of neediness amongst individuals.[88] At the same time, it reflected a particular trait in the human psyche that manifested itself in the natural admiration of those deemed superior. As Haller put it,

---

[83] Haller, *Restauration*, Vol. 1, p. 75, note; see also 76–77.
[84] Haller, *Restauration*, Vol. 1, p. 76.
[85] Haller, *Restauration*, Vol. 1, p. LXVII; LXIX; on Kant, see esp. pp. 72–79. On the context of Haller's critique of Kant's peace plan, see Johann Baptist Müller, *Konservatismus und Aussenpolitik*, Berlin: Duncker und Humblot, 1988, pp. 14–29.
[86] See esp. Haller, *Restauration*, chap. 12, pp. 337–355.
[87] Haller, *Restauration*, Vol. 1, pp. 360, 375.
[88] Haller, *Restauration*, Vol. 1, p. 364: « the greater or more pressing the need, and the less it can be overlooked or satisfied, the greater will be the dependency and servitude. »

No one on this earth tolerates being ruled by an equal or even an inferior. One only wants to see someone superior above one's self, and from a common labourer up to the minister or general, every one serves willingly only those who are truly superior.[89]

Haller was of course familiar with what Hobbes had described as men's predisposition for glory seeking and the emphasis he put on it in explaining the breakdown of natural society. Glory seeking, amour-propre and jealousy of status, Haller agreed, could indeed become a major problem for preserving social peace, but not in the way Hobbes had presented it.[90] Jealousy and glory seeking, in Haller's reading, were psychological manifestations typical of societies of equals, whereas in natural and thus unequal societies the stirring of jealousy and glory seeking was held in check by the principle of natural admiration for superiority. It was only in civil society, where authority no longer depended upon an individual's strength, private wealth and natural superiority, that the psychological dynamics, which Hobbes had attributed to the state of war, would become an active force of human behaviour.

Far from being generally opposed to any higher and natural authority, jealousy rules rather amongst equals or those who consider themselves equal, and envy becomes silent to the degree that the difference and superiority becomes visible. [...] If all men were equal in force they would not only find themselves in a state of general neediness, but also, as the misanthropic Hobbes says, in a state of general war, whereas between unequals there is pleasant peace. In all of nature war erupts only wherever equal forces meet and clash with one another.[91]

This, Haller argued, also explained why social peace was so much harder to maintain in republics than in monarchies.

Haller listed another principle of natural society that both Hobbes and Rousseau had overlooked and which he believed contributed further to the stability of natural society, namely the principle of the natural magnanimity of the strong towards the needy:

Finally, and this is the most important aspect, nature has ordered with admirable wisdom, that the sense of one's own superiority inevitably ennobles the character and brings to the fore precisely those virtues that are most appreciated by those inferior. (...) Who wants to hurt an infant, even though almost every human has greater strength? Are the superior the ones who envy the happiness of the

---

[89] Haller, *Restauration*, Vol. 1, p. 366.
[90] For a detailed account of Hobbes' notion of the state of nature, see Ioannis D. Evrigenis, *Images of Anarchy. The Rhetoric and Science in Hobbes' State of Nature*, Cambridge University Press, 2016.
[91] Haller, *Restauration*, Vol. 1, pp. 368 and 376.

small, or is it rather the small that envy the mighty? Who is likely to better care of property, the needy or he who has no use for others' goods?[92]

Haller's comments on glory seeking, the natural admiration of superiority, and natural magnanimity were evidently meant as a response to Hobbes. Rousseau posed further challenges, notably in his 'Discourse on Political Economy' where he rejected the economy of the household as a viable model for modern politics.[93] While the economy defined the natural household of the extended family under the natural authority of a physically stronger housefather, politics was about a society of equal adults under the rule of law. Both models were fundamentally different and should be kept strictly separate.

Once the natural household had become too developed for it to be governed by a single housefather, Rousseau had argued, the weak natural bond of sociability became strained so that the affection a housefather felt for every individual member of the family could no longer serve as a guiding principle for natural justice, instead giving rise to favouritism.[94] Hence, rather than trying to impose the principles of the rule of a household onto the setting of a large society, the economic society of the extended family had to be transformed into a civil society. Instead of listening to their heart, rulers of large societies, due to their inability to directly oversee all members that were under their care, had to be guided in their action by general laws, not personal sentiment.[95]

Haller gleefully noted that Rousseau himself considered the task of placing law above men to be virtually impossible. Haller argued, however, there was no good reason why this should be considered a task at all. Nor was it in any way evident that the freedom Rousseau claimed men had enjoyed in the state of nature could only be preserved through the establishment of a civil society. According to Haller, it was perfectly possible to explain fully the nature of the state, including the relationships between its members entirely within the framework of private law.

The key here, Haller claimed, was to realise that humans in fact had never left the state of nature and that all states remained private social

---

[92] Haller, *Restauration*, Vol. 1, pp. 378–79, also 385.

[93] Jean-Jacques Rousseau, 'Discourse on Political Economy' in *The Social Contract and other later political writings*, ed. by Victor Gourevitch, Cambridge University Press, 1997. For a detailed discussion of Rousseau's article, see Bruno Bernardi (ed.), *Jean-Jacques Rousseau. Discours sur l'économie politique*, Paris: Vrin, 2002.

[94] Jean-Jacques Rousseau, 'Discourse on Political Economy', pp. 4–6.

[95] This argument was reiterated by Wilhelm Traugott Krug in his essay *Das Repräsentativsystem. Oder Ursprung und Geist der stellvertretenden Verfassungen mit besondrer Hinsicht auf Deutschland und Sachsen*, Leipzig: Köhlersche Buchhandlung, 1816, p. 27, note.

institutions. Given men's natural propensity to enter into and to maintain unequal relations, there was no reason why Rousseau's model of a simple household could not be extended to fit even more complicated social arrangements. Haller's point here was, however, distinctive. If a large household became too difficult to control, it would naturally break up into a set of new households who then would form unequal relations amongst themselves. According to Haller, the household that was most successful in satisfying its needs, hence acquiring the ability to offer services to those who had failed to do so, could then be called a state. In most cases, households would be governed by a single person. If they were governed by several they would be called a commune, and if a commune gained independence it would be called a republic. At no time in this process was there any need to introduce public law or even to codify private law, since the framing of laws remained the private prerogative of the patrimonial state. As a consequence, there did not even exist anything that might be called a people, let alone a nation.[96] The same applied to corporations and to what the neo-Romans had called civil servants. Corporations were private associations whose privileges were granted to them by the state, while civil servants were simply individuals employed by the sovereign in order to assist him with the management of his personal affairs.

One can see why German students calling for constitutional monarchies and German unification felt that Haller's theory of the Patrimonial state should be best answered with an autodafé. For most of them, Haller's *Restauration* advocated power politics of the worst kind. Yet, for some of his more moderate critics, like the nineteenth-century German political economist Wilhelm Roscher, this was most definitely not how Haller wanted things to be understood. Even if Haller's patrimonial politics, when applied to a modern setting would lead to either anarchy or despotism, he deserved to be counted amongst the friends of law and of liberty.[97] Haller's arch-adversary Krug, too, conceded that "Mr v. Haller means well and is well disposed towards humanity. He is no friend of despotism, even though his political principles would in the end lead to this".[98] It is significant that Haller devoted considerable

---

[96] See especially Haller, *Restauration*, Vol. 1, chapter 12 'Natürlicher Ursprung aller geselligen Verhältnisse' and chapter 13 'Von dem Ursprung aller Herrschaft nach einem allgemeinen Naturgesetz', pp. 337–387.

[97] Wilhelm Roscher, *Geschichte der National-Oekonomik in Deutschland*, München: Oldenbourg, 1874, pp. 780–81.

[98] Wilhelm Traugot Krug, *Die Staatswissenschaft im Restaurazionsprozesse der Herren von Haller, Adam Müller und Konsorten*, Leibzig: Gerhard Fleischer dem Jüngern, 1817, reprinted in Krug, *Politische und juridische Schriften*, Braunschweig: Verlag von Friedrich Vieweg, Vol. 1, p. 329.

sections of his work to reveal how the idea of the patrimonial state might be seen to be supportive of individual liberty and as providing solutions to reason-of-state politics internationally. Early modern reason of state, Haller argued, reflected the inner tensions that confronted European monarchies once they started remodelling themselves along the lines of the Roman republican empire. Although the politics of the patrimonial state, too, could be said to be centred around the notion of reason of state, it was one, Haller insisted, that was stripped of all the elements usually associated with Machiavellianism.[99] Instead, reason of state as applied to the patrimonial state was simply and exclusively about securing the independence of the princely household and should therefore more appropriately be labelled the "art of prolonging the life cycle of the state" [Lebens-Verlängerungs-Kunst der Staaten], or the "art of maintaining the prince's status" [Thron-Behauptungs-Lehre].[100] Machiavelli, according to Haller, was thus largely correct in his account of princely politics, even though he lacked a coherent notion of the state and focused mostly on the means by which the prince could assure his subjects' obedience. Unlike his humanist critics who later accused him of immorality, Machiavelli was still aware of the fundamental distinction between princely and republican rule, and it was only once European kingship was confounded with the semi-republican institution of Roman imperial rule that the accusation of Machiavellianism could arise. Under the system of the patrimonial state no such confusion was possible. Given that the prince simply ruled over a certain number of individuals, who themselves did not constitute a people or nation, princely politics could never be considered to be directed against a commonwealth or in violation of any common interest. Princely actions were ultimately judged by history alone, since the inability to secure the necessary material independence and shore up the loyalty and friendship of those under the prince's protection inevitably led to decline and to the loss of independence.[101]

Politics understood as governing one's own affairs, rather than the affairs of the commonwealth or a nation, Haller believed, also meant that the prince could not exercise command over what was not strictly his. One immediate consequence of this was that the state had no right to levy direct taxes, nor could he force those under his care into military service, thereby rendering impossible the kind of total republican war that had been unleashed during the French Revolution after the institution of the *levée en masse*. Furthermore, individual households could

<hr>

[99] See esp. *Restauration*, Vol. 5, Chapter 45, 'Makrobiotik der Patrimonial-Staaten oder von der Erhaltung und Befestigung der Unabhängigkeit', pp. 3–15.

[100] Ibid., p. 3.

[101] See esp. Haller, *Restauration*, Vol. 3, pp. 22–31, 384, note 36.

at all times renounce their private agreement with the state, sell their lands, and seek the protection of another prince. Patrimonial rule, Haller argued, thus offered in principle the same liberties that Liberals believed could only be established under a constitutional representative government, with the added advantage that under a patrimonial state any tension that might arise between the needs of the state and the subjects' rights to the exclusive enjoyment of private property would be kept to a strict minimum: "No one, on the basis of his alleged superiority, can discard some else's rights or rightly lay claim to his property. One cannot deprive another of his standing and belongings in order to become free in his place".[102] The clear separation of the different spheres of interests was particularly noticeable with regard to the economy. 'Good economy', *gute Oekonomie*, as applied to the prince, amounted to little more than traditional household management.[103] By avoiding excessive spending, the setting up of an efficient administration, the development of princely industry and the improvement of infrastructure, the state could increase its income in indirect taxes, improve the agricultural output of its domains and thus not only solidify its economic foundation, but also support charitable institutions aimed at those parts of the population most likely to voice their dissatisfaction with the state. Economic activity should be left unchecked, with a few exceptions like the production or import of salt.[104] In Haller's largely free trade scenario, which he described as directly in opposition to that of eighteenth-century Cameralism, the princely household would maintain a relation of friendly competition with all other households under his protection.[105] While Haller left open the possibility of state decline through the lack of economic competitiveness, he seemed confident that by following a consistent policy aimed at increasing the princely domain through acquisition the state

---

[102] Haller, *Restauration*, Vol. 1, p. 387. Haller argued that patrimonial rule was thus fundamentally different from the patriarchal model espoused by Filmer, see *Restauration*, Vol. 2, p. 14, note 10.

[103] Haller, *Restauration*, Vol. 3. Chapter 46 'Gute Oekonomie. (Finanz-Macht)', p. 16ff. For the continuing relevance of the household model for early nineteenth-century German economic thought, see Keith Tribe *Strategies of Economic Order: German Economic Discourse, 1750–1950*, Cambridge University Press, 1995.

[104] Haller's economic ideas were first developed during the early 1790 when he acted as President of the Economic Society of Bern. See e.g. his *Gutachten über ein einzuführendes Getraid-Polizey-System*, [Bern]: s.n., 1791; and *Abhandlung über den freyen Kauf und Verkauf der Butter im Canton Bern*, [Bern]: s.n., 1791.

[105] Haller's idea of competing households was strikingly similar to what Rousseau had advocated. See, Istvan Hont, *Politics in Commercial Society. Jean-Jacques Rousseau and Adam Smith*, Cambridge MA: Harvard University Press, 2015, chapter 5. For the post-revolutionary French background, see David Todd, *Free Trade and its Enemies in France, 1814–1851*, Cambridge University Press, 2015, esp. Chap. 1 'The reactionary political economy of the Bourbon Restoration', pp. 20–54.

could confirm its position as the dominant actor in grain production, thereby rendering it less vulnerable to any potential rival forces arising from trade and industry.[106] Not surprisingly, Haller identified modern finance, and here notably the instrument of public debt, as the main threat to the economic and social stability of the patrimonial state in that it inevitably led to a confusion of politics and the economy.[107] Besides its evident economic effects, the raising of new taxes needed in order to service the debt, as well as the influence it gave to the prince's creditors, state debts prompted expectations that would ultimately transform the naturally sociable relationship between state and subjects into a political one. State debt, Haller warned, would thus become the financial vehicle through which the terminological confusion inherent in Roman Law would be infused into the household setting of the patrimonial state.[108] It was the inability of Louis XVI to service the French debt, Haller reminded his readers, that had prompted the convocation of the Estates General, thereby setting off a series of events that culminated in the Jacobin terror.[109]

Haller admitted that his vision of a politically and socially fluid Europe populated by continuously competing patrimonial states did not correspond to any eighteenth-century or early nineteenth-century model of perpetual peace. As he explained, no institutional or legal framework could guarantee the absence of war or state decline. Early-modern perpetual alliances, originally termed alliances of perpetual peace, offered no solution, in that they gave weaker parties in particular a false sense of security, thereby softening their capacity for continuous vigilance: "perpetual peace will thus turn into the perpetual absence of resistance, friendship will turn into submission".[110] Even more harmful were those numerous projects that relied upon on the presumed natural peacefulness of modern representative republics.[111] The patrimonial state, which

[106] Ibid., pp. 17–18, 24.
[107] The significance of the issue of public debt in late eighteenth-century French and European political thought is discussed in Michael Sonenscher, *Before the Deluge: Public Debt, Inequality, and the Intellectual Origins of the French Revolution*, Princeton University Press, 2007.
[108] Ibid., p. 34.
[109] Haller, *Restauration*, Vol. 3, p. 41.   [110] Haller, *Restauration*, Vol. 3, pp. 150–151.
[111] Krug sketched out his ideas on perpetual peace in 'Ewiger Friede', *Allgemeines Handwörterbuch der philosophischen Wissenschaften nebst ihrer Literatur und Geschichte*, Leipzig: Brockhaus, 1827, Vol. 1, pp. 744–747; 'Ueber politisches Gleichgewicht und Uebergewicht, Universalmonarchien und Völkerverein, als Mittel, die Völker zum ewigen Frieden zu führen', *Politische und juridische Schriften*, Braunschweig: Verlag von Friedrich Vieweg, 1834, Vol. 2, pp. 73–90. For a collection of late eighteenth- and early nineteenth-century German comments on perpetual peace, see Anita and Walter Dietze (eds.), *Ewiger Friede ? Dokumente einer deutschen Diskussion um 1800*, Leipzig and Weimar: Gustav Kiepenheuer Verlag, 1989.

Haller saw as the answer both to the theoretical challenge posed by Rousseau and to the political problems facing modern Europe, had at least the advantage of limiting the fall-out from military conflict. Moreover, by eliminating any abstract notion of the state that both sovereigns and subjects could appeal to, it escaped the on-going political and ideological crisis inherent to modern representative republics, thus opening the possibility for what he called 'true perpetual peace':

True perpetual peace consists in the continuous preservation of the principles of good and evil, right and wrong. As long as these are upheld, wars will become less frequent, shorter, and more humane; here, all disputes and conflicts over mundane matters can easily be settled. Where these principles are contested, however, as the current situation of Europe shows, there can be no peace, and even the cessation of armed conflict, which is mistakenly called peace, presents nothing but perpetual and unbearable wrangling.[112]

It is unclear to what extent, if at all, Haller's *Restauration* had any influence on early nineteenth-century conservative notions of perpetual peace, although some of the key points of his critique of the modern representative republic as an agent of peace come close to arguments subsequently formulated by left-wing authors, and most notably by Proudhon. Nor is there any indication that he had any particular role in the debate on the Holy Alliance. Paradoxically, it was Krug who defended the Holy Alliance as a welcome step towards the realisation of the rule law, liberal politics, and a more during international peace, while Haller himself remained noticeably silent on this topic.[113] To contemporaries Haller could look like an advocate of outdated politics, a defender of a Europe that had been destroyed by the French Revolution. Imagining a world devoid of modern natural jurisprudence and of political economy, and capable of removing national debts and international commercial rivalries, seemed altogether utopian, and so impractical as to be irresponsible. At the same time, there can be no doubt that Haller's perspective merits reconstruction, especially today. Haller had a profound sense of what a republic was and the forms of economic activity that were compatible with a stable politics. Political arguments, that we label Roman or republican, would have been identified by Haller as antithetical to the true Roman and republican traditions. It is equally the case that his critique of Liberalism, and his explanation of why liberal polities were doomed

---

[112] Haller, *Restauration*, Vol. 5, 369, note.
[113] Krug, *La sainte alliance. Oder Denkmal des von Oestereich, Preussen und Russland geschlossnen heiligen Bundes*, Leipzig: H.A. Köchly, 1816; Krug, *Geschichtliche Darstellung des Liberalismus alter und neuer Zeit. Ein historischer Versuch*, Leipzig: F.A. Brockhaus, 1823, pp. 141–159.

to repeat a cycle of economic decline, political crisis, and intermittent war, remains valid for explorations of alternatives to the modern representative republic. For Haller the central question was whether the state could commit itself to peace and political order, or became an institution in politics that was unstable to its very core.

10   Pierre-Joseph Proudhon's *War and Peace*
The right of force revisited

Edward Castleton

One of the well-known difficulties for partisans of natural jurisprudence from Grotius onwards was related to their inability to describe a world beyond reason of state. This conceptual incapacity was rooted in a persistent fact: because states remain in a state of nature, there can be no basis for their sovereign jurisdiction over territory since, on the international place, right was essentially indistinguishable from might. It was perhaps inevitable then that academics interested in studying the peculiar features of the resulting "anarchical society" of states should eventually take an interest in the ideas of early "anarchist" theorists who wrote about international relations such as Pierre-Joseph Proudhon.[1]

It is common knowledge that Proudhon developed a theory of federalism in the final years before his death in January 1865. The starting point for this theory, his 1861 work *La Guerre et la Paix*, was perhaps the most extensive and sustained nineteenth-century attack on the "sorry comforters" first targeted by Kant (and into whose fold Proudhon included Kant, himself).[2] In this controversial work on international law, Proudhon defended the legitimacy of the "right of force" in interstate conflict – a position seemingly at odds with his current reputation as one of the nineteenth century's most prominent European "socialists", or, for that matter, "anarchists". Most commentators since *La Guerre et la Paix*'s publication have dwelled on this surprising theory of right.[3]

---

[1] Most notably in Proudhon, *Du principe federatif et de la necessite de reconstituer le parti de la Revolution* (Paris: Dentu, 1863).

[2] *La Guerre et la Paix, Recherches sur le principe et la constitution du droit des gens* (Brussels: Hetzel, 1861). Henceforth abbreviated as *LGLP*. Although there have been several French critical editions published since the twentieth century of *La Guerre et la Paix*, they all have republished the Paris edition of the same work (Paris: Dentu, 1861), which, for reasons having to do with the imperial censorship of the time, varies slightly from the Brussels edition, which appeared simultaneously. For this reason, quotes from and references to this work below will be exclusively from the original two-volume Belgian first edition.

[3] For examples of such readings amongst Proudhon's contemporaries, see Ernest Desmarest's review in *La Critique française*, 7, 15 June 1861: pp. 521–534; and Félix Stappaerts's review in *La Revue britannique*, 11, 1861: pp. 412–424. Twentieth-century

Yet far from being a vitalist glorification of the regenerative virtues of conflict, *La Guerre et la Paix* was an argument for the right of force's supersession. In this work, traditionally conservative arguments favouring the right of the most powerful to rule over their natural inferiors – arguments rehabilitated by critics of the French Revolution, such as Karl Ludwig von Haller – were spun differently and turned into a teleological theory of progressive legal, moral, and social evolution anticipating a bright, market-driven future once the balance of power between hegemonic states contained inter- and intra-state instability. This chapter will examine the arguments of *La Guerre et la Paix* in close exegetical detail in order to suggest, by way of conclusion, how they contents might fit into the larger history of ideas about international relations, commerce, and peace.

Proudhon published his 1861 *La Guerre et la Paix* in Belgium, where he had fled after the imperial government's 1858 condemnation of his *De la Justice dans la Révolution et dans l'Église*.[4] In this work, Proudhon sought to demonstrate the persistence of two conflicting conceptions of justice: one "transcendent", rooted in notions of hierarchy and traditional Christian theology, and the other, which Proudhon preferred, "immanent", emerging instinctively in the individual conscience from the stimulation of unmediated social relations. The anticlerical nature of *De la Justice* proved intolerable for official censors. Leaving for Brussels to avoid certain imprisonment, Proudhon became more interested in international politics. *La Guerre et la Paix* was the fruit of three years of reflection on this topic, but Proudhon also saw it as the pendant of the earlier 1858 work, insofar as he considered it to be an application of his larger philosophical conception of immanent justice to international affairs.

exegetical readings of *La Guerre et la Paix* have particularly emphasized Proudhon's opening phenomenological speculations about war and the "right of force" at the expense of grappling with the bulk of the 1861 work. For some examples, see Alexis Philonenko, "Proudhon ou le silence des dieux", in his *Essais sur la Philosophie de la Guerre* (Paris: Vrin, 1976): pp. 99–158; Édouard Jourdain, *Proudhon, Dieu et la Guerre: une philosophie du combat*, (Paris: L'Harmattan, 2006); and Alain Panero's lengthy introduction to the most recent critical edition to *La Guerre et la Paix* (Paris: Nuvis, 2012): pp. 5–74. With mixed success, Prichard, in his *Justice, Order and Anarchy*, pp. 112–134, attempts to correct for this exegetical imbalance by giving some attention to the immediate geopolitical context in which the work was written. See also Henri Moysset's introduction to his interwar critical edition of *La Guerre et la Paix* (Paris: Rivière, 1927): pp. i–xciv; and Aaron Noland, "Proudhon's Sociology of War", *The American Journal of Economics and Sociology*, 29, 3, July 1970: pp. 289–304.

[4] *De la Justice dans la Révolution et dans l'Église, Nouveaux principes de philosophie pratique adressés à son éminence Monseigneur Mathieu, cardinal-archevêque de Besançon*, 3 volumes, (Paris: Garnier frères, 1858).

La Guerre et la Paix began with a consideration of the anthropological origins of thinking about military conflict in light of what Proudhon called a "phenomenology of war".[5] Proudhon proceeded from these anthropological conjectures to criticize the errors of misguided jurists who applied international law to questions of war and peace.[6] Proudhon's alternative jurisprudential account began where *De la Justice* left off. Justice was a fact of conscience, a hard-wired sentiment, which resulted from stimulation wrought by the interface between individual action in the world and human sociability. This "immanent" faculty – directly related to the measurement of the relative merit or demerit of others with respect to oneself – generated rights. These were rights not to things, legitimated in accordance with the need for self-preservation, but emanated from the diverse qualitative powers specific to humans, evidenced in differences in ability, such that there were according to Proudhon, "as many varieties of the application of justice, [. . .] as many kinds of rights as faculties are in the subject, and, in the sphere of its action, objects capable of furnishing justice with terms of comparison".[7]

The faculty of justice was also always at work in human conflict, notably in war, which was not just force and antagonism but additionally also as an internal, immaterial phenomenon that was part of humans' psychic experience of the world. This psychological truth explains the importance accorded to violence in primitive religions, which confounded legislation, state power, morality, and justice. For crude peoples, war, like authority, was endowed with divine, primordial characteristics.[8] Because it was only through action in the world that human faculties develop, natural inequalities and diversities in ability necessarily lead to conflict, which then, through their assertion in struggle, are generative of rights and a legal order. War engenders rights

[5] "Phénoménologie de la Guerre" is the title Proudhon gave to the first book of *LGLP*, v. 1, pp. 29–111.

[6] This is the subject of the second book of *La Guerre et la Paix*, "De la nature de la guerre et du droit de la force", v. 1, pp. 113–310.

[7] This kind of psycho-anthropological argument confounding rights and faculties was not [. . .] was not entirely novel and long predated the nineteenth century. Leaving aside the more well-known case of Giambattista Vico, concerning whom the scholarly literature is voluminous, the eighteenth-century tradition of a "primitivist" critique of post-Grotian natural jurisprudence has been notably discussed by Michael Sonenscher, *Sans-Culottes: An Eighteenth-Century Emblem in the French Revolution*, (Princeton University Press, 2008): pp. 166–195.

[8] Proudhon's list of authorities confirming his "anthropothysic" theory of the theocratic, syncretistic contents of primitive religious consciousness was a highly eclectic one: it freely lumped together [. . .] lumping together Joseph de Maistre and Ludwig Feuerbach, both of whom were agreed with one another about the relation between religious sacrifice and warfare and its liturgical attenuation in Christiandoctrine. *LGLP*, v. 1, pp. 50–51.

but, contrary to the just war tradition of legal thought (in which the "justness" of belligerents was necessarily unilateral and the justice of one's cause could be separated from the outcome of military conflict), war, itself a form of legal process, was sanctioned by the verdict of victory, since "victory has no other end than to show which side has the greater force and to consecrate its right".[9] Much as there were other rights generated by the superior abilities or capacities of some over others (those generated through the exercise of work, intelligence, or even love, to take some examples), the right of war, according to Proudhon, derives from the "right of force", the most elementary and positive right. Seen this way, insofar as justice was in many ways nothing more than a retrospective "consideration of the use of force", war was "the demand and demonstration of the right of force".[10]

Contrary to the intuitive common sense of the masses confirming these assertions, the opinion of jurists and political theorists from the seventeenth century to the present day generally refused to grant any "moral phenomenality, any spirituality" to the mere "material demonstrations" that were "acts of force".[11] For them the right of war was "a fiction, a euphemism, which it would be puerile, ridiculous, absurd to take seriously", "a sort of legal fiction, suggested by the unfortunateness of the times".[12] For such writers (and Proudhon named specifically Grotius, Hobbes, Pufendorf, Barbeyrac, Wolff, Vattel, Kant, and Georg von Martens), the idea of a "right of war" had no real juridical content, since force could not create right and right and war were antithetical to one another, war being "by nature, foreign to right" and its "violent, injurious suspension".[13] Such reasoning was true for Grotius, for whom war was "the effect of the absence of justice, the absence of any judicial authority".[14] The same set of assumptions also held true for others writing in Grotius's wake, such as Emer de Vattel, for whom war was "the state in which one pursues one's right by force" and for whom, like Grotius, "if war was just on one side, it was necessarily unjust on the other",[15] or Kant, for whom war was "extra-legal" since right was what allowed mankind to leave a state of nature dominated by force.[16] The entire school of "sorry comforters"–Proudhon did not employ the

---

[9] *Ibid.*, v. 1, p. 222, and for just war theories, *ibid.*, v. 1, pp. 117–118.

[10] *Ibid.*, v. 1, pp. 208 and 222.

[11] *Ibid.*, v. 1, pp. 32–33. The juxtaposition between the common sense of the masses about the meaning of warfare and the unnatural assertions of an elite intelligentsia with regards to the same is made throughout *La Guerre et la Paix*. See, in particular, v. 1, pp. 115–125.

[12] *Ibid.*, v. 1, pp. 32–33.   [13] *Ibid.*, v. 1, pp. 116–117.   [14] *Ibid.*, v. 1, p. 128.

[15] For this reduction of Vattel, *ibid.*, v. 1, pp. 128–129.

[16] For this reduction of Kant, *ibid.*, v. 1, pp. 160–161.

expression, but he had read Kant's *Perpetual Peace* carefully in the translation done by his friend, Claude-Joseph Tissot[17]–reasoned similarly, assuming the validity of a perverse anthropology in which a personal right to self-preservation becomes a real right successively enshrined in civil, political, and international law.

Following from Proudhon's "phenomenology of war", the reverse process in the development of legal consciousness was the case. Most primitive societies only respected corporeal force, which was their basis for ascertaining both merit and right. For them, force was the first source of right and all primitive legislation stemmed from the reverence it inspired. The right of war was legitimately granted to the strongest member or members of early communities, whose centralization of jurisdiction in a single sovereign distinguishing some peoples from other peoples in the interests of protection marked the beginnings of international law. This concentration of power then inspired the development of public law, whose rules were determined by the sovereign authority endowed with a monopoly of violence over its citizenry. The origins of civil law followed from there.[18] These early societies were furthermore characterized by high degrees of inequality, with aristocrats, patricians, and other oligarchs on the one side endowed with legal authority, and slaves and plebeians on the other endowed only with an extra-legal existence. Jurists and publicists from Grotius onwards discussed the idea of "natural right" regularly, juxtaposing it favourably to the vagaries of divine right, whereas, following from Proudhon's phenomenological anthropology of law, there was no real difference between the two forms of right, since "force", in primitive consciousness, was identical with divinity dressed in crude symbolic forms. Indeed, according to Proudhon, "What we have for a long time called '*right of nature*' should be eliminated from the terminology of law".[19]

Proudhon singled out Hobbes – the most consequential writer on the question of war and peace – for particular criticism.[20] From his reading of *De Cive*, Proudhon thought that Hobbes was particularly guilty of ignoring war's importance to the life of nations, inasmuch as it generated its own laws, necessary for the felicity of peoples and the survival of the human race. According to Proudhon, Hobbes had rooted his theory of

---

[17] For evidence of Proudhon's reactions to Kant's political writings, see his manuscript notes on Tissot's translation, *Principes métaphysiques du Droit, suivis du projet de paix perpétuelle*, (Paris: Ladrange, 1853) found in MS. Z°550, ff. 1–2 and MS. 2859, ff. 44–46 recto-verso, Bibliothèque d'étude et de conservation, Besançon, as well as his marginal annotations to his copy of this edition held at the same library.

[18] For these points, *LGLP*, v. 1, pp. 213–214.

[19] *Ibid.*, v. 1, p. 213.　　[20] *Ibid.*, v. 1, pp. 171–196.

legality in the passage from the primitive needs of self-preservation and the utilitarian exercise of "right reason" to the imperative to transcend conflicts through the intervention of an external authority taking the form of the state. Proudhon had no time for Hobbist speculations about the utility of "right reason", which in his eyes was "nothing other, at root, than a demonstration of the necessity of justice by the reduction to absurdity of the hypothesis of the non-existence of justice".[21] Hobbes's theory boiled down to arguing that justice had to be state-sanctioned, a claim obviously at odds with Proudhon's view that there is a positive principle of justice contained within the rational and moral faculties of mankind: an internally hard-wired emotional capacity to recognize the dignity of oneself vis-à-vis others and vice versa, allowing humans to recognize instinctively what was just beyond the purview of their own immediate interests. Because Hobbes was unable to conceive of "force" and the respect it demanded as something existing internally within human conscience (since mankind was bereft of any innate, natural sociability capable of spontaneously generating its own forms of justice), he had to externalize authority through the invention of the state, construed as an expression of indirect representative sovereignty resulting from a union based on fear and the desire for self-preservation. For the narrative purposes of this political theory's construction, war was like the conjectural state of nature which it characterized and which, in turn, necessitated the creation of the state so man could leave it. Justice, as a result, was grounded in no more than the monopoly over the use of force accorded to the artificial state person, and Hobbes's system amounted to "nothing else than the theory of temporal power, considered independently of any religious, spiritual and moral element".[22] This abstract idea of the state person persisted in Western political thought, and was notably adopted by natural jurisprudential advocates of a *jus gentium* like Christian von Wolff or Emir de Vattel (all of whom were Hobbists, whether they admitted it or not), who projected onto states the same "natural law" they claimed was applicable to individuals – minus differences related to those "voluntary" (as opposed to immutably "necessary") aspects of interstate (as opposed to individual) relations.[23] Such highly speculative assertions ignored the larger teleological course of human history in this regard, since Proudhon was convinced that individual sovereign states were destined, regardless of any reference of the "right of nationalities" to exist as autonomous entities, to increasingly

---

[21] *Ibid.*, v. 1, p. 185.   [22] *Ibid.*, v. 1, p. 194.
[23] On Wolff-Vattel, see *ibid.*, v. 1, pp. 150–158, and for the Hobbes-Vattel parallel, *ibid.* v. 1, p. 244.

interpenetrate one another with population growth, concomitant state development, and war, such that they would all become intertwined and absorbed within each others' affairs to the point where any presumed individual, discrete national sovereignty was irreversibly attenuated and no longer conceptually relevant. To this extent, the post-Hobbesian "collective person", whether called a "nation" or a "state", was merely an attempt to set up an artificial roadblock to the realization of the "right of force".[24]

Due to the same jurists and publicists' refusal to recognize the legitimacy of the right of force, the right of war appeared in their works as the product of a pure fiction: a *jus gentium* ultimately incapable of ever giving states sufficient sanction for conducting military operations. Having initially refused to recognize that all right is based on force, jurists and publicists working in the wake of Grotius and Hobbes invariably attempted to find ways of justifying the use of force to protect their conception of the "law of peoples".[25] Apart from appeals to the superior rationality and morality of governments, jurists were unable, according to Proudhon to find any convincing guarantee for the *jus gentium* they sought to promote and codify, short of imagining the emergence of some higher supranational authority: "In short, the theory of modern publicists, founded on an analogy, leads to the hypothesis of a universal monarchy, republic, or confederation, precisely that which nations protest against with the most energy [...] Outside of this omniarchy, the right of nations, according to them, remains a *desideratum* of science, an empty statement. With regard to one another, nations *are in the state of nature*".[26] Because, for Proudhon, "civilization only develops through the influence political groups exert on one another in the plenitude of their sovereignty and independence", the desire for such a supranational authority was, much like Charlemagne's ninth-century imperial pretentions, a regression: "the negation of the sovereign independence and autonomy of states, the negation of all human freedom, something which states and nations will be eternally agreed to reject".[27]

---

[24] For these points, see *ibid.*, v. 1, p. 229.

[25] Indeed, it was for this very reason that Proudhon considered basically all writers concerned with theorizing the *jus gentium* to have been – whether they admitted it or not – Hobbists, mired in all the same difficulties with which Hobbes's political theories were plagued. See *ibid.*, v. 1, pp. 118–119, pp. 205–206, p. 244.

[26] *Ibid.*, v. 1, p. 110. Used facetiously by Proudhon, the term "omniarchy" was a Fourierist neologism for the supreme dignitaries who would govern over a harmonious Phalansterian world.

[27] *Ibid.*, v. 1, pp. 111–112.

In order to be a distinct juridical sphere, the "law of peoples" had to concern itself with collective agents – either "nations" or "states" – that were distinct from mere citizens. This focus had important implications:

That which distinguishes, from the standpoint of right, collective being, whether called a state or nation, that which establishes a line of impassable demarcation between the social person and the individual person, is that the immolation of the first can, for a higher reason, be juridically necessary, whereas the immolation of the second, outside the case of a crime bearing capital punishment, can never be. [...] In many circumstances, it is necessary for this collective person, who also has its soul, its genius, its dignity, its force; before which individualities bow as before their sovereign, it is necessary, I say, for it to disappear, absorbed by a superior existence. The movement of civilisation, the perfectibility of states, is at this price.[28]

For this reason, Proudhon concluded that the proper practical sphere of inquiry of any *jus gentium* should be reduced to "when, how, and under what circumstances one should proceed with the fusion or incorporation within a larger state of one or many other smaller states; fusion that is nothing more than, for the latter – and sometimes for the former – a suicide; and reciprocally when, how, and under what circumstances one should proceed with the reverse operation, that is to say a dismemberment [of a larger state]".[29] Because externally the sanction of justice on an international level could only be deduced from the exercise and demonstration of the right of force, likewise, war and its consequences had historically been the affirmation and ultimate guarantor of any genuine *jus gentium*, the latter being necessarily a product of the rights of war. According to Proudhon, it was in the logic of societies to expand, while the states that governed them sought to achieve the maximum level of independence from their neighbours.[30] As European states developed following the decline of the Roman Empire, their growth was constrained by equally or more powerful sovereign states. By the second half of the nineteenth century, "[t]he degree of civilisation being roughly the same everywhere, everywhere there was also an energetic repulsion to fusion, which is to say that the hypothesis of a European monarchy is anti-European".[31]

---

[28] *Ibid.*, v. 1, pp. 249–250 and *ibid.* pp. 248–250 more generally on this distinction between collective and individual persons.
[29] *Ibid.*, v. 1, pp. 250–251.   [30] *Ibid.*, v. 1, pp. 313–315.
[31] *Ibid.*, v. 1, p. 325. For these reasons, Proudhon claimed, major peace treaties were usually constructed with the dominant hegemonic power in mind: for example, Charles V for Westphalia; Louis XIV for Utrecht; or Napoleon for the Congress of Vienna Settlement. *Ibid.*, v. 2, pp. 140–141.

But in modern times the right of force applied to governments, not to the peoples they ruled. If the façade of diplomatic manoeuvres could be disregarded as mere artifice, the object of interstate disputes was always sovereignty.[32] Indeed, the absorption of other states was often enough a zero-sum affair, entailing the "moral death" of one nation through its territorial appropriation by another.[33] Contemporary cant about a supposed "principle of nationalities" could not mask the historical fact that there was no right of nationalities to exist if they could not be robustly asserted and defended by sovereign governments. As Proudhon argued with regard to the question of Italian unification in the wake of the recent 1859 Austro-Sardinian War: "The people which cannot manage to constitute itself politically, which is incapable of rebuffing the aggression of others, grants them, precisely through its weakness, a right to supremacy. It cannot pretend to be independent; it would be a danger for others, a principle of dissolution, if it did not obey".[34] And he added a few pages later (in part to defend the right of the King of Naples to resist the peninsular machinations of the kingdom of Piedmont-Sardinia): "Ideas which cannot fight, which find war repulsive, and which flee the glean of the bayonet, are not fit to lead societies; men who do not know how to die for their ideas are not made for government; a nation which refuses to arm itself, which, against its dominators, would only grimace, is unworthy of autonomy. The right of nationalities exists only under this condition: force creates it, and victory gives it its sanction".[35]

However, if states could disappear entirely as discrete sovereign entities, Proudhon was at pains to point out that in order for their conquest to be complete and definitive, there necessarily had to be some degree of assimilation between peoples after conquest "the first duty of the conqueror, [...] the right of the conquered people".[36] Proudhon reassured his readers that the end of a state's sovereignty by conquest did not necessarily entail the destruction of its citizenry. Because the right of force was "the prerogative of sovereignty, the symbol of justice",[37] the consequences of its use fell squarely upon sovereign governments (and not the citizenries they governed) since war in modern times was the prerogative of states alone (unlike, for example, in the feudal era when

---

[32] Consistent with his larger assertions about the juridical ubiquity of the "right of force", Proudhon asserted that very words "sovereignty" and "power" were "two terms which, taken one for the other, remind one of the identity of the two notions, right and force". *Ibid.*, v. 1, p. 136.

[33] For Proudhon's use of the expression "moral death", a Christian theological concept describing how post-lapsarian humans criminally participate in the Fall every time they actively sin, see *ibid.*, v. 1, p. 315, and *ibid.*, v. 2, p. 78.

[34] *Ibid.*, v. 1, p. 334.   [35] *Ibid.*, v. 1, p. 346.

[36] *Ibid.*, v. 1, p. 322.   [37] *Ibid.*, v. 1, p. 303.

it was still shared in various degrees with barons, nobles, and other distinguished social ranks granted military authority). As an outcome of modern military conflict, defeated peoples only faced the possibility of assimilation with the victors, which was distinct from the threat of extinction states faced.[38]

To Proudhon, any credible "law of peoples" had to concern itself with the absorption, incorporation, annexation, and reorganization of states insofar as their development revealed itself through the results of interstate conflicts (and independently of the various justifications used by sovereigns to justify their behaviour). This *jus gentium* presupposed a legal order whose rules were imminent to the history of international relations but which could only be grasped retrospectively. Unfortunately, the jurists and theorists who developed the concept of a *jus gentium*, seeking to subsume the right of war within it, condemned themselves to irrelevance by ignoring the origins of both the law of peoples and the right of war in an irrepressible "right of force". Consequently, they never could address matters of any pertinence to contemporary international relations. They avoided asking difficult questions such as what the normal size of a state should be, or whether its delineation should be determined by such diverse criteria as geography, ethnicity, language, religion, customs, or some general, overarching normative standard of civilisation which might even, in certain cases (like the American antebellum South) justify the temporary enslavement of some by others.[39] Although aware of the problem of the absence of a supranational sovereign, such jurists and theorists waffled when it came to suggesting practical solutions for world peace and were reluctant to make categorical claims about

---

[38] On these points with regards to the *jus gentium*, see *ibid.*, v. 1, pp. 248–251, and as specifically applied to racial relations in the United States on the eve of Civil War, *ibid.* v. 1, pp. 280–281. This was not crucially the case of ancient times, in which, subjected to the criteria of a more primitive moral compass, the right to the use of force confounded individuals with states (there being no distinction in peoples' minds), and policies of genocide regularly carried out against defeated peoples were ubiquitously considered to be legitimate. See *ibid.*, v. 2, pp. 289–293.

[39] For the specific enumeration of what the international jurists did not examine, see *ibid.*, v. 1, p. 251. In a passage reminiscent of Thomas Carlyle's polemical denunciation of the "dismal science" of political economy in his 1849 "An Occasional Discourse on the Negro Question", Proudhon justified the brazen racial inequalities that characterized Southern society on the eve of the American Civil War by arguing that the forced migration and enslavement of Africans might serve a salutary quasi-pedagogical function when cast in world-historical terms, gradually bringing inferior peoples into the sphere of a superior civilization in an integrating fashion preferable to their immediate emancipation, which would only throw freed slaves into wage labour and the miseries of the urban proletariat. Provided the behavior of the slaveholding master class was strictly regulated by the government, slavery, Proudhon argued, would more surely lift black Africans out of their intellectual and cultural inferiority than their sudden post-emancipation integration within an industrial workforce. See *ibid.*, v. 1, pp. 276–282.

anything relevant to achieving interstate stability. They never directly addressed whether there could be genuine equality between states; whether it would be desirable for the different nationalities populating the globe to fuse together to form a single multiethnic mass governed by a universal monarchy; or, alternatively, whether it would be better to see either a hierarchy or a confederation of states established in the interest of maintaining international order.[40] They avoided imagining whether the only basis for the balance of power between independent sovereign states could very well be the anarchical absence of a supranational state or tribunal capable of regulating the relations between them, much less whether the existence of a supranational force could even be functional or desirable.[41] They were likewise vague about what should be done with newly acquired colonial territory acquired and the indigenous peoples who would have to be displaced, as well as the role slavery should have in modern civilized societies.[42] Finally, they failed to speculate on whether diplomatic alliances might preclude the sovereign autonomy of individual states, itself rendering problematic the very idea of official international relations between sovereign governments.[43] All of these seemingly abstract questions of principle were directly pertinent to solving important contemporary issues like the merits of fusing Ireland and Britain; the separation of Holland and Belgium; Polish, Hungarian, and Italian demands for independence or unification; German federalism; Panslavism and Scandinavism; the breakup of the Ottoman Empire and the territorial parameters of Greece; the proper rules for extradition; and myriad other issues related to the Vienna Congress System and its multipolar attempt to regulate the post-Napoleonic international order, to say nothing of what attitude to adopt to Southern Secession in the United States.[44]

The "law of peoples", in Proudhon's redefinition, was, however, distinct from the different forms of public law derivative of it:

[T]here is this difference between international law and political law that the first essentially implies the eventuality of the absorption of some states by others, and consequently, in case of conflict, the legitimacy of their immolation; whereas in political law, neither state sovereignty, nor the liberty of citizens can perish; far from it, the masterwork of the constitution is to make the two grow incessantly side-by-side and one through the other. In international law, if the balance of power cannot be amicably obtained, there will be suppression, through war, of one or several rival states; in political law, on the contrary, order is imperiously required without it costing the sacrifice of a single freedom, nor a single life:

---

[40] For these points, see *ibid.*, v. 1, pp. 251–252.
[41] *Ibid.*, v. 1, p. 252.   [42] *Ibid.*   [43] *Ibid.*
[44] On these "contemporary questions", see *ibid.*, v. 1, pp. 262–287.

proscription, which is, so to speak, the soul of the law of peoples, becomes herein contradictory.[45]

Nevertheless, eliding questions of public and international law, Proudhon asserted that "[a]t the same time that political constitutions are based, in the last instance, on force, they also have for their sanction force: in this public law comes to be confounded with international law".[46] Because "it is the right of force, [. . .], the respectability inherent to force, as a human faculty, which forms the first basis of right, the first rung of the legal and political order", constitutional principles such as legal equality had to be continuously defended by individual citizenries, since such equality could always be repealed through the exercise of the sovereign force of the states which backed public law.[47] For postrevolutionary citizens, Proudhon asserted that the only way, short of civil war, to protect and guarantee whatever political liberties they had was through the attenuation of concentrated sovereign power in the government. This meant encouraging the creation of constitutional monarchies in which violable ministries were rendered accountable for their policies and sovereign authority was sufficiently depersonalized and removed from the act of governing. It also meant allowing the middle classes to enter the electorate through universal suffrage while promoting policies conducive to social mobility and encouraging greater access to education and wealth.[48] Short of adopting such measures, nations were as doomed to foreign conquest as those that could not defend themselves militarily against external threats:

Any nation, in effect, incapable of organizing itself politically, and in which the power is unstable, is a nation destined to be consumed by its neighbours. Like

---

[45] *Ibid.*, v. 1, pp. 291–292. Attempts to confound national constitutional law with international law were particularly attractive to liberal nationalists. Proudhon identified this sort of amalgam at work in the excerpts he read in the *Revue Contemporaine* (31 January 1860) of the 1859 treatise, *D'un nuovo diritto europeo*, of a juridical proponent of the principle of nationalities, of the Northern Italian jurist Terenzio Mamiani, an ally of Cavour. See *ibid.* v. 1, pp. 283–287.

[46] *Ibid.*, v. 1, p. 300. See also *ibid.*, v. 1, p. 292. Proudhon suggested that internal national conflicts played a role in shaping national legal consciousness analogous to the way interstate conflicts determined the balance of power responsible for the international legal order. Historically, force had revealed its importance in shaping legal evolution in the form of class conflict (for example, in conflicts pitting patricians or aristocrats against plebeians). Although the right of birth had been replaced, particularly since the French Revolution, by more democratic forms of collective organization determining the criteria for the distribution and shape of political power, force, now understood in terms of number and not heredity (or, as Rousseau would have it, some sort of "general will"), found new expression in the electoral rights of majorities over minorities. *Ibid.* v. 1, pp. 292–296.

[47] *Ibid*, v. 1, p. 294.   [48] *Ibid.*, v. 1, p. 299.

those which do not know how or do not wish to wage war, or who are too weak to defend themselves, it does not have the right to occupy a place on the map of states; it annoys, it is necessary that it be subjected to suzerainty. Neither religion, nor language, nor race, are anything in this regard: the preponderance of interests dominates all and makes the law. The right of force, the right of war, the law of peoples, political right, all are here synonyms: where force is lacking, the government cannot hold, and nationality even less. Terrible right, you say, right to regimicide [*régnicide*] in which one hesitates to recognize a form of justice. Oh! No ! No vain sensibility. Do you remember that the death of a state does not entail that of its citizens, and that there is no worse condition for the latter than that of a state decrepit and destroyed by factions? When the fatherland is unyielding to liberty, when public sovereignty is in contradiction with that of the citizen, nationality becomes a disgrace, and regeneration via foreign intervention a necessity.[49]

The relation of the "right of force" and the "law of peoples" to domestic political constitutions and external relations between sovereign states did not explain how international conflicts might ever end, however. In the last two books of *La Guerre et La Paix*, Proudhon switched gears and attempted to offer an alternative explanation of how the source of warfare, a seemingly atavistic, imperishable right to dominate others, could, once its stimuli and motivations were better understood, be diluted to the point of its transformation into peace. Proudhon argued that Grotius had hinted at the real cause of war when he repeatedly reduced the sorts of conflicts characterizing interstate relations to the defence of persons and their possessions (independent of reasons of state), dwelling as much on matters of property rights, marital rights, inheritance, criminal law, and trade as on relations between sovereign governments.[50] If Grotius confounded civil (or private) law with national (or public) and international law without adequately explaining how the defence of individuals and their proprietary interests applied to constitutional arrangements or interstate conflicts, his intuition was on the mark. "Demands or denials of property", Proudhon asserted, "this is what is at the root of all human struggles, as much between states as between individuals".[51]

Because of this truth, from the standpoint of "social economy", what appeared sufficiently moral from a national and international political standpoint lost much of its legitimacy.[52] Recast in this manner, the

---

[49] *Ibid.*, v. 1, pp. 300–301.   [50] *Ibid.*, v. 2, pp. 158–162.
[51] *Ibid.*, v. 2, p. 161. Somewhat confusingly, Proudhon elsewhere, *ibid.*, v. 1, pp. 301–304, claimed that civil law was itself historically derivative of public law, itself the result of the *jus gentium* produced through the exercise of the right of force and its subsidiary, the right of war.

cause of all war could be understood as "the lack of subsistences", itself identical with "the RUPTURE OF ECONOMIC EQUILIBRIUM". Likewise, "[t]he end and object of war, seen from this new point of view, would thus be, for the aggressor, to recover from the penury which torment it with spoils; for the aggressed, to keep that which it considers to its property, in accordance with whatever title it claims to hold it".[53]

According to Proudhon, there was a basic existential fact at the heart of the human condition which explained this: in order to live, one needs to eat, but in order to eat, one needs to work and produce things to meet one's subsistence needs. Superimposing a labour theory of the divided human condition and its relation to the laws of supply and demand onto what had been up until that point an argument about the feebleness of discussions of war and peace, Proudhon argued that labour was responsible for the physical development and intellectual perfectibility of mankind. Thanks to humanity's dual nature, humans at once had an unlimited capacity for consumption – an "indefinite", "negative faculty" related to their acquisitive desires – and a limited capacity for production – a "finite", "positive faculty" related to their constrained capacity to act in the world.[54] This tension was exacerbated on a collective level by the disparity between population growth and seemingly limited natural resources (minus whatever productive advances could be made by labour to overcome such scarcity) such that "abundance" and "wealth" had become antonyms.[55] As humans attempted to overcome this disparity through heightened commercial activity, they regularly fell into cycles of overproduction, market gluts, and unemployment. To avoid falling into these cyclical patterns, humans needed to find innovative ways for creating new needs satisfying their insatiable cravings for consumption, which for Proudhon necessitated the promotion of higher levels of education and culture in order to better foster a beneficial distribution of knowledge, services, and products. They also needed to create a demand for labour in keeping with population increases; improve production and technological development; and ensure some equilibria between services and capacities, on the one side, and wages and the products of labour, on the other.[56] In this manner, balancing supply and demand was also about balancing mankind's divided self.

What applied to the individual, however, could also be applied to collective entities such as entire societies and the states that governed them since, according to Proudhon, "It is necessary [...] that the state, like the individual, live, that is to say, that it consume; the sovereignty

[52] *Ibid.*, v. 2, p. 162.   [53] *Ibid.*, v. 2, p. 163.   [54] *Ibid.*, v. 2, p. 167.
[55] *Ibid.*, v. 2, pp. 168–169.   [56] *Ibid.*, v. 2, pp. 175–176.

that it arrogates or claims for itself or claims is to no other end than to assure its consumption needs."[57] Thus, labour inputs constituting the total production levels of a society should be examined in terms of their relationship to what was collectively necessary for that society to reproduce itself (as measured in terms of market outlets, population subsistence needs, and the overall balance of labour and capital) and its government to maintain, expand, or satisfy its sovereignty. Thus, the sources of warfare could be reduced to such matters as questions of subsistence, territorial needs, trade imbalances wrought by a dearth of adequate market outlets, the desire for colonies and waterways for geostrategic and commercial purposes, and all the other assorted economic disequilibria affecting the relationship between production and consumption and the distribution of products within a nation embedded in an inegalitarian world of diverse nations. These different factors all reflected the tension between the independence of sovereign states and their growth (measured either demographically, commercially, or territorially). Proudhon gave a term to the problem of the internal organization of national economies, which caused all war: he called it "pauperism", "a violation of the economic law which, on the one hand, obliges man to work in order to live, and on the other, balances his products with his needs."[58] As a "lack of equilibrium between man's products and his income, between his spending and his needs, between the dreams of his ambition and the power of his faculties, consequently, between the conditions of citizens", "pauperism" was "essentially psychological", engendered by the "exaggerated sentiment that we have of our own dignity and the little we accord to that of others" and "the desire for luxury", itself a product of the "idealism of our desires".[59]

---

[57] *Ibid.*, v. 2, p. 162.   [58] *Ibid.*, v. 2, p. 196.

[59] *Ibid.*, v. 2, pp. 195–196, p. 194. For the claim that "pauperism" was the "original cause of all war", *ibid.* v. 2, p. 163. In this regard, French society in the Second Empire was particularly exemplary of the ravages of *"paupérisme"*. As symptomatic evidence of national sickness, Proudhon particularly singled out the luxury goods industry, contemporary artistic and literary productions, and excessive government spending, all of which phenomena were conducive to increasingly ostentatious displays of disparities in wealth as well as such economic trends as rising rents and costs; urban development; the growth of finance and its reshaping of corporate culture (as expressed in the joint-stock companies responsible for the vast public works projects Napoleon III encouraged); and speculation on the precious metals responsible for backing currencies (itself exacerbated by the Gold Rush in California). For this enumeration, see *ibid.*, v. 2, pp. 197–200. All of these trends were mirrored in the sociological behaviour of French society, finding expression in the insatiability of upper classes; the moral and physical degeneration of the lower classes; and the anxieties of the middle classes tempted to imitate the consumption habits of the rich while irresponsibly running the risk of falling into the ranks of the poor. See *ibid.*, v. 2, pp. 201–205.

The problem was that the pursuit of wealth by both individuals and collective entities hoping to balance production and consumption was illusory, since wealth was a false ideal as an end in itself. For one thing, since there was no way of retrieving a mythical primitive abundance in which the scarcity of resources would not exist, humans' promethean nature led them to create new needs as they produced new ways to satisfy them. Contemporary reformers' pretence of making the lower classes more moral by improving their well-being and giving them access to heightened levels of material comfort, Proudhon argued, would only encourage new levels of concupiscence.[60] For Proudhon, "wealth", much like the term "value" used by political economists, was nothing more than a conceptual term representing a relationship – whether between production and consumption; supply and demand; labour and capital; output and its remuneration; or, more abstractly, needs and those actions necessary to meet them.[61] Rather than mistaking what was a material relationship for a moral panacea, Proudhon suggested that serious reflection upon the divided nature of mankind should lead individuals to redefine how they live their lives: "before an unlimited capacity for consumption and a necessarily limited capacity for production, the most exact economy is demanded of us. Temperance, frugality, daily bread obtained through daily labour, my own destitution quick to punish gluttony and laziness [in others]: this is the first of our moral laws".[62] If humans should appreciate when their subsistence needs were being met, they should also work more and spend less. This kind of lifestyle change would generate the opposite of "pauperism", that acute sense of wont which inspires cupidity and aggression and which was responsible for war. Proudhon used the term "poverty" to describe the desirable acceptance of the constraints imposed upon a perfectible humanity's ability to develop in a permanent condition of scarcity. A "reciprocal, rigorous limit of our production and our consumption" ensuring that man "obtains through labour that which demands the needs of his body and the culture of his soul, *neither more nor less*", "poverty" was a "law of our nature which, by obliging us to produce that which we need to consume, does not however grant to our labour more than the necessary".[63]

When it came to suggesting how humanity might ever arrive at this moral end, Proudhon conveniently proffered a teleological narrative of

---

[60] For this point, *ibid.*, v. 2, pp. 188–189.
[61] *Ibid.*, v. 2, pp. 189–190. According to Proudhon, the most generic expression of these different relationships representing "*la richesse*" was intuitively understood to be, on an individual level, the average workday cast in terms of labour (measured in time expended) and the results of labour's efforts (measured materially in terms of output).
[62] *Ibid.*, v. 2, p. 171.   [63] *Ibid.*, v. 2, p. 169 and *ibid.*, v. 2, p. 195.

legal and psychological evolution and changing conceptions of right which, while linking his existential and economic assertions about the divided nature of mankind to his earlier discussions of the "right of force" and the origins of war, rendered such a happy outcome plausible. This shift could be measured historically by examining changing conceptions of warfare from antiquity to the post-revolutionary age. Likely indebted, in part, to his reading of Giambattista Vico just over twenty years earlier, Proudhon described how war, in a primitive "heroic" age of human history, was indistinguishable from pillaging, pirating, privateering, robbing, looting, marauding, and despoliating.[64] The agent of expropriation changed over time, first from individuals (who were not much more than bandits), to cities (in classical antiquity), and finally to states. This shift in the locus of belligerence began in ancient Greece, between the end of the pre-classical era of Dorian tyranny to the time of Alexander the Great. It was consolidated through the rise and expansion of Rome, whereupon conquest became explicitly linked to political incorporation and initially national prerogatives became universalized through imperial designs. The shift in agency caused a concomitant shift in the experience of "pauperism", which was less and less felt as a matter of individual wont and more as a matter of collective desire as expressed first in local and socio-professional trends, then in state policy. For "[a]t the same time peoples became industrious and workers, war became the prerogative of governments".[65]

As the sphere of war was allocated to the sovereign state, there was a concomitant shift in the experience of the feeling of personal dignity and individual worth which changed how humans respected their peers. Mankind's perfectible understanding of its rights developed through a psychological phenomenon entailing the recognition of human dignity as experienced in all humans' faculties, attributes, and prerogatives. If rights evolved with mankind's perfectible faculties (since "each faculty, power, force, carries with it its own right"),[66] new rights emerged as societies changed. Towards the end of *La Guerre et la Paix*, Proudhon additionally asserted that the overarching *telos* behind all conceptions of

---

[64] For this account with regards to world history up until the time of Alexander the Great, see *La Guerre et la Paix*, v. 2, pp. 220–251. Proudhon discovered Vico when he was preparing to write his 1840 work, *Qu'est-ce que la propriété?* (and at the same time he was reading or rereading other pre-revolutionary authors such as Grotius and Rousseau). For evidence of Proudhon's reading of Vico in late December 1839-early January 1840, see Nouvelles Acquisitions Françaises (henceforth NAF) 18256, Bibliothèque Nationale de France (henceforth BNF), Cahier 2 in-4°, pp. 33–47.

[65] *Ibid.*, v. 2, p. 218.   [66] *Ibid.*, v. 1, p. 269.

right since the French Revolution tended towards a moral end of civilization necessitating the secularization of authority, as the Gospels, grace, revealed dogma, and sacerdotal authority were progressively replaced by the rights of man, liberty, justice, and "public conscience" understood as "the only interpreter of right, the only judge of the temporal, and the only sovereign".[67] The end of legal evolution was the identification of "pure liberty" with "pure right", this equivalence being "the ideal of civilisation, the most elevated expression of force".[68] Facilitating this tendentious process of moral secularization was the emergence in the nineteenth century of a new sense of "economic justice", which aspired to a "just redistribution of products and services" depersonalizing social relations through the application of more equitable criteria to the valuation of products for the remuneration of labour.[69]

This change in consciousness also brought new scrutiny to the internal economic constitution of modern states endowed with monopolies on violence since "one can judge the peaceful dispositions of governments by the state of their finances, the agro-industrial condition of peoples, the number of mortgages, the parallel growth of parasitism and the proletariat, the ever bigger disparity in wealth".[70] The spread of ideas about equality before the law during the eighteenth century and their enshrinement in nineteenth-century constitutions made conquest less appealing since pillage no longer had any obvious benefit beyond those

---

[67] *Ibid.*, v. 2, p. 453.

[68] *Ibid.*, v. 1, p. 305. War, however, played a critical historical role in facilitating this teleological process of realizing freedom on earth.

[69] On "economic justice", *ibid.*, v. 2, pp. 194 and 437. This way of conceiving human relations, Proudhon asserted, was utterly foreign to the world of classical antiquity. Confounding their understanding of "fatherland" (*patrie*), patriotism, sovereignty, and honour with their sense of self-identity, the more communitarian Ancients might have understood the laws of both nature and warfare better than the Moderns. But if they elided the two, they were unable to develop any systematic theory of international law, which only really began with the publication of Grotius's *De Jure Belli ac Pacis* in 1625, a point reiterated on several occasions, in *ibid.*, notably v. 1, pp. 237–238 and v. 2, pp. 105–106. This was because they were unaware of the laws of political economy (by which Proudhon meant the laws of production and exchange), through whose lens the phenomenon of warfare could be grasped beyond the confines of a merely subjective conception of law such as was implied by the "right of force". An economic consciousness of human relations allowed the Moderns to assess more objectively the causes of war and how to remediate them, even if they were more natively egotistical and driven by highly individuated material concerns. Proudhon suggested that this shift in consciousness could be seen in the growing indifference of modern peoples with regards to who exactly ruled them, a process facilitated by the fact that for many citizens of the most advanced modern societies, their only direct relation with government came with taxation. *Ibid.*, v. 1, pp. 315–316. This indifference had a positive effect insofar as it made citizens less and less inclined to sacrifice their lives to satisfy their rulers' interests.

[70] *Ibid.*, v. 2, p. 252.

gains directly made by sovereign governments whose affairs determined modern interstate conflicts. The attractiveness of conquest, which in modern times increased state expenses more quickly than governments could raise revenue, had been eclipsed by the desperate rearguard efforts of states to augment, at less risk, the size and scope of their governmental powers without engaging in international conflicts. War had become excessively costly and did not offer any way for states to recoup their expenses and cap their bloated deficits. It had also, through technological developments (notably regarding the use of artillery), become more lethal.[71] The last period of genuine warfare in Europe was that which had occurred between 1792 and 1815.[72] After 1815, a new constitutional era had been ushered in with the Vienna Settlement, bringing to the fore the preponderance of economic interests in the social life of nations. The last true obstacle to ending war which remained was a neologism Proudhon called "*gouvernementalisme*", by which he meant the state control of commerce, production, administration, education, and other functions necessary for a healthy social order.[73] Having distinguished between the "political problem, concerning the formation, demarcation, and dissolution of states, [. . .] that which war is assigned with resolving" and the "economic problem, relative to the organisation of productive faculties and to the redistribution of services and products, [a] problem with which neither war, nor the state, nor even religion, have up until now occupied themselves" Proudhon added that "following the demonstration that we have made of the causes of war, the economic problem antedates and is superior to the other, and [. . .] it overshadows it".[74] In this manner, Proudhon shifted focus from

---

[71] On this subject, inspired by the relatively recent (24 June 1859) battle of Solferino, *ibid.*, v. 2, pp. 46–52 and v. 2, pp. 92–96. For a reading of Proudhon's *La Guerre et la Paix* which emphasizes this aspect in the larger context of nineteenth and early twentieth-century theories about the relationship between technology and war, see Daniel Pick, *War Machine: The Rationalisation of Slaughter in the Modern Age* (New Haven, CN: Yale University Press, 1993): pp. 42–47; as well as Prichard, *Justice, Order, Anarchy, op. cit.* pp. 57–58 and pp. 127–128.

[72] Proudhon suggested that since 1815 the role of soldiers had also changed, as they had become not much more than glorified gendarmes. *LGLP*, v. 2, p. 384.

[73] For the use of the neologism, see *ibid.*, v. 2, p. 197 and v. 2, p. 322. According to Proudhon, governments (by which he really meant imperial France) were effectively at war with the principle of equality before the law through their conscious efforts to buy off their citizenries by offering them government jobs, or by granting them other regular forms of income. If sovereigns sought to exploit their own nationals by offering them secure public employment, it was because the interests of the state had become autonomous from the society over which the state supposedly governed, a bifurcation that potentially could call into question the legitimacy of the scope of state authority itself.

[74] *Ibid.*, v. 2, pp. 377–378.

the international perspective of relations between sovereign states to the national one of their internal constitutions. He did this to underscore how the political and administrative organization of individual states had to be made subservient to the economic needs of their societies before the likelihood of war could ever be diminished. As he wrote rather colourfully: "On domestic order depends external tranquillity: this is as certain as an axiom from mathematics. The intuition of the people is miraculous in this regard: destitution makes it smell war from afar, [...] like the hungry ogre sniffs out fresh flesh".[75] If the future Proudhon continuously projected into the backdrop of *La Guerre et la Paix* intimated the emergence and generalization, in the interest of world peace, of societies whose governments lacked either hereditary or elective princes, monarchs, chief magistrates, or any other form of personified sovereign, it also demanded a radical reorganization of economic life necessitating this political transformation.

For Proudhon, this desirable economic reorganization was clearly different from that envisaged by Napoleon III when he endorsed the 23 January 1860 Cobden-Chevalier trade agreement between Britain and France. Proudhon thought that contemporary proponents of "free trade" invariably distracted attention away from a more equitable internal distribution of goods and services towards the illusory promise of growth through exports. Such propagandists were supported by British interests, which sought to overcome the hurdles posed to profitability by protective tariffs and pre-existing domestic markets in those foreign countries they sought to penetrate.[76] But Proudhon did not stoop to the contemporary Anglophobia shared by French socialists, republicans, legitimists, Bonapartists, and clergy alike. Instead, towards the close of *La Guerre et la Paix*, Proudhon provocatively measured the respective political and economic strengths and weaknesses of Britain and France while imagining a futuristic scenario in which the two countries went to war over global dominance, repeating the past scenario Europe witnessed during the Napoleonic era after the 1805 and 1807 battles of Austerlitz and Friedland.[77] Although France benefitted from a larger territory and population, it had neither the commercial, industrial, agricultural, or maritime strengths of Britain. Its government was a militarized monarchy, whereas Britain was a constitutional one, which, although saddled with a larger national debt, benefited from larger levels of capital investment and profitability.

---

[75] *Ibid.*, v. 2, pp. 252–253.
[76] For these points, *LGLP*, v. 2, pp. 262–263 and pp. 270–274.
[77] *LGLP*, v. 2, pp. 301–314.

Because the territorial annexation of one nation by the other was inconceivable in the case of military conflict between Britain and France, the
definitive end of a war between the two would have to spell the total
overthrow of the existing ruling order in the losing country. By targeting
one or the other nation's core weaknesses, the eradication of the system
of rule from which this order derived its power would consolidate
defeat. Either Britain's plutocratic wealthy would have to be expro-
priated of their fortunes, or Paris would have to be razed and France
decentralized into a federation of regencies based on the Old Regime's
provinces. Readers were left to draw whatever implications they might
from such imaginative equanimity. In either outcome, Proudhon suggested that the losing country would emerge a better place, since, in
both scenarios, victory was assured by the destruction of those major
internal social vicissitudes undermining the political capabilities of the
combatants.

Such conjecture aside, Proudhon never went into specifics on the sort
of economic restructuring he wanted, possibly because he did not wish
to distract readers with a potentially off-putting blueprint for a future
social order.[78] This omission might explain why many contemporaries
were left unconvinced, having been introduced to the *deus ex machina* of
political economy, by *La Guerre et la Paix*'s final words: "HUMANITY
NO LONGER WANTS WAR".[79] They were struck most by Proudhon's
counter-intuitive rehabilitation of the "right of force" and the defence
of the Vienna Settlement, which came with this rehabilitation and
which notably justified the partitioning of Poland from 1772 onwards.[80]
Indeed, *La Guerre et la Paix* closed with an elegy to Vienna Settlement, at
peril since the Bonapartist coup d'État in France and the end it brought
domestically to those constitutional arrangements enforced and guaranteed in Proudhon's own country by the original 1814–1815 treaties.[81]
Externally, the post-Napoleonic treaty system had been undermined

[78] For what this blueprint might have looked like, see my "Association, Mutualism, and
  Corporate Form in the Published and Unpublished Works of Pierre-Joseph Proudhon",
  History of Economic Ideas, forthcoming.
[79] *LGLP*, v. 2, p. 456.
[80] For a contemporary review, which focused particularly on *La Guerre et la Paix*'s treat-
  ment of current international affairs, and notably the principle of nationalities, see J.-J.
  Weiss, "La Politique étrangère de Proudhon", *Le Courrier du dimanche*, 16 June 1861.
  For another, focused exclusively on Proudhon's comments on Poland in *La Guerre et la
  Paix* (in LGLP, v. 1, pp. 267–270), see the criticisms of Élias Regnault published in *La
  Presse*, 25 August 1861 and the polemic between Proudhon, Regnault, and Alphonse
  Peyrat which followed in the same newspaper. The entirety of this exchange has been
  republished in "Regnault et Peyrat, à propos de la Pologne", *Archives proudhoniennes*,
  2013, pp. 63–113.
[81] *LGLP*, v. 2, pp. 438–456.

by an expansionist French foreign policy: first with the 1830 conquest of Algeria during the final months of Charles X's reign; then with French machinations in the Lowland countries which, subsequent to the 1830 breakup of the United Netherlands, failed in absorbing the new state of Belgium in the years immediately; and, finally, with the recent 1860 annexation of Nice and Savoy granted by Victor Emmanuel II in exchange for French military intervention the year before.[82] Proudhon's praise for the Congress of Vienna was an obvious provocation, both to Bonapartists and patriotic, anti-imperial republicans claiming to represent "*la démocratie*" alike. But it was also part of an argument for why international stability depended since Napoleon's defeat at Waterloo on the internal dissolution of governments through the devolution of concentrated state power – first and foremost in imperial France – and the world-historical necessity for state power to be subordinated to the balance of supply and demand within societies and to "economic justice". Immediately following the publication of *La Guerre et la Paix*, Proudhon found himself on the defensive, however, and became embroiled in a series of newspaper polemics justifying the history of Poland's successive partitions and criticizing the Francophone press's overwhelming bias in favour of Italian unification. This lead him in his final years to develop a theory of "federalism", but it did not provoke him to go into much more detail about what might concretely constitute "economic justice".[83]

How does *La Guerre et la Paix* stand within the larger history of ideas? Certainly, Proudhon's unconventional positions on the law of war were idiosyncratic when viewed from the standpoint of the larger history of legal theories about military conflict. On the one hand, Proudhon clearly endorsed the standard eighteenth-century view that warfare was a legitimate means for resolving political disagreements between sovereigns, and that victory was a "verdict of battle" of which the proper legal procedure was war.[84] On the other hand, Proudhon seemed to be subverting this same way of thinking about international law and its relation to the rights of war. Proudhon not only explicitly reversed the understanding, basic to natural jurisprudence, of war as a form of civil justice, founded in property law and acquisitive claims, by inverting it. His work

---

[82] *Ibid.*, v. 2, pp. 142–143.

[83] On the consequences Proudhon's polemics over the Polish question and his criticisms of the principle of nationalities more generally had on the development of his final theory of the state, see my article, "Une anthropologie téleologique anarchiste? Fins et origines des peuples et des hommes selon Pierre-Joseph Proudhon", in Vincent Bourdeau and Arnaud Macé (eds.), *Nature et pensée sociale au XIXe siécle*, (Besançon: Presses universitaires de Franche-Comté, 2017, forthcoming).

[84] On this topic, see James Q. Whitman, *The Verdict of Battle: The Law of Victory and the Making of Modern War* (Cambridge, Mass: Harvard University Press, 2012).

also seemed representative of the general shift from the idiom of *jus in bello* to that of *jus ad bellum* characteristic of the nineteenth and twentieth centuries, which subverted older theories about the "verdict of battle".[85] To this extent, Proudhon's arguments might be thought to stand somewhere between older eighteenth-century arguments about war as a form of legal procedure and post-revolutionary teleological arguments justifying war as a form of punishment. Framed this way, *La Guerre et la Paix* can be cast as a sort of compromise between older and newer ways of theorizing international conflict, one which allowed the tension between normative assertions and historical justifications to resolve itself (as so often it did in the nineteenth century) through the inscription of theories of social change within a larger linear narrative of the progressive history of human consciousness.

Proudhon's critique of international law also seems at odds with the general evolution of juridical thinking about international relations over the course of the nineteenth century. During this time, with the triumph of legal positivism, there was a penchant for assuming that international law applied uniquely to sovereign states. International relations within a "states-system" were often treated by professional jurists in the rather conservative terms of a normative legal order emerging from treaties and the various interstate obligations they entailed for dynastic sovereign rulers.[86] Yet the same "states-system" responsible for promoting this putatively counter-revolutionary trend in legal thought – the post-Napoleonic Vienna Settlement which encouraged the promotion of the mutual independence of states and respect for the rights of the territorial sovereignty of rulers – was also one which Proudhon ardently defended. But he did so in a way crucially different from those supposedly "conservative" jurists who pushed for a "states-system" approach to understanding international relations because they were convinced that positive agreements between sovereigns were more important than the dangerously abstract principles of natural law responsible for sparking the French Revolution. For Proudhon the Vienna Settlement, far from being reactionary, had set in place a system of Great Power multipolar

---

[85] Working from Carl Schmitt's insights, Whitman, in his *Verdict of Battle*, cites as reasons for the shift from the contained conflicts of the eighteenth century to something decidedly worse in the twentieth century, buttressed by the criminalization of warfare, developments in military technology, the decline in influence of an aristocratic class in Western societies, the rise of democratic nationalism, and a penchant for teleological rhetoric starting in the nineteenth century, which frequently degenerated into a millenarian desire to see some providential plan at work in armed conflict.

[86] See Edward Keene, *Beyond the Anarchical Society* (Cambridge University Press, 2002), and Martti Koskenniemi, "The Legacy of the 19th Century", in David Armstrong (ed.), *Routledge Handbook of International Law* (New York: Routledge, 2009): pp. 141–153.

hegemony more amenable to the revolutionary potential of commercial growth and the moral progress it brought than the dangerous distractions of national self-determination.[87]

When seen in light of the long evolution of political thought from the mid-seventeenth century to the mid-nineteenth century, Proudhon's *La Guerre et la Paix* seems rather novel. Proudhon sought to move beyond the intractable interrelation between the jealousy of trade and the jealousy of state while arguing against nineteenth-century advocates of the principle of nationality who had transformed once anti-political theories of the pre-political state into a political theory of the state requiring extensive overlap between the expression of popular sovereignty, ethnicity, and geographic territory. In the process, he mobilized certain arguments common to eighteenth-century moral and aesthetic theory to serve the opposite of their original anti-commercial orientation. Thus, in *La Guerre et la Paix*, argumentative elements of pre-revolutionary anti-Hobbist proponents of natural sociability were harnessed by Proudhon in the service of a progressive, perfectibilian conception of the anti-national and anti-statist benefits to be had from the spread of commercial society and its capacity to personalize authority in commutative relations of market exchange.

Translating backwards into the terms of early modern political thought, one could argue that Proudhon rejected the strict conception of justice contained within the idiom of natural jurisprudence (wherein rights, attributable to everyone, were reduced to questions of self-preservation), in contradistinction to more traditionally Aristotelian conceptions of distributive justice (wherein formal equality was rejected in favour of meritocratic compensation for unequal qualitative differences in moral worth as measured in terms of talent, performance, etc.). But in rejecting the minimal self of natural law, Proudhon redefined prior Aristotelian notions of justice in terms of those very same commutative relations fostered by exchange in market economies which jusnaturalists sought to underscore. The result was a theory in which the development of the division of labour itself could reconcile qualitative differences between individuals with their equal legal status, while the distinction between fact and right could be blurred in both international relations and the distribution of property as human perfectibility in commercial society unfolded. Proudhon's theory of "poverty" as a desirable existential condition, when translated backwards into the language of early modern political theory, gives a new moral spin to

---

[87] A point reiterated in his Si les Traités de 1815 ont cessé d'exister? Actes du Futur Congrès (Paris: Dentu, 1863).

the concept of *indigentia* critical to jusnaturalist narratives. It is also at odds with Marx's ideal of creating a terminal social condition in which humans would be "rich in needs". This is because, for Proudhon, insatiable needs, irrepressible as a feature of human nature, perpetuated mankind's insurmountable existential condition, since there was no way of getting beyond the daily, intractable struggle of balancing production with consumption in conditions of scarcity. Because mankind's natural desire was to remain indolent,[88] to be motivated to work humans needed to feel the "sting of need".[89] Consequently, what made man abject also made him moral.

Translating forward into our own language of political thought, one might argue that this conceptual mishmash of pre-revolutionary and post-revolutionary positions marked the starting point for the dual hostility to state and nation professed by past and present proponents of the ideological doctrine commonly known as "anarchism". Nonetheless, subsequent "anarchist" critiques of nationalism generally have not entailed a larger systematic reflection on international law; the necessary relationship of warfare to the progress of human morality; or the interrelation between the nature of right, the evaluation of authority, and their dual relation to evolving conceptions of justice. Nor have they typically had recourse to teleological speculations about the future of both war and the state in a manner, which confidently has justified the right of conquest, to say nothing of the political eradication of entire nations, or even slavery, the blessings in disguise to be had from a balance of multipolar power limited to a select group of hegemons. They generally do not make bold claims about the desirability for a highly fortified sense of personal morality to complement post-revolutionary commercial sociability or celebrate the virtues of work for work's sake. To assert Proudhon's genealogical place on the far left of a conventional ideological spectrum, they tend not to underscore how, after 1848, Proudhon's focus on curtailing state growth in accordance with the economic needs of society led him to denounce the autonomization of the political, a process the mirror opposite of the autonomization of the economic central to Marxist thought; that dynamic development one day supposed to call "capitalism" as a "mode of production" into question. Nor do they often underscore the related fact that because Proudhon aspired to formulate a theory for creating more equitable expressions of authority and not a theory for overcoming the supposed alienation which occurs in modern divisions of labour, his attitude

---

[88] *LGLP*, v. 2, pp. 174–176.   [89] *Ibid.*, v. 2, p. 184.

towards the market was more ambivalent than superficial reference to his famous 1840 statement, "property is theft", might let on.

As for the subsequent geopolitics of anarchism, if, exceptionally, Kropotkin, James Guillaume, and other notable "anti-authoritarian" members of the First International rallied to the *Union sacrée* during World War I, it was because they were preoccupied, much like Bakunin before them, by the geopolitical threat posed by the unification of Germany.[90] When during the 1930s, the German radical Rudolf Rocker composed in exile what was by far the most systematic anarchist treatment of the principle of nationalities and state sovereignty since Proudhon's later writings, it was in order to juxtapose unfavourably "nationalism" (whose conceptual originators in the history of political thought were Machiavelli, Hobbes, Rousseau, Kant, Fichte, Hegel, von Haller, and Mazzini amongst others in a diverse and ecumenical group of contemptible culprits) with "culture".[91] At the opposite side of the political spectrum, in 1940 a young German law professor close to Carl Schmitt, Wilhelm Grewe, pointed to the geopolitical interest of Proudhon's *La Guerre et la Paix*, underscoring the close interrelation between the history of European power politics, conceptual innovations in international law, and the latter's inextricable relation to justifying territorial appropriation by dominant hegemons.[92] Whereas the view from the Germanic side of the Rhine made Proudhon's "right of force" seem particularly attractive to belligerents oblivious to the anti-nationalism it implied, elsewhere anarchist thought in the era of Hitler was clearly much more saturnine than in that of Napoleon III.

---

[90] On this subject, see René Berthier, *Kropotkine et la Grande Guerre* (Paris: Éditions du Monde libertaire, 2014) as well as Marc Vuilleumier's introduction, "James Guillaume, sa vie, son œuvre" to the re-edition of Guillaume's *L'Internationale, Documents et Souvenirs* (Geneva: Editions Grounauer, 1980), tome 1, notably pp. xli–xliii.

[91] Rudolf Rocker, *Nationalism and Culture* (Los Angeles: Rocker Publications Committee, 1937). On the other hand, Lessing, "Jean Paul" Richter, Herder, Schiller, and Humboldt figured more favourably in Rocker's survey, a their libertarian place alongside such conventional prophetic heralds of anti-political thought as Godwin, Proudhon, Bakunin, and Kropotkin.

[92] Grewe, "Krieg und Frieden. Proudhons Theorie des Völkerrechts", in *Zeitschrift für Politik*, 30 (6–7, June-July 1940): pp. 233–245, and for his larger critical project initially written during this same period, Grewe, *The Epochs of International Law* (Berlin: De Gruyter, revised translation, 2000) in which Proudhon is mentioned on p. 211 and pp. 532–533. On the reception of Proudhon's ideas in the Third Reich (notably with regards to both Schmitt and Grewe), see Frédéric Krier, *Sozialismus für Kleinbürger: Pierre-Joseph Proudhon – Wegbereiter des Dritten Reiches* (Cologne/Weimar/Vienna: Böhlau-Verlag, 2009), and on Grewe's criticisms of international law within the academic framework of his time, see Bardo Fassbender, "Stories of War and Peace: On the Writing of International Law in the 'Third Reich' and After", in *European Journal of International Law*, 13, 2002: pp. 479–512.

Despite Proudhon's hostility to the principle of nationalities, his scepticism regarding the implausible panacea of super-states, and his criticisms of those who condemned "aggressive" war, many aspects of his paradoxical arguments about international relations would be later re-appropriated in the early twentieth century by French advocates of the League of Nations and defenders of the sovereign autonomy of small, militarily weak nations and the Wilsonian right to national self-determination.[93] They would also be rehabilitated throughout the twentieth century by assorted regionalists and advocates of a federalist "personalism", themselves initially partisans of a continental federation of states, foreshadowing the postwar European Union, which they also subsequently supported.[94] Other interpretations of Proudhon's international thought were possible, of course. In the wake of World War I, radical social theorists who did enthusiastically cite La Guerre et la Paix, like Georges Sorel and his disciple in revolutionary syndicalism, Edouard Berth, referenced this work less in light of its ideas about international relations and their future than in the name of the vitalist glorification of the regenerative therapeutic virtues of class conflict (as opposed to the unredemptive and destructive perfidies of interstate warfare). The result was a highly eclectic ideological cocktail reconciling Proudhon, Marx, and Lenin.[95] Proudhon's arguments have yet to find fashion among contemporary twenty-first-century advocates of "realism" in international relations, however. The latter are unlikely to be drawn to "realism" out of anti-nationalism. They have generally been content to assert the unavoidable ahistorical permanence of great power hegemony, the balance of power, and the supposedly iron laws of both at the

---

[93] All of Proudhon's writings on international relations which appeared after *La Guerre et la Paix* were published in critical editions by Marcel Rivière edited by militant pacifists and advocates of the League of Nations, Jules-Louis Puech and Théodore Ruyssen.

[94] The best example of a "personalist" interpretation and appropriation of Proudhon's theory of federalism (additionally the best history of the posterity of Proudhon's international thought) is to be found in volumes 2 (*Le fédéralisme de P.J. Proudhon*) and 3 (*Les lignées proudhoniennes*) of Bernard Voyenne's three-volume *Histoire de l'idée fédéraliste* (Nice: Presses d'Europe, 1973). For criticism of the appropriation of Proudhon's ideas about federalism by partisans of European unification, see Christophe Réveillard, "Proudhon et le fédéralisme: l'origine française de la conception intégrale", in Pierre-Jean Deschodt (ed.), *Pierre-Joseph Proudhon: l'ordre dans l'anarchie* (Paris: Cujas, 2009): pp. 135–155.

[95] Sorel was writing a book on Proudhon's La Guerre et la Paix before his death in 1922. See Sorel, "Proudhon (un article italien de Georges Sorel)", Archives proudhoniennes, 2000: pp. 23–42; Sorel, "La guerre et la paix, essai d'exégèse proudhonienne", Mil neuf cent, 19, 2001: pp. 151–207; and Sorel, "Ébauche d'une étude sur Proudhon, à propos de La Guerre et la Paix », Mil neuf cent, 20, 2002: pp. 129–152. For Berth, see his Guerre des États ou Guerre des Classes (Paris: Marcel Rivière, 1924); and Du "Capital" aux "Réflexions sur la violence", (Paris: Marcel Rivière, 1932).

expense of examining the role played by the social distribution of wealth within a "states-system". That said, it has become almost impossible in our own teleophobic age to imagine, like Proudhon, how subordinating sovereign states to the demands of market-driven behaviour could ever usher in equitable social relations fashioned in accordance with a more just expression of the laws of supply and demand.

11 From King's prerogative to constitutional dictatorship as reason of state*

Duncan Kelly

I

Locke's analysis of prerogative in the *Second Treatise* shows very clearly that his argument can be made to fit into conventional and contemporary liberal doctrines about the separation of powers only by doing violence to his text. This, perhaps, is one of the principal reasons why his legacy for modern political theory has been so unusual and so ambivalent. In fact, in the Anglo-American world Locke's centrality as a foundational figure for modern liberalism is of very recent vintage, hardly predating the First World War.[1] Before then, he was typically thought of as a Whig, whose succor for a long tradition of Anglo-American radicalism was well established, but whose direct connection to founding revolutionary debates was minimal.[2] It is possible that his defense of prerogative could have aligned him with patriot royalist accounts of the American revolution and its aftermath, which defended the unifying power of the British crown and its veto power, particularly through its North American courts.[3] That is not my immediate concern, but in any event, hardly any modern treatment of liberalism does not somehow see him as foundational for either a philosophical or a political conception of the

---

* Thanks to the editors and contributors to this volume, as well as John Dunn, Udi Greenberg, Joel Isaac, Jamie Martin, Sam Moyn, Paul Sagar and Richard Tuck for conversation and comment on its themes.

[1] Cf. Duncan Bell, 'What is Liberalism?' *Political Theory*, 42, 6 (2014), pp. 682–715; Tim Stanton, 'Authority and Freedom in the Interpretation of Locke's Political Theory', *Political Theory*, 39: 1 (2011), pp. 6–30.

[2] John Dunn, 'The Politics of Locke in England and America in the Eighteenth Century', in J. Yolton (ed.) *John Locke: Problems and Perspectives* (Cambridge University Press, 1969), pp. 45–80. In general, see Mark Goldie, 'Introduction', *The Reception of Locke's Politics*, (ed.) Mark Goldie, 5 vols. (London: Pickering and Chatto, 1999), vol. 1, pp. xlix–lix; 'The Roots of True Whiggism, 1688–1694', *History of Political Thought*, 1: 2 (1980), pp. 195–236.

[3] Eric Nelson, *The Royalist Revolution: Monarchy and the American Founding* (Cambridge, MA: Harvard University Press, 2015), pp. 14ff, 243 n. 59; Brendan McConville, *The King's Three Faces* (Chapel Hill, NC: University of North Carolina Press, 2007), p. 8.

doctrine. Only a very few, and John Dunn most importantly, have thought that Locke's analysis of prerogative power and the account of prudence and trust that his argument presupposes, might serve as a realistic guide to understanding the ambiguities of modern politics as a predicament, rather than as a system or structure of liberalism.[4] My aim in what follows, though, is to signal an earlier intellectual genealogy of Locke's prerogative that runs through certain strands of modern German political thought most obviously, and which attempts to understand Locke's prerogative as a form of constitutional reason of state in this vein. I do this both in order to signal a longer pre-history of the current resurgence of interest in the subject by writers concerned with the nature of emergency powers under liberal democracy, and to frame an account of the interpretation of constitutional reason of state by Carl Friedrich in particular. For he is a hinge between Anglo-American and European political theory in this context, and someone who revised the history of Western political theory in the twentieth century in order to invoke the idea of a constitutional reason of state that could support a militant and Protestant form of modern democracy. In order to set out the full extent of this claim, however, my argument begins with Locke's account of prerogative itself.

II

Pasquale Pasquino has offered an account of Lockean prerogative as if it was part of German state theory (*Staatslehre*), and therefore concerned with the interrelationship between the various organs of state and their functions. Focusing on the interplay between different functions highlights the fact that power can be shared between offices, even though the branches of power are normally considered distinct. For example, king and parliament might hold executive power together.[5] Nevertheless, one can see this most obviously by simply noting that Locke in fact speaks of five different branches of political authority, namely executive, legislative, judicial, federative and prerogative power. The two less-well known branches refer first, in the case of federative power, to the power of making war and peace and conducting foreign alliances, while the second, prerogative, refers to the 'discretion of him, that has the Executive

---

[4] John Dunn, *The Political Thought of John Locke* (Cambridge University Press, 1969), esp. pp. 148–156; more generally, *Political Obligation in its Historical Context* (Cambridge University Press, 1980); *Rethinking Modern Political Theory: Essays 1979–1983* (Cambridge University Press, 1985).

[5] Pasquale Pasquino, 'Locke on King's Prerogative', *Political Theory*, 26: 2 (1998), pp. 198–208, at p. 199.

Power'.[6] Such discretionary prerogative, he continues, consists both of a 'Power in the hands of the prince to provide for the publick good, in such cases, which depending upon unforeseen and uncertain Occurrences, certain and unalterable Laws could not safely direct'.[7] Of course in common law, the king had prerogative power to determine cases of necessity. But prerogative under normal conditions is extraordinary power granted to the executive, acted upon only under conditions of necessity as determined by the executive, but justifiable only in the interests of the public good and public safety. As Locke reiterates the commonplace, one can hardly fail to go wrong by following 'so fundamental a rule' as *Salus Populi Suprema Lex*.[8] It unites the politics of prerogative both domestically and internationally.

There is, of course, a puzzle here relating to theory and practice, or more prosaically to functional necessity and logical completeness. Prerogative for Locke is a matter of taking a conventional practice, but understanding its justification as a functional prerequisite for achieving the ends of political society, namely peace, justice and good order.[9] It cannot be theorized in advance, because the empirical requirements of actual politics are too varied and too complex to be tied down to a causal argument about when and where a situation of crisis and emergency is likely to arise. Equally, prerogative cannot be legally constrained, because prerogative is often *de facto* illegal, to the extent that the actions of those with prerogative power literally break the law when they deem it necessary.[10] The curiosity here is that although it cannot be theorized and constrained through legal means, prerogative itself had a conventional legal status in England when Locke wrote. The issue of the king's prerogative, his 'negative voice' and associated veto, were all constitutionally quite ordinarily accepted by royalists, just as much as the Whigs, who asserted the right of parliamentary control over it, re-described it. The revolution pivoted around it.[11] Locke considered both sides, in

---

[6] John Locke, *Two Treatises of Government*, (ed.) P. Laslett (Cambridge University Press, 198), II. §159, p. 374.

[7] Locke, *Two Treatises*, II. §158, p. 373.   [8] Locke, *Two Treatises*, II. §158, p. 373.

[9] Dunn, *Political Thought of Locke*, pp. 150f.   [10] Locke, *Two Treatises*, II. §160, p. 375.

[11] Compare the pamphlets in J. L. Malcolm (ed.) *The Struggle for Sovereignty: Seventeenth-Century English Political Tracts*, 2 vols. (Indianapolis, IN: Liberty Fund, 1999), vol. 2, pp. 771–844, with the Resolutions of the House of Commons on suspending power in 1673, reproduced in W. C. Costin and J. Steven Watson (eds.) *The Law and Working of the Constitution: Documents 1660–1914*, vol. 1, *1660–1783* (London: Adam and Charles Black, 1952), pp. 163–166. For the general shift in thinking about prerogative in English law, see Alan Cromartie, *The Constitutionalist Revolution: An Essay on the History of England, 1450–1642* (Cambridge University Press, 2006), esp. pp. 234–274; and on the centrality of prerogative as filtered through contemporary political theory, Quentin Skinner, *Liberty before Liberalism* (Cambridge University Press, 1998), pp. 51ff, 69f, 72f.

effect, but found them equally wrong. Prerogative could not be bound by law or constitutionalism, but only assessed in terms of its legal credibility according to the standards of trust and public good that had conferred executive authority upon the holder of prerogative by the assumed, or tacit consent of their subjects in the first place in terms of the development of a constitution.[12] If 'imployed for the benefit of the community and suitably to the trust and ends of the Government', it is *'undoubted prerogative'*. If there is a question of where responsibility lies, either with prerogative or executive power, then its resolution is judged against subsequent action according to the 'good or the hurt of the people'.[13] That was an historical, developmental story of gradual acceptance and local development, focused in the first instance on the peculiarities of English constitutional history, where 'prerogative was always *largest* in the hands of our wisest and best Princes'.[14]

Nevertheless, although the peculiarities of English history might have sanctioned a certain local deference towards a particular acceptance of prerogative, prerogative power is nonetheless exercised in the same way irrespective of time and place, and the result is nearly always the same because its extra legal status always sets the individual face to face with the sovereign. If those views conflict, the ultimate judge of the rightness of prerogative is to be found in what Locke famously thought of as an appeal to heaven. In this world, though, because the structure of political societies reflects human needs and because political societies are emphatically human and thus artificial creations, prerogative presupposes an accepted structure of power relations, and is authorized by the trust of people in their rulers to act in their own best interests. This by no means offers the promise of such action, and indeed the problem of promising and fealty in Locke's political thought is also somewhat opaque. All promises are to be kept, always, as indications of *bona fides*, or what he elsewhere thought of as *fides vinculum societatis*. Promises even bind the deity, and this looks like an incredibly stringent requirement, especially given the fact that promises and oaths, in the form of treatises and alliances, are the bulwark of many political agreements. Breaking them may yet plunge a state into a situation of war with another. But it may also be the case that prerogative dictates, and therefore trumps the

---

[12] Dunn, *Political Thought of Locke*, p. 151.
[13] Locke, *Two Treatises*, II. §159, p. 374. See also §157, pp. 372f, where the origin of the legislative 'constitution' is re-described as the act of constituting, that is, as an act of prerogative itself. On this, and therefore on Locke's playfulness and allegedly 'entertaining' qualities as a writer, see Harvey Mansfield, *Taming the Prince* (Baltimore, MD: Johns Hopkins University Press, 1992), pp. 188f.
[14] Locke, *Two Treatises*, II. §165, p. 377.

federative power, which in turn is typically going to require an executive decision. So prerogative can make problems for international relations. That is unsurprising. What is perhaps more surprising, is where Locke leaves his argument domestically. Within the state, prerogative action by executive sovereignty can, in principle, be entirely appropriate, agreed with, and consented to, even when it breaks the letter of the law, so long as it is in line with the basic constitution, the constitution of political society itself, which exists for the purposes or ends of peace and commodious living. The rule of the King was premised on trust, such that parliamentary rights of oversight could be claimed if the monarch was deemed to be acting contrary to the public good. Ultimately, though, this was because the people themselves were the judge of whether any such impropriety of action had occurred. Executive action, whether undertaken by prerogative or not, can always be appealed against by the individual citizen, or the entire body of citizens, through a right to resist that has intrinsically formal elements (such as, the inability of a rational and free agent to knowingly sell themselves into a condition of slavery, or to be asked to give up their life without a struggle).

Beyond those formal elements, citizens can also look to the only source of agency that has a final judgment in these matters by lodging an appeal to heaven. Their case may (and in Locke's mind surely will) receive ultimate judgment at some point hence, but it can be used to justify an action in the here and now given purity of belief and intention, but without any practical guarantee of success. The appeal to heaven and its revolutionary upheaval can therefore return otherwise stable political societies to legal or jural states of anarchy and uncertainty (just as Hobbes had also supposed), even though it may yet have little effect on the realities of social order and power. Conversely, the appeal to heaven may gain revolutionary assent, because of illegitimate rule by no-longer trusted authorities, and political transformation can occur. In both cases, though, the issue of prerogative assumes conventional historical and sociological acceptance of constitutional foundations, unless something goes very much awry. In Locke's rendition, nevertheless, such a revolutionary sounding end is presented with such 'blandness' as to have allowed for both radical and reactionary interpretation, but remains the logical outcome of an argument that grounds political authority upon trust, rather than contract. What it suggests, in fact, is that Locke saw no practical or preconceived limits to prerogative at all, save that its exercise was prudential and undertaken according to the requirements of trust and rational agency; as he suggested, where historically prerogative had been limited, this was because the people had deemed it necessary and desirable. They had not '*incroach'd upon the prerogative*', but because the end of government is the 'good of the Community', there could have been no encroachment as the ends of individual and government are the same.[15] A free and rational individual would not 'put himself into Subjection to another', and prerogative is therefore simply 'Peoples permitting their Rulers, to do several things of their own free choice, where the Law was silent, and sometimes too against the direct Letter of the Law, for the publick good'.[16] This makes his account both more conventional on the one hand, but also more open-ended, and potentially more rapacious, than any extant reason of state argument on the other, making light of the apparent obviousness of his point: 'Prerogative is nothing by the Power of doing publick good without a Rule'.[17] It is based on a form of political trusteeship akin to the Ciceronian account of *fides publica* in a Roman setting, even as Locke's prerogative presses the 'ineluctable possibility' of a social or political dilemma with no prospect of resolution, thereby cutting across the grain of a conceptual framework otherwise untroubled by the fact of diversity, and concerned instead to focus on the possibility of a coherent worldview.[18] It also offers a distinctive combination of authority and utility as justification for a politics of legislative supremacy based on trust, with prerogative as something like a trump, though his account would find sharp criticism in the later political thinking of David Hume and Adam Smith for its seeming lack of historical depth.[19]

The peculiar, and somewhat idiosyncratic feature of Locke's account thus lies in its attempt to simultaneously ground prerogative upon a conventional and historically developmental foundation, but only in order to allow that foundation to be bypassed in the name of preserving the public good, which is in turn premised on those conventional and developmental foundations. It looks distinctly circular in its reasoning, and Locke was well aware of the puzzle. As he expressed a similar thought pertaining to the problem of liberty, he could no more refuse to believe in the absolute and all-seeing power of the Deity any more than he could refuse the thought that he had complete free will.[20] But, rather like discussions of Presidential or executive prerogative and the question

---

[15] Locke, *Two Treatises*, II. §163, p. 376.

[16] Locke, *Two Treatises*, II. §164, p. 377.   [17] Locke, *Two Treatises*, II. §166, p. 378.

[18] Marc de Wilde, '*Fides Publica* in Ancient Rome and its Reception by Grotius and Locke', *Legal History Review*, 79 (2011), pp. 455–487, at pp. 477, 479ff. For more on the Ciceronian content of Locke's account of freedom, see Duncan Kelly, *The Propriety of Liberty: Persons, Passions and Judgement in Modern Political Thought* (Princeton University Press, 2010), pp. 47–53.

[19] István Hont, 'Adam Smith's History of Law and Government as Political Theory', in R. Bourke and R. Geuss (eds.), *Political Judgment* (Cambridge University Press, 2009), pp. 131–171; Kelly, *Propriety of Liberty*, pp. 136f; more generally, Knud Haakonssen, *The Science of a Legislator* (Cambridge University Press, 1989).

[20] John Locke, Letter 1592, to William Molyneux, January 26, 1693, in E. S. de Beer (ed.) *The Correspondence of John Locke*, 8 vols. (Oxford: Clarendon Press, 1976–1989), vol. 4, pp. 623–628.

of slavery during the American civil war, the issue of whether prerogative in times of emergency could reset or overturn the basic constitution itself was primary.[21] Moreover, the foundation has two further components. Because it is based on reason, derived from natural law, Locke claims that political authority is predicated upon rational action on the part of the governing powers, whether 'fiduciary' in the case of the legislative, or sovereign in the case of the executive or prerogative power. The utility of this argument from authority comes from its secondary status as what we might call the art of prudence. If government is a relationship of trust between rulers and ruled, that trust is based on conventional acceptance over time that rule of a particular sort is suited to considerations of time, place and space on the part of those who are subject to it. Their continued acceptance relies upon the continued acceptance of both legal, and extra-legal action, continuing to meet their expectations of prudential political management. If and when it fails, and an appeal to heaven is lodged, then Locke's further considerations upon the right of resistance to arbitrary rule become operative, even if its effects are also potentially conservative.[22] While it remains rooted in the here and now, though, prerogative is, according to Locke, wholly distinct from arbitrary power.[23] Again, he seems to provide something like a proximate (though not obviously direct, in ways like Matthew Hale or William Blackstone) source for debates about prerogative and emergency powers that were crucial to nineteenth, rather than eighteenth century American debates during the civil war.

Prerogative thereby presupposes a claim about its utility both for the general constitution and for the individuals who live under a particular constitutional order. That utility is grounded in prudence, and prudence is an attribute that is derivative upon the primary relationship of trust. Such a perspective connects Locke's theological politics to the artificial realm of worldly politics. Conversely, the notion of an appeal to heaven when aligned to claims about the legitimation of authority in natural law, takes Locke's political theory out of the secular realm and back into the sphere of theology, in order to try and avoid the apparent circularity of his argument. For some, this ambivalence or elision signals a typically evasive manoeuver on Locke's part, while for others, it is simply a muddle. If it is both evasive and somewhat muddled, though, it does not necessarily render it useless for political thinking. Not only because political thought and action is often evasive and muddled, nor because

---

[21] Mark Neely, *The Fate of Liberty* (Oxford University Press, 1992).
[22] Quentin Skinner, 'On Trusting the Judgment of Our Rulers', in Bourke and Geuss (eds.), *Political Judgment*, pp. 113–130.
[23] Locke, *Two Treatises*, II. §163, p. 377.

those theories that either turn these matters into questions of moral sensitivity, or offer answers predicated upon sovereign will, typically cannot say much about the complexities of political calculation in the real world. Ultimately, the authority of prerogative over the individuals in any society can only be valid and binding to the extent that they themselves recognize it to be so, in a fashion rather like the somewhat circular political theory of legitimacy outlined by Max Weber, where legitimacy is simply what people believe it to be.[24] Authority is historically constituted, rather than theoretically prescribed. But the evasion that seems to typify Locke's political thinking about prerogative gives him a flexibility that is both more pervasive than traditional reason of state thinking, and less free-floating because governed by the demands of constitutional norms.[25]

The general shape of the doctrine of reason of state is well established, and its general contours shaped by the opposition between the good (*honestum*) and the useful (*utile*) governing the politics and policy of the early-modern state. Through early formulations ranging from Machiavelli and Botero, reason of state came to be associated with the interest of the prince. Concomitantly, as Noel Malcolm has reiterated, a central trope of the earliest reason of state doctrines concerned religion, and even the most Tacitist writers were keen to disavow the idea that religion was simply a tool to be used by the prince. Such *politique* approaches to religion as a tool of the state were quite problematic for the predominantly Jesuit origins of the idea of reason of state.[26] Both sorts of interest of or reason of state arguments thought religion was necessarily useful for a ruler, but its utility for the latter stemmed from its connection to truth and universal justice, rather more than simple expediency as civil religion. The central issue confronting both sorts of arguments, however, was the question of the exceptional situation. Either reason of state is a norm of policy underpinned by agreed upon criteria (prudence, wisdom, honor) which is subject to general assessment, or it is focused on the albeit temporary suspension of these general criteria as dictated by a different, higher-order claim based on the interest of the state. Locke's attempt to combine executive and federative power in the hands of a single ruler, subject to the demands of trust and the judgment of prudence, was an attempt to fix some kind of political order out of this otherwise constant 'flux', showing how crucial it is to recognize the primacy of trust

---

[24] Cf. Dunn, *Political Thought of Locke*, p. 155; David Beetham, *The Legitimation of Power* (Basingstoke: Macmillan, 1992).

[25] Locke, *Two Treatises*, II. §171, pp. 381f.

[26] Noel Malcolm, *Reason of State, Propaganda, and the Thirty Years War* (Oxford University Press, 2005), p. 97.

and authority, rather than merely contract, at the root of his argument.[27] Thus, although he is not typically thought of as a 'reason of state' theorist (his awareness of Gabriel Naudé notwithstanding) rather as a theorist of prerogative, the ambiguity of the distance between these visions left a space that could be fruitfully inhabited by certain sorts of critics of liberalism at the beginning of the twentieth century. This would in turn form the modern backdrop to the prioritizing of Locke's position in the still very recent construction of a philosophical-liberal canon, and highlight the central issue. For theorists of *raison d'état*, focusing on promises and *fides publicum* was little more than superstition and irrealism; for theorists of prerogative like Locke, *raison d'état* looks like it might have no justifiable foundations, and therefore is little more than permanent prerogative without the foundation of trust.[28]

The flexibility and possibility of acting between these two poles is precisely what attracted early twentieth-century German political and legal thinkers to Locke's analysis of prerogative, first because it helped make sense of certain contemporary arguments about the relationship between global politics and national imperialism. Second, because Locke's antiparliamentary model of prerogative, with its constitutional justification but simultaneous denial of authority to the sphere of the legislature even as it claimed the mantle of the people, chimed well with a desire to defend constitutional monarchy as the medium of representative sovereignty with prerogative powers. This, of course, very quickly transitioned into a debate about the authority of presidential powers under the Weimar Constitution. During both the *Kaiserreich* and Weimar Republic, however, this distinction between foundational natural power (of the people) and artificial (hence representative) legal authority would be critical to determining the location of political authority in a world of increasingly powerful bureaucratic control.[29] Third, the utility of Locke's arguments for the previous two issues was itself bound up within a wider argument about the possibility of putting him into the framework of arguments about emergency politics, and using him to show the realities of prerogative for contemporary debates about constitutional and legislative dictatorship in particular. Fourth, and finally, this revised concern

[27] Locke, *Two Treatises*, II. §§157, 171, pp. 372, 381f; Dunn, *Political Thought of Locke*, p. 162.
[28] Dunn, *Political Thought of Locke*, p. 161; see also Ian Harris, 'The Legacy of "*Two Treatises of Government*"', *Eighteenth-Century Thought*, 3 (2007), pp. 143–167; Kelly, *Propriety of Liberty*, p. 36; Richard Tuck, *Philosophy and Government 1572–1651* (Cambridge University Press, 1993), pp. 93, 151; *The Rights of War and Peace* (Oxford University Press, 1999), pp. 168, 172–179.
[29] For a classic synthesis in English, see John Röhl, *Germany without Bismarck* (London: B. T. Batsford, 1967).

with Locke as a modified reason of state theorist, relevant for an age of constitutional dictatorship, expresses an irony in the history of modern political thought. Namely that Locke, in developing a Ciceronian-style prudence and a powerful, executive and federative apparatus alongside the cultivation of a theory of regulated freedom, was more, rather than less, important to the radical anti-liberalism of early twentieth-century political thought. It suggests in fact that these early attempts to colonize Locke as something like a constitutional reason of state thinker in modern German political thought might be the hidden but proximate source for the subsequent elaboration of Locke as a 'liberal' political figure that would emerge in the twentieth century, when liberalism began to be more resolutely defended against its obvious and often malignant detractors. It also seems to confirm that until that time, Locke was read rather less as a prototypical liberal than as continuing the grand traditions of modern political thought from Hobbes to Rousseau, focusing on the implications of wealth, virtue and self-interest for modern, secular politics after any primitive form of Golden Age.[30]

III

If reason as the expression of natural law rightly understood trumps the conventional authority of legislative power, then Locke gives prerogative rational foundations. Locke also normalizes those foundations with reference to history, suggesting that the actions of princes and politicians over time, since the beginnings of political society even, can most often be seen as the enactment of prerogative power, because prerogative power is the normal, rather than the exceptional, force of authoritative rule undertaken for the public good of the people.[31] It is neither mysterious nor miraculous, but rather conventional and prudential, something to be judged according to human standards of reason rather than revelation.

Yet when connected to questions of international relations, the federative power of the Lockean state dealing with relations between sovereign entities, the prudential qualities of executive leadership, rather than the rationally constrained activities of domestic prerogative, become blurred. One might see in Locke's politics here the primacy of foreign policy writ large, because if national safety and the public good is the basic requirement of domestic legal order, such national safety must also be

---

[30] Locke, *Second Treatise*, II. §111, pp. 342f.

[31] See also David Wootton, 'John Locke, Socinian or Natural Law Theorist?' in J. Crimmins (ed.) *Religion, Secularization and Political Thought: Thomas Hobbes to J. S. Mill* (London: Routledge, 1989), pp. 38–67.

determined first in an international state of nature. Equally, the origins of political society and the history of prerogative show that early societies stood 'more in need of defence against foreign Invasions and Injuries' than a proliferation of domestic laws.[32] As David Bates points out, what Locke really provides is a dual system of political and legal authority, embodied in the singular figure of the executive, but which has no clearly demarcated boundaries when and if they come into conflict.[33] So while Locke's text does not outline a standard separation of powers doctrine, it is a text that comes close to showing what happens when prerogative butts up against systemic threats and breakdowns in societies based on a constitutional separation of powers. That perhaps is its central lesson for modern political theory.

For example, the federative power determines whether a state of enmity pertains within the civil state, or between particular civil states. That power is held by the executive, but is not governed by the demands of reason as prerogative is; instead it is focused by its relationship to the individuals subject to it. Where prerogative ultimately is measured by success, that success is governed by the criteria of preservation and development that motivate the foundation of the rational, political state in the first place, the question of judgment is difficult, but clear. There is a standard of judgment, rooted in trust, and governed by natural law. With federative power, there is no rational-legal calculus. The motivation instead is solely prudential. And when the federative power has to deal with internal enemies of the state, under conditions of civil war most obviously or via multiple claims to domestic sovereignty and legitimate kingship, the boundaries between prerogative and federative powers are at worst unclear, or at best, constitutive of two distinct logics embodied in the singular titular figure of the executive, comprising the legal and the political spheres.[34]

So when Erich Kaufmann, the German jurist to whom Pasquino referred when suggesting ways to understand the relational quality of Locke's theory of different powers and their authority, came to consider Locke's prerogative in the context of a new global politics of imperialism spearheaded by the United States of America, the claim was clear. For Kaufmann, Locke's account of prerogative is the component that most signifies the idea or perhaps even spirit of a state and its self-understanding, embodying its 'necessarily historical principles' [*notwendigen historischen Prizipes*], where prerogative comes to help

[32] Locke, *Second Treatise*, II. §107, p. 338f.
[33] David Bates, *States of War: Enlightenment Origins of the Political* (New York: Columbia University Press, 2012), pp. 94ff.
[34] Pasquino, 'Locke on Prerogative', p. 201; Bates, *States of War*, pp. 125–133.

realize the rational foundation lying behind state formation in Locke's wider treatises about government.[35] Tying together prerogative, as the human embodiment of national sovereignty, both in and through time is precisely what German thinking about constitutional monarchy had attempted to develop during the nineteenth century. Both Locke and nineteenth-century theorists of constitutional monarchy, could agree upon the blunt definition of prerogative as simply 'him that has the executive power in his hands'. In fact, the entire history of government, which combines a focus on both authority and utility, could best be made sense of in this way. In the beginning, not only was the 'world', quite literally, America in the sense of a still-to-be developed political society. But as political societies developed from families and tribes, through to princes and subjects, one might very well say that 'government was almost all prerogative', and that in England specifically, prerogative was an attribute of the 'wisest and best' princes.[36] If true, then Locke's vision of 'discretionary authority' might 'best be understood as a *repetition* of the very origin of the state' out of a mixture of convention, prudence, consent and history.[37] For Kaufmann, following Ranke, this explains why Locke's preference for William III as the best hope for a new restoration ('our great Restorer') both pointed forward in time, while presenting his argument as a response to revolutionary politics. At the same time, however, Locke is effectively just repackaging his earlier account of prerogative, allowing for the continuation of an older theory under new circumstances [*auf Grund parlamentarischer Beschlüsse zustande kam, in der Staatslehre Lockes zugleich als Fortsetzung der alten*].[38]

In Kaufmann's text, the principal motivation behind his concern with Lockean prerogative was a wider argument about the relationship between violence and imperial or colonial politics. Of course, in the later nineteenth and early twentieth centuries, Germany had been a latecomer to the imperial scramble for territory, and had moved to absorb parts of Africa and the Middle East into its territorial orbit. This much is quite well known, and usually forms part of a story about late-industrialization and the political economy of economic backwardness in historical perspective.[39] Partly because of the horrors of later German concerns with space both in itself, and in terms specifically of

---

[35] Erich Kaufmann, *Auswärtige Gewalt und Kolonialgewalt in den Vereinigten Staaten von Amerika* (Berlin: Duncker & Humblot, 1908), p. 30.

[36] Locke, *Two Treatises*, II. §162, p. 376.

[37] Bates, *States of War*, p. 101, cf. p. 111. Emphasis in original.

[38] Kaufmann, *Auswärtiges Gewalt*, p. 31.

[39] See David Olusoga and Casper W. Erichsen, *The Kaiser's Holocaust* (London: Faber and Faber, 2010); Shelley Baranowski, *Nazi Empire: German Colonialism and Imperialism from Bismarck to Hitler* (Cambridge University Press, 2011), pp. 55f.

Lebensraum, the theory of spatial ordering and imperial politics prior to National Socialism has been widely considered. Indeed, imperial politics seen through the lens of a *Großräume* theory and the political economy of international competition was entirely mainstream in German speaking academic study from the 1890s onwards, if not before.

Kaufmann related his own concern with Locke to contemporary American imperialism, noting the similarities of justification between the requirements of executive autonomy in the *Federalist Papers* to Locke's analysis, and concerned himself with how that autonomy could be used to underpin the fighting of wars over territory in the first place. For Locke, of course, the vision of America as something approaching *terra nullius* could justify not only colonization in the abstract, but also the appropriation of persons, spaces and places in practice. That Lockean justification, however, was soon used by America itself to justify outward acts of colonization and territorial occupation and acquisition in its own expansion west, south and into the pacific. But it was contemporary American empire, in the form of a German theory of the so-called three world empires (of Britain, America and Russia), which really came to matter.

This theory was part of the claim about how German political economy could help to direct policy and politics towards the end of achieving parity with the predominant global imperial powers. In the period of Leo Caprivi's chancellorship from around 1890–1894, the idea of a German power, under the banner of a new idea (*Mitteleuropa*) began to take shape, and was given form by industrial and political economists. Alexander von Peez, an Austrian industrialist, wrote in 1895 explicitly about the need for a great Europe [*All-Europa*] to counter the rise of a great America [*All-Großamerika*]. In the same year, Max Weber gave his highly charged inaugural lecture on the national tasks facing German politics and political economy, with these discussions (particularly concerning inner colonialism, emigration and Poland) quite obviously in the background.[40] Well before it became a clarion call for yet another restoration during and after the Great War, German hegemony within Europe, as part of a wider global system of geo-political balance and competition, was well considered.[41] With the Navy Law established

---

[40] Max Weber, 'The Nation State and Economic Policy', [1895] in P. Lassman and R. Spiers (eds.) *Weber: Political Writings* (Cambridge University Press, 1994), pp. 1–28, esp. pp. 20–22.

[41] For general accounts of the background, see Kenneth Barkin, *The Controversy over German Industrialisation, 1890–1902* (University of Chicago Press, 1970); also Sebastian Conrad (ed.) *Das Kaiserreich Transnational* (Göttingen: Vandenhoeck & Ruprecht, 2006); Woodruff Smith, *The Ideological Origins of Nazi Imperialism* (Oxford University Press, 1986), chs. 4, 6.

under Bernhard von Bülow, German *Weltpolitik* set its foreign policy agenda most clearly, and academic considerations of geo-politics and an imperial balance of power received political consideration as the so-called 'new course' of German economic policy was directed towards these ends.[42] Otto Hintze suggested likewise, writing in 1907 that the 'meaning of German "*Weltpolitik*"' was explicitly 'not the struggle for world domination, but rather a striving to maintain an equality of power in the global state system of the future'.[43] Weber thought similarly. But one obvious corollary of the so-called theory of the three empires, by the time it was popularized by Heinrich Dietzel's *Weltwirtschaft* and Schmoller's own analysis at the turn of the century, was with the earlier protective *Dreibund* policy.[44] This aimed to tie the security of Austria and Italy together with Germany and act as a bulwark against France from the West and Russia from the East. Now, though, the centrality of German reconsiderations of imperialism as *Weltpolitik*, had moved on from an understanding of the relative failure of territorial acquisition as the primary method of counterbalancing the imperial powers of France, Britain and Russia.

Weltpolitik was considered as a German path around the dilemmas of economic competition that resulted in military and territorial struggle, at least as it was highlighted by the 'neo-mercantilist' politics of the three world-empires in Schmoller's account.[45] Political economists entered the mainstream of political debate, building upon arguments made famous during the previous century through the idea of jealousy of trade. By making a distinction between retaliatory and reconciliatory

---

[42] Alexander von Peez, 'Mittel- Europa und die drei Weltreiche Grösser-Britannien, die Vereinigten Staaten und Rußland', in *Zur neuesten Handelspolitik. Sieben Abhandlungen*, Wien 1895, pp. 7ff; cf. *Mitteleuropa und die Balkanhalbinsel*, Berlin 1904. For discussion, Peter Theiner, 'Mitteleuropa: Pläne in Wilhelminischen Deutschland', *Geschichte und Gesellschaft*, Sonderheft 10 (1984), pp. 128–148, at pp. 130f.

[43] Otto Hintze, 'Imperialismus und Weltpolitik', in *Staat und Verfassung: Gesammelte Abhandlungen zur Allgemeinen Geschichte*, (ed.) Fritz Hartung (Leipzig: Koehler & Amelang, 1941), pp. 447–459, at p. 459: '*Der Sinn der deutschen "Weltpolitik" ist jedenfalls nicht Streben nach Weltherrschaft, sondern Streben nach Aufrechterhaltung des Gleichgewichts der Macht in dem Weltstaatensystem der Zukunft*'.

[44] Heinrich Dietzel, *Die Theorie von den drei Weltreichen* (Berlin: H. S. Hermann, 1900); Gustav Schmoller, 'Die Wandlung in der Handelspolitik des 19. Jahrhunderts', *Schmollers Jahrbuch*, 24 (1900), pp. 373–382, esp. pp. 373–374 on the three world-empires theory. Carl Schmitt, *The Nomos of the Earth*, [1950] trans. G. L. Ulmen (New York: Telos Press, 2003), pp. 234f, would later reintegrate these claims into his postwar work about the decline of European public law. For detail on these connections particularly, see Jamie Martin, 'The Theory of the Three World Empires: Carl Schmitt and the Emergence of the Global Economy', unpublished paper.

[45] Rosa Luxemburg, *The Accumulation of Capital*, [1913] trans. A. Schwarzschild (London: RKP, 1971), pp. 295ff, viewed the proposals with a cynical gaze.

policies, writers like Dietzel were able to show the paradoxes of retaliatory mercantilist economic policy, which effectively meant shoring up German colonial expansion in order to compete with the mercantile empires of Britain, Russia and America. Yet as Dietzel suggested, competition between the empires had hardly led to economic closure. In fact, as others have since confirmed, if anything integration levels in the European and world economies were extremely substantial in the immediate decades prior to the Great War. He offered, in effect, a neo-Smithian argument about free trade, whereas Schmoller, by contrast, sought to show that autarchic imperial blocs were the normal consequences of imperial competition, leading him to seek refuge in an early intimation of a plan for *Mitteleuropa*.[46] In ways similar to the updated analysis of socialism and reform presented in Germany by writers like Eduard Bernstein, Dietzel's account involved an internal critique of the logic of his predecessors, but unlike Dietzel, this didn't necessarily cohere with support of German expansionism for its own sake.[47] Empires had not become pathologically closed, or relentlessly private; global competition was not the death knell for nationalist political economy, rather its presupposition; and the contradictions of capitalism as both a national and a world system were not necessarily catastrophic for both. Moreover, the prognosis for the world economy, itself a developing concept in turn-of-the-century Germany, was in Dietzel's analysis moving towards greater openness rather requiring an up-scaled version of a quirky and quasi-Fichtean series of closed commercial empires. His rather abstract models, however, prompted criticism from British economists like Arthur Pigou and Francis Edgeworth.[48]

Dietzel claimed that proposing higher tariffs on imported goods, for example, as several of those who followed Schmoller had wanted, would obviously harm the exports of competitors, but simultaneously bring reprisals that could damage domestic producers too. It was a simple logic but powerfully expressed, and one that showed how day-to-day economic competition had to be carefully considered in light of longer term political calculations, if one were to reap steady rewards. In a study of the apparent myths of American competition with Germany, Dietzel made

[46] See Theiner, 'Mitteleuropa', esp. pp. 144f.
[47] Cf. Roger Fletcher, 'Cobden as Educator: The Free-Trade Internationalism of Eduard Bernstein, 1899–1914', *American Historical Review*, 88: 3 (1983), pp. 561–578 discussion in Manfred Steger, *The Quest for Evolutionary Socialism* (Cambridge University Press, 1987), pp. 158ff; Friedrich Naumann, *Demokratie und Kaiserthum* (Berlin: Oldenbourg, 1900).
[48] Arthur C. Pigou, 'Professor Dietzel on Dumping', *Economic Journal*, 15: 59 (1905), pp. 436–443; F. Y. Edgeworth, 'Vergeltungzölle', by H. Dietzel, *Economic Journal*, 14: 56 (Dec., 1904), pp. 608–609.

the point clearly. There was more to gain from commercial reciprocity and free trade, than protectionism and tariffs.[49] And the tenor of that conflict, between Schmoller-style protectionism and self-sufficiency that went forward into the celebrated wartime idea of *Mitteleuropa* as reiterated by Naumann, and the free-trade internationalism of writers like Dietzel, structured the framework within which economic policy as a form of political strategy took place. In part, it was an idea about the possibilities of European cooperation, but also in part it remained the principal mechanism of analysis for gauging the future political options of Germany in a battle amongst vast empires of both land and sea, like Britain, Russia, France and America.

As others have commented, levels of business level interdependence and integration were high, and well established, particularly within Western Europe, but also between Europe and America, in the years before the Great War, and prompted quite open political support for anti-protectionism.[50] What was required was structural balance so as to avoid being taken advantage of, rather than forms of economic nationalism that could threaten the profits of heavy industries like coal and steel. In turn, that meant increased military production (especially the navy), and aggressive searching for the best open markets. It sat foursquare in the field outlined by Friedrich List's national political economy as it had developed during the nineteenth century.[51] That also meant, given List's use of American history and experience for the construction of his account of so-called *Smithianismus*, that German engagement with *Weltpolitik* was filtered through an American lens.[52]

When added to the terms of my discussion of Lockean foreign policy, one might say that this was the moment when federative power took shape through economic strategy allied to a more conventional defense of prerogative power and all that entailed. During the war, particularly in debates over the safety of trade routes and the economic policy of the Allied blockade, questions of retaliatory measures such as unrestricted submarine warfare were tied to questions of economic survival and closed commercial states. At the liberal origins of an international, or a global political economy, stood the question of whether or not

[49] Heinrich Dietzel, *Der Deutsch-Amerikanische Handelsvertrag und das Phantom der amerikanischen Industriekonkurrenz* (Berlin: Leonhard Simeon, 1905).
[50] Carl Strikwerda, 'The Troubled Origins of European Integration', *American Historical Review*, 98: 4 (1993), pp. 1106–1129, at pp. 1110f.
[51] Thomas Hopkins, 'The Limits of "Cosmopolitical Economy": Smith, List and the Paradox of Peace through Trade', in T. Hippler and M. Vec, (eds.) *Paradoxes of Peace in Nineteenth-Century Europe* (Oxford University Press, 2015), pp. 77–91.
[52] See Keith Tribe, *Strategies of Economic Order* (Cambridge University Press, 1995), esp. pp. 36–9, 44–47, 55ff.

radical nationalism or open economic competition would prevail. Its justification as either a defensive or an offensive strategy was molded by war and imperialist competition, but its framework relied upon the idea of prerogative power nonetheless. This was the backdrop to the revival of histories of liberalism in German political thought, some of which directly traced the genealogy of nineteenth-century liberalism to the updating of jealousy of trade style arguments derived from David Hume and Adam Smith.[53]

By so doing, German political and economic discussion could readily have integrated Locke into a wider discussion of international competition and the possibilities of peace, and in ways typically associated in the history of political thought with the eighteenth-century concerns and authors with whom this volume of essays is predominantly concerned. In fact, the nineteenth and early twentieth century German interpretation of Locke in this context in some sense mirrors earlier eighteenth century French revisions to Machiavellian forms of politics as jealousy of trade. If Kaufmann's text was only the most explicit uptake of Locke on this front, one can trace earlier iterations of his importance to the rewriting of histories of political thought in the work of Johann Kaspar Bluntschli (where Locke's account of compact, history and prerogative makes him 'almost identical' with Rousseau, which in turn makes him nearly the same as Hobbes), as well as seeing his account of prerogative and its supervening function in relation to executive and federative power revised and updated later in the work of Carl Schmitt (signaling Locke's difference from Rousseau and from Hobbes).[54] The signal ambivalence of Lockean prerogative is that domestic politics was to be limited with reference to custom, prudence and history above all, but this seemed to have no limits in a rapacious world of foreign affairs and international competition for resources. Locke's oft-recognized colonial priorities appear then

[53] Heinrich Dietzel, *Das neunzehnte Jahrhundert und das Programm des Liberalismus* (Bonn: Röhrscheid & Ebbeck, 1900). esp. pp. 21, 24, 26f. Cf. Johann Kaspar Bluntschli, 'Weltmacht und Weltreich', in J. C. Bluntschli and K. Brater (eds.) *Deutsches Staatswörterbuch* 11 vols. (Stuttgart and Leipzig: n.p. 1865–1870), vol. 11, pp. 183ff, where his theory of an international confederation of nation states as the future union of civilization and humanity, is concisely presented.

[54] Johann Kaspar Bluntschli, *The Theory of the State* [1885], 3rd Ed., trans. from the 6th German edition (Oxford: The Clarendon Press, 1901), esp. pp. 67f (on Locke's political theory as part of an age of absolutism), 295f (on Rousseau and Locke's symmetry), 471f (on Locke's colonialism and Carolina), 500ff (on the 'personality' of the state, represented by the monarch who governs according to reason and prudence). Cf. Carl Schmitt, *Die Diktatur* [1921] (Berlin: Duncker & Humblot, 2006), pp. 10f (Locke as theorist of the prerogative of reason); 24 (on the anti-plebeian Locke and his justification of revolution); 40f (on Lockean prerogative as classical 'aequitas'); 115f (difference the Rousseau and Locke, and of Locke's less systematic theorizing between than Hobbes's).

to have a much wider ambit when seen in the context of late-modern imperialism as a form of reason of state, where few limits to prerogative powers exist in the international realm, and the possibilities of inter-national peace are to be limited solely with reference to a balance of power.[55] This was analogous to his self-consciously 'strange' doctrine of punishment, wherein the right to kill the highwayman who threatened your life for money (by returning you to a natural state of war with them), equally compelled you to seek redress for an actual crime of theft if you have merely asked someone to look after your money for a while and they refuse to give it back.[56] In the international sphere, it looked like Locke was no different from many of the standard and canonical figures in the history of Western political thought. The state acted like a self-interested individual on the world stage, rapacious and destructive internationally unless artificially chained, while its domestic constraints were grounded in prudence and trust.[57] But were there other reasons behind this inter-est in Locke, though, that went from the international back to the nature of domestic prerogative?

IV

One of the boldest statements of the extra-legal force of prerogative made by Locke concerned its capacity to move at a pace and with a force unconstrained by the 'old custom', moved instead by 'true reason'.[58] Those old ways, of course, refer to traditional mechanisms of parliamen-tary representation and political calculation, which remain grounded in historical reason, but whose agency can be trumped by the prudential calculation of emergency requirements. Yet if prerogative is necessary when those rational purposes that establish and constrain the normal running of political society are most under threat, then the anti-rational and anti-legalistic justification for prerogative can only be reconciled to the requirements of political society in terms of its consequences. To put this another way, Locke had consistently suggested both rational and prudential foundations for the establishment of political societies, and a secular and conventional argument about the relationship between utility and authority that underpinned them over time. That secular argument in turn assumes the validity of prerogative to the extent that it is able to continue the aims and ends of political society when there are domestic

---

[55] See David Armitage, 'John Locke, Carolina and the *Two Treatises of Government*', *Politi-cal Theory*, 32: 5 (2004), pp. 602–627.
[56] Locke, *Two Treatises*, II. §9, 13–14, pp. 272f, 275ff.
[57] Tuck, *Rights of War and Peace*, esp. pp. 6–15.
[58] Locke, *Two Treatises*, II. §158, p. 257.

threats and uncertainties that require extra-legal action. This is usually taken by the executive power, and that executive power can also typically combine with the federative power, so that prerogative can both respond to domestic and international uncertainties and threats, as defined by the figure of the executive or the holder of prerogative. Both executive and federative powers require the 'force of Society for their exercise', such that prerogative is derivative upon it, while legislative power is 'fiduciary' and thus breakable.[59]

Clearly, prerogative cuts both ways. It can, of course, be used by the executive power to safeguard the state internally, as well as motivating action externally to counter the enmity that occurs when there is a state of war between states. In both cases, this rests on the judgment, opinion and the prudential experience of the person who holds executive power.[60] As Bates implies, prerogative therefore also serves as a surrogate for prophecy and mimics, though the analogy is not direct, the wisdom of the Creator. Politics and prudence are not worshiped as if they were divine, for they are human judgments. But the theological foundations of Locke's worldview do allow him to claim that prerogative, just as resistance and revolution, must be justified by deeply felt conviction about the right course of action by participants. For there is always a further judgment to come, after the crisis has passed, and that is at the court of the Creator, who himself cannot be deceived. Hence Locke's assertion that in cases where ultimate ends and beliefs in the rightness of a cause cannot be mediated through words and peaceful means of political accommodation, the appeal to heaven is a last resort. His model, somewhat awkwardly, was the Old Testament figure of Jephthah.

If boundary disputes about words and actions cannot be rationally resolved by the executive power in the state, Locke's idiosyncratic use of Jephthah gives an historical illustration of the appeal to heaven. Showing the divine right of the Israelites to attack and subdue the Ammonites, but to do so in a secular fashion through regular channels of politics and diplomacy, justice and right are seen to be on Jephthah's side.[61] The appeal to heaven exists, because although it is never certain who genuinely has justice on their side in a case of deep and legitimate disagreements, there is always the possibility of a final, otherworldly judgment whose oracular power cannot be deceived. This is the necessary appendage to that 'strange doctrine' of punishment, which goes beyond the norms of collective life and is retributive because governed by the

[59] Locke, *Two Treatises*, II. §122, p. 349.   [60] Locke, *Two Treatises*, II. §147, pp. 365f.
[61] Samuel Moyn, 'Appealing to Heaven: Jephthah, John Locke, and Just War', *Hebraic Political Studies*, 4: 3 (2009), pp. 286–303, at pp. 289, 292; see too Andrew Rehfeld, 'Jephthah, The Hebrew Bible and John Locke's "Second Treatise of Government"', *Hebraic Political Studies*, 3: 1 (2008), pp. 60–93, esp. pp. 70ff.

demands of a state of nature.[62] The quid pro quo is that the benefits of moving towards society and away from an original state of nature and towards the formation of a new political arrangement are so compelling and motivational, that executive authority and prerogative are the very things that keep civil societies, in the main, from continually falling prey to this elemental reversion. The Jephthah narrative for Locke seems to suggest that even in cases where sovereignty and civil society no longer exist, or where a putative state of nature does exist either within or between states, there is never a wholly normless or meaningless world because we are all elements of divine Creation. What is difficult is knowing whether and when we are acting in accordance with the requirements of natural law, because Locke's argument about the epistemological uncertainty of words and meaning leads directly to an uncertainty about political as well as ethical consequences.[63]

This underscores the message behind his use of Jephthah, namely that the people judge the rightness of actions in civil societies where government rests upon trust, but that judgment is itself subject to a higher-level judgment. In order for this system to work, citizens must be prepared to regulate their conduct accordingly both in public and in private, to act with the propriety that both natural and civil laws require. Ultimately men can judge their actions for themselves in terms of justice and right, but they can never be completely certain about their ground because such certainty is denied to man, and only granted to (because by) God. This uncertainty shapes the basic requirement of prudence on the part of the executive with prerogative power, to maintain and develop over time a sense of what is and is not appropriate or beneficial to the maintenance of a civil society, much of which is predicated upon custom, inheritance and history.[64] It also explains how Jephthah works for Locke, given that on Locke's own terms, Jephthah stands on the wrong side of arguments he made elsewhere in the *Second Treatise* about conquest, the deferral of justice and the revolutionary chaos of the appeal to heaven.[65]

---

[62] Tuck, *Rights of War and Peace*, pp. 166–181, on Locke's apparent defense of Grotian political conclusions against the criticisms of Samuel Pufendorf.

[63] Kelly, *The Propriety of Liberty*, pp. 37–41; Hannah Dawson, 'Locke on Language in (Civil) Society', *History of Political Thought*, 26: 3 (2005), pp. 397–425; Dunn, *Political Thought of Locke*, p. 161.

[64] Samuel Moyn, 'John Locke on Intervention, Uncertainty and Insurgency', in S. Recchia and J. M. Welsh (eds.) *Just and Unjust Military Intervention* (Cambridge University Press, 2013), pp. 113–131, clarifies Locke's claims about Jephthah as a response to the problem(s) of uncertainty.

[65] Rehfeld, 'The Hebrew Bible', pp. 73ff; for a brief account of Locke's relationship with political Hebraism, in the context of wider arguments about toleration and agrarian laws in early modern European political thought, see Eric Nelson, *The Hebrew Republic* (Cambridge, MA: Harvard University Press, 2010), pp. 135ff.

If 'old customs' are to be rejected then Locke's prerogative has some quite broad implications. Indeed, his anti-parliamentarism is also very strong, and certainly one can see in it both a Whiggist attack on parliamentary corruption, and a related worry about parliamentary representation with its predominance of sectional interests. For if Parliament cannot neutrally represent the needs of political society, then the executive with prerogative power will have to. After all, the monarch has the prerogative to summon parliament and rightly so, Locke thinks, for only the monarch can stand above the fray and act for something like the 'good of the Nation'.[66] And as with Hobbes's more obviously *de facto* theory of sovereignty and obedience, for Locke, Parliament often stands in the way of sovereign decision by challenging it domestically. The way he sets this up, however, is by saying that although legislative power within the state is supreme, politics needs to leave the space for uncertainty that executive and prerogative power can fill, and it must do so according to the reasoned foundations of political society. Equally, he notes that the 'natural' executive power of men in society is divided when it becomes political and is given form in the corporate legislative body, but where political power is ineffective, natural power remains – whether in the necessity of prerogative, the appeal to heaven, or the right to strike down a clear and present enemy.

For those who would take Locke to be foundational for a broadly liberal, even democratic political order in the mid twentieth century, this meant thinking of a way to constitutionally justify what remains an anti-parliamentary prerogative. If Locke was concerned to make prerogative safe against parliamentary supremacy, then according to twentieth century critics and defenders of liberalism alike, Locke had alighted on a crucial problem. One of the most important, if understudied, figures in terms of this particular development of Locke's analysis of prerogative was Carl Friedrich, whose account of Locke formed part of a wider rethinking of the history of modern political thought, but whose intellectual formation developed out of the sorts of debates about prerogative in German politics and economics that have just been alluded to. His was a program for an austere, regulated, and strongly controlled form of modern democratic politics, one not likely to be subject to the changeable whims of parliamentary politics and stiffened through executive 'choice' and prerogative.[67]

---

[66] Locke, *Two Treatises*, II. §167, p. 378; cf. Mansfield, *Taming the Prince*, p. 199; Mark Goldie, 'John Locke's Circle and James II', *Historical Journal*, 35: 3 (1992), pp. 557–586.

[67] Locke, *Two Treatises*, II. §159–160, pp. 257f.

V

One notable feature of recent political theory has been a return to Locke's theory of prerogative for its insights into contemporary dilemmas brought about through presidential and governmental emergency powers.[68] Obviously, the catalyst for thinking about the politics of emergency has arisen in response to a perceived threat of war, particularly the idea of a so-called war on terror. Several writers focusing on this have begun to tease out the implications of Locke's prerogative for this purpose, and to see its rather indirect relation to classically rationalist analyses of the constitutional separation of powers. There is some irony in this resurgence of interest, for many writers interested in emergency politics the specter of Carl Schmitt has instead been central. His focus on the existentially threatening qualities of truly political decisions has been revived, allowing critics to focus on the limitations of what might be termed a variant of procedural liberalism. Those who seek to show that a modern, if retrospectively constructed, tradition of liberalism, already provides the necessary resources for thinking about the prudential requirements of emergency politics, turn instead to Locke's account of prerogative to show that liberalism need not require anti-liberalism in order to be realistic about threats and dangers.

What such debates have not focused on, however, is the fact that this series of questions about Locke's resonance and relevance to the problem of emergency powers is hardly new at all. In fact, it received quite considered airing in particular during the early decades of the twentieth century, in the work of German speaking legal historians and philosophers, even in the work of Carl Schmitt. And through this German legacy, in fact, a wider though often occluded husk of Lockean political theory emerged both in Europe and in America thanks to the work (perhaps most obviously) of Carl Friedrich, the émigré Heidelberg political scientist who would become an incredibly influential institution builder and Professor of Government at Harvard University, making it (according to legend) something of a 'new' Germany on the East Coast of America. Indeed, because Locke clearly became foundational for the history of philosophical and political liberalism in the Anglo-American world only after the Great War, with the rise of increasingly radical and militant criticisms of liberal and parliamentary democracy, culminating in the rise of totalitarianism, Friedrich's criticisms of mass democracy and its

[68] For two recent examples, see Clement Fatovic, 'Constitutionalism and Contingency: John Locke's Theory of Prerogative', *History of Political Thought*, 25: 4 (2004), pp. 276–297; Ross Corbett, 'The Extra-Constitutionality of Lockean Prerogative', *Review of Politics*, 68 (2006), pp. 428–448.

totalitarian threat were designed as an alternative defense of democratic politics. Those who were influenced by Friedrich at Harvard, writers otherwise diverse in their views like Judith Shklar (whose doctorate on political faith Friedrich supervised), seem nevertheless to have also taken up Friedrich's concern with the question of the limits of liberalism by synthesizing legal and empirical political issues within the framework of a drastically chastened liberalism, asking the question as to how executive politics might be adequately restrained in order to defend democratic freedom.[69] Yet unlike Shklar, for example, Friedrich's account of his problem relied on a repatriation of Locke into a much broader re-envisioning of the entire tradition of Western political thought. By making Locke part and parcel of a constitutionalist idiom of reason of state, Friedrich reconnected him with the wider concerns about the possibilities and limitations of perpetual peace that dominate this collection of essays, particularly because of the way in which he combined Locke's political theory with a renewed interpretation of Immanuel Kant after the Second World War. He folded both writers into a discussion of the religious bases of constitutionalism in the 1960s, after having reflected upon the idea of constitutional reason of state in the 1950s, and having discussed the possibilities of what he termed 'inevitable peace' in the 1940s. His work was clearly part of the wider development of both militant and Christian forms of democracy in Europe during the post war period. And although chronologically out of sequence, Friedrich's account of John Locke as a constitutional reason of state theorist offers the best way into his discussion.

In the Colver Lectures given by Friedrich in 1956 and published as *Constitutional Reason of State: The Survival of the Constitutional Order*, the discussion of Locke only takes little more than two pages, and is part of a broader discussion of Milton, Rousseau and Kant, writers who, according to Friedrich, signify a 'moralist slant' in reason of state thinking. Within its boundaries, though, Locke plays a small but significant role. Friedrich considers Locke as such a constitutional reason of state theorist, in opposition to his other dynamic category of 'absolutist' reason of state theory, 'because of his notion of the people as the constituent power' and Locke's attempt to 'balance the twin rights of revolution

---

[69] Judith Shklar, *After Utopia: The Decline of Political Faith* (Princeton University Press, 1957); 'The Liberalism of Fear', repr. in *Political Thought and Political Thinkers* (ed.) Stanley Hoffmann (Chicago, IL: Chicago University Press, 1989), pp. 3–20. On Shklar in context and her connections to Friedrich, see Katrina Forrester, 'Hope and Memory in the Thought of Judith Shklar', *Modern Intellectual History*, 11: 3 (2011), pp. 591–620, esp. pp. 598f.

and king's prerogative'.[70] Here, the question motivating this chapter is revealed by Friedrich, namely, what is the difference between a reason of state theory and one that talks of a balance between the dual right of revolution and of king's prerogative? In contemporary political theory, Friedrich's text has gradually become part of a wider body of literature concerned with historical accounts of the ways in which forms of emergency power might be constitutionally limited, and how political theorists should think about that question when using Locke as a liberal voice.[71]

The striking difference in historical concerns motivating and lying behind Friedrich's work and those of contemporary political theory, however, indicates something of the peculiarities of conceiving Locke as a theorist of constitutional reason of state. When Friedrich was writing, the background lay in crucial debates about executive authority and military government, particularly in the Philippines, and whether military government could be constrained as a form of constitutional dictatorship, or whether it was in danger of being a totalitarian dictatorship.[72] For Friedrich, in fact, his attempt to transpose a vision of constitutional reason of state from post-war Germany into New Deal and then Cold War America would be crucial, and bureaucratic responsibility was key.[73] This recognition lay behind his sympathetic though critical history of the political thought of neo-liberalism.[74] Equally, whereas contemporary political theorists talk of the precautionary principle and the problem of how to trade off, or discount, current liberties for the sake of either future liberties or future security within the state, those of Friedrich's generation considered emergency powers in the aftermath of Nazism, alongside vision of the Cold War as a conflict between totalitarian dictatorship and constitutional democracy, with a pressing threat of nuclear annihilation.

[70] Carl Friedrich, *Constitutional Reason of State* (Providence, RI: Brown University Press, 1957), p. 82, and n. 10; cf. Dunn, *Political Thought of John Locke*, pp. 161f, nn. 2, marks Friedrich's questions, but for a similar rendering through an exposition of Locke's theory, W. von Leyden, 'La loi, la liberté et la prérogative dans la pensée politique de John Locke', *Revue philosophique de la France et de l'Étranger*, 163 (1973), pp. 187–203, at pp. 195f, 199.
[71] John Ferejohn and Pasquale Pasquino, 'The Law of the Exception: A Typology of Emergency Powers', *International Journal of Constitutional Law*, 2: 2 (2010), esp. pp. 1–21, esp. pp. 4, 5, 7ff, 15.
[72] Carl Friedrich, 'Military Government and Dictatorship', *Annals of the American Academy of Political and Social Science*, 267 (1950), pp. 1–7, esp. pp. 4, 7, on the liberatory potential Friedrich saw for constitutional dictatorship.
[73] Udi Greenberg, *The Weimar Century* (Princeton University Press, 2015), p. 19.
[74] Carl Friedrich, 'The Political Thought of Neo-Liberalism', *American Political Science Review*, 49: 2 (1955), pp. 509–525.

By suggesting, in wholly conventional fashion, the need for executive power to act under emergency conditions according to some predetermined and yet vague criteria such as the common good, they were
of course merely updating an argument from the very foundation of
Western political thinking, namely the institution of the Roman dictator.
They were updating it for an atomic age, however, and with a slightly different concern. In Clinton Rossiter's memorable terminology, a 'constitutional dictatorship' could future proof democratic moeurs and values,
by trading off future security and present liberty. With Weimar Germany
in mind, Rossiter was keen to assert the necessity of the rule of necessity, seeking only to constrain it through democratic procedures. Then,
the threat was unconstitutional dictatorship and arbitrary tyranny. When
Rossiter's book was published, the overriding worry was a credible threat
of nuclear war, and how to constitutionalize dictatorship in the face of
a nuclear winter. The structure of that argument, however, is similar
to those typically presented today under a threat of extreme terrorism.
Now, as then, a central question concerns how best to safeguard current values with the recognition that under conditions of nuclear war,
or terrorist atrocity, emergency government that lies necessarily outside
the normal course of law is going to have to take place.[75] This assumes,
of course, a series of questions about the value of current values and
about how to trade them off against a future where certain risks can
obtain probabilistic calculation, but the reality of uncertainty makes dis-
counting of either individual preferences, or communal values, a drastically difficult procedure even where certain values (being 'democratic'
or 'American') are seemingly taken as read. It means, as with Locke's
analysis, that prerogative and constitutional dictatorship presumes a certain constitutional 'maturity', a sense of their being something worth
defending in the first place, hard won over many years, that can justify
such a constitutionally limited dictatorship to a democratic populace,
and simultaneously help make it administratively manageable through
bureaucratic means.[76]

What makes Friedrich's book of particular fascination, though, is not
the originality of his interpretation of Locke (for it is not hugely original), but where the language of Locke as a reason of state thinker comes
from, and how it is effectively to be parsed with the generally accepted
claim that Locke is not a reason of state thinker, but a theorist of

[75] Clinton Rossiter, *Constitutional Dictatorship* (Princeton University Press, 1949), esp.
pp. 401ff, 406, 408, 418.
[76] Rossiter, *Constitutional Dictatorship*, pp. 396, 398f, 406, 408. The connection to Locke's
ideas about freedom being dependent upon a 'state of maturity' is striking. See Locke,
Two Treatises, II. §§ 59, 57, pp. 307, 306.

conventional prerogative. Friedrich develops his own claims in part thanks to what he takes from the work of an earlier teacher, Carl Schmitt. This can be gleaned from the appendix published alongside his Colver Lectures. It reproduces Friedrich's review of Friedrich Meinecke's celebrated history of the idea of reason of state. When Friedrich's review was first published, Meinecke's book had been out for nearly four years, but there was very little critical commentary. Friedrich was at pains to show his fealty to the intellectual grandeur of Meinecke's vision and historical writing. But he took aim at the conceptual imprecision of Meinecke's study, for its failure to really tie down what exactly reason of state is, and what its limits (if any) actually are. This he attributes to the peculiarities of Meinecke's own method of *Ideengeschichte*. What is less clear from the review as printed in 1931, and reprinted in 1957, is that it basically recapitulates in an albeit shorter compass the precise criticisms of Meinecke that were made in a review by Carl Schmitt, which appeared within a year of the appearance of *Die Idee der Staatsräson*, in the *Archiv für Sozialwissenschaft und Sozialpolitik* of 1926. So, when Friedrich chastises Meinecke for not being clear enough about the more general failure of political theory to adequately disentangle political from legal concepts, which allows for the dangerous possibility of moralizing political ideas and flattening out their history, he is simply repeating Schmitt's analysis of several years earlier.[77]

Schmitt's account was, as one might expect, more stylized and more polemical than Friedrich's rendition, and castigated the moralistic ambitions of Meinecke's history, given its attempt to show the possibility and probability of a distinctively German solution to the riddle of reason of state. Meinecke historicized reason of state and German nationalism into a form of cultural destiny after the French Revolution and the Wars of Liberation, where the possibilities of political and cultural nationhood were reconciled as a form of 'good' or safe and constitutional *Staatsräson*, because the moral calibrations of political calculations could combine in the figure of the prudential statesman. Such a statesman would be capable of balancing and reconciling the otherwise oppositional forces of power and ethics, or good and evil. This claim misunderstands the nature of the political, according to Schmitt, which, he argues, can never be subject to such moral foundationalism because it has to deal in practice with the possibilities of violent conflict and is therefore occasionally to be governed according to prerogative powers, according to the

---

[77] Friedrich Meinecke, *Die Idee der Staatsräson in der neuere Geschichte* (Berlin: Oldenbourg, 1924); Carl Schmitt, 'Zu Friedrich Meineckes *Idee der Staatsräson*', *Archiv für Sozialwissenschaft*, 56 (1926), pp. 226–234.

decisions of an executive representative or sovereign. In Schmitt's mind, of course, this figure was, at least during the period of the Great War and the Weimar Republic, the figure of the *Reichspräsident*, but Friedrich was elsewhere at least clear (as many contemporary political theorists are not), that Schmitt's focus on the ambiguities of the Weimar Constitution was not straightforwardly destructive.[78] It was during these Weimar era debates that Schmitt's anti-Americanism would develop, alongside his concern with the question of whether any sort of constitutional mechanism could be elaborated for safeguarding a constitution under conditions of emergency. Friedrich, in his earlier work on constitutional government and politics, simply reiterated Schmitt's points about its weaknesses, but then reframed the need for a regulated and strong form of executive authority and bureaucratic competence to oversee an otherwise ramshackle and disordered form of mass-democratic politics.[79]

Discussion of Schmitt's account of the representative power of the sovereign executive president has typically focused on its Hobbesian foundations, outlining some of the oddities in his political theory that conflates Hobbesian sovereignty with debates about representation found in the writings of the Abbé Sieyès, in order to show how the history of political thought could be pressed into a contemporary defense of the power of the representative *Reichspräsident* under Weimar and after.[80] By doing so, Schmitt allowed the figure of the sovereign to bring about a form of political unity, by making the multitudinous people into a singular artificial person known as the state, represented by a sovereign and a government, so that although political authority is said to rest with the constituent power of the people, in practice, the people cannot act because they can only be made to live (metaphorically) through the actions of their representatives. These are by now well-known component parts of Schmitt's Weimar period writings, thanks to his focus on the question of dictatorship and prerogative in terms of Article 48 of the Weimar Constitution. The wider history of dictatorship upon which those particular claims were based, however, is intriguing because of the extent to which Schmitt's analysis of dictatorship, reason of state, and prerogative bears a striking resemblance to Locke's

[78] Carl Friedrich, 'Dictatorship in Germany', *Foreign Affairs*, 9: 1 (1930), pp. 118–132.
[79] Carl Friedrich, *Constitutional Government and Politics* (New York: Harper & Brothers, 1937), p. 220.
[80] Duncan Kelly, 'Carl Schmitt's Political Theory of Representation', *Journal of the History of Ideas*, 65, 1: (2004), pp. 113–134; Wilfried Nippel, 'Carl Schmitt's "kommissarische" und "souveräne Diktatur". Französische Revolution und römische Vorbilder', in H. Bluhm, K. Fischer and M. Llanque (eds.) *Ideenpolitik: Geschichtliche Konstellationen und gegenwärtige Konflikte* (Berlin: Akademie Verlag, 2011), pp. 105–140.

argument.[81] For even though Locke has a weaker presence in Schmitt's writings than Hobbes, and even though Schmitt was mildly scathing of Locke's 'either-or' approach to politics, he says that, much as with Bodin, Locke's synthesis of executive and federative power through the framework of prudential prerogative was in fact a form of commissarial, or restorative, dictatorship. Doing what is necessary, following prerogative and prudence, is a form of Lockean *aequitas* according to Schmitt, and Locke here becomes a legitimately liberal figure because of this focus on restorative dictatorship, rather than the anti-liberal and much more radical 'sovereign' forms of dictatorship that emerge through Rousseau and filter into modern politics during the French Revolution.[82]

Given this, perhaps it comes as no surprise to learn that (at least before the outbreak of the Second World War), Friedrich had been planning to translate Schmitt's book on dictatorship into English. Because that failed to transpire, whether because of radical disagreements about National Socialism in the mid 1930s, or because of a lack of funds for such work, we have had to wait nearly a century for Schmitt's book to appear in translation. Now it has, it should become easier for Anglophone readers to see the extent of Schmitt's reconstruction of the history of political thought for Friedrich's enterprise, even if it is true that in the 1940s and 1950s, Friedrich was moving away from Schmitt's analysis of the problems of dictatorship as either commissarial or sovereign, and looking instead at the administrative implications of executive or legislative dictatorship in America and in foreign policy (particularly in the Pacific), compared to the politics of totalitarian states.

It looks as if Schmitt's attempt, at least during his wartime work, to resuscitate a historically grounded theory of liberalism whose attention to restorative forms of what he called 'commissarial' dictatorship could help to remind modern liberals of the techniques of political management available to them from within their own history, might in fact be tied to a sensitive awareness of Locke's centrality to a certain strand of modern politics. As his own politics became more profoundly authoritarian, Schmitt's account of prerogative increasingly became non-Lockean. For example, and as Ernst Fraenkel's celebrated account of the Nazi state suggested, the so-called prerogative state under National Socialism was definitively not an update of Locke's ideas.[83] Reading

---

[81] Duncan Kelly, 'Carl Schmitt's Political Theory of Dictatorship', in J. Meierhenrich and O. Simons (eds.), *The Oxford Handbook of Carl Schmitt*, (Oxford University Press, 2014), pp. 217–244).

[82] Schmitt, *Die Diktatur*, pp. 115f, 118f.

[83] Ernst Fraenkel, *The Dual State*, trans. E. A. Shils (Oxford University Press, 1941), pp. 3, 60, 67, 461 (on Haller).

Fraenkel, one also finds a reversion to Franz L. Neumann's account of the Nazi *Behemoth*, showing how National Socialist political theory was, for left-wing anti-Schmittian political theorists, much more akin to the restoration arguments of Karl Friedrich von Haller, the subject of another discussion in this volume.[84] What seems clear, at least, is that although Locke's political ideas became fundamental to the post-war Anglophone development of liberalism as a political theory, that development was undertaken without much recourse to his account of prerogative or reason of state. By contrast, German political thought from the development of the Anglo-German antagonism through to the rise of National Socialism, seems to have found, something useful in Locke's account of prerogative as a form of reason of state, one that could justify both economic competition and political prudence in a modern nation-state.

If Friedrich utilized Schmitt's criticism of Meinecke's idealized or idealistic interpretation of a tradition of reason of state, we might wonder why he did so. As today, many writers are interested in and pricked by the force of Schmitt's arguments, without wanting to be seen in any meaningful way to endorse his polemical vision. But Friedrich thought Schmitt was onto something perhaps even deeper, something he could use for himself. So in 1926, at the Institute for Politics in Grenville, South Carolina, Friedrich delivered a lecture on the Weimar Constitution. The lecture shows Friedrich's attempt to delineate precisely what the structural problems of the Weimar Constitution actually were, and unlike Schmitt's rather more pointed focus on Article 48 and the question of presidential dictatorship either in theory or in practice, Friedrich's first-order question concerned the viability of federalism within the Reich or Republic, given the predominant structural position of Prussia. Thus, like Schmitt, Friedrich connected contemporary debates about the imbalances of German federalism to questions of *Realpolitik* and Prussian hegemony that had concerned both right and left since the failed revolutions of 1848, when exactly the same questions had been raised.[85] The classical federalist problem (both for political science as well as the history of political thought) of whether Germany was a union of states in the form of either a

---

[84] Franz L. Neumann, *Behemoth, The Structure and Process of National Socialism* (New York: Harper & Row, 1944), pp. 461f; cf. Duncan Kelly, 'Rethinking Franz Neumann's Route to *Behemoth*', *History of Political Thought*, 23: 3 (2002), pp. 458–496.

[85] August Ludwig Rochau, *Grundsätze der Realpolitik angewendet auf die staatlichen Zustände Deutschlands* (Stuttgart: Karl Göpel, 1853), p. 2. Carl Friedrich, 'Lecture on the German Constitution 1919' [1926], Harvard University Archives, Box 8, HUGFP 17.60. I am grateful to Udi Greenberg for alerting me to the text, and for discussion about it.

Bundesstaat or a *Staatenbund* had not yet been resolved.[86] But by the time of the unified and unitary Weimar Constitution, Friedrich, unlike Schmitt, saw the constitution and its preamble through the lens of its aim to foster 'universal peace and social progress', rather than simply expressing the will of the German people. He did so even as he recognized that its radicalism (particularly with regard to property and trades union rights) was grounded in the 'social revolution' that laid the groundwork for the constitution in the first place.[87]

In fact, Friedrich roundly defended the democratic potential of this republican constitution. A unitary constitution where each particular part (the *Länder*) didn't need to ratify every point meant that rather than signaling confusion about dictatorship and presidential prerogative, the infamous Article 48 had in fact curbed the possibilities of secessionist civil war such as had happened earlier in America fifty years previously. Moreover, because the President was also subject to recall with a two-thirds vote in the Reichstag, Friedrich argued that it 'bears witness to the fundamental conception of democracy, that the people are the sole source of authority'.[88] This idea of democracy, with the people as its sole and authoritative source or foundation, points towards a deep root in Friedrich's political thinking, but one that has a more interesting story than its bare presentation suggests. It became clearer as Friedrich moved from Weimar Germany to America, and started to write extensively about democratic politics after the Second World War. By that time, according to Friedrich's presentation, a radical disconnect between the needs of contemporary politics and the claims of democracy as popular sovereignty had opened up. He explained: 'One of the most important questions of political theory in historical perspective is why democratic ideology, the philosophy of the cooperative commonwealth, should be thus associated with a philosophical outlook which the climate of opinion in our time doesn't favour'.[89] This claim, from Friedrich's book *Inevitable Peace* (1948) is found in a text that is devoted to outlining the extent of the Kantian background to contemporary debates about human rights and its limitations.

As various other chapters in this book have made clear, the dimensions of the eighteenth century debate about perpetual peace were very

---

[86] Daniel Ziblatt, 'Rethinking the Origins of Federalism: Puzzle, Theory and Evidence from Nineteenth-Century Europe', *World Politics*, 57 (2004), pp. 70–98, esp. pp. 77ff; Murray Forsyth, *Unions of States* (Leicester University Press, 1981), esp. chs. 4–6.

[87] Friedrich, 'German Constitution', pp. 4, 10.

[88] Friedrich, 'German Constitution', p. 9.

[89] Carl Friedrich, *Inevitable Peace* (Cambridge, MA: Harvard University Press, 1948), p. 77.

clearly bound up with arguments about jealousy of trade, international competition and the nation state. These are precisely the sorts of issues that István Hont's work outlined, in order to show the longevity of concern about the relationship between capitalism, competition and war on a global scale since the eighteenth century. If his own work often hinted at the legacy of those problems for twentieth and now twenty-first century politics and economics, so too, perhaps ironically, did Friedrich's own agenda mirror those concerns, but with a much more overtly politicized form of ideological fervor. In 1948, he could write without fear of hyperbole that almost everyone expected there to be a third world war. Not yet a Cold War, but a global civil war nonetheless, because such a war would first be about ideas, and those ideas would be ones that mattered not because of the detail of their original context, nor through some sort of dialectical reasoning. Instead, he argued, we would have to assess the 'influence' of particular ideas on the institutional development of the United Nations, as a way to understand the battle of ideas that sought to hold in check any future battlefield conflict between democratic nations.[90]

Claims of influence have been philosophically decried in much postwar intellectual history, and although Friedrich's aim here was quite limited methodologically, he both had his own agenda as well as an axe to grind about the utility of history for contemporary political thinking. He well knew the success of contemporary writers like Max Lerner, whose *Ideas are Weapons* (1939) had become important politically for having said that 'ideas in politics are much like poetry: they need no inner logical structure to be effective'.[91] For Friedrich, however, this was far too cynical, denying the claims to truth and right that political thought at its best necessarily tried to uphold. From that perspective, it was easy to say that it remained important to try and get back to Kant's original intentions and arguments about perpetual peace, because they had been undone in the Anglo-American world by thirty years of antipathetic scholarship like that undertaken by George Santayana, whose attempt to tar an entire nation's historical philosophy with the brush of wartime despotism distorted the real picture.[92] Friedrich then proceeded to delineate the terms of his understanding of Kant, showing that he could not fit into the mold of this egotistical heritage, and that his attempt to theorize freedom and

---

[90] Friedrich, *Inevitable Peace*, p. 11.

[91] Max Lerner, *Ideas are Weapons: The History and Uses of Ideas* (New York: Viking, 1939), p. 357.

[92] Friedrich, *Inevitable Peace*, pp. 16ff; he was referring to George Santayana, *Egotism in German Philosophy* (New York: Charles Scribner's, 1917), an attack begun during the First World War.

peace and their possibilities was a critical attempt to move beyond determinism in order to think creatively about the future, but also to recognize historical tendencies (such as war most obviously) that had acted as proxies for the development of autonomy at times when people had not 'freely' chosen the right path of their own volition.[93] A tremendously optimistic reading of Kant even by his own standards, this perspective nevertheless allowed Friedrich to open up a parallel genealogy of the history of political thought, into which 'voluntarists' (like Locke, Kant and Rousseau) could be placed and compared alongside 'determinists' (like Hobbes, Machiavelli, and Spinoza).

This done, he was able to propose and outline a defense of democracy under the United Nations as a modern update of Kantian voluntarism, and to contrast the sort of 'welfare state' that a Kantian history could support with that of the determinist, or more obviously reason of state inspired counter narrative. The 'right' law underpinning the 'freedom from fear' emblazoned on that early UN flag, and which seems to point directly from Friedrich to Shklar, also suggested to Friedrich that Kant's critique of Hobbes in *Theory and Practice* (1793) was located in the sphere of autonomous right, even if he retained Hobbes's account of the absolute quality of sovereignty.[94] But as with so many twentieth century histories of the history of political thought, Friedrich's parallel genealogies (akin to the frame of reference motivating Michael Oakeshott's traditions of *Societas* and *Universitas*, for example) permitted him also to pick sides and choose the precursors of a contemporary democratic tradition with a philosophy of cooperation that he saw as under threat.[95] Here, Friedrich moved back in time, towards the Calvinist political thinker of group and associational life, Johannes Althusius, whose major text on politics he helped resuscitate.[96] He did so for two principal reasons.

First, in assaying the ways in which Calvinism and Lutheranism impacted upon political thought, Friedrich argued that they helped to make 'secular', rather than 'analytical', the demands of and for divine authority. Put another way, Luther and Calvin were not Hobbes and Bentham, obviously, but the political theology that lay behind the wider, secularizing tendencies of modern ideas of natural law they helped empower, even if its extent remained 'elusive', signaled a need to recognize these wider foundations of legitimate political authority. At this

---

[93] Friedrich, *Inevitable Peace*, pp. 64, 82f.

[94] Cf. Friedrich, *Inevitable Peace*, pp. 87f; Tuck, *Rights of War and Peace*, esp. pp. 218–225.

[95] Michael Oakeshott, *Morality and Politics in Modern Europe* (Cambridge, MA: Harvard University Press, 1958).

[96] See Carl Friedrich, 'Preface', to *The Politics of Johannes Althusius*, trans. Frederick S. Carney (London: Eyre and Spottiswoode, 1964), pp. vi–xii.

point, Friedrich was in line with the sorts of claims about the theological foundations of politics that both Carl Schmitt and Leo Strauss had made famous.[97] However, at the same time, the most obviously elusive writer who signaled the transition of a deistic or theistic tradition these was, for Friedrich, John Locke. Friedrich therefore constructed a voluntarist and theologically grounded tradition of thinking about political thought generally, and the roots of democracy particularly, that wove its way through these figures. And in his particular iteration, this ran from Althusius and Locke to Kant, and from Kant thereafter to contemporary democracy generally, and German democracy especially. It signaled in his mind both a clear and Protestant foundation to the roots of democratic politics, roots that were intrinsically Germanic on the one hand, and generalizable on the other. Here then was a model of democracy that Protestant Germans could sign up to rather than pillory, as had been the case during the Weimar Republic, while it was a model that could also take favorable roots in terms of wider, transatlantic connections too. When pressed hard, in fact, Friedrich could claim that these Germanic, Protestant and natural law foundations were as central to the development of modern Western democracy as they had been, even as they had been forgotten and buried, to German democratic development too.

That leads to the second point of interest, one amplified in a telling recent account of Friedrich's political theory, which shows the true extent of his transatlantic vision of Protestant, Christian democracy and its tremendous influence. As Greenberg shows, for Friedrich, democracy is the 'realization of Christian principles', similar to the way that Max Weber had called *Kultur* a 'secular substitute for Christianity'. Those Christian principles were, alleged Friedrich, transposed into democracy as the realization, rather than merely the secularization, of politics properly understood.[98] In fact, just a few years after the publication of Otto von Gierke's celebrated little book on the political ideas of Althusius, Friedrich was once again trying to revive Althusius's work more broadly, by writing about the foundations of a group or associational forms of communal life found in his texts. Friedrich focused in on Althusius's notion of the covenant, around which five principal forms of association life could pivot. These were the private realms of the family and the *collegium*, and the public spheres of the town, populace and commonwealth, and when set in combination, Friedrich mirrored the associational

---

[97] Heinrich Meier, *Leo Strauss and the Theologico-Political Problem* (Cambridge University Press, 2006).

[98] Greenberg, *Weimar Century*, p. 30; cf. Peter Ghosh, *Max Weber and the Protestant Ethic: Twin Histories* (Oxford University Press, 2015), p. 94.

bases of German democratic politics with the Puritan origins of American democracy at the same time.[99] It was an original twist on the originality of Althusius's account of sovereignty, an account that had been rendered more accessible thanks to the work of Gierke, but which for Friedrich would surely have been better known from its similar rendering in the pages of Schmitt's account of dictatorship.[100] The extent of Friedrich's missionary zeal was *non pareil*, however, and as these foundations were developed intellectually, he was building practical and educational institutions under Weimar with Rockefeller Foundation funding, which would help make his theories practically influential.

Friedrich had little sympathy for mass democracy in its widest extent, retaining a patrician intolerance for the 'masses' that never subsided. In order to maintain a well-functioning democratic and representative form of politics, he thought it would be necessary to train a cadre of academically and ideologically committed bureaucrats to effectively manage an otherwise irrational system. Without 'responsible bureaucrats' to check the conflicting demands of the people on one side, and politicians on the other, the only other solution was likely to be dictatorship, as the German example had readily shown by the 1930s.[101] This was also why new institutions (and funding for them) were so important. Having invested heavily after 1924 in the construction of a new *Institut für Sozial-und Staatswissenschaften* [InSoSta] in Heidelberg, the Rockefeller Foundation had invested around $1.5 million by the mid 1930s into the sorts of projects Friedrich was aligned with, including an academic exchange program (DAAD) that brought American scholars like John Dewey and Charles Merriam together with German figures like Arnold Bergestraesser and Alexander Rüstow, as well as Friedrich himself. Friedrich would travel between Germany and America, easily operating within the academic and policy nexus between government and the universities. During the 1940s, he was advisor to General Lucius Clay on the de-Nazification process in Germany, having supported Roosevelt and the politics of the New Deal as well as American engagement in the Second World War. Unsurprisingly, earlier debates about a war economy and the problems of constitutional or other forms of dictatorship thereunder had also been of more general concern to many other émigré figures alongside Friedrich, and prominent intellectuals like the Austrian

---

[99] See Greenberg, *Weimar Century*, pp. 31ff; Carl J. Friedrich (ed.), *The Politica Methodice Digesta of Johannes Althusius* (Cambridge, MA: Harvard University Press, 1932).

[100] Schmitt, *Die Diktatur*, p. 124.

[101] Carl Friedrich, *Responsible Bureaucracy: A Study of the Swiss Civil Service* (New York: Russell and Russell, 1932); Greenberg, *Weimar Century*, pp. 48, 36–40.

334 *Duncan Kelly*

Gustav Stolper also came to figure in American debates about post-war planning.[102]

By this time, Friedrich had also moved to develop a similar institution to InSoSta at Harvard, and it garnered support from Senator Lucius Littauer. Students arriving at the school from the late 1930s onwards, 'received a thorough political indoctrination to prepare them for unelected leadership and defense of the covenant', and it was political theory that was the key to this study. The power of ideas in Friedrich's mind was, once more, precisely what mattered, and through the study of ideas, the logical corollary of policy positions that buttressed a managed democracy predicated on the pillars of Althusian political thinking found transatlantic form as well as content. Friedrich was hugely influential at Harvard, combining his teaching there with a continued presence in Heidelberg, where he helped to train generations of eminent scholars and bureaucrats.

In 1964, Friedrich reiterated the central propositions of his work in an oddly neglected, but capacious synthesis entitled *Transcendent Justice*. In it, he outlined what he saw as the religious dimensions of a modern constitutional order, whose roots in political theory spread from Cicero to Locke in particular, and whose 'prime function' was 'accomplished by means of regularized restraint'.[103] Focusing once more on the language of *concordia* or federation in Althusius's discussion of politics, the unity of Friedrich's idea of the German state as a 'commonwealth', which had begun back in 1926 (if not before), was once again made primary. The modern democratic state, if understood as a harmonious and regularized (because restrained) form of federation, had parts that together became the kind of 'symbioticus' Althusius had predicted. Once more, this gave Friedrich the intellectual foundation from which to develop his particular claims about Locke and Kant as the transmission mechanism through which this Protestant vision was updated for the modern world. When Locke talks of freedom as independence, of the politics of regulated conduct and of noticing the important prerequisite of constitutional government as the absence of arbitrary power, he becomes part of the deist and theist roots of modern politics that Friedrich traces.[104]

---

[102] Gustav Stolper, *Das Mitteleuropäische Wirtschaftsproblem*, 2nd Ed. (Leipzig: Franz Deuticke, 1918); Hansjörg Klausinger, 'Gustav Stolper, Der deutsche *Volkswirt*, and the Controversy on Economic Policy at the End of the Weimar Republic', *History of Political Economy*, 33: 2 (2001), pp. 241–267; Ira Katznelson, *Desolation and Enlightenment* (Columbia University Press, 2003), pp. 106–151; also Ira Katznelson and Bruce Pieterykowski, 'Rebuilding the American State: Evidence from the 1940s', *Studies in American Political Development*, 5 (1991), pp. 301–339.

[103] Carl Friedrich, *Transcendent Justice* (Cambridge, MA: Harvard University Press, 1964), p. 17.

[104] Friedrich, *Transcendent Justice*, p. 78.

Friedrich's work suggests how a form of constitutional reason of state might be a plausible attempt to steer a middle way through the history of political thought, whose binary opposition between reason of state on the one hand, and justice on the other, had been polemically focused upon by Carl Schmitt, and which has in turn been so crucial to the perspectives on modern politics opened up by Hont, particularly in his discussions of the rise of modern nationalism.[105] If force without authority is simply a state of aggression and war, as Friedrich thought and as Locke implied, then it is to Kant's account of perpetual peace that we must look to seek the 'transcendent' rather than the 'particular' or English foundations of modern natural law that renders this point most sharply.[106] Because a new language of rights fixed those foundations, it was to that history, and in particular the 'humanist' and revolutionary history of that language that Friedrich turned his attention.[107]

The attempt to rethink the intellectual and political origins of modern constitutional government and reason of state based on these languages of rights and their revolutionary foundations has remained the focus for much of the most interesting work in the history of modern political thought. In this, István Hont's energies and inspiration were pioneering. But if he ultimately traced a different set of objectives from a history that ran from Hobbes and Locke to Smith, Rousseau, Hume and Kant as the foundations from which the economic limits to modern politics could be built up, his concern to show the crucial role of political theory and its history in shaping contemporary concerns in some ways mirrors that of Friedrich. Both were interested in the development of a language of reason of state that could connect the seventeenth and eighteenth centuries to the present, and if the bulk of the chapters in this volume have focused on the historical context of those developments in the eighteenth century, we should not forget the important ways in which those developments were subsequently repositioned and repurposed for political ends, and how crucial (if rather underappreciated) the Germanic focus on Locke's political theory has been.

It posits an alternative genealogy of Lockean prerogative that has much to tell us about the structural limitations of contemporary liberal political theory, clarifying in particular how Locke could only become a central figure to the history of liberalism if he could be made into a reason of state theorist, because only by so doing could his politics be seen to have limits rather than permitting a potentially limitless prerogative. That early German writers saw this ambivalence as justifying wide-ranging

---

[105] István Hont, *Jealousy of Trade* (Cambridge, MA: Harvard University Press, 2005), ch. 7.
[106] Friedrich, *Transcendent Justice*, p. 81.
[107] Cf. Tuck, *Rights of War and Peace*, 'Conclusion'.

attacks on liberalism generally, and as justifying imperialism particularly, shows how far from contemporary liberalism Locke seemed at the turn of the last century. By contrast, whereas more recent political theorists who have focused on the imperial dimensions of liberalism have found Locke guilty of being both a defender of colonialism and the founding father of early-modern 'liberalism', he could only become the founding father of modern liberalism once the ambiguous ideas behind his politics were given new and fixed coordinates. Locke's occupation of a genuinely ambivalent position within the theory and practice of modern liberal politics is, it seems, intimately related to the ambivalence surrounding his account of prerogative. Only when prerogative had been made safe as a form of constitutional reason of state could Locke be made safe for modern liberalism. And the history of how that happened is surely an important part of any history of the history of modern political thought.

12   Afterword
Peace, politics and the division of labour

Michael Sonenscher

Much of this collection is about how, particularly in the eighteenth century, thinking about politics also involved thinking about the economy. In part, the overlap was a product of the assorted legacies of the Portuguese, Spanish, Dutch, British, French or Ottoman empires of the sixteenth and seventeenth centuries. In part, it was a product of the seventeenth-century military revolution and the many dimensions of competition involved in war and preparations for war. Both added a range of new concerns into the old Roman maxim that money was the sinew of war by bringing the subjects of trade, finance and debt into closer political proximity to the mixture of prudence and patriotism usually associated with the thought of Plutarch and Machiavelli, the two political thinkers generally taken to be responsible for the original maxim.[1] They did so not only because of the additional commercial, fiscal and financial pressures involved in funding the costs of war but also because of the new political possibilities that these same pressures seemed, sometimes tantalizingly, to offer. From one perspective, the combined demands of war and empire entailed escalating public expenditure, relentless commercial competition and the arrival of those systems of permanent taxation that, as one early nineteenth-century commentator put it, had turned "feudal France" into "fiscal France" and now threatened to do the same to much of the rest of Europe and America.[2] But from another

---

[1] On the maxim, see Raymond Aron, *Peace and War: A Theory of International Relations* [1962] (London, Weidenfeld, 1966), p. 245, referring to Machiavelli, *Discorsi*, ch. 10 and Antoine de Montchrestien, *Traité de l'économie politique* [1615]. More broadly, see the chapter on Charles Davenant and neo-Machiavellian political economy in Istvan Hont, *Jealousy of Trade. International Competition and the Nation-State in Historical Perspective* (Cambridge, Mass. Harvard University Press, 2005) and, more recently, Sophus Reinert, *Translating Empire: Emulation and the Origins of Political Economy* (Cambridge, Mass. Harvard University Press, 2011) and Duncan Bell, *Reordering the World. Essays on Liberalism and Empire* (Princeton University Press, 2016).

[2] The phrase was coined by Paul-Edmond Lemontey, *Histoire de la Régence et de la minorité de Louis XV*, 2 vols. (Paris, 1832), vol. 2, p. 276: "Le cardinal de Fleury trouva cet élément [referring to banks and their functions] tout prêt lorsqu'il acheva la métamorphose de la France féodale en France fiscale."

perspective, the new institutions and financial instruments produced to meet those same demands also seemed to offer a prospect of prosperity and peace that, it was claimed, amounted to an achievable alternative to existing conditions of misery and war.

In different ways, both of the eighteenth century's two most famous peace plans – those produced by the abbé de Saint-Pierre and Immanuel Kant – focused as much on the economy as on political society as the key to peace. Although their initial diagnoses were radically different, their final prognoses were, in reality, not far apart. With Saint-Pierre, the interdependence produced by trade and industry meant that there was a world to win. With Kant, the same economic and social interdependence meant that there was a world to lose.[3] For the first, the moral and causal priority lay on the side of the rewards, while for the second, it lay on the side of the risks. For both, however, the properties of trade and industry seemed, in the first instance, to be largely responsible for the line separating modern politics and its prospects from the darker legacies of ancient and gothic politics. Most of the contributions to this collection are examinations of the various moral and causal claims underlying these ostensibly divergent, but still fundamentally convergent, assessments of risks and rewards. If, as Hume put it famously, trade had become a reason of state, it was also possible – at least on Saint-Pierre's or Kant's terms – to think that one-day trade might, ultimately, trump reason of state. The problem, both then and now, was to work out whether trade would be able to do so because of its own properties, or because the properties of certain types of government – possibly liberal, or democratic, or corporate, or federal – would be able to neutralise the menace and, instead, realise the promise that trade seemed to offer. At first sight, the outcome, together with the putative solution to the problem, seems obvious. Politics have become democratic, governments have become representative, and economics have become commercial, industrial or capitalist. But it is not clear whether there is any necessary connection between any, or all, of these qualities, nor whether any, or all, of their putative connections now add up to a basis for thinking about commerce and perpetual peace that is substantively different from anything that was conceived in the eighteenth century. Democracies, it has been said, do not go to war with one another, but it is an open question whether this is because democracy favours peace or because peace favours democracy.[4] Causation is sometimes more complicated than it seems.

---

[3] See the contribution by Isaac Nakhimovsky to this volume.

[4] On these subjects, compare John Dunn, *Western Political Theory in the Face of the Future* [1979] (Cambridge University Press, 1993) to, equally classically, Michael W. Doyle,

Today, the concept of a commercial society is usually associated with the thought of Adam Smith and, more specifically, with the many different types of division of labour underlying the political and economic life of the modern world. Before Smith, however, the concept of a commercial society was used mainly to refer to a less foundational set of social arrangements. In this now forgotten version of the concept, a commercial society was the outcome of a historical sequence that, like its more familiar counterpart, began with hunting and gathering, turned subsequently into a pastoral and an agricultural way of life, but then became something rather different from the market-driven set of social arrangements involved in Smith's version of the concept. Instead, the commercial part of the idea of a commercial society referred simply to commerce in the old sense of the word, as social intercourse or social interaction, so that a commercial society was, accordingly, a society whose members had acquired the resources and culture that enabled them to escape the imperatives of survival and could, instead, enjoy the fruits of the arts and sciences and, more particularly, of their commerce with one another. In this usage, a commercial society was also, and in a rather necessary sense, a cultured, or cultivated, society because it was the type of society that could house artists and scholars as well as merchants.[5]

This usage has largely disappeared. Arguably, its last major occurrence was Marxism and the idea of the many-sided, polycultural human that lay at the heart of Marx's vision of communism as the setting in which life after states would one day be lived. But Marx's philosophy of history was, originally, only one outcome of a broader cluster of conceptual reappraisals of the pairing of economics and politics that began with Smith's unconventional version of the concept of commercial society, but also included Rousseau's concept of the general will and Kant's concept of unsocial sociability. Underlying them all was the thought that a world made up of states was a world in which peace at home was likely to be matched by war abroad and, more bleakly, by the further thought that the second condition was the price of the first. From this perspective, states were the problem, not the solution. Not only did they consume, and not produce, but the power that they could project seemed, paradoxically, to depend as much on their capacity to consume as on their

"Kant, liberal legacies and foreign affairs", *Philosophy and Public Affairs*, 12 (1983), 205–35, 323–53. For a recent overview, see Luigi Caranti, "Kantian Peace and Liberal Peace: Three Concerns", *Journal of Political Philosophy* (2016), doi: 10.1111/jopp.12097.

[5] For one example, see Johann Heinrich Gottlob von Justi, *Die Natur und das Wesen der Staaten* (Berlin, 1760), pp. 8–9, cited by Ronald Meek, *Social Science & the Ignoble Savage* (Cambridge University Press, 1976), p. 131, n. 1.

ability to coerce. From the vantage point of the late eighteenth century, rich countries seemed to have established a permanent superiority over poor countries and the old, providentially based, self-correcting historical cycles formed by the rise and fall of empires seemed to have gone for good.[6] In this context, the military arc traced across the globe by Napoleon Bonaparte amounted to bellicose evidence of what a modern state could do, just as the enormous dimensions of the victorious early nineteenth-century British and Russian empires seemed to indicate the likely shape and content of the global future. Both, in their different ways, had developed a capacity to mobilise huge numbers of people, like the empires and republics of the ancient world, but were also able to equip them with unprecedented quantities of financial and military resources. From the vantage point of the early nineteenth century, the hundred years separating the wars of the age of Louis XIV from those of the age of the Napoleon revealed, for the first time, what the combination of ancient politics and modern economics could do and, by doing so, generated a range of questions about the properties of states and the prospects of peace that are still alive today.

The initial effect of these questions was a switch in analytical and historical focus that has yet to be fully explored. If, in the eighteenth century, thinking about politics came to involve thinking about the economy so, in the nineteenth century, thinking about the economy also came to involve thinking about politics. Here, the initial impetus came from the concept of the division of labour. In a narrow sense, the concept referred to technical specialisation and occupational differentiation. In a more extended sense, however, it could also be used to refer to institutional specialisation and political differentiation. This usage was a prominent feature of the thought of Emmanuel-Joseph Sieyès and his claim that the division of labour was, simply, a representative system. More significantly, however, it also became the basis of Georg-Friedrich Hegel's concept of civil society and the many different extrapolations from Hegel's concept that came to be made during the nineteenth century.[7] From one perspective, this more extended sense of the concept seemed to show how political institutions could be reformatted to match the combination of specialisation and integration that the division of labour implied. From another perspective, however, the same usage helped to raise a

---

[6] On this subject, see Istvan Hont, "The 'Rich Country-Poor Country' Debate in the Scottish Enlightenment", in his *Jealousy of Trade*, pp. 267–322 and his "The 'Rich Country-Poor Country' Debate Revisited: The Irish Origins and French Reception of the Hume Paradox", in Margaret Schabas and Carl Wennerlind (eds.), *David Hume's Political Economy* (London, 2008), pp. 243–323.

[7] On Sieyès and Hegel, see Sonenscher, *Before the Deluge*, p. 89.

further set of questions about the nature and necessity of states, governments and laws.

These questions overlapped with the growing late eighteenth-century interest in federalism and federal systems of government, most obviously in the United States of America in the context of the long debate between federalists and anti-federalists after 1783, but also in Europe itself in the wake of the models of federal government set out most influentially in Hume's essay on *The Idea of a Perfect Commonwealth* and Rousseau's *Considerations on the Government of Poland.*[8] Both models were quite similar in structure to the concept of monarchy that Montesquieu had presented in *The Spirit of Laws* in 1748, where monarchy was defined as a system of government in which one person ruled along with a number of subordinate, dependent and intermediate powers.[9] In Montesquieu, the combination of a single monarch and a number of intermediate powers was predicated on inheritance and property. In Hume and Rousseau, however, the same type of dual system was predicated on elections and eligibility. Just as, with Montesquieu, a monarchy could accommodate many different types of property and inheritance, so, with Hume and Rousseau, a federal system could accommodate many different types of election and eligibility. Elections to local office could follow one set of procedures and rely on one type of criterion for eligibility, while those to regional or federal office could follow other procedures and different criteria without calling into question the integrity or viability of the system as a whole. As Rousseau emphasised, federal systems could combine the properties of big states and small states in ways that were compatible with both.[10]

The same flexibility applied to the economy. A federal system of government could, in principle, accommodate the differences that might otherwise affect rich countries and poor countries, just as it could also accommodate a broad range of different types of specialised economic activity within a single common market. In part this was simply a matter of size, a common currency and the potential for economies of scale supplied by both. In part, however, it was also an effect of variety and the

---

[8] On Hume, see, particularly, Ryu Susato, "Hume as an *Ami de la liberté*: the reception of his Idea of a Perfect Commonwealth", *Modern Intellectual History*, available on CJO 2014 doi:10.1017/S1479244314000687 and, on Rousseau, see Michael Sonenscher, *Before the Deluge, Public Debt, Inequality, and the Intellectual Origins of the French Revolution* (Princeton University Press, 2007), pp. 233–37.

[9] Charles Louis de Secondat, baron de Montesquieu, *The Spirit of the Laws* [1748], ed. Anne Cohler, Basia Miller and Harold Stone (Cambridge University Press, 1989), Bk. 2, Ch. 4, pp. 17–18.

[10] On Rousseau and federalism, see Patrick Riley, "Rousseau as a Theorist of National and International Federalism", *Publius*, 3 (1973), pp. 5–17.

broader array of fiscal and financial institutions, along with the related range of economic and social policies, than more unified systems could accommodate. In this sense, a federal system had the potential to borrow, tax and spend at a number of different local, regional or federal levels, just as it could also manage the resulting flows of income and expenditure through a parallel hierarchy of different levels of decision-making, scrutiny and accountability. From this perspective, both the division of labour and a federal system of government shared the same modular structure. Additional units could be added or subtracted without necessarily having a radical affect upon the nature of the whole. This, in turn, raised a further set of questions both about earlier conceptions of sociability and about established conceptions of sovereignty. In place of the older, eighteenth-century, debates about sociability and whether or not humans were naturally sociable, this more modular approach to politics could rely instead on a more limited range of claims about sociability and the further idea that a multiplicity of partial associations could add up to a single, integrated, whole.

The common ground shared by the concepts of federalism and the division of labour was not limited to Hegel's concept of civil society and the range of activities and occupations that civil society was said to house.[11] It also came to be connected to the concept of industrialism, particularly as it was developed by both the supporters and critics of the Saint-Simonian movement in France. To both its supporters and critics, Saint-Simonianism, with its concern with a range of differentiated institutions centred on, or representing, the interests of science, industry, finance, agriculture, the professions and the arts, was simply a modified version of Hegelianism.[12] The conceptual cluster was reinforced by the developing interest in the various types of association singled out for special consideration in the various nineteenth-century movements variously called positivism, associationism, cooperativism, mutualism or anarchism.[13] In different ways, all of them raised a question

---

[11] On the connections between Hegel's concept of civil society and subsequent concepts of federalism, see particularly the fine, but oddly neglected, monograph by Rupert Emerson, *State and Sovereignty in Modern Germany* (Yale University Press, 1928), especially pp. 39–46. See too David F. Lindenfeld, *The Practical Imagination: the German Sciences of State in the Nineteenth Century* (Princeton University Press, 1997), pp. 175–204. There is no authoritative study of the concept of civil society in nineteenth-century European thought. See, however, Sudipta Kaviraj and Sunil Khilnani, *Civil Society. History and Possibilities* (Cambridge University Press, 2001).

[12] For an initial presentation of the similarities and differences, see Warren Breckman, "Politics in a Symbolic Key: Pierre Leroux, Romantic Socialism and the Schelling Affair", *Modern Intellectual History*, 2 (2005), pp. 61–86.

[13] On these subjects, see J. E. S. Hayward, "The Official Philosophy of the French Third Republic: Leon Bourgeois and Solidarism", *International Review of Social History*, 6

mark against earlier claims that civil society, in the old pre-Hegelian sense, also required a state. In doing so, they played a significant part in the emergence of the concept of pluralism and the models of political decentralisation now usually associated with the thought of late nineteenth- and early twentieth-century political theorists like Otto von Gierke, Harold Laski or the Belgian sociologist Guillaume de Greef.[14] Common to them all was a willingness to apply the concept of the division of labour to a far broader range of human activities than the original concept had done. This conceptual elasticity was particularly evident in the thought of a now largely forgotten early nineteenth-century German philosopher named Karl Friedrich Christian Krause, whose *Urbild der Menschheit* (Ideal of Humanity), published in 1811, attracted a growing following, first in Belgium and France before 1848 and then, more considerably, as *Krausismo*, in Spain and in many parts of South America in the second half of the nineteenth century.[15] As one of Krause's admirers put it, humanity's destiny was bound up with "a cultural division of labour" and the promise of a future age of social and cultural harmony based on the many potentially self-governing associations involved in modern economic and political life.[16]

Before Marxism, there was Krausism. Both were indicative of the broader range of critical assessments of earlier conceptions of the state that straddled the period of the French Revolution and the Napoleonic Wars. Before Kant, it was usual to think that individuals were rather like states: single, solitary and equipped with a limited bundle of putatively

---

(1961), pp. 19–48; J. E. S. Hayward, "Lamennais and the Religion of Social Consensus", *Archives de sociologie des religions*, 11 (1966), pp. 37–46; and, more fully, his London University, 1958, Ph. D Thesis on "The Idea of Solidarity in French Social and Political Thought in the Nineteenth and Early Twentieth Centuries".

[14] For a particularly helpful way in, see David Runciman, *Pluralism and the Personality of the State* (Cambridge University Press, 1997). On the connections between de Greef and pluralism, see particularly Guillaume de Greef, *La constituante et le régime représentatif* (Brussels, 1892) and, more generally, Dorothy Wolff Douglas, *Guillaume de Greef, The Social Theory of an Early Syndicalist* (New York, Columbia University Press, 1925). There is still room for fuller examination of nineteenth and early twentieth-century discussions of the concept of sovereignty. For one possible starting point, see Martin Loughlin and Neil Walker (eds.), *The Paradox of Constitutionalism. Constituent Power and Constitutional Form* (Oxford University Press, 2006).

[15] On Krausism and Spain, see Juan López-Morillas, *The Krausist Movement and Ideological Change in Spain, 1854–1874* (Cambridge University Press, 1981). There is no comparable study of the reception of Krause's thought in Germany, Belgium and France. See, however, John Bartier, *Naissance du socialisme en Belgique: les Saint-Simoniens* (Brussels, Mémoire Ouvrière, 1985).

[16] Heinrich Ahrens, *Cours de droit naturel* [1838], 6th edn. (Leipzig, 1868), p. 253. On Krause and Ahrens, see most helpfully Georges Gurvitch, *L'idée du droit social* (Paris, Sirey, 1932), pp. 442–470, 497–505.

344   *Michael Sonenscher*

natural rights.[17] After Kant, it became equally usual to think that states were rather more like individuals: composite, cohesive and equipped with particular personalities as well as a bundle of rights. Neither set of metaphors has been particularly illuminating. Both, however, still help to throw light on the subjects of states, war and peace. They do so both negatively and positively, and it is worth concluding by trying to list both.

The negative side of this metaphorical legacy is not hard to identify. It is bound up with organic or corporate conceptions of the state, and, by extension, with the retrospective shadow cast by the wars of the twentieth century over the common intellectual ground once shared by British and French political thinkers like Mill and Tocqueville and their German, Swiss or Belgian counterparts.[18] The positive side is more varied. One effect of the extension of the concept of the division of labour to encompass political institutions and social arrangements was a new emphasis on history as a process of divergence, rather than convergence, with as much to do with individual character and personality as with collective rationality and shared rules. From this perspective, the latter was simply a precondition of the former, just as its most salient intellectual precursor was Herder rather than Kant.[19] This, in turn, injected a new set of criteria into moral assessments and political choices. Within limits, difference and diversity could count as much as equality and humanity, just as race and nationality could give way to gender and capability.

A second effect of the same extension was the addition of a potentially large number of intermediate levels to the relationship between states and their members. In this sense, the concept of civil society injected a further component into the concept of federalism and the idea of a federal system of government. This, in the third place, helped to make it easier to think about international relations negatively as well as positively, by focusing on finding ways to reduce the number of possible causes of conflict, instead of simply trying to increase the number of possible areas of agreement. A common market made up of several regional or national markets could, for example, turn questions of trade and tariffs into questions of regional development and employment policy, just as the earlier establishment of systems of elected offices could take the question of the royal succession out of the sphere of international relations. Whatever else modern wars have become, they are no longer, in any literal sense, wars of succession. The idea of a political society

[17] See, classically, Richard Tuck, *Philosophy and Government, 1572–1651* (Cambridge University Press, 1993).
[18] For examples of this common ground, see Georgios Varouxakis, *Victorian Political Thought on France and the French* (Basingstoke, Palgrave Macmillan, 2002).
[19] See the contribution of Eva Piirimäe to this volume.

as a compound of different, partly functional, associations also made it easier, in the fourth place, to think about detaching some associations from the rest without having to call the integrity of the whole entity into question. The idea was applied to the legal profession in the early nineteenth-century German Confederation, just as it came to be applied both to the nineteenth-century *Zollverein* and the European Coal and Steel Community in the twentieth century.[20] The same emphasis on specialisation and functionality could, finally, be applied to the concept of the state itself by highlighting the relationship between states, laws and legality as the basis of the type of institutional international legal system that began to be discussed in the second half of the nineteenth century.[21] From this perspective, legal positivism could begin to look like a real alternative to the old nexus of states, governments and laws, just as the same emphasis on specialisation and functionality pointed towards the idea of the state as the only legitimate source of the use of violence.

There was, in short, more to commerce than *doux commerce* and more to the idea of the division of labour than technical specialisation, industrial productivity and absolute or comparative advantage. The intellectual history of the nineteenth century was saturated with discussion of the additional attributes and further properties of this apparently familiar range of subjects. In one sense, they amount to the intellectual legacy of the period that preceded the European revolutions of 1848. In another sense, however, they could also be part of a range of conceptual resources that has yet to be fully explored.

---

[20] For the legal profession, see James Q. Whitman, *The Legacy of Roman Law in the German Romantic Era: Historical Vision and Legal Change* (Princeton University Press, 1990). There is still room for studies of the latter two examples within a comparable framework.

[21] See Bo Stråth, *Europe's Utopias of Peace, 1815, 1919, 1951* (London, Bloomsbury, 2016) and the discussion arising from Martti Koskenniemi, *The Gentle Civilizer of Nations: the Rise and Fall of International Law* (Cambridge University Press, 2001) in Ian Hunter, "About the dialectical historiography of international law", *Global Intellectual History*, available at http://dx.doi.org/10.1080/23801883.2016.1155863.

Index

Meinecke, Friedrich, 44, 325
Melon, Jean-François, 6, 53, 79–81, 114
mercantile system, 108, 235, 239, 242
mercenaries, 31, 61, 114, 121
Mexico, 91
militias, 119, 122–3, 194, 203, 206
Mirabeau, marquis de (Victor de Riqueti), 6
monarchy, 59, 63–4, 175, 198, 302–3, 341: constitutional, 283–4; universal, 65, 278
money, 81, 93. *See also* balance of money
Montagu, Edward Wortley, 119
Montesquieu, baron de (Charles-Louis de Secondat), 40–1, 64, 115, 116, 341
Mounier, Jean-Joseph, 234

Napoleon I (emperor of France), 217, 225–6, 228, 244, 246
national character, 164, 169, 171, 185
nationalism, 157, 297, 315, 316, 335
naturalism, 159–61, 181
natural right. *See* law: natural
Navigation Acts, 24, 105
Necker, Jacques, 234
Neville, Henry, 39

Otis, James, Jr., 42–3

Paine, Thomas, 225, 226
parliamentarianism, 308, 320
Pasquino, Pasquale, 301
patriotism, 18
peace, 215–91: and balance of power, 54, 66; and commerce, 101, 104, 150; democratic, 10, 19; and empire, 213, 221, 228; and finance, 16, 84, 98–9, 106; international, 156, 162, 196; and technology, 7–8, 147. *See also* perpetual peace
perpetual peace, 2–3, 9–11, 92, 246, 322, 338: Haller on, 252–3, 269–70
Peru, 91
Pictet, Marc-Auguste, 237, 238
Pictet de Rochemont, Charles, 237, 238, 241–2
Pinto, Isaac de, 16, 79, 82, 83–95, 98–109
Plato, 24
political economy, 198
Polybius, 113
Portugal, 103
Pownall, Thomas, 41–3
prerogative, 301–8, 309–11, 315, 316–21, 323, 324

Prévost, Pierre, 238–9
Price, Richard, 6, 234
primogeniture, 206
productivity, 6, 84, 88, 285, 345. *See also* industry
property, 87, 194, 206, 268, 284. *See also* balance of property
Protectorate. *See* England: Commonwealth
Proudhon, Pierre-Joseph, 18, 270, 272–99. *See also* La guerre et la paix
providence, 138, 140–1, 142, 159
prudence, 306, 319
Prussia, 64, 67, 248, 258
public finance, 84, 93–4, 97, 98–107, 108: credit, 99, 101, 196; debt, 41, 89–90, 164, 269
Pufendorf, Samuel von, 131, 262
Punic Wars, 113, 114, 118, 122–3

Raynal, abbé (Guillaume-Thomas-François), 182
reason of state, 49, 62–3, 111, 266–7, 307–8, 324–5: constitutional, 19, 63, 301, 322–3, 335
regulation, 151, 153, 290–1
religion, 32, 134, 142–3, 249, 307, 318–19. *See also* Catholic Church
representation, 43, 194, 252
republic, 121, 208, 252, 256, 258: universal, 278. *See also* democracy
republicanism, 24–30, 172–3, 192–3, 214, 215
rich country–poor country problem, 219, 227, 230–2, 237, 243
right of force, 272, 275, 280, 281, 283–4
right of war. *See* war: right of
rivalry. *See* competition
Rocker, Rudolf, 297
Rome, 28, 32, 111–24, 256, 288
Rossiter, Clinton, 324
Rousseau, Jean-Jacques, 6, 111, 245–6, 341: and *Anti-Machiavel*, 75–6; and Beccaria, 139, 147; and French Revolution, 244–5; Haller on, 250, 252, 260, 261, 265–6; and Hobbes, 15, 260, 316; and Kant, 246, 252; reception in Germany, 246–71; and Saint-Pierre, 74–5

Saint-Lambert, Jean-François de, 84–5
Saint-Pierre, abbé (Charles Irénée Castel de), 2, 74, 176, 338: on *Anti-Machiavel*, 69–73; and Hobbes, 12, 14–15; and Rousseau, 74–5
Say, Jean-Baptiste, 242